How to Win Nature and Enjoy Good Life

How to Win Nature and Enjoy Good Life

Baby Steps to Follow Mother Nature

Prabhash Karan

Author of

Nature Is My Teacher

Of Human Nature

and Good Habits

Life, Living and Lifestyle

Health and Medical Care

Library of Congress Control Number:		2018913690
ISBN:	Hardcover	978-1-9845-6687-4
	Softcover	978-1-9845-6688-1
	eBook	978-1-9845-6689-8

Print information available on the last page.

Rev. date: 04/17/2019

To order additional copies of this book, contact:
Xlibris
1-888-795-4274
www.Xlibris.com
Orders@Xlibris.com
695351

To my Daughter, Priyanka Karan, with love

How to Win Nature and Enjoy Good Life

Baby Steps to Follow Mother Nature

Contents

1 LOVE AND RELATIONSHIPS 1
- 1.1 MARRIAGE 19
- 1.2 FAMILY 111
- 1.3 CHILDREN 143
- 1.4 FRIENDS AND SOCIETY 239

2 ENJOY GOOD LIFE 273
- 2.1 LIFE IS GOOD 281
- 2.2 LIFE IS BEAUTIFUL 295
- 2.3 LIVE YOUNG, LIVE LONG 309

3 ENJOY GOOD FOOD 357
- 3.1 HOW FOOD WORKS 495
- 3.2 DIET AND NUTRITION 563
- 3.3 HERBS AND SPICES 635

Nature Is My Teacher

Baby Steps to Follow Mother Nature

Contents

1 THE NATURE 1
1.1 Mother Nature 11
1.2 The Universe 21
1.3 Planet Earth 33
1.4 The Weather 59
1.5 Natural Resources 69
1.6 The Air We Breathe 79
1.7 The Water We Drink 107
1.8 The Future of Nature 153

2 ORIGIN OF LIFE 191
2.1 Gift of Life 223
2.2 Human Life 229
2.3 Human Evolution 301
2.4 Self and the Rest of the World 311
2.5 Time Goes By 323
2.6 Life Changes Over Time 339

3 HUMAN EMOTION AND LIFE EXPERIENCE 349
3.1 Worries, Anxieties, Fear, and Regret 381
3.2 How to Deal with Stress 419
3.3 Depression 461
3.4 Kindness and Devotion 495
3.5 Charity and Humanity 503
3.6 The Power of Hope 521
3.7 No Pain, No Gain 527
3.8 Education and Experience 535

Of Human Nature and Good Habits

Baby Steps to Follow Mother Nature

Contents

1 HUMAN NATURE 1
1.1 Nature vs. Nurture 19
1.2 Personality 31
1.3 Patience and Confidence 57
1.4 Discipline and Good Habits 69
1.5 Courage, Attitude, and Ambition 93
1.6 Aim in Life 125

2 MIND AND MENTAL HABITS 161
2.1 Mind and Body 175
2.2 Mind and Memory 217
2.3 Power of Meditation 295
2.4 Greed, Envy, and Jealousy 327
2.5 Humor and Laughter 343
2.6 Talk and Sing 351

3 NATURE AND NATURAL HABITS 377
3.1 Be Wise 381
3.2 Be Happy 421
3.3 Be Honest, Simple, and Natural 453

Life, Living and Lifestyle

Baby Steps to Follow Mother Nature

Contents

1 ACTIVE LIFESTYLE 1
1.1 Play and Exercise 9
1.2 Joy of Yoga 81
1.3 Lose Weight 97
1.4 Walking and Running 205
1.5 Quit Smoking 233
1.6 Sleep 259

2 LIFE, LIVING AND WORK ETHICS 331
1.5 Etiquette, Courtesy, and Behavior 341
2.1 Science and Technology 363
2.2 Organize Yourself 395
2.3 Work and Workplace 411
2.4 The Job We Do 443
2.5 Home Sweet Home 481
2.6 Personal Finance and Money Habits 489

Health and Medical Care

Baby Steps to Follow Mother Nature

Contents

1 ENJOY GOOD HEALTH 1
1.1 Men's Health 17
1.2 Women's Health 39
1.3 Children's Health 99

2 MEDICAL CARE 225
2.1 Medical Science 229
2.2 Human Organs 291
2.3 Arthritis 361
2.4 Headache 383
2.5 Blood Pressure 393
2.6 Heart Attack and Stroke 413
2.7 Diabetics 465
2.8 Cancer 493
2.9 Old Age and Death 581

Preface

Nature! Mother Nature! She is so ancient yet so novel! So mysterious yet so marvelous! A deep connection between evolution and civilization! She is my life, she is my universe. From birth to death, Mother Nature cradles me in her bosom. She is always in my mind. She is so dear. Nature is my teacher.

Simplicity is her beauty! Nature that envelopes all of us is so dear, so loving! She provides us the grace, the beauty, and the fluency of our lives. The love, care, and affection of all our lives are imbibed from her spirit. She breathes life into us. Grow up in the sun, grow up in the shadow, we live the life given to us by her goodness. It is very hard to avoid her; and even harder, not to. She is the creator, protector, and promoter of our mortal life. Our purpose in life is worthy of her benevolence. She elevates us to that, that we are. We all are her children. *Mother* has been and will always remain synonymous with *love*, *devotion*, and *dedication*, and its personification as a nurturing mother is so primitive. Giving nature the attributes of a mother, life-giving and nurturing, is as old as the evolution of human being as a thinking animal. It was then, it is now, and it will always be. We are at home and in harmony with her—in our labor, at our leisure, and at our pleasure. She is the reservoir of all happiness. We follow her in baby steps, wherever she leads us to.

Modern research reveals that innate genetic programming accounts for as much as 50 percent of our happiness. Fifty percent! Our satisfaction with life is, to a large extent, already embedded in our genes by Mother Nature. Genetic researchers claim that the fact that genes help us to be happy is not an accident, rather it is a result of evolutional and natural selection. (Other combined factors—such as education, finance, marital happiness, and the status quo—accounts for less than 10 percent of happiness. The remaining 40 percent or so, is dependent on how we cope with the adverse situations in our life.) In Mother Nature, a whole planet of happiness waits for us at every step. Most of us enjoy it, the wise rejoice it. It is the human friction with nature, a Midas touch of Mother Nature! It is the eternal mother-child relation—so normal, yet so essential that the absence of either is an exception. Trust in nature is the prime expression of our life. In trusting nature, we trust ourselves. Life is beautiful. So cool! Mother Nature is so simple, yet so beautiful!

Nature Is My Teacher; Of Human Nature and Good Habits; Life, Living and Lifestyle; How to Win Nature and Enjoy Good Life and *Health and Medical Care* constitute a series—that tells the same tale in separate episodes. The names are different, the contents are different, yet the idea is one: to discover and rediscover the beauty of nature, and explore the wisdom of Mother Nature. All five books are subtitled, "Baby Steps to Follow Mother Nature," signifying its obvious meaning, a hand-holding guide to life. Also, all books are introduced with the same preface—just to establish *one origin* reflecting a strong relationship among the books. Each book is a companion of and complement to the others. *Nature Is My Teacher* primarily deals with the physical, notional, and real world in general. *Of Human Nature and Good Habits* deals with the everyday experiences of the good life. *Life, Living and Lifestyle* deals with work, play, sleep, finance, and the practical experiences of good living. *How to Win Nature and Enjoy Good Life* deals with love, relationship, marriage and family life. *Health and Medical Care* deals with health and health care services, and primarily, how to prevent diseases, stay healthy and thrive. The book—five books combined—provides a comprehensive familiarity about our planet, our environment, our cosmos, our bodies, our minds, our health, our food, our illnesses, our medics, our life, our job, our living, and our lifestyles. The book deals with social physics, customs, myths, biases, and the biology of life. It gives a fascinating glimpse of some of the topics that we vaguely know or are told for the first time. The author pen-points these points in detail.

It's not a story until it's told! The topic is not only a fact, figure, and statistics, but also a story. The book tells us a complete story about how a slight alteration can make a significant renovation in life. The life of a modern man is moving at a frantic pace like never before. People now live in a society cultured with instant gratification: fast food, fast cash, miracle cure, extreme need, and *I-want-want-it-all* and *I-want-it-now.* They are rushing, all the time, not knowing to where. They are marinated so much with the culture of speed, that there's hardly any pause for the cause, and there is no recess from the race. There is no time to think it through—the very purpose of life. People fail to comprehend how easy it is to cure all these maladies and still live a life of modernity. The book provides steps—in baby steps—with case studies to resolve the issues. The methods suggested in the book are very basic and very easy to follow. Each topic, each page, and even each paragraph relates an idea that you may have encountered in your daily life. Some ideas are trivial and straightforward. The only need is a slight adjustment to our stereotypical thinking and a little tuning of our lifestyle.

We are *one-third born (nature), two-thirds made (nurture)!* If you think about it seriously, this is a huge statement. We have to nurture while being inclusive of nature and vice-versa and transform our God-given talent for our benefit. A small adjustment in lifestyle (nurture) can make a huge difference and improve our quality of life meaningfully. The adjustments are so minor that we hardly experience any inconvenience. A tiny tip, a little mindfulness, and a little planning will lead to a lot happier life. Our hunter-gatherer ancestors essentially lived on day-to-day hunts and day-to-day harvesting of roots and vegetables. From that evolutionary standpoint, we humans are not really designed to think ahead about the distant future. Yet, in many ways, our health and happiness are essentially the sums of our today's activities, including the countless choices we make about what we eat, what we do, what we plan for tomorrow and even how we spend our time now (i.e., moving versus sitting). Small moves—eating healthy, sleeping well, leading a simple life—can transform our lives profoundly. A big resolution adds up from many micro-resolutions. These micro-resolutions fit into our daily life, stay sustained over time, and lead us into good habits (e.g., do your duty, don't tell lies, be natural, have self-assurance, choose whole-foods, eat less, be mindful of what you do, and don't sweat over small stuff). Many good ideas and habits are explained in detail and are made easy to understand and to implement. Many are easy to accrue and adapt. Once accrued and adapted, they work like clockwork and help us to achieve a sea of changes. Good habits stay good for good; break it now, it is broken for good. The book makes a comparative study of both good things and bad things, in order to comprehend the problem with dos and don'ts, and make a good life even better, especially with the ever-helping hand from nature. Nothing triumphs over nature! Here are the statistics: if you consider all human physiological reactions so far discovered in the whole universe, which is approximately 1,000,000, the existing targeted reactions by all medicines and medical treatments are only 250, or percentage-wise only 0.025 percent. With only a 0.025 percent score, while the human boast of medical marvels (human genome, CRIPER, antibiotics, and vaccines), nature remains reserved, with 99.975 percent. You got the point. So, if you are wise, you better follow Mother Nature, for the better of you. Also, when you better your life, you also help others—your family members, friends, and colleagues—to better their lives as well. Thus, one of the ideas of the book is to influence as many people to better their lives as possible so that its impact on society, in the world, as a whole, is significant. Compared to its book value, the value of the book is unrivaled. The book is a tribute to our society and our humanity, at large.

Invent nature! Inventing nature is so exciting—precisely because of its enormous varieties and complexities! When we are in harmony with nature, we live naturally within the moral gravity. We maintain our self-dignity and our standing is at par with our conscious moral terms. Our labor becomes lighter, our leisure becomes a pleasure. For instance, a school of neurologists and neuroscientists, says that it is simply a mind-fulfilling just by staring at the sky. Keeping that in mind, what we have attempted in the book is to connect and build a bridge, between our existing lifestyle and our natural love of life. The connection helps us see the green of the trees, the blue of the sky, the birds fly, the rise of the sun, the gargle of the ocean, with a new look. The book transports you to nature, gives you a tour of wilderness, and inspires you to the many wonders of life. It makes you feel that these were there before your eyes all these days, yet, you missed them all. The joy of life lets you feel the traction of living. It is so close to the earth, yet so open to the world.

The views expressed in the book are solely of the author. The author is not an inventor or an originator, but a simple messenger who delivers the message. The book does not validate or endorse any scientific, medical, ethical, or religious view, advice, or recommendation. The book is *for information only.* Also, the information presented here does not claim textbook accuracy; rather, it is a general guide. The book gives a *good faith* summary of *a good life*. Some facts may be inadequate, inaccurate, deprecated, or outdated, therefore, any error, omission, and exclusion are on the part of the author, for which a plea is acknowledged in advance.

You cannot fight the facts. Facts are nothing but the interpretation of data, and they are not always linear. They are not a product of assumption, speculation, opinion, or notion. By expanding their explanatory power, the fascinating facts explained in the book reinforce the topic with research results, discoveries, surveys, and statistics. Today, there is so much information, so much communication, and so much evidence that one can no longer plead ignorance. Considering how vital these facts are, willful blindness is nothing but an incredible ignorance. Facts and statistics help us explain and compare the "as-is" with the "as-should-be." Sometimes, statistics are as mystifying as they are enlightening. Thus, in order to keep the motion of the topic steady, the key data are skimmed and highlighted broadly to the context and then rounded "up or down" to make it generic, casual, simple, and, more importantly, easy to understand and remember. For instance, our sun is 93 million (92,960,000) miles away from Earth, and the Moon, one-quarter million (238,855) miles. Quantitatively, if any data are of any special importance, they are put in a numeric rather than text format. (Half is not exactly 1/2. The numeral 1/2 is more significant than "half." Radiation from 1 chest CT scan = *350–400* standard chest X-rays or *1,400* dental X-rays or *70,000* backscatter airport scans or *nineteen* years of smoking of one pack of cigarettes per day. Text format: Greed is one of the *seven* deadly sins in Catholicism.) The "percent" and percent sign "%" are used interchangeably, % is used more for clarity. The data address the measure of the context and help us understand the topic in perspective. Some text of the topic is sub-texted for clear understanding like: The U.S. jails (jails are for short-term, minor crimes) and prisons (long-term, serious crimes) are primarily male-gender environment.

The book is an index and an introduction to many of our day-to-day concerns. By design, some vital information is repeated, sometimes immediately and, at other times, in different contexts, with the hope of meeting at some point, the person reading the book at random. Some sentences are repeated according to their importance. Some information goes beyond the scope of the chapter. Some technical terms, never heard of before, are translated into generic names. The book is targeted neither to professionals nor to experts but to ordinary people who need a "how-to" manual on everyday problems. Written by a reader like you, for a reader like you, the book may not teach you how to drive, but it will prompt you to safe driving. It may not prescribe you medicine, but it will prompt you to prevent illness in the first place and in the event of illness, to seek information and medication. The reader's intelligence is never discounted, never ever. Far from it. Instead, it is appreciated.

Many of the ideas put in here are so basic that the reader has experienced them already: some familiar things you, the reader, will know from your gut feeling. For instance, it's often convenient, and even a good idea to be irrational or simplify a decision, and then create a rule for your own use only that works for you most of the time. You can stick to it. One size never fits all. The social order at a national level, may not fit at an individual level, because every individual is unique and discrete. Many ideas are illustrated in the book from which you may pick and choose. Identifying your own thoughts with an additional endorsement from the book nevertheless reinforces your belief system and your own views, and thus fosters your self-assurance and helps you to improve your confidence and will make your bad day better. For a test-drive, crack open any book, at any chapter you like, and read any paragraph, now. Try it, test it, trust it. Overall, the initiative here is to make an idea work for you. Be optimistic, act realistic. If it works, hold on to it. If it's worth sharing, share the idea and spread the knowledge. In fact, the broad readership of the book comes predominantly from word of mouth.

This book is indebted to hundreds of books, publications, journals, and articles. It is an enormous undertaking in trying to synthesize all the information delivered to the reader in a story-telling format, and at the same time, as accurate and as up-to-date. Again, make no mistake, the author is merely a messenger, not an inventor, originator, or any of that sort. Although filled with exciting ideas and fascinating facts, this book is not an academic work in the sense that everything here requires to be acknowledged or footnoted. It contains numerous comments, notes, and quotes. They are not attributed, and at times they are somewhat condensed; otherwise, they would interrupt the flow of the go. While the main topic is emphasized, some details are encapsulated, making it a more readable tale—a tale of arts, science, life, and nature. Readers are invited to join the debate and are respectfully requested to send their comments, complaints, and compliments. Readers, please note here that for the book's next revision, any correction, suggestion, addition, deletion, or information, submitted to the author, will be highly treasured. The contents may become the property of the author, in which case it is assumed that the reader gives the author the right to use it suitably with or without compensation. All trademarks used in the book are the property of their respective owners and do not relate to any endorsement of any kind.

The book is topic oriented and detailed and covers everyday aspects of life. Out of more than a hundred standalone topics, readers are suggested to read only those that interest them now, not the entire book. Try any chapter, any page, or at least any paragraph—right now. At the end of the "Preface," you get an overview. Each paragraph usually starts with a declarative sentence that announces the idea of the topic that follows. You then promptly feel the pull of the topic. While the book targets a wide audience giving readers a choice between numerous isolated, interrelated, and even unrelated topics, a typical reader is requested to read only a few topics. That's worth having the book handy—to read a few pages now and then and refer back to it later. Even the author, who updates the topic periodically, finds some topic interestingly afresh.

This book is a quick and easy *handbook, reference manual, good-will guide, how-to guide,* you name it. It talks about the topics ranging from the creation of the universe to human evolution to modern-day civilization to current hypes to age-old myths and mysteries that mystify us. Why is the sky blue? Why do we typically submit to the situation, saying "yes," or to go with the flow? Why do people often fail to recognize their own voice? How do one's prayers affect others? Why do twins think and act alike? Why do half of all resolutions fail, and one-third of New Year's resolutions do not make it to February (especially for weight loss)? Why don't wearable fitness devices necessarily make you fitter? Or, you don't need to use soap every day in your shower. Or, how to navigate through the shifting views, say, recommendation and confusion about aspirin, breast cancer, colorectal cancer, fat, eggs, vitamins, and dietary supplements. The book explains it all. The book is a myth buster, a zeal enhancer, and a life changer. Good health is always associated with good habits. Good habits are surprisingly few and basic; so, anyone can practice them without even trying. Knowing this helped the author when he tried for the first time. Written with uncomplicated clarity, various topics ring a bell. The book is a collection of explanations, propositions, and suggestions. The book possesses the power to change your good life better, for good. It will make you a new you!

Enjoy reading!

1 Love and Relationships

> It is better to have loved and lost than never to have loved at all.
>
> —Alfred, Lord Tennyson (1809–1892), the poet laureate of the United Kingdom during much of Queen Victoria's reign and one of the most popular poets in the English literature

Love wins, hate ruins. Human, by nature, loves more readily than hates occasionally. Most people would rather give affection than get affection. Affection affects. Love and affection are among the few fine emotions nestling in the human bosom. It is the passionate intensity caring for another person. It is love that makes life alive, the world rally around. It is the love through which we feel an intense emotional attachment, a strong positive admiration, and a combination of a variety of feelings, states, and attitudes, ranging from generic pleasure to intense interpersonal attraction. Love is the single most important one, out of many passions. Love is hard to describe, it is often bewildering and unknowable—you may never know, even in your lifetime. But it is easy to sense. It is the love in the greater sense—our sensitivity to loved ones, our feeling of brotherhood and our goodwill to other people of the world, with compassion and personal connection. It is a global platform that allows people to plug and play, compete and collaborate, share and care. Love is the sunny side of human emotion.

Love reveals. Love is an intense feeling of deep affection. It is one intimate, tender, personal wondrous state of rewarding. Love is like the universe—the more you know, the more mysterious it unfolds. Unconditional love in general is of human nature. It connects the threads of the universe that give us enough understanding of how to use them; it is up to us to use them. It is our affectionate feeling of affection. On the contrary, the lack of relationship is the source of all melodies. We do not see love in terms of "making a relationship work," rather "an event of the sole," which is surprisingly to do with who you are with: *I am most alive when I am with you.* Get together with—who *gets* you! A man does or does not love a woman because she is beautiful or not so beautiful, intelligent or not so intelligent, and vice versa. He loves you—because, he loves you. Rabindranath Tagore (1861–1941), the Nobel laureate poet from India, once said, "I do not love my child because he is good, but because he is my little child."

Love is one primitive and very basic human trait, as basic as fear, anger, and joy. Biologically, love is not trivial. Love is rooted in very deep, old, and cold-blooded organisms that involve basic needs, wants, and cravings. We, as a subset of a species, feel glad being accepted and feel sad being rejected. Love and hate swift through our nervous system. The level of cortisol, the stress hormone, ups or downs when we assume we are being loved or hated, accepted or rejected. (Cortisol is one life-sustaining adrenal hormone essential for maintenance of homeostasis [the tendency toward a relatively stable equilibrium]. Called the stress hormone, cortisol influences, modulates, and regulates many of the changes that occur in the body in response to stress including blood sugar [glucose], fat, protein, immune response, anti-inflammatory action, blood pressure, heart and blood vessel tone and contraction, and central nervous system activation). That explains how evolution programs our human sociability: love thy neighbor. We are meant to be social and be comfortable to love one another. Love and warm physical bond in infancy are essential to becoming healthy adults. Therefore, it is so obvious and natural that a child draws his first lesson in love and affection from the family, perhaps, with little foolishness and a lot of curiosity.

A family is not only an essential unit of society but also at the root of culture. A little child wins everyone's heart and gets unconditional love and acceptance from the family. This provides him a lifelong connection and a link with the rest of humanity. Love begets love. Love is the reward of love. The family is the first setting in which a child learns to deal with siblings, to socialize with others, and to live with mutual respect and honor. Siblings matter a lot. Siblings remain longer than anyone else throughout life. Strong and loving relationships help to absorb the odds of growing up and aging, especially when conflict cuts to the bone. In a family, the child learns to display affection and controls his desire. Gradually he absorbs the values of culture to which he belongs. A family is also a stepping-stone for the perpetual source of encouragement, assurance, and emotional support, which enables a child to be escorted enough and to be ventured enough into a greater world and to try out to be what he wants to be.

The need for love especially arises from a person's quest for refuge from an environment that he perceives to be unfriendly, if not hostile. The world is indeed large, too large for us to feel comfortable with. So, a man tries to shrink the world that does not always treat him with indulgence to a small niche of himself surrounded by close ones whose company is comforting—like a little girl who picks up a teddy bear or a ragged quilt instead of many other from a roomful of toys in every night before she goes to sleep. Love is thus a little haven of refuge for him where his mother, father, and sister will treat him with admiration and praise him even if he is not so admirable or so praiseworthy. This is human life.

Love is a feeling of intense desire and attraction toward another person with the emotion of passion, romance, and sex. The love of the man for woman and the love of the woman for man—is one nature's vicious prophecy. The fact that love is only a heterosexual relationship that has sex embedded in it does degrade it. Young lovers need each other because they love each other, but after a while, as they mature, they love each other because they need each other. A sexual relationship is bereft of true love. Sex provides the emotional bonding so much necessary for relations to last and enables one to put up with small frailties in the loved person. Sex is like the salt in the food but not the food. Too much sex in love is like too much salt in the food, which could be a spoiler. Love is essential; sex is optional.

Love is largely reciprocal. It is a two-way dialogue. Love dies of neglect. One of the great myths about love is that love is self-sustaining. It is not. Love must be fed and nurtured, constantly renewed. Of all the human qualities, a warm heart is the one most valuable. Hate in the heart is the one least desirable. Make sure hate does not reside in your heart. Hate does not *hide;* it exposes its ugliness soon enough. Hate is dangerously *elastic.* Love others, and you will be loved. In sex, love is the chemistry where sex are the chemicals. When the chemicals kick into your brain, you feel emotional, filled with exhilaration and passion. Mental chemistry is a huge mystery. In love, you feel you are here, together, and for forever.

Unlike many other countries in the world, in the United States, the bond in the relationship of many features of life—parent-child, husband-wife, teacher-student, doctor-patient, employer-employee—is, in general, artificial, not strong enough for a deep connection or healthy enough for human friction. It is, in part, the source of rage, resentment and mental distress at home, workplace and society. People hardly value other people's worth, recognize their service, or appreciate their potentiality. They lack appreciation, hardly express sincere gratitude or courteous enough for a simple "thank you." In a relationship, when people feel loved and understood by the partner, both feel fulfilled; here, one doesn't try to be everything to everyone but everything to someone. In tangible matters, those who mind don't matter, and those who matter don't mind. Studies show us again and again that our relationships and attachments matter for our long-term mental health and physical health. Psychologists categorized them in three major types of attachments: (1) anxious attachments (feeling anxious in getting close to people and worrying about not being trusted), (2) avoidant attachments (feeling uncomfortable in being close to people and having difficulty in trusting), and (3) secure attachments (being comfortable on depending on people and being close to them). Around 20% of the people are anxiously attached. Anxious people feel to be close; they love to be intimate, but they are preoccupied with current relationships and are very responsive to small cues of threat in that relationship. They have a very sensitive alarm system. About 25% of people are the avoidant type. Avoidant people still want to be in a relationship but are not comfortable with too much closeness—somewhat that interferes with their independence. The majority, 54% of the people, are the securely attached type. They are warm, tender, and love to stay close. They are not typically preoccupied with current the relationship. They do not mind things too much; they don't have a sensitive alarm system. They possess the quality needed to be in the relationship. Overall, worries, anxieties, and insecurities relating to relationship generate not only heartaches but also heart attacks.

One physical manifestation in a relationship is—kissing. Observing the animal kingdom (kissing is commonly observed in chimpanzees and bonobos), some scientists hypothesize that the practice of kissing evolved from feeding rituals from mother animals to their offspring, where mothers chew and break down food in manageable bites before passing by mouth. Thereupon traditionally, kissing has evolved into a universal sign of love, affection, and gesture. While it is common that adults kiss babies or small children, romantic kissing isn't something every adult does or likes. Decades of ethnographic studies of 168 cultures found that 54% of the cultures have no record of romantic-cum-sexual kissing. Some cultures find it repulsive for reasons like mouth smells, they never brush their teeth, or they don't swap spit for fear of getting sick. According to kiss experts, just a ten-second French kiss can transfer 80 million germs from one person's mouth to the other's. For adults, kissing has been evolved in fulfillment of three vital needs: sex, romance, and attachment. Romantic kissing is in vogue in more than 90% of all modern societies, and for good reason. It is one very fun way to build immunity. Parents safeguard their babies from being infected starting from womb.

Women treat romantic kissing far more important when they are close to ovulation—in other words, when they're more likely to get pregnant. Kissing allows a mate to assess through trial, taste, or smell. It boosts her libido (sex drive). The biological reason behind that is that the male saliva transfers a dose of testosterone of the male to the female, which in turn further boosts her sexual desire. The flow of biological reactions during romantic kissing plays a key role in boosting the levels of neurotransmitters like dopamine (like dope, involved in craving and desire) and serotonin (that elevates mood and the ability to stay obsessed and passionate). It boosts happy hormones and elevates the level of oxytocin, the so-called love hormone, whose release during orgasm triggers attachment between couples. Romantic kissing stimulates the brain to release hormones that leave them, both male and female, a sensation of being coupled, connected, and bonded to each other. It reinforces the relationship. The male and female both endorse the idea that frequent kissing brings healthier sexual satisfaction. A long kiss goes a long way and lasts long as well. Romantic kissing is as universal.

Kisses for the breakfast early in the morning! Males and females kiss differently at a different time at a different pace and appetite, and act differently at different sexual intimacy. The male kisses in a way to gain a sexual favor, while the female kisses more to assess her mate, to test the waters, so to say. One survey was conducted online asking 308 males and 594 females, ranging in age from eighteen to sixty-three, mostly from North America and Europe. From it, researchers concluded that kissing does help people assess their potential mates and then maintain the relationship. In a long-term relationship, the frequency of kissing is one good barometer of well-being and emotional bond. Females are far more likely than males to insist on kissing before, during, and after the sex. Having sex is a big booster for males but not so much for females. A study indicated that women's happiness decreases a bit after having sex for the first time, while men's satisfaction rises. It is primarily due to sexual double standards, where society views sex more positively for the men and more negatively for the women. While premarital sex is now seemingly getting acceptable for women, men's self-image is climbing, in part due to the cultural advantage of masculinity. Men having sex may feel more empowered because they are living up to these expectations of what is considered manly. Interestingly, women are more attracted to men when they have only a 50% chance that the man will like them best, rather than those of 100% certainty.

Life has many variables, yet there are some constants. Love and affection are few constants that are innate to human life. A hug, a handshake, a sip of wine together, or a small talk may speak volumes. One study emphasized that hugging and kissing are more important to the happiness of men than that of women. In another study, while researching the biological basis of love in pain management, researchers found that love is the best medicine—by far. Love is one primitive reptilian system that does work really well in reduction of pain. Pain is one of the earliest primitive experiences going all the way back to single-celled organisms. Pain aids an important purpose by signaling us to avoid something potentially injurious. But if we have to listen to that signal every time we feel a twinge, ache, or headache, we will not be able to function properly. So, through evolution over millennia, we have developed a reward system that serves us to seek and alter our behavior so that we can win the rewards to counterbalance the pain. A mother gives a kiss to a crying baby. Love is typically a similar reward system that is activated by addictive drugs such as cocaine. The brain cannot differentiate the nature of the reward, whether it comes from a drug or from love. Soldiers carrying pictures of their lovers in the battlefield is just as common. Passionate love has the power to regulate pain and allied melodies. Love is a wonder drug.

The love game is easy to play! Truly, simple and normal people know more about love than those who try to describe it in high rhetoric, install it on a high pedestal, and invest it with a celestial glow. They try to create an impression of love. They do it so hard that they soon exhaust their talents. It turns unreal. The counterfeit hardly redeems. Hot love turns cold soon. Only true love survives. Love's labor is never lost; true love lives ever.

High level of love hormone in new parenthood fosters lifelong attachment between parents and a young child. While young, parents can perhaps show their love more by meeting the child's need than by repeatedly telling the child that they loved him. When a little boy is learning to tie his shoes, the father should rather insist that he should do it by himself than by doing it for him, even when the child finds it hard for him. Occasionally of course, parents may chip in when something gets too tough for him. The mother may help the child by doing the job and saying that she loves him. The child also reciprocates by saying he loves her. And when he says so, you stay rest assured that he means it. Sometimes you're going to have a hard time being kind and to even love—being too loving might make you the kind of person who can get played. So yes, you have to be careful about over-love. Strengths of love do not become the weaknesses of love.

Love is not imaginary; it is not real either. It is like a complex number—a part is real, and the rest is imaginary. For this reason, some scientists—biologists and anthropologists—thought it was futile to trace love's evolutionary origin, that is, when it was encoded in our genes and for what adaptive purpose. Some believed that the model of love, the classical description of love, was not older than six or seven centuries in origin. The concept came to the brain when men had workable language and had enough time to indulge in effusions of love in literature, poetry, and plays. The task was assumed by the poets and novelists to build upon the fiction of romantic love. They have tried to promote love through art, culture, literature, and plays. Romantic love was a form of fiction. It was primarily the invention of the troubadour (who writes the verse to music) poets of the twelfth and thirteenth centuries—they were the Beatles of the Middle Ages—who tried to capture the illusory ideas of romantic love in sentimental poetry. Many of the sentimental ideas of romantic love such as love at first sight and that true love involved suffering and sacrifice originated from such literature.

Contrary to that, there is no dearth of cynical dismissal of the value of love and regarding it as an effusion of fake emotions, unmitigated, pure sexuality with the veneer of an intense self-denying attachment. Half of the couples cohabit before getting married. They tend to have poor confidence in their union, more negative interactions (like withdrawal), and greater risk of divorce ultimately. Internet, speed dating, and instant social networking are such manifestations. About 23 million Americans use 4,000 online dating services each month, leading to 1/3rd of total marriages. These marriages are however more stable, according to one 2013 study. In the trade of love, dating is one important business model.

Rating the dating! Compatible daters who are interested in dating pay a close attention to each other and continue dialogue more alike. One study analyzed dialogue and the words in use especially the function words. Each word has its weight and energy, and its use appropriately gives the speaker an edge for right expression. Functional words (*the*, *I*, *this*, *that*, *a*, *an*, *though*, and, *there*) are small invisible filler words that tie our sentences together and that we hardly pay any attention to. We pay more attention to key or content words (*home*, *office*, *job*, *love*, *person*, *money*) that summon a specific symbol and substance of what's being talked about. Using the computer model to process massive data sets and discern patterns, the study could tell more (who was lying, male or female, rich or poor) about the relationships. The more use of similar functional words, the higher the probability of compatibility. Crunching daters' data, matrimonial websites use different models of behavioral matchmaking like the following:

- Use the algorithms based on past behavior and then extrapolate from similar users' behavior.
- Note when users contact people who do not fit their stated performances and then adjust for which performances seem least crucial.
- Look at the user's rating of the daily matches, which helps improve the matchmaking accuracy of its algorithm.
- Make matches using users' liking the same activities and recognize patterns among those to which users send messages.
- Match people by what they do, not just what they say.
- Support the prevailing opinion that older men prefer younger women and the older women, younger men.

However, today's online dating—call it iDating—may seem great for meeting a great many people in a hurry, but the digital romance may not necessarily be the one you want. Only, when you sit down, when your all five senses are at play, you know what you want. The dubious science of iDating, with all mathematical algorithms based on modern-day psychiatry cannot just identify pairs of singles likely to have a successful love because love takes time! You can't hurry the love!

A dater knows where the date flinches, almost immediately whether or not he or she likes the date. Initial and instant perception is a big deal to do with whether the date is ultimately decided as a date. A decision on a romantic relationship is most likely to have formed within seconds of seeing each other. Brain scans indicate that a certain region of the prefrontal cortex is almost always activated when a person has an immediate attraction for another. Biological evidence clarifies the doubt and clearly establishes that love exists as an independent emotion apart from lust. In an experiment that was carried out where some people were shown pictures of their lovers, while they looked at the pictures, their brains were scanned. The scanning indicated that some particular parts of the brain were lighted up. But these were not the same parts that were lit up by a feeling of lust. Here's the conclusion: love exists as an emotion independent of lust. Yet all would not agree. There are scientists who would still not recognize love's biological evidence. Love, they say, is sloppy, loony, mushy, nebulous emotion, not definitive like anger or fear. The latter can be quantified in the subject's pulse rate, breathing, and even muscle contraction. When they try to track down love, they get a hazy, nebulous image, which could be anything, even distress caused by indigestion.

Once you recognize love is the spirit and sex is the body in which the spirit is contained, then you are faced with the sharp question of which comes first—love or sex? This is like the proverbial chicken-and-egg dilemma. Sex is not a momentary itch. Darwinians would tend to put sex first because reproduction was the principal objective for the coming together of the two sexes. Looking at the adaptive imperatives, it would seem more probable that sex came first. But then how did love follow? The impulses of romantic love, which are often derided as bundling together of mawkish sentiments, not only came in the wake of sex but also survived the onslaughts of bantering and slugging and shelling of severe critics. If love was indeed a figment, as it is made out by some, it would not have survived as a universal human emotion common to cultures and creatures across the world, and so long.

Love and sex may not be synonymous. Perhaps it is also true that love without sex does not create as strong a bond as sexual love. But sexuality alone does not provide the mental and spiritual satisfaction that can be spawned by true love. That is why for a child, the family becomes the source of unconditional love and also of an awareness of the value of love. It provides a link to the child to an external world as his consciousness develops.

As for the chastity and love, the two are often described as antipodal in a sense, for example, that love outside of marriage is deprecated and seen as lack of chastity. Sex is sexier when it is immoral. Our moral hackles are often raised when we are confronted with love outside of marriage. The roots of such prejudices are so deep that our literature is full of stories in which a lack of chastity is ultimately visited with punishment of God. Sometimes the punishments are too severe to fit the crime. Such fatal errors are more popular than friction and are as elusive as ever. We are fascinated by the sex but afraid of it.

It is not just a physical relationship that can breed true love. Even friendship without any physical relationship (Facebook friendship) can ignite intense love. Love is a special type of affection based on admiration, warm attachment, compassion, and devotion. Yet some people believe that self-love is what is of importance and interest to us, being a matter of unending passion, and that all other love manifests from self-love. Intellectuals often indulge in this kind of sophistry. Science has so far not developed any mechanism to verify the truth. So, it is just enough to say that there are opposite views as well on this.

Beauty is the wisdom of women; wisdom is the beauty of men. The beauty of today's question about the relationship between man and woman is whether men can beautifully handle an intellectually equal woman sensibly. The oft-repeated jibe from feminists is that men still have a lot to learn when it comes to entering into the relationship with intellectual women. A large percentage of people believe, according to a survey, that men can handle intelligent women, but still a significant percentage believes that they are unable. A common complaint of intelligent women is that men tend to be patronizing and condescending in their attitude toward women. Deep inside their hearts, they believe women are inferior beings. But they will not betray their prejudices lest they are regarded as unprogressive. According to some women, many of the so-called progressive men who seemed to have liberal ideas about women harbored doubts about women's real worth. A man chases a woman until the woman catches him. He figures out then that those career-focused women would give hardly any priority to him. Perhaps this may be the reason why some marriageable girls hide or deliberately downplay the fact that they are higher educated than the men they meet because education could be a kiss of death. A situation where an intelligent woman was married to a husband that would let her grow in her own way as an independent woman would be extremely rare. Here is a typical confession of an unknown intelligent woman: "I gave up on dating powerful men because they wanted to date women in the service professions. So, I decided dating guys in a service profession. But then I realized that kings are to be treated like kings, and consorts tend to be treated like kings, as well."

One extreme prejudice, dated but not dead yet, nurtured in secret for many men: when an ant gets wings, it loses its head and jumps on fire. They apply this metaphorically to women. When a woman gets money and power, they jump out of their skin. They tend to become a man, and then there starts the Greek tragedy. But the mind is changing among the members of the young generations. Such derogatory concepts are hardly countenanced by the young minds today in advanced societies. Old prejudices are giving way to a much more liberal view—one exit makes way for another entry. The women are also increasingly proving their competence at all levels, in academics, in management, at workplaces, in military, and at games and sports. The younger men are often discovering that letting the wives grow as an independent being according to their potential is rather bettering their love across than by subduing them. Both men and women of this generation, a good percentage of them if not most, seem to embrace a more cordial and equal relationship in life than their earlier generations.

Counseling as to how a woman should handle her man and how she can understand him bombards the modern woman in unending streams, quite often making her confusions worse confounded. There are texts, surveys, and literature galore in the shelves of bookstores advising women how to understand the whole in proper perspective along with whether their husbands love them or not. Some of these go to ludicrous proportion. According to some of these tips, there are numerous ways of knowing whether a woman is loved by her man. The way he looks at her in a party amid numerous other guests can also tell the woman of her man's feelings. What happens if the woman is away from home on important office work on her birthday? Does the husband celebrate her birthday in her absence with a cake and candles? What message does it bear for the woman in case he doesn't do that? Does it or doesn't it signify the low of his love for her? What if after honeymoon love goes out of fashion like an old song and if that happens very swiftly? These and so forth!

No doubt many intelligent women find such tips to be shallow, cheap, and irritating. Today, a woman's worth is not determined by her looks or by her price like an ornament for sale. If her husband's love for her is ebbing away, no one has to point it out to her through such external indications. Likewise, no one has to counsel the intelligent woman to decide how to handle her man. Typically, such counsels, however, do not apply to men. If anything, these tips and guidelines bring home the message to women that in society they have still to play the subservient role in which keeping their men satisfied is deemed to be very important. These are the vestiges of the mindset of a typically male-dominated society (mostly in developing countries), which the modern woman will find anathema and which, fortunately, young men of the modern generation are fast coming out of.

As to the duality of love and sex, man, as a social animal, resolves it by neither overrating nor underplaying the role of sex in love. Sex is hostile to love. Sex is not hostile to keeping the bond of marriage intact, which is more important. Also, what is important is that men and women need to come in terms with their roles—their own and that of their partner. Love each other. What the heart thinks, the brain acts and the mouth speaks. This is the secret of keeping the marriage from dissolving. Where there is love, there is pardon. Love forgives the lover even his lust. The larger test is to keep the love intact through understanding, adjustment, and care for each other. Love stories, poems, and tearstained sonnets are all well and good, but they often sound counterfeit and cannot stand the reality of very personal love. Love survives all the oblique references, the satirist's haranguing, and the witty broadsides. Plus, it makes the world go around. Long live the love!

> Little deeds of kindness, little words of love,
> Make our earth an Eden like the heaven above.
>
> —Julia F. Carney (1823 – 1908) an American educator, poet, author, and editor.

Love out loud! Love and let love! Love someone who doesn't deserve it. Especially, love the unloved people—they need love the most. Ill to none, trust to some, love to everyone! Love thy enemy! No loathing but loving. Love them as you've never been hurt. "Hatreds never cease by hatreds in this world. By love alone they cease. This is an ancient law," said Lord Buddha. And love Mother Nature. She is the reservoir of all love.

1.1 Marriage

If there is such a thing as a good marriage, it is because it resembles friendship rather than love.

—Michel de Montaigne (1533–1592), one of the most influential writers of the French Renaissance, known for popularizing the essay as a literary genre.

[Michel de Montaigne had a direct influence on the then writers all over the world, including René Descartes, Blaise Pascal, Ralph Waldo Emerson, Friedrich Nietzsche, Eric Hoffer, and possibly on the later works of William Shakespeare, who was Montaigne's best reader. Shakespeare's plays "The Tempest" and "Hamlet," contain some elements of Montaigne's thoughts.]

Let me not to the marriage of true minds
Admit impediments. Love is not love
Which alters when it alteration finds,
Or bends with the remover to remove.

—William Shakespeare (1564–1616), English poet and playwright (38 plays) widely regarded as the greatest writer in the English language. Shakespeare is second most spoken name after Jesus while Lincoln is the third.

Marriage is honorable. A grown man needs a wife, a grown woman needs a husband, and so they marry. They marry to stay together and live together happily ever after. Marriage prospers and contributes to bliss. An ideal marriage is an equal opportunity for both. A marriage is a legal union of a man and a woman as husband and wife. In some countries same-sex marriage is considered a legal union—creating a logical family rather than biological family. The civil union gives them the strength as the primary bond to society. Marriage is the base of the family, and the family is the base of society. Marriage, as an institution, is so important in some society that it is considered as immutable as birth and death. In Indian mythology, birth, marriage, and death are "writings on the wall." Marriage is a tangible state of marital bond and interplay of love, sex, and beyond. Proverbially, happy is the marriage where the husband is the head and the wife is the heart. In the husband there is wisdom; in the wife there is grace and kindness! An ideal wife is a woman who has made an ideal husband. It's a match made for each other! In the U.S., about 2 million people say "I do" each year. "There is nothing nobler or more admirable than when two people who see eye to eye keep house as man and wife, confounding their enemies and delighting their friends." (Homer)

There are many beautiful theories to choose from the evolutionary biology explaining why various species, especially the *Homo sapiens*, have adapted a lifestyle where males and females pair up for the long term. One theory of love implies—never having to say anything! It's innate! Why do we long for love so much, even to the point that we would die for it? The stories of Romeo and Juliet and Samson and Delilah are not just dramas of tragedy but they also portray our real life. Love is real and very physical; romantic love lays bare the mysteries of our most treasured emotion. Love—it's what makes human a human. It is perhaps through marriage only that a man and a woman can remain attached to each other constantly, perennially. They pair up, brim with optimism, and vow to be fair and generous mates. For a marriage to be successful and lasting, the passion and intensity of love on the first day of marriage should never fade. D. H. Lawrence, the British author, says, "A man and a woman are new to one another throughout a life-time, in the rhythm of marriage that matches the rhythm of the year. Sex is the balance of male and female in the universe, the attraction, the repulsion, the transit of neutrality, the new attraction, the repulsion, always different, always new." Like the cycle of the seasons, the relationship moves from high to low and back and always renews itself. Domesticity and eroticism pull them in and keep them there. Love is a feeling that you learn to assume.

Sex is not love. Newlywed couples vow to love each other, to remain loving each other forever, and to keep their love from fading. But the love fades. Sexual desire and romantic love do fade over time. Scientists used to measure sexual desire and found that it fades around the seven-year mark. Romantic love fades even faster, around the three-year mark. Only 15% maintain lifelong romantic marriages. So, rekindle your love; feel good more like a romantic mate rather than a roommate. There are lots of good things in a long-term relationship: better health, longevity, mental condition, and overall well-being. Besides, a loving partner always offers a companionship, comfort, and emotional support in need. A romantic relationship is considered as one of the fundamental sources of happiness for the most part of our lives. With respect to wealth, especially extra wealth, research suggests that wealthier people tend to be more narcissistic about romantic love; they love wealth and get more pleasure out of their own accomplishments than relationships. In general, for people in a higher social class with wise reasoning style, wealth sets some kind of independent mindset that allows to reason them to 'shrug off' their romantic relationship.

Still, even if it is not for love, sex and wealth, you need something that makes the world go around. Marriage is that thing; it offers social, legal and genetic interest to the married couple for the common good. Marriage is a social norm and is regulated by laws, rules, customs, and beliefs. The ceremony that marks its beginning is the wedding. A wedding is an event just for a day; a marriage is an achievement for the rest of life. Marriage has a much deeper significance and consequence in human life. "My advice to you is to get married. If you find a good wife, you'll be happy; if not, you'll become a philosopher," advised Socrates [469 BC–399 BC], the classical Greek philosopher.

Marriage is not an overrated idea. It is the next half of your life. It is one long conversation punctuated by disputes yet nonetheless enjoyable. To solve these disputes politely and to make the marriage of two harmoniously, the patience of at least one is essential. A pragmatic man will always believe that the quality of a marriage is determined by its ability to solve such disputes. That sounds like success, yet to make the marriage happy, it is not so much how compatible you are but it is as much how good you are to deal with those incompatibilities.

Of marriage, the choice of partners is often made through negotiations, and in some cases, such as in traditional and orthodox society, parents take an active role in the negotiation. Marriage negotiation is universal irrespective of societies and religions, rich and poor, then and now. It is acknowledged and practiced in all cultures because it sub-serves the basic social and personal need of two human beings. Marriage provides not only the legal structure of the union but also the structure within which social norms are fulfilled and personal needs are satisfied. Some of these needs are the sexual gratification of the two individuals, a division of labor, the emotional need of love and affection, raising family, and beyond. Marriage makes them complete. In America, they are categorized into three chronicled models of marriage:

- *The institutional marriage:* Since nation formation until around 1850, the prevalence of individual farming households was the driving force for arranging the marriage that revolved around things like food production, shelter and protection. Lucky couples are those who found an emotional connection with their spouse.
- *The companionate marriage:* From around 1850 until 1965, American marriage increasingly centered around intimate needs such as to love, to be loved and to experience fulfillment in sex life. It was an era when people started moving from rural to urban life, and men started working outside their home, thus amplifying the extent to which the two sexes occupied distinct social spheres.
- *Self-expressive marriage:* As the nation became wealthier and its social institutions became stronger, Americans with higher self-esteem and personal growth, had the luxury of looking to marriage primarily for love and companionship. Since around 1965, the countercultural currents of the 1960s was

> primarily responsible for marriage being increasingly a self-discovery. Marriage became less of an institution and more of an elective means of achieving personal fulfillment.

Choosing a wife or buying a gun, trust none. Yet in ancient cultures, marriage was never a matter of free choice. The personal needs of the two individuals had to be accommodated within and be consistent of social structure and norm. Often, a parent, relative, or an elderly person in the neighborhood acted as the matchmaker who had to arrange the union so as to ensure compatibility not only between the two individuals but also between the two families. In some societies that encourage such arranged marriage, dowry is a common feature. Typically, the bride (sometimes groom) has to bring some wealth, in cash or material, with her when she comes to the house of the bridegroom.

In many countries, until recent times, marriage meant a legal transfer of a bride from her father to a husband. The bride had no control over her own affairs and even over the properties and dowry that the bride brought. The concepts of marriage underwent much change with the gradual emancipation of women during the previous two centuries. There were legislations bringing about equality between man and woman, and modern marriages now can be looked upon as a voluntary union between a man and a woman. Marriage is a social institution, and one human enterprise. Yet, there are vestiges of archaic ideas standing in the way of women's true freedom from the manacles of a male-dominated society. In many developing parts of the world, women are literally domesticated and are asked to stay home and rear children.

They are hardly given any liberty to function, or to refresh after their change of status following the marriage.

The rituals accompanying the marriage vary from religion to religion, sometimes from society to society within the same religion. Among the Hindus, the rituals of marriage are very elaborate. Matrimonial horoscopes are consulted in details, and the date of the ceremony is often determined through astrological calculation so that the very auspicious day is chosen for the ceremony. The prospect of marriage is given the same status of birth and death. In other religions, the rituals may be less. But all religions treat the union as permanent—one blessed by the divine being. Christianity treats the marriage as one indissoluble union between two souls. It is considered to be a part of the sacraments by some churches. In Islam, it is treated as a gift from the Supreme Being and is founded upon mutual love and mercy in the name of God.

Different cultures treat dissolution of marriage differently. In Roman Catholicism, marriage is treated to be sacrosanct and not to be allowed to be terminated easily. In the Muslim religion, it is not considered to be so rigid; if the union is not a happy one, it is better to terminate. But termination is often unilateral, the option being vested with the husband who can pronounce irrevocably the dissolution of the marriage by mere repetition of a particular word three times. No doubt it is a primitive idea, and it is unjust to give the option to only one side of the union unilaterally without the consent of the other. The trend in modern societies is that marriage needs not be treated so sacrosanct as to be totally indissoluble, but such dissolution should be by mutual consent if the couple finds the union has become unworkable.

"A lady's imagination is very rapid; it jumps from admiration to love, from love to matrimony in a moment," said Jane Austen. Matrimony is not to be entered into impulsively, unadvisedly, or lightly but prudently and seriously. "I kissed a hundred frogs before I kissed my husband" is one typical expression of a frustrated woman. But with the advancement of IT, modern-day matrimonies are a different ball game altogether. Gone are the days of dependency and those husband-facing wives. In digital life, love is redefined: casual and easy. It is the tale of the time. The narrow purpose of marriage is now a matter of chance and convenience, matrimony is a matter of give and take, and divorce is not an outrage.

They remain married—till death take them apart. Yet, marriage, which is still being expected to be an everlasting union, is really an achievement for both. Marriage is the merger of two equals. It's not a hostile takeover. Yet, marriage remains one very interpersonal battlefield. Innate conjugal affairs matter. We must need to take into consideration such behavioral differences of both sexes. The two sexes act different primarily due to how their brain works, not so much how their body works. The key to a better relationship, therefore, is the acceptance of this very difference as normal, useful and helpful. For example, if a woman wants to improve her man to the best of her sincerely, her unsolicited act is hardly appreciated or welcomed by the man. Another example, while women's emotions are vertical and come in waves—high and low, and then high and low again—men's emotions are horizontal—close and then distance and then close and distance again. Besides, whatever may be the brain functions, both man and woman are required to understand one thing that relationships are *mentally expensive*: partnership and intimacy takes a lot of space in the brain, even though much of it happens unconsciously. Strain relationship or uneven union, leaves the partners mentally cluttered, and thereof, with lesser capacity for focused thought. Therefore, an everlasting union is really an achievement for both.

Also, another factor is space. Too close a Skype-like connection is sabotage: if a long-distance relationship is overly connected, you actually feel further apart. The magic of the distance disappears. Laptop wives and desktop husbands are actually the spoiler in the game of love. Psychologists call it an intimacy-desire paradox. Yet the key here is the right kind and the right degree of intimacy. Contradicting the notion, one social study (published in 2016 in the *Journal of Personality and Social Psychology*) found that couples' levels of responsiveness—how attentive and sincere they are committed to each other and how superior and special they make each other feel—are directly linked to how much they desire each other sexually. The point here is the quality of intimacy: intimacy doesn't have to breed boredom or hinder desire. Similarly, if both belong to the same profession, situation, or environment, the mystic magic of unknown disappears. Too much familiarity, in fact, breeds contempt; hyperconnectivity leads to resentment. It is a double-edged sword. Therefore, for a marriage to click and be successful, it is necessary for both partners to keep a measured distance, to have personal space, and to understand each other's physical and emotional need and refresh it quite often.

Good understanding is the objective. Not working equal but working together and not thinking alike but thinking together are the kind of mantras to a healthy and constructive marriage. It works on the principle of equal partnership. What is now important is the capacity for adjustment and trying to understand each other's point of view. Both have to see each other at the same eye level. Don't make a fuss—that you'll be sorry later. It should not be like that, that within the marriage you owe everything and without the marriage you owe nothing. Both should be responsible outside as well as inside the marriage in order to reduce the illusion to evade marriage. Love is the answer. Love stops when manipulation starts. Love starts when manipulation stops. When it comes from the heart, it goes to the heart. You remember in reflection. You never renew an old account with intention or make a side-eye with suspicion. Mentally, one way to love someone is to backtrack, imagine that the love could be lost. Love comes unnoticed, but you will only notice when it leaves you *unnoticed,* and forever.

When people fall in love and then advance the relationship and finally decide to marry, the expectation essentially is that the love, marriage, and happiness that follow will last, as the vow says, "Till death do us part." But the flame of love recedes. Love stops where care stops. Expectations about marriage have risen according to their financial, emotional, and spiritual needs. Marriages have been polarized:

- The best marriages of the day are better than the best marriages of generations ago.
- The worst marriages are now worse.
- Overall, average marriages are comparatively weaker.

The differential differences are mixed. The divorce rate in the United States remains approximately half the marriage rate (45% divorce, 10% separate but do not divorce), which very certainly does not justify marriage as an institution. While some divorces are obviously justified for emotional and physical reasons, addictive behavior, intolerable infidelity, or irreconcilable incompatibility, some happen largely from the lack of effort to keep the life of love alive. Failed marriages that have been marred by negative or hurtful situation can often be rescued with trust, love, and actions of affections. [Info: According to 2017 study from University of Washington, more divorces happen in March and August than in any other months, across the counties irrespective of unemployment and the housing market.]

Why do we marry the wrong person? The short answer is because there is no right person. The marriage of reasoning of two persons, in hindsight, is not reasonable at all. Marriage is often narrow-minded, snobbish, expedient, and exploitative. People marry for all sorts of reasons: for love, for custom, for wealth, for power, for glamour, for status, for carrier, for sex, for present circumstances. That is why and if possible, what we really need is the marriage of feeling. The marriage of feeling of two persons is an emotional tension drawn to each other by an overwhelming instinct and intensity that tells us to our heart that that's it, that's right. Once decided, once the mental investment is made, a general tendency is to continue the endeavor; the longer you stay together, the harder it gets to break up. Sometimes, we grown-ups find ourselves declining suitable candidates not because they are wrong but because they are too right—too mature, too understanding, too balanced, and too reliable; with all our sincerity, such rightness feels foreign to us. Therefore, we marry the wrong person because we do not associate being loved with feeling happy. In our mind, we need to swap romantic love with tragic ones because every human by nature will anger, annoy, madden, frustrate, and disappoint us. And based on that and thereupon, and in spite of, we need to decide and commit. The person best suited apparently may not be the person who agrees to our every value and every liking. Sure, there will exist a sense of emptiness and incompleteness, but none will grow disproportionate and unusual, leading to a divorce. Better safe than sorry. Here, the notion of perfect compatibility is far-fetched; selection is essentially a matter of identifying the sorts of suffering we would endure and negotiate the differences intelligently and intellectually. It is our capacity to tolerate the differences with generosity. We all are human, and there are limitations to what we can get out of life and marriage. Yet researchers say, moderately higher expectation yields a higher return. One study covering 135 newlywed couples (interviewed twice a year for four years) revealed that across the board, newlyweds who had high standards are pretty happy and satisfied with their marriages, but those who had high standards but didn't compromise and work together or are more hostile to each other are bad. Compatibility is not a precondition or agreement, but an achievement.

Getting married and staying married is hard—and it's becoming even harder in recent decades. Now, here is the thing, everybody needs to understand that. When you pick your spouse, you pick a story, and that story becomes your life you live. You only realize then, sometimes after years of living together, that some parts of you and some parts of your spouse have virtually disappeared, say, behind the motherhood, fatherhood, caregiving, or a responsible profession. There appears new expression of longing and yearning—for connection, for togetherness, or for a sense of aliveness, which has nothing to do with sex, excitement or self-fulfillment. You feel alive, vital and vibrant. The relationship is complex. On the downside specially, people let each other down, people do not care for others, people break their promises. Betrayal comes in many forms: the spouse may be absent, neglectful, indifferent, contemptuous, cheating or rejecting sexually for years. Maturity in marriage is, therefore, essential, not only by the measure of sexual exclusivity, but also by the ways people respect, trust, love and care.

When you marry a person, you marry the whole person with all fortunes and faults. You take the good, you take the bad, and you take the ugly. So, it's important that one should focus more on the potentialities of the spouse rather than the shortcomings. As a matter of civility, each should take the vow that at least a few things should go unsaid today and every day. Then the secret would remain secret and the marriage would thrive happily. Privacy is one paramount importance in the marriage. The secret of happiness in almost any relationship is knowing what not to ask and what not to say. Conjugal intimacy thrives on privacy. Things that happen in the night are not explained in the daylight. What happens in the room, stays in the room. Ignore small stuff. Quarrels amplify misunderstandings. When pressure builds up, marriage experts always advise the demand-withdraw cycle: one spouse introduces some kind of change to avoid the current crisis either by skipping or distracting attention from the subject (avoiding) or by leaving the room or refusing to talk (withdrawing). Withdrawal is some kind of stonewalling. A sense of proportion should be maintained always. Each partner is to be a supporter rather than a slayer, a forgiver rather than a prosecutor. Don't be indifferent; be reasonable. Be rational than emotional. Don't create a mountain out of a molehill. No blame game, be honest in disagreement. No fight in the night. Keep the night tension free, for tow good reasons: a good night sleep and a good morning; otherwise, you spoil both the days. And if you fight, fight fair! Disagreements are inevitable and welcome. So, learning to fight fair is essential. Arguments quickly descent into hurt feelings by the way a point is made across, especially, an eye contact. Researchers from the University of British Columbia tell us that in the midst of an argument, looking the other person in the eye won't get them to agree with you. Making eye contact does exactly the opposite; it backfires. Also, one advice from an expert, a good marriage is not simply the "chemistry" but a good friendship, and thereof, how the partners handle the conflict, which requires some baseline adjustment. And more interestingly, take note of the statistical fact that most conflicts that are managed are never resolved. And not surprisingly, research shows that those who report communicating more effectively with the intimate knowledge of the partner show the highest satisfaction into their conjugal relationships. Here are some common relationship problems that psychologists suggest couples should avoid:

- Criticism (you finger point to your partner)
- Aggression (avoid too much fighting and continuous microaggression, claiming superiority, which is very hard to qualify and quantify)
- Defensiveness (counterattacking or whining)

- Contempt (acting like you're a better person than your partner)
- Stonewalling (shutting down communication or passively telling, "I don't care")
- Skipping small stuff (do not bog down too much on small stuff)
- Reasonability (treat your heartache as headache and not more)
- Knowing each other (know and let know the real you, both of you, and always remember you stay married out of want, not out of need)

Every couple argues, even the happiest and the most stable ones. Some arguments may be even good for building the relationship. But when quarrels become heated and when blame, criticism, or name-calling spew forth—sometimes unintentionally—plenty of research shows that too much of it is not good for any marital happiness. Criticism erodes love. Don't criticize but talk the disagreements while calm. It's not easy to calm down and think straight in the middle of the heated exchange, but people who do have a happier marriage. Listen carefully to what your other half says. Both need to learn listening. Listening is an active love. Highlight difficult subjects not when you are angry but when you feel close and confident. It will then come transparent how a small adjustment was enough. A stitch in time saves nine. A very simple act can save a marriage and can lead to a desired transformation over time. Social research curiously notices that the level of conjugal conflict does not vary much over the course of marriage. So, the good news is if you can get along with the current status quo, you are more likely to continue along the same trajectory. And try this! Be around with your spouse, engage in simple activities, and spend quality time. It is the physical presence that nourishes affection, intimacy, and unconditional love. Unconditional love and unconditional acceptance have no substitute in a conjugal relationship. [LOL: Never laugh at your wife's choices because you are one of them. Never be proud of your choices because your wife is one of them.] There is a lot of stability in conflict as a matter of fact. A little marital stress is a beneficial traction to the conjugal lifespan. And also, this is to remind you all that just because a relationship is not tranquil does not mean it is unhappy, and equally, a marriage devoid of fighting does not mean happily ever after.

Yet another spin! It's a fact that the wider the gap between what partners feel to be the ideal level of closeness and the actual closeness, the more likely he or she experiences depressive symptom and poor quality of relationship. This is true across the board demographically and at any level of intimacy. And also, it does not matter if the partners are closer or not—if they aren't happy, they aren't happy. You can't help it; they typically generate more negative effects. Then again, closeness in a relationship doesn't necessarily follow the more-closer-the-better rule. If the desired closeness and actual closeness align over the years, the partners are more likely to report a stronger relationship and better mental health. Partners who tend to feel "too close" or "not close enough" are more likely to break up.

The prevailing theory is that at the initial stage, "romantic love" serves more or less the same purpose as booster love that romanced them together, and then it is replaced by "companionate love," which is more a regulated, less passionate love that binds two people together with shared welfares and interests. Now neuroscience researchers found some twist in that. In one study, they took fMRI brain scans of participants while viewing images of their spouses of long-married partners to whom they claimed still madly in love with even after an average of twenty-one years of marriage. They matched these brain scans with those of lovers who have just fallen in love. In several key ways, the scans looked alike. They observed a lot of activities in the ventral tegmental area (VTA), which is part of the reward center. Partners in long-term relationships do experience such sexual enjoyment, excitement, and engagement that are intensity associated with romantic love. Hence, in these cases, "romantic love" is replaced with "companionate love." Both can coexist.

Love's labor never lost! A happy union helps to live longer. In one study, social researchers interviewed more than 19,000 married Americans up to age 90 who took part in the General Social Survey between 1978 and 2010. They expanded their work with other existing studies that have linked marriage to a number of health outcomes, from a healthy heart to slim waistline to longevity. They tracked their health and survival records through 2014 and compiled on common denomination after taking into account for age, gender, race, education and geographic region. The findings, published in the journal *Health Psychology* in 2018, reveals that people who self-reported that they were "pretty happy" or "very happy" marriages, were tend to be about 20% less likely to die during the study period of four decades, compared to the people who said they had "not so happy" marriages. In one study, heart patients who were happily married when they underwent coronary artery bypass surgery, were more likely to survive twice as much for fifteen more years, compared to unmarried patients. One meta-study, published in the journal *Heart* in 2018, combined over 30 studies involving more than two million people, reveals that (a) people who aren't married are at a 42% higher risk of developing cardiovascular disease and a 16%, coronary artery disease compared to married people; (b) people with happy marriage are more likely to live a longer life, in general; (c) the statistics of survival rates is reinforced when parsed by gender and marital satisfaction: (i) among the happily married, as high as 83% of men and women were alive fifteen years later compared to 36% of men and 27% of women who were singles; (ii) among unhappy couples, about 60% of men and 30% of women had survived; (iii) unhappy women who testified dissatisfaction in their marriages had no better survival rate compared to women who had no marriage at all. So, be wise, marry, live happy, and get some romance in conjugal life.

The science of love and relationships boils down to a few fundamental lessons that are simple, obvious and not very complicated—*strong emotional connection, positivity, empathy and sincerity:*

- *Strong Emotional Connection:* To maintain a strong emotional connection that is vibrant over the years, fall in love again and again, renew your love again and again, answer one critical question again and again, 'Are you there for me?'—with emotional responsiveness again and again.
- *Positivity:* To keep things in a positive note, psychologists always encourage couples to engage in small (not big or spectacular), simple, routine points of contact that demonstrates appreciation. Never act out.

- *Empathy:* Where human spirit is at its purest! For empathy, listen to your mind, not just your heart. Using high-resolution brain scanners, psychologists have shown that the brain releases three essential neuro-chemicals in the areas relating to empathy, of a person who experiences high satisfaction in a happy relationship. In a happy relationship, both tend to empathize each other and drive the issue, if any, to a reasonable solution instead of proving someone right. Each plays their own role in controlling their stress and emotions (keep the mouth shut) and try to understand each other's perspective from the heart.
- *Sincerity:* Ultimately, a sense of sincerity to build a happy relationship for a joyful and long life, is the motto. Man is mortal, is always in the mind. A tenure of sixty-plus years together is possible—not theoretical—but practical. Once got the idea, everything falls in place; relation stays strong, resilient and vibrant, till last years of life.

Monogamy is a problem! Lifetime monogamy is not a natural state. Very few animals mate for life. Evolutionary anthropologists tell us that only 9 percent of all mammal species—males and females—share a common territory for more than one breeding season, because male mammals could theoretically have more offspring by giving up on monogamy and mating with lots of females. Similar counter study on primates, other anthropologists claim that approximately 25 percent primate species—males and females—are in monogamous status. They bond for a lifetime in fear of the threat of infanticide (killing of children) which leads males to stick with only one female, protecting her and their offspring from other males. The human mating system is extremely flexible, only 17 percent of human cultures are strictly monogamous. The vast majority of human societies embrace a mix of marriage types, with some people practicing monogamy and others polygamy. There are even some societies where a woman may marry several men.

Sexual selection! Primarily based on beauty, female chooses the most appealing male "according to their standard of beauty." To trace the origin of human mating, one source of clues, lies in our closest relatives, chimpanzees and bonobos. They live in large groups where a female mate with lots of males when she is ovulating. Males fight each other to get a chance to mate, and they've been, in the process, evolved to produce extra sperm to increase their potentiality to be a father. From several other characteristics too, males have been evolved toward the competitive standard, despite the cost. A female mountain gorilla mate with a dominant male gorilla, sometimes for pleasure, other times to keep other females in the group from being able to mate and get pregnant. Thus, the concerned idea that the preferences of "capricious" females would dominate the evolution of entire species was obvious but squarely debunked—because, the beauty was no way considered a proxy for the health and advantageous genes in aesthetic evolution. While the best chance of surviving and multiplying has been considered at the core of evolutionary theory, many evolutionary biologists justly believe that there are so much of other forces also at play that the modes of evolution are much more mysterious and mischievous than that of simple natural selection. The human lineage has never been evolved to be strictly monogamous. Yet, even in the polygamous relationships, individual man and woman formed a stable relationship and long-term bonds—a far cry from the arrangement in the chimpanzees and gorillas. While some anthropologists disagree about what force drove the evolution of monogamy, especially over last six million years, they do, however, agree on something important: once monogamy evolved, the male care emerged far more likely. The male carried the offspring, groomed their fur and protected them from attacks. In our human lineage, fathers went even further. They had evolved the skill to hunt and scavenge meat, and provided food to their family. The steady supply of protein and calories that human children then started to receive, was the watershed moment in human evolution. It explains why the human have the brains far bigger than other mammals. Because, the brains are calorie-hungry organs, demanding 20 times more calories than other muscles weight wise, only the steady supply of energy-rich meat could meet the demand, thereby, helping the human brains to evolve bigger and better—and all the mental capabilities that come with it. In fact, because of monogamy, where fathers played a key role as a savior, protector and beyond, it then became normal for monogamous primates.

Today people of both sexes do have many options. Here, psychologists coined a term called, “psychological organ.” The theory is that it is more like a regular organ, except it exists in the brain. Human brain has been evolved over time to assess the environment and adjust mating preferences accordingly. In other words, humans have developed a flexible mating strategy: neither a strong will monogamist, nor a freewheel polygamist. (Technically, polygamy means multiple spouses and polyamory means multiple loves, having more than one consensual sexual or emotional relationship.) One’s strategy can change according to the circumstances relating to like, relationship, children, money—and the stake involved to pursue the type of mating. Level of wealth changes partnering preferences accordingly. Under resourceful abundance, a short-term mating is typically a viable option for both sexes. Romantic behavior changes quickly around the money and thereof, the mating option. Today, people of both sexes have many such options. At the forefront is Facebook! Facebook is a fertile breeding ground for infidelity. Facebook is foreplay that facilitates adultery and infidelity. The network provides you the platform, the means, and the cover to communicate with people—that you have no reason, no purpose, no business, to relate to. If you let stay in the net, you get caught in the net.

Historically, fidelity remains one important element that augments and endures the marriage. Men with plural girlfriends may be a cause of a woman for not loving her man. Man, by nature, is assumed to be as faithful as his options offer. In the wake of the substantially poor economic situation, lower-to-medium-income people tend to find a way to cultivate fidelity, sobriety, monogamy, and thrift. Very appealingly, monogamy is a convenient legitimacy that prevents a man from wasting time and effort on hunting new prey, deceiving a partner, or curing a broken heart or beaten ego. If you are smart, this is it—monogamy makes sense. Besides, a marriage vow should be "Yes, we can" instead of "I do," and chastity pledge should be "Just with you" instead of "Just say no." Remember, marriage is neither for better nor for worse—marriage is for good. It is a diamond promise—forever!

A typical taboo is that man is more promiscuous by nature than a woman. Man's unfaithful love is a part of a genetic male development that evolved to help man spread their genes far and wide. For a woman, the development is different; she needs to go through enough hassle just to have a baby and then, not to mention, nurture it. She is genetically programmed and evolved through natural selection to want just one man who will stay with her, love her, and support her to raise their children. To put it amusingly, a man wants one thing from a lot of women; a woman wants a lot of things from one man.

According to one survey in 2017, about half of all people in the United States and Western Europe will have at least one one-night stand. While accepting opportunities and having casual sex, the feeling of morning after tends to vary based on gender: women are more likely than men to regret casual sex, when men are often happy. While not accepting the evening before and not having casual sex, there is a big difference in how men and women feel differently: very few women regret saying no, while nearly one-third of men could have said yes instead. Actually, the notion that men are more promiscuous than women by nature and, as a consequence, that there exists a huge gap between men's and women's attitude toward casual sex, is simply not true. To prove the point, evolutionary psychologists conducted the experiments on men and women on a college campus. Students were approached in public with an indecent proposal of casual sex by "confederates"—men and women—who were hired for the study. A confederate perhaps says something like, "I see you here quite often and seem to be very attractive." The confederate then would ask one of three questions:

1. Would you mind going out with me tonight?
2. Would you come over to my dorm/apartment tonight?
3. Would you like to go to bed with me tonight?

Almost equal numbers of men and women agreed to proposal 1 to go out on a date. In proposal 2, women were much less likely to agree to go to the confederate's dorm/apartment. As for going to bed for proposal 3, zero women agreed, while roughly 70% of males agreed. The experiment also noted that men and women accepted offers of casual sex from famous people or considered offers from close friends whom they were told were good in bed. Another study found that women more than men were likely to agree to casual sex with a celebrity. Under these circumstances, the gender difference in venturing into casual sex evaporated nearly to zero. Social experiments like these are ample for old-school Darwinians to revise their theories in order to accommodate the possibility that our mating behavior is less hardwired than they have so far been presumed. Women's—not men's—short-term mating psychology may be assumed as to acquire good genes from physically attractive short-term partners. Overall, the conclusion can be drawn that while a gender difference can be manipulated, if not eliminated, by controlling cultural norms, it merely suggests that an explanatory power of evolution cannot always sustain itself when applied to mating behavior. Surveys bear this out. [Hint: In 2014, researchers from New York University and Cornell University dismissed the conventional notion that casual hookups—sexual activity outside the context of a romantic relationship—will drop you low with low self-esteem and depression. Another social study, the result of which is published in the *Archives of Sexual Behavior*, analyzed survey data from 30,000

Americans from 1973 to 2014 and reported that the number of Americans who had sex with someone of the same sex had doubled between 1990 and 2014 for both men (4.5% to 8.2%) and women (3.6% to 8.7%). Socio-sexually unrestricted people report a higher level of well-being after having casual sex compared to not having sex at all. In U.S. college campuses students aren't necessarily having more sex today than previous generations, but the culture that permeates hookup has changed. Developing a conjugal attachment to a casual sex partner is the breach of the social norm. There even exists a dichotomy between meaningless and meaningful sex, and students have to prove to "perform the meaninglessness." They have to prove that they are not emotionally attached to their sex partners, and that they care less about the other person. This leads to seemingly a contradictory situation, where people want to have sex with partners they're not interested in, and where friends are getting meaner to each other after developing a sexual relationship. The hookup culture is getting ever complex surrounding casual sex. The effect of casual sex is very subjective and is congruent with the individual's general personal preference: if you want to have casual sex, go for it; otherwise, if you don't want to have casual sex, certainly not—don't go for it.]

Studies to the contrary notwithstanding the assumption that men have substantially more sex partners than women are not disputed but rather passed as taboo. In the U.S., some statistics revealed men have a median of seven partners and women four. But such statistic is quite often an attempt to dramatize and distract from the context. Besides, men do quite often overstate the number of partners they have while women understate. So, in some surveys, when participants were apprehended by the fake lie detector, the gender difference in reported sexual partners vanished. In fact, women reported even slightly more sexual partners (a mean of 4.4) than did men (4.0). Analyzing what matters, one study indicates that when it comes to infidelity, interpersonal factors (sexual compatibility and relationship satisfaction) as well as behavioral traits (risk-taking, promiscuity) are the key factors than demographics. The study found that the rates of infidelity are similar along gender lines: overall 23% of the men and 19% of women admitted cheating in their current relationship. Sexual incompatibility, poor sexual function, and performance anxiety are main factors associated with the propensity to cheat. Cheaters typically tend to have higher incomes, more education and less spiritual values. The notion to explain why men give a good portion of their total mating effort to a short-term mating is that men are evolved toward promiscuity while women evolved away from it. About promiscuity, the researchers hypothesize that according to the established social norm, it is more damaging to the female reputation than to the male reputation.

What is the right amount of sex? It has long been established that sex is one of the few top human activities people crave for and that there is a link between having sex and feeling satisfied with yourself and the world. In 2004, one study covering 6,000 American adults on incomes, sexual activity and happiness, led economists to conclude that increasing the frequency of satisfying intercourse from once a month to once a week increased the happiness and joy to an extent equivalent to having an additional $50,000 in the bank account. But when they were randomly asked to double the frequency of sexual acts, the additional sex did not help them any happier.

Sex is not necessarily a volume business. On the contrary, their well-being declined, in the measure of energy and enthusiasm, as did their pleasure of sex. Men and women both expressed that their additional act of intercourse was not much of a fun. In terms of pleasurability, it seemed mechanical as if you are having sex for an external reason rather than for an internal urge that you like and want. It undermines the temperament and mood. While psychologists and therapists are constantly experimenting to figure out whether more sex makes us happier or not, nearly all of them warn against using frequency as a meaningful measure of sex lives, marital competence, manhood or womanhood. In one survey in 2015, researchers analyzed data on sexual behaviors of 25,510 Americans ages 18 to 89 and found that for about 2/3rd of them, which are either married or in a romantic relationship and those who want to keep a happy and healthy marriage and a well-functioning relationship, having sex only once a week hits a sweet spot of their play and pleasure. This may come, however, as a comedy or tragedy depending on how you feel about your sex life. Other study found couples generally get more sex in their first marriages than second. Finally, here's the advice from the expert: if you want to be happy enjoying sex, concentrate on the quality rather than quantity. And that too, never expect the pleasure over the moon, every time you have sex! Sex is like salt in the food, but it is not the food.

One survey involving more than 2,000 married women between the ages of 18 to 49 asked one question: Just how much sex do you get once married? The result was, "Well, it depends." Overall, about one quarter (23%) of women had sex one to three times per month; another one quarter (21%) get more than ten times a month. Age-wise, younger

18–29-year-old women had at least eleven times a month, and 30–49-year-old had 1 to 3 times a month. A vast majority (80%) of women said their sex lives were predictable, which had a pleasant ending. Nearly half said their spouse were their best sexual partner ever, and roughly half said they were mostly happy with their sex lives, and one-third said they were very happy. Yet contentment doesn't predict any overall sex drive. Many women said they regularly felt "in the mood," but many admitted that when it came to free time, sex wasn't "always on the mind" but would rather prefer an hour of sleep (40%), read a book (16%), or watch a movie (21%). In another small survey, researchers found that couples had sex, on average, once a week during the first six months of marriage and about 3 times a month by the fourth year of marriage. For many couples, though, the decline did not make much difference in how content they felt about their marriage. In Sweden, one survey in 2013 of 3,000 people by the *Aftonbladet* tabloid found that the Swedes are having less sex. In 2017, Swedish city councilor called for official sex break—an hour break in which people can go home and have sex—to boost health, wellness, and childbirth. In the U.S., another poll conducted by the National Sleep Foundation highlighted that about one-quarter Americans 25 to 60 years of age and married or living with romantic partner regularly feel too exhausted for sex. Nearly a quarter said their work schedules kept them from getting enough sleep and relaxing. Anyway, that's roughly the picture. In the meanwhile, masturbation, solo, continues to be universal. Among men, there is no problem; among women, there are about half solo and a quarter with a partner. Same-sex movement, for both men and women, appears to be on the rise or at least less taboo. And finally, as universal, people are always curious about the sex of others.

More or less! Sex feels better with "little more than a little less." In the doubt of more-or-less measure, here is the comprehensive summary of American sex life in a nutshell from the National Survey of Sexual Health and Behavior (NSSHB), which takes survey periodically on the issue. Recently, they randomly surveyed cross-sectional and population-based sample of 14- to 94-year-olds across the United States. It was considered to be the most complete study of its kind in nearly two decades. While some sexual features are innately rooted in evolutionary heritage, such as how quickly it takes men and women to become aroused, what scientists found is that Americans still continue to view sex *primarily in negative terms, unnatural, and less open, frank conversation.* Legal status, social bias, and basic interpersonal sensitivity weight in, as well, and muddle the mud. The technical point that centers on one operative term—*consent*—which is the legal standard for permissible sexual interactions, takes its toll in various ways. In situations where it may be legal to wear down someone, but doing so, it may not lead to explore a healthy relationship between two persons, be they of the opposite sex or of the same sex. As a matter of fact, in most healthy romantic activities, the situation turns in such a way where consent is unclear. Now, where things may go wrong, it will not only go wrong, but sometimes go ugly. *No-fault* victimization happens. As it gets complicated, the whole affair of sex act stays persistently deplorable, which affiliates them, both man and woman, to a sexually dysfunctional society, which is again, primarily due to limited views of sexuality, and the lack of basic knowledge and understanding concerning the complains and the complements of sex. The survey found that while 85% of men believed that they had had fully satisfied their partner following a sex act, only 64% of women concurred. This leaves a solid 21% difference in perception, of what researchers call an *orgasm gap.*

Conjugal love and physical intimacy are essential to our health and well-being. Neglectful, dehumanizing or quicken sex, may not be harassment but causes serious harm. Sympathy sex is worse than no sex. Rough sex is a rape, and a regret. When it comes to sex life, the basic oath to uphold is: "First, do no assault or rape anyone." Sex could be terrible or sex could be wonderful. It is, therefore, the partner's responsibility to be sensitive in each other's companion. This is the closest moment with your loved one. Sexual contact is one key personal communication of acceptance and social inclusion from those, with whom we are so intimate. Therapeutically, it is very easy a therapy—a therapy without therapist—for enhancing health, wellbeing and thrive. Having good sex makes you feel better, the morning after. Good sex is delightful. The experience is so powerful a signal of inclusion that it improves emotional connection, and balance relation. Intimate relation, conjugal love and satisfying sex, increases the wellbeing, strengthens bonds and increases the feeling of acceptance to even superior level. Good sex is a wonderful high.

Sex is so basic and the guiding principle is so simple, not very complicated. Sexual acts ought to be agreeable, pleasurable, and mutually enjoyable. Partners should advance earnestly and happily, not because one merely grants permission to the other. Try to treat your partner as if he or she possesses a precious heart and an infinite soul. Then everything else will follow suit. Remember, there exists something deep feeling about an individual giving you access to his or her body and accepting access to yours. Having sex is one such important event of emotion and satisfaction. Experts believe that the satisfaction gap is primarily due to the man's contentment to please himself without concerning his partner. Here, they recommend that if it is not working for you, ladies, speak up! Your (s)expectation is in your brain. A lights-out performance leading to orgasm can be a thunder-rumble of storming, not a pitter-patter of raining. Faking out an orgasm means you're partially to blame for bad sex. So, do communicate! At least send some non-verbal signals like move your body away if it doesn't suit you, or lean in if it does. Good communication yields better sexual interest. If you love your partner, then the sooner you speak up, the better. Some factors are at play in low libido: (a) lack of interest in sex, (b) lack of emotional closeness or openness with partner, (c) fatigue associated with a primary caregiver role, (d) having children under 5 in the household. The libido issue is with the man and with the woman, which is also affected by a number of other factors like stress, depression, medication, health, affairs, previous sexual trauma, pain with sex and relationship dissatisfaction. To fix libido, if any, many men and women are now turning to over-the-counter products, including lubricants, arousal gels, lubricants, massage oils, nutritional and herbal supplements, and vibrators. Drugstores are jolly well selling them right next to the Band-Aid and toothpaste.

In general, nothing is wrong with you or with your sex drive. Many drug makers are simply trying to pathologize sex, cash on you, and treat you for something that isn't an illness. For instance, the FDA announced in 2018 that it had asked several manufacturers to stop marketing laser devices for procedures billed as "vaginal rejuvenation," warning that the procedures are injurious, dangerous, and deceptive. Low sex drive could be for other reasons. One serious one is antidepressant drugs. Antidepressant drugs and drugs to cure bipolar disorders can be life-changing, and can be even life-saving; but, the long-term side effects of these drugs are *cloaked in mystery*. Especially for women, libidos are either dampened or eradicated, leaving them pathetic and vulnerable to their ability to find an appropriate mate—raising the divorce rate and allied social disorders. There was a Mayo Clinic study in 2017 that looked at data from almost 100,000 postmenopausal women ages 50 to 79. The study inference that if you are not enjoying sex as much as you used to, your sleep pattern could be one possible reason: women who sleep better enjoy sex better. The study also has a broader association with their previous 2015 study in which college-aged women who had good night's sleep had a higher level of genital arousal the next day. For the most part and for a variety of reasons, it is only a lack of sexual desire. Usually, sexual desire comes first, like hunger (a biological one), driving an individual to fulfill the desire. It is conceptualized as it emerges naturally and "spontaneously." Some people experience it this way: desire first, then arousal. Others, especially women, experience the desire as a responsive (in response to) rather than in expectation of erotic fantasies: arousal first, then desire. Both styles are natural, normal, and healthy. Neither is linked to any disorder of arousal or of orgasm. Some women may have a "low desire" that their ability to enjoy sex with their partner is dull and that they don't feel a persistent urge for it. In some extreme cases, their desire isn't what it is "supposed" to be. This is where default desire defaults. Yet, they don't necessarily judge themselves as broken, and seek medical treatment; instead, they need to have a thoughtful exploration of what creates lack of desire between them—perhaps a leap of assurance, a lift of confidence in their bodies, and a feeling of acceptance in an explicitly erotic stimulation. Interest in sex peaks during major religious celebrations, cultural festivals and long holidays—in Christian countries, around Christmas and New Years' time, and in Muslim countries, around Eid-al-Fitr. When people are happier, less anxious and family oriented, the mood manifests in sex, which correlates to the fact that there results in an increase in birth rates, nine months later (i.e., more babies are born in September in the United States). Couples, make your holidays merry and sexy!

How much sex should an average adult have every week? The short answer is at least once a week. Sex and health go hand in hand, and yet, Americans are having lesser and lesser of it. While the decline has been nearly across the board, gender, race, marital status, region, and perhaps across the globe, here are some prevalence from several reports in recent time:

- Average American adults have sex 54 times (married couples 56 times) a year, a little over once a week, during 2010 to 2014, which is 9 times fewer in frequency per year than that the average of 2000 to 2004. Highest drop is in couples with higher levels of education. The percentage of Americans having sex at least once a week fell from 45% in 2000 to 36% in 2016. Yearly sales of condom drop 4% in 2016, and again 3% in 2017.

- Fertility rate— children born to a woman in her lifetime —is at a record low since the Great Depression. As of 2016, the average fertility rate in the United States is 1.8, and in the world, 2.5 (which has halved in the last 50 years).
- Nearly 20% of 18- to 29-year-olds did not have sex at all in 2016, which is almost 50% rise since 2000. A similar trend is in vogue in the U.K., Japan and other developed countries.
- In developing countries, having a TV set in home is responsible for a 5% drop in sexual frequency, according to a survey of 4 million individuals from 80 countries.
- Complicating factors like #MeToo movement is taking its toll. Therapists notice shifting dynamics in both male and female patients—nobody knows where the boundaries lie.
- For a large number of women, sex is actually painful instead of joyful: one in five women, ages 18 to 29, experience chronic pain during sex; they report sex is a source of fright instead of delight.
- In the households where men do more traditionally male labor and women do more traditionally female labor, a higher frequency of sex happens. Any deviation in gender-role dynamics or sexual chemistry thereof, causes a disruption: mates do not find each other attractive.
- For both men and women, besides many health implications, the higher obesity rate is one libido-dampener—from self-image to social status to feeling attractive. Obese men are more likely to be impotent.

- Worries, anxieties and depression are leading causes of low desire; general happiness among adults over 30 years of age, has dropped considerably since 2000.
- Erratic work schedules, 24/7 on-call, longer working hours and higher work-related stress, makes it harder for couples to spend time together.
- Economic pressure forces young people to fall off the sexual activity. More than a third of 18- to 34-year old Americans live with their parents, where the situation tends to a stellar of sex life.
- Millennials in their early 20s are sexually inactive, twice as much than their prior generation, the sharpest drop happened from 2014 to 2016. Teen sex which has been on a downward trend since 1985, is now flat.
- The lesser frequency is primarily due to a cultural shift in recent years with more options for different kinds of pleasure—like internet and social media, playing video games, and watching movies and porn at home.

Here are a few helpful facts that you perhaps need to know how sex affects your physical and mental well-being:

- One prescription for better sex life is: Just do it. Have sex, even if you're not in the mood of sex. Sex triggers hormonal responses in the body, which brings you back in the mood. Get your partner in confidence. Chances are that you will get over it quickly once you start. So, make sex a priority and make time for sex in spite of your busy schedule.
- When it comes to satisfying sex life, how young you feel may be just as important as your actual calendar age. The interesting point here, in particular, is how old

you feel. It is as strong a predictor of sexual satisfaction in midlife and even in later life.

- Sex boosts your mood, relieves pain, sheds weight, and does many good things beyond.
- Sex acts like a drug. The dopamine released during a sexual act is known to be the chemical responsible for the high. It affects the same regions of the brain as drugs do.
- Sex acts like an antidepressant. Sex with condom or without condom differs. One study covering 300 women found that those who had sex without condom had fewer depressive symptoms than those women with condom. Researchers hypothesize that various chemicals in the semen, including estrogen and prostaglandin, which have antidepressant properties, are absorbed into the body after sex and create a stimulant effect.
- Sex can be a downer as well. The feel-good chemicals may go full throttle during the act, but some (about one-third) women don't get that. They often get post-sex blues (technical term: postcoital dysphoria), and they experience sadness after sex at some point in time. Regret or feeling oppressed can be a reason.
- Sex relieves pain. One 2013 German study conducted an experiment with participants composed of 60% who had migraines and 30% who had cluster headache. Having had sex during a headache episode, they reported partial or total relief.
- Sex calms you down. It relieves you from a stressful situation. Sex refreshes and boosts memory.
- Sex aids to falling sleep. It is more likely to men than women. Neuroscientists think that the part of the brain

known as the prefrontal cortex winds down rapidly after ejaculation. With this, and along with the release of serotonin and oxytocin, the body undergoes a condition typically known as *rolling-over-and-falling-asleep* syndrome.

- A woman who sleeps more tends to have more sex. Each additional hour of sleep increases the possibility of next day's having sex by 14% or more.
- People report they are happiest when they are having sex. But there is a catch. People can't or even don't have sex very often. So, even if you consider them really, really happy when they have sex, but as they don't get it that frequently, it actually doesn't affect their happiness overall.

Now, here are some social issues. Social research shows that if husbands and wives are assigned housework along the traditional lines of gender, the couple tends to have more sex than those who split the chores irrespectively; otherwise, a frequency of having sex 5 times a month may reduce to as low as 1.6 times if husbands do stereotypically all female tasks (making meals, rearing a child, scrubbing floors). Classically, if husbands do not do traditional female tasks, couples tend to have more sex: 4.85 times a month compared to 3.3 times a month.

Win some, lose some! A spin to the love life! Does more equal marriage mean less equal sex? Is there any trade-off? According to census data, in the U.S., 64% of couples with children under 18, both husband and wife have job; 23% of married mothers have higher salary than their husbands. Here comes the derivative of love with respect to income. The individual income status carries more gender fluidity: who makes the money, who does the house chores, who braids kids' hair, and who owns the home? A substantial part of adults under 30 desire, to what social sciences name it, an egalitarian marriage, meaning that both work and take care of the house on equal footing and that the relationship is built on equal power, shared interests, and friendship. But then the very equalities that lead to greater emotional satisfaction in peer marriages, as sociologists label them, may bring an unexpected snag on their love life. One study found that if men do all of what the researchers classically characterized as feminine chores like cleaning, cooking, and laundry—the kind of things modern women often press their husbands to do—then couples are likely to have sex 1.5 fewer times per month compared to those husbands who did what are considered predominantly male chores like taking kids out to play or fixing the car. The less the gender difference, the less is the sexual desire. It asserts strict sexual scripts that hurt their love life. In contrast, if there are more traditional calls in the division of labor, meaning a major share of the husband's masculine chores compared to feminine ones, the greater will be his wife's report of sexual satisfaction. Couples, in which the husbands do plenty of traditionally male chores, report a 17.5% higher frequency of sexual intercourses than those husbands who did none. These findings, sociologists believe, might have something to do with the fact that the traditional behaviors that men and women enact feed into associations where people prefer an established social structure of conventional masculinity and femininity. Male and female, as a species, are sending out cues continuously that appeal attractiveness to a potential partner, and it involves in an ongoing reminder of the difference, the sense of mystery, and the excitement that comes with the magic that the other person is someone special. When you know his all or when you know her all, curiosity lessens. Less curiosity lessens the sex. Mating, in and of itself, addresses such desire in an individual's role, where, in case of egalitarian partnerships, it is not necessarily the ones that drive the lust. She asks her husband to be forceful and rougher in bed. Alas, the result is comical. As a matter of fact, most of us get turned on emotionally at night by the very things we, the husband and wife, do during the day.

For men, study on sexual behavior found that more men do stick to pretty much one routine and are more likely to orgasm the when sexual act is vaginal intercourse, while women tend to get orgasm when they are engaged in a variety of sexual acts. The point here is that sex is more than just vaginal intercourse, and it does take time to learn to orgasm or ejaculate with a partner. There are five basic acts identified by the sex studies: (1) penile-vaginal intercourse (PVI), (2) solo masturbation, (3) mutual masturbation, (4) oral sex, and (5) anal sex.

While it seems to be considerably adventurous, vaginal intercourse remains the most popular sexual act. Humans are a few species that mate face to face. While men are, in general, more likely to reach orgasm during missionary style, women are not; they are far more happy if their partners adapt more than just one of the five basic techniques. Besides, nearly 90% of women say they are comfortable when they, or their partner, use all five. This is the paradox about sex, and one disturbing fact is that a startling number of women—almost a third—report experiencing some sort of genital pain during their sexual encounter, as against just 5% of men. Why are so many women experiencing pain during sex? Nobody knows. That's both answer to the problem and the cause of the problem. Imagine sex as a study of "love and hate." If you can visualize it (of yours and others), lovemaking is actually a sort of disgusting, with all the sweats, saliva, fluids, and smells. This is so much so that a group of researchers carried out an experiment on how people do enjoy sex at all. They noticed that people are able to get over the hate factor associated with the sexual act once they get turned on. Sexual arousal overrides the natural disgust response and allows them, especially the women, to willingly engage in behaviors that they otherwise find repugnant and feel pain.

When your partner has an affair! According to the 2018 national survey by the American Association for Marriage and Family Therapy, 25% of married men and 15% of married women have had extramarital affairs. Emotionally, an affair is an adventure. Man and woman have different reasons. Married man looks for more sex, typically any sex. Married woman looks for an affair to initiate, typically by temptation. Both man and woman portray an affair as a fun, and pretend it as a fun. Because there is no obligation involved on either side, both crave for intimacy and fantasy, which is not available in a plain relationship. Man is not typically interested in an adventure, rather desperate for affection. Biologically, man can get easy desired and aroused, while woman can't, even with the help of pills and therapy. Relationship is a complex game to play, after all. It is always easy to talk theoretically about marriage than to navigate it through. Very happy couples have sex 74 times a year (1½ times a week) on average. Unhappy couples lack it: one survey in 2017 reports that 15% of men and 27% of women had not had sex in the past year; and, 9% of men and 18% of women, in last five years. The decline of sex in marriage is due to a combination of many factors: health issues, presence of children, boredom, sleep, work schedule, stress and unhappiness in relationship. But the primary factor is age: sexual frequency declines 3.2% a year after the age of 25. Lack of sex leads to a lack of closeness, which leads to even less sex, and then eventually, both turn to resentment and blame each other. Sometimes, one is torn apart by a partner's secret use of pornography, causal relationships, virtual affairs, or even just ogling or flirting with another person. Lack of sex is so common in marriage that it leads to such blame and shame; and, by the same token, to be fair, an episode of affair doesn't have to lead to an end of marriage. Of course, betrayal cuts to the bone, but the wound can be healed. Once a mistake is made, an individual should be allowed to learn from that. People are fathers, mothers, in charge at workplace and holding responsible positions in society. Many of them genuinely care about the well-being of their partners even when they are in active affair. Some sooner, some later eventually, come to a sense and become sober forever. A marriage may not be perfect—whose is?—but the supportive nurturing of each other and working through the course, both can make the marriage even stronger. A good relationship is precious and doesn't happen overnight. It takes commitment, forgiveness, compromise, and most of all—an effort.

Your attention, please! Attention deficiency for both man and woman can take a toll on marriage. Common symptoms are forgetfulness, distraction, and disorganization. They are so common and so simple to make that they can be easily misinterpreted as laziness, selfishness, and outright lack of love and care and concern. Some of these disorders could have their origin at childhood. Half of the children with ADHD do not fully recover and continue to struggle with symptoms as adults. Others develop symptoms of their own as they grow up. Children with ADHD experience more disability after mild brain injuries than those without the condition. In the U.S., at least 4% of adults have this disorder. Spouses with attention deficit are often unaware of their own mistakes and get confused by their partner's simmering frustration. It's not because they don't love their spouse or they're lazy but because they are mentally distracted. The treatment for frustration tolerance can be physiological and challenging. Although some treatments often start with medication, typically it doesn't solve the couple's problem. Talk therapy is essential to clear accumulated resentments. Behavioral therapies for both partners are vital.

In conjugal love, a woman's tears matter. Man, be careful if you make a woman cry to tears. According to one new research, tears can send chemical signals to influence the behavior of another person, in general. From experiments, researchers ascertained that men who sniffed drops of women's emotional tears became less sexually aroused and, in extreme cases, might feel as if they had a cold shower. Evolutionary function of chemo-signaling in tears is very significant in humans as a species. Some experts are in the opinion that tears could have evolved to evade men's aggression toward women who are weakened by emotional and physical stress during menstruation. Because it generally coincides with menstrual cycles and because there are several other evidences that women cry much more during menstruation, it makes a biological point that it is not a convenient time to have or enjoy sex. So, while the man is guilty of sexual arousal, a woman's tears come so convenient in the time of need to reduce any sexual desire.

Surprising discoveries of an eighty years' study of health and long life in *The Longevity Project* indicate that when it comes to marriage, there are many caveats. In marriage, arithmetic addition of husband's happiness and wife's happiness is a good predictor of a couple's future health and longevity. But it is interesting enough to note here that it is the husband's happiness (not wife's happiness) that matters the most and is the better predictor of health and well-being for both the husband and the wife. The wife's happiness matters much less to her own future health and well-being. Their mutual compatibility, however, is a strong predicting factor for their children's longevity. For child's longevity, it is the single most social predictor while compared to early death due to parental divorce during childhood.

For centuries, the primary purposes of marriage were considered from a social and economic standpoint. The couple's emotional and intellectual needs were secondary. Enough attention was paid to the survival of the marriage as an institution. But in today's relationships, couples are seeking marriage as a convenient partnership. They want partners who can make their life more interesting. Individuals are now voicing more expressed relationship to gather knowledge and experiences, a process called self-expansion. Research illustrates that in such relationship, the more self-expansion people experience from their partner, the more committed they are and over time and for the sake of lasting relationships, the personal gains are often compromised.

Almost all marriages are happy at the start. It's trying to live together afterward that often brings the travails. When a marriage works, nothing on earth can take its place. A good marriage is good for your health and wealth, and a better marriage is even better; you thrive. But when it fails, the whole world collapses, upsetting all members of the family including the children. Children get hurt the most. And when that happens on a massive scale, the community itself is threatened. The rise of divorce rates during the '60s and '70s was a matter of great concern for people all over the world. As women were getting integrated into the workforce, a significant adjustment took place in the model of marriage. Before the '60s, marriage was an inescapable option for most of the women because of their economic dependence. Considering marriage as full-time employment, as women did, was no longer to hold good for the working woman. Perhaps it may not come as a surprise that in the U.S. in 1970, 40% of women worked outside the home, and now in 2015, it is 60%. Between 1960 and 2011, single mothers as the sole or primary provider have increased from 7% to 25% and that of married mothers from 4% to 15%, making it now a total of 40%, while the fathers as the sole or primary providers have decreased from about 90% to 60%. Women have moved fast into some traditionally male-dominated jobs like pharmacists, physicians, surgeons, dentists, teachers, lawyers, civil engineers, and software engineers, while men have not moved fast enough into traditional female-dominated jobs like kindergarten, prekindergarten, and elementary school teachers; social workers; librarians; and registered nurses.

Men need to push forward to train and to perform equally good the traditionally female jobs in health, education, administration, and literacy, the so-called HEAL jobs. Besides, if men traditionally of blue-collar jobs do not seize the opportunities in these pink-collar jobs, they will continue to lose ground in the area of dynamic labor market.

Within a generation, more families will be financially supported by women than men. Today women have advanced in education and roughly in parallel with men in the growth of the knowledge economy. The rising employability, earning power, and education of women are transforming the meaning of love, sex, and family. In the age group of 25 to 29, women hold a bachelor's degree or higher, 35% more than men. Typically, a single childless woman earns 20% more than their male peers. Recent attitude toward a childless or child-free (as some like to say) society is one huge demographic shift. Women are not obliged to start a family or, for that matter, stay in a marriage that doesn't make them happy. Almost 2/3rd of all divorces, survey estimates, are initiated by wives.

Worldwide, women earned 13 trillion in 2009 while the world GDP was 45 trillion. Women control nearly half the wealth in the U.S. The percentage of marriages where the women are taller than the men has increased by more than 10%—a trend that signals an unbelievable shift in marital and gender norms. There has also been a rise in the percentage of marriages where the wife is older than the husband. Sociologists and economists now indicate that financially independent women can be more selective in choosing their husbands and that they can have better negotiating power within the married life. In a materialistic sense, it is not just that the women win but the net effect also tends to be congenial and benevolent for both. Especially for happily married moms, they are more likely to remain happy in marriage if they have, in this order: first, sexual satisfaction; second, commitment and generosity from husband like expressing affection; third, good attitude toward raising kids; and fourth, social support from family and friends.

Matrimony today is a different game than it used to be. Marriage counselors suggest that you ask your faithful friends about your prospective life mate and listen to them. The aim is to find someone you know you'll love and care, even when you don't like him or her as much. Yet in the matrimonial match, years of research repeats one old saying: "Birds of a feather flock together," specially, when it comes to education and look. People like to marry people who have similar levels of education and look. Self-sorting occurs. Jack has his Jill; Jill has her Jack. Better-looking people tend to marry other good-looking people who are also better educated than average. Though social psychologists have not yet been able to account all certain factors that may explain why people pair up by education, it could be, for instance, that people just end up marrying people they meet conveniently in the college or grad schools. Many others meet in the workplace, where people with similar backgrounds end up being together. Or it could be the same standard of education that guarantees many other desirables like similar income and compatible lifestyles, such as common hobbies, interests, and abilities. In cases where educational achievements vary widely, it is the wife mostly who has less schooling than her husband.

Like education, race plays a role, perhaps even bigger. In the United States, in the past four decades, approval of interracial romance has swung in the opposite direction: from 3-to-1 opposed to 3-to-1 favored. Love may be blind, but marriage is not color-blind, at least not yet. A new survey of more than 1 million online daters showed that while taken as a group, whites, women, and older people are the choosiest and want to stick with no other colors than of their own. In the United States, from another survey, social researchers are surprised to know that single men

- are, on the whole, as likely to want to get married at par with single women;
- are more likely than women to be open to dating women of different race or religion;
- are prone to fall in love at first sight;
- are more likely to have joint bank accounts; and
- are more ready to have children.

For instance, statistically, men's greater inclination toward parenthood is due to the fact that

- more than 50% of single men age 21–35 want kids while only 46% of the women do;
- women want more independence than men do;
- women want to have their own bank accounts, certain parts of their single lives as their own, and personal space;
- more men (80%) than women (70%) do not care about race; and
- more men (83%) than women (62%) are flexible on religious beliefs.

Not only that, the statistics suggest men are more pro-marriage than has been typically believed, and women are less so than the stereotypes would believe it. One could argue it could be the inertia—single people like to be single! Whatever may be the case, here are a few points worth considering. Social researchers carried out one analysis based on online dating-messages that 200,000 users sent, seeking opposite-sex partners over one month on a popular, free online-dating service. The findings, published in the journal *Science Advances* in 2018, reveal that (a) men's sexual desirability peaks at age 50, and women's at 18 and then the desirability, for both, declines from there; (b) the age gradient for women declines steadily from age 18 to 65; (c) the result aligns with other surveys by OkCupid in 2010, where the survey found men from ages of 22 to 30, focus on women who are almost exclusively younger, and as they get older, they search for even relatively younger and younger women; (d) the result also aligns with evolutionary theories of mating where youth yields better fertility; and finally, (e) men are less interested in earning potential or power, they are more interested in physical attractiveness, while women are more interested in education and earning potential. The idea of the bachelorhood that began in the 1950s is still in vogue; because, physically, by virtue of both health and look, a man remains a man for much longer a time than a woman, woman. A man is old as he feels; a woman is old as she looks.

Women's right is a human right. Slowly it has dawned upon women that all those things they had learned about the women's right and gender difference were indeed products of age-old prejudices and are now actually not true. During the last so many decades, there has been a gradual change in the educational and socialization patterns of women and women's right everywhere. Studies have revealed that women are really no different from men when it came to showing their mental skills. The so-called gender differences for verbal and mathematical skills are now realized to be thoroughly misconceived.

My life as a wife! Post world wars, America produced the so-called modern independent women. Never before in history (across the board globally) have women had such degree of freedom of choice with respect to higher education, career achievement, social behavior, dress, and sexual orientation. Modern women are active in most activities. They control about 83% of all consumer purchases and dominate consumer electronics, health-care services, and cars. Ironically, with the achievement and attainments of women in higher education and income, the area of conflict within the household has aggravated. There are plenty of data that shows (a) positive correlation between success and likability for the men, while in contrast (b) negative correlation between success and likability for the women. This means that when a man gets more successful, he is better liked by men and women, but when a woman gets more successful, she is lesser liked by men and more so by women. A new study from the American Psychological Association in 2013 highlights that the wife jolly well likes it when her husband is successful than when the husband is not. A husband's self-esteem takes a beating if the wife does well across the board. He would feel as if he is personally is threatened and could alter his perception about his future romantic relationship. And interestingly, he feels worse about himself subconsciously whenever his romantic partner has scored a win—even if that is the woman he loves.

Most men would not feel secure with an intelligent woman who could steer her life and career in an independent manner.

Many of them felt rather intimidated and threatened in their presence. They would prefer an intelligent woman who can speak intelligently as a girlfriend but not as a wife. Men would rather marry their secretaries than their bosses. It's typical thinking of a man that when a woman has a scholarly aptitude, there is usually something wrong with her sexuality. At home, they would rather like to have someone who is tamed to accept husbands' authority. However, the social status that men will be the "senior partner" is vanishing fast as there are as many successful women as men. This translates to the fact that men now need to get used to marry up and women, to marry down. Yet women still are moving up and trying to marry up, while men are still moving up and trying to marry down. The two sexes' moving in opposite directions has resulted in a plethora where professional women are missing out on husbands, family, and children. There began huge loneliness in these unmarried women that no married man knows anything about.

The percentage of both parents working full-time has increased from 31% in 1970 to 46% in 2015 and that of the stay-at-home mother has decreased from 46% to 26%. Working parents are now a new norm. Even under the circumstances, as long as women are accustomed to playing a subservient role within the household, the areas of conflict are limited. This situation, in which women are gradually attaining a higher position in institutions and in the corporate world, warrants greater adjustability on the part of both and an acknowledgement of the fact that the marriage is a genuine company of equals, not an aggressive takeover. Yet a survey of more than 1,200 U.S. mothers tells us that most of them resent being at home because their husbands handle far less than their fair share of the housekeeping and childcare; they feel like single moms. On the counterpart, men with their traditional gender role, although slow to overcome their prejudices, have their age-old ideas about gender differences start to adapt themselves. The very idea that men and women shall and should be equal partners is only a generation or two old. Social change takes time, and there's hardly any time to adapt, merely a generation at the most. Subscribing to gender equality, the total hours men spent on paid work have decreased from 42 hours a week in 1965 to 38.5 hours in 2015, and the hours spent on housekeeping has doubled to 8.8 hours a week and that on childcare has tripled to little over 7 hours a week. Yet the sarcasm part is that while 56% of fathers claim they share housekeeping equally, only 46% of mothers acknowledge.

Marriage is now multi-cultic! Historically, marriage has been evolved with laws, cultures, restrictions, and superstitions intended to protect social customs and marriage as an institution. Today, families are created in different forms. With marriage expanding in an unimaginable way—intercaste marriage, interfaith marriage, international marriage, interracial marriage, same sex marriage—what might the next phase in this evolution be, god knows! [Info: According to the conference held in 2016 called "Love and Sex with Robots" at Goldsmith University in London, experts are making the bold prediction that marriage between humans and robots will be legal (beyond a reasonable doubt) by 2050.] What is the future of marriage then? Marriage culture is changing fast. His husband, her wife, birth certificates with missing father (donated sperm) and missing mother (surrogate mother), children of missing father and mother (abandoned child), brother, real brother, half-brother, and brother from another mother are all getting into the social norm. He changed his hat, and she changed her wig. Whatever the reason may be—marriage gap or divorce divide—the ultimate result is a rising rate of divorce among married couples. Statistically, a 40 to 50 percent of first marriages, 60 to 70 percent of second marriages, and over 70 percent of third marriages end up in divorce. In the U.S., the rates of marriage and of remarriage are among the highest in the Western world. One study suggested that Americans should get married between the ages of 28 and 32, if they want to avert the divorce, at least for the first five years. The rate of divorce declines as they grow from teenage years through the late twenties and early thirties, and thereafter, it goes up again as you move to late thirties or early forties (after about 32, it goes up by about 5 percent each year). By the late twenties and early thirties, people are now old enough to reason if they do really want to get along with each other to start a family and a lifelong partnership, which makes sense. [Psychology trivia: Would you rather date someone who dumped his or her last partner or someone who was the dumpee? Study finds that man gives a woman a lower rating when they learn that she dumped her last partner, perhaps fearing—after ex is axed, he is the next. But a woman rates man more highly when she learns that he had done the dumping part, perhaps seeing it as a sign of desirability.]

You cannot fight the facts. Facts are nothing but the interpretation of data, not always numerical. They are not a product of speculation, opinion, or theory. Yet sociologically speaking, high divorce rate stamped with facts, does not mean that people have lost faith in the institutional marriage.

Rather, they have ever higher expectations of it. It defines new idioms of "marriage love." Apparently, it is no longer the ring, the wedding, or the certificate that demonstrates the committed relationship but a joint bank account, a joint purchase of car and home, shared pin codes of credit cards, and passwords of email accounts. In a postmodern society, such actions constitute the ultimate materialistic demonstration of trust. The matrimony of conjugal relation has paid a high cost for going against a deeply ingrained cultural assumption that love and money, sentiment and commerce, closeness and caution are opposites whose blend can only result in their mutual contamination. Yet practical life and legal necessity have forced a rethinking of these assumptions. Is contractual arranged marriage any less of a marriage? Does a marriage contract betray any mutual trust? What are the rights a rent-a-womb mother has over the child she bears? Contemporary legal and moral issues like these are being constantly accused, argued, and tested. If the twentieth century is considered as the age of romantic marriage, one based on expectations of love and intimacy, then the twenty-first century is the age of postromantic marriage, one based on duty, responsibility, partnership, and, yes, convenience.

So, is the marriage better or worse now than they used to be? This puzzling question can be answered in two ways. Because of marital decline, marriage has weakened; higher divorce rate reflects a lack of commitment and decline of moral character that has damaged not only couples themselves but also their children and the society in general. Yet considering the marital resilience, the experience of disruptive marriages can also be an indication that the life cycle of marriage has evolved to self-expressive matrimony and to a respectable individual autonomy, love, and companionship, particularly for women who are more liberated now compared to confined as it was only a few decades ago. Americans today contemplate marriage increasingly for self-discovery, self-esteem, and personal growth, and with respect to love, in good part, as a mutual exploration in exciting selves.

Undoing "I do" is never easy! Once upon a time, not long ago, the man worked, the woman didn't, and that appeared to be the norm of harmonious family status. To a woman, "Will you marry me?" was the theme. Today much of truism has changed for the woman but not so much for the man. While attitudes about a woman working have been evolved considerably, social pressure on a man to be a breadwinner is still very strong. A woman who is unhappy in their marriages is more likely to begin divorce proceedings if she is working than if she is not. Before, whether or not a woman worked had no bearing on the chance that her husband would leave the relationship. But now under the circumstances, unemployed men, on the other hand, stand a greater chance to face a dual dilemma: (a) their wife will leave them or (b) they choose to leave even if otherwise they are fairly satisfied with their relationship. Because men have been culturally shouldering the role of primary breadwinner and because as their prestige and self-esteem are often contingent on their role as provider, unemployment hits them really hard. That is one primary reason why men without full-time jobs are more likely to divorce. In 2016, one survey of 6,300 heterosexual couples found that while all other factors remain equal, men who are not working full-time are 33% more likely to divorce in the following twelve months of unemployment than those husbands who have full-time jobs. In 2015, 42% of mothers were the sole family breadwinner and an additional 22% were co-breadwinner (responsible for 25–49% of total family earnings), according to a report from the Center for American Progress. Many contemporary social studies establish that unemployment, more than unhappiness in the relationship, predicts a divorce. Higher unemployment correlates to higher google search for pornographic materials, which social scientists interpret, people are hit hard to their core. It is still unacceptable for many men to stay as househusband and take care of housekeeping. In 2010, barely half of U.S. adults were married. [Fact: In the global job war, according to a Gallup poll in 2011, out of the 7 billion people worldwide, there are 5 billion people over 15 years old, out of which 3 billion need a full-time job, while there are only 1.2 billion jobs available. Competition for jobs is fierce. Layoffs and downsizing are facts of life. The "job for life" is long gone. According to the International Labor Organization in 2014, 75% of workers do not have a permanent job; most people work without a contract or are self-employed. It is one cruelty resembling the game of musical chairs where every year you have to face the music and every year chairs will be disappearing even at a faster rate.]

To marry or not to marry is a dilemma that rattles an individual as ever. How do you marry someone who won't stay? How do you get rid of someone who won't go? The conservative view is that the worst of reconciliation is better than the best of divorce. One of the reasons why there are so many broken marriages in modern society is that men have not quickly adapted to the new situation. Another reason may relate to evolutionary development: the division of labor in hunter-gatherer communities was complex and crucial to their economic success, where women had to stay away from collecting honey and hunting because neither was helpful for rearing young children, and for that reason, women were not given the opportunity to develop these skills. One-third of their life was tied up caring for young children. But now, things have changed. Men, for instance, often have a tough time adjusting to a woman's equal or sometimes greater earning power. A man hardly seeks advice on how to adjust marriage and a career. So many of them find it difficult to come out of their old mindsets, their old concepts about manhood, and their role in the family. In consequence, the working wife often finds life extremely frustrating, having to balance the needs of the workplace and that of the household. A woman can hide her love for the lifetime but not her frustration or anger for a day. At work, she thinks of the children she has left at home. At home, she thinks of the work she has left unfinished. Such a dilemma is unchecked within her. Therefore, what we need is a family-friendly society, especially from employers, which will appreciate the new role of the working women in and outside the home and help them balance both the ends. Men should also come out of their age-old prejudices and rewire their notion and ideas of manhood.

However, though women are still managing more housework and childcare than men, the greater hours of paid work that men do, typically, counterbalance women's additional hours of unpaid work. In many ways, it is also true that women themselves are their own enemies. At home, they want men to do some work and also at the same time want to tell them how they should do it. That goes a little too stretched for a husband. (Male birds are better parents in guarding the nests and upbringing the chicks.) When dads chip in child-rearing—helping kids brush their teeth and preparing meals—it flickers conflict, with the mom and dad critical to each other over how best to handle a task. So, when couples say they want to share parenting equally, that never happens. When you have two parents highly motivated in parenting, there are occasions to step on each other's toes. When women allow men to share domestic work, they should not insist that it should be done in their way and not crib about it when it is not. Frictions occur when such adjustability is missing. Men may be somewhat sloppy in the domestic work initially, but they are not always—they catch up. So, for all fathers and mothers, for all fairness and fair-mindedness, do communicate openly about parenting. Now, the good news is that when fathers are involved, for example, in playing with their children, the quality of the co-parenting relationship between the parents is rather warmer and cooperative, and with fewer disagreements. It doesn't necessarily spark domestic ecstasy. In gender consideration, it is interesting to note here that researchers find a typical gender difference in parenting—it makes men happier than women.

Surveys in 2015 on the roles of parents who work both full-time and part-time show that more pregnant women are staying in the workforce longer and that more moms are going back to work fairly immediately after birth and perhaps more hurriedly than ever. More dads are compromising about the time they spend with their kids even though opinions of working dads and moms are divided: 48% working dads say they spend too little time, 48% just enough, while 66% working moms say they spend just the right amount of time, only 26% too little.

At any rate, the paradox of conventional wisdom happens: the women hope men will change after marriage, but they don't, and the men hope women won't change, but they do. Thereby, the comedy of fears changes the dynamics and, obviously, the lifestyle of each, especially, when the marriage does not follow the conventional route. In the U.S., a study in 2010 found that there are about a third of marriages where wives are better educated than their husbands and that wives are the primary breadwinner in 22% of couples, what was merely 7% in 1970. Some sociologists are projecting that a matriarchal society is very near and the rise of women as the "richer sex" will turn men into boys while demoralized single men will take refuge in perpetual adolescence. A study found that men in their fifties whose wives earn more money are associated with poorer health. It is more so for the men in their sixties where 60% are less likely to be in good health when compared with men earning more than their wives.

Marriage looks easy like yoga until you try. It is an oversimplified message on a very complex subject. An ailing marriage can be a source of ill fortune. There is huge loneliness in a failed marriage. It is less in both husband and wife. Long before, the question was a singleton, how to save the marriage as an institution. Now people all over the world, not just America and Europe, started to make marriage more permanent and divorce more difficult. Getting divorced just because you do not love your spouse anymore is almost as silly as getting married just because you do. Love may be a dealmaker, but considering all other factors associated with the marriage, love does not translate to a big deal after all. Also, there remains a fact which everyone agrees, love is often bewildering and unknowable. You may never know, even in your lifetime, if you have made the right choice, or what would have been otherwise. So, give it a *benefit of doubt,* and also see the things from others point of view! You may not love your spouse anymore, but quite often, your spouse still loves you. Love still lingers in the injured heart. The bidirectional love may not be 100% on either side, varies on a sliding scale and regenerates over time. Also, to remind you that one single event in life (cancer, accident) could be a game changer. Your "go get 'em" attitude could vanish with a single CT scan. Love is a yes-no-maybe-so situation. You do not always marry the person you love, neither you always love the person you marry. Instead of running hurriedly to the court, you, if not both, try to resolve it coolly. Marriage and divorce that were once dictated by the potency of romance—the falling in and out of love—are now increasingly replaced by economic factors. One study showed that when the unemployment rate goes up in bad economic times, the divorce rate actually goes down. Sociologists theorize that it could be one or combination of a few things, like:

- Even though they are unhappy, they can't afford to divorce.
- Bad times drive couples closer together and make a stronger bond.
- Whenever a separation is made between husband and wife, neither is safe.

It is typically a lose-lose proposition. And therefore, divorce appears to be less of a viable option. No matter who says what, divorce is a man-made crisis, and it can be resolved humanly.

Try this! Try this in a very deeply personal way! Studies have shown that writing down *introspectively* on a regular basis (even on a temporarily on-demand basis)—at least weekly or monthly—can lead to a lowered blood pressure, better heart condition, improved liver function, and even accelerated healing of postoperative wounds. One study encouraged subjects to write for a short period each day about emotional experiences and found that most had been drifted to the topic of love and felt better afterward. Men and women both felt love, but they expressed differently. A man's romantic ideal is more likely to exist somewhere in the past in the form of a flesh-and-blood person he loved, whereas a woman's romantic ideal is more likely awaiting somewhere in the future in the form of a fantasy that will soon turn to be a flesh-and-blood reality that doesn't just exist. Writing poems and love stories feature the same merits that define a good relationship: honesty, generosity, open-mindedness, curiosity, humor, and self-deprecation. Social experiments have established that writing pleasurable personal experiences can recover mood disorder, improve health after a heart attack, reduce symptoms among cancer patients, and even boost memory. The benefits of so-called expressive writing are really remarkable. Many professional writers assert that writing a personal story can lead to a behavioral change and improved happiness. Try also this! If you can truthfully write down all the reasons why you stay married and all the reasons why you go for divorce, you will see a lot of overlapping, and staying in marriage surely wins. Divorce is not in the genes. It's an avoidable error. Marriage is a serious business; people have started realizing that lately.

Today in America, getting married is not as popular as it used to be. While a majority of unmarried people (60%) still want to get married, marriage rates have hit a historic low. Just over 50% of adult Americans are married, down from 72% in the 1960s. In 2015, the median marriage age rose to 28.7 years for men and 26.5 years for women, the highest ever been for both then, up from 27 and 25 in 2003, respectively. Census figures released again in 2018, show the continued uptrend: the median marriage age was nearly 30 for men and 28 for women, again the highest ever been for both. Cohabiting has become a norm in most Westernized countries: in 2018, 15% of people ages 25 to 34 lived with an unmarried partner, up from 12% a decade earlier. In America, in 2018, more people under 25 cohabited with a partner (9%) than were married (7%); two decades ago, those figures were 5% and 14% respectively. People are cohabitating more and getting married late. Also, today's limited employment prospect means they may have to move away from each other to find work. Fear of divorce is very real. These factors are keeping people from getting married. Typically, home and hearth are woman's horizon, yet polls reveal that it is often women, rather than men, who view the marriage as a trap. They are seriously concerned about divorce: 2 out of 3 say they are concerned about potential social, emotional, and economic fallout of divorce, fearing that a legal union would lead only to extra work and additional responsibilities on their part, without any additional benefits. In the short term, that makes sense, but they are exceptions than rules, and that does not turn the tide against marriage as an institution. The institution may be losing its status as a social obligation but its desirability.

A question frequently raised in the studies carried out on divorce and its impacts is whether a divorce has differential effects on men and women. And the finding is that it is in almost every way different. First of all, in 2 out of 3 cases, the divorce is sought by women. Second, in most cases, after the divorce, the children are in the custody of their mother. Third, a woman seeking a divorce, generally, knows her mind quite well, but what she doesn't anticipate is the demand on her time and resources that life after separation and as a single parent will make on her that most women initially find it difficult to cope with. A breakup doesn't mean severing all ties with the spouse. Both husband and wife, the wife in most cases, have to keep dealing with the ex on a large number of issues. One potential downside in dealing friendly with the ex, is that it holds you back from going into a new relationship, romantically. Financially, the breakup is bound to have huge implications. In spite of the financial support from the husband that the terms of the divorce may enjoin, the woman is largely responsible for the economic support of the children, and thus, their financial position is bound to take a beating. The prospects in such cases are not very bright either for the woman or for her children. The status of a single father is even worse. One Canadian study covering 40,000 people for 11 years, finds that single fathers die young, twice as high as other parents. They lack healthy lifestyle, less likely to eat fruits and vegetables, more likely to binge drink, and more likely to have cardiovascular disease and cancer. About 8% of American households—representing 2.6 million—are headed up by single fathers in 2013. Studies after studies reveal that the effect of the little bundle of joys of *parental happiness* is very little for single parents (even worse, those with three or more children) compared to that of their married peers.

Parents—both father and mother—have now come to realize that. Of late, more unmarried parents decide to live together, resulting in decline of single motherhood in the United States. According to data from the Census Bureau analyzed by Pew Research Center, the prevalence (a) of single mothers, which was 88% in 1968 and 68% in 1997, is now 53% in 2017; however, (b) of single fathers has stayed the same at 12%.

Being married is a status. It expresses your personality. It is one very civil way to demonstrate to the world and to the family, friends, children, and grandchildren that you lead a responsible personal life. Though over time whatever its social, spiritual, romantic, or symbolic appeal is not as it used to be, yet marriage still remains reserved. Only a little flexibility is needed for how marriage is defined. When it comes to raising children, study found that while some people—more than half—say that marital status is irrelevant in achieving happiness, respect, ethical security, career goals, or even fulfilling sex, a landslide of them—more than three quarters—say it is best done when married, doing the things together. Yet surprisingly, very few say children are the most important reason to get married.

In the United States, for six decades, there have been huge social transformations in the marriage differential between the rich and the poor. The more rich (and perhaps more educated) you are, the more you stay married. It is socially accepted and usually the fact that married people are happier than single people. This arises out of observation of the lifestyles of married and single people. Married people are generally noticed to be less stressed and less prone to diseases like headaches and psychological disorders. They generally do not smoke or drink heavily. The married people are usually happier by disposition. Some people, however, say that it is naive to draw a simplistic correlation. The reason is that married people look happier and may be indeed happier because they were genetically disposed toward happiness in the first place. They are generally content with what they have, and because of this disposition, they are more likely to get married and stay married. No matter how much the Americans value marriage as an institution or personal gratification, the very fact remains that they live single more than ever. In 1960, Americans remained married for a period of average 29 years out of 37 years of their life between the ages of 18 and 55, which is almost 80% of their prime life. By 2015, the average married life dropped to only 18 years. Even if the boost of post-wedding happiness fades after about two years, married couples remain more blissful than singles. As a matter of fact, people in relationships are so convinced that marriage is the only way to go (while singles do adamantly refuse). Typically, people who don't see their marital status are likely to change and tend to idealize relationships while people who are still open to other possibilities remain skeptical. Psychologists believe that the mystifying behavior among both singles and couples is based on the theory of cognitive dissonance, a phenomenon that was first described in the 1950s, which defines that if you are deeply committed to a belief system and have acted in such a way as to think that is irreversible as a result, it's often easier to alter your subsequent actions than it is to question the original idea. Basically, it tells that when you have made a choice and yet not 100% satisfied or have felt uncomfortable, you bend your attitude a little bit so that your choice now fits better with your new attitude (or to explain it in a very simple term, suppose you paid a high price for something, a bottle of wine or a car or even a fraternity initiation that fails to deliver its full 100% worth, you bend your attitude a little bit to accept it). In the case of a relationship, the more the couple feels that their relationship is going to last, the more they imagine more glad, more happy stories about their current relationships being married, and side by side, imagine more sad and more unhappy stories on being single. Conversely too, the more single people imagine that they will remain to be single for another long time, the more they imagine more glad, more happy stories about being single, and side by side, more sad, more unhappy stories on being married. That also explains why single people tend to find that their friends drop them when they marry and also explains why couples who break up often find themselves excluded by their married friends. It's all how people imagine their relationship.

Studies indicate that married men are less antisocial. Married men are less irresponsible, less aggressive, and less likely to do something illegal and as a whole are more social and more mentally healthy than single men. Whether it's the marriage that makes men less antisocial or whether fewer antisocial men get married is a chicken-and-egg dilemma. Actually, it is both. In general, marriage is respectable for men, at least in terms of lesser antisocial behavior. The data support that men are not random who enters into the state of marriage. Some men who are less antisocial get married and then become more social after they get their wife and then family. The data also establish a link that married people—both man and woman—live healthier and longer. While opposite-sex marriage could be a healthy estate, the seeming benefits can extend to other same-sex marriage, couples living together, the gay couple, and the divorced, for instance. Yet studies claim that married couples have more health benefits than those who are single, divorced, or widowed. From a medical standpoint, married people have measurably lower levels of cortisol, a stress hormone that, when produced in excess, can cause inflammation and chronic disease. Contemporary life science experiments have linked that married people are less likely to develop cancer, to get pneumonia, to develop high blood pressure, to have surgery, or to have heart attacks and strokes while the unmarried are by far. The results have positively influenced both policy and politics and also national marriage-promotion efforts stressing the health benefits of marrying and staying married.

However, other studies have discounted this, saying that the marriage advantage does not extend to those in troubled relationships, where it can leave a spouse less healthy than if the spouse had never married at all. In what researchers call an ambivalent marriage, where couples are not bad enough to leave but still have noticeably negative attributes, they do not get the many benefits of good marriages. Never-married people have better health than those who married and divorced. The study went one step further and cautioned that a troubled marriage could take a toll on the heart as much as that of a regular smoking habit. The final conclusion of these studies is that while the previous studies exaggerated the importance of the institution of marriage and underestimated the quality of the marriage, the fact now remains that it is the relationship, not the institution, that matters. When the relationship falters, health suffers. Many married people are known to have admitted that their physical health depends in large measure upon the health of the relationship. Just because two folks argue does not mean they don't love each other. By the same token, just because they don't argue does not mean they do love each other. Quarrels are dowries that married folks bring to each other. But it is true that the health and happiness of a married couple depend not on how much they quarrel but on the manner in which they quarrel. There is obviously a difference between a healthy debate on misaligned interests and acrimonious exchanges on trifle issues. If the relationship has soured, the heat will be palpable in the manner they argue and from their body language. Often insults and sarcasm are hurled at each other, causing an excess release in the stress hormones.

Today for women, making the decision to have a child is monumental. More than ever, they are actively pursuing their career. For them, balancing the goals of career and the needs of the home is a delicate and difficult act. Timing to have a baby is an important decision, naturally, and then bringing them up as well! Late children are early orphans. So, it is essential for women to plan early enough where they want to be at age 40 or 45 and then work backward. Alternatively, as it is happening, they want the baby without marriage, instead. It's in vogue and has become the social norm in most developed countries. A study asserted that these babies born to unmarried mothers are not at all the product of casual sexual encounters or that those unwed mothers' chances of marrying the baby's father are 50% or greater. In the U.S., more millennial mothers are single than married. Researchers who have been tracking for several decades about the decline of marriage as an individual's milestone or goal in life—love marriage and then baby—found that in 2014 only one-third of mothers in their late twenties are married and the number of millennial single mothers is actually rising. According to the Pew Research Center, a quarter of millennials will never marry, partly because they don't have enough income and partly because the marriage is becoming less and less respected. It is now at a historic high.

Marriage is a big deal. It still is. It still remains the best avenue for most people for making their dreams come true. Analyze this. About half of the unmarried mothers live on their own, and other half live with the man at the time of the birth of the baby. This explains why there was a spike of 13% increase in couples living together in the U.S. from 2009 to 2010, the beginning part of the financial meltdown. It was so much of a surprise that census researchers went back to double-check the data. One simple fact is that people are living together because they do not have enough money to live alone and that they are not going to get married until they have enough money—a catch-22.

Once it used to be indecent or even called illegitimacy. Now it is the new normal, perhaps even moral. Following a steady rise for five decades, the number of children born to unmarried women has crossed a threshold—now at an all-time high: more than 50% of births to American mothers under thirty occur outside marriage; about 40% of all births in the U.S. occur to unmarried women, up from 5 to 10% in the '60s. More than ethical, single moms who are having worse health conditions and getting married afterward didn't help them either. Single mothers are facing poorer health in midlife than married mothers. Researchers hypothesize that it has to do with the stress of raising children alone while at the same time struggling income against stiff economic challenges.

Sexual revolution or sexual renaissance! In the U.S., the years between 1968 and 1974 were the time when women's movement took place. The movement focused on feminine mystique on transforming women's personal consciousness. This was also the time for changing expectations about women's role. Young women who would have been or wanted to be housewives changed their role abruptly. This was also the time where men were still trying to come to sense with the new realities of life. Men dragged to respond; many clung to their old-fashioned role as long as they could. Naturally, this was a very turbulent and disturbing time for the families in which a very large number of young children saw their homes breaking up. For women, it was not only the slow dying of the old concepts of gender differences that brought women out of their homes but other economic factors as well. During the '80s, the earning capacity of young families declined considerably. This compelled both to share the economic burden. At the same time, given the option, most women wanted not to neglect the household but manage both the pressure of workplace and the home. None perhaps wanted the child to be reared by a stranger. But it was indeed difficult to juggle both the home and the workplace. The inevitable consequence was a decision to defer the coming of the child.

Many such women thought they would opt for the baby after some years of work, which would give them both financial stability as well as a reasonable status in the workplace. But what was the ideal time for having the baby? Many often realized that they could have both, the work and the baby. Many of them believed they could wait till they were forty but ultimately came to grief when they found that it was too late. Sadly, biology was unforgiving, and so was corporate and industrial culture. There are certain truths about the woman body that nobody told them.

Studies after studies caution that women who give birth after age 40 face a higher risk of having an autistic child, regardless of the father's age. Another study found that pregnant women are as much as 3 times as likely to miscarry when the father is over 35 compared to as when he's 25 or younger and that the risk of autism among children is up to 6 times as much when the father is 40 or older as opposed to when he is 29 or younger—here the mother's age was not relevant. Women who give birth after age 33 are more likely to live longer than those who stopped before age 30. The overall risk for a child developing autism or schizophrenia to a father older than 40 is in the range of 2%. The probable reasons are, researchers say, the change in the quality of sperms that occur as men grow older. Use of steroids of any type pose a special threat: it hinders testosterone production in men, leading to a terrible withdrawal problem. [Hint: The quality of sperms is measured two ways: (a) concentration of sperm and (b) total sperm count per ejaculation. Sperm count (or sperm concentration) is the number of sperms per milliliter in man's ejaculated semen, which is over 15 million sperms per milliliter for a normal healthy man, according to the WHO. Total sperm count is the sperm count (or sperm concentration) multiplied with volume. A man needs to produce at least 18 million sperm cells for a woman to successfully conceive. Infertility may have some side effects like a higher risk of developing brain, prostate and testicular tumors, as well as melanoma and lymphoma. One study of 5,177 men finds that those with low sperm counts are 20% more likely to have low testosterone levels, more body fat, higher blood pressure, more "bad" cholesterol and persistent metabolic syndrome that increases the risk of developing diabetes, heart disease and stroke. Both counts are rapidly declining in Western countries. In one estimate, it is a drop of up to 38% in concentration. Another study in 2017 reveals that sperm counts among men in Western countries, including men in North America, Europe, Australia, and New Zealand, have dropped substantially from 1973 to 2011 by more than 50% in both sperm concentration and total sperm count. Sperm count is still considered the best measure of male fertility. There are numerous factors—from lower levels of physical activity to exposure to environmental chemicals—contributing to biological factors. But one that stands out clearly matches up with increased TV viewing. Men who view TV 20 hours or more a week may risk on an average 44% lower concentration than that of men who view less. Most physically active men enjoy up to a 73% higher sperm count than those who were more sedentary. Study asserts that more active and less TV is associated with higher sperm concentration and higher sperm count for the young men, overall.] Sperm boosters: (a) exercise, but not too much; (b) avoid sedentary, stay fit and slim; (c) limit TV viewing; (d) avoid STDs; (e) quit smoking; (f) limit alcohol; (g) eat food that contains zinc, like red meat, oysters, nuts and beans; and (i) keep testicles cool - avoid tight underwear and hot baths. [Info: To check if sperm level increases wearing boxers, after a period of wearing tighter underwear (briefs), researchers from the Harvard Public Health, carried out one experiment collecting data from 656 men who were part of the infertility treatment program at Massachusetts General Hospital between 2000 and 2017. Based on the typical cycle of sperm production, researchers asked participants to wear boxers for about three months, after a period of wearing tighter options like briefs or jockeys. Researchers find that 53% of men had roughly 25% higher sperm concentrations, 17% higher total sperm counts and 33% higher motile sperm counts compared to men who wear tighter types of undergarments. In their report published in the journal *Human Reproduction* in 2018, researchers underlined that tighter underwear style results to increase scrotal temperature, a hindrance to sperm production.]

Coming back to the very same important question again, what is the ideal time for having a child? Fifty years ago, such a question was irrelevant. But now, it is no longer so. The median age of first-time mothers increased steadily during the preceding 30 years to 25.1 years in 2002 in the U.S. It is an all-time high for the nation. Fertility of a woman peaks between late teens and early thirties; it is relatively constant during the late teens, twenties, and early thirties. But that's not to say conception is guaranteed; even for a healthy thirty-year-old woman, the odds of getting pregnant during any specific ovulation cycle are just 20%, which means that 4 out of 5 women have to try the next month. While it is not clear for the most part why fertility starts falling at 35, research suggests that mitochondrial function within the egg might diminish with age, causing chromosome abnormalities. Even if the egg is perfectly healthy, other lifestyle factors ranging from smoking to obesity to stress to age could play a role in the overall quality of the "intrauterine environment."

Today many women are relieved from the financial dependence of their husband. This socioeconomic change reflects in all aspects of marriage including the time to have a baby. Building up a career is no more a male prerogative today. But the truth is that after a certain time, the hands of the clock cannot be moved back. It is one thing, for instance, of a 29-year-old woman whose fallopian tube had a blockage. The doctor could set it right; but for a woman who has crossed 40, it is totally a different matter. Surveys found that more than ½ of 35+-year-old career women are childless. Between 1/3 and 1/2 of 40+-year-old professional women are childless. The number of childless women aged 40 to 44 has doubled in the past 30 years from 1976 to 2006. Nearly half of women (47.6%) between 15 and 44 had no kids in 2014, up from 46.5% in 2012. Nearly half of women between 25 and 29 were childless in 2014, which is an all-time high. As of 2013, the general fertility rate—measured by the average number of babies of women between 15 and 44 have over their lifetimes—had fallen for 6 straight years to 1.86.

In 2010, among corporate executives who earn $100,000 or more, half the women did not have children compared with only 10% of the men. The open secret is the fact that the more successful the woman is, the less successful she is to find a husband or have a child of her own, while for the men, the reverse is the case. The woman has a lot of money to make a home, but no child. They usually know that their fertility declines with age, but they just don't realize how much and how fast. After 42, the chance of her having a baby using her own eggs, even with advanced medical help, is less than 10%. At age 40, half of her eggs are chromosomally abnormal; by 42, it jumps to 90%. These are the women who opt to wait to have a child, but they waited too long. The outcome is shocking and devastating—a glaring failure to bear a child! Medical technology does not help; even after many years of fertility treatments, the only pea on the pod is absent. You remain in a family of two. The silence settles down, but the grief continues through the dark nights of constant sorrow and deep cramps and meanders you go through every single night for the rest of your stupid life.

To be a woman, childlessness is a private sorrow. Childlessness signifies a rolling loss into the future. It means no children and no grandchildren. Childlessness pressures many women to remain unvoiced about their struggle. They hardly resist tears at the sight of a new mother pushing a stroller or control anger toward friends who innocently invite them to a baby shower, or even argue with their own parents, who have not accepted that they will never be grandparents—for when a child is born, so born the grandparents. The grief comes in layers of bitterness, and the regret, beyond the silence of sorrow! Like a chronic back pain, the guilt never goes away. She is the killer of her own child. She slowly learns to deal with it. She larks in the dark and cries alone in the night. The child could have been nature's gift; the child could have been a baby of her own!

What then is the solution? Should women return to the '50s? Should women settle in marriage soon after graduation and have a baby? Of course, not! The hands of the clock cannot thus be put back. But the early twenties, everybody acknowledges, is not the ideal time for the baby. This is the time to put in hard work at the workplace for the advancement of career, like the menfolk. So, specialists recommend the late twenties as the right time. This is the time when women should take a break from work for having babies. There will be enough time to catch up and focus on the career later.

These factors along with the steep competitive world facilitated by new technology have given rise to many difficult choices for the younger generation. By being better informed about the experiences of others and of the consequences of their decisions, they still find the choice of getting married and having children a difficult one to make. Job, marriage, and children are three big-ticket items. To take a decision whether a woman should have her family when she is in her early twenties or in her late twenties, one has to reckon with many factors. Options regarding her investments and starting and changing careers are wider when she is in her early twenties. Approximately, twenty-four is a prudent age for women to marry. A younger mother has more time in the bank (including the life herself), more time to conceive successfully, and more time to start, restart, or change careers when she is ready. For example, when her child is eighteen, she will be only forty-four with grandchildren at eyesight. But on the downside, she will have lost a few years in her career, so she will either have to nurture a new life while nurturing a fledgling career or return, years later, to an entry-level position while her school friends have moved on. One survey indicated that married moms with kids who lost their jobs between 2007 and 2009 had a 31% lower chance of finding a new job than married fathers with kids. Approximately 40% of working mothers say being a parent makes it harder to advance in their careers, compared to 20% of fathers. The proportion of stay-at-home dads though doubled in the past decade, but it still remains low at 3.4%. Stereotype hiring decisions still appear to toll the motherhood penalty.

That's the story of the haves who have money and resource. Now is the story of the have-nots. The financial instability—like unemployment, job loss, and recession—has dramatically reshaped women's childbearing desires. Survey shows that 3 out of 4 women said that with the dismal economy the way it is, they couldn't afford to have a baby now. Less than half said that they plan to postpone or reduce their childbearing—again because of the economy. The number of men who opted to have vasectomy procedures spiked during the Great Recession from 3.9% of men in 2006 to 4.4% in 2010, meaning an unintended 150,000 to 180,000 men per year had vasectomies in each year of the recession. According to one study released by the Urban Institute in 2014, 1 in 3 Americans faced debt collectors: they had debts and unpaid bills that had been reported to collection agencies. Nothing stresses a marriage like money trouble. When MONEY surveyed more than 1,000 married Americans in 2014, they found that money was the biggest cause of conflict for couples, with 70% of respondents arguing about finance, above and beyond of other matters including even sex. In fact, 60% of the participants said they checked their bank balances more often and were mindful about it.

The far-reaching development that has fueled much of the changes is that of women flooding the workplace and thereby the emergence of the new-age woman. This leads to a natural query as to why women are compelled to work in today's situation, while even a few years back, it was an option, not a compulsion. Reasons for the changed equations in the nuclear families are many. But the very important one can be found by looking at the changed definition of womanhood in today's world. Women today are eager to carve out an identity for themselves in more meaningful roles apart from the ones they continue to play at home. Tomorrow it will be even more.

They want to feel more fulfilled and to expand their board horizons. Men too have become supportive of this sunny idea. And thus, it has given rise to the new-age woman who takes pride in her ability to multitask and often excels both at home and outside.

However, apart from these elusive issues, there have also been more imminent economic ones. A look at the rise in price index vis-à-vis the rise in average income tells us that today, in most of the U.S., it is no longer possible to support a middle-class family on one income alone. This isn't a question of having enough of the luxuries in life. It is in most cases a question of having enough to get by the basics. Only in the last generation, the home price has risen twice as fast for families with young children. This is due to the lack of confidence in the public schools, leaving millions of families to settle that the only way to ensure their children's safety and quality education is to take up a home in a good school district. That means, in most of the cities, paying more for the family homes. For instance, an average home mortgage has been doubled in just less than twenty years. There are plenty of mothers who, for the sake of their families, try to find a way to stay home at least for a few years. But there are plenty more who decide that the cost is just too high, and the choice of whether to stay home is no choice at all. This has made most mothers come out of the traditional domain of household work and prove the point by earning to support the family as well.

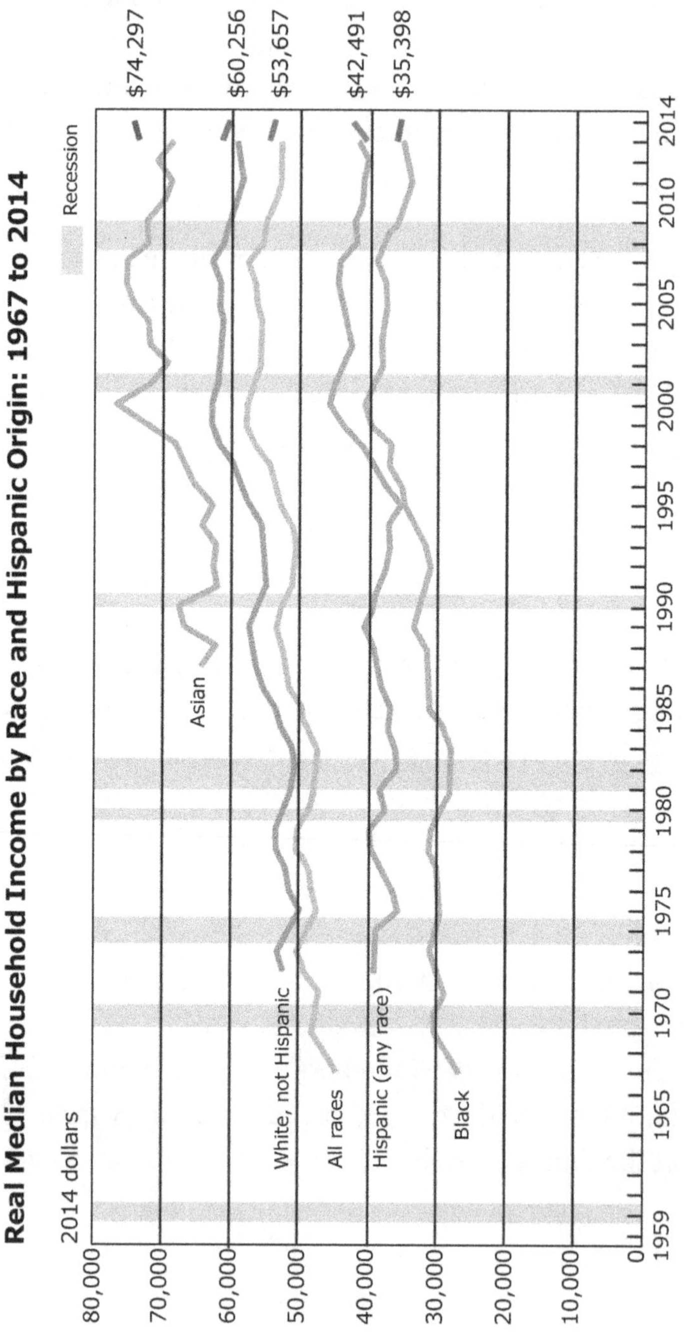
Real Median Household Income by Race and Hispanic Origin: 1967 to 2014
2014 dollars
Recession
80,000
70,000
60,000
50,000
40,000
30,000
20,000
10,000
0
1959
1965
1970
1975
1980
1985
1990
1995
2000
2005
2010
2014
Asian
White, not Hispanic
All races
Hispanic (any race)
Black
$74,297
$60,256
$53,657
$42,491
$35,398

U.S. Median Household Income

Faint heart ne'er won a fair lady. Skepticism thrives in the women's concept of the male attitude. Men are generally a set of people who are bloated by their own sense of superiority, insensitive, selfish and more often than not, incorrigible. Now, from another perspective, there are reasons to say that masculinity is a delicate attribute. Historically, manhood has social status, something a man earns, through brutal tests of physical endurance or by risky demonstration of toughness. Manhood is the logical extension of masculinity. Real men are made, not born. Modern men may not exhibit physical action or aggression to prove their manhood, but the masculinity—boyhood to manhood—is hard-won. Some men, especially those with vulnerable economic status, typically retreat into 'hyper-masculinity,' where it leads to low status, loss of respect, and at the extreme, hatred, and even violence. They get the message that being vulnerable is unmanly and that needing others' help is a sign of weakness. Culture (especially, the American culture), tries to zip the masculinity out of them and creates an absurd profile, all but in the heart of a lonely man! Thus, once owned, masculinity can be easily lost as well. One misstep, for instance, losing a job, a failed challenge, or a scandal, is enough to undo it all. This phenomenon explains why man is so sensitive about his masculinity. It is always in his mind. Women do not have that problem. Womanhood is largely evolved something innate, immutable: girls become women through puberty; once achieved, womanhood stays. Womanhood is more stable than manhood.

The concept of masculine superiority has been abetted and aided by the rise of a radical and often rabid form of feminism in the '70s and '80s. In the minds of many young women today, the feminist movement is one that has essentially been won. The ease with which it has been taken today for granted is one measure of this success. More than 60% of new mothers are now integrated into the workforce. Few young American women today face the same kind of barriers that their mothers faced when, for example, applying for a scholarship. To these young women, the old gender stereotypes and the constraints are all nonexistent. They say that they deserve more than equality with men because it is they who, with their unique disposition, can strike a balance between the lure of success and money at the workplace and the love for home and family. According to them, gender differences are not to be effaced; rather, it is to be celebrated. It is not that they would like to enter into the man's world unnoticed. But they want their presence to be felt like the other gender whose equality and dignity are recognized.

Today that presence is felt globally. Male academic ability and aptitude are lagging. In elementary schools and in high schools, boys earn three-quarters of Ds and Fs. The malaise starts in the classroom where girls overtake boys at every stage of education from the early years through middle school, high school, and college. Young men at college campuses are now a minority. While girls are characteristically more focused and self-disciplined, boys are distracted by sports and games or even derailed by drinks and drugs. To be successful in education, students from an early age need to be able to sit quietly, listen to teachers, and focus on studying. They need to be emotionally stable, to be aware of the context, and to be able to communicate smoothly. But for some reasons, hereditary, genetic, or culture, many boys fail to get the message. In college, men are far behind—only 40%

of bachelor's and 40% master's degrees go to them. The fall of men could be due to the rise of women for several factors including gender status. The push for gender equality—or call it gender neutrality—is a noble project and is for political correctness, but in effect, it might have gone overboard. Some critics of gender innovations maintain that for all the feminist emphasis on removing limitations, the government, school, and other institutions are imposing a whole new set of prejudices and barriers—for example, some social thinkers strongly believe that boys do better in classes when taught by men while girls do better when taught by women. Yet overall, near leveling of the same playfields does not require the fall of men.

Men are falling out of the labor force so casually. As high as 96% of the American men ages between 25 and 54 worked in 1954; today, that percentage is down to 80. Earnings dropped by 28% over the past 40 years. Men yet dominate the top-tier corporate ladder because of the fact that many women take time off to raise children; otherwise, women are gaining momentum nearly everywhere else. Approximately 12 out of 15 fast-growing professions are dominated by women in 2010. The women are flooding into new jobs and new opportunities. Once unemployed, women are more going back to school and pursuing new careers while men are waiting around for lost jobs and are hardly coming back. Men are strangely immune to new options. Women in their twenties earn more than men in their twenties. In one survey, the median female income is 140% of the median male income. However, some sociologists are in the opinion that: (a) this is merely a convergence in economic fortunes, not female ascendance; (b) it is one-time surge of women into the workforce, for example in U.S.

between 1965 and 1990, not the freedom of females; (b) men suffered more job losses than women; and (c) the progress of women in many arenas has actually been stalled.

It is not that the women are winners in the global gender war or that they are doing great simply because men are doing worse. Far from that! The salient point here is women are adapting to today's economy more flexible and resiliently than men. Even evidences are that women are better able to adjust to divorce; their income rises by 25% after a marital breakup. Only a generation ago, men and women adhered to a certain ideology, what it meant to be a man or a woman. Today young women claim to have abandoned both feminist and pre-feminist preconceptions. They are more like clean slates and are desperate to embrace any social rules that give them the freedom to excel. Meanwhile, men fail to get the memo; they still adhere to the masculinity rule, which limits their vision and their ambition.

Man and woman experience the world differently and so vastly—thanks to each gender's exposure to sex hormones. Evolutionary psychologists have long claimed: (a) men seek women with beauty, youth and good health; (b) women seek men with the most resources—wealth, power and status—so as to invest in their children; and (c) the general preferences in human mating are universal and are based on biology. But new research promotes that these preferential attributes may be malleable: if men and women attain financial equality, in terms of earning and economic power, then these mate-seeking preferences by gender tend to diminish under established societal circumstances. Researchers analyzed two large pools of people who were surveyed for what qualities they wanted most in a mate: one survey was in the late 1980s and involved 8,953 people from 37 different cultures; the other was current and involved 3,177 people from 10 countries via the Internet. Within different cultures, researchers looked for relationships between the gender gap with respect to male female mate preferences. They finally established an interesting relationship that the better the equality of status between the genders, the better the equality of traits that both men and women sought in potential mates. Furthermore, they also illustrate that the more equal men and women are as follows: (a) the less emphasis men place on the beauty of women, and (b) the less emphasis the women put on money, power and position. Among the 10 countries surveyed, Finland had the least and Turkey had the most gender gap. Top four gender-equal nations world wise are in Scandinavia and the bottom are in the Middle East and Africa.

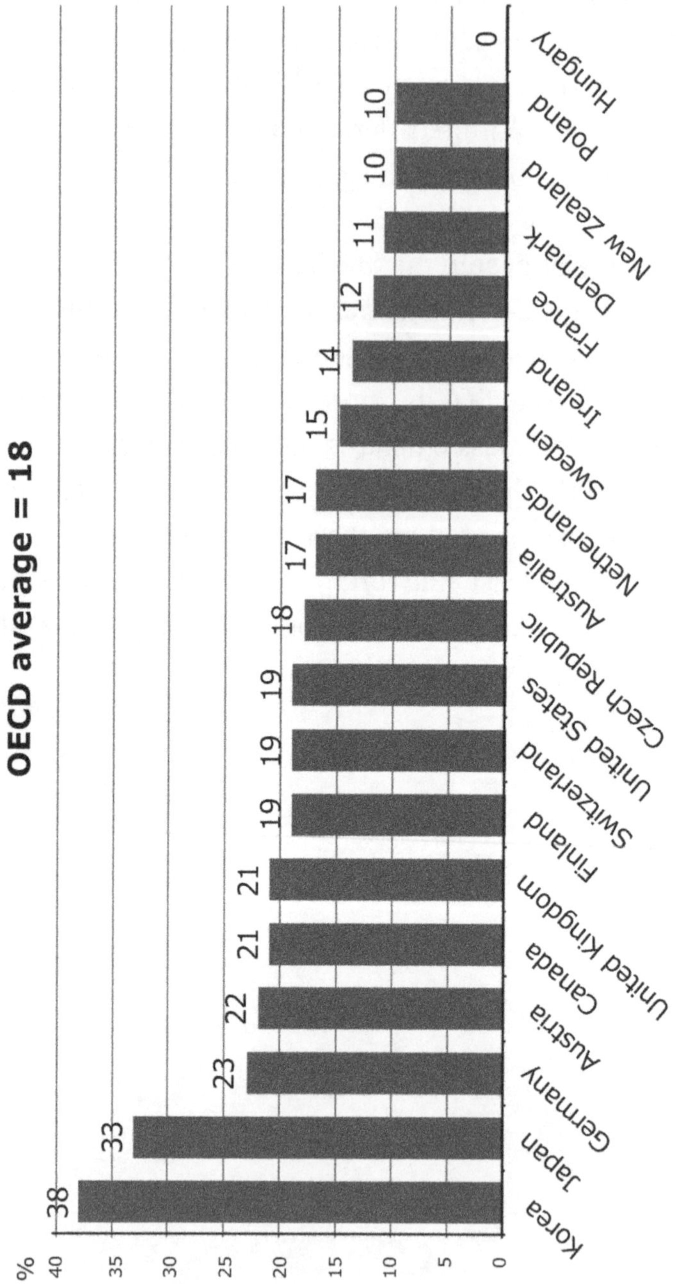

Organization for Economic Co-operation and Development (OECD) Gender Pay Gap 2008

America ranks 17th place in the world in gender equity. One study analyzed United States census data from 1950 to 2000, (a) when the employment of women surged in several fields, (b) when women moved into historically male jobs in larger numbers in white-collar fields than of blue-collar jobs, and (c) when women occupied in many other occupations in large numbers. They found all promising only good but less pay—after controlling factors like skills, education, work experience, race, and geography. Out of the 30 highest-paying jobs like chief executives, architects, and computer engineers, 26 are male dominated, and in reverse way too, out of the 30 lowest-paying jobs like housekeepers, food servers, and child-care services, 23 are female dominated. Another ranking is done by the World Economic Forum, Switzerland, who gathers and analyzes more than a dozen metrics to rank 144 countries with respect to access and opportunity for men and women: in 2017, the U.S. ranks at 49th place above average for gender equality worldwide, dropping four spots since 2016, due to low performance on the "political empowerment."

When a couple finds that their wedlock was like a heavy chain around their feet or when they find their going gets impossible, they sometimes decide to split. Or after the shattering clash of the couple, it becomes very difficult to pick up those pieces of peacemaking and remake the home.

Tell the truth—don't be cruel while breaking up the relationship! It's not fair. If you are breaking up the relationship, honestly, you owe an explanation to your partner. Be serious and spend a considerable amount of time in soul-searching, journaling, talking it to your really good friend or having conversations you're your family members, and may be to a relationship specialist and a lawyer, just to get your act right, morally, socially and legally. Do not make mistake on the spur of the moment and then repent all the moments. Relationship is very hard to make, very easy to break. People need to understand that. This is where most people fail. Without proper communication and serious discussions, after break up, most people fail to comprehend what went wrong and why it happened. Ideally, your explanation shouldn't surprise your partner, because you've discussed it in the past, and you have tried to work it through, but it didn't work. Now, if you have to, you have to. In that case, please do it face-to-face and preferably at your partner's home, or at any familiar place. Often, divorce brings sad consequence to both and especially to children.

In the nineteenth century of the United States, about a quarter of all children experienced the death of one of their parents. Not until the '60s did the main cause of missing one of the parents shift from death to divorce. In 1993, 2.3 million couples got married, and 1.2 million couples got divorced, and about 4 out of 10 first marriages ended up in divorce. Roughly 1 million divorces a year translate into at least 1 million kids under 18 becoming children of a divorced family. The world's highest divorce rate is throwing millions of children into poverty and inconveniences. Millions more are scarred by bifurcated lives and loyalties. Children are the worst recipients of such consequents. Survey shows children of divorced parents have poorer interpersonal and social skills than their peers. They battle loneliness, sadness, anxiety, and low self-esteem. They find difficulties in forming and maintaining friendships, expressing their feelings to others, showing their own sensitivity to others' feelings, comforting other children, and getting along with people who are different. They have, in general, lesser cognitive abilities such as memory and attention and poorer math skills. Research bears the fact that in the long term, children of divorce are more at risk of being unhealthy, having mental illness, being poor, not graduating from college, and getting divorced themselves.

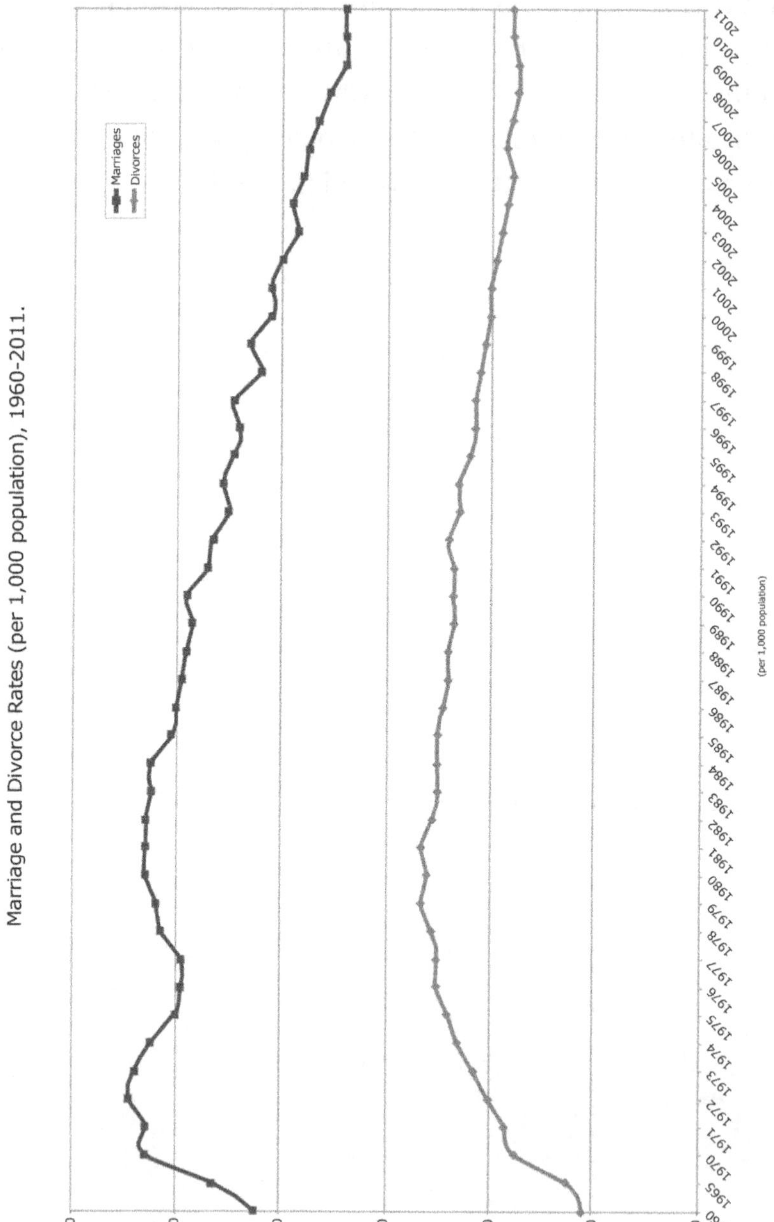

Marriage and Divorce Rates

Staying married is both satisfying and disappointing, as the institution has ever been. Marriage is most satisfying only if you invest a lot of effort; it is most disappointing if you don't. Good marriage requires solicitations. In a bad marriage, friends are often able solicitors—the invisible glue. If you have good friends, the relation goes on for years, intending to leave and talking about leaving instead of actually packing up and leaving. But not a divorce lawyer! Divorce lawyer is not a marriage lawyer. If you are in a divorce lawyer's office, it's already too late. And certainly not the Facebook! Facebook is a dread dumping ground! If you're unhappy with your conjugal relationships or marriage matters, stay away from Facebook. Vast majority of stuff you find there are unhappiness masked with happiness. Good old friends are your best choice. The friends and families of the divorced couple are also sometimes at a loss to decide which side to go. Sometimes, a situation arises where no words are quite right. Generally, the man takes back the friends he brought in, and the woman takes with her friends she brought in. But this is not a set rule. Sometimes people use their own moral principles to decide which side to take, and normally they take side with the one they perceive to have been wronged. "For though we love both the truth and our friends, piety requires us to honor the truth first" (Aristotle).

Marriage makes; marriage breaks! Very often, divorce leads to abandonment by friends. Maybe only a few of the families who were friends before the parting would choose to remain friends. This may happen to the man as well as to the woman. Sometimes the loss of friends can be a harsher consequence for the man than the woman. Quite often, the closest friend of a man is his wife. She is the link through which he remains connected to the world. Losing a wife can mean losing his connectedness to the world. Sometimes he, at an advanced age, does not have the capacity to make new connections. For a woman, it is also not easy either. There is hardly a noble way for her to live alone. Historically in the United States, divorced women have the highest poverty rate among all-aged women. Even if she gets by financially, but emotionally, she is never left alone. Her family, her friends, and her colleagues never let her forget her husbandlessness, her childlessness.

So what to do about "I do"? The institution of marriage has weathered many storms, the heaviest perhaps in the last fifty years. But it survives today because it is within marriage that all the strains in man-woman relation can be resolved, not outside it. The strength of marriage is tested by the ability to tolerate an occasional exception. Both partners in marriage must understand that marriage is an equal partnership in which each inspires others and brings fulfillment to both. Early on, boys and girls are to be brought up in a manner conducive to strengthening the bond of their own union when they get married.

Above all, love is a universal binding force. Love understands tolerance, patience, obligation, and correction. It saves the institution of marriage from the battery of all storms. The basic underpinning of the edifice called marriage is love. Love overcomes all damages. After fight and injury, love still lives in injured hearts. Love reminds us that all marriage was once new, and it will continue to renew.

Evolutionary science reveals that human are hardwired with natural selection, whose purpose is to help marriage thrive. Natural selection—each slight variation, if useful, is preserved—favors marriage to thrive because thriving marriage increases the chance of reproduction, family cohesiveness, and other factors that allow the life to continue. Marriage is an act of nature for life to go on. So, make it a matter. Adam and Eve are also the progeny of Mother Nature, after all.

1.2 Family

> The happiest moments of my life have been the few which I have passed at home in the bosom of my family.
>
> —Thomas Jefferson (1743–1826), the principal author of the Declaration of Independence (1776) and the third president of the United States (1801–1809)

The family is one of nature's masterpieces. It is the building block of the human race. It is the basis of the microcosm of the humankind. Broadly defined, a family is a primary social unit living together in one home in society. Characteristically, a family is made up of one or two parents and their children, where the group shares common ancestry, certain conviction, or common affiliation. The group of people are hierarchically related by blood, as great-grandparents, grandparents, parents, children, uncles, aunts, cousins, and beyond. Sometimes a family grows not only with the parents and their unmarried children living at home but also with children that have married, their spouses, and their offspring and perhaps elderly in-laws and dependents as well. This arrangement is called an extended family. A big family is a big fun. It gives you a feeling of belongingness. Society is, so to say, an extended family at large. The family provides the economic and protective needs of individuals, especially the children and elderly. A family is not only the fundamental unit in society but also for the children the very soil from which they absorb and assimilate the culture of the society. Children learn most of the social skills in the family. It is also the family as a platform where children learn mutual respect and tolerance for each other. Charity begins here. The belief instinct gives them the ability to understand that other people have voice and value as well. A family adopts and accommodates a child and gives enough emotional support that empowers the child to venture with confidence into a greater world. The glory of close family envelops the child in supporting all it needs and beyond. "Perhaps the greatest social service that can be rendered by anybody to this country and to mankind is to bring up a family" (George Bernard Shaw).

One purpose of ethics is to understand the degree of difference between right and wrong, moral and immoral, civil and evil. Good family teaches good things—good ethics, the virtue of good work, humanity, honesty, clean living, marital fidelity, and above all individual responsibility and accountability. It is the place for the foundation of ethics where children first learn integrating ethics in daily life and get a handle on how to limit their wishes, abide by the rules, judge rights and wrongs, and consider the needs of others. Though these values are largely social, communal, and cultural yet ethics as a social contract coming to children mostly from parents, these attributes are learned within the family. Their process of growing up happens largely by osmosis, through interaction with others around them. In the family, living together brings them in contact with one another and bonds the minds together. Primarily, the family performs certain indispensable functions for its members. It provides food, cloth, shelter, and security—the basic necessities of living. Of equal importance is the physical, emotional, and psychological security. You do a lot to keep your family safe at home. Living together primarily under the same roof generates human friction, conversation, attachment, and relation. Love and warmth of the relationship are the source of the emotional strength with which the young members move out to negotiate the complex situations and challenge of the world outside. "If you want to bring happiness to the whole world, go home and love your family." said Mother Teresa. A family is not built in a day. A good family is a good fortune that one is born in. Building up the family's fortune needs patience like moving the earth by the needle. But losing it can be as swift as a raft rushing downstream.

An edge of the old man! Historically, in many cultures, the families have ever been patriarchal or male dominated where the oldest man has an edge over other members. The head of the household is typically a male member, in most cases the eldest who remains the most respected person in the household. He is responsible for all major decisions. Once gets old, this old man, having a cargo of experience, is a family asset. In modern society, the entrepreneurship we draw from our seniors is one of our most valuable resources. Contrary to the outdated and antiquated idea that older people remain separate from the society and be at rest, statistically and on the contrary, businesses in the United States founded by the seniors over the age of 50 are major sources of employment across the nation. The idea that older people are consumers rather than producers—the takers, not the givers—is not always true. The traditional family is a natural family where, in general, women have had a rather low status. In Roman times (500 BC–AD 100), the family was patriarchal; yet, the status of women was somewhat improved, even though they were not allowed to manage their own affairs. The typical family as it existed in medieval Europe was male dominated and extended.

A woman's whole life is a history of affection. As many philosophers describe it, the woman, in any form—mother, sister, or wife—is believed to be the embodiment of sweetness and affection. The traditional family usually allocates roles for the mother as the homemaker and the father as the bread earner. The picture of a perfect family is framed with a loving woman at the center. She is positioned to have the caress and the consoling tenderness to allay all pains and to teach hope and faith in life and love. She is the link that holds a large family together.

With the advancement of human civilization, science, and technology, the definition and operating principle of the family kept evolving according to the new-fangled environment and convenience of society. Men, in such a family, had their roles restricted to earning the livelihood and securing a stable future for the children. Both men and women had their own duties and responsibilities, which were largely delegated, complementary, and nonoverlapping. Grandparents, parents, and several brothers with their wives and children lived in the same household as a family. However, industrialization and the accompanying urbanization spawned many alterations in family structure by causing a sharp change in life and occupational styles. The modern family that begun to emerge after the Industrial Revolution was different from the older classic. Patriarchal rule began to give way to more equality between the sexes. Similarly, family roles, once considered exclusively male, have started breaking down. Caring for the home and children, once the exclusive duty of the female, became more of shared responsibility, and increasingly, the earning of money and the pursuit of public life, once the elite domain of the male, also began to be shared by the females. In the U.S., the world of stay-at-home moms and job-trapped dads had ended sometime around the '70s. Now the good news is that the stay-at-home dads have since been increased and doubled in the past decade by the conscious choice that dads are proud to defend.

However, an exact demarcation between premodern and modern family is hard to draw. While some authorities consider the modern family to be identical with the Western family since the Industrial Revolution, some others think that after globalization in which the world is united by the same set of rules, there is no rationale in equating the modern with the Western. So, the word *modern* has to be understood in the context of each society wherever it exists today. In any case, the modern family, the way it is commonly defined, emerged when many people, particularly unmarried youth, left the farm and went to industrial centers in search of employment, which led to a termination of many extended families. Their parents were left to be on their own, while these young people later married and had families comprising husband, wife, and children, which came to be known as nuclear or conjugal families. This family is the basic unit of organization virtually in every socicty today. Comparing this new form of family organization against the traditional one, known as the joint or extended family, still prevalent in many parts of India, China, and elsewhere, provides interesting contrasts and insights into several problems of modern society. In India, for example, the joint family may have property held in common by male members of the family. By default, the eldest brother is considered as the head of the household. Though it follows a patriarchal and male-dominated hierarchy, it works well in the setting of these communities.

The nuclear family, on the other hand, consists of only the husband, the wife, and their children. The nuclear family lives in either a single house or an apartment. In modern society, there happen to be more nuclear families than extended families. We see nuclear families even in agricultural societies, and these units are the primary units of producers and consumers.

Another trend also changed the structure of the family, as some couples chose not to marry legally and instead elected to have their children outside wedlock. Many of these casual relationships would turn out to be short duration, and this, along with the rise of divorce, led to a rapid increase in the number of one-parent households as a common subset of the nuclear family in developed countries. One-parent family (predominantly single-mother family) is becoming more of a norm and more socially accepted. Apparently troubling already, however, the extent to which a one-parent family is as successful as the traditional nuclear family is a matter of conjecture. In the United States, as much as 40% of all births in 2010 are to unmarried women. Therefore, this is a huge paradigm shift in a social development that has been worrying social scientists for the last half a century or so. The partial sidelining or disappearance of the father figure from some modern families, largely due to rising divorce rates and out-of-wedlock births, is seen as an alarming trend. In addition, the once-simple concept of a family tree has now grown complicated in the wake of adoptions, sperm donations, surrogate mothers, and relationships outside wedlock. In the U.S., it means that in the turn of the twenty-first century, more than one-quarter of children are living in single-parent homes as against only a nominal fifty years ago.

The trend of fatherlessness, if not controlled, is a sign of coming trouble. So is in the case in families where both parents lead equally important professional lives with no time to spare for their home, family, and children. The interplay of various dynamics in society, while they have given material comforts and access to a lifestyle unimaginable previously, has also pushed society a step closer to the tragedy. Though irreversible, these changes and the reasons behind them need to be studied in great detail to avoid getting blinded by the lure of short-term gains, so much so that one can't see the looming disaster.

CDC finds from research that the more traumatic events—so-called adverse childhood events like physical, emotional or sexual abuse, or exposed to mental illness of parent or parental divorce, neglect and domestic violence—people suffered in early childhood, the more likely they suffer from chronic stress-related health problems like obesity, heart disease, and premature death, later in life. Trauma does not have time limit. One survey asked 17,000 patients, predominantly white and upscale, to describe if they had experienced any of the ten categories of childhood trauma like if they had been abused, if their parents had divorced, or if family members had been incarcerated or declared mentally ill. Then the study calculated their adverse childhood experiences (ACE) scores depending on how many of the ten experiences—each 1 point—they had endured. The data automatically established a link between childhood trauma and adult outcomes, which was very striking. Adults who scored 4 were 7 times more likely to be alcoholics, 6 times tend to have had sex before age 15, 2 times diagnosed with cancer, and 4 times to get emphysema (damaged lungs) as compared to the people with ACE score 0. People with ACE score over 6 were 30 times more likely to have attempted suicide. To illustrate it from another perspective, while the baseline was that only 3% of students with an ACE score of 0 had learning or behavioral problems in school, it was 51% higher with a total ACE score of 4 or more. Results from yet another intriguing experiment suggested that parenting by father, mother, or both can affect differentially in the growth of nerve cell (neural) in the child's brain and that males and females respond differentially to parental influences. Childhood stress has lasting neural impacts, making it harder to self-control, focus attention, delay gratification, and do many similar things that contribute to a happy and successful life. Social dysfunction ruins life in effect.

In 2006, out of all births to women under 30, roughly 50% were outside the wedlock. The prevalence is 80% among black women while it was only 6% in 1960. The percentages have risen across the ethnic spectrum. A large part of the present-day social strife and tensions are owing to the huge number of fatherless kids. They are a hidden threat to America. "Of all the rocks upon which we build our lives, we are reminded today that family is the most important," said Senator Obama in 2007, "and we are called to recognize and honor how critical every father is to that foundation . . . But if we are honest with ourselves, we'll admit that too many fathers are missing—missing from too many lives and too many homes. They have abandoned their responsibilities, acting like boys instead of men. And the foundations of our families are weaker because of it." The speech demonstrates itself the need of father in a single-mother family. Out-of-wedlock births have sharply increased in the last few decades because many poor and poorly educated young men cannot earn enough to support the family. Women's liberation movement started in the late '60s; it opened more opportunities for women to pursue a wider range of education, job and business, changing the perception of the family breadwinner. In addition to the rise of conventional contested divorces, the convenience of no-fault divorce, simple divorce, online divorce, divorce through mediators, also led to more kids living between homes. The dad-mom-kids model family started disappearing in the later decades of the 20th century. American society started recognizing the truth in a hard way. Moms and dads are now struggling to figure out what it means to be a *good* parent. "More children will go to sleep tonight in a fatherless home than ever in the nation's history," TIME said in their cover story that hit newsstands on Father's Day 1993, "Talk to the experts in crime, drug abuse, depression, school failure, and they can point to some study somewhere blaming those problems on the disappearance of fathers from the American family. But talk to the fathers who do stay with their families, and the story grows more complicated. What they are hearing, from their bosses, from institutions, from the culture around them, even from their own wives, very often comes down to a devastating message: We don't really trust men to be parents, and we don't really need them to be."

The trend of fatherlessness is one unfortunate social development of our generation. Apart from the very obvious drawbacks of the absence of a father figure in a child's upbringing, there are larger social issues to reckon in a society that produces a vast part of progeny born and brought up in single-parent families. Talks and interactions with fatherless children have revealed their yearning for normal family life, the way they see it around with other friends and peers. Very often, they indicate a terrible longing for a father figure in their life, someone they could play with and in whose company, they could feel the assurance of safe and sound. Studies of young criminals have found that 3/4th of all juveniles in state-reform institutes come from fatherless homes. It has also been presumed that school failures may have as much to do with disintegration of families as with the quality of schools. Disintegration of the family entails a lot of emotional trauma for a child due to sudden absence of the psychological support of the father who quite often serves as the role model for the child. Some psychologists suggest that boys without fathers do risk growing up with low self-esteem. This low self-esteem manifests itself in the form of trouble in developing meaningful relationships for themselves. Thus, a society with large number of fatherless households should have plenty to worry about for its future.

Like households of no father, households of too many fathers pose equal but different sets of problems. According to a study, more than a quarter of all U.S. mothers having more than one kid have kids fathered by different men. The occurrence among African American women is almost half, among Hispanics a third, and among whites a quarter. Such multiple partner fertility (MPF)—as called in academic circles—is another layer of concern and confusion, as because many studies have shown that growing up in such a family, where different men cycle in and cycle out, is not good for children's emotional health and overall well-being. These families having domino dads, with each one's departure putting pressure on next arrival, pose a phenomenon that goes through vicious cycles. Rearing children of different fathers is a major issue in the intergenerational transmission of disadvantage, especially while a family has to juggle for decades all the diverse duties and demands of fathers in at least two households and four or more pairs of grandparents. This is another perspective of American life today how families are being created in many different ways.

Like parents, sibling matters. A sibling makes another sibling happy or unhappy. One study finds that adolescents—both boys and girls—who have at least one sister are less likely to report such feelings as this: "I am sad, unhappy, depressed" or "I am feeling lonely, no one loves me." Besides, instant playmate, gender plays a role here. The reason may be that girls and women are, in general, more likely than boys and men to talk about not only the emotions but also the detail of the talk. The way women talk may not be better than of men, but it is different—it may be too detailed. Men, very similar to women, talk more frequently to their sisters than to their brothers. That explains why sisters make them happier.

Siblings influence siblings in so many ways. One 2014 study by Duke University discovered as follows:

- In a family where the older child is obese, the younger child has a 5 times greater chance of being obese (irrespective of whether the parents are obese or not).

- Siblings are the earliest teachers who shape each other's character. They help to navigate social situations. The older sibling learns social skills in interacting with the younger, and the younger learn cognitively by imitating the older.
- If the family is large, siblings are less likely to divorce.
- Close sibling connection lowers loneliness and depression and boosts self-esteem. In large families, relationships are close—two-thirds brothers and sisters are their best friends. During adulthood, the sibling relationship remains one very powerful bond.
- Approximately 5 to 8% of siblings die early. Preteens, who experience the death of a sibling, have higher anxiety and depression levels than those who do not, and as a result, they exhibit a higher degree of attention deficit disorder. Yet, at the same time, show resilience and emotional maturity that others don't. "All of my goodness, and all of my weaknesses come from the experience of my elder brother's illness and death. Hardly a day goes by that I don't think about my brother," the hidden grief of a little sister.

On the contrary, sibling rivalry, squabbling, and intruding may lead to confusion, depression, anxiety, and stress among teens. Two very common types of conflict are (a) equality and fairness issues (things like who's watching TV or whose turn it is to walk the dog) that appear to escalate to a high-risk depressed mood over time and (b) personal domain conflicts (like taking items without asking or scuffling through personal items), which are primarily related to lower self-esteem and higher anxiety. Sibling squabbling is one unavoidable part of growing up; however, the negative effects of lingering conflicts can be avoided by appropriate arbitration of parents. Again, sibling inequality could be the result of faulty parenting techniques as well. The family size and economic influences are major factors in deciding the upbringing of each sibling. Inequality, it begins at home. This is where parents treat children differently on the basis of their behavior, intelligence, and conduct as they grow up. Studies were carried out in three main characteristics of siblings: (1) physical, (2) intellectual, and (3) personal. In the first two areas, siblings are really quite similar. Physically, siblings may tend to differ somewhat, but on average, they are lot more similar. Intelligence-wise, they are pretty much similar as well. But in terms of personality, siblings are way different—sometimes strangers to each other. Siblings are similar only about 20% of their traits. For the most part, psychologists believe, parenting is important, siblings not.

There can be vast socioeconomic differences between siblings of the same family. The differences have their origin in the different ways of upbringing that parents often subconsciously adapt. While almost all parents love their children equally, they are often not able to manage the different resources required for their different needs. Each family has a pie of resources in the form of parental time, energy, and money. A larger number of siblings means a lesser amount of resources for each. It is also a fairly common phenomenon to have a favored child who gets a larger share. It is practically impossible not to have a favorite child, and the perception of favoritism poses an additional danger in sibling rivalry. The danger bubbles up when the favoritism persists long and steady and becomes a lasting part of family dynamics. Evolutionary psychologists contemplate parental investment in their children as the division of a finite pool of resources of love and care, rather than infinite. Parents can't make the difference between love and favoritism. In a family of three or more children, the middle ones are more likely to get, for instance as it is noticed, less of the educational resources and therefore less likely to perform well academically. So, when it happens, it is certainly an abnormality in parental duty, and parents need to understand that so that wrong parenting practice does not unfairly bestow one child while deprive the other.

Birth order is another order of importance. Centuries ago, irrespective of the status of the family—royal or rural—the oldest son had huge duties, responsibilities, and incentives to stay on track and live up to family's expectations. This was primarily because, by tradition, he was set to inherit almost everything in order to maintain the status quo of the family tradition. [Interesting statistics: Firstborn Indian children are taller than the next siblings.] Today one may think of any firstborn effects in the modern family, but they do. More parental time and attention may be given to firstborns just because there are no competitors yet. Expectation-wise, parents are systematically more upset, data shows, when their oldest child returns home with ill results like bad grades. Repeating with subsequent children, they typically ease off the pedal. Experts who study birth order statistics establish that firstborns, on average, do edge out later-borns in several high-performing careers, like corporate CEOs, professors, and judges. There are more country's presidents and Nobel Prize winners among firstborn kids or singleton kids. Intelligence-wise, firstborn children, who generally get undivided parental resources at the beginning, outperform by about 3 IQ points over second-born siblings. Another theory suggests that firstborn kids are often in the role of playing a mentor or teacher to their younger siblings, and the experience of being a mentor itself is what is producing the outcomes. Older kids are typically overachieving bossy types primarily due to parents' stringency, while younger kids are typically underachieving spoilers due to parents' leniency. Even though parents do not intend to parent differently because it's very costly and unpleasant, oftentimes it happens that way.

Yet if you analyze it critically, typical birth-order count gives wrong statistics. Take, for instance, that the majority of presidents were firstborns: it is wrong for the reason that firstborn girls were not counted as being older siblings. So, along with women's liberation and the rise of feminism and when sisters are counted on the common denomination, it turns out to be that 52% of presidents are actually middleborns. Psychologists argue, for so many other reasons, that many middleborns have hidden strengths and are agents of change in business, politics, and science. They have clear benefits of the lifestyle, which is very different from the firstborn's spotlight. When parents expect very specific things that they want them to do, it can be a point of pressure for kids. So, it is not an advantage point of being, for example, a firstborn. Besides, in this respect, one hidden benefit middle children enjoy is that they grow up with a sense of independence and think freely, quite independently outside the box (parents). They do not carry the burden of firstborn "superiority ego" but rather look at others as peers with an open mind. The youngest child, for instance, often smaller and less powerful than everyone else, try consciously to outstrip other siblings either by imitating the parents or with the help of the parents and become a more capable member later in life. However, one study analyzed data sets of 5,240 Americans, 10,457 Germans, and 4,489 British people and noticed that, in line with earlier researches, oldest kids score higher on IQ tests, but besides that, it does not show any significant statistical difference in birth order with respect to the five standard aspects of personality: emotional stability, agreeableness, conscientiousness, extroversion, and imagination.

Among the many conflicts and complications that may add to family troubles is sibling rivalry. Such rivalry and comparison and repeatedly making one sibling feel humiliated and insignificant can be very damaging for his self-respect and will teach him little other than humiliation and shame. Brothers and sisters fight, typical. But when the bickering turns into physical or emotional abuse, it's bullying. In order to feel good about himself, a child must feel successful in his own eyes, and such a feeling can only be enhanced if parents accept each child for what they are and praise them when they deserve it. One way to achieve this is to train kids at home "to work at home." It will allow kids not only to come in contact with their parents and siblings more easily but also to learn the dignity of labor, which will also help them to act with dignity to other home members.

Do parents play favorites among children? Do they exhibit a preference for one child over the other? Yes, typically they do. Sometimes, it is even not necessary that mom and dad have the same favorite, and typically, they don't. Study reveals that almost 70% of fathers and 65% of mothers endorse preference. For fathers, it is often the girl, most likely the youngest; for mothers, it's the boy, most likely the oldest. Since it may not be a good idea to freely acknowledge favoring one child over another, "don't ask, don't tell" may be the way it typically goes. Some things play better when left unsaid. Most parents conceal such bias so perfectly that it has been a socially accepted norm for ages and generations. As a matter of fact, from the evolutionary standpoint too, playing favorites, also known as differential parenting, is hardwired into us as species. Survival of families through generations happened principally by the way of "survival of the fittest" principle—fittest genes were passed (as natural selection where each slight variation, if useful, is preserved)—and we have since been programmed to favor a child who stands the fittest chance of survival. So, do parents discriminate among their own children? Yes, they do. Maybe, what they fear, rightly so, is that some child is less likely to succeed in life. It strains the family relationship. For example, take a case of overweight children who often don't fare as well in school, at work, and at home. Parents discriminate, probably not knowingly. Like how any chronic condition is stressful, parents of obese children might feel frustrated just like parents of kids with learning disabilities; therefore, parents retire and opt to favor the able ones. Or maybe, parents try to be fair, but sometimes children pick up on subtle differences in the way they are treated. Or maybe, it is Darwinian's *survival of the fittest* for the fittest child, in a literal sense.

It surely matters, the look of the baby! For adults, facial expressions do prompt assumptions about how honest, trustworthy, kind, or mean one is. In criminal justice, inmates thought to have trustworthy faces have a higher chance of receiving lenient punishments of life in prison, according to one study. For about last two decades or so, many criminologists, economists, and social scientists have demonstrated the prevalence linking facts with figures. The main point for men and women is that there is hardly any reason to feel ashamed of exploiting the compliment of beauty. And by the same token for lack of beauty, there is hardly any reason to be embarrassed about it. Even adult look matters to the baby, mutually. Not only does a baby gaze longer at a more comely adult face, researchers say, but so does the parent gaze longer at more comely babies as well. Researchers have added a startling assertion that parents take better care of pretty children over the ones who are not so pretty. Good-looking children, especially boys, get more care from their parents and are kept closer in the family.

Experiment on the wide-ranging effects on playing favorites (differential parenting) shows that it can have an impact on mental health on not just the individual sibling but also among family members. Typically, mothers who come from unstable family are more likely to treat their children differentially than mothers who had privileged upbringings, and the more severe conditions a mother faced, like being a single mother or struggling with acute depression, the more difficult it is for her to treat her children equally. However, even when the parent-child relationships are skewed in this way, proper communication can moderate many negative consequences. In a family, certain siblings (handicap) may need more attention or support than others, and in that case, parents should discuss with their children why they are treating siblings differently in order to avoid any misunderstanding children might feel. Children then don't mind. They only notice when they feel that the differential treatment is unfair and when things aren't explained to them in context. Children are people too!

However, this is just an observation, not entirely predictable how birth order and parental bias may play out our personalities, behaviors, or family dynamics. Since the one-child policy was introduced in China in 1976, the singleton generation does not have birth order or differential parenting issue. But they have other issues, many of them. While it is a fact that positive sibling associations moderate the relationship between stressful life events by internalizing and controlling behaviors, a survey of the single-child population, now ages 15 to 25, found that 58% are lonely and selfish. Lack of burden denies them the depth of life. Even though Chinese study claim that these kids tend to score higher on intelligence tests and are better in making friends, the fact remains that the one-child generation is hugely struggling with issues especially with relationships and marriages. About 1 in 5 marriages ends up in divorce, which is about double the figure a decade ago and is expected to rise even higher. Singleton babies never learn how to "eat bitterness," handle stress, or deal with disappointments and frustrations in ways that would better prepare them for life. Kids are spoiled rotten at early years. Parented by grandparents for the most part, instead of mom and dad, they are twice as likely to be overweight. They are less generous, exhibit lack of faith, possess no social skills, are less completive, and yet expect instant gratification. They pawn the whole family when they fail. The negative anticipations and expectations for the parents who deny their child of siblings do only strengthen the general condemnation against the one-child policy. The situation is so dire that in China today, some employers have gone as far as to stipulate "No singleton child—please" in job postings; the singleton child is singled out not only in the job market but also in other social areas as well. One branch of government, the Chinese People's Political Consultative Conference, pleaded to the party leadership to abandon the one-child policy. In a top-down governance setting in China, this is a surprising bureaucratic assertiveness. Driven primarily by the fear that an aging population could threaten China's economic progress, the Communist Party leadership have ended their thirty-five-year-old one-child policy on October 29, 2015, and declared all married couples would be allowed to have two children. The decision was a paradigm shift from the imposed policy in the late 1970s, which was formally instituted in 1980. In 2017, they further relaxed the law to abolish all birth limits: let people have as many children as they want. It was again a startling reversal of the policy. Also, Chinese government who only a short while ago imposed punishing fines and compelled hundreds of millions of Chinese women to undergo sterilization and abortion operations, is now making the new campaign so harsh that it has raised a fear among citizen that China may go invasive extreme again by tightening access to abortion and making divorce more difficult, in getting women to have more children. The birth of a child, to put it bluntly, is no more an affair of the family, but an affair of the state. Another very troubling fact is that there are 32 million more marriage-age men than there are women in China (perhaps due to deliberate killing of girl babies at birth, or more commonly abandoning after birth). The one-child policy, some researchers say, was one of the most radical approaches in limiting population growth. In the near future, China will have another condition, which perhaps Chinese people may call the next one-child-generation syndrome.

When the wine is drained out, it is no more a bottle of wine; it is just a wine bottle. Many a modern parent is like a wine bottle where children have parents, only for namesake, not for parental founding with love and care. Children suffer from the lack of love and care, affection and attention from their parents on a daily basis. Children of job-busy parents focusing on their own needs and failing to find sufficient energy to participate in social activities become problematic sometimes. The circumstances often force them to create their own difficulties and make them very visible as an attention-seeking technique, just to come into their parents' focus, hoping to be loved, cared, and appreciated. From here on stems the sad rise in children with anorexia, phobia, and bulimia; the rise in number of neurotic children; the rise in suicidal children; the rise in children falling prey to drug and sex abuse; etc. In many cases, parents of these problem children happen to be ignorant or weak, exhausted, or immature, who focus on their own immediate needs. They, like other good parents, love their children and encourage them the best from life, but they are, for many different reasons, not on top of things and are unable to foster the optimistic development of the child's personality.

Demise of the traditional family with one person as the head of the household brought many problems in its wake. Today, both parents in the nuclear family get exhausted juggling the roles of bread earner as well as homemaker, and consequently have little time for their kids. Public authorities, especially the governmental ones, have assumed many of the functions that a family used to provide, such as educating the young, caring for the senior and the sick, and providing for recreation. For those younger, being in day care for about ten hours a day has become the norm. For those older, a rising number of them have been hospitalized or admitted to residential care, not because they are sick but because they are old and their own families are not ready to provide the necessary support and care, as they are too busy, occupied primarily by the job they needed.

The shifting paradigms of modern life have been both cause and effect of the redefined roles of both parents. Today in the U.S., a majority of men are more involved in rearing children and housekeeping than their fathers ever were. Gender gaps are gradually disappearing; men are definitely contributing far more household work—cleaning, laundry, cooking, etc. Many couples have developed their own divisions of labor, depending on work schedules and preferences. Dads are now putting 50% more time on housework than they did twenty-five years ago. It is now a reality of today's world that has far-reaching implications for society as well.

Some scholars suggest that fatherhood is by nature very different from motherhood. Men parent differently from women, and in many ways, that matters enormously. Men and women are suitable for different roles at different times. While parenting of a young infant is the natural activity for women, the father's role becomes more important once the child grows older. Mothers typically are more worried about an infant's well-being and his or her basic and immediate needs. They discipline their children on a moment-by-moment basis. Bit by bit, pop by pop. Fathers on the other hand are more concerned about children's long-term success. They are more concerned about the fact that children should turn out to be socially viable as they consider their children's character to be a reflection of their own. Women's voices are supposedly more soothing for infants, and they are better able to read the signals a child sends before a baby can even talk. But then slowly as time passes, the strengths that fathers may bring to bear on child-rearing become more important. In this context, the phenomenon of men getting more involved in household activities is definitely a positive change, as the involvement of both mother and father would ensure better all-round development for the children.

Historically, men had to apply themselves and work hard to make sure that they rose within an organization, leaving home to be taken care of by their wives. However, today, they must contend with plenty of other factors like a shaky economy, buyouts, layoffs, and mergers. Employers for family life are still a mere lip service, and practically little is conceded to the male employees to ease it. Men too, like women, have been gradually troubled by the struggle to balance home and family. Men have now two places to prove their worth, the workplace and the homeplace. A survey shows that those who got to the top in the corporate ladder almost always were men with wives who didn't work outside home.

It is a problem more for the older generation of women who still think their domestic role is more important for them than taking up a job outside the home. To them, contentment comes more out of playing dutifully her domestic roles. It is not so with the younger women who start their professional life immediately after finishing their studies. They have many other scores to derive their satisfaction and to identify from. So, they are not so cautious of relinquishing the powers at home.

Couples require more mutual support and proximity once they attain middle age after the children complete their studies and reach adulthood. Children develop new relations of their own and share their love with others. Women suffer more from these changes as they are usually the ones who have given more in the upbringing of the children. A great deal of understanding and adjustment between the parents are needed at this stage to deal with the emotional distress so caused.

For most parents, children are the key to happy family life. Sociologists regard the raising of children as the crucial function of the family. For women, the universal challenge is that the prime years for having children coincide with the prime years for building career. Therefore, some say it is advisable to plan their life backward, decide where they want to be in life, and then choose the appropriate course of action because the condescension that nonworking mothers face in a career woman's world can be especially hard on women who don't have a list of work accomplishments in their résumé. And taking an early break now becomes tougher in some fields than in others. The consequence, professional mothers put their career in front of motherhood. Moreover, in a society where it is common to have a baby on hold for a career or where career is equated with identity, young mothers feel like outsiders. Now the technology and technological companies came up with an innovative idea: women employees freeze their eggs for the future. Freezing a woman's egg was originally intended for childbearing women due to some medical conditions like facing infertility as a result of cancer treatments like chemotherapy. Now corporations seize this opportunity, offering female employees the financial incentive to freeze their eggs. While the biological clock is on hold, the employer gives the employee a choice to focus on their careers instead of a child. The procedure is uncertain, emotionally draining, and inherently risky. Couples endeavoring to have a baby using frozen eggs are often told that frozen eggs are just as good as fresh ones while, clinically, an in vitro fertilization (IVF) with frozen eggs has a significantly lower prospect of live birth. The "shells" of the frozen egg get hardened, and bypassing the hardened shell needs injecting the sperm through the shell and directly into the egg. With age, a sperm becomes more prone to errors, aggravating the risk of autism and other disorders. For this reason, some bioethicists even argue that the sperm of all eighteen-year-old boys should be frozen for use in later life, perhaps to be an older father. That is biologically true, but that is hardly a reality! Certainly, everybody will agree to the fact that women try to get pregnant at a younger age, if possible, rather than banking eggs and hoping to get pregnant later in life. Yet maternity leave is far-fetched, let alone the paternity leave. Glassdoor, a company that catalogs salary details, published one report in 2016 with the help of the London firm Llewellyn Consulting stating that the United States has the least generous benefits out of fourteen European countries, based on six key factors: annual leave, sick pay, unemployment benefits, maternity-related entitlements, paternity-related entitlements, and parental-related entitlements. The most generous countries by score (in the scale of 0 to 10) are Denmark (7.8), France (7.2), and Spain (6.4). The least generous countries are the United States (0.3), followed by Ireland (2.3) and Switzerland (2.3). Once again, the whole business of America is business. The postindustrial government created by the corporation, for the corporation, and of the corporation shall not perish from the United States. The employer comes first; the employee comes next. Customer first, citizen next! Corporation dictates; consumer takes. But in a good-governed nation, these business models are seriously flawed. Making the market decide is not right. Everybody needs to understand that.

Striking a middle path, there are many who decide to have children late but take a long break after childbirth. Even then, making a return once the children reach a certain age may prove to be difficult. Employers unanimously agree to the fact that there is a definite bias against hiring women who have been out of the work for a long time: firstly, they doubt the latter's commitment, and secondly, the fact that they have been out of touch in their field goes against them. Women, once they join after taking a break, need flexibility on a regular basis, which very few jobs and employers offer. Salary is another area that needs careful negotiation when trying to make a comeback.

Faced with a barrage of uncertain consequences in the professional and personal life after childbirth, many couples, particularly women, keep delaying this stage, by years, to buy some more time on the professional front. This fact, along with the stresses of modern life, often results in a difficulty to conceive, so much so that some couple, in spite of planning to have a baby, may not be able to do so for many, many years. It indeed comes to a very traumatic situation for many after realizing that all the professional accomplishments and the financial security they had planned to provide a better future for their family and children were actually useless. Some keep pursuing their professional goals and ambitions without realizing that soon it might be too late to plan for children. Technology has got a solution for those experiencing such trauma with options for artificial reproductive technology. However, as in the case of any other artificial procedure, risks cannot be eliminated. There are limits to what medical science can do for infertile couples, and one always runs the risk of the process, giving rise to a faulty outcome.

The risk differs from couple to couple. While for some the decision is planned, for others it is not, and in some other cases, when planned, it might be too late. But in any case, any such decision always involves many trade-offs apart from money. Having a baby takes a toll not just in financial terms, but also in terms of a major part of youth lost, which could have otherwise been devoted to pursuing, say, better career options. An infant means less mobility and greater aversion to undertaking risks, at least till such time as it grows up to a more adaptable age. Bringing up a child is also an activity that requires plenty of physical stamina from parents. Moreover, for many women, having a baby means allowing her career to be put on hold at least for a while. It also implies plenty of earning potential lost and several such sacrifices that young mothers today are uncertain about. Most importantly, the decision, in many cases, takes a toll on the marriage itself. A baby brings with itself plenty of responsibilities and workloads, and trying to do justice to all of them often creates friction between spouses and puts added pressure on the marriage. The demanding work hours needed to make ends meet can deprive the family's breadwinner of time with the children and create a strain in the marriage. In 2015, over 42% of mothers were the sole family breadwinner and an additional 22% were co-breadwinner (responsible for 25–49% of the total family income), according to a report from the Center for American Progress. So, with the stress of full-time motherhood—a constant feeling of running on a treadmill—a mother trying to balance home, children, and work all at the same time is like a candle burning on both ends. The challenge is to make sure that both partners have enough time for the family and for each other and enough money to support the family. Paradoxically, that never happens; time and money often have an inverse relationship, and the need to do better professionally, to be better financially, often eats into the time one needs to spend at home with the family. Balancing risk versus reward is so delicate.

Yet for all these sacrifices, being young parents also entails certain intangible advantages. Foremost are the romantic images associated, and there are few things as satisfying and fulfilling in spite of the trade-offs involved. Apart from this, young parents also have greater patience and energy to dedicate to the activity of child-rearing. Young mothers run a lower risk of encountering fertility problems. To have gone through the physical travails of pregnancy at a more youthful age is a relief for them. Thus, in spite of the downsides, women perceive plenty of benefits in being a young mother as also a young father. The thought of being relieved of one's responsibilities as a parent at a relatively early age is definitely another incentive. While parents themselves growing up with their children, young parents can very well look forward to being able to see their grandchildren, which is one very humane and quite a pleasing thought for all parents.

However, not just for the present generation but also for the generation of the baby boomers, who graduated in the early 1970s and who were the first to break the conventional societal norm of stay-at-home moms and job-trapped dads, the ideas and plans about nurturing a career and raising a family together, with both spouses balancing each to perfection, often ran into trouble. After having children, they often felt distressed at the realization that the going was not as easy as they thought it would be. The wife often had to give up full-time work and stick to a part-time job while compromising on her professional advancement in the interest of her family. The baby boomer men were the first ones who desired their marriage to be a genuine partnership of equals. But the pressures of family life often weighed too heavily on them and forced the women either to quit their jobs or to experience serious turmoil in their marriage. This was one of the key important social phenomena, first experienced in the developed nations, which later also caught on in the developing nations that ushered in many more transformations in many societies of many countries. Together, they gave rise to the modern way of living.

Unlike all correct answers of any arithmetic problem matches with one answer, all wrong answers are wrong in their own unique way. All happy families are happy alike in one way, while all unhappy families are unhappy in their unique way. Clearly, the ideal picture of a happy family is hard to attain in today's age. The traditional mottos of a happy family remain an elusive dream for most. But in spite of the disturbing trends, the family as an institution is considered by everyone to be indispensable for the happiness of the present generation and the next generations. The members of happy family care for each other, share each other, and enjoy together. As in some ways, happiness outflows from other people, family happiness is a sort of key to that togetherness. Together, they have many a common hope for the future and love and care for one another in a larger degree than unhappy families. It passes on to their children the family values toward others—tolerance, compromise, support, flexibility, and importantly, the continuous process of mutual accommodation, without which family life is impossible. Family tradition counters the risks of alienation and confusion. The happy family provides a steady, reliable, and safe harbor in a confusing world. It is the first institution where children start learning parents are powerful role models, and the lessons learned remain with them past the times they become parents themselves.

What better thing is there for a human soul than to enjoy family life, to be with each other in silent memories? When we look carefully, we realize that our happiness generally stems from our family happiness. The family is the strength in an individual's life and carries personal and emotional connotations. Erosion of faith in family life in any form has to be checked, and full trust must be restored in order to have confidence in such a happy family life. Unhappiness and trauma caused through separation and then by one-parent families can only result in more depressed and unhappy children where their chances of turning out to be socially viable are remote. Therefore, this problem of society needs to be addressed by first taking a good look at its very basic unit, the family, and by trying to apply corrective measures thereon. A family in peace prospers; a prosperous family is a living paradise.

Family carries a very personal and emotional association. It is also essential that we learn to view all of humanity as part of the earth's family. It is a link to our past and a bridge to our future. While we have the pleasure of cherishing our own children, we should appreciate our wider responsibility to the world's children. Only then will we value other children as our own with the same opportunity to reach their full potential. Only then will we be secured of our own future and the future of our planet and we, in turn, find our own places in our family. "As the family goes, so goes the nation and so goes the whole world in which we live" (Pope John Paul II). All under heaven is one family. The family is the beginning of civilization.

We have never chosen the family; the family is chosen for us by nature. It's a gift to us. When the tear falls, the smile spreads, the love blooms, the success thrives, we all come to each other in our own family—a little world, a little world within our Mother Nature.

1.3 Children

> Do not train a child to learn by force or harshness; but direct them to it by what amuses their minds, so that you may be better able to discover with accuracy the peculiar bent of the genius of each.
>
> —Plato (428 BC–348 BC), the ancient Greek philosopher

The more new parents do parenting, the more they respect their own parents. To experience the emotions of parental love, we must raise children ourselves—for indeed the emotions that go into bringing up a child cannot be adequately expressed but can only be felt. We raise ourselves in raising a child. Raising a child is a process of creating an individual out of the raw material that nature hands out to us, with only a few inborn traits. The rest is shaped by the surroundings and the circumstances. Children use, like other inborn abilities, all their senses to realize the world, and therefore, raising a child is a resourceful effort, a creative endeavor, and an art. "It is a wise father that knows his own child" (William Shakespeare).

You are always on my mind! To be a parent, a child is always on the mind. How sweet is it stealing a kiss from a sleeping child? Parenting is one of the very responsible and very satisfying tasks that persons as parents get delighted. It is also the one of which parents receive the least formal training. Parenting is never without error. A parent who teaches children learns twice. Individual experience of how to bring up a child typically comes from his own parents and his own surroundings and upbringing. This may be in a pattern from the parents' parental experiences being repeated and passed on to their children. Parents teach children that teach the world. In a greater sense, the parent should teach the children in such a way that it will not be necessary to teach them when they become adults or when they will be parents themselves. A child is a small parent. Thus, when parents teach their children, they teach their children's children. It is hereditary. One can hardly measure the wealth of sympathy, gentleness, kindness, and generosity hidden in the soul of a child.

Children have hidden talents! They learn to read at age two, play music at four, do math at six, and speak foreign languages fluently by eight. By eighteen months of age, they have fairly a sophisticated understanding of human emotion, overall. For example, if a child as young as twelve to fourteen months old sees an adult with a problem—like being unable to reach a book on the floor because she is sitting on a chair—the child on the floor will try to help her. Researchers in cognitive development, show that human babies prefer helpers and oppose intimidators of all kinds. Toddlers have moral sense so much so that even though they tend to like high-status winners, they don't like who win by force. In one experiment, researchers gathered children ages 21 months to 31 months for a series of puppet shows. In the first scene, one puppet walks the stage repeatedly, from right to left. In the next scene, another puppet walks the stage from left to right. In the next scene, came a conflict: two puppets bumped in the middle, blocking each other's way. One of two scenarios happened, either one puppet bows down and moves out of the way, allowing other puppet to pass, or one puppet pushes the other away and moved ahead of him. After the show, researchers presented the two puppets to the toddlers and asked which one they liked. Everybody loves a winner, toddlers too; yet, they don't like those who win conflicts by using force. They not only observe the social interactions happening around them, but also actively participate and evaluate them. When they didn't like the *winner* because it had pushed the other puppet away, in which case, the toddlers re-evaluated their preference and acknowledged the loser. This report was published in the journal *Nature Human Behavior* in 2018. Toddlers like the winner; yet, they value even more how it was own. In addition, researchers further evidenced that while human's closest primate, the bonobo, always shows preference to the winner—even when the dominance comes from beating others up, human toddlers, on the other hand, prefer only those who are dominant, yet, not mean. Children are little humans, they have hidden emotions as well.

The child's ability to observe and respond to someone else's distress can be seen in children as young as twelve months old. Babies eighteen months old seem to willingly condole stoic people and recognize that obvious sorrow is appropriate after an unfortunate experience. They also display an understanding that a neutral or passive response does not always mean a person is unreliable. The study shows that even infants can make out a difference between an event that happens and the emotions that follow, and thereby, based on the event, they can very well infer what the appropriate emotions should be. Another study found that babies born in the U.S. are more likely to be social and impulsive than those from other countries (Chile, South Korea, and Poland), and they are more mindful to enjoy inspiring activities, less likely to be unhappy or irritated, and are easier to comfort when upset. Psychologists theorize it to the idea that toddlers' temperaments are much influenced by their parents' values:

American society is predominantly not very tolerant of negativity, which is one important way leads to the fact that American parents discourage their children from expressing negative emotions.

It's a crawl-walk-run approach and largely a creative process. It's an art that most people acquire at varying degrees once they become parents. No one can pontificate on the right way of parenting or argue on the best practice. However, there is one area in which the opinions of all caring parents converge: all parents want to convey their standards and values to an extent to have their children grow up to be a human whom they will appreciate, a human who will contribute to society more significantly—even a hard-core criminal wants his child to be a good citizen of the world.

Parents may give birth to children, but it is the children who give birth to a fresh life to the parents. Most parents feel their children make them happy, by far. Yet some researchers have come to question—mostly on the ground of how they define the parenting happiness based on the findings—that

- parents—both mom and dad—are slightly happier than nonparents;
- there is a difference between happiness measured at a day-to-day level and happiness measured at a larger level, where on a day-to-day basis, even though parenting may be a grinding experience, parents report significantly more meaning in their lives than nonparents;
- parents who are economically stable are happier than parents who are struggling, obviously;

- parents who have biological or adopted children are happier in general than parents who have stepchildren; and
- parents' happiness is not a static thing; it changes its impulse throughout many, many situations during the lifetime of a child.

Usually, parents who are blessed with the kind of children they have, have children who are blessed in the kind of parents they have. It is noticed that children who appear to be the more mature and competent tend to have parents who were more supportive, more affectionate, more conscientious, and more committed to their roles as parents. These parents control and demand more mature behavior from their children. The welfare of the children is an important consideration in the happiness of the family. To many sociologists, one primary function of the family is the raising of children. As the family goes, so go the children. The institution of the family belongs to the society at large. Children are indispensable for the progress and prosperity of society. In this light, the role of the family to do a good job in preparing and upbringing children assumes importance. A child is educated not only in school but also in family and in society.

A butterfly is nothing but a caterpillar a few days ago. A newborn marks the beginning of a new life; it brings with it hope for a newer, better life and a dream of possibilities. At a certain stage of life, people feel a need to procreate and have children as it makes them a complete family cycle. Becoming a parent, they feel an obligation to perform their duty as sincerely as possible. Children with their personality and unique gifts also convey to the household a new perspective.

Their innocence and complete unawareness of worldly complications provide a much-wanted freshness into our mundane occupations and transport us into a completely different world for a while full of natural, innocent queries that we adults forget to ask ourselves in the midst of our busy existence. They are our link to nature, one of the very few remaining ones, as all the others are gradually sacrificed to our needs of so-called better life. They awaken our natural parenthood, rekindle our love and sacrifice, and often make us experience a level of fulfillment that no material achievement can make up for. Childbirth sets forth an immediate adjustment of roles as people become not only husband and wife to each other but also father and mother to the newborn child.

More and more research over the last several decades suggest that experiences in early life, even prenatal life, can have a remarkable influence on the development of physical, mental, and emotional qualities. Early learning is important and essentially social, but artificial learning though smart toys, computers, tools, and devices, where they take the role of parents, is not social. A group of studies reinforce the actuality, suggesting that children who get more parental physical touch and affection during infancy turn out to be more social, kind, and compassionate and care more about others. Children who get more affection during early life gain the most benefits in later life. Researchers found that kids who were held physically more by their parents, whose cries received quick responses in infancy, and who were disciplined without harsh punishment were more understanding; they were better able to comprehend the minds of others later in life.

One study illustrated the importance of early parenting and nurturing. Using brain scans, it showed that children who make their own schedules, evaluate their own work, and set their own goals truly build up their prefrontal cortex, and with that, they subsequently become more capable of making their own decisions and are kind of taking more control over their own lives. Supportive parents can directly influence healthy development of such kid's key brain regions involved in cognitive functions like memory and learning and other emotional aspects like worry, anxiety, and fear. It causes anatomical changes in the hippocampus (the part of the brain responsible for retaining and regulating learning and memory); it grows nearly 10% larger on both sides of the brain compared to that in kids with less empathetic mothers. There is also a direct influence of stress hormones on the hippocampus. High toxic levels of stress hormones can cause the hippocampus to shrink, resulting in depression, and recovery can cause new cells to sprout and to grow back. Growing up, adolescents face a number of personal, social, and emotional challenges like getting accepted by the peer group, separating from the parents, and accepting firsthand who they really are. One research found a startling difference in outcome when children are exposed to their very best peers who are little better and to those who are way better: children are encouraged and discouraged respectably. The reason is one very interesting psychological phenomenon known as reference bias. An intellectually equal peer can honestly advise and boost the vigor, while a highly intellectual can, unconsciously but seriously, make them feel inferior by drawing a faulty conclusion that involves induced anxiety-provoking transitions like worry, anxiety, and fear. During the developmental phase, different regions and circuits of children's brain mature at different rates. The important brain circuit amygdala responsible for processing fear is precocious and gets developed way ahead of the prefrontal cortex, the area responsible for reasoning and executive control. The brain of an adolescent is wired with an enhanced capacity for worry, anxiety, and fear but yet relatively underdeveloped when it comes to rational reasoning. One study showed that children who are often spanked do feel depressed and devalued, and their sense of self-worth suffers. Harsh punishments can bounce back because they promote false, lying, getaway, drop-you-low, and other allied and associated behaviors. Adolescents start to avoid or disappear on parents. Physical punishment in early life is associated with mental health problems, including fear, anxiety, depression, and drug and alcohol abuse later in life. Neuroimaging scans show that physical punishment may alter certain parts of the brain involved in the performance of IQ tests and certain parts of the brain involved in the regulation of stress and emotion. In the U.S., according to a survey in 2016, the trend is appreciating; the percentage of mothers in middle-income families who reportedly spanked their kids dropped from 46% to 21% over the last twenty-three years.

Relations among the members of the family undergo restructuring with the birth of a baby. Even the roles of the older children within the family undergo change. They have to be more responsible and often have to assume a caring and protective role for the juniors. The parents of the couple, who have become grandparents, have to assume a role appropriate as the grandparent, which is being conventionally more indulgent toward the kids than that of the kids' parents. While the parents of the children have to assume a strict role for the discipline of the kids, their parents, by their indulgent attitude, provide a counterbalance to the atmosphere of strict and rigid standards. The kids acquire a lot of informal education within the family through these relations while receiving their formal education through social institutions like schools or churches. Parents train their children to their studies in a playful manner judiciously and in tune with the natural bent of their respective characters. If moms argue with their friends, their kids will follow soon. In parenting, there is a mountain of evidence that kids mimic their parents' behavior, positive or negative. For example, when mothers report high levels of negative qualities with their close female friends, kids tend to report a similar type of negative qualities with their own close friends as well.

In one very long study, the researchers started with 243 kids from low-income families in Minnesota and followed them through long many years until they turned thirty-two. They recorded mothers' interaction with the kids during their first three years of life, and as the kids grew older, they periodically inquired the kids' teachers about the kids' social skills and current academic performances. Once the children grow adults in their twenties and thirties, researchers questioned them again about their current education, social skills, and relationships. The study found that those children with mothers who had more sensitive kind of parenting during their first three years of life had better academic achievement, more successful relationships, and superior social skills compared to those whose mothers didn't. The impact on academics appeared to be stronger, and the overall effects of parenting could even be seen past age thirty.

Apparently, kids may not pay adequate attention to their parent's teachings, but they can very well reproduce parent's characters faithfully. So, in contrast, therefore, we need not worry that children never listen to us; rather, we should worry in a way that they are always watching us. What we wish our children to become is what we should strive to be before them. The hard job children face today is learning good manners without seeing one. They benefit from the tales we tell them over dinner or during bedtime. They learn from the things we explain to them what we do. They learn to smile from our smile, they learn to love from our love.

Baby is a bundle of personality! A mother's relationship with her baby is not something that is easily decipherable. Her attitude to her baby is usually one of pure joy at creation. No kid is really old enough till his mother stops worrying. While the baby's dependence on the mother is fairly obvious, a mother's emotional dependence on her baby is more subtle. But the father has a more particular and personal role to perform. The child feels the difference between the father's outlook and the mother's outlook on life. Mothers are more likely to see themselves in their daughters, and fathers are more likely to see themselves in their sons. Compared to mothers, according to leading researches on parenthood, fathers do talk bluntly and tend to expect more from their children. While fathers talk directly and more honestly with their children, they try to resolve genuinely if there are any shortcomings. Fathers are less likely to pamper, or comply to their child's childish behavior. They like to promote discipline and self-reliance, more maturity, and more resilience. If you enquire children which parent is more likely to help them confront about their lives, about themselves, about their unpleasant truths, most children, especially daughters, will say, "Dad." From their side, they—both sons and daughters—appreciate that their father understands their need and can give them help in ways much different from those of mother's. The father adapts a crucial role, once child's very early years of life is crossed, more so if the child is a boy, because boys in their adolescent years often identify with their fathers and see a role model in them to emulate. Little thing like shaving is often seen as a masculine rite of passage, an inherited ritual passed from father to son. A big thing like when a son succeeds his successful father, it is the proud father who is born-again more successfully. In the animal world too, it is observed that young son-monkey prefers spending more time with father-monkey. Like father, like son.

A girl is not born as a woman but becomes a woman. The mother has a huge influence on that. Like mother, like daughter. Then again, a woman-mother is hugely influenced by the way her own mother acted. Women whose mothers had played with them and read to them are now more likely to play or read to their own children. It is the same pattern held for praising children, showing affection, and spanking as well. However, fathers are typically unrelated to how they were treated by their moms. The only exception noticed is spanking: fathers who had been spanked as a child are now less likely to spank their own children. Dads may inherit some habits from their own dads instead of their moms or adapt some practices from their wives or from someone else entirely.

The relationship between mother and son face special stigmatization than any other parent-child relationships.

Mother-daughter relationship is very typical. Father-son relationship is very common. Even father-daughter relationship is valued and socially accepted. But the mother-son relationship is viewed with little skepticism, perhaps due to the stereotypical taboo of strain mother-son relationship where a dominating mother interferes with her son's natural life and denies to let him come to adulthood of his own. Otherwise, in a normal, healthy, loving relationship where she is emotionally supportive of her son, she gets familiar with his individuality, his sensitivity, and his vulnerability along with his strengths and potentials, and she tends to teach the emotional intelligence to her son, the effect of which translates to better mental health later, and as the son reaches manhood, the outcome can be various.

Interestingly, kids transform their dads to a great deal. Fatherhood changes men's lifestyle to a decreased rate of tobacco, alcohol, and crime. Fatherhood promotes good behavior. A study monitored 191 at-risk boys from age twelve to thirty-one and noticed that once the boys became fathers, something was changed: their bad habits weren't quite as bad as before, they were involved in fewer crimes, and they used less alcohol and tobacco; fatherhood was a kind of transformative experience for them. On the contrary, men who did not have children were 17% more likely to die over a period of ten years than men who were fathers, and interestingly, the more the children a man had, the less likely he died of any heart-related problems.

Besides the romantic feelings of the parenthood, watching an infant grow up, develop his motor skills, and gain knowledge of the world with the help of his senses, is a source of pride and pleasure, fiction and fascination. Looking at a toddler, those wide innocent eyes, those instant smiles, those naive activities, one often wonders what goes on behind them, how much of the knowledge of the world these infants are born with, and how much they are learning through these experiences. Babies younger than nine months know almost nothing of the world and their surroundings, yet infants are more intelligent than we might believe. They view the world primarily with their emotional component and live entirely in the present. They construct their knowledge exclusively through observation. Their process of growing up happens largely by osmosis, through interaction with others around them. It is primarily through playing, working, and observing with other elders and youngers. A child discovers what he can do and who he can become. He develops identity and ability; if identity is taken away, his ability falls short. His knowledge is built up by many factors in upbringing. A well-brought-up child can be a result of several influences, some of which may not even be known or seen by the parents.

As soon as babies are born, they are capable of doing a number of important things. A still-developing brain receives a flurry of challenges. Sounds, smells, sights and touches, and other physical and emotional experiences flood in and wait to be processed. They are the groundwork for everything from language to emotion to protection, and especially, how to socialize with others. By six weeks, a baby starts smiling. As soon as the mother sees her baby smiling, the reward center in the mother's brain is activated, which spreads to the baby's brain to react similarly and simultaneously. By three months, babies begin initiating grins and eliciting reactions and attentions. From a cognitive standpoint, they can recognize faces and moving objects. Humans, by nature, are remarkably skilled at facial recognition: we can differentiate family members and friends from strangers in far less than a second. Babies can differentiate their mother from other people.

Babies recognize their mother's voice since they were in the mother's womb. From very early on, they are drawn into language and attempt to learn how to talk. By four months they are able to process language. While they can differentiate syllables and new sounds, there are ways for parents to help their children develop their language skills faster and more efficiently. Language, conversation and communication are our lifeline. Any attempt to engage the baby in a conversation led to better language scores. One simple way is to be around them and talk to them a lot and respond when the baby attempts to talk. Even if the baby is not forming the words correctly, parents just acknowledge that like some communication has occurred. Their synchronous movement with own kind of language—a language of affection—in repetitive syllables (babababa, mamamama, dadadada, gagagaga) are important signals to tell parents that babies are now in a state of learning. It sets up one important developmental social feedback loop—also known as *conversation*. Some words are challenging but teachable. A smile and a little pat encourage the baby to continue. Moments like these are precious. Don't let them die or fade away. So, encourage natural learning. Studies show that vocal and written language is acquired quite well before the age of six, but trying to force them to read before the age of four is counterproductive because the brain is not yet ready. Children reach plummet of language fluency at age 10, after which it is "nearly impossible" to reach native-level fluency. Learning ability starts dropping at age 17 or 18, and it is very hard to learn new language after childhood, primarily, due to changes in brain plasticity, changes in lifestyle, unwillingness to learn new things and lack of user-friendly grammar. Young children who learn two or more languages are better prepared to learn abstract rules and to reverse the rules that they have already learned. Cognitively, they are also better to figure out what people are thinking, which researchers believe, is probably due to the fact that they have to figure out which language to use every time they speak to somebody. They perform better in comprehension of a topic and in education, in general.

Kids are built-in intelligent sometimes with unbelievable potentiality. Ever wonder why children are so intuitive to figure out how to work with a TV remote? Or why they "totally get" computer or smartphone faster than adults? It turns out that kids are more open-minded than adults when it comes to problem-solving. They can even outperform adults in day stock trading. In one study where researchers tracked half a million stock market accounts in Finland over a 15-year period between 1995 and 2010, kids under 10—repeat, kids under 10—picked profitable stocks—profit up to 12% per day—in 72% of cases compared to that of 50% of adults. Kids have hidden treasure, no kidding.

A Nielsen study found that children in the U.S. aged 6 to 11 spent more than 28 hours a week using computers, cell phones, televisions, and other electronic devices. Another study found that children on the whole wasted 12 hours of free time a week, including 8 hours of casual play and outdoor activities during 1979 to 1999. According to the journal *Pediatrics* in 2015, the preschooler gets an average of 48 minutes of exercise per day instead of the recommended 60 minutes. School-age children (6–13) are now overscheduled and overloaded. One can easily assume that children's free hours have further reduced over the last few decades because many schools have eliminated the recess in favor of academics. Now only a few states require the recess or follow a recommended guideline on physical activities.

Recess in the middle of school hours is good for children and is backed by a large body of empirical research. Researchers from the American Academy of Pediatrics (AAP) recommend that children should participate in 60 minutes of "moderate to vigorous activity per day," and that recess should be a part of the academic curriculum. They argue recess is one necessary break for child's social, emotional, physical, and cognitive development—in essence, it should be considered as child's personal time, and should not be withheld for any academic or punitive reason. Yet, 30 percent of kindergartens do not offer recess. While aerobic physical activities can benefit the students to learn, absorb, and remember more, cutting it in the school is hurting students' performance, which shows up in grades. In one small study of 48 students between the ages 9 and 10, researchers from the University of Illinois at Urbana-Champaign showed that those with higher levels of physical fitness perform better on mental tests: students in the top 30% of their age group for aerobic fitness were better able to learn and recall, in a lab setting, made-up names and fictitious addresses than those in lowest 30% for aerobic fitness. This contrast was even more noticeable when the kids were tested in the most challenging way, say, after studying alone. All it suggests is that aerobic fitness boosts children's neurological processes potentially in significant ways, which is pretty much in agreement with previous research among elderly people that suggested that improved blood flow followed by physical exercise can keep neurons healthy and efficient, which can maintain the nervous system and improve the cognitive function. This study hinted the same benefits might occur in younger brains. In general, children are movement based; forcing them to sit still is pushing against human nature (even adults aren't wired that way either). Other research found that the active time is used to energize the brain, which makes all those still moments better learning: kids who are more active have faster cognitive processing speed, show greater attention and perform better academically on standardized tests than children who are less active. Yet "Sit still" is the mantra of many classrooms.

So, give the child a room to roam, a space to pace! Total parental controlling is pointless, neither total sheltering. A child should be surrounded by the children not by the adults. In the USA today, children are constantly guarded, monitored, and secured by the parents and are super protected by the laws. Kids spend 90% of their leisure time at home, often watching TV or playing computer games even when they are normal, healthy, and physically active. They are watched closely by the parents at home, by the teachers in school, and by other authorities in other activities. Overprotective parenting has gone to new absurd level security while the government is acting as a super nanny.

Young students consistently demonstrated performing better on academic tests if they participate in some kind of physical activity during the school day. Brain scientists think that exercise alters the biology of the brain in such a way as to be more malleable and receptive to new information, a process that they refer to as plasticity. Even for adults, in one experiment, learning a second language, is made easy if they exercise while learning: it amplifies their ability to memorize, retain and recall new vocabulary. In general, the brain begins to lose some of its innate language capability after childhood and displays lesser plasticity in areas of the brain related to language, and as a result, for most of us, it gets harder to learn a second language after childhood. Study of elementary-age kids by the medical researchers shows that kids who are not part of after-school exercise program tend to gain on a particular type of body fat that can have a deleterious impact on brain health, memory and cognition. Yet, prevention, protection and remedy can be just as simple and easy as playing outdoor.

Today's parents, who themselves had a completely different experience in their childhood, acknowledge that they had nearly unlimited freedom, whether they could ride bicycles and wander through woods, parks and alleys, unmonitored by their parents. In growing up, children need to go out to the world as a thrilled discoverer, as a wonderful explorer, or as a confident entrepreneur. Later, these experiences merge with their skills to engage themselves constructively, for their own good, for social good and for good, in general. Free play aids children to maneuver their inter-personal skills, guided play further advances their other skills, curiosities and abilities. Children will play and children will learn. Playing and learning are to be recognized and supported by the parents. But the irony is parents are the players and spoilers in the children's play. They are really depriving their own children, stealing their beautiful childhoods, especially in the light of opportunities to learn social skills and how to stand alone, handle situations, and steer their own life. It hurts them; the children soon suffer from anxiety, depression, and various other mental ailments, which in fact have gone up drastically in recent decades.

Given a lot of autonomy, children learn to settle their own differences, to make and break their own rules, and to respect the rights of others. They are able to resolve disputes, plan their time and manage their games. When they get a lot of autonomy, it feeds their self-esteem and mental health. They learn on their own without the protection of parents that friends can be kind as well as mean and that life is not always a fair game. Nowadays, kids are play-deprived. Simple games like marbles, stickballs, leapfrog, hopscotch, and hide-and-seek are dated back hundreds of years. The children of only the previous generation have had these games in their own settings. Yet that culture has just vanished almost overnight. A lot of popular and much-loved games have vanished from the school playgrounds. Some schools replaced tug-of-war with "tug of peace." It is not just in America but all over the world. A child's cry and a spontaneous scream and laughter that once filled the neighborhood, streets, alleys, and playgrounds have completely vanished. In its place, the games with rules, limits, and restrictions are utterly lifeless. For children thrown into this culture, it is a different socializing process.

Let kids play! The play is the work for the children. Play plays a key pediatric role in enhancing the development of infants, toddlers to teenagers. Playful learning supports children's *intrinsic* motivations to learn and discover, instead of *extrinsic* motivations to perform and score. Let parents be there, not to control the play or solve the puzzle for the child, but to help with *scaffolding* or to point out any clue indirectly. Let parents be there, not to provide fancy toys necessarily, but to encourage playing at home with household items. Let parents be there, even for little things like, for instance, if 3-month-old smiles, smile back in turn. These kinds of parent-child relations and activities may look trivial, but they are not. They are so essential a milestone development of language, social and emotional skills. So parents, to empower your kids in this anxious world, to grow them as a confident kid, give them a *lot of autonomy*—give them a real sense of willingness and choice, take the training wheels off, let them handle unsupervised play, let them deal with peers and let them self-directed learning. Don't interfere. To begin with, the influence that has always been considered affecting children is the presence or the absence of parents in their lives. In the initial years, they are fascinated by and in awe of everything they see around, which is a very novel experience for them. Children view the world while cradled in their parents' lap and love every new experience. For instance, children as young as three understand that sharing is important, but they really don't care until they are at least seven. If you watch at situations that show what kids fight about, it is mostly about sharing. You tell them to split a resource equally, youngsters, though agree in theory, don't share, in practice.

How to raise a parent! Essentially, children need parents, and parents need children. A parent doesn't have to be perfect to be a perfect parent. Perfections matter, but that comes later. The objective of a parent is to empower their children to succeed on their own. Parents need to avoid the overparenting trap and parenting from fear. Encourage children 'do it yourself' concept and motivate them, for example, to clean up after themselves, fix their own beds and resolve their own issues. Create an environment and teach them how—*they themselves, can teach themselves*—to resolve any problem in any situation. Psychologists at the Yale School of Medicine have developed one *parent-only* training program to train parents to change their message—calling accommodation is actually counterproductive for children with anxiety disorders—and to encourage their children to face anxieties rather than flee from them. The training highlights parent's own responses as the integral part of childhood anxiety and the new approach is to make children feel heard and loved, while using supportive actions to build their confidence. While parents provide their love and support from afar but don't take over, it helps the child to make out their own way of coping and ride whatever wave of anxiety they're having. By the end of the pilot training, nearly 70% of the 64 children had no anxiety.

Let the kids be the kids. When kids whirl through childhood, they love their parents with a passion so natural and innocent that parents at times find it difficult to comprehend. Instant softening and loving that kids give to parents without ever knowing what they are doing is something parents should be indebted to their children. These are the years when children cling on to their comforts of their home and their parents while trying to grasp the novel experiences of the world. Hence, being around for the children, engaging in simple activities with them, and spending quality time has no substitutes. It is the physical presence that nourishes affection, closeness and intimacy, and unconditional love and acceptance. Again, it has no substitute in the parental-child relationship. It is an established fact that children from poor families have lower noncognitive skills than those from rich families. Many social scientists believe that these lower noncognitive skills affect not only the children's academic performance in school but also a host of other capabilities later in life, including social skills in the family life, society, and workplace. In one study, scientists tracked children's behavior from kindergarten through fifth grade in order to find the effects of family income and working parents. The study revealed that poverty created measurable stress in children's lives and in the lives of their classmates who are also more likely to come from poor families. If mom and dad work two jobs, it's hard for them to spend quality time with children and help to develop these noncognitive skills. For example, in the U.S. on typical weekdays, dual-income-parents get very little time to spend with their children, usually four or fewer waking hours. This becomes a source of guilt for many parents. They try to substitute that by buying their children toys, gadgets, clothes, and other possessions. On average, an American child receives seventy new items per year. Yet meaningful inheritance parents can give to their children is a few minutes of their time each day. Storytelling is interesting. [Hint: Aesop's fables are great. An audio collection of 500+ stories is available online.] Stories ignite the imagination, cross barriers of time, leap over cultural walls, and allow children to exchange the experience of similarities and dissimilarities between themselves and others. Or there are also some mind-twisting riddles or jokes. [Hint: Something like asking children, "Why did the chicken cross the road?" Answer: To get to the other side. Q: Which side is the handle of a teacup? Hold the cup in front—ask if it is the left side or the right side. A: Outside. Q: Is zebra a white animal with black stripes or a black animal with white stripes? A: A zebra is an animal with black and white stripes.] Assist them—*to think how to think*—practically, logically, and fundamentally outside the box. Talking to children, reading with them, and playing with them give them far more joy than any favorite toy you can ever buy.

Parents are the first line of teachers that a child learns to emulate and appreciate. They are the primary and influential role models. For example, parents can teach math to their children by creating math culture at home—a culture around math. Math is a logical, functional, and practical application of not only how but why. Math is the hidden secret to the understanding of the world. It unlocks the mysteries and inner workings of all things; it follows the patterns of the arts, science, finance, and engineering. It allows us to go beyond our intuition to uncover these secrets and mysteries from nature to natural happenings, from physics to astrophysics, from the shape of our body to the shape of the cloud. It is in the musical notes of a symphony that gives the rhythm. Math is so beautiful! It is, perhaps, one reason why many philosophers who possessed great scientific minds were mathematicians. Math is interesting, and in the household, examples are plenty. Starting a ritual when the child is two years old using numbers like two pencils plus another three pencils can be a fun-filled bedtime math-solving ritual, fostering a love for math. If your child says 1 plus 2 is equal to 12, appreciate that and then find out his strategy why he came out with his answer (perhaps, like adding 'a' with 'm' equal to 'am') and then with your equal enthusiasm, give him your analogy. Never denounce him rather encourage him for the effort and give him next challenge. Give them a little math practice each day, even if they find it painful. In the long run, they will thank you for it. FUNdamentals of numbers along with its four basic FUNctional operations (+, −, ×, %) is one essential part of mathematics. In mathematical simplification, the order of operations has the acronym BODMAS which stands for: brackets ((3+2)), order (3^2), divide (3%2), multiply (3x2), add (3+2), subtract (3-2). You can ask curiously why March 14 is celebrated as Pi Day by the math fans every year. This is because the date (3/14) resembles the ratio of a circle's circumference to its diameter—pi (π)—which begins with 3.14. After analyzing the academic performance of 7,725 students, researchers said that to be good at math and science, a teenager needs to spend one hour a day for homework. It is not that long, but long enough. [Hint: A survey by a British math writer revealed that the number 7 is the world's most favorite number.] Kid-friendly math according to age will encourage a math-shy kid to love math in later years. One problem a day keeps the fear away. A math problem could be a fun thing that kids seek out because they are otherwise bored by the dry math worksheets in typical school settings when they could be exposed to a chock-full of real-life stories and be entertained with fun-filled illustrations.

However, all learning is not and should not be *fun.* The more we try to make learning fun, the more we *dis-service* children's ability to deal with difficult topics. Math is one prime example. Math is a language of science, engineering and technology. Like any new language—which is best acquired through memorizing vocabulary, understanding detailed, and accompanying thorough in-depth practice—math requires practice. Practice makes perfect. Becoming proficient in any skill, requires the development and improvement of neural patterns which is acquired through much of practice and repetition. With enough practice—not just any practice but dedicated and intensive practice—most of us can achieve a level of proficiency that an expert would envy! Many scholars claim that the traditional way of learning by rote (memorization by repetition) has its merits: some learning requires just plain effortful practice, especially for children. It allows the neural patterns of learning to take form. Citing an example, they argue that to *internalize* the multiplication tables, children need to memorize. It enables them to do math faster, while those using blocks or fingers to work out the problem, are slower and less accurate. Unfortunately, as they point out, the way math is taught in the United States often downplays the practice in favor of stressing the conceptual understanding of the theory, principle and formula. Parent, teacher and educational authorities together need to research the situation and come up with the solution, which would be beneficial for the children, progress for the society and elite for the nation.

Some physiologists assert that 1, 2, 3 is easier than A, B, C. Teachers find math more easily addressed than reading. In a home setting, do one-time math stories, other time other stories or anything that parents might tell them interestingly. Do you know where I work? Do you know where your grandpa was born? Children who score high on the do-you-know test, exhibit higher self-esteem and a greater sense of control over their lives. The do-you-know and general knowledge proficiency is one single biggest predictor of emotional health. Kids typically assimilate these and other tiny pieces of information given to them often casually and thoughtlessly. They gradually get familiar with the normal everyday world and learn to appreciate the fact that the world is interesting and work has dignity and labor is necessary. It is pleasing and perfectly natural for both parents to do some work, so long as they are not completely deprived of their share of their parents' time and attention. This way of involving children in parents' life would help them understand that by being away from them for long hours, parents are trying to facilitate a better future for them. Keeping these channels of communication open with children is very important even in the middle of a hectic work life that happens to be the reality for many parents. Social researchers show that it is only ten minutes of productive conversation at practically any time of the day, for example, in the setting of any family dinner, that children get an important benefit. Research after research have shown that children who normally eat dinner with their parents and siblings at home, do better on a number of mental and physical health issues: (a) higher self-esteem and more positive outlook; (b) higher reading scores, better vocabulary, and better school grades; (c) lower rates of substance abuse, school behavioral problems, depression and teen pregnancy; (d) fewer eating disorders and better body image; (e) eat more fruits and vegetables and drink less soda; and (f) lower rates of obesity in childhood and in adulthood.

In general, happy and successful children have parents who basically do not do things for themselves that satisfy their own needs rather than the needs of their children. The parents' job is to motivate the child to develop a sense of self that is self-determining, natural, and at par with reality. If you treat your walking toddler as if he can't walk, you obstruct his effort and diminish his confidence. Once he has done something well himself, congratulate yourself for the job well done and move on. There are actually two stages of parenthood, and it's hard to differentiate when the transition goes from one to the other. When kids are really young, one to two years old, you can't be too loving; you just need to support and pay attention to the child's need. But at some point, somewhere around two or three, you need to change yourself because kids need independence and challenge. Otherwise, prolonged sheltering and unnecessary lingering intervention make him feel bad about himself (if he's young) or angry at you (if he's a teenager). What he wants to do at this stage of life is to establish his confidence that he can do the thing of his own. Success is not the absence of failure. The little challenges that start in infancy present him the opportunity for "successful failure," the failure he can live with and grow from. To rush too quickly or to rescue him too early is nothing but to deprive him of these challenges, which he needs later in life to handle similar demands of life. Let him feel the depth of life. Doing things for him unnecessarily or prematurely reduces motivation, increases dependency, and damages the child's own confidence. So, give your child an autonomy to do something interesting with a full sense of willingness and choice. Take gentle care for the girls; because, the confidence levels of girls between the ages of 8 and 14, as research asserts, tend to fall as much as by 30 percent. At age 14, while girls hit their confidence level all time low, boys' confidence is still 27 percent higher; and the effect lasts long. Girls might be over-thinking, people-pleasing, or might be a bit reluctance to speak up in the class, or try out any new sports, or in extreme cases, may put themselves in harm's way. When such emotions typically kick in, the confidence effectively comes to a grinding halt. Yet, research affirms that girls' confidence can be restored, encouraged, nurtured, or even freshly created during such turbulent years, just by turning off the negative thinking from their head, and then gently convincing them to embrace—the risk and the failure.

Raising confident children begins with your confidence in yourself and your ability to take appropriate and effective action. Here, confidence is contagious in the sense that kids get what it takes to get up and do something they find a challenge through learning and discovery. As a parent, you play a role to create an environment and support a system around children that lay the foundation for fulfilling their potentiality later in life. But don't overprotect them; they may otherwise start to take more risks because they feel safer. Few indicators in encouraging confidence can be motivation, emotional stability, direction and values, positive mindset, self-awareness, flexibility in behavior, enthusiasm to discover, thriving health and energy, readiness to take a risk, and finally a sense of purpose. You create a foundation to build these skills from a young age, and children will strengthen their skills day by day.

Too much praise is a burden! It's unnatural! Overpraising and over-nurturing do more harm than good because children experience an inflated perception of their abilities. They suspect flattery. It's a neurobiological fact. When parents praise their children's intelligence, parents believe they are enhancing their children's self-esteem. But that's not what happens. Sociologists found that about 3 out of 4 American parents think it is important to appreciate their kids that they're smart. Now as a social norm, everyone does it routinely. Kids are saturated with messages that they're smart and that they're doing great. It is a protection that the children do not sell their talents short and a constant reminder to excel. "You're so smart" just seems to roll off the tongue. An effusion of accolades regardless of the excellence displayed with expressions such as "We are proud of you" can do exactly the opposite of what is intended, and it does not provide any warranty against underperformance. It does, unfortunately, pave the path to failure. An excess of praise takes away the child's natural control of success and distorts his motivation. It undermines the inherent bulwark against adverse situations where things can go wrong or how to handle failure. On the contrary, the unique openness of children may allow them to experience a larger spectrum of reality.

The psychology of winning and losing! By and large, the appraisal on admiration shows that it can be effective as a positive, motivating force. There are over 15,000 scholarly articles written between 1970 and 2000 on self-esteem and its role in kids (and adults alike) to everything from education to self-control (from sex to career advancement). Anything likely to harm the kids' self-esteem is eliminated. Competitions are discouraged. Soccer coaches stopped bothering about goals and handed out trophies to everyone. Teachers withdrew their red pencils. None is berated for underperformance, and every child is showered with praise. They press the lemon little too hard, go a bridge little too far! Participation trophies and prizes are given to almost all children. Children are showered with confetti of cheap prizes and are persistently assured that they are the winners. Parents and teachers alike never realize that the chickens will come home to roost someday. In the beginning, they react positively to praise. They tend to appreciate hearing that they're talented, smart, and so on. It is a part of the larger cultural conspiracy: to succeed, you just need to show up. But such noble endeavors with some elements of dishonesty are often counterproductive: high self-esteem, of its own, does not improve the performance, the grades, or career achievements. One study in 2016 in which eighth-grade students in the U.S. and South Korea were asked whether they were good in math. Among the U.S. students, 39% said they were excellent compared to only 6% of the Koreans, but in the actual reality, Korean students scored far better in math than the over-confident American students. Confidence is good, but overconfidence does not assist the students to acquire the required strength to cope with the actual situations and, especially, to handle the failure. By the age of four or five, children aren't fooled by all those praises. They break down at the first encounter of difficulty and get demoralized from the failure; they'd rather cheat than to risk the failure again. The problem is further complicated when the parent ignores the child's failure and still insists that their child will do better next time. But it flips. The flipside of too much praise is students may start focusing on the reward rather than actual learning. What's more telling is that failure leads to a devastating and confusing situation for a student whose confidence is based on an inflated ego rather than actual abilities. While the ability cannot beat the ego, now the task is how to teach a student the failure that failure is a part of the process, failure is the pillar of success. As a matter of fact, now the task is how to *teach* the American parents that failure is the pillar of success. Here, culture comes into play. Culture is the culprit! American parents believe that failure is debilitating, believe that children see failure as concerned to their performance, and believe that scores and ranking are important rather than education, knowledge, and learning. But you need to value the education as a culture, as a country! Therefore, the very fact remains: if your child is struggling in some area, acknowledge it and try resolve it; don't hide it. Help them without hurting their feeling. In helping them in an assignment, for instance, a parent need not be a student either. Over-parenting is robbing their children of adulthood. National survey in 2019 indicates that (a) 75% of parents of children ages 18 to 28, had made appointments (for doctor or haircuts) of their adult children, and had reminded them of deadlines for important college curriculums; (b) 11% would contact their child's employer for an issue; (c) 16% had texted or called to wake them up so they didn't sleep through a class or test; and (d) 8% had contacted a college professor or administrator about their child's grades or a problem they were having. The prevalence is across lines of class, race, income or education.

Let the parent be the parent, let the teacher be the teacher, and the student be the student. And then, let the learning happen! At the college level, heavily praised students, when confronted with a harder task, often drop out altogether rather than suffer from a mediocre grade. They do the requisite work in general, but without scholastic potential, they do not get motivated promptly to do it well. For many taken to the task, college begins to feel like a pressure cooker. According to surveys by the Center for Collegiate Mental Health in 2018, and by the American College Health Association in 2017, a record numbers of college students are seeking treatments for anxiety and depression: the number of students (a) visiting counselling centers increased by 30% from 2009 to 2015; (b) felt depressed in last 12 months is about 40%; (c) felt overwhelming anxiety, over 60% and (d) seriously considered suicide, about 10%. Intimidated by heavy course load, students now face a hard time in choosing major, because they are afraid to commit to something they cannot succeed. At the workplace as well, they still believe mere attendance is all it takes to get a promotion, which is obviously a demand far-fetched. The simple fact is that we humans are all rational being, and in full control of our destiny, and if we accept that truth and take the responsibility—no name-and-shame policy—we naturally see ourselves in a good life; otherwise, we fail.

You got a friend in me! Narcissism is on the rise! Narcissism is one irrational fascination with oneself. It is unreasonable, excessive self-love and an erotic gratification resulting from admiration. On the whole, millennials are more likely than their parents to make an artificial claim that they are above average practically in every way, from their academic achievements to their entrepreneurship to their drive to get ahead. They are special, unique. Parents give them unique names. Pop culture is fast and furious. Pop songs are focused on the self. Social media offers a platform for them to portray themselves more exclusively and positively. They are out of touch to 360-degree of people. America's vanishing adults without facing hardship in childhoods! In one survey in 2016, researchers evaluated that they scored higher on the Narcissistic Personality Inventory. Another survey questioned 565 children aged seven to twelve years, the age when signs of narcissism first start to emerge, and then questioned their parents afterward. The researchers found that overvaluing the awesomeness is partly responsible to affect narcissistic tendencies; whereas, withholding praise and affection, on the other hand, lowers a kid's self-esteem a bit temporarily but does not affect narcissistic tendencies. Self-esteem is a feel-good phenomenon about yourself, while narcissism is a craving to be felt good about yourself. People who kill people and people who kill themselves often have their roots in towering narcissism, strong sense of grievances, and a fatal desire for fame. Therefore, earnestness in praise is essential. One single mistake parent usually makes assuming children aren't intellectual enough to see and feel their true intentions. Just as grown-ups can sniff out the true meaning of a cloaked compliment or a disingenuous apology, children, too, scrutinize praise for hidden intentions. According to life science research, young children under the age of seven only take praise at its face value, while older ones are just as judgmental as adults. Research showed that if the parents' praise comes with the feedback about the behavior and the choices children made, it helps children to cope better with difficult situations five years later compared to superficial praise that focuses more on the children themselves like, "You're a good boy." Praise is important but not the superficial ones. It should have some merits on real ground, some skill, or some talent they have. Otherwise, while children get insincere praise, they take it meritless; over time, they discount or completely ignore not just the insincere praise but the sincere ones as well. This is quite pathetic.

So, parents, be firm but real and loyal! Be loving but understanding. Parenting advice is pretty simple and is often monochromatic. However, a one-size-fits-all approach may not be the best way to handle all things always; rather, a parent's flexibility may be the key to a well-adjusted kid. Then again, nimble parents who tailor their parenting approaches to each child's individual personality can transform the child who will be half as likely to have symptoms of fear, anxiety, or depression compared to the peers of parents who don't take children's temperaments into consideration at all. When it comes to independence and space, for example, parents should let their children's outlook be their guide. Being overly involved in grown-up children's lives can do more harm than good. Helicopter parenting decreases children's feelings of autonomy, competence, and confidence. In a way, parents send unintentional messages to their children that they are dependent and incompetent, and subsequently the problem snowballs and get worse. Yet, it succeeds. Authoritative parents like parents of helicopter parenting, parents of strict discipline, parents of strong religious belief, regardless of their income and social status, tend to be more authoritarian who expect discipline and obedience from their children, and do subscribe to corporal punishment. One study, using children's developmental milestone data of thousands of American teenagers for years, researchers find that the children of *authoritative* parents are (a) more likely to graduate from colleges and graduate schools; (b) less likely to use drugs, smoke or alcohol; and (c) begin experiencing sex at later adult ages. Once again, parenting is a delicate balance: independence is good, but too much may go a wrong way.

Serious empathy deficits! Empathy is one mutable trait which can be taught like education. Cultivating empathy on child-rearing has traditionally been low. Fostering cognitive empathy in children's early life is possible. It needs more of a rational approach—than of an emotional approach that one might intuitively think. According to new research, that each of us is born with a given number of neurons that participate in our empathetic response, is *not* true. The social skill can be learnt from early life experience, which then can be nurtured and practiced more effectively. Each of us is born with a certain endowment, and it can be dramatically regulated—up or down—depending upon environmental factors. To practice, you don't have to be a *yes man* to every request, neither have to be a *world savor* to world's every problem. Instead, you recognize which is most important to you, something from your own life experience that determines which is most close to your heart that deserves your time and resource. With that idea in mind, a healthy degree of empathy can be instilled in children's early life by their parents, teachers and caregivers (in child care and pre-K settings). For instance, if a child is fearful of a dog, instead of saying 'Don't worry, he won't bite you,' acknowledge and accept child's fear as genuine, and then say something like, 'Are you afraid of the dog? Let me hold your hand. Don't worry, I am with you.' Such a secured endorsement, in and of itself, validates your child's difficult emotional situation, instead of you being judgmental. It helps them to learn cognitive empathy.

More than test scores and earning certificates, children especially need to understand and appreciate the people around them in order to be better able to work together, innovate, and solve a problem. About 20% middle-school students consider suicide as a solution to peer cruelty, 70% of college students admit to cheating in class, and 33% report having felt so depressed that they find trouble to function normally. Social scientists call it a selfie syndrome due to, in part, the rise of social media and, more importantly, due to the decline in our moral and ethical parenting styles. Today's children are more self-absorbed than ever. Here are few hard, cold data about millennials, the selfie generation (birth years ranging from the early 1980s to the early 2000s or those aged 20 to 36 in 2017, roughly about 80 million in the U.S. population):

- The occurrence of narcissistic personality disorder (men are more narcissistic than women) is about 3 times as high for youngsters in their twenties compared to that for the generation who are now 65 or older. Tragically, 58% more college students score higher on a narcissism scale in 2009 compared to that of 1982. They got into the situation perhaps because in the 1970s, parents desired to improve kids' chances of success by instilling self-esteem. It turned out the opposite way—not so great for keeping a job or a relationship. It was an honest mistake all along. Test scores on empathy also fell sharply; they struggle understanding others' points of view intellectually.
- Millennials might have got so much pampers and so many participation trophies while growing up that the lack of burden denied them the depth of life. They are drifting away from traditional institutions—social, religious, and cultural. They have lower political aspiration than any previous groups.
- They have student loans, higher level of unemployment and poverty, and lower levels of personal income and savings than their two immediate predecessor generations had at the same age.
- One study showed that at the workplace, millennials as much as 40% believe they should be promoted every two years, regardless of performance.
- According to studies, they are obsessed with fame: compared to their parents, about 3 times as many middle-school girls want to grow up to be a famous person or want to be a senator. Yet only 60% are

capable to judge what's right; their mental and social development is stunted (many children ages 18 to 29 live with their parents than with a spouse and are covered against parents' insurance until they're 26). Never before in history have so many youngsters been able to grow up and reach age 23 so dominated by peers.

- They are not responsible enough—only 60% of them under 23 want to have a job with greater responsibility compared to 80% in 1992. Astonishingly, these are not just rich-kid problems. Poor millennials have an even higher rate of narcissism, materialism, and technology addiction in their ghetto-fabulous lives. They are "digital natives."
- Today, the average middle-class American household displays pictures of mostly themselves compared to family photos, parents' portraits, and school pictures in the 1950s. They have fewer civic engagements.
- A 2014 survey showed people 18 to 34 years old did not check the voice mail and preferred telephone greetings like, "Please do not leave a message."
- In 2014, only 26% of millennials were married.

The fruit is rotten before it had a chance to ripen. Childhood is one important part of children's life. Children are missing that. By the way and the pace that our lives are changing today, children are often denied a fair share of their childhood, either because parents today tend to worry too much about the child's tomorrow, or because children are denied the simple joys of a young life due to lack of resource. One way or the other, when children are denied a normal childhood, they hardly experience normal adolescence and adulthood. For instance, children, when pushed into an early adult experience, act mature apparently but remain immature actually. They cling to childhood longer, sometimes all their lives. [Classic examples: Michael Jackson (1958–2009), the King of Pop, was bodily and emotionally abused in early years by his father during incessant rehearsals, though he also credited that his father's stern discipline played a major role in his success. The American celebrity actress Elizabeth Taylor (1932–2011), who had early years as a child star, reflected that "apparently, I used to frighten grown-ups, because I was totally direct."]

Children today are exposed to an unprecedented dose of adult reality. [Dear children: If you want to understand your parents more, ask them to talk to you about their own childhood, then you will realize where their fears and their expectations about you come from.] Today's young kids are more familiar with and are more likely to value individualistic personality traits like fame, achievement, and wealth than kids of the past decades. Instances of child labors, child soldiers, child computer prodigy (one kid got Microsoft OS certification at age five), kids chasing master's, kids becoming MD at the age of fourteen, TV child idols, and child stars are not unheard of. By pushing young adults into adult territory too fast too soon, the unusual trajectory of growth followed by these young minds leads to very complicated adult life. Survey shows that the median age of the workforce at the top tech companies is fifteen years below the national average. To count the chicken early, scoring high academically or beating athletically in the school should not be the aim to start a childhood, particularly as it tends to exhaust the youngster early enough that they fail at a time later when they should go full throttle of energy.

A U.S. child psychologist rightly observed, "The shift from the perception of the child as innocent to the perception of the child as competent has greatly increased the demands on contemporary children for maturity, for participating in competitive sports, for early academic achievements, and for protecting themselves against adults who might do them harm. While children might be able to cope with any one of those demands taken singly, taken together they often exceed children's adaptive capacity." Thus, the first victims claimed by the pressures and tensions of modern life are children denied of the pleasure and joy of childhood that are rightfully theirs. Parents should not kill the pig to clean the pig.

Navigating these treacherous currents of difficult childhood, one reaches the even more complicated territory of adolescence. These are crucial, formative years in a child's life, perhaps even more so than childhood in terms of maturing of the mind and the body to set the stage for the adult to take shape, where one becomes the individual one is destined to become. However, adolescents in today's world are happier than adolescents in previous decades according to one survey in 2015, perhaps due to the cultural shift toward individualism that might favor them an opportunity in self-focus and self-interest. Adolescence should be a time of growth, challenge, and discovery. It is during this phase, the early teens, that the final physical changes take place, which transform an individual from an adolescent to an adult. These years also coincide with the onset of puberty. Puberty is one of the important and profound biological and social transitions in whole of the life span. The role of hormone and physical changes that characterize the onset of puberty is well researched and documented. Apart from the changes in height and weight, changes occur in the hormonal secretions and sexual characterizations. The phase of development of the child when these changes occur is called the pubescent phase. The phase ends not only with physical maturing but also with sexual maturing. In girls, prepubescent changes typically begin an average of two years earlier than in boys. At this stage, the girl suddenly grows taller and heavier than boys of the same age. The pubescent phase of a girl is also characterized by the beginning of menstruation. The other sexual development in girls is the development of breasts. In boys, the growth of the body is accompanied by deepening of the voice and appearance of facial hair.

The social context of an adolescent is more wild and more complex than that of the infant or the child. These are the years of exploring the world outside the confines and security of home boundary. Children at this age start to think and reason differently and begin to develop a close relationship outside the family with networks of their age. One noteworthy social phenomenon of the adolescence is the noticeable importance of peer groups. Peer groups gain huge importance in the lives of young adolescents and continue to do so for at least the next ten years, till the teenager is molded into a more assertive and mature individual who gives precedence to his thoughts and instincts, rather than succumbing to any peer or parental pressure. Also, disputes, disagreements, and differences with parents emerge for the first time during these years as young people develop their own views that are not fully shared by their parents. They reform their own mental conviction and figure out what they believe and why. Adolescents spend quite a bit of time to hang on in each other's company, which helps them gain a sense of identity that is distinct from that of the family. Sailing through these formative years may at times prove to be rather tough, for trying to gain acceptance from people of the same age group, coming from varied backgrounds could prove to be an uphill climb the mountain for some and an easy breezy afternoon walk for others. Children learn how to win. Children learn how to lose. They generate the power of their own to fight through their business of life. Microaggression or submission in daily conflicts helps them the caches for the future. Silently, they sort themselves into popular, accepted, or rejected categories.

Acceptance and rejection from peers at this stage in life can be a huge morale and confidence booster as well as a dampener at the two extremes. The difference is huge. One case study may be worth mentioning here that the racial gap in achievement between African American and white college students has been stubbornly persistent for a long time. In the U.S., hate-filled racism is real, and the racial disparities and other biased outcomes in the social functions, in the criminal justice, in medicine, and in many professional settings can be described by unconscious attitude and stereotype racial bias that is silent and subtle. Social studies indicate that if one can restore and increase the African American's sense of belongingness—as opposed to feeling lonely and rejected—it can have an immediate effect to cut the grade point average (GPA) gap in half, resulting in long-term higher academic performance and better health outcomes. Acceptance or rejection from the peers is a game changer, a big deal.

A teenage brain is 'work in progress,' which continues to progress into the mid-20s. Middle school is typically a growing pain and challenging. It is a time of chaotic emotions and confusing relationships that have surprisingly lasting effect on the future. Adolescents venture to rely on peer groups for support, security, and direction at the very time when such things are urgently needed because at the same time, other peers are also venturing in similar transitions. To be socially inclusive, they—both boys and girls—jointly use social media like Instagram, Snapchat, Facebook or texting. They are predisposed to be influenced by their friends as a group, and remain particularly vulnerable in areas like smoking, drinking, experimenting with drugs, and bullying. Survey shows that teens who best resisted peer pressures during junior high are less likely to engage in criminal behavior or to have alcohol or drug problems. This possibly is the reason behind the belief that children after a certain age do not welcome parental advice. Occasionally, they may pay attention to what another adult says, but once they reach adolescence, children don't want to subscribe to their parents' line of thinking. During this phase, they acquire social skills not so much from adults but from their interactions with each other. They mostly discover through trial and error which strategies work and which do not and later reflect consciously on what they have learned. However, contrary to this cultural stereotype, there are some social thinkers who believe that the family still remains quite influential in the case of adolescents. They testify that no social institution has as great an influence in a child's life as his family does. In choosing their peers, adolescents typically gravitate toward those who exhibit attitudes and values consistent with those maintained by their own parents, and ultimately, they do adapt themselves as well. Adolescents continue their close and supportive relationship with their parents, and their relationship with peers tends to support their parental ideas rather than going against. However, looking at practical cases from real life, what one might conclude is that this way of subscribing to parents' views by choosing peers accordingly is largely subconscious. On the other hand, the visible trend largely points to the fact that consciously, the teenage or adolescent years are those of a subtle rebellion in terms of wanting and trying to accept and live a way of life that is unlike what their parents think to be appropriate.

Here is one illustration in the context of taking a driving lesson from parents. Parents do not scare the child with raw data like car crashes are by far the number 1 killer of teens. Scare tactics perhaps scare them but do not help them to learn the lesson of driving safely. The best way is rather to adapt positive behaviors, to provide positive reinforcements, and to make the child feel competent of the skill—for example, how to scan the periphery, to look from side to side on the roadway, and to recognize road hazards and not allowing another teenager as a lone passenger. [Hint: Research shows that if a new driver has one other teenager in the car, the risk of a fatal crash increases by 2 times and, if more teenagers, by 5 times.] Parents can scold their children, telling them that they are behaving badly or doing poorly in education or that they should improve or pay more attention to their studies, but that doesn't work because (a) human behavior flows from hidden soul that needs constant care and craftily pushing rather than bluntly pushing around and (b) of the fact that warning lacks the reason about shortcomings. Typically, kids continue the same trajectory because they have fallen into the pattern of action from which they are unable to escape. So, parents need to extend their helping hand, cleverly obliquely, to get out of the negative cascade of actions and shoehorn them toward the positive flow of actions. Under the circumstances, parents' supportive advice works far better than that of their peers.

Thanks for arguing! A decent argument with mom wins the day: a mother-child deliberation benefits the teens to fend off the peer pressure. A household argument to resist peer pressure is the key quality that helps children to understand and be assertive through calm reasoning rather than whining or yelling. It does not seem to be a good thing if parents always gain the upper hand in arguments (e.g., tiger moms) with their own sons and daughters. Study shows that adolescents who quickly back down in the course of an argument with their mothers have a harder time resisting peer pressure to use drugs and alcohols than teens who are able to calmly, persuasively, and persistently argue their points through with their moms. Sometimes doing so may create unintended consequences. When the kids are at age thirteen, two-way conversations are quite possible and predictable than that of at age fifteen or sixteen when the teens have more likely been influenced by their peers already. At the school curriculum level, study shows that arguing improves students' reasoning skills as well. Reasoning skills that emphasize debate-type dialogical discussion with others are more effective than arguing on paper, say writing an essay in isolation.

However, this is mostly a passing or a transient phase and, in most cases, ends coinciding with the end of adolescence. Children going through this phase require very tactful handling by the parents in order for children to turn out as responsible adult citizens. It is at this stage in life that the child also gets exposed to the various problems of bullying by playmates, sexual abuse, drug abuse, as well as depression as a result of peer pressure. Schoolchildren in the U.S. are replete with anger, anxiety, grief, trauma, and physical and mental problems. Instances of teenagers physically assaulting each other and having tumultuous relationships with classmates are not uncharacteristic at this age. At times, there are vicious assaults and attempts to brand a child as a nonconformist—almost like an "outlaw"—which can prove to be mentally disturbing.

Today, in the United States, a typical teenager in school is not only stressing on grades, prom, or heartache but also tackling amid larger paralyzing issues like violent relationships, broken homes, and illegal immigrations. They are simply not ready to work on math or a poem. One of the things one can see a lot, one did not see as much before, is depression. About 1 in 5 U.S. kids experiences some form of mental illness—depression, mood disorder, substance abuse, suicidal behaviors, eating disorders, anxiety, stress, and more serious mental illness as bipolar disorder, as well as experimentation with tobacco, alcohol, drug, and sex. The well-being of mental health and acting in response to problems, if they arise, require a range of adolescent-friendly health-care and counseling services in the home, school, playground, and social communities.

A balanced set of rules prevalent at home for the teenagers to abide by, as well as providing healthy limits around their behavior, can help curtail the intensity of some of the adolescents' problems. About 80% of teens who experience good relationship with their parents are also happier with life in general. Maintaining a family environment congenial to open communication between parents and children will further encourage the latter to take their problems to their parents when the problem gets too difficult to handle, as that might be the only solution in some cases. Parents need to prepare them to face the day. A homely home environment is the key. It encourages a free exchange of thoughts and ideas between parents and children and also gives the former some knowledge of what's happening in the teenager's life, which is important to monitor, if not from close proximity, at least from a distance.

Parents believe honesty is one moral compass that they want to instill in their children. Aesop's fables like "The Honest Woodcutter" and "The Boy Who Cried Wolf" speak the value of honesty and the danger of dishonesty, respectively. In contrast, child psychologists suggest that children start lying as early as, age 2 and that lying at young age is often considered as a normal. Lying is not only normal, but also an important milestone in children's developmental intelligence. In one experiment, children are asked not to peek at a toy hidden behind them while the researcher leaves the room under false pretense, and then after few minutes, return and ask the children if they peeked. This simple experiment was designed by the developmental psychologist Michael Lewis in the mid-1980s and has been tried on hundreds of children. The outcomes, and follow-ups thereafter, are consistent, which are interesting and worth considering: (1) a vast majority of children peek at the toy within seconds of being left alone; (2) at least one-third of 2-year-olds (toddlers), half of 3-year-olds and over three-fourths of children over 4, lie peeking at the toy; (3) toddlers who lied turned out to be higher verbal IQs than those who didn't, by as much as 10 points; (4) children are good at lying—so good that it is hardly detectable even by experts, including teachers, police officers and judges; and (4) children who don't peek at all are the smartest of all, but they are rare.

By the age of four, almost all kids experiment with lying. Parents should expect that. When children begin to lie, although lying is something to be discouraged, there is actually a positive takeaway. It reflects one very important milestone in children's cognitive development. One may, otherwise, call it an "intelligent judgement or intelligent disobedience. It is the same skill set that allows them to lie, is the same skill set that allows them to make social interaction. Children come to understand first hand that other people have different beliefs than they do. They experience in perspective of their moral understanding, and the features of the specific situation. They enforce the executive function, which is an important accomplishment. (Cognitive skills like the ability to control impulses, staying on task, memorizing, remembering and making good decisions are collectively known as executive function.) Parents need to listen carefully to their answers or the arguments. Is that real or just a reason not to feel guilty? Parents should not threaten lying children with any consequence of immediate punishment. If they do, the threat of punishment only turns kids into more frequent lies and falsehood. But the question is what happens over time? One advice to parents is that they should take it easy on children for first few occurrences, and then if they suspect that a lie is forthcoming, motivate a child to tell the truth by telling something like: "You make me really happy if you tell me the truth." Another way to motivate is to set stable rules, but leave a door open for some negotiation. That may lead to two possibilities: (1) telling parents the truth that may lead to anger and arguments, or (2) just outright lying. Arguing over actual rule is one better alternative than lying. Some anger and arguments with parents are actually good, not bad.

The key to passing through this phase of the childhood without any bad consequence to either the child or the parent, lies mostly with the parent. Teaching a child to stop lying is a challenge. Experts in the field of Psychology and Child Psychiatry advise parents a few ideas:

- Prime the child with truth and get the habit of truth, for a practice. Praise the child and encourage to say something, say, that happened at school that is true. When the child complies, praise enthusiastically.
- Cite an example, give a model of truth. Tell a story, or something happened to you when you were a child or something happened in recent memory. You need not be dramatic. Help children to visualize what is truth and, especially, what is *not* truth.
- Emphasize the moral value of the truth and deemphasize the punishment. Wait and see. No rush. When you get a chance, or are able to make a chance, give encouragement a boost.
- Parents need to intro-scope children only on a *need-to-know* basis. Children understand that. And thus, what is required of the parents and averting more lies afterward, is to respect the child and his burgeoning aspiration to be independent.

Let parent be patient, a good listener, not a trespasser of child's solitude. Only then, parents will understand that the urge, that distinguishes an adolescent from the rest of the adults at home, is normal and natural. When adolescents seek autonomy and independence, from their side too, it's no small a task—to detach from those who have superintended their life nearly in every aspect so far. Now, once the teenagers have had their time and space to establish their own preference, interest and taste, their allergic response to their parents, dies down. Plus, from the perspective of neurological development, as they grow up, their evolving cognitive capacity allows them to think beyond the parent-child relationship, especially, how they themselves want to be.

Soft parenting! In earlier generations, children wished to make their parents happy, but today, it's the other way around—parents wish to make their children happy. Well-known, parents want the best for their children and see their children succeed even if it means giving them a gentle nudge. Gentle, yet strong! But sometimes, the judgment is clobbered, and parents' actions can actually impede children's progress. For some parents, those nudges often turn into a huge push: parents actually do things for the children—from tying the shoe to doing homework to making beds—what children should be doing for themselves. To make children happy, parents also lie. Sometimes, they lie so much that some sociologists have dubbed the practice as "parenting by lying." In the U.S., 80% of parents lie to their children just to sway children's emotion or behavior. This is alarming and paradoxically surprising. Parents seemingly justify the act in terms of a goal they want to achieve. While parents may often be afraid that there will be a lot of crying now, the right thing to do is for parents to be consistent in principle; the child will adapt eventually. When parents themselves live by the principles of honor, faith, and service, then their children will follow suit as well.

Rules blindly imposed on teenagers, at an impressionable and rebellious age, stand far greater chances of being flouted. The solution here would be to involve the children in the rulemaking process and get them to decide and agree on the dos and don'ts. They may like to provide their own thoughts and inputs, which, if paid heed to and discussed thoroughly, stand far greater chances of being obeyed. Working parents, who stay away from home and children for long hours, often try to compensate for time not spent with them with material rewards. But this may be fraught with the possibility of being interpreted as a sign of guilt and weakness, which would be exploited later. Instead, compensation should come in the form of quality time spent with them whenever possible, which would benefit children in every way. For mothers with young children, especially, it is hardly possible to be both an ideal mother and an ideal worker because it's just possible to be either one of the two; both are equally fictitious.

Some teenagers are famously reckless. Take for an example the motorcycle-related fatalities which account for 1 in every 8 deaths on the road. Teenagers speed motorcycle or car too fast, experiment with the drug, play with the gun, and try illicit sex and many more dangerous activities. CDC reports that more than 16,000 young people die each year from unintentional injuries. So far, the evolutionary psychologists thought that young brains are not just developed enough to make smart decisions, but the opposite. New research suggests that in a few teens, the brain matures not slowly but too quickly, which the psychiatrists, with trial research, find that these few teens have enough white-matter pathways that appear more mature (to venture risk) than those in risk-averse teens.

White matter contains myelinated nerve fibers—essentially the brain's wiring where the neural strands connect the various gray-matter regions (where actual nerve cells reside). They are, otherwise, independent to one another. Myelin is an electrically insulated pipe-like material that forms a layer around the neuron and is essential for the good functioning of the total nervous system. Myelin varies in composition and configuration, but it performs the same insulating function (like the outer layer of an electrical cable). In appearance, the myelinated axon is white and is typically called the white matter of the brain. White matters are in the frontal lobe of the brain region, which is responsible for decision-making. As nerve impulses travel faster in matured white matter resulting in increased processing speed, maturation of white matter is an important factor. The pattern of brain's pathway structure changes as children grow: between grade school and grad school, the brain's information highways get remodeled to become more efficient due to the emergence of executive function.

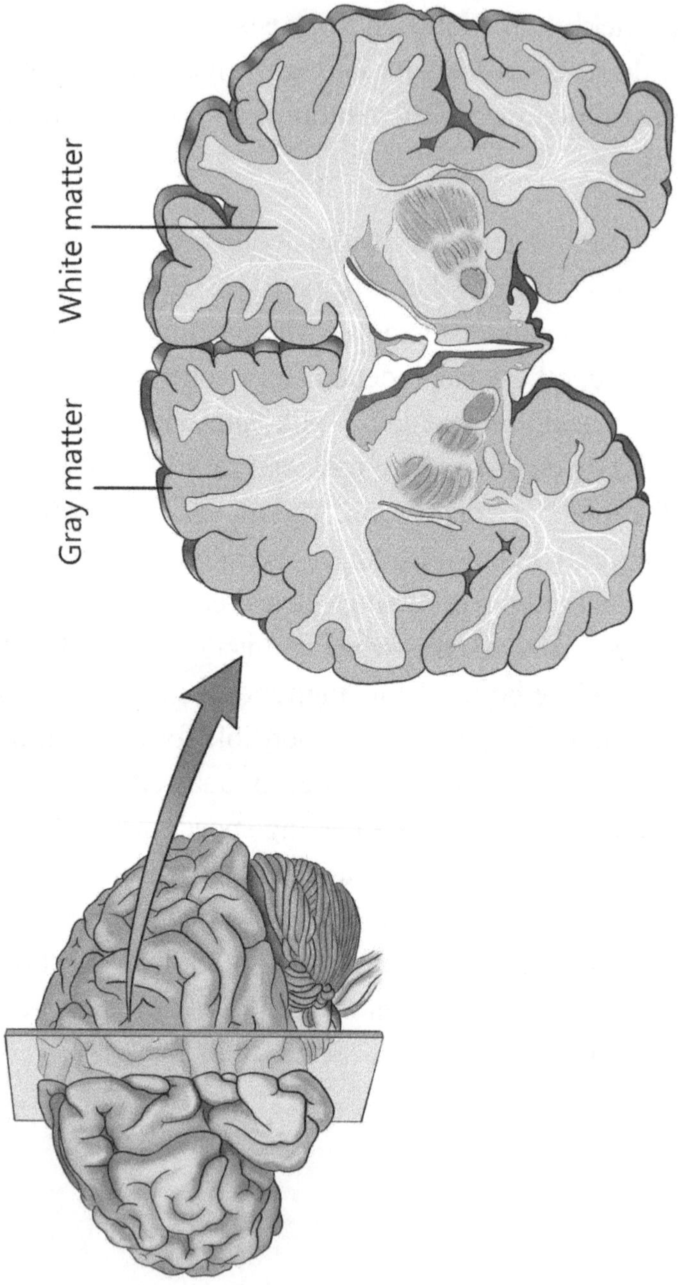

White Matter and Gray Matter

Teenagers are typically cynical: the whole world is against them, grownups are messed up, parents impose curfews, rules and schools don't make much sense, and they have a ton of power to undo and redo the world. They often put themselves in characters of dystopian fiction, in a strange land that makes them believe so, only in the world they know. Their brains are so responsive to emotionally arousing stimuli that when they feel sad, especially, they often put themselves in a situation where they feel even sadder: feel fear of missing out, listen to sad music, post damaging messages in the social media, watch melodramatic TV shows, and read dystopian novels. Quite often, the sadness kindles their developing brain with some big emotional ideas like fairness, justice, loyalty and mortality. As their brain develops, so do the executive functions. Teens now try to recognize the difference between logical reasoning and hypotheticals, and start to understand the real world that things are not always black and white, and that there are whole lot of ethical grey areas out there.

One study tried to find a connection between exercise and white matter in children and noticed that children who are more physically fit have more volume of white matter in their brains than those who aren't as physically fit. White matter is essential for attention and memory retention and is vital for linking different parts of the brain together. With respect to maturity, there is some gender-based difference in the timings: girls' brains mature faster than boys' brains. In one study, scientists tracked 121 people from the age of 4 to 40, scanned them using MRIs, and documented the ebb and flow of new neural connections, and they found that some brain fibers that bridged far-flung regions of the brain tended to remain stable while some shorter connections, most of which were redundant, were eliminated, and that entire reconfiguration occurred sooner in girls' brains than in boys'. From another study involving nearly 1,000 children aged 8 to 22, it revealed that the small differences between girls and boys before puberty become larger at around age 12 or 13 and that patterns remain throughout the adulthood. The more mature the brain is, the more risk-taking to new experience the teenager is. A matured brain is synonymous to what actually lead some kids to seek out a new, novel, and sometimes, potentially harmful experiences.

When do children become criminals? Sadly, it is when an early life closes early! By age 23, at least 1 in 3 of all youths in the United States is arrested at least once for something like shoplifting, underage drinking, robbery, assault, and murder. Social media with fake news and manipulated pictures and videos accelerating the incarceration drive of teenagers and young adults especially the blacks and browns. This is happening across the nation arresting children in groups and gangs. Juvenile detention is very alarming. Most teens are from minorities, more than whites. Low-income juveniles are routinely denied the right of legal representation, which is supposed to be guaranteed by the constitution. The poor kids get a stereotype injustice—an assembly-line justice—that can hunt them for the rest of their lives. In 2009, overall 1.6 million were arrested on drug charges. The war on drug has succeeded by imprisoning millions in jail. For comparison, the U.S. has 760 prisoners per 10,000 citizens, while Britain has 153, France 96, Germany 90, and Japan 63. The higher incarceration rate of the U.S. should not be the case.

Let no guilty escape! You did the crime, now you do the time! True. But punishment should fit the crime. In the name of punishment, the U.S., being 5% of the world population, has 25% of the world prison population. Here, while the male prison population is about 90%, the 10% female population are of important consideration. Female prisoners represent more than 30% of the world female population and are growing at an even faster rate than that of the overall prison population. The number of women prisoners has increased faster than that of men in 2014; it has increased almost 14 times from 8,000 to 110,000. Women accounted for 26% of total arrests in 2014, compared to 11% in 1960; the most common offenses involved drugs, which doubled for men but tripled for women, according to the Bureau of Justice Statistics. U.S. jails (jails are for short-term, minor crimes) and prisons (long-term, serious crimes) are primarily male gender environment. Pregnant women face their own gauntlet of humiliation especially when shackled during labor and delivery and while rearing their newborns. It cuts a very sorry figure indeed despite any legitimate evidence that they pose any threat. Most of the newborn babies are separated from their mothers immediately after birth. It has a destructive impact on families. Two-thirds of female inmates are mothers (some are teenage mothers) and have their little children. Children are typically shipped off to foster homes where they bounce for years, which only make their path to successful adulthood more difficult. The current prison system—today's Jim Crow—has increased mass incarceration eightfold since 1980 to the point of diminishing return. Incarceration is the further cause of desperation. Due to widespread incarceration of the mentally ills, U.S. jails and prisons have become the warehouses. By some estimates, nearly half of inmates have a mental illness. Without any functioning school, an enormous burden is placed on correctional officers, who are also human, to act as mental health providers when they're not adequately trained. Suicide is the leading cause of death in prison due to dangerous living condition, especially the lack of mental health care. Criminal treatment of mental illness is insane. They are all but crimes against humanity. Laws are designed only to break "man's will to live alive." Citizens are imprisoned and tortured repeatedly on a regular basis. Torture is not American culture. Yet torture is ramped. Inmates are out of the jail and into the jail. They are so immune that the jails do not feel like a jail but a holding cell.

In general, crime is considered as a matter of public safety. Now, some social scientists argue that it is also a public health issue. Because, crime spreads like a disease, similar to a blood-borne pathogen spreading from person to person, ultimately affecting the entire community. They experimentally illustrate that after the crime, regret comes almost as fast as anger, and that the control of first 5 minutes can make all the difference: between committing a crime and not committing a crime, between an open life and a fallen life. To steer away from the situation, a child needs our kind attention, willful deliberation and planned welfare service. Offering beneficial social services, and programs supporting multiple visions of recovery from prison, pregnancy and murder, works better than using one rigid approach. Given the option of work or crime, they will opt for work. Encouraging teens to take part in welfare programs do lead to better care than using the criminal justice system to coerce them. Programs that use sympathy and reward, rather than apathy and punishment, are actually more effective. Instead of creating a divide between those who would prosper and those who would be fed to the great hydra of prison, parents and teachers need to peach in and escort these teens to cross the barrier. To teach them accountability, responsibility! Once they learn responsibility, they earn liberty—never imprison again!

The teenage years can never be crossed without experiencing sensitive issues and topics. A big number of these are related to the sensitivity of some kind of attraction toward the opposite sex. Handling of these emotions by parents requires a lot of tact and thoughtfulness. Sometimes, the way we talk to boys and girls about sex stereotypes them and hurts their feelings. The issue must be dealt with a sensitive and nonjudgmental attitude. The parents must project that they are entirely neutral in the matter, encouraging the children to discuss the matter more freely and openly. Physiologists advise that a paternalistic approach is justified, yet parents should aim to keep the talk as soft as possible. It gives them leverage of negotiation to see things from both points of view; otherwise, hard paternalism, on the other hand, is coercive and intimidating. After all, parents are duty bound to guarding their children against making bad decisions.

At what age should you talk to your child about sex? There is no specific time and age at which a child is suddenly ready for "the talk," of course. But knowing when the moment is right is down to the moment of connection between the child and the parent, the parents expressly. If the parents are putting off the chance because they think it is not relevant yet, then a real chance is hard to come by. Paradoxically, for children between the ages of thirteen to seventeen, by the time parents got around to the sexuality sermon, 40% of the kids had already had intercourse. Lack of discretion in bringing up children, more so by working couples, may lead to unwanted impacts on children's upbringing. Some pampered and difficult children can arm-twist their parents to obtain all they want, and the more they get, the more their belief gets reestablished that theirs' is the right way to act. They often experience mood swings and throw tantrums, which makes life further difficult for their already harassed parents and forces them to give in to these demands. These kids run the risks of growing up to become extremely introvert; that makes them almost incapable of communicating with others.

Kids in adolescence are like people at the crossroads often not knowing which way to take. They are in search of an identity. They often have an amorphous picture of the role they would play in life. The parents may help the kids at this stage to clear their self-doubt and gain a sense of direction and progress, which will be consistent with the values the kids have imbibed from the family and the society. It is necessary that the kid develops self-respect, self-esteem, and self-acceptance at this stage, which is possible only if he is treated with love and respect. Emotions do not come out of repressed desire or needs but directly from our thoughts, beliefs, attitudes, and ideas. So, hearing bad remarks from others, saying humdrum statements to ourselves, and being in the company of low friends all generate negative emotions and add up to the crisis of identity over time and represent the poor psychology of life overall, which, otherwise, can easily be altered for good life. Such a crisis, painful sometimes, is also necessary to forge a stronger, more commanding self. The virtues of gentleness, sympathy, patience, and kindness are also acquired at home. For ethics, principles, morality, and goodness, home is the appropriate vehicle for conversation. Children who get good experience and who get love and care from parents also learn to care as they grow up. Good manners and simple respects get them a long way in life.

A child at an early age should acquire an idea that distinguishes between the good and evil. Thus, one of the first lessons in child upbringing should be to make children feel self-esteemed in and around themselves, for it helps them to continually recognize and integrate with their newly acquired value as they progressively grow and mature. Self-esteem is an important part of their fulfillment and happiness in every aspect of life: how they function at school, at work, and the way they strive to achieve. Their self-esteem develops in proportion to the level of trust reached in a parent-child relationship. A parent who trusts children educates children. Blood is thicker than water. Trusted parents, who set examples in kindness, honesty, friendliness, hospitality, and generosity before their children, will later find children behave to them in a similar way.

The world is different and difficult from the family. The world doesn't care about your child's self-esteem. It is tough out there. Children evaluate themselves by assessing their worth in the eyes of others. The world is demanding and expects you to accomplish something. If children are exposed to critical, sarcastic comments about their capabilities and harsh words, they will suffer a loss of self-esteem and confidence. They will be left with a feeling of inadequateness and even worthlessness. They start developing a negative self-image and forever, keep believing that irrespective of the worth of efforts they put in, their work can never be worth enough. Such a negative perception of the self can easily be prevented from forming in the first place through positive involvement of the parents. And that makes a vast difference in the child's life.

During the time of adolescence, children enlarge their natural sentiments of pity, friendship, and generosity. They advance and adventure for an understanding of human behavior and a host of human characters and gain insight into the strengths and weaknesses of human value as a whole. The parents can play an effective role during this formative period. One critical quality in this regard is whether and how they communicate their love to children, the disciplinary methods they use, and their own behavior as role models. Psychologists have long identified two essential components of parenting: structure and warmth. Adolescents may have authoritarian parents (higher standard on both structure and warmth), indulgent parents (lower on structure, higher on warmth), or neglectful parents (lower on both). Authoritative parents achieve both: they hold a higher standard for behavior they expect and get, and offer love and affection as a treat. Children are different from one another, in personality and temperament. Some are active, others quiet; some shy, others bold; some self-assured, others less so. Parents must keep in mind to respect these individual differences, which form the cornerstone of a good parent-child relationship.

Not any single area of interaction alone can account for parents' influence on a child's behavior and social skills. One study has classified four such areas:

- To the scale to which parents try to control the child's behavior

- The pressure imposed on a child to perform well at high levels of social, cognitive, or emotional development
- The transparency of parent-child communication
- The parents' nurturance of and love toward the child

While the parents accommodate children's independence in general, responsible parents hold firm positions and provide clear reasons for them. Along with communicating their expectations from their children and putting in place firm discipline tactics, it is also imperative that the parents let their children understand that parents are humans too, and thus, they are not infallible. Hence, for example, when a mistake is made, it is important for parents to apologize and yet not sound guilt ridden about it, but the apology should come forth in a manner that is prompt, straightforward, and sincere.

These of course are the all-too-well-known best handling tactics for bringing up children coming down from ages. But today, the childhood itself is in crisis, and the issues parents confront now cannot be discounted as mere generational prejudices that our fathers and forefathers used to face. For instance, childhood obesity escalates as junk food sellers bombard children with slick ads all over. They portray a happy meal, heaven in hand. A child cannot escape that. Today, children spend more hours engaged in multi-electronic medias—TV, games, videos, and other online entertainments—than they spend in school. The mass media and communications are not a natural or neutral invasion. They take advantage of child psychology and change their course of advertisements solely to their profits. American children in the age group of 8 to 18 watch TV 4 hours a day on average.

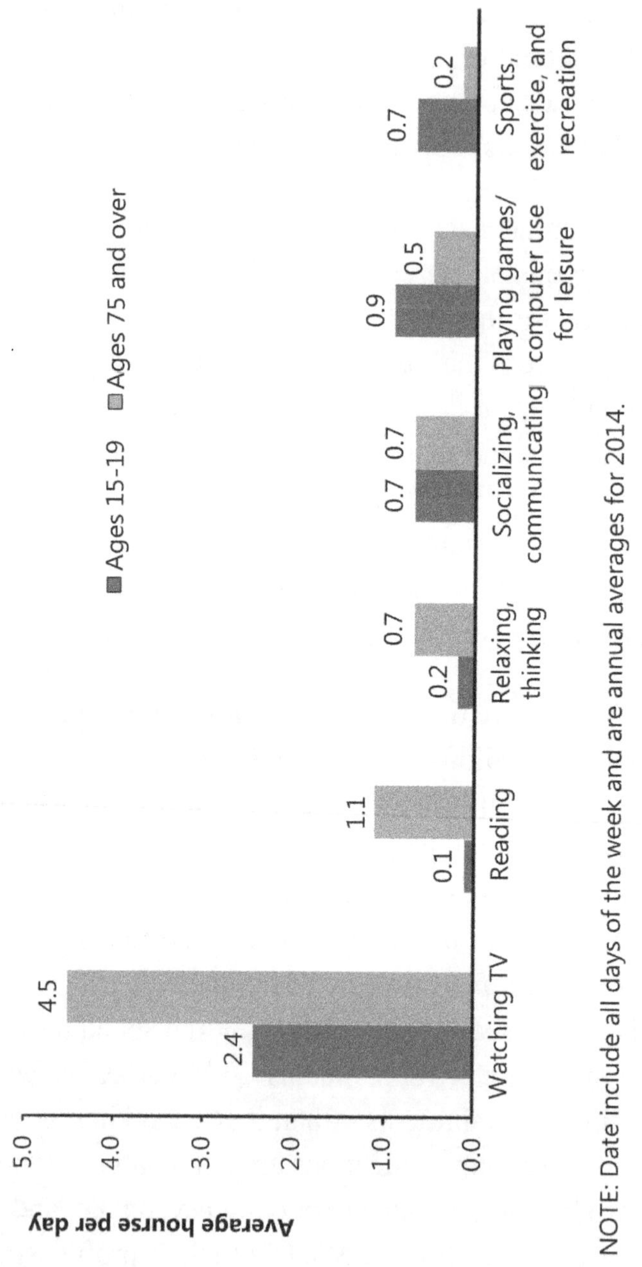

Average Hours Spent Per Day Watching TV, Reading, Relaxing, Computer Games and Sports

Hundreds of studies indicate that much of what children experience from video game and porn, involves aggressive behaviors, horror of violence and sexual imagery. Gaming feeds the young mind an endless "novelty" and "surprise factor," always desperate to make it to the end of the game. Teen porn exploits with "arousal addictions" and the thrill that course through. For children and adults alike, sex and violence grab our attention not only because they are everywhere, but because of our evolutionary root:

- *sex* is a paramount need for humans as species, as every mating is an opportunity to keep the species from getting extinct; and
- *violence* is a survival guide that has been attuned to safety that prepares humans to defend themselves.

So, sex and violence are innate characteristics for the human. Also, one study indicates that intense video-game playing may release dopamine which is responsible for addictive behavior due to dopamine squirt, and at the same time, the absence of boredom. Overexposure makes children become further desensitized to violence and inert to human feelings in real life leading to the possibility of psychiatric disorders. Social scientists note that current generations of college students are the class to grow up having played video games for a good part of their childhood. Those games having significant content on competition, frequently destroying objects and killing people, could desensitize their own feeling and the feelings toward others as well. Yet children's media remains largely unregulated. Video games designed on modern warfare are now a big business. Another area of concern is harmful psychotropic drugs that are less effective to cure and more damaging to children than parents had been led to believe. For instance, sex video games do harm a boy's brain. It reduces their empathy toward the female as a victim of violence. Boys treat women as secondary characters who are typically used as sexual objects by the players (in some games, the women are depicted as prostitutes or strippers). Clinical brain scans show boys' diminished empathy toward female victims. Video games, especially, differ from other incidences of violence in the sense that, here the player is taking an active role, which in effect, we let ruin our children. By any measure, our current failure to provide enough protection to our children in the face of corporate-caused harm, only reveals nothing but the sickness in our societal soul.

In today's complex world, situations on the domestic side do not always remain ideal. Ups and downs and agreements and disagreements will always remain a feature of all domestic households, and children will always take lessons from difficult situations and will prepare themselves accordingly. But what the parents can always try to avoid is the situation getting out of hand or the disagreements and discords becoming more frequent than they should. About 35% of women around the world have been raped or physically abused, according to statistics the World Health Organization (WHO) released in 2013, after analyzing data from 141 studies in 81 countries. About 80% of the time, this violence occurs in the home, at the hands of a spouse or loved ones. Domestic violence of any form is never okay and is not acceptable. Yet the World Values Survey from 2010 through 2014—a major and an extensive study of social functions and cultural attitudes in about 100 countries conducted on a regular basis since 1981—gathered that one-third of men say it "may be acceptable" for a husband to "beat his wife" and that one-third of women approve that a husband who beats his wife may be justified, at least in some of the times. The cultural approval of spousal abuse is so pervasive that in some countries, a vast majority of women say it's acceptable as a social norm. Domestic violence hurts women's overall health. It takes a toll on their young children who develop various complications and abnormalities later in life. Examples are abundant in our modern-day society, and they often present themselves as serious societal problems that become the subject for contemplation of thoughtful minds. American society is a case in point, being riddled with every conceivable problem starting with broken homes and unstable parents, and its children, the most vulnerable segment of society, have fallen victim. Problems ranging from obesity to depression to large cases of sexually transmitted diseases among teenagers have taken center stage, and the Americans are looking everywhere to find solutions to help their progeny.

While Western societies, in general, are facing a rising number of issues on the social and domestic fronts in the U.S., the incidence of HIV infections and sexually transmitted diseases (STDs) among teenagers has been on the rise. "The human immunodeficiency virus (HIV)," as defined by the World Health Organization (WHO), "is a retrovirus that infects cells of the immune system, destroying or impairing their function. As the infection progresses, the immune system becomes weaker, and the person becomes more susceptible to infections. The most advanced stage of HIV infection is acquired immune-deficiency syndrome (AIDS). It can take 10–15 years for an HIV-infected person to develop AIDS; anti-retroviral drugs can slow down the process even further. HIV is transmitted through unprotected sexual intercourse (anal or vaginal), transfusion of contaminated blood, sharing of contaminated needles, and between a mother and her infant during pregnancy, childbirth and breast-feeding. HIV continues to be a major global public health issue, having claimed more than 39 million lives so far. In 2013, 1.5 million people died from HIV-related causes globally." After investigating the archived samples of HIV's genetic code, researchers now identify its origin in Kinshasa, the Democratic Republic of Congo, and its beginning was sometime in the 1920s, long before HIV was officially recognized in the 1980s. In the U.S., there are 1.1 million people who live with HIV: 78% male, 44% black, 33% white, and 24% female. A medical team from Columbia University developed one handheld device that can be plugged into a smartphone and be used as a diagnostic tool to test for HIV and syphilis very quickly. Using a finger prick of blood, the device searches for three infectious disease markers and completes the diagnosis in just 15 minutes. The mobile devices are being used at remote places like rural Africa and are saving millions of lives from sexually transmitted diseases.

Sexually transmitted diseases (STDs) are primarily contagious infections. They get transmitted through sexual contact from person to person. There are about thirty different sexually transmissible viruses, bacteria, and parasites. The most common ones are as follows: gonorrhea, syphilis, chlamydia, trichomoniasis, chancroids, genital herpes, and genital warts. Syphilis and HIV are transmitted from mother to child during pregnancy and through medical operations involving blood products and tissue transfers. According to the WHO, approximately 1 million people acquire STDs every day globally (out of total population of 7300 million).

In the U.S., a national study found four common ones (that 1 in 4 is infected with at least one of the diseases) among girls and young women:

- human papillomavirus (HPV),
- chlamydia,
- genital herpes, and
- trichomoniasis.

According to the CDC, the prevalence in 2008 is as follows: 3.2 million teenage girls were infected with one or more of the four diseases, the leading two being HPV (18%) and chlamydia (4%). Each disease can be serious in its own way. According to 2018 CDC report, young people aged 15 to 24, account for almost half of 20 million new STDs reported each year.

Here are few cold hard-core facts and serious statistics for teenagers and young adults. HPV is very common, so common that almost every sexually active adult—man and woman—get it at some point in life. Therefore, if you are sexually active, it is more likely that you are infected with HPV. Gynecologists recommend that teenage girls have their first gynecologic visit when they are 13 to 15, and if they haven't done so yet, at least get an HPV vaccine. As many as forty different types of HPV may infect men and women in their genital areas. Almost 70% of healthy Americans are infected with HPV with at least one strain of the virus, out of which 4% could lead to cervical cancer. Most HPV do not show symptoms and go away of their own, but some can cause cervical cancer in women and other less common genital cancers—like cancers of the anus, vagina, and vulva. Some HPV shows up in the form of warts in the genital areas of men and women, called genital warts. They may not be a life-threatening disease but can cause worry and anxiety, and the treatment can be very painful.

The current guideline recommends that women over thirty should do a pap smear every year. The procedure involves scraping and analyzing the cells in the cervix to check if the cells are normal for three years in a row. Other panels of experts recommend that women over thirty should take HPV test as well in addition to the Pap test, as the HPV test has proven to be quite accurate in detecting the presence of high-risk viruses in the cervix that could go on to become cancerous. Obviously, dual screening promises fewer cancers. careHPV testing procedures (visual inspection with acetic acid) diagnose HPV, identify potential cancerous lesions, and provide treatment all in one visit. Doctors or trained nurses, using visual inspection, can quickly treat and remove the harmful tissue. Like a Pap test, a careHPV test is very effective if done every year; it has a huge benefit. One unusual study found a link between HPV and increased risk of heart attack and stroke in women. One meta-analysis reviewed fourteen studies and suggested a possibility of diagnosing HPV by identifying HPV DNA sequences. The study claimed that urine HPV test has as much as 87% overall sensitivity (the proportion of positive results identified). Urine tests are also 94% correct in identifying negative tests. So bottom-line advice is this: urine tests may be a very good option for women who are not consistently doing cervical screening or who live in remote countries.

In spite of educational campaigns and public health efforts to combat them, sexually transmitted diseases (STD) continue to rise, with 19 million new cases annually, according to the Centers for Disease Control and Prevention (CDC). Probable reasons are higher levels of reporting, better screening techniques, and perhaps, reduction in protected sex. Dispensing new vaccines accompanied by more awareness campaign can help diminish rates of infection. Educational campaigns and healthy discussion are paramount to guide young people through a health-focused approach to prevention, as opposed to scary delusion. Scare tactics are a bad idea; social scientists call it an information aversion behavior. It produces worries and anxieties. Instead, many health screening services are now explaining politely how dreadful the diseases can be and securely drawing their attention to routine tests as much as possible.

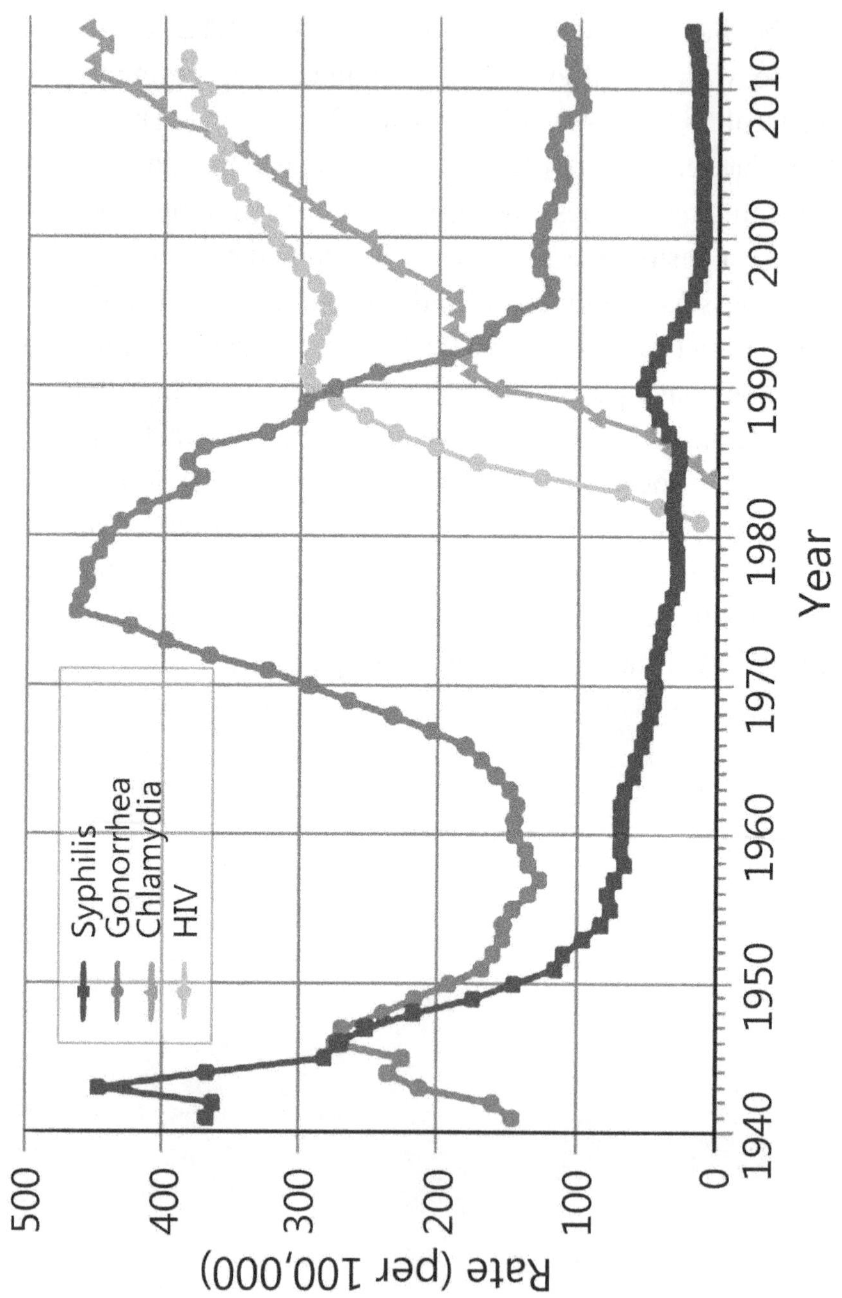

Sexually Transmitted Diseases in the United States

A word of caution to teenage girls for Pap test and pelvic exam! Doctors recommend that teenage girls are probably better off continuing still with their pediatricians who have been seeing them since they were babies. Pediatricians are better equipped to deal with the issues surrounding puberty, menstrual disorders, contraception, screening for cervical cancers, and sexually transmitted diseases (STDs). Most teens do not actually need a full pelvic exam, complete with speculum, and they do not need an initial Pap test until their twenty-first birthday.

During adolescence, kids are often exposed to half-baked information and wrong ideas on various issues. Parental intervention to provide sex education is critical as it is one of the sensitive topics where incomplete or flawed information could lead to harboring misconceptions for years to come. Parents should approach the topic in an open and frank manner and should not expose any embarrassment while telling the child about the man-woman relationship. Their body language should be very relaxed and casual and should at no point convey that they are uncomfortable about discussing the matter as this may lead to the conclusion on their part that sex is something to be guilty and ashamed of. The parent should read the child's mind in the eyes. A child coming back to the parents for information or cross-checking is definitely a healthy sign, but it will be decided by the clarity of the message and the warmth of the manner in which parents initiate the discussion and communicate the message especially for the first time. However, one good news is that more and more young adults born in the 1980s and 1990s are choosing not to have sex, according to the *Archives of Sexual Behavior*. They are twice as likely to remain virgin compared to Gen Xers—born in the 1960s and '70s. The safer-is-better state of mind is also reflected in drinking: underage drinking is at an all-time low. On the whole, our teenagers are better behaved—less likely to smoke cigarettes, try alcohol, binge drink, have sex, and carry weapons; not to mention, they wear seat belts and use condoms, according to CDC.

Today, 15-year-old daughters are 15 times more likely to be using illegal drugs as their mothers did when they were 15 years old. Marijuana is by far the most common teenage drug. In a national survey, almost 10% of girls aged 12 to 17 said they had used illegal substances in the past month. By the time they are 18 to 25, it is 16%. Boys and girls are at similar rates. A survey in 2015 revealed about 6% of college students smoke marijuana daily or nearly daily. Statistics reveal that even though substance-abuse rates in kids have been dropping for more than a decade, still $1/3^{rd}$ of eighth-, tenth-, and twelfth-graders have used some form of the drug (including alcohol) at least once. Some signs like thrill-seeking and impulsivity, depression, anxiety disorder, ADHD, or significant mood swings are to be watched by parents carefully—particularly when the child is under peer pressure. Teaching kids some practical cleverness like how to avoid peer pressure, for instance, is more successful than scare tactics. However, honest efforts led by peers may work better than those led by teachers.

Another trend that has staged entry in the last decade or so is related to the world entering the age of internet, a giant global computer, and the creation of a huge virtual world. Rapid progresses in information and communication technology have given birth to new devices, which when placed in the hands of children have given them access to unwanted information and have often robbed them of their innocence. Innovation has spurred broad societal changes. As cellphones became universal, teenage users have found a new form of privacy and an easy way of communication, which was unknown to them only a few years ago. Experts recommend the best age for teen to get a smartphone is about 14, around the start of high school. They also call on smartphone manufacturers to develop digital lock that limits how long children can use their smartphones. As half of U.S. teenagers are addicted to their mobile phones (according to a Reuters report in 2017), the call for better parental controls is welcomed by academics studying youngsters' use of technology. An average American checks phone 47 times a day. So, install a time-tracking app to monitor how long and how often you use the phone. It might depress you first—but it's a one way to start to curb your impulsion. Use apps to block other apps. Delete social medias. Replace phone-time with your own-time: spend prime time with your loved ones, read a novel, take a walk, or watch the blue sky, see how clouds are floating away. Or, do all those things you're supposed to do, or you haven't got time to do. Now, you got the idea!

We sometimes worry that we are collectively becoming a little too blasé about our scrutinized lives. Advantages of technological solutions are balanced by the mistrust of technology taking over our lives. In public, the demons are always lurking somewhere beneath the surface of our high-tech surveillance. The mobile device you carry that you think is a mobile phone, guess again, is a tracking device that happens to make a phone call as well. It tracks you not only wherever you go but also whatever you do with it. A mobile number is even more important than a social security number as it is linked to so many databases and connected to devices you interact with. In private everyday life, while it may seem harmless to attach a chip to our preschoolers' clothes, think again. Do you really want to raise a generation of kids that are accustomed to being tracked—like cattle or warehouse inventory—reducing the very little privacy of their own? With the tech taking over everywhere in the homes, schools, and public places, worry rises. Challenging the practices of an industry built on data collection, parent groups, and privacy, advocates have now started campaigning for wide-range legislation protecting children's personal information. A kid is a private citizen; everyone needs to understand that.

Innovations in science and technology are not making us less smart. Personal devices are gradually becoming the future of work as well. The only thing we need to do is to curb our appetites for technological device and delivery (on demand: I want it, all and I want it now) that are becoming more and more immediate all the time and to motivate the critical importance of personal contact and communication collectively. Communicating in cyberspace can preclude our social connectedness to the real world. Parents and children plugged into their devices cannot provide such interaction. Children using the internet and internet alike are not always welcome. One study surveyed computer use among half-million fifth- through eighth-graders in North Carolina and found that the extent of home computers and high-speed internet access was responsible for the significant decline in math and reading skills. A CDC study found a strong association of regular gaming and internet use with increased risk for depression, higher body mass index (BMI), and other negative physical and mental health issues. Studying internet addictions, researchers found that people who compulsively browse, socialize, and play online have higher rates of moderate to severe depression than people who are not compulsive. They also spend proportionately more time on sites having sexual contents.

Is technology making us lonelier? Perhaps. From stone carving to palm-leaf writing, from pencil to printing, from computers to the internet, and more recently, our smartphones, each has evolved communication in its own way. Digital communication today is so invasive that most of us don't even think about its presence or bother to worry about its role in society. It has vined everywhere. We expect more from machine technology and less from human prodigy, more from digital life and less from real life. Things are evolving fast and furious and sometimes so vulnerable—especially in mobile communication—that it's getting into a zone of ever-growing dangerous level of made-to-measure relationship with each other. People would rather, as the trend goes now, text than talk because people want to be in control. Controlling a relationship has become a major theme in the world of digital communication. Sometimes, it makes us feel together yet alone because it is a controlled relationship, which is a kind of relationship where you cannot feel a kinship. Technology wedges a layer of validation in between us. This is not a full conciliation of a person; this turns into a part object out of a full person. Such potential effects of technology on social learning are enormous for young generations.

One important thing we are losing is an ability to just be self-alone in a restorative way. If you cannot make out how to be alone, all you can ever be is alone yourself. If we don't coach our children how to be alone, all they can ever be is alone themselves because we are not going to get rid of any of the technologies, a backlash or a correction, whatever you want to call it. So, it is the parents' responsibility to make it useful for the children and for the social good overall. Today our world is connected more than ever. Some parents apparently believe that. About 7% of babies and toddlers have got their very own email accounts. By age 4, 75% of children have their own mobile device or tablet. In one experiment, while children aged 10 to 16 months play with electronic toys, researchers observed that the interactions between parents and their children were low and that both parents and children use fewer words and aerial vocalizations than they do with traditional toys. In the case of picture books, while reading and being read to, it instantly opens unlimited stories and evokes more words and dialogues than traditional toys. While researchers are gathering data on how electronic media affects children's brains and children's learning habits, they caution that distracting features of electronic media may cause "cognitive overload," which gets in the way of learning. The internet is just the beginning. The more we acknowledge ourselves that the technology is immature, we need to mature them to fit our need, the better off we will be in the long run.

Children are to be seen as much, not to be heard that much. The automobile has brought in an era when teenagers could go on dates far away from watchful parents, and the internet with social networks has given them, even very young children, a virtual life distinct from their parents' or elder siblings'. No one really creates a new technology understanding how it may be used or how it may change society. Social networks now dominate our social life. Media technology drives us to lead a digital life, from smartphone to smart home. Today, technology strategy is our social strategy. Children have increasingly started to rely on personal technological services like cell phones, iPods, Facebook, Twitter, and WhatsApp by defining themselves and creating social domains apart from their families, changing the way they communicate with their parents and peers. The mobility, the intimacy, and the convenience afforded by the cell phone have increased its popularity. Today 96% of 18- to 29-year-olds own a cell phone. [Hint: A 2010 UN study emphasized that the cell phone is one of the most effective advancements in history to lift people out of poverty. For instance, the Indian government is providing a cell phone to empower every household living below the poverty line. The world is congested with mobile airwaves, and users are divided in an uneven manner, with 1% of consumers consuming half the traffic and the top 10% consuming 90%. The forecast was that global mobile will surge by 1,700% from 2011 to 2016. And it did.]

[Warning: While on the subject of the cell phone, be aware of radio frequency! Radio-frequency waves can heat up human cells and possibly damage the human body. The shorter the distance from the radio signal, the more powerful the waves are. Here is one legal warning in the safety manual for Apple's iPhone: "When using iPhone near your body for voice calls or for wireless data transmission over a cellular network, keep iPhone at least 15 mm (5/8th inch) away from the body, and only use carrying cases, belt clips, or holders that do not have metal parts and that maintain at least 15 mm (5/8th inch) separation between iPhone and the body." Similar warnings can be taken against carrying cellular and smart phones in a body-hugging, closely sewn pocket. This may be considered as safety violation per Federal Communications Commission (FCC) guidelines: not exceeding maximum specific absorption rate of 1.6 watts per kilogram of body tissue from the radio-frequency energy exposed by carrying the phone outside a holster and within 0.98 inches (2.5 cm) of the human body. So, do not carry them in pant pockets; never ever carry them in breast pockets. Always carry it in holsters.

Cell phones emit nonionizing electromagnetic radiations. These radiations are emitted as waves of energy that are theoretically too weak to break the chemical bonds or disrupt a DNA that causes cancer later. Despite years of research on the issue, there is still no clear answer. Scientists have no idea or have no known biological mechanism to explain why and how non-ionizing radiation might lead to cancer or other health problems. After review of many studies on cellphone safety, the Food and Drug Administration (FDA) have issued one statement in 2018 saying, "not found sufficient evidence that there are adverse health effects in humans caused by exposures at or under the current radio-frequency exposure limits."

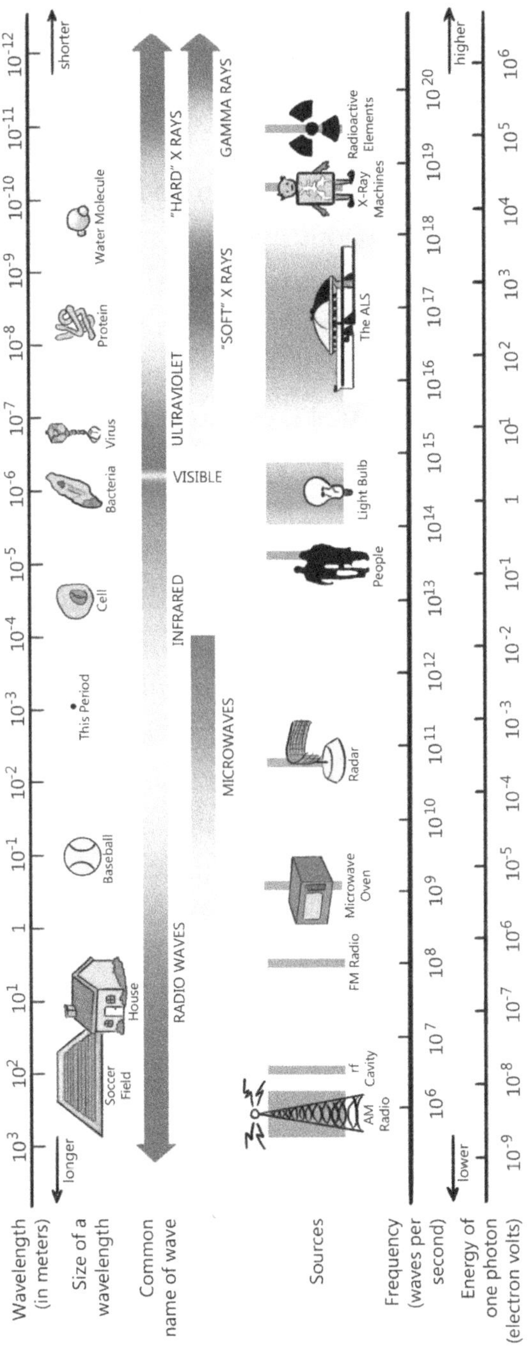

The Electromagnetic Spectrum

One research shows that the more time college students spend on their cell phones, the more anxious they become and the more their academic performances suffer. A National Institutes of Health (NIH) research has found that less than an hour of cell phone use can speed up brain activity in the area closest to the phone antenna, as observed in brain scans. If comparing the moments when the cell phone is activated versus when it is inactivated, there is a surge in brain glucose metabolism in the area of the brain near the antenna. This signifies that the human brain is too sensitive to the electromagnetic radiation emitted from a cell phone. The radio-frequency signal, though weak, has a measurable effect on a person's overall health. In recent years, instead of strength, concerns have been drifted to frequencies that oscillate not 60 times a second but millions to billions of times—those used by cell phones, cordless phones, Bluetooth, and wireless networks. For example, even though there is no direct evidence as of yet about broadcasts at lower energy levels than cell phones, the recommendation is to keep the Wi-Fi out of schools. The World Health Organization (WHO) now changed their position and identified the radio frequencies used by cell phones, Wi-Fi, and other telecommunication devices as "possibly carcinogenic"—especially an increased risk among heavy cell phone users for a rare type of brain tumor called a glioma. They classified cell phones as category 2B—a designation the panel was given to 240 other agents including the pesticide DDT, cleaning chemicals, engine exhaust, lead and various industrial chemicals, pickled vegetables, and coffee.

In another study earlier by thirteen countries called Interphone—the largest and longest study to establish a link between cell phone use and brain tumors—there was no overall increased risk found but reported that participants with the highest level of cell phone use had a 40% higher risk of glioma. While a hands-free headset during a conversation or communication via text message can be options for lowering radio-frequency exposure, it is generally advised that if people want to use cell phones, they should consider using an earpiece just to keep the phone unit away from the head. About radiation exposure, another similar but different risk is probable from the use of laptop by men on the lap. Argentinean researchers obtained ejaculated semen samples from twenty-nine healthy men and placed some of the samples underneath a laptop computer seemingly simulating a situation of using a laptop on man's lap and then placed the other samples at the same temperature but away from the laptop. Using Wi-Fi, laptops were then connected to the internet. Four hours later, the researchers observed that the sperm in the samples stored under the computer showed less movement than that in the control group. They also noticed laptop sperm showed a 9% DNA damage, which was more than 3 times higher than in the control group. While the large epidemiological study is needed to establish any rule, there is no need to panic and assume that a laptop is turning man sterile. Ergonomically, however, it is always a good idea to place a laptop not on the lap but on the desk.]

Instant technology—go viral! It's true for other products as well. It follows Metcalfe's (he co-invented Ethernet) law: the value of a telecommunication network is proportional to the square of the number of connected users of the system (n^2). Basically, the more people start using something, the more valuable it becomes. Gadgets that are meant to revolutionize communication have created undesirable and far-reaching social impacts that have emerged as a major cause of concern. Kids trying to keep up with peers have been demanding the newest gadgets, and parents are often happily obliging; one main reason parents give the new devices is the convenience of being able to contact their children instantly practically whenever they want. In addition to calling, texting and e-mailing, they have become widely popular but comparatively less intrusive methods of keeping in touch. One study by Common Sense surveyed roughly a thousand teenagers about their habits back in 2012, when most teenagers said their primary method to communicate with peers and friends was in person face-to-face. Fast forward six years, similar survey in 2018, reveals most teenagers prefer texting (35%), followed by selective social media (16%), video chatting (10%), and less than one-third face-to-face.

The new gadgets allow the kids to have much more of private life, most of which their parents are not privy to. Teenagers who are connected via social media have better relationships with their parents and lesser behavioral problems, according to one survey in 2013. However, with the younger generation discovering newfound independence assisted by these gadgets, it has become imperative for the parents to keep themselves involved in their children's life to watch that they don't go completely astray. However, as it is inherent with any cultural issues involving parents and children, several gulfs have emerged. Baby boomers (born during post-World War II, 1946–1964) who declared decades ago that their parents had fallen steps behind now sometimes find themselves in similar unpleasant situations with respect to their own children.

A study by a telecommunication company revealed that a large number of parents learned how to text message from their children and that more than half not only agreed to the fact that it benefited them to communicate with their children in need but also transpired at the same time that the children often didn't have emotional space and didn't want any surprise hearing their parents' voice at the other end. A text message is preferred by these children as they get to hear from their parents without having to talk to them. As a matter of fact, the entire generation has suddenly stopped talking over the phone and switched to text-based media, starting with instant messaging. Today, calling someone on the phone is almost like a violation of privacy, while texting is not so. Interactions with several teenagers reveal that they try to keep a healthy relationship with their parents, but they want to keep the parents away from any involvement in their life and in their peers' life. They hardly return calls; so, the only way hapless parents can hope to elicit a response is by sending a short text to keep track of their whereabouts.

Also, being fully aware of the destabilizing effect of cell phones, iPods, and handheld video games on family relations, parents, who themselves are digital immigrants in the land of technologies, often try to persuade their digitally native children to keep their gadgets away. In an effort to find out how cell phones and mobile devices affect child-parent relationships, Common Sense Media conducted 1,200 interviews in 2016 with children between the ages 12 and 18 and with their parents. They report that 50% of teens say they feel addicted to their devices, 59% of parents say that they are worried about their children's addiction, and a significant number of families seem to be struggling. Children, are you addicted to your phone? If you feel or if your parents tell you that your phone is hurting your health or relationship, then the answer is yes. If you can't help these compulsive behaviors, that loss of control is the hallmark of an addiction. Try to be idle away from your device for some time; it's a good thing. Your brain needs time to wander alone without distraction. Parents, try to spend time with children face-to-face, skin-to-skin; if children lack an inclination to carry out the interaction, find some ways. Never before had parents have so little time with their children. Enforcing family rules with teenagers can also be a very tough job as they strongly resist any attempts by parents to intrude in their privacy or to cut them off from their peers even for a short while. Studies conducted recently found that 1/3rd of 16- and 17-year-olds send texts while driving. Researchers established a link that teens that send more than 120 text messages a day are more likely to be unstable and more likely to have sex or use alcohol or illegal drugs than peers who text less.

However, the cell-phone or text-message story may not be all bad all the way. Studies reveal that these gadgets are also perceived as things that cement relationships and keep people together. It offers the new generation the convenience of being engaged with the world to share every life experience the second it unfolds on a 24/7 basis. Information, news, and communications that were so opaque only a few years back are so transparent now. While parents of teenagers have been complaining about the destabilizing impacts of cell phones, there are some others who claim that their relationship with their children became closer and reaching out became much simpler with the use of cell phones. Recently, there was hue and cry about kids' sexting. A survey in 2012 indicated kids' sexting may not be as big of a deal. In reality, only 7% of children between age 10 and 17 had sexted or appeared to have received sexual content in the past year. Among teenagers, it is 1 in 4. However, among college students, *sexperience* is different. Four out of 5 receive sexually suggestive messages. More than ½ receive intimate images, 2/3rd send salacious messages, and 3/4th *sextexts* are sent to romantic partners. One 2014 survey claimed that those who sexted during their sophomore years were 32% more likely to have had sex in the following year than those who did not. Another survey analyzed 39 studies covering 10,300 young boys and girls under age 18. The result, published in 2018 in the *JAMA Pediatrics*, reveals that sexting, sharing of sexual messages, images and videos, have become increasingly commonplace: sexuality is now a normal part of adolescence. In 2018, three out of four teenagers had a smartphone. With the exploration of technology, parents now need to be proactive, not reactive, about digital safety. They need to have open conversations early on and often, not just when a problem arises or incident happens.

Adolescence is a time when children first start sincerely to learn about the outside world and want to try out novel experiences, some of which may be risky or outright dangerous. The young mind craves excitement in a way that adults find difficult to understand. Watching teenagers learn to drive, for instance, can be extremely nerve-racking for parents, knowing that even the very mature teenager can take ill-advised risks, and the inexperience of the hand behind the wheel can be deadly. In fact, statistics reassures of the fact that the risk is real. Car accidents are the leading cause of death for 15- to 19-year-olds: a survey found 40% designated drivers drink before driving. State programs have been put in place to reduce the number of such accidents and have proved to be effective. But ultimately, the effort to keep teenagers away from all kinds of dangers, not only in driving, has to be initiated at home. While the government can offer to do its share by passing laws and bylaws and ensuring enforcement, it can never give to the children what parents can in terms of a good upbringing, which can form the guiding factor in a child's life for years to come.

As for a good upbringing, it can be neither easily nor objectively defined. Once individuals become parents, they acquire a natural ability to raise children. In fact, we all possess it in varying degrees, and abilities are brought to the fore only when we become a parent. Though the details of it may be subjective, the basics are fairly simple: spend time with children, take them around, play with them, and talk to them. The years of togetherness and bonding with parents stay with a child for years. And once you fulfill these basic duties of parenthood, there is no need to feel guilty. Pampering your child can never be a substitute for lack of attention and time, and your parental instincts will tell you that disciplining is as much a part of a good upbringing as loving and caring. While praising them for the good things they do is important, so is disciplining their behavior with love and affection. Through discipline, a child gets guidance about what kinds of behavior are acceptable and what are not. Setting such boundaries actually help them and guide them to learn more about how to behave in broader society. And surprisingly enough, the children too love family discipline in due course.

If you want to give one important gift to your child, then let it be enthusiasm. Enthusiasm is one precious gift. Respond to their intrinsic motivation and support them with wholehearted enthusiasm, especially in their newly accrued skills. When children get the message that their parents love them and care for them and are willing to spend time with them to help learn what is appropriate, they get a feeling of belongingness and the security that helps them stay on the right course. The bottom line: love has to be the basis of a healthy discipline. The desire to be loved is a powerful motivator for children to behave in ways that would win acclaim from their parents. Once parents truly praise children for all the good things they do, it encourages them further to do more good things to win more praiseworthy confidence. Children need attention and affection.

Parents need to bear in mind that the years of adolescence are not easy ones. They are the years when children experience lots of ups and downs and emotional turbulence. Adolescents may swing from euphoric self-confidence and a narcissistic strength in which they feel invulnerable to despair, disappointment, and depression. An adolescent mind is rebellious to suppression of beliefs, thoughts, and expressions. It is, therefore, so important for parents to keep open the channels of communication with their children. Offering explanations helps them work out matters for themselves. Encourage them to channel their confidence acting like being powerful by recalling a few instances when they themselves felt powerful in the past in other occasions. Share your personal experience as well. Parents who share their experience with their children will see them develop a similar trait. Children will learn to discuss and think in a more reasonable manner. Over time, they become confident and learn clear communication. Honest and open discussion with parents is essential as it encourages children to come to their parents when they are in trouble resulting from, say, bullying or the lure of sex and drugs.

A society ridden with problems can result in complexities for teenagers and adolescents. However, a stable home environment and a happy family, in most cases, can see them through almost all the problems. The absence of it, on the other hand, can add to the teenager's struggle and may leave a painful impression on his or her mind, and that would take time to heal. It is common in a single-parent family due to the uncertainty of the future.

The uncertainty dawns upon a children's life when their parents decide to part; that can drive children to an extreme form of behavior and also unsettle their faith in marriage and family when they grow up. A study on the subject revealed that the divorce and its aftermath leave scars that can linger in the afflicted children throughout adolescence and through adulthood. This affliction can diminish the kid's interest in his studies and other normal business. It can also lead to juvenile delinquency and depression. While divorce is a painful experience for all the family members involved, the children especially become more obvious victims. The impact on kids is obvious during the first year of divorce, and then it seems to be enduring—more for boys than for girls. Preschool kids seem to be most vulnerable to the consequence than adolescents. Experts often advise potential parents to postpone separation if their children are in the vulnerable stages in life—baby, toddler, or early adolescence. Divorce, if avoidable, should be avoided until children cross these impressionable stages. Marriage counselors notice that one reason why marriage is popular among the highly educated is that most couples see it as the optimal way to give an advantage to their offspring. Unhappy couples generally wait until their kids have left them their empty nest.

The children of a lesser god! The harsh reality that remains is that while for the adults the divorce is the ending of a troubled relationship, for children it is the beginning of uncertain relationship. While statistics say that about 3/4th of divorced parents live happier than they did when they were married, the same cannot be stated about the children. Children of divorce require ages to recover from the trauma. Throughout the adolescence and a part of adulthood, they keep battling the ghosts within themselves, those that keep them from building social and personal relationships in their own life. Pathologically, children of divorce suffer from depression, learning difficulties, and other psychological disorders more frequently than those of intact families. The happiness of family life, once lost for these kids, is hardly regained. Its profound effect shows up mostly when these children reach maturity. A sense that love is lost often haunts them as they grow up adult and try to build a meaningful relationship of their own. Their adult life is plagued by doubt, pessimism, and cynicism. They are usually not successful individuals in life, being devoid of initiatives that, in their view, only create a new set of disasters. They often commit mistakes and make awful errors of judgment. The love they lost in childhood is a melancholy nostalgia they carry in their mind too vividly, which is contrary to the notion that children somehow manage to come to terms with the reality and that even if it is harsh on them for a while, they recover from it.

Children from harsh backgrounds become unmanageable, aggressive, and sleepless, and putting them back on track is a task that could take immense perseverance, and the time, measured only in years. Children who witness the separation of their parents when they are in the adolescent stage of their lives face a somewhat different set of problems. The huge loss of an intact family brings with it the possibilities that parents find separate partners and go to subsequent marriages. Each of these conditions throws a child's life into turmoil and brings back painful melancholy. Not only that, watching their parent's courtship, especially for teenagers, it might be a rage to their future, and they too may become aggressive sexually at an early age. In fact, this probably happens in America more frequently than the Americans are willing to admit. It contributes to the rising prevalence of sexually transmitted diseases (STDs) among teenagers. One study gives circumstantial evidence that the girl who lives at home without her biological father gets physically mature—onset of puberty—sooner than those who live with their biological fathers. Parents who have ended their first marriage and remarried don't have enough time for them and for the children before they can figure out where life is taking them. Kids engage in all kinds of activities, the implications of which they are often too young to comprehend. Thus, while in some cases they may marry late or never marry at all, in other cases, they may end up marrying rather early or may rush into relation with hardly any forethought.

At the threshold of young adulthood, relationships are very important. Survey shows most children want to make the relationship of their parents as models for their own. But the traumatic memories of their parents failing to keep intact the relationship do not inspire any moral or psychological assurance regarding their own marriage. For a healthy transformation into adulthood, children need to see the interplay of personality of father and mother, male and female. Their social imagination is by far more active, and they are helped by observing the friendliness of one sex to the other. Survey supports the fact that approximately 45% of teens consider their parents—not their friends or celebrities—their sexual role models. More teens trusted parental advice than that from their friends. Friends' influence accounts only 32% and celebrities' 15%.

If father and mother are at loggerheads, it will be hard for a child to envisage with satisfaction the founding of a home of his own. Parents should behave themselves; they should never take their fights or similar bizarre behavior in front of their children. Once it happened, if at any time, they should resolve their differences in front of the child so that the child understands the whole cycle of the story. The experience and the memories of a happy home beget the desire to produce a similar one for oneself. A child needs to see the considerate behavior of his parents to one another, their good humor in the face of vexations, their solidarity and mutual loyalty. If these images are positive, a child develops a healthy, kind, and loving attitude to the other sex. Those whose childhood and adolescence are devoid of these happy experiences become cynical about human bondage and evermore keep doubting their capacity to live in a happy relationship. For the child, the divorce carries one meaning that the adults had failed in the crucial task in their adulthood. The child's confidence in building a stable, happy relation for him is badly mauled by the failure of the parents. These children follow a different, much longer trajectory for growing up. More teens trusted parental advice than that from their have to rework their way through life and rethink the role they want to play as spouses and parents.

Yet all these findings and endless stories of misery cannot revive a failed marriage, and divorce is the inevitable conclusion when two adults living together decide to live completely away from each other. Some optimists would say that when there is no way of salvaging the situation, then separation is the best course and that while it is hard on kids, they do eventually recover. In some cases, they say, it is the way to go for fear that distances between couples become irrecoverable. With children, while the situation will obviously be not as happy as living in a good family, it will not be the hardest blow either, and for every problem that they face in life, their background may not be the culprit. The cloud does have a silver lining. There is still reason to believe that this generation will not perish and will not witness a complete collapse of the family as an institution. Despite their eyewitness experience of failed marriages, they sincerely want suitable, faithful, and lasting relationships. They want to do better for their children as parents and are definitely not willing to accept the notion that the institution of marriage will wither away. Some studies suggest that overall, in spite of being beset by all the problems, American children seem to be resilient and are doing fine, and the situation is not as bad as the parents make it out to be. Though they may not be correctly indicative of the situation yet, this fact is borne out by some statistics as well. In spite of parents fretting about their child's health and safety and about their encountering problems of drug use, sexual abuse, and other crimes, statistics from some sources point to a remarkable improvement in these situations. Teen birth rates are at record lows while teen crime rates are plummeting. Kids are beginning to comprehend the harmful effects of smoking and are trying to abstain. About 90% of young Americans are now earning high school diplomas and getting much of the basic health care they need (immunization rates are high, for example, with 90% of kids getting vaccinated against hepatitis B and a record 80% against chicken-pox).

A social system that is ailing makes the kids vulnerable in more than one way. One area of concern is the not-too-negligible number of kids turning to commercial sex for food and shelter and often also to drugs or other things that they cannot otherwise afford. Any system that makes its future generations turn to demeaning ways of earning a livelihood cannot be sustainable in the long run. It points to some serious flaws in their upbringing, which society for its own welfare cannot afford to ignore.

The plethora of research and findings reminds one of the age-old saying, "Prevention is better than cure." Several ways of possible prevention have been suggested, which could certainly help control the situation. The mind is in prevention before something happens, not immediate attention after it has happened. Prevention stops right there, where it starts. Of course, the ultimate way of prevention has to be addressing the problems of the society at large, but an overhauling of the social structure or bringing about a change in people's values, morals, and commitments is not easily achievable. Instead, what would be more useful is trying to help parents do a better job of bringing up their children. This can nip most of the problems in the bud, and the outcome could be a healthier, more productive society.

One such counsel that the parents would do well to follow is that of preventive parenting. Using some personality tests, behavioral scientists found that only about half of babies had easy temperaments from birth. Most of the rest show significant moodiness, disobedience, or other behaviors that place them in a so-called difficult category. If they are left to themselves without any intervention, the majority of the kids become intransigent and hyper-excitable. Some of them, mostly girls, become withdrawn and run the risk of becoming depressive later. The strategies that the parents have to adapt to normalize the condition vary, which is dependent on the personality of the child and the aberrations of behavior. But assistance of professionals of child psychology is warranted before any kind of intervention is made. It is also imperative that the parents take the child into confidence in this process, and thus they work together. But if the anomalies are left untreated, it may lead to unseen unknown consequences. For example, when a child is suffering from depression or is suicidal, going to the specialist seems to be the only way. Depressive disorders, if untreated, may result in suicide in about 20% of cases.

Summing up, one can reasonably conclude that there is definitely a cause for concern. To know more about our children and to ponder about what the future would be like in two decades, ask preschool teachers. That is why children who are the future inheritors must turn out to be dutiful, wise adults, capable of being entrusted with such burdensome responsibilities. Yet there are horrendous realities that we face today. Schoolyard argument that gets resolved with guns is often a norm now. Though most kids fret at the idea of parents getting involved in their dealings with friends, colleagues, and classmates, it might be the wise thing to do in situations where kids get themselves entangled in affairs that they do not have the capacity to resolve. Though some amount of peer pressure can be good, it may be difficult to judge how much the right amount is. Also, even nice kids have the habit of turning nasty in a pack. Bad habits are contagious. Bad group habits seem to take a toll on the sense of morality and accountability of a child. It puts on parents an added responsibility of having to monitor the kind of peers their children are a part of. Breaking bad habits and solving problems from child abuse to drug abuse to sex can be handled, provided parents take enough efforts to reach out to their loving children and create an atmosphere of trust, support. and happiness at home as an institution. The joys of the parents are secret, and so are the sorrows. They cannot utter the one, nor will they utter the other.

Children are the most valuable resources of this planet—one-third of our population and all of our future. They hold our history, our heritage. They are nature's gift to us. To bring them up to our expectation, is our duty and obligation. Children are the light of our lives. Parenting is our pride. Happy is our family where children are our objects of affection!

1.4 Friends and Society

> Words are easy, like the wind; Faithful friends are hard to find.
>
> —William Shakespeare (1564–1616),
> the English poet and playwright
> widely regarded as the greatest
> writer in the English language

Most Americans are home alone (2.6 people per household), drive alone (1.6 per car), and stay alone. In 1950, only 4 million Americans (in 5% households) lived alone; in 2011, they were 33 million (in 28% households). In 2016, about 1/3rd of Americans over 65 lived alone, including half over 85. People are segregated by age, nationwide and worldwide. In another study by AARP (American Association of Retired Persons) Foundation in 2018, about 35% of adults over 45 are lonely, the prevalence remains unchanged since 2010—meaning almost 48 million in total, are lonely at any given time. Many fears are born out of fatigue and loneliness. Fear is the sound of silence. In the age of technology, social media, and instant gratification, it's all because we are gradually losing our ability to feel uncomfortable: particularly, silence is hard to bear. Being alone means you and your mirror, a continuous self-probing. The aloneness is amplified in festive times by watching or reflecting the cheerful parties while you still remain the party of one! Even having pets has shown to improve the health of the lonesome. Lonely people are more likely to get sick, suffer, and die at an early age. One meta-study in the U.K. analyzed 23 studies involving 181,000 healthy people in 2016 and found that loneliness is associated with 29% increased risk of coronary heart disease and 32%

stroke. Loneliness can be insidious and wreaks havoc on our metabolism. It changes the way our genes work and may alter the internal process through which a normal, healthy person responds to external situations. One major social study covering 3.4 million people in 2016, found that loneliness increases the risk of heart disease by 29% and stroke by 32% and overall a 30% higher risk of dying in the next 7 years. The phenomenon that you feel safe and secured in a crowd, goes back to the herding behavior in animals. Even merely feeling the presence of other people elevates the feeling of safety and you are less vigilant, yet safer.

Yet, the Bureau of Labor Statistics' Time Use Survey reveals that an average American spends less than four minutes a day "hosting and attending social events (parties and other organized social occasions)." It hardly totals to 24 hours a year, barely enough to cover Thanksgiving dinner, and some children's birthday parties. While it is true that introspection, self-reflection, and to some extent solitude are important parts of a psychologically healthy life, but from practically every piece of research, it is even more true that the need and cause of human happiness depend on other people, your friends and families. In one analysis of 148 independent health studies, social scientists notice that (a) people who cultivate a culture of social relationships with a wide network of friends, have a mortality rate 50% lower than those with weak ties; and (b) people are more beneficial from a large network of friends rather than family members. Yet, another two studies covering nearly 280,000 people in almost 100 countries, find that friendship becomes increasingly vital to the general well-being at older ages: (a) relationships with friends are better predictor of good health and happiness, than relations with family; and (b) relationships with friends are additional support, among other aspects, associated with more satisfying marriages, over and above good marriage, where couples are already content with the support from each other.

What's more, the lack of social relationships is disgracefully dangerous to health and well-being. Lonely people are more likely to get sick, suffer and die at an early age. One study in the U.K. analyzed 23 studies involving 181,000 healthy people in 2016, and finds that loneliness, is associated with 29% increased risk of coronary heart disease and 32%, stroke. One study published in *Health Psychology* in 2017 finds that among people who fall ill after being exposed to cold virus, those who are lonely are more likely to report severe sneezing, runny nose, sore throat and other symptoms. According to census data presented at the 125th Annual Convention of the American Psychological Association in 2017, it underlines the connection between loneliness and the premature death. Loneliness can be insidious and wreaks havoc on our metabolism. It changes the way our genes work and may alter the internal process through which a normal, healthy person responds to external situations. Major social studies covering 3.4 million people in 2016 finds that loneliness increases the risk of heart disease by 29% and stroke by 32%, and overall a 30% higher risk of dying in the next 7 years. The effect is as significant in middle age comparable to other risk factors of early death as obesity and smoking. Loneliness—but not living alone—is associated with dementia. Worse than suffering is suffering it alone. In another study, researchers from University of California, San Francisco, tracked 1,600 participants with average age of 71 and find that lonely people are more likely to develop difficulties with activities of daily living and they die early. After controlling factors like socioeconomic status and health, the loneliness is accountable for higher mortality: nearly 23% die within 6 years, compared with 14% of those who weren't lonely. Loneliness is the sad reality of modern life. Human needs social connection, not isolation!

Human friction, not separation! No one thrives in isolation! One growing trend in this increasingly lonely country is noticeable! Americans of all ages are coming together in *intentional communities* in municipalities, towns, and cities—living close to the people but not too close. The community is made up of mini-apartments, housed in like a large apartment complex, fully equipped with own baths and kitchenettes, access to a larger shared chef's kitchen, library, coffee lounge, game room, common room, community-wide dinner, happy hour events or the shared holiday parties. Residents occupy studio-like apartments, but move and socialize in larger shared spaces throughout the building. The business of relieving loneliness is at the core of business model of this mission. Here, neighbors know each other. The arrangement comes handy when an individual needs community—because, the partner is away, baby is sick, to share an event, or just need a company—it's there. It caters even to millennials who are classically transitory, eight months on average stay.

If you do not learn how to be alone yourself, then you will be forced alone in the midst of other selves. One survey found that participants who reported feeling lonely even in the midst of friends and family members were more likely to develop dementia than those who reported not being lonely. They are not alone, yet alone. A person who feels lonely views the social world as lonely and threatening. It is a tricky situation because confessing and accepting loneliness carry a social stigma. Accepting loneliness means as if you're accepting that you've failed in the most fundamental domains of life: attachment, belongingness, love, and care. It hurts your basic instincts to save your face and makes it hard to ask for help. A lonely person thinks negatively about their friends and other people as a whole.

One pervasive factor at play is the shame. In our amorousness-fixated culture, loneliness means failure—a failure in relationship that itself drives isolation. Yet the fact is that loneliness is a lot more common than people think. More than a quarter of adult Americans experience loneliness, independent of race, education, and ethnicity. Loneliness is not any shame or a rogue state; it is a part of our rich fabric of shared lives. Loneliness may not necessarily be the result of poor social skills or lack of social support, but can be, in part, as a result of perceived ambiguous social cues. To revert the trend, essential is "maladaptive social cognition"—people to re-examine their interaction with perceived social cues and communication with other members of the society. People also need to appreciate the upside of loneliness: many experiences a drive for artistic creation, intense alertness to the outside world, heightened sensitivity to compassion and empathy.

Many studies across large populations have repeatedly shown that those who describe themselves as lonely or having little social support are more likely to die prematurely as a result of high blood pressure, stroke, heart attack, insomnia, infections, and cancer. One study in 2014 monitored 3,432 heart attack patients recording their levels of social support one month and then one year after the heart attack. One in five had low social backing; they didn't have friends or family for emotional or financial support. In their recovery, they showed very low mental functioning, worse quality of life, and more depressive symptoms (within six months of heart attack, depression increases the chance of death from 3% to 17%). In the context of human life, love and care and relationship are essential, and particularly after an illness, it has an enormous effect on their recovery and quality of life afterward. Sometimes ill health leads to social isolation, but the risks of being socially isolated are phenomenal and are associated with twofold to fivefold increase in mortality rates. These correlations have emerged from study after study and in country after country.

The antidote to loneliness is to be disposed of with someone, a friend. A friend who finds a friend finds a treasure. A ready smile and a quick joke are a Midas touch from a loved one, your spouse, your children, or your friend. An Australian study spreading over ten years found that older people with larger friend circles were 22% less likely to die during that study period than those with smaller friend circles. Life without friends is death without a witness. Strong social ties promote mental health and physical health especially when we age. A study involving 3,000 nurses with breast cancer found that women without close friends were 4 times as likely to die from the disease as women with ten or more friends. Another study covering 45,000 people who had heart disease already or were at high risk of developing it found that living alone increased the risk of early death by 24% in the age group of 45 to 55, 12% in 66 to 80, and no change in 80 and up. Age disparity is due to the fact that for the middle-aged people, for whom living alone is much less a social norm than that of the elderly, the lonely living can trigger psychological problem that can affect their health. Another study involved 1,604 participants, average age 71, and followed them every 2 years for 6 years and evaluated certain day-to-day abilities that measured overall health like walking, bathing, dressing, eating, and stair-climbing. By the end of the study, after all things considered at par, they found that lonely people displayed significantly more disability: 59% tend to lose the ability to perform tasks of daily living, 18% mobility problems, and 31% difficulty in climbing stairs than those who did not report being lonely. Even more alarming, the lonely people were 45% more likely to have died by the end of six years of the study period than those who weren't lonely. Just having friends is so protective.

Here is the spin. What is really happening for a negative effect—the physical and social lack of contact with others or the emotional toll of feeling alone? Untangling these two influences is important because therapies targeted to change perceptions of loneliness aren't likely to work if the real problem is not having friends or family who can support. Based on one survey that tracked 6,500 British people over 52 years of age, from 2004 to 2012, researchers found that most socially isolated people were 26% more likely to die during the study period compared those with most active social lives, after controlling the factors that affect the mortality like age and age-related illness. In contrast, however, the feeling of loneliness, although often linked with isolation, is not significantly linked with the risk of death after controlling other factors at per. The finding concludes that the subjective experience of loneliness—often due to the psychological manifestation of social isolation—is not the primary mechanism that links between social isolation and mortality. Loneliness is not the cause but the experience of loneliness is.

Studies suggest that feeling lonely can trigger changes in brain chemicals and hormones and produce unhealthy levels of chronic inflammation, which has been associated with Alzheimer's, heart and cardiovascular disease, arthritis, and other illnesses. Studies show that lonely people who are socially isolated have 50% increased risk of premature death compared to people who have strong social ties, which is equivalent to the mortality risk of smoking 15 cigarettes a day. People with strong social ties live nearly 4 years longer than those who feel disconnected from others. They are less likely than others to get sick, perhaps because they have a lower stress level. A corollary to that, researchers studying Parkinson's disease say that group visits, in which patients are pooled together for longer sessions with a doctor, may be just as effective, if not more, in treating the neurological disorder. After observing more than 800 men and women in the context of their social networks, researchers found that socially isolated men aged 70 to 79 appear to be at greater risk of heart disease than men with more robust social networks. The reward of friendship, in and of itself, is a friendship. When you need someone to open your mind, it's better to actually have a friend.

Friendship helps. As a matter of fact, friendship helps in a better way on psychological and physiological well-being than even family relationships. It has its evolutionary root as well. One of the reasons why some primates have bigger brains than others is due to their social behavior not only within the family but beyond. Called the "social brain hypothesis," it states that the more the primates moved around in bigger and more complex social groups, the more they required bigger brains to manage and process social networks efficiently.

Did you invite your friend home lately? Are you the life of the party? Eighty years of study on health and long life in *The Longevity Project* indicates that a reliable social network is one important predictor of longer life. Social affairs include sociability: neuroticism, life purpose, catastrophic thinking, marital happiness, job satisfaction, religious faith, and social support. In sociability, women differ from men in many ways. Some interesting findings are the following:

- Women, in general, are more likely to have stronger social networks than men, and that perhaps is the reason why widows outlive widowers.
- Widows may outlive still-married women.
- Neurotic widowers are likely to outlive their fewer neurotic peers. The reason may be that more neurotic widowers are more likely to take care of more of their own health when their wives are gone.
- Men who are suited for marriage and marry a long and satisfying marriage do live especially long compared to men who get and stay divorced or who remarry and divorce again.
- Men seem to get together with male friends and especially get drunk together more than women—male bonding over drinking is a ritual as old as drinking itself, which serves as a social lubricant for men, making them more sensitive to social behaviors like a social interaction to a greater extent among men or

feeling connected with one another in a way that a soda or coffee can't.

Other studies about the trend show that in developed countries, men and women, both in large numbers, are choosing to live alone and loving it. In affluent societies, where social lives are affordable and accessible and where families are no longer a burden or financial necessity, people are simply evolving into creatures with different fallacies. Some even theorize that women have easier time living alone than men.

Stretch the friend circle wider. When a good thing happens to you, you feel better when you experience it in the midst of your friends. The "entourage effect" helps you to feel powerful and influential that makes you feel even better. In America, the number of closest friends—the ones with whom one can discuss important matters—shrank over the past twenty years from 3 friends to 2 friends, while the number of Americans who have almost none to trust rose from 1 in 8 to 1 in 4. They increasingly rely solely on family members (80%) and spouses (9%). Other studies also support that a strong social network has a direct effect on a reduced risk of Alzheimer's disease, lower blood pressure, and greater longevity. A simple meet and greet has its benefit.

The University of Virginia conducted a study about the confidence level of the person when they get support from friends versus when they are left alone. They took thirty-four students with a heavy backpack on the back for a hike to the base of a steep hill. Some students were standing next to friends, while others were standing alone. All of them were asked the same query: give an estimation of the steepness of the hill. The students standing next to their friends gave lower steepness of the hill compared to those who were standing alone. The closer the friendship, the lesser was the difficulty level. The moral: the stronger the friendship, the higher the confidence. Friendship means so much of a morale booster.

Friendship is a term used multipurpose to denote a cooperative and supportive behavior between two or more people. It is an association of two persons close to each other by a feeling of love, affection, and personal regard. It is a relationship that involves mutual understanding, affection, and respect. Friendship is based on civil goodness; it hardly exists in evil wickedness. Friends help each other particularly in the time of need. Two faithful friends belong to one team, a team with a power of 2 (2^2). Friendship is powerful: the strength, we repeat, is not the sum of two but the power of two (2^2). Or it is a team where 1 stands beside 1, representing 11. It may sound like a witty ambiguous wordplay, but in reality, it remains unambiguous—it is a team with more power than two individuals combined, even when the friend is absent. It elevates your power as well; plus, the booster power from your friend. Friendship brightens your beings. In the setting of team performance, in research, at work, in music, at play, or in performing arts, it is very common. In one study, when individuals and teams were given a complicated card game (Wason selection task, a logic puzzle relating to the psychology of reasoning), only 14% of individuals solved the problem as against 75% of the teams—which is more than 4 times. It is much more than one thinks. Especially when you are lost, and you are found by a friend—you got a friend!

Friends do welcome each other's company and exhibit loyalty to each other. You may forget whom you laughed with, but you will never forget whom you wept with. Joy fades out, but sorrow lingers. Old friend matters. It takes time to both build up trust and be longtime friend. Much of the strength in a friendship is developed from honoring the differences rather than simple enjoyment of likings. A good old friend is one nice thing you can have and one nice thing you can be. Old wine and old friend improve with time. The old friend is the last dog that dies.

A friend in need is a friend indeed! At a time of need, a real friend just simply walks in while the rest of the world simply walks out. By the same token, if you are a good friend, then when your friend is in trouble, you don't ask him if there is anything you can do—you just do it—you just do whatever is appropriate for you to do. A friend is a scout; a friend is a counselor. But a true, faithful friend is not so easy to find. Today, you have hundreds of friends because you pay the bill; tomorrow, you have none because you are ill.

A wise man is one who understands the value of true friendship. He is, by and of himself, a good friend. He supports and stands by his friend. He is not one who will leave his friend in danger to avoid trouble for himself. He understands the value of mutual trust. He is a man who will never look forward to reward when helping others. He will do so selflessly. He knows discretion is the first sign of maturity; an enemy is, therefore, preferable to a friend who lacks discretion. They are all immature small people. He distances away from people who try to belittle him and his motto. Small people always do that. He ignores them. There is no honor in small people.

You may not love him for his look, for his personality, or for his wisdom, but you love him because he sings a song that you only can hear. Or maybe you know his "triggers." Triggers, as they are known in psychological circles, are behaviors or characteristics of other people that are likely to annoy him like perfectionism, timidity, obliviousness, or skepticism. These are the things—"the if-then profile"—that really set him off. Friends who are better able to predict with reasonable likelihood how his friend will react or who can describe his friend's qualities, like witty, athletic, or tech-shabby, are better able to maintain a healthy friendship. No one friend possesses or offers all the qualities that you need, in need. Some are great listeners but aren't available when you need them. Others are faithfully loyal but lack the quality to get you out of a jam. And so on. You get different things from different friends; but at the same time, it's also no guarantee that you get what you want even from a sizable group of friends. Friendship is an umbrella term that has many attributes:

- *The Builder:* they are motivators, always push you towards the finish line.
- *The Champion:* they stand up for you for what you believe in.
- *The Collaborator:* they have similar passion and interests, one important aspect for many great friendships.
- *The Companion:* they are there for you, whenever and whatever the circumstances are.
- *The Connector:* they connect you to others.

- *The Energizer:* they are your "fun friends," who boost your energy and give you a positive spin to make a good day, great.
- *The Mind Opener:* they expand your horizons and encourage your will and wish for innovative ideas, opportunities and prospects.
- *The Navigator:* they give you good advice like a counselor and guide you in the right direction.

Friends get along, to go along! They walk together side by side, talk together truth and right. Friendship is a single soul dwelling in two bodies, sharing the pain and pleasure together. Thus, it divides the pain and doubles the pleasure. Each is complementary to the other. A friend knows all about you, loves you just for you. Each hears the other in the noise, in the silence.

Truly, faithful friends are hard to find, but difficult to leave, and perhaps impossible to forget. Our true friends are those who accept us as we are. They are the ones who enhance our self-esteem and ways that make our lives pleasurable. Not only that, friends are also the agent who broaden our horizon and contribute to our growth. Friends are considerate to one others' idea. We matter to them; they matter to us. At uncertain situations and at various levels of difficulty, they supplement the quality of our emotional life. They are the folks who when they walk with you try to stride their steps to suit yours. And you are the folks who invite them to your life and win them for life. Here are some suggestions how to win friends and influence people, according to some experts:

- sync with the people you're with—the chameleon effect—literally, copy their body language, gestures, and facial expressions;
- spend time with the people you're hoping to befriend with—people tend to like people who are familiar to them;
- compliment the people sincerely—people associate adjectives you use to describe other people, with your personality, a phenomenon called spontaneous trait transference;
- try to express positive emotions—because, emotional contagion propagates impulsively as people are influenced by the moods of other people;
- be warm and welcoming, people judge others based on their warmth and competence;
- reveal your pitfalls and flaws from time to time—called the pratfall effect—people like you more after you make a genuine mistake that you never try to hide, which reveals your characteristics that you aren't perfect;
- emphasize shared values—called similarity-attraction effect—people are more attracted to people who are similar to them;
- touch casually— tapping someone's back or touching their arm or wrist—a kind of subliminal touching that occurs when you touch a person so subtly that they barely notice it; and
- see the other person how they want to be seen—because, people want to be perceived in ways that align with their own beliefs—a kind of self-verification, seeking confirmation of their own views, positive or negative.

A growing body of research suggests that happiness and sadness—as well as lifestyle factors like smoking, drinking, obesity, fitness habits and education—might be contagious which can spread across social networks, both online and in real life. We choose friends not only because of social features similar to ours consciously, but also because of biological and even genetic features similar to ours, unconsciously. A new study suggests that when it comes to certain genes, 'birds of a feather flock together' applies to a great extent. The research shows a potential insight into subtle genetic influences—friends of a similar type of gene—that tend to affect how we become friends.

In every day's life, genes and social environments are intertwined in many aspects. For instance, an individual is actively seeking to hang around with someone, may actually turn out to be an impersonal force—which is at play that pools them together. After studying 5,000 pairs of adolescent friends, researchers find (a) that friends are more genetically similar than random pairs of people; and (b) that about two-thirds are as similar as an average married couple. The phenomenon is due to (a) the primary effect—called social homophily—where individuals form the bond based on shared characteristics, most of which can be traced back to genetics, combined with (b) the secondary effect—called social structuring—where individuals are pooled together for their shared social environments (school, college, club, office and social function), most of which can also be traced back to genetics. The social tendency gives rise to a harmonious sense of belonging, shared purpose and easy coexistence. However, at the same time it gives rise to the basis of tribalism, xenophobia, in-group bias and racism. The combined effect gives an urge to *otherize* those who differ from us. At the personal level, we are over here, they are over there. It is not simply what is ours and what is yours, but, more subtly, who we are versus who they are. Such predisposition is based on the human tendency to define one's identity in contrast to another cast as different and untrustworthy. Others are best—ok—kept them at a distance. We love ours, we hate others. Here, friendship skews a bit of a conspiracy, where it creates a common enemy. In-group bias and xenophobia go hand-in-hand. At the global level, in the globalized world, it is *us versus them.* When world people flow across the border and the citizen sees it an imminent threat to their lives, livelihoods and entitlements, they demand border-wall, prioritize their country first, or what you might call the trespassers, *them.* One survey reveals that two-thirds of supposed friendships are actually unrequited likes. Under the circumstances, friendship gets surprisingly fragile. One in-depth survey of 540 participants by Oxford University, reveals that (a) people fall out of friend-circle about two times a year; (b) after a year, 40% of those ruptures remain unhealed; and (c) the overall conflicts of friendship does not differ very much between men and women—even though women are more likely to clash with their close friends, and more likely to express feelings of anguish over the breakup.

Gene factor can have a huge impact on our later life choices. It goes both ways. The same gene that may link friends is also connected to the risk of other behaviors, say alcoholism and drug use. What happens to me may not only depend on my genes but also depend on the genes of my friends—biologically as a group. Molecular biologists found an interesting relationship between two specific genes. One is

DRD2 involved in producing a type of dopamine receptor that results in bonding friends to each other and, on the downside, increased risk for alcoholism as well. If you have this gene, more likely your friend has it too. You're not only susceptible pathologically to this behavior but also prone to be surrounded by the people who are susceptible to similar behavior. From an evolutionary standpoint, it makes sense at the time of mate choice that it can affect both romantic connections and friendships. Friendship and social networks tend to affect our act, behavior, and personality, sometimes even more than genes. For example, researchers found that people who have friends who are obese—even if they do not live near each other—are more prone to gain weight themselves. Having obese friends is linked to a greater chance of being obese than having obese siblings.

Second-hand obesity! One study asked about 9,000 adults ages between 18 and 65 whether or not they wanted to lose weight and at the same time asked to list at least four people with whom they spent the most of free time face-to-face or interacted via phone, social media, texting, or email. The findings, published in 2016 in the journal *Obesity*, revealed that obese people spent more time with obese people. It is not "nurture between introvert and extrovert. The famously charismatic extrovert Steve Jobs teamed up with introvert and shy Steve Wozniak. The two types needed each other at the Apple Inc.]

Friendship is flexible: you choose a friend, or your friend choose you as a friend. The expectations from friendship, once matured, doesn't change much across the course of life. Make friends even you are adult—because, it's important.

Now the question is how to have good friends. The best way to have good friends is to be one. Don't wait for other people to be friendly, show them how. Be yourself a friend first. Be interested in them. You will have more friends just by getting interested in others, rather than trying to get others to be interested in you. A person who does not open his doors to others will never find the doors of others open for him. Ask yourself a very private question: Who among the friends are your real friends? One very influential research flatly argued that only about half of perceived friends are mutual. Or in other words, someone you think is your friend may not be so, and vice versa. It is one startling finding in modern life and personal relationship that has prompted many debates among sociologists, psychologists, neuroscientists, philosophers, and organizational behavior experts because it is one alarming concern for the validity of one's relationship, especially when the friendship has an enormous effect on one's health, wealth, and well-being. Friendship is really hard to describe. Friends are perhaps the people you take time to understand and allow time to understand you, or perhaps a fostering notion of whiling away time in each other's company and doing nothing.

We come in contact with many people in our lives; people come and people go, many we call our friends, be they neighbors, colleagues, business associates, or simple acquaintances. One survey asked people how their inner friend circle changes when they open up to friendship, especially when they fall in love. The finding illustrates that people typically have five close friends at any given time, and then when one gets, in a romantic relationship, instead of having the typical five individuals on average, they only have four including the new love in the friend circle. The circle shrinks. Or in other words, if one new love comes into your life, you have to give up two others. Also, there are concentric circles of friendships. The innermost circle consists of only one or two people, typically a spouse and one best friend with whom you are most intimate with and relate daily. The next circle can have at most four people for whom you interact on a regular basis, weekly or so. The outermost circle contains relatives and more casual friends with whom you have formal connections; they are not your friends and easily fall in the realm of an acquaintance after a long gap. People have a limited amount of time and emotional capital to invest in friendship effort, so a person has only five openings for the most intense type of relationship.

"Be slow in choosing friends, slower in changing."—Benjamin Franklin. A false friend can turn into an enemy, so quickly. So, take your time, move slowly and realize, what lies deep in other person's heart before you make any emotional investment of your *self* that true friendship requires. Be even slower in breaking-up, or reconciling after breaking-up. A reconciled friend tends to be a lethal enemy. His hatred may be concealed and may be more concentrated. So, don't switch a friend; rather, while choosing a friend, avoid negative people at the first place. Some of the people are uninteresting, incurious, lazy, absorbed in the small stuff, doubting everything, and tepid in emotion and thus are incapable of being a friend. They are toxic. And also, you don't have to make friends with everybody. Leave those unhealthy friendships out of your life, on principle. In one survey, as much as 84% of women and 75% of men had encountered a toxic friend at some point in their lives. The majority—8 out of 10—say they hold onto unhealthy friendships because they cannot just break up. These friends are self-absorbed narcissists, downers and emotionally draining, self-righteous, and overly critical types. People of low moral character, tyrants and scoundrels can have friends, but they can only be *friends of utility.* They are silly, immoral, and just plain bad. They are the boulder on your road. They lower you down to their level. Avoid them on principle. Tell them quietly, "Bless your heart!" and move on. They go low; you go high. Ignore those who try to diminish you. They are backseat drivers. Avoid all the grumblers, complainers, blamers, and nitpickers. They are all low; some are naked, have no clothes. "I am just being honest" is an excuse for "just being mean." "We all are friends here" may be a prelude to a fraud. "I am sincere" may be a lie is to surface. Suspicion is the cancer of friendship; therefore, a friend of doubt is dangerous. Reject them outright. A prudent enemy is preferable to an unfaithful friend. "Surround yourself only with people who are going to take you higher," said Oprah Winfrey, an American media executive, actress, talk show host, television producer and philanthropist. Health researchers studied the health habits of people who live in so-called—blue zones—the countries or country's regions of the world where people live longer on average, and reveal that positive friendship is one very common theme: friends provide an ongoing influence on healthy behavior in a way that even a super-diet can't substitute.

True friendship is not for 'profit or loss.' Not for 'give or take.' Nor for cooperation that you scratch my back, I will scratch yours. It is not a business relationship; it does not seek repayment, nor keep a score. True friendship is in spite of all. True friendship requires trust, wisdom and basic understanding. There are times when a person cannot talk his problems to others, sometimes not even to the spouse; still, he can take his faithful friend, in confidence, in such terrible matters, often ensuing terrific results. Friends who are close like literal family members can bring you not only the joy, but also a pile of frustration, because it is the way closeness works. Your good friend will tell you on your face when your face is dirty. He will stab his finger on your chest and caution you the danger. When that happens, you realize he is simply right. His moral and vocal support has some sense. If you are wise, you come to sense. With the same token, your good friend will also tell you when your face is clean. It is like one hand cleans the other hand. Having stable close good friend in your teenage years benefits you later years. One study followed 169 participants for 10 years, starting at age 15 and interviewed them and their closest friends, one-on-one, at then at age 15 and again at 16, and thereon every year. Researchers asked questions like, how much they trust, how good communication and how alienated they feel to each other in the relationship. The original participants were additionally asked to assess their levels of anxiety, depression and self-worth. During the course of study period, researchers noticed that these teens tend to be open with one another about difficult topics, more engaged with one another and helping each other. In conclusion, researchers revealed that the teens who had close, emotional ties at age 15 and 16, showed improvement in coping with anxiety, depression and self-worth up to the age of 25. Those who had the most stable relationship, seemed to do the best.

We all have virtues as well as faults. There are imperfections in all of us. If we put the foibles under a scanner trying to dwell too much on those, that can be only at the cost of the relationship. A friend is one who has the ability to overlook these imperfections for the sake of goodness. He judges his friend less on his mistakes than on how he handles the mistakes. He may like to see you as a man as perfect as possible. If the foibles are such as are not good either for the man or his neighbors and friends, a true friend may be interested in wiping the blots in the character of the friend, but he should do it subtly so as not to offend his friend's sensitivity. If your friend has to reproach you for some grave error, he must not do that in public; he can do that in private, taking you in confidence. On the other hand, if you have real good qualities worthy of other peoples' notice, your friend should praise you openly and unstintingly so as to bolster your self-esteem. A close friend adds value to our personal advancement and to our personal pleasure, making music a little sweeter and laughter a little louder.

Males have different chemistry of bonding among other male friends than that of females. Researchers have revealed that men tend to link and bond on such nonpersonal passions such as news, politics, game, or job. When women make friends with other women, what they seek is to build up relationships on a comprehensive, holistic level. When men get together with other male friends, they would like to talk mostly on public space about their passions, which brought them together and which created the bonding, while on the other hand women talk more in private space where they would like to share many things personal, their pains and pleasures, their expectations and disappointments. Sometimes problems that she cannot share with her husband can be unburdened before friends, and she is often more comfortable discussing her illness with her female friends than with her doctor. For working women particularly, life in modern society is a tightrope walk. The stress of balancing the often-conflicting demands of the home and the workplace is enormous and complex. Some of these emotional problems can be alleviated, if not eliminated, through the association of her friends.

Emotional stresses, if pent up within oneself, can wreak severe damage of the psyche. Within the circle of friends, these stresses find an outlet. In one survey, researchers found that men do suffer more than women after breakups because males are less likely to disclose problems to other male friends. Their analyses indicate that when a relationship fails, it tends to have a greater impact on men's own sense of self-worth. Breakup feeling is further compounded in the shed of isolation. In contrast, women are slightly better off. They are more likely to have close female friends whom they typically talk with and whom they can turn to for support. For these reasons, friendship outside the home counts a lot for modern women. The value of such type of association in reducing the stress and enhancing the peace and pleasure in day-to-day living is indisputable. In recent times, women are increasingly realizing the value of such bonding and spending time within a close circle of friends. Social research shows that the path to recovery from a breakup will be better if you don't try to forget but rather expose yourself to the very conditions about your ex that you can think of. Social scientists hypothesize to explain it to the fact that our brain gets bored when we loop the brain with the same information over and over again and eventually cease to take note—which helps to forget and move on with life. This may be true even if the information overload may be torturous at first. Be rational rather than emotional!

The rapid disintegration of American social life had begun quite some time ago. Today social ties are less than half as strong as they were in the 1950s. The society is not a community anymore but merely a collection of isolated family units. Everybody plumes on improvement of society, but nobody really does. Society is a joint-stock company that exists only as a mental concept; in actuality, they are only individuals bunched and labeled as communities. Maybe, someday, we all cross again the invisible lines between our homes and achieve greater unity in the neighborhoods as we live.

Today, life is so fast that even deer go gets behind. We are running to race ahead there. God knows where! We leave our near and dear behind, elbowing out the crowd just to go ahead. We forget dead and wounded. We don't hear much from our failed friends anymore—like the battered soldiers at the end of a lost war, sick grandmother in an assisted home, and ordinary folks who got laid off from the jobs and after unsuccessful months resigned to their diminished status. In the human highway, remember, one day our vehicle will also stop silently, and no one will ever notice our disabled vehicle roadside. It will be towed away soon, in teardrop silence.

Society is a collection of individuals in one-to-many relationships. There is a conflict between the demand of an individual that tries to assert to the society and the demand made upon the individual by the society. "My fellow Americans, ask not what your country can do for you, ask what you can do for your country," said John F. Kennedy. Such conflict has existed from the time man started to become civilized. Moral gravity still pulls the intense sociability of human beings rather than on divine law or an idea of individual autonomy. Superseding the Old Testament that put fresh emphasis on the individual, the New Testament was truly the symbol of personal salvation because it took individualism to a logical extreme by asserting that the individuals not only could change the world but also bore the responsibility to do so. Different societies have seen and treated this conflict in different ways. Many would assert that every inch of progress made by mankind has been made possible by the efforts and genius of individuals. Perhaps, the assertions are, in most part, true. But at the same time, we shall not be telling the whole truth unless we add that it is the society that has preserved every inch of this progress. Different societies have looked upon this duality in different ways. There is a remarkable difference in the perception of this duality between Western and Eastern thoughts. Looking at the political histories of both, we realize that Western societies have treated the rights of individuals as sacrosanct and inviolable and pivotal to the progress of mankind, while in the East, it is generally treated to be subservient to the claims of the society. It is generally thought that an excess of individual right will lead to anarchy, and a society cannot make any progress in such anarchic environment.

Freedom is not free! It costs. Absolute individual freedom costs an individual absolutely. Full freedom is fantasy. When a person is seen to be thinking, working, and expressing himself apparently without any obstruction or societal pressure, a number of forces are at play in his subconscious mind of which his conscious mind is not aware of or have no control of. There is a plethora of societal prejudices that he has already imbibed from his environment and that are at play inside him and that makes the idea of an absolutely individual initiative an illusory. These prejudices are what he has absorbed from his parents during childhood and which contain the collective ethos and prejudices of the class and the social milieu. The quality of a man's true individuality has to be understood in this context and not without.

Yet there is a general distinction of the concept of individual freedom in the thoughts of the West and the East. In a person brought up in Western culture, there will be more preference for individual freedom and initiative than societal control. The Western mind sees an individual primarily as an individual entity and then as a unit in society. The Western man will tend to give more importance to individual right and privacy. The Eastern mind may treat the needs of harmony and the duty to society as more important. In the west, the bird is freed; in the east, the bird is caged. Skeptics in the West have questioned the motive behind this so-called harmony as the mowing down and bulldozing of dissent to defend authority. It is stated to be more of a triumph of the authority in power than the true demands of progress and harmony. Such debates are perennial. However, due to this difference in culture, we have seen the supremacy of market economy and capitalism in the West, while in the East, more societies have settled for a system of collective control and control over individual initiative.

The conflicts between the ideas of a free society and a society controlling, marginally or substantially, the affairs among its members will go on forever. When a free society rises up, it not only ennobles its members but also entails giving up some of their personal liberty for the need of the whole. A free society does not administer the affairs among its members but administer a moral and lawful justice among the people who conduct their affairs freely. Justice is better served in a free society where even though unpopular is equally safe. Yet an absolutely free society appears to be a myth, perhaps not warranted. There is no society, either in the East or in the West, in which the state does not control the affairs between the individuals in some way. In the U.S., there is always a hitch going on between government and citizen about the First Amendment, an amendment to the Constitution of the United States guaranteeing the right of free expression that includes freedom of assembly, freedom of the press, freedom of religion, and freedom of speech. For a democratic nation, they are the guardian of the gate. A bird needs to fly, a man needs to flee. Democratic participation, free expression, and the rule of law, which are largely realities in India, are still aspirations of many developed nations and especially in China (for free speech, family planning, and land acquisition per se). When we talk of a free society, we use the word *free* in relative terms only. We may, at best, say that a certain society is freer than the other.

Karl Marx (1818–1883), the German revolutionary socialist, did not consider society merely as consisting of individuals: "Society does not consist of individuals, but expresses the sum of the interrelations, the relations within which these individuals stand." Even a person like John F. Kennedy (1917–1963), the U.S. president who was steeped in the ideas of Western liberal democracy, had underlined the need for protecting the material interests of the poorer people by state intervention: "If a free society cannot help the many who are poor, it cannot save the few who are rich."

While the debate concerns at the macro level of nations and countries, activities at the micro level of people and their immediate neighborhood, their families, and friends are equally significant. Whatever may be stated in favor of individuality, it cannot be denied that a man living in a dense social network will tend to flourish more because of the security and social support that his environment provides. Even a man of great genius and creativity needs the appreciation and support of people around him. If he is isolated from the environment and if the support and appreciation are not forthcoming, it may not help his genius to bear fruit. You could have a place of honor in the community, but in a democratic society, you play your role like playing an instrument in a symphony. "Democracy is a charming form of government, full of variety and disorder, and dispensing a sort of equality to equals and unequal alike" (Plato [427 BC–347 BC], Greek philosopher). And, for this very reason, India is considered as one of the greatest democracies in the world today, where elections are regular and fiercely contested, speech is (mostly) free, the courts are independent, and people are guaranteed—of their expression, belief, faith and worship—by the constitution and by the institution.

When we talk of a more ordinary person, such collective support is more crucial. Life is integrated with friends and society; otherwise, it's lonely. Today societies both in the East and the West are characterized by fragmentation. Overall, households are gradually downsizing. As the conflicting interests of different groups and ethnics assert more and more, the social fabric becomes more and more vulnerable. Even within the limits of the small neighborhoods, people are growing isolated from one another. There are haunting tales of individual isolation in urban societies. The death of an elderly lady inside a lonely house went unnoticed by the neighborhood until her son came to look her up in the weekend. Her neighbors did not have any inkling of the tragedy that happened next door. There was another story of a ghastly murder of a woman, mother of two kids, by her husband! The neighbors came to know about it only after the two kids ran out of the house howling in horror. Yet the neighbors hardly had an inkling that there was such a tension between the couple so as to culminate in such a tragedy. Stories of such nature are widespread.

A lonely man is an angel or an animal. Loneliness comes to life at different stages in different forms. In adulthood, you are classically alone. Every so often, loneliness adds loveliness to life. It adds a rare hue on sunsets that makes a quiet night feel a little better. Inside yourself, there is a greenroom where you live all alone, and that's where you change and renew your spring that never dries up. Yet most of the time, loneliness symbolizes your dire lack of love. It is something less of you, the defeat of you. Loneliness comes from solitary living. There are many statistical data about the wonders of medical science and the longer life span, but we do not have perhaps any data on how many people are dying out of mental trauma created by isolation and loneliness. In 1950, only 4 million Americans (5% of households) lived alone; in 2011, there were 33 million (in 28% households). They are primarily women of middle age 35 to 64. But surprisingly, young adults of age 18 to 34 have now been the fastest growing segment of singleton population. The unprecedented rise of solitary living is one of the biggest social threats that America neglected to identify, let alone assist. Elderly people especially are alarmed by such situations and are worried about what was lying in store for them. For them, there is the nagging, disturbing thought as to why the concept of community is gradually perishing. They seemed not to be living in a community but in seclusion in hundreds of little, isolated homes.

Loneliness can be contagious. A new study from a panel of researchers specializing in the psychology of social networks suggests that loneliness can diffuse through groups of friends and family members. In the analysis of nearly 4,500 participants about how frequently they felt lonely, researchers found that close friends and family members of the person who reported persistent loneliness were 52% more likely to feel loneliness themselves. A person who feels lonely perceive the social world as lonely and more threatening. A lonely person thinks negatively about other people as well. So, if you are his friend, and if he starts treating you negatively, then over time, he and you would stop being friends. In fact, this is what happens in the real world—tossing more people out in isolation.

Loneliness hurts. Let us illustrate it with one example. Loneliness negates the rational benefits of physical exercise. Loneliness and isolation can undermine the benefits of exercise at a cellular level. On the contrary, having been in a relationship with friends and family indirectly helps to get the full benefit of exercise. And perhaps even more fascinating is how a relationship affects the exercise or any activities for that matter. While neurogenesis remains somewhat mysterious why and how isolation affects exercise, some experts' view is this: an exercise is a form of stress and so is social isolation, each release stress hormones independently. So, performing exercise may seem to be an independent physical activity, but it is not. It is, in fact, a behavior braid with social and emotional concern that influences how we work out and with what physiological (physical and psychological, i.e., body and mind) consequences. For example, it may take longer or more effort to come at per for the lonely people to maintain the state of the brain with exercise.

Typically, we feel sad when no one talks to us. The biological impact of such social isolation is much more than what we ordinarily understood. Some researchers, who have been carrying out surveys in such matters, indicate that lonely people are more likely to get sick and die at a younger age. It works in a subtle way insidiously and wreaks havoc on our metabolism. It changes the way our genes work and may alter the internal process through which a normal, healthy person responds to external situations. There is hardly any prescription for mental sickness in such a profoundly sick society in America.

Loneliness kills. It's the next big public health issue. Living alone is associated with increased risk of mortality: social isolation (precisely, lack of social connection) and living alone increase the mortality risk by about 29% and 32% respectively. Studies have also indicated that in America, people are spending less and less time in social events and get-togethers now than they used to do only thirty years ago. Developments of technology have given them so-called unlimited comfort within the four walls. The internet has given access to the world wide web of openings. There is a continuous tide of information from all corners of the globe. So, people need not look outside. They do not have the time or the temper to look anywhere outside for any mental nourishment. Our make-believe society is engaged in making and decorating the cage in which humans can be kept imprisoned happily. What perhaps is not realized is, At what cost is this isolation?

Friends and society exist in the animal world too. Researchers observed that chimpanzees share food, come to each other's help in fighting external forces, and travel through the forest side by side, and when one dies, the other seems to grieve. Female baboons keep a close relationship with a few for many years. Those with friends tend to live 4 times more to age 15 years compared to those who don't. Horses pick a few friends and groom or play with them or lean their head to one another. Heart rate slows down during those quiet moments. Male dolphins start friendship at a young age and maintain them throughout life. Friendship is natural. Friendliness trait gets passed on across the species in the milieu of Mother Nature.

2 Enjoy Good Life

Life is a ticket to the greatest show on earth.

—Martin H. Fischer (1879—1962) a German-born American physician and author, famous for his teaching on the art and practice of medicine.

The show begins. There you are, in the front row, at the center—the most memorable moment on Earth. But you are not intelligent enough or swift enough to enjoy the full view of the show. Life is just a moment. Yet it is great to be here. At least once in your lifetime! So, while you are here, be happy and help yourself. If you are wise (or otherwise), think seriously; it's a privilege to live on this earth. Start TODAY, right here where you are. Enjoy a good life!

Do not postpone the joy. Enjoy. Joy delights in joy. Life passes away quickly like a candle in the wind, in the blink of an eye. Its span is nothing but a tiny slice of time. You only live once (YOLO). Enjoy!

How we enjoy our days, of course, sums up to how we enjoy our lives. Nature has strewn around us so much beauty, so much treasure, and so much pleasure. Only, we have any time to take a look. Our goal should be to live at par with nature. So be wise. Be in tune with nature, and be at home in leisure and domestic pleasure. Turn the fear into cheer. It is a beautiful world out there. Be cheerful. Enjoy the pure, simple, natural life. It's a great privilege and boundless pleasure to be here once in our lifetime. It really is!

Our life is always full of events. There is no finish line. It is better to acknowledge as much and then decide to be happy in spite of it all. For some time, it may appear that life is about to begin. Real life! But there is always some obstacle on the way, an ordeal to get through, some job to be done, some time to wait, a debt to be paid, a new home, and so on. Life is a pile of damned things, one after the other. But the fact remains that these things are life. So, enjoy every moment you get a chance while working, while playing, while talking, while praying, and even while sleeping. Stop waiting for the payday, for Friday evening, for Sunday morning, for spring, for summer, for fall, or for school to end to finish the college, to start a new job, to get married, to have a baby, to die, to be reborn. It's a moving target; but the fact of the matter is that happiness is a direction, not a destination. There is no better time to be happy than now. Live and enjoy the moment. Let us be happy one day and every day.

If you want to enjoy your life, enjoy each day every day. The best part of the day is the first part of the day—the morning hours. It's a beautiful morning! The world stirs to life each morning. A typical day! Imagine—it is a gentle spring, the hillside is dew-pearled, the lark is on the wing, and the snail is on the thorn. The sky is red, waiting for the sun to crawl up, and you are right there! That is so cool—life is so beautiful.

Typical repentance goes like this. When I had youth, I had no money. Now I have money but no time; or when I get the time, if I ever do, I may have no health to enjoy. Many people get crazy over earning more and more money. They depreciate the best part of their life earning money only to appreciate illusive pleasure in the least part of their life. They think more of security than opportunity. Ten years down, they will be disappointed. If ever there was a time of opportunity, that might just be it; but they lost it. True, money is an important factor in life, but it is not the sole factor. The labor that we do should not make us feel more wretched at the end of the day. It should make us feel content and happy. It is a labor of love. Life is not an endless, uninterrupted pulling of the oars in the galley. Put it away. Get rid of it. Get free! Growth is evidence of life. To grow and thrive, life has to be a combination of and a balance between the work, which is meaningful and purposeful, and the leisure which is delightful in the harmony of nature.

While we enjoy our lives better, we also appreciate better what others want for their lives. While we enjoy our lives in our own way, we must allow others to enjoy their lives in their way as well. A lot of complication in life may be avoided if we learn not to attach maximum importance to our own right. It is good only as long as it does not intimidate another person's right. It is akin to the concept of liberty and freedom. You have the right to swing your arm as long it does not smash the nose of others.

Let us remember one thing: that there is no such thing as enjoying life to the fullest. It's all relative and circumstantial. For a person with a disability, simply enduring can feel like a tremendous victory. For a person with knee problems, simple walking can be a sheer joy. Sometimes it's being human, enjoying being a little silly. Enjoyment can be found in noise, pageantry, and pomp. However, enjoyment is not always a reckless, hedonistic gratification of human senses. Social studies say, on average, there are fewer fatalities in the last week of the month and least at the end of the month; but then, thereafter, there's a huge spike on the first day of the month, the payday, and then it tapers off by a week. Impale in financial choice leads to impulse in mortality. This is just one example. Enjoyment can come out of a high-decibel and noisy life; rambunctious rollicks, raucous notes, and desperately wanting to be happy are merely signs of lower psychological health. A happy life need not be made of happy moments out of every moment of the day. Life can be as enjoyable in silence, in its placidity and serenity, and in quiet communion with nature. It can be in a gentle conversation with others. There is a plethora of media ads and publications on the subject, where they list the secrets of happiness. The truth, however, seems to be that few people admit being happy in life. Among the happy people, there seems to be no commonality as to the way of achieving their happiness. Each person seems to be happy in his own way. Each has to find out for himself the source of happiness. The skill is to avoid pain and to find pleasure. Many problems that we encounter every day—stress, anxiety, depression, chronic pain, addictive behavior—actually stem from the brain's hardwired disposition to seek pleasure and avoid pain. The art of living is the feeling that we are alive. We can hope, we can love, we can laugh, and we can cry. A happy mind inspires a happy life.

The Dalai Lama was once asked why one needed to be happy. He replied, "If one is happy, not only is he happy himself, but he will make others happy, and the ripple effect makes many others happy. On the contrary, if one is unhappy, one will make others unhappy and the same adverse ripple effect thereafter." Social scientists and economists who make public policy of the states are in the opinion that the measure of happiness is how successful society is. So be happy, and let others be happy as well.

Seligman, the social scientist, has defined three kinds of happiness. The first, he says, is the "pleasant life—smiling, feeling good, and being ebullient." Such prototypical happy people are ebullient, hugely guffawing, and full of fun. But not all people are genetically predisposed toward this type of happy-go-lucky state of mind. Second, people are capable of a higher form of happiness, which he calls "good life." Applicable to most of us, it consists first in knowing what one's strengths are, and then "recrafting" the life so as to use those strengths consciously in different activities, such as in love, friendship, and parenting. This attitude can come out of a total commitment to life in which one gets fully immersed and involved. Third, there is a still higher and ultimate form of happiness. It consists of first identifying one's strengths and then using those in the service of something that one believes to be higher than one's self. This kind of happiness is, obviously, not for common people; it is for people of a higher caliber, like great statesmen, reformers, and thinkers. In general, the higher form of happiness arises from a purpose-driven meaningful life, which can sometimes coexist with acute depression of the mind. One doesn't have to be conventionally happy to achieve such satisfaction. To them, useless life is an early death. Seligman says Churchill and Lincoln were two profound depressives who dealt with it by having good and purposeful lives.

Many problems that we encounter every day—stress, anxiety, depression, chronic pain, addictive behavior—actually stem from the brain's hardwired tendency to seek pleasure and avoid pain. Yet happiness is not the absence of unhappiness. Pain, sorrow, hunger, and conflicts are so part and parcel of our lives that if we miss them, we miss a part of our life. Unhappiness, too, is not the absence of happiness. Both happiness and unhappiness can even coexist together. And also, circumstances do not always define our emotional status. For example, it is true that poverty can be utterly degrading and depressing, leading to unhappiness. But wealth is also not such an important factor in determining happiness either. People in rich countries are not noticeably happier than the people of poorer countries. Even at the individual level, a misfortune like cancer or some life-threatening terminal diseases do not make a person more prone to unhappiness than the rest of the population. Happiness, love, and joy are all mysteries. They should not be rationalized and, for that matter, should not be quantified. The moment we do so, the very sense of feeling fades away. If we recognize that happiness is not an uninterrupted, perpetual state of mind, then we can easily realize that happiness can only come out of realizing that we can't always be happy. And also, it does not matter if you are happy always. Ambitions are worth struggling for, but not dying for. Certainly enough, desire is necessary to keep life in motion; but what is required to save a life from vicissitudes and catastrophes is a sense of proportion.

It is true that humans who have a greater sense of what is truly important—a greater awareness of their relationships and their true worth—are more capable of being happy.

Natural joys within us are the true happiness of life. At the same time, an awareness and an acknowledgment of the happiness of life is essential for attaining the state of contentment. It is a state of resignation and a quiet philosophical acceptance of the existence of the opposites of life. The more we merge with nature, the more we fulfill ourselves and adapt any opposites. The true source of a higher level of happiness is a recognition and appreciation of all these opposites—like birth and death, joy and sorrow, light and dark, hope and despair. There can't be a better school for learning these realities than nature itself. It is so vast that such opposites, appearing like ripples on its surface, fade away into nothingness within moments.

What else could be more soothing and embalming to the grated soul than nature? Look at the apparel of nature in its many hues. Look at the color of its trees and plants. Green! Isn't it a color that evokes a feeling of cool comfort? Isn't it a color that nature has spread so predominantly all over the planet? How many among us wouldn't feel the thrill of walking over a carpet of soft green grass or straying deep into the forest with foliage arching green above our heads? Doesn't it bring within us a feeling of inner strength swelling inside us, to enable us to negotiate all the tumultuous paths of life? So, enjoy all the seasons of nature; protect and preserve our green earth. According to one research from an environmental health perspective, living near greenery helps one live longer. In the study, researchers tracked 108,630 women who completed questionnaires on their health and lifestyle twice a year, from 2000 to 2008. And they tracked—using satellite imagery—the range of seasonal vegetation where individual women lived. The study had taken into account such factors as age, race, body mass index, physical activity, smoking, education, socioeconomic status, and behavioral factors. During the study period of eight years, 8,604 women died. Researchers then compared mortality rates between those living in the top one-fifth for greenness in the 250 m^2 area surrounding their homes with those living in the bottom one-fifth, and they found a 12% lower mortality rate. As we focus more and more on the green of nature, we realize what tremendous positive energy it is invested with. Green is thc lap of Mother Nature for all her creatures—caring, protecting, and giving. It is the soft bed on which all the species of her creation feel restful from the turbulence of life around. When we have a realization of this positive energy emanating from nature, protecting and sustaining life, we can't help but feel a moral obligation. Consume less, share more.

If you understand how important the nature is, then you will understand how important to win the nature and, even more, how important not to lose. In naturc, we have to dissolve ourselves—to be in and to win! We are not in the nature, we are part of the nature. To better our lives, we have to be a part of her! We arrive at this world with nothing and shall depart with nothing. Whatever we get during our stay is adequate. Celebrate life while we are alive! Each day is a new day, a new hope. Greet the day! Enjoy a good life!

2.1 Life Is Good

Not life, but good life, is to be chiefly valued.
—Socrates (469 BC–399 BC), classical Greek philosopher

Life is good. It has been, and it will be. Life is understandable, comprehensible and predictable. Don't let anyone fool you it's not. Life, for and itself, is good; and furthermore, you choose a good life. Choose to feel good, not bad—it's a choice. When you feel good, the world feels good with you. Life is beautiful. Don't ever ignore the "feel good" factor. Everyone is responsible for their share of joy. Feeling good is only a choice away. Life is fine all the time!

Health and sleep are better appreciated when they are interrupted. Likewise, you appreciate that life is good only when you contrast it with when it is not. Feeling good or otherwise, is the reflection of our inner selves, our physical and mental well-being. Research on well-being concentrates on three core factors: health, relationships, and a sense of purpose in one's chosen pursuit. A sense of purpose is something that really comes from inside—spontaneous happiness—not from external circumstances. We feel good when we are happy and when we are able to make other people happy. Enjoy together. Joy is a great spirit, an optimistic attitude, and a heart full of love. Joyfulness keeps the body young and the face fresh. Yet joyfulness, as we know, cannot give an uninterrupted state of mind. A good time has to alternate with not-so-good time.

Feeling good is inseparably linked with being in a joyous mood. There may be occasions when we feel good in spite of being not so good. Sometimes, when we are lost, we feel deeply uncomfortable, unhappy, or unfulfilled. We are more likely to step out of our ruts and start soul searching or try to trace a true meaning of our lives. It happens to few. But for most of us in real life, the thinking is that when we are depressed, it is less likely we try out new things—and that when we are happy, we venture out to the world with a sense of exploration. Occasionally, it may arise out of a sense of being valued by others. If we analyze our lives, we shall realize how often we feel miserable—because we pay too much attention to how miserable we are. There is a famous quote of George Bernard Shaw that goes: "The secret of being miserable is to have leisure to bother about whether you are happy or not." Precisely because our ideas of success and failure and the assumption thereof underlying these two judgments are flawed. So, do not measure successes or failure by only materialistic value. Your feelings determine the feeling of richness (and poorness) of your life. Be alive so long you live. Listen to your mind, body, and beyond. Do not live in the frustration of abstraction. If you are happy and you know it, clap your hands!

Our life is being consumed in the modern rat race. In pursuit of wealth and prosperity, we are chasing El Dorado, trying to bite a larger slice of the cake to get ahead of the people around us. In the pursuit of an extraordinary life, we sacrifice our ordinary life, navigate in sinking rapids, and land up in a hot mess. Yet, the simple fact remains simple: true prosperity comes when we discipline our mind and enjoy our normal life. Content inside! Contentment comes from within and is relatively independent of external conditions. Isolate the major turning points both by achievements (education, career, marriage, children, wealth) and by failures (divorce, financial ruins, illness). Discard the myths of happiness, acknowledge the peaks and valleys of life, and realize that people are far more adaptable than they think. Research finds that the more people have, the less content they seem to be. A sense of authority and power is an intoxicating stimulant a mortal can feel good about. Where a simple living is not reconcilable with the pursuit of a life of plenty and pleasure—and when life runs greedily after abundance, consumption, and luxury—do we have the time to pause and ask ourselves if we feel good?

Are you happy? Why do things feel so good for some people and for others so bad? What does it mean for the brain to experience pleasure, or pain? How does our brain react to food, sleep, sex, drugs, gambling, charity, power, exercise, and importantly, the work we do, rather we love to do? Scientists and physiologists have since traced the origin of pleasure in the human brain. Un-guilty pleasure, because of its natural relationship to us, is good; but guilty pleasure in the pursuit of every pleasure is bad. We are still experimenting how and why we get pleasure and, thereafter, sometimes become addicted to certain foods, chemicals, and behaviors. Studies find that there are some variants in genes that control the function of dopamine signals within the pleasure circuit. The neurotransmitter dopamine is the brain's pleasure signal for all subtle varieties of human happiness. It is the "pleasure molecule" that stimulates the chemistry of joy, laughter, addiction, and even anger. Hypocretin—another brain chemical, which is primarily responsible for sleep and appetite—is also associated with neurons that are found in the same vicinity where dopamine acts to influence feelings of pleasure and reward. The two agents work together, and their level is responsible for why some people are more impulsive than others. Scientists assert that our pleasure circuits—which are a combination of genetics, stress level, and life experience—begin as early as in the womb. Normally, normal people experience natural pleasure naturally. In contrast, addicts have some genes that turn down natural function of dopamine-signaling, resulting in the brain's inability to experience natural pleasure naturally. Addicts—and, for that matter, some people who have such gene variants—have their dopamine systems muted. This leads to the blunted pleasure circuits, which, in turn, affect their pleasure-seeking activities. While most of us are able to achieve a desired degree of pleasure with moderate indulgence, people with blunted dopamine systems are hijacked to overdo. For instance, in order to get equivalent drinking pleasure while others would get so easily—maybe with two drinks in a party and laughter with friends—an addict needs six drinks, possibly the additional indulgence of other kinds of drugs.

Addiction, by definition, is a compulsive behavior related to a substance or to an activity that an individual continues to engage in, despite the negative consequences. It is a broader and complex phenomenon not limited to mere activation of pleasure pathways. Children and adults alike are hooked to addiction from foods to drugs to internet porn to violence. Neuroscience finds that alcohol, cocaine, opioids, and other allied drugs destabilize—rather hijack the brain's pleasure systems and trick the brain to think that a drug high is essential for survival. As natural rewards such as food and sex also affect the brain's reward systems in the same way as drugs do, therefore, they can be considered as a "natural addiction." But this is, in fact, a weird form of circular reasoning as it muddles the original purpose of the brain's pleasure pathways. These areas in the brain are not likely to have evolved specially to enable us to get high on cocaine or heroin. Ironically, that would have been evolutionary sabotage. They evolve in such a way as to get us to pursue food and sex relentlessly in order to guarantee our survival as a species. In fact, these brain regions are designed to make food and sex fun. Generally, the vast majority of people are not food, sex, or drug addicts. Also, a vast majority of drug users, including those who use cocaine and heroin, are medically not addicts after all. For instance, studies have shown that approximately 97% of people who take opioid painkillers like OxyContin, and who do not have a prior addiction, do not become addicts. In 2015, the FDA requested drug manufacturers to conduct studies on the safety of OxyContin for pediatric patients as young as eleven years of age. Now here is the recommendation: OxyContin is not for kids. The CDC reported more than 16,000 prescription drug overdose deaths involving opioids. In 2017, the CDC again reported that 25% of overdose deaths are from heroin, three times the proportion of 1999 (8%). Now, two decades in the epidemic, and more than 140 Americans die every day from opioid overdose, the U.S. Government declares opioid crisis a public health emergency. The dose does the damage, overdose does the death!

Is that man on the park bench, dozing or overdosing? Both. Widespread rise of painkiller abuse, overdose deaths, and child poisonings are on the rise in the United States. In 2015, the deaths from drug overdose had overtaken that of automobile crashes as the leading cause of accidental death since the CDC started tracking drug-related deaths in 1979. The overall increase in drug deaths is largely due to the surge in overdoses involving prescription painkillers. The total prescriptions dispensed in 2015 was about 4.4 billion, an average of 14 per American. About half of Americans take prescription medications. One study claims that same increase in prescription drug use by adults may also be fueling a related trend in children under five: from 2001 to 2008, accidental drug poisonings of young children increased to 22%.

Although drugs like heroin and oxycodone are often grouped under the umbrella term opiates, they are clinically semi-synthetic opioids made with chemicals, not from morphine, codeine, or opium, nor from the poppy plants. They are derived from another naturally occurring opiates which are deadly. Yet, the synthetic opioid is a hundred times more deadly than fentanyl, the prescription painkiller, which is fifty times more deadly than heroin. And now available in 2016, there is an even deadlier opioid called carfentanil, which is more potent than morphine. Carfentanil is a hugely powerful drug that is normally used to tranquilize large animals, like elephants. In the U.S., its use is so widespread and the overdoses are so rampant that the U.S. Drug Enforcement Administration had declared a public health emergency. Mostly illicit imports from China or available online, carfentanil is being sold and consumed to tranquilize humans, and this has deadly consequences. Instead of having four to five overdoses a day, people are having twenty, thirty, forty, and maybe even fifty overdoses a day. It's a very serious life-threatening situation. However, the good news is that the

Chinese government is taking enforcement on the issue in 2017.

Studies show that some dopamine-producing cells in the brain are activated by both painful and pleasurable stimulation, which explains why some people get pleasure in the painful situations of others (cruelty scenes) and sometimes of their own (intravenous drug users)—and for that matter, why, though gently, people enjoy eating chili or spicy food. Researchers theorize that dopamine is not so much of the pleasure itself, but the expectation of pleasure (gambling) or the prediction of pleasure (mother expecting child is returning home after a long timeout).

Anyone can be an addict at any time. Fundamentally, addiction is not a moral failing. It is not an ailment of weak-willed losers. Biologically, the only model of addiction that makes sense is a disease-based model. When you are ill, you take medical care; equally, when you are addicted, you need medical care. Say, for a food lover—just liking the food a lot doesn't make one a food addict. In contrast, people whose brains have trouble registering food satisfaction may lead to eating disorders, including the risk of weight gain and so on. Likewise, just liking the sex a lot doesn't make one a sex addict. For a sex addict, just like a heroin addict, one is only at a point where one is having sex not because he is seeking extra pleasure from it but because he needs to have it just to fall asleep at night, get by the day, or to ensure not having any withdrawal symptoms.

Yet the "disease model" (based on the evidence that the brain changes with drug use) is not acceptable to many other cognitive neuroscientists and developmental physiologists.

They argue that from the biological aspects of desire, addiction is not a disease; rather, addiction is a learned something. It stems from a motivated repetition of the same thought and behavior till they become habitual. Like any other developing habits, addiction is also a process stuck in a neurochemical feedback loop that is present in all human brains. Treatments based on "disease model as physical disease" often fail and are obstacles to cure. Given the realities of the brain plasticity, the treatment can be retooled to reverse the process (e.g., by replacing bad habits with good habits) to achieve lasting recovery. Out of the hell, get well!

Share the joy—double what you enjoy. Nothing perhaps can make us feel happy or as good within ourselves than when we share our joy with our family and friends, or when we perform an act of benevolence to another person or to a community. There is more to happiness in making others happy. Feeling good comes from the former and is unrelated to whether you yourself are comfortable enough from your circumstances. When you look back on your life, you will see that the events that stand out are the ones when you have done something good for others. Feeling good also comes from giving somebody a pat on the back in appreciation of some good work done by him or her. This presupposes the existence of a positive mind. How good it would have been if all on earth were capable of appreciating the work done creditably by somebody else. Often, we are blinded by jealousy. Often, we indulge in criticism, find faults, belittle the good, and overplay the mistakes.

It is possible to switch over from one such negative attitude to more of a positive attitude by our conscious effort—broadcasting "yes" to the world. Let us take a look at the life of Benjamin Franklin (1706–1790). He admitted that he had to work hard to overcome his tendency to find faults in others. For an experiment, he vowed to look for the good in others instead of judging and criticizing them, and he consciously desisted from saying unkind things about other people. The experience of the experiment had a profound effect on him, and he credited these efforts for much of the diplomatic skills he was not born with. He started using measured phrases, such as "It appears to me" or "If I am not mistaken." The moral of the story is this: don't just look for the bad in people—look for good in people. It's a habit. If you look for the ill, you surely will find some, but at the expense of your expensive time, energy, and your evil interest to find it and, above all, your unnecessary mental agony. Over time, you may be stigmatized in your society and may run the risk of losing your civil status. On the contrary, look for the good in them; you will be far better off and be at peace with your mental amity by relieving the nasty captive psyche. Not only that, you should practice, at the same time, to advise others to practice the same and explain the benefits of being a well-wisher. Showing a real appreciation is one superior quality of human bondage creating a strong relationship. Another hidden secret of appreciation in almost any relationship is knowing what not to ask and what not to say.

In general, successful people achieve emotional self-mastery. Feeling good is compatible with self-mastery—or at least, self-esteem; conversely, it is incompatible with a lack of self-esteem. Whatever the external factors in favor of creating a good feeling, a person without self-esteem will never attain good feelings. If a good feeling is like grass sprouting on the mind's soil, self-esteem is like water to the soil. Without water, grass never grows. A mind deprived of self-esteem is incapable of feeling good. Surveys show that both man and woman of the young generation value self-esteem more than sex and food. While man values self-esteem more than money, friends, and alcohol, woman values self-esteem more than only alcohol. Collectively, however, these findings ascertain that the view of self-esteem is an essential need. Self-esteem takes root in mind since childhood. Unless a child is successful in his own esteem, he will not adjust healthily growing up. It is an inner feeling in which a child feels confident of himself. Once it is formed, it grows like a snowball with accretions of more and more experiences reinforcing the proofs of their worth.

A moral is not an imaginary. A moral is a real. Moral, based on motives and reasons, is a maxim by which we act; it has a universal appeal. It is the basic principle of most religions. It is the bridge of experience between the human and spiritual world. Feeling good has a moral connotation. As sensible thinking people, we have our own notion of right and wrong, moral and immoral. Doing wrong or acting immorally—besides hurting the recipients of such wrongful or immoral actions—causes mental agony to our own selves. If we are sensitive enough, we can have an idea about morality just by the feelings it generates within us. Ernest Hemingway said, "About morals, I know only that what is moral is what you feel good after, and what is immoral is what you feel bad after."

Life is good. Here are a few simple rules of a good life:

- Make your heart free of hatred. "With malice toward none, with charity for all, with firmness in the right as God gives us to see the right . . ." (Abraham Lincoln)
- Relieve your mind from those tiger-facing worries. Worry has no better friend than fear. It thrives on fear. Fear kills us. When under constant fear, when our finger is on the trigger, we ought to feel distressed. Stop worrying and start living. Be happy. Lead a clean life. Try not to be unhappy. Commit to it. The attitude of unhappiness is not only painful but mean and perhaps ugly.
- Life is simple. Life is really simple, but we make it complicated. Everything should be as simple as possible. Live, love, and laugh!
- Avoid arguments. A gentleman never argues. Nip the argument in the bud. Avoid argument by all means as you would avoid rattlesnake; because, in most situations, it drifts to bogus arguments. Bogus arguments lead to more bogus arguments, and the cycle goes on, especially in politics and religion. Sometimes, it turns into a face fight. One not only calls other's view as crazy, stupid, and silly, but also calls that individual crazy, stupid, and silly. While most of the arguments happen within the circles where most people are intellectually equal to you, you hardly win, no matter what. And, even if you rightfully win with your valid and strong argument, it's hardly deemed as a win. So instead, try to persuade and reconcile with passion. Slow down the high wind category 5 to a debatable category 2 or discussion category 1. The most effective way to persuade others is to frame your points in line with the other's moral framework. Here

is why. Generally, our unconscious moral framework makes us argue (or agree). The arguments we normally make are the arguments that we normally use to convince the people who we assume to be like us, not our opponents who don't agree with us. So, if you want to win the opponent, stop for a moment and asses the person: what is the moral framework of the person whom you are arguing with? And then frame your points using ethical reasoning on that person's moral framework. Then you learn a great deal about the issues, about your opponents and about yourself.

- Don't complain. It's a bad habit. What you focus always expands. Therefore, your complaint about the problem will grow only bigger. So, jolly well, focus on your own plan, do not complain.
- Don't just look for the bad in people. It's a habit. If you look for the bad in people, you surely will find some, but it is at the cost of your precious time, energy, your enough effort to find it, and above all, your unnecessary mental agony and aggravation.
- Give more. Give more than you take. It is more blessed to give than to receive. As the wallet empties, the heart fills. In fact, try to give more than you can. Yes, you can afford it.
- Expect less. Present consumerist society has made us believe that happiness lies in having things. Having things, most of which are unnecessary, creates a surfeit of happiness that is actually a burden—like ingesting in excess what you can't digest.

Sometimes, it will not be easy for you to always live up to these simple rules of life, but you can try to be moral and natural. You can enjoy the trust of nature, the respect of good men, and the love of children. You don't have to swing your life between horrible and miserable. Human beings—no matter how they live and where they live—are preset to be happy. Life is good. It is only on our deathbed that we realize what a wonderful life we have had. Why can't we realize it a little earlier?

2.2 Life is Beautiful

> The best and most beautiful things in the world cannot be seen or even touched—they must be felt with the heart.
>
> —Helen Adams Keller (1880–1968)

> [Helen Keller was an American author, lecturer, and political activist. She was *not* born deaf and blind. As a baby of nineteen months, she contracted an illness that left her deaf and blind.]

Life is beautiful! Life is a sheer joy. A beautiful life is a heavenly gift to a blessed few to enjoy. Do not postpone the joy—enjoy! Enjoy life as if you were going to die tonight at midnight. Joy delayed is joy denied. Enjoy each moment of life, acknowledging that this moment will never return to you. Each moment is a little life. So, try to live all the moments of your life with all the joy you can enjoy. It's all yours! Greet the day every day. Studies show that if you give extra money to a poor starving person, he will not use it all for the food alone, but a part of it is for pleasure as well. Everybody wants to live a beautiful life now, not all to invest in the future.

We are sorry for the past and worry for the future. But true living never has to be all regrets of the past or all prospects of the future. We are simply what we are now—we live in the present, we recall the past, and we can only anticipate the future. Sociologists researching time perspective note that people who have a sentimentally good view of past events are happier and more satisfied with their lives. The distant past events may still have echoes today, but the future cannot bury the past. All of us should have this perspective: "If I have to live my life all over again, I would live it as I had lived. I neither repent the past nor fear the future." Yet the paradox of human nature is that most of us usually put off the good living in anticipation of the better living. Many of us are daydreaming of some magical rose garden over the horizon instead of appreciating the roses blooming in our garden now. We overlay the future with the past. We repeat history. But the truth of the matter is that if we are haunted by history, we will be history soon.

Years ago, one ad for Amtrak train ride from New York to Boston was something like this: "The best part of going to Boston is going to Boston." Exactly like that: The best part of living a life is the "living" part of life, which is happening now. The joy of living in the present is the essence of life. Living life is kind of a similar concept; do not rush. Life is less of a race and more of a journey. In the journey, happiness is a direction, not a destination. So, keep going.

Mother Nature all around us is a vivid expression of beauty. Yet we have no eyes to see it. Tragic indeed! The beauty of life is on the air, on the road, on both sides of stretched lands within our view. It is everywhere in every turn. They are the small things in life. Life is a symphony of small things. In view of extending healthy life and enjoying a good life overall, it's the small things—sunshine, flowers, smiling pedestrians—and just a few small changes that keep us young. In view of longevity on how well the body ages at the biological level, it's all small changes, like sleeping well, walking, eating well, occasionally fasting, and being mindful about positive feelings on aging and focusing on upbeat things. A positive mind-set can make us resilient in measurable ways, up to 86% more in better cardiovascular health. Positive cues come from many sources, like when we anticipate with pleasure, express happiness to ourselves and others, and reflect on happy memories. Life is a bundle of small joys. It is in the upbringing of a baby, in the way baby blinks at us, in his smiles, in his toddling way up to us. It is in the nice gestures of a friend, an act of help or kindness to a fellow traveler in the walk of life. It is in the blossoming of small flowers in the shrubs beside our walk, whose names we don't know. We don't have to wait all the time for the magical paradise that will take our breath away. Pockets of life, strewn everywhere!

Life is half spent before we envision what it is. Life is a vision for the wise, a play for the fool. It is a comedy for the rich, a tragedy for the poor. The perception that life is beautiful is not the same for everyone. Life is interesting if you're interested. Life is beautiful if you are attracted. Some will say life is so beautiful; others will say life is so awful. The rest, nearly most of us, will always be there in between "life is half full" and "life is half empty," one day thinking how beautiful life is and the next day thinking what a misery it is. The beauty of life will not reveal itself to a man who does not understand the opposites, the dualities, and the contradictions in nature and in life. In life, joy and sorrow are two sides of the same coin. They come in turns. Sadness succeeds gladness; high succeeds low. One cannot recognize a joy if one has never tasted sorrow. Uninterrupted happiness is an absurdity in life. A beautiful thing is hardly perfect—so is life!

We explore, experiment, and experience our lives continuously. The fact is that life is beautiful and dreadful, delicious and hideous, sweet and bitter. As we try it, so we experience it. We need not take life seriously all the time, because by taking life too seriously, we become unable to appreciate the beauty of life. Some may advise not to take life too seriously, for you may not be able to come out of it alive. Life is beautiful; life is dutiful. As we enjoy the beauty, so we perform our duty, and there is a balance. As a matter of fact, we lose the essence of life when we reason either too much or too little about our obligation, reality, loyalty, and duty. Contrary to these, there are our errors, exceptions, omissions, and ignorance. They all have been in our daily lives so long and so common that they are part and parcel of our lives; and without these, our lives would be unbearable. Nobody wants to fail. We try our level best to be better, if not perfect. We are mindful not to make any mistake and try to avoid failure. Still, mistakes happen. And when they do, we deal with them; and sometimes we face them head-on. So, do expect mistakes at any time, at any stage. To err is human. Overall, life is mystic and optimistic. Optimism is not only for the young who embrace positive delusions. Whether you are nineteen or ninety-one, male or female, of ethnic or non-ethnic origin, you are likely to have an optimism bias. It's quite natural. In fact, 80% of the population does. Synonymous to "American dream," many believe optimism is unique to Americans; but studies show that the rest of the world, east to west, is just as optimistic.

Humans are emotional creatures. They are biased in different situations. The bias that influences judgment from being balanced is a complex neural interplay between emotions and beliefs. It is a way we get things systematically wrong. Neuroscience and social physics suggest that we humans have typical mind-set that is more optimistic than realistic. We expect more the "better" than less the "worse." We anticipate that things turn out better than they typically wind up being. We, in general, overestimate our expectations: children gifted, happy family life, and higher life expectancy (a margin of twenty years or more); and we hugely underestimate our shortcomings, like losing a job or being diagnosed with cancer. Theoreticians call it an optimism bias—a bias that the future will be better than the past and the present. It is a bias that we all have. The farmer expects the best crops next year. Optimism bias is across the board: age, sex, race, religion, and socioeconomics. Schoolchildren are rampant optimists ("I will be president when I grow up"), and so are the grownups. Optimists are often punished at the end.

Optimism is radical. It is one hard choice, one brave, rebellious, daring and vital. It is the one that you need the most in the face of despair—just as a car most needed when you have a distance to cover, otherwise, it is just a piece of unmovable object laying in front of your house. In life, 99 percent of everything is crap, only 1 percent—which is your optimism—is worth the damn effort.

The fallacy of optimism is that collectively, we may grow pessimistic—grouse about high unemployment, about the downhill of our country's economy, or the incapability of our government to improve education and reduce crime. But privately, we are optimistic about our own personal future. We remain incredibly resilient: "I will have a job. My family will be safe." One survey in 2007 found that while 70% of families were collectively pessimistic (less successful than their parents' days), 76% of families were optimistic about better prospects for their own family.

Can optimism change realism? Can ability alter actuality? Yes, it can. An average human brain processes about 60,000 thoughts a day and 70% of them are perceived negative. Yet, similar to the conventional wisdom that success creates success, optimism creates optimism, cultivation of optimistic significantly increases the benefits of health, wealth and happiness—overall well-being and thrive. For instance, studies find that people with the highest levels of optimism—after adjusting for poor mental health conditions and for sociodemographic characteristics—have up to double the ideal cardiovascular health than that of their pessimistic counterparts. On the contrary, those with pessimistic expectations—such as those clinically depressed—negative expectation shapes the outcome in a negative way. In one study, to induce an "expectation of success" in one of two groups, the researcher primed college students with words like "smart," "intelligent," and "clever" just before getting ready to perform a common test. Each word has weight and energy of its own. To induce an "expectation of failure" in the other group, the researcher primed them with words like "dull," "stupid," and "ignorant" just before taking the same test. The result was this: the students who were primed with success messages performed better. Expectation gets you the expected result. It basically transforms the way you perceive the world without altering the reality itself. Positive expectation turns a virtual reality into a real reality, a skeptic into a believer. It addresses hello to the world. Say loud, be proud, "I got to be me!" Normally, and by nature, we do not anticipate failure (to be ill, lose a job, or file for divorce), but when these incidents do actually occur in real life, with the optimism buffer, we get over these with more resilience than is easily broken down. Study after study endorse the fact that optimists outlive pessimists. One study that tracked nearly 100,000 women for over eight years found that people who had a higher score on an optimism personality test developed 9% less heart disease and died 14% less compared to those who scored low. In another study published in *BMC Public Health* in 2016, Finnish researchers followed 2,267 men and women 52 to 76 years old for eleven years. While 122 people died from coronary heart disease, they found that a pessimistic attitude increases the risk of death from heart disease after controlling factors like smoking, obesity, and diabetes. Over time, an optimistic attitude helps one to bounce back quickly to the normal level of welfare, and it gets even better when people perceive difficult events more positively if they have had experienced them before in the past. That is why little failures early on prevent the glaring failures later on.

Yet surprising discoveries of eighty years' study of health and long life in *The Longevity Project* indicate that as for optimism bias, it has its downside as well. If you are too optimistic, especially in the face of illness (the classic case of Steve Jobs, who was overoptimistic about the nonconventional procedure of his pancreatic cancer treatment), or if you do not consider the possibility that you might have any disaster, then those setbacks will put you in situations that are even harder to deal with. The stress of failure—because you have never planned for it—is harmful. In fact, statistically, optimistic and cheerful children are less likely to live longer lives. The primary reason is that with optimism bias, they perceive all good things would happen to them and feel like nothing bad ever would; they predispose themselves to be heavier drinkers, smokers, and go with risky hobbies, extreme sports, and dangerous habits. Pessimism is a glass half empty; optimism is a glass half full. Optimum optimism is a glass just full, but the extreme optimism is a glass twice as big which hardly is. The moral is this. Do anticipate problems in life; deal with them as and when they arrive. And move on.

Studies show that people who can correctly predict the probability of coming events tend to be mildly depressed. The rest of us, not so wise, systematically fail to interpret the melodies. For quite some time, scientists were mystified by the existence of this unshakable optimism. It does not make sense. How can an individual remain optimistic in the face of harsh realities? Recently, with the progress of noninvasive brain imaging, neurologists have gathered evidence that suggests that our brains are hardwired to be optimistic, even unrealistically. Neurons efficiently encode "expectedly good information" but inefficiently encode "unexpectedly bad information." Therefore, optimism thrives. Thus, unfortunately, with all its apparent advantages, these optimistic illusions come at a price. Overly positive assumptions can lead to a disastrous miscalculation—loss in the stock market, fall sick. Assumptions do not tally up the total. Moral: with due underestimating of the potential risk, it helps us to practice safe sex, save for retirement, buy insurance, or undergo medical screenings.

Safety first, safety last! Any port in a storm! If you are not able to understand the true importance of safety, you end up making your life a life devoid of all concerns, being recklessly adventurous and happy-go-lucky. Obviously, that is not the purpose of life. That is not the ideal way of living. Yet at the same time, a life always on tenterhooks—perpetually worrying about the future, always expectant of bad news—is not the life either. It invalidates the zeal of life. Life has to be lived with a little sense of detachment, which will make our disappointments and disillusions a little more bearable to us. The extent to which we can bear the disappointments depends upon the values and the ideals we are attached to. No one can live through his life without falling into frustrations and sorrow; we have our own personal miseries to bear. But if we have before us some great idea, some purpose of life, some great cause to uphold, we can overcome those frustrations and disappointments more easily. A person who has a reason to live can bear almost anything.

For that, you need to summon yourself. You have to commit, for example, to spend some time—say half an hour every night—reading, thinking, reflecting, and praying about why you exist on this earth. It is time of your own. It is solitude (not loneliness). It looks modest but very challenging to maintain, because every time you spend time in doing that, you are not apparently productive. You are conflicted about whether you can really afford to take that time off, but you are stuck with it, as you have committed already. Ultimately, you figure out your purpose in life. Once your life is purpose driven, you can make decisions about allocating your time, energy, talent, and other resources. Highly influential people with big goals to achieve commonly allocate and reallocate these resources very effectively.

Another way to see that life is beautiful is to see it from an entirely different perspective: life is not a project to be completed but an engagement with a larger purpose, an approach for a "well-planned life." A teenager or a young adult cannot sit down and define the purpose of life because he is not yet knowledgeable enough to know himself or his purpose. He cannot see the future in retrospective of love, faith, wars, illness, and any chances that may loom. He may know concepts like marriage, parenthood, or old age, but he does not really understand their meanings until he is engaged in them. The adult person leading such a life—the *summoned life*—starts with a very concrete and result-oriented situation. I'm living this calendar year doing a specific job in a specific place, dealing with a specific problem. At this point in my life, I am engaged with that specific job with opportunities and options. The main questions are now what these summonses can do to me. What is needed? What is my role for social good? These types of questions are answered primarily by sensitive observation and situational awareness, not back calculation or manipulation. For a person leading such a summoned life, the individual is small and the context is large. He is part of the whole. He does his part only. Life reaches to a point not when that individual project is complete but when the self is dissolved into the larger context—for example, doing one's job dutifully or performing an active philanthropic engagement. A candle that lights others, consumes itself!

To be born again or born better is not an option. Also, there is no point in asking the question of whether life is worth living or not. This could have been a question of an embryo, but it is too late for us. Having already been born, we have to make the best of our lives, make this life truly worth living by our deeds. Sometimes, even though the small deeds we do, we can show our worth. By caring for life, by caring for the lives of others, by lending a helping hand to the needy, we can show our true measure. Life should be such as others would value. Life need not be long; but it should be elastic and generous enough, with kind feelings for fellow beings. What matters most is not adding years to life but adding life to the years. Add value to your life, and lead your own life. Majority of people do not lead their own lives; they are led by others—by the government, by the media, and by the employer. They barely survive. Really!

Quality of life is not to be measured by our material possessions, the money, the gold, the fame. It is not what we possess that constitutes the abundance or luxury; rather it is what we enjoy and what gives us happiness. You are your wealth! True wealth is your health, your peace of mind, your internal happiness. Feel free to be happy. Social scientists challenge one concept that we are unhappy if we don't get what we want. It is not true. They assert that our "psychological immune system" lets us feel *truly* happy even when we don't get what we want or things don't go as expected. Typically, *synthetic* happiness is less enjoyable than natural happiness. You can be happy for no reason. Ultimately, this well-being is your real prosperity. Open your heart to prosperity. It is not what we ingest but, rather, what we digest. It can be as simple, for example, as a simple train ride or a small talk. Crack a joke, stay fifteen minutes longer in bed, or get early to the airport and watch people moving. Our real wealth is the wealth of our minds.

Life is beautiful! Yet, much of the beauty is lost in our unfulfilled desire. In this short life, we want to achieve too many things. We want money, we want fame, we want power—quite often without thinking whether it is within our reach or not. Often, our ambition is out of bounds as to our available resource, ability, and capability. When we fail to achieve, we blame our fate, or we blame others for betraying us or not helping us enough. In this way, we come to grief and frustration. We complain about pain; criticize about mosquitoes, snow, and silly people; and we lapse into doubt and cynicism. We die every day for some reason or other. Quite the reverse, happy are those who come alive every day. One five-year study indicates that there seems to be a 35% decrease in the risk of dying among people who reported being happy every day. They are excited on a typical day and contend with whatever they have, compared to those who are sadder or more anxious. So, be alive and lead a balanced life. He lives long who lives well.

Live and let live! There is a group of people on earth whose desire is to love human beings and be loved by others. How more beautiful our life could have been if all people on earth fell into this category! As we move from a life of self-absorption to a life full of love and feeling for others, our own desire to prosper in a materialistic sense will diminish naturally. Among others, there are two typical ways one could be happy. One is by diminishing one's wants. The other is by augmenting one's means. Suppose all of us take the second course instead of trying to curtail our desires and restrain our wants, what a terrible world of cutthroat competition it would be in which all would try to augment their means and resources for attaining their goals by undermining one another. You get an inch by pushing another by an inch. Those who are perennially seeking power, wealth, and fame may have more creature comforts in life. They may live in luxury with scores of people at their command to serve them, but the beauty of life—which issues from proximity with nature, a sense of modesty, loving others, and living for others—will always elude them.

We have to go back to Mother Nature again and again to feel the beauty that is latent in life, to have a vision of the everlasting. Through her, we reach the beauty that is imminent in the eternal and infinite. It is she who stimulates a feeling of the abundance of life. Let us recall a poem by Lord Byron:

> 'Tis the perception of the beautiful,
> A fine extension of the faculties,
> Platonic, universal, wonderful,
> Drawn from the stars, and filtered through the skies,
> Without which life would be extremely dull.

So much beauty is there in man's creativity. It is creativity that is emulated from Mother Nature (for example, music). If we look deep into nature, we find the harmony of music. Our hearts sink in music. Music is beautiful in its pain and in its capacity to liberate us from all bondage. Music is in the land, in the water, in the air. It is in the morning, in the evening, in the wings of the linnet. "I could hear the voice of the water that taught me how to sing," said Pablo Neruda. The musician, the poet, the artist, the sculptor, and the very common man draw their lessons and inspirations from Mother Nature. Their creations do not always speak of an experience of happiness and pleasure but, rather, speak of the pain of life. As a life's worshipper, an artist's philosophy is complete.

We celebrate life in all its aspects, in the dualities and opposites. The purpose is not to capture happiness and mirth only—but to reflect equally in pain. It is to celebrate life and its beauty in its totality, not just one side of life. Variety is the spice of life. Variety is charming. Variety turns survival into living. It is not true that life's beauty has to be perceived only in its joy. "Our sweetest songs are those that tell of saddest thoughts," says Percy B. Shelley. Melancholy crosses genres, and sadness gives us an understanding of who we are. The pain of life is an antithesis of beauty. It does not reflect the malice of life. What constitute malice of life are our baser instincts, such as hatred, selfishness, cruelty, and dishonesty. The superior value of life underlies the grand perception of life as the most wondrous creation from Mother Nature. Give her a bright smile. Life is beautiful.

Beauty comes to life in silence and touches those who adore the grand design of Mother Nature. In nature, look around. All is beautiful. It is alive, tender, and delightful. We don't have to do anything more to make our lives beautiful. Life is beautiful already. We don't have to wait for the beauty to reveal itself to us. It is already revealed. Beauty is here, beauty is there, beauty is everywhere. What we need are fresh eyes to see it anew. Beauty is in the eye of the beholder. A little awareness and a little mindfulness! Our life is very short, like lilies of the field whose bloom is brief. Yes, our life too—brief but beautiful.

2.3 Live Young, Live Long

> The way you think, the way you behave, the way you eat, can influence your life by thirty to fifty years.
>
> —from Deepak Chopra's *Ageless Body, Timeless Mind: The Quantum Alternative to Growing Old*

> [Deepak Chopra (1946–) is an Indian medical doctor, writer, and a public speaker on subjects such as spirituality, Ayurveda, and mind-body medicine.]

Worldwide, between 2000 and 2050, the population of people aged 60 years and older is expected to increase from 605 million to 2 billion. A group of sixteen researchers across the world looked at the mortality trends from 2000 to 2010. They were encouraged by the fact that mortality is falling very rapidly by one-sixth for everyone below age 70. Americans are likely to live longer because the two leading causes of death—heart disease and cancer—have become less deadly. A child—boy or girl— born in America in 2014 is forecasted to live longest, with an average life expectancy of 78.8 years, 0.1 years longer than that in 2011. Gender wise, a girl can expect to live up to 81.2 years, a boy 76.4 years. Eight of the other ten leading causes of death have become less deadly in 2012 as well. In poor countries where premature death is prevalent due to weaker health systems and infectious diseases, the news was even better. Deaths fell by an even larger percentage, about 24% over the last ten years. Overall, early deaths may fall as much as 40% in the next twenty years globally. By 2030, one billion people will be over the age of 65. By 2050, more than 800,000 Americans will be over 100. In 2014, Americans who made it to 65 could expect another nineteen years of life, including nearly fourteen years of relatively good health, the CDC estimated. It is a century of success story pushing the limits of longevity from 59 years (in 1925) to 70 years (in 1955) to 75 years (in 1985) to 79 years (in 2015) and perhaps to 81 years in 2045. However, after a steady rise, the overall life expectancy 78.9 years for a baby born in 2015, fell to 78.8 years in 2016, and 78.6 years in 2017, on average. For American men, it fell two-tenths of a year, from 76.5 to 76.3; and for women, one-tenth, from 81.3 to 81.2 years; and the overall death rate increased from 724.6 (2016) to 733.1 (2017) to 731.9 (2018) per 100,000. In 2017, the key contributing factors were drugs, alcohol, and suicides, especially among middle-aged white Americans living in rural areas.

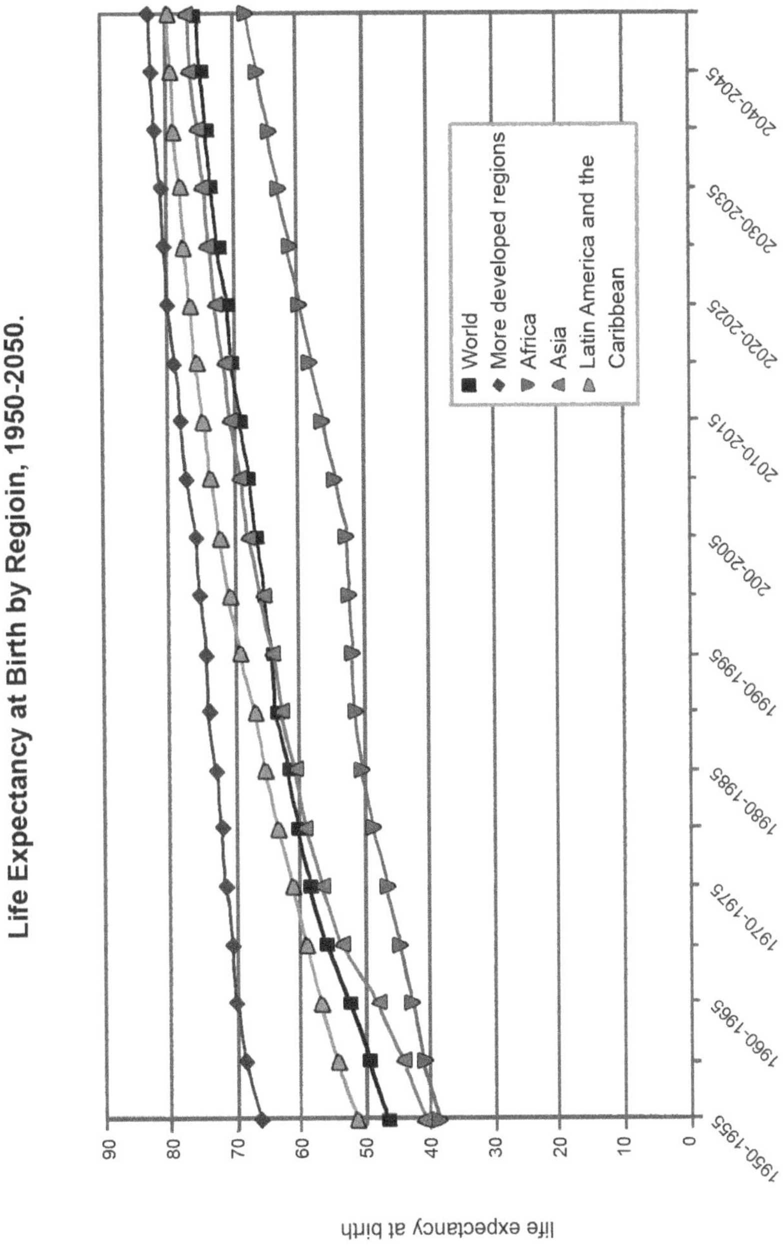

Life Expectancy at Birth by Region

A snapshot of the world population as of December 31, 2019:

7,650,000,000	Current world population
328,000,000	Current U.S. population
254,000	Births per day
107,000	Deaths per day
147,000	Net population growth per day
105,000,000	Births per year
44,000,000	Deaths per year
61,000,000	Net population growth per year

Well-come to long life! Wellness is at the core of long life. While doctors consider most diseases as curable, genetics consider life extension as solvable. For long life, about 10% to 30% comes from your genes, and the rest is from your lifestyle. In terms of longevity, especially in the United States, the diseases that are most likely to kill people, are neurological disease, heart disease and cancer. In other countries, however, there are other potential diseases in addition like, tuberculosis, malaria and many more infectious diseases. One extraordinarily comprehensive worldwide study clearly demonstrates it, how people live their lives: whether they smoke, what and how they eat, and whether they abuse drugs and alcohol. Life spans in countries worldwide, about three-fourths of life expectancy are attributed to these risk factors. Life expectancy is influenced much more due to the sociocultural environment, especially what people eat, than to their genes or the physical environment. Therefore, your genes are not your destiny. Studies clinically demonstrate that when you live healthy, eat better, do exercise, and sleep well, your body function well and your brain cells actually grow or stay the same, and your cardiovascular illnesses and some cancers get treated, reversed and even cured. The simple idea here is that instead of scaring people with "fear of dying," inspire them with "joy of living." Convince them that good life is possible and within reach, and importantly that they can feel better, and live younger. When you live younger, you live longer!

The age of aging is aging! Want to live an age of hundred years? Learn from the centenarians who forget to die. They are old but far from frail, ailing, bedridden, or sick—one might think. On the contrary, the majority of them are relatively able, mentally stable, and available on active duty. While typical elderly people fall victim to chronic diseases, such as heart disease, stroke, cancer, and dementia, and end up at nursing facilities in their mid to late life, these centenarians, on the contrary, appear to be remarkably resilient. The centenarians who live with vim and vigor say the key is a simple lifestyle and few common diets. They avoid the chronic diseases of aging, and if they get sick, they normally bounce back from typical health problems and remain relatively well until their final days. Only 40% experienced one of these illnesses (heart disease, stroke, cancer, and dementia) in their lifetime, but they seem to have pushed it aside without long-term complications. In 2013, a team of researchers from Harvard University had high hopes that Americans had every reason to be optimistic about longevity. They do live longer and healthier. The only period during which they are in ill health is effectively being shortened and pushed until just before the end of life. Americans used to be very, very sick during the final six to seven years of their lives, which is now far less common. They are living young—adding healthy years, not debilitated years—and are enjoying youth till their old age. They live to the last. To name a few places where people live the longest and healthiest lives: Sardinia, Italy; Okinawa, Japan; Nicoya, Costa Rica; Loma Linda, California; and Ikaria, Greece. These places are called as 'Blue Zones'—the name comes from the color blue which happened to be used by the researchers to draw circles on the map to identify some of the oldest and healthiest people in the world.

While global life expectancy averaged out to over 70 years, nearly 75% Americans died in 2013 were over 65. In 2016, the life expectancy of a 65-year-old American was 84; the top cause of death over 65 was heart disease (26%), followed by cancer (21%). More than ever, more Americans, especially women, are celebrating the big 100. According to a 2016 report released by the National Center for Health Statistics in the United States, there were 15,000 centenarians in 1980; 50,281 in 2000; and 72,197 in 2014—women accounted for about 80%. One survey of 2,330 adult Americans reveals that three-fourths of Americans want to live to 100, and more than one-third believe they will live past 90. But the tragedy hits from the financial situation: out of people under age 65 who want to retire by 65, about 40% say they will not have the finances to live to 100. It shows how ill prepared they are for the eventuality.

Obviously, living clean is the key to living long. People who have prioritized healthy habits are more likely to outlive those who haven't. By tracking personal lifestyle and health data of 16,958 Americans aged 17 and up from 1988 to 2006, the National Health and Nutrition Examination Survey III Mortality Study identifies four crucial habits associated with longer life: (1) quit smoking, (2) drink alcohol in moderation, (3) exercise regularly, and (4) eat healthy. Otherwise, the cumulative impacts—bad habits accumulate and contribute collectively—can prematurely age a person by as much as twelve years. Here are some other key factors on how to live young and live long:

- *Genetics:* The Long Life Family Study (LLFS), sponsored by the National Institute on Aging and other groups, investigated genetic issues to figure out which genetic, environmental, and behavioral factors control longevity. Because it happens in certain families, it does mean genetic. Geneticists and biologists have been pursuing the secret to longevity inside out, at a cellular level and at a molecular level, first in animals and, more recently, in humans. They aim to recognize genes associated with slowing normal aging and avoiding chronic illnesses, which ultimately push the limits of life span. Some claim that they found it. They used genetic screening to identify 150 gene variants that may be the precursor to whether people will live to be centenarians. With 77% accuracy, they have found the potentiality of genetics for longevity and clues to the secrets of long life. The findings are widely reported. Yet contemporaries in the field of genetics are skeptical about the study, saying that the small size of the sample and varying technologies used to analyze the DNA would have undercut the outcomes. Whatever. Optimistically, the research in the field may, however, one day lead to drugs that would aid people to live to be centenarians.

One surprising study—interesting to note—surveyed 477 Ashkenazi Jews between the ages of 95 and 109 and found that people who made it to almost centenary (average age of 97) were, just like their shorter-lived peers, engaged in normal kinds of lifestyle habits that researchers deemed unhealthy, like the usual daily stress, lack of exercise, drinking, smoking, and eating junk food. (Junk food—colloquially called so—is typically a fast food along with soda and sweets.) The study concluded that exceptional longevity might have been encoded into their DNA—the software of life—that protected them from some of the adverse effects of unhealthy living and that their gene variants could have undermined and negated the ill effects of some of the bad habits. One study published in the journal *Cell* in 2016 argues that there is hardly any correlation between the genes that had already been identified as contributors for longevity to that of people who live long but are also relatively free of disease. They identified a set of ApoE gene that is linked to a higher risk of Alzheimer's disease and early death. From another study reported in 2016 in the journal *Current Biology*, scientists say that a person's youthful or aged appearance can partly be traced to different versions of one specific gene—called MC1R—which is responsible for inflammation and repairing the damaged DNA. People having some forms of the MC1R gene look about two years older for their age and are vulnerable to the higher risk of certain diseases associated with living longer, like heart problems, cancer, and cognitive decline. While genetic variations contribute to longevity (up to 30%), heredity is of particular importance.

To live long, experts recommend adults need to cut down on protein overall. One aging disadvantage comes from growth hormone IGF-1 (insulin-like growth factor 1). Having sufficient IGF-1 is essential for early development, but too much from high-protein foods later in life accelerates aging. IGF-1-deficient people are typically short in stature, but they rarely get age-related diseases like cancer or type 2 diabetes. Limiting animal protein is one primary way to lower IGF-1.

Siblings typically look alike. Many parental characteristics are inherited: color, height, weight, stroke, diabetes, and tendency to develop heart disease. Sometimes even personality. Life span, logically, seems to fit with the rest. Doctors and scientists have been studying for decades to find out if there is really any genetic link to life span—and if so, to what extent. Researchers analyzed data of twins of the same sex. The number of living twins worldwide is estimated to be approximately 125 million in 2006 (roughly 1.9% of the world population). Out of that, only 10 million are identical twins (roughly 8% of all twins), and the majority 92% is "fraternal" or "non-identical." Studying these twins revealed that life span is nothing like common traits (like height, facial features, or size), which are strongly inherited. Individual life span (only 3% of cases) is inherited from parents. Identical twins die at different times—on average more than ten years apart. The variance factors include genetic predispositions, nutrition, disease, subtle injuries, accidents, and for women, their health during pregnancy. Genetically identical beings—from worms to flies to humans—living in the same environment die at random times. The reason is not yet known. While on the subject, it is interesting to note here that one study noticed mothers of (naturally) twins—excluding in vitro fertilization—are more likely to live longer, have more children over their lifetime, and have offspring closer together, compared to that of women who had singletons.

- *Environment and Behavior:* The lifestyle environmental and behavioral components contribute to as much as 70% of good life. Good habits—such as healthy food, a good night's sleep, steady physical and mental exercise, easygoing attitude, not smoking, and staying lean—can keep the elderly vibrant through their golden years. Such factors can be brought under control even before it starts through fitness and strength. Seniors 65 to 75 who regularly exercise with resistance weights can improve the cognitive ability of memory and decision-making. However, they may not stay chronologically young but can stay, at least, in good health. Reduced calorie intake is another key factor. Experimenting on east and animals, researchers' initial findings direct to caloric restriction. Their hypothesis is that reduced calorie intake extends life span significantly.

- *Outlook Psychology:* Cutting-edge research on the aging process shows that your outlook can change how you age at the cellular level (at telomeres). Your mind can restore the body, rejuvenate the physique and make it measurably younger, or at the very least, slow down the aging process. Here's how:
    - Age slow. Maintain a low stress level. Exercise, take walks, and live naturally.
    - Control the levers of aging. In the course of a lifetime, the telomeres burn like a candlewick. Cardiovascular disease, immune system problems, and diabetes expose the chromosomes vulnerable to damage and accelerate the aging process. Prevent the disease.
    - Meditation slows the aging process.
    - Try solitary contemplation at a quiet place and enjoy a good time.

  An optimistic outlook overall is good for health, according to one study by the *American Journal of Epidemiology*. They established significant associations between increasing levels of optimism and decreasing risks of death, particularly from cardiovascular diseases, like heart disease, stroke, and respiratory problems.

- *Feel Young:* Feel young, live young! The secret to feel young and live young, and thereof, live long is: to feel in control. Studies reveal that overall, when people, especially elderly adults, feel more in control, they feel better in a youthful state of mind. Feeling free and independence is the key. Psychologists present their case with evidence in the American Psychological Association (APA) annual convention in 2018, highlighting the facts that:

- The power of feeling in-control gives people a sense of agency that boosts their mental health and drive down their subjective age (lower than their chronological age), which in turn motivate them further with a feeling—that their action matters—so they make even better effort in healthy choices of lifestyle, make better diet choices and do exercises, and thrive;
- Feeling younger than chronological age is linked to a lower risk of dementia and better health of mind and cognizance, suggesting that a sense of subjective age matters, and it is just as important;
- Surveying 116 older adults, ages 60 to 90, and 106 younger adults, ages 18 to 36, for nine days, researchers find interesting insight that the day they feel in control or in controlled perception—which may be as simple as to go for a walk or read a book or invite a friend—they feel empowered which drives them to accomplish more other things;
- Similar to feel in control, they include other supportive activities like exercise (typically walking) and socialization.

- *Brain Aging:* Aging is inevitable, but aging well is not. Keeping the brain healthy is an essential part of good health. Normally, memory declines with age, causing a diminished ability to think and reason. For centenarians, the balance between wear and tear and subsequent repair may be the key to their healthy brain aging. By analyzing genomes of centenarians, researchers plan to isolate a few genes—and the biological processes attached to them—which will help to protect from the damage by balancing between wear and tear and subsequent repair. Those might then be harnessed to give non-centenarians the same edge, at least in theory. The hypothesis explains a growing body of evidence: *use it or lose it.* It pretty much suggests that older people can improve their odds of remaining mentally alert by keeping their minds engaged.

One survey in the United States, England, and eleven other European countries finds a straight-line relationship in retiring people. In the U.S., the U.K., and Denmark, people retire late—65% to 70% of men still work when they are in their early sixties. In Spain, the figure is 38%; and in Italy and France, it is 10% to 20%. Sometimes, however, as their memories and thinking skills are declining, they are more likely to retire than people whose cognitive skills still remain able. Of course, not all jobs are mentally demanding. In blue-collar jobs, health does not permit this. Staying in the job for a few more years, learning a new language, picking up a hobby, and maintaining a rich network of social connections are all to keep the brain's neurons active. Personal and social skills—getting up and dressing up in the morning, going to the workplace, and dealing with people, knowing the value of being helpful and trustworthy—go hand in hand with daily activity. If work helps to maintain cognitive functioning, it is interesting to find out what aspect of work is doing that. Is it the social engagement and interaction or the cognitive component of work? Or is it the aerobic component of work? Inversely, is it the missing part when they retire that could increase loneliness? The whole idea here is to come up with a lifestyle reconfiguration that will give elderly people a way of life that they will enjoy.

- *Gender:* On average, women live longer than men by five years, across the board. The reasons are as follows:
    - Female fetuses are tougher in utero. Compared to the number of female fetuses, as many as two and a half times male fetuses are conceived but female fetuses are so tough infection to prenatal infection or other issues in the womb that by the time they are born, the ratio is almost 1:1.
    - Women are less likely to be risk-takers. Unintentional injuries: one-third for men, one-sixth for women.
    - Women, in general, tend to have heart disease ten years later in life than men. Even though heart diseases are the leading cause of death for both men and women, men start to develop it earlier and die from it as early as in their thirties and forties. The reason for that is women are protected until menopause, since their bodies still produce estrogen, which helps to keep arteries strong and flexible.
    - Women maintain stronger social networks. The presence of friends and the absence of loneliness are good medicine for longevity. People with

stronger social connections have up to 50% lower chance of dying than those with few social ties.

  - Women take better care of their health, in general. Men, who often repudiate illness, are 24% less likely than women to have visited a doctor within the past year.
  - The woman's immune system is a lot stronger than man's, in part because, throughout the course of evolution, human bodies have prioritized procreation (to produce offspring) over immunity; and as a result, women are less susceptible to illness and suffer less severely than men.
  - While age reduces brain metabolism rate, in general, women still retain a higher brain metabolism rate throughout their lifespan, and they have a younger brain age—about four years younger, on average—relative to males.

The findings are based on statistical models of characteristics distinguishing men from women. Interestingly, it suggests one phenomenon colloquially referred to as "man flu"—meaning that man turns a sniffle into flu and a headache into a migraine. Men are more prone to infection and less able to get rid of it. Men are the weaker sex, really.

- *Food:* The quality and quantity of food matters. First, the quality. Go high quality. Try almost plant- and fish-based. Take low fat, less sugar and more fruits and vegetables. Quality of food is so important that we devoted one entire part "Enjoy Good Food" with its three chapters. Second, the quantity. Go less quantity. Cut back the quantity, overall. Remember, after the invention of agriculture and potteries around 7000 BC, human started eating double as much. Practice intermittent fasting. If you are over 60, it's for you. Here's why? Every cell—of human, animal, plant, or yeast—has one nucleolus (plural nucleoli). Seen through the colored transmission electron micrograph, the nucleolus is fairly large dark blob at the center, and the most prominent substructure of the cell. Structurally, if you imagine an eyeball as a cell, then pupil is the nucleolus; and functionally, if you imagine the whole human body as a cell, then the brain is the nucleolus. The nucleolus is the cell's ribosome factory. A ribosome is a sphere-shaped structure consisting of RNA, produced in number and contained within the nucleolus. Ribosomes act like micro-machines that make proteins which are used for multipurpose activities ranging from hair forming to memory forming— and thus, keeping the cell running and functioning. These ribosomes micro-machines collectively use about 80% of a cell's energy for their work. Metaphorically, nucleolus is like a construction engineer with blueprint (DNA) in hand and a fleet of micro-machines at his disposal. He has all the resources. He coordinates all activities, does quality control and makes sure things going well—so well to influence cell's health and life span. If eaten more, available nutrients and growth signals are more, and the nucleolus makes more micro-machines or ribosomes. Physically, it gets bigger to contain them, but for the higher growth and for some mysterious reasons, this process unfortunately shortens the cell's life, and thus organism's life. If eaten less, available nutrients and growth signals are less and the nucleolus can wane. So, when the food is restricted, and thus when the metabolic pathway is slowed down, nucleolus shrinks, making fewer ribosomes, and the cell lives longer. Researchers have experimentally seen that for genetically identical twins, because of their eating habits, some live a short life and some live a long life. They are now sanguine that smaller nucleolus is the cellular hallmark of longevity. They are also optimistic that a modest dietary restriction along with exercise, can help people even over age 60.

- *Income:* Money can buy you something that is more precious than even money: the time of your life, your life span. Globally, life expectancy grows and shrinks according to income trends. In one comprehensive study of life expectancy and income—income based on income tax returns by Americans from 1999 to 2014—the economists at Stanford University reveal that the greater the income, the longer people live. However, the relationship levels off after a certain threshold of income. Overall, people who belong to the top 1% income tier live nearly fifteen years longer than those who belong to the bottom 1%.

- *Exercise:* The guidelines of the World Health Organization (WHO) on physical activity for an adult is very attainable: 75 minutes of vigorous exercise or 150 minutes of moderate exercise per week. In order to optimize the sweet spot for recommended exercise time per week, one study was carried out by

National Cancer Institute who compiled data from six large, ongoing health surveys, covering more than 661,000 adults, most of whom were middle-aged, and that covered people who exercised nothing at all to people who exercised 10 times as much the current recommendation. After comparing 14 years' worth of death records, results published in *Journal of the American Medical Association (JAMA) Internal Medicine* in 2018, researchers establish that: (a) people who did not exercise at all are at the highest risk of early death; (b) people who met the recommended level of exercise (150 minutes per week) had longer longevity and are 31 percent less likely to die prematurely compared to those who never exercised; and (c) people who tripled the recommended level of exercise (450 minutes per week or a little more than *an hour per day*) hit the sweet spot for exercise benefits that had even longer longevity and 39 percent less likely to die prematurely compared to those who never exercised. According to one research covering 1,228 men and women of diverse racial and ethnic backgrounds, being active slows brain aging up to ten years. The study was published in 2016 in the journal *Neurology*. Exercise and being more active is one effective way to protect memory and evade cognitive problems. To stay young, you have to keep the cells young. The research finds that just moderate-intensity physical activity helps to keep the cells young. By analyzing the muscle biopsies from cyclists' legs before and after the cycling session, researchers measured the blood levels of muscle function with lactate, which the muscle cells produce when exercised, and noticed the

> production of a compound called nuclear respiratory factor 1 (NRF1), that controls the shortening of the telomeres. Exercise boosts the levels of NRF1, which in turn protects the telomeres from being shortened. Each session of moderate exercise is a layer of protection to the telomeres being refreshed, thus helping the DNA and, in turn, the cells to remain younger.

Man is mortal. Mortality rate is 100%. Everyone dies. But the idea here is to stay young and live long. You cannot stay young forever, nor can postpone death! Yet you can very well live long enough and be able to blow out the candles on your hundredth birthday cake. Today, women in general have 1% chance of reaching age 100 while men only have 0.1%. [Info: In a multiyear study of postmenopausal women in the U.S. by the Women's Health Initiative (WHI)—which covered nearly 28,000 women—half survived to reach age 90. Researchers reveal that delaying childbirth is associated with longer life. Compared to women below 25 when they gave birth first, women above 25 were 11% more likely to live to 90; and women who had two to four children are more likely to live longer than those who had one.]

In the U.S., there is a 2% chance that the anticipated life span of people born in 1910 could reach 100. However, in general, the anticipated life span of the average American rose year after year, almost without exception, to 78.1 years in 2006 from 61 years in 1933. Compared to earlier centuries, the trend of longer life, less disease, and more fitness has been registered in the last century. But the point is that it's not just how long one lives but how well one lives. New studies show that the rising tide of life expectancy is not at all at par with

American health as a nation: there exists a widening gap in life expectancy based on the interwoven socioeconomic status. Longevity, in general, is not evenly distributed across the population. In every country, there are average life spans for different subsets based on wealth, education, race, geography, culture, and even faith. To see life through these lenses, studies show a variety of hypotheses as to what it takes to live a long life:

- *Wealth:* The rich inherit the property; the poor inherit the poverty. The rich die old; the poor die young. The rich have the pass; the poor have the sanction. The rich start ahead, stay ahead; the poor start behind, stay behind. The gap of life expectancy between rich and poor has always been growing, and now it is growing even faster. The same is also true between the highest and lowest educated people; it is, however, narrowing between men and women, and between blacks and whites. In the U.S., out of several reasons why poverty and chronic diseases like obesity go together, there are two common reasons: (a) in many poverty-dense regions, people do not have access to affordable healthy food, even when they can afford it, and (b) the lower-income group tends to have a more sedentary living environment compared to that of the higher-income group.

  Wealth is health. Wealth buys health, and it seems plausible. It is truer in the recent and coming years. You need a head start financially (born better). Whether measured at birth or at age 65, today, the socioeconomic status has become a more important indicator of life expectancy than ever. After decades of sluggish growth, the middle class in the U.S. appears to trail, not to mention the poor. According to a study published in 2016 in *The Journal of the American Medical Association*, the gap in life spans between the rich and the poor widened from 2001 to 2014. For the top 1% in income, men live fifteen years longer than the poorest 1%—women, ten years. The rich Americans have gained three years of longevity just in this century. They live long almost without any regard to where they live in the U.S., while the poor have big differences where they live. In the last three decades, there has been slow income growth at the bottom and rapid income growth at the top—giving rich people a better chance to live longer. The wealth disparity effectively infiltrated all parts of people's lives, including health. The creation of vast fortunes at the top hollowed out the middle class in Western industrialized countries. In the United States, the share of adults in the middle class has been shrinking: from 61% in 1971 to 50% in 2015. Americans radically underestimate the level of wealth inequality.

What the customer wants or what the market decides is not always right. The market is not the determinant of human destiny. Because you have the money, you have the right to consume anything you want! The consumer is not always right. Too much consumerism is not ethical. Many things—though legal—are not just. Here comes the role of morals, religion, and God. The rich need to change their lifestyle. In the throwaway culture of a rich country, even human lives are disposable. With the power of money, people dispose people, people trade people like slaves. Good governance needs a plan in what should be the role of money and market in society for the common good. The more things the rich buy, the more influence they exert, and vice versa. If their money stays local (say, to vacation homes, expensive cars, or private jets), then the inequality wouldn't matter much. But if the money goes increasingly inclusive—governing essentials of public life, human rights, health care, education, and other social benefits—the inequality hurts. The corrosive influence of money and politics affects society. For example, it may increasingly get difficult to apply for bank loans; cell phone, cable, or internet service; credit cards; or even shop online without agreeing to private arbitration. The corporations have systematically insulated themselves from lawsuits, leaving law-abiding citizens in a system where arbitrators overwhelmingly favor business. In a democratic process, government oversight should be a protector, not a predator. Businesses typically opt out the legal system (i.e., bar people from joining together in class-action lawsuits) and misbehave without reproach. Good citizens are systematically deprived of one of their most fundamental constitutional rights: their day in court.

In fact, the rich 1% controls the other 99%, practically in every aspect of a citizen's life and lifestyle. In a 2014 estimate, the richest eighty-five individuals own half of the wealth of the world. In the U.S., the richest 1% owns more than the bottom 90%; and the richest 20% own 84% of all wealth. In 2018, the top

10% Americans held 80% of the stocks. The rise of inequality has dented not only the American dream but the growth of the economy. Now, lifting GDP growth is terribly difficult. The economists modeled two alternate scenarios—one with less inequality, another with faster GDP growth. They found inequality mattered more. Since 1980, the real economy has doubled in size; the government uses a substantial share of that bounty to share as much as $5 trillion to help working families, disabled, older people, and unemployed people pay for home, medicals, and their children's education. Yet for half of all Americans, their share of the GDP growth has shrunk significantly, leaving 117 million adults stuck on the lower half of the income ladder. In the bottom 50% of working-age adults, there has been close to zero growth. By 2014, while the average income of half of the American adults barely budged—lingering around $16,000 per year—the top 1% spiked to an astronomical $1,304,800 per year, or eighty-one times as much. Inequality in the U.S. is destabilizing. The wholesale marketization of everything—from health to education systems, from art to inventions, from playing fields to killing fields—sharpens the sting of inequality and its social and civic obligations. It is all about money. A small group of people concentrates power with almost complete control over other people's money, other people's labor, other people's health, and other people's lives. That is a very serious concern, and we have to diminish, if not eliminate, the corrosive influence of money and politics in our system.

Some inequality is vital to generate incentives, of course. How much inequality is too much or too little? Is there any "right" amount of inequality? The government needs to administer the unemployment, the stagnation of wages, and trade and commerce. Each age has its own inequality. History repeats and capitalism routinely generates arbitrary, unreasonable, and unsustainable inequalities that ultimately undermine the meritocratic values on which our democratic society is based. Feeling of fidelity undercuts the feeling of industry. History rhymes everywhere. Today, the state has now reached a point where inequality actually hurts economic growth. The rich don't earn money, actually; they make money. They make money at the pace of, as some economists in 2014 estimate, at the rate of three times the rate of the general economy. They (the 1%) make money with creative accounting through financial instruments, including tax evasion and inversion that are legal, but only at the cost of 99% of the general population. Their ingenious legal and financial engineering, undercut our democracy and turn our economy from long-term sustainable growth to a casino for a few instant winners. These winners are smart enough to consolidate their winnings and get themselves powerful and protected enough to quell with their own government. They are opportunists, obstructionist and enemy of the state. They snatch money by throwing dust in your eyes. One percent's windfall is 99 percent's downfall. Deceptively legal money gives rise to billionaires. One survey of wealth managers who manage billionaires' money, reveals powerful (yet pathetic) lives of their clients: richest people all over the world are so different from the rest of us that it is almost unimaginable. They miss life. For them, rules, regulations, laws, national borders are nothing—they might as well not exist. They seriously believe tax evasions, financial scams and other illegitimates are their earned legitimate right. Driven by the anticorruption drive and "tax terrorism" in many countries, they siphon out of their wealth to a safer place and never even blink to migrate to other countries. According to New World Wealth, out of global population of 15 million people having more than $1 million in net assets, nearly 100,000 changed their country of residence last year. While countries like India, Russia, Turkey and Venezuela lose their talents and wealth, countries like the United States, Canada, Australia and the United Arab Emirates gain them. The Panama Paper revelations in 2016 is one prime example of extreme ownership of illegal wealth. They get away with the destructive creation of such counterproductive financial tricks. They jump off the sinking ship first. They are the passengers who hurdled out of the sinking *Titanic* into the "money boats" (a few lifeboats taken over by a handful of millionaires) and left everyone else behind. They own corporations that evict tax using loopholes. Sometimes, the loophole is so big a hole that the whole corporation slips through. Interviewing the multimillionaires and billionaires who gained their fortunes not from inheritance but from actual effort reveals that they are proud of their success and try to equate their personal business success with public virtue and, to an extent, their moral and civic virtue with the size of their bank account. With the arrogance of wealth, the world's elite super rich live large and are less sympathetic and less close to the rest of the 99%.

Social studies on behavioral economics—how wealth (or the lack of wealth) can affect behavior—find that increased wealth and status lead to an increased self-focus and, consequently, decreased compassion, altruism, and ethical behavior. Those at the very top (0.1%)—the plutocrats—sway the political spectrum of mobile society like America. Economists caution that worsening inequality further is an inevitable outcome of free-market capitalism. Capitalism's inherent dynamic force of monopolization threatens the very fabric of democratization of societies. Uneven returns still continue from the economic recovery of 2010–11 with higher gain at the top and bigger pain at the bottom. The rich have so much money that they assume themselves richer than God—creating a gap between them and everyone else. A huge gap. It cuts a sorry figure indeed!

Wealth inequality is factual and very real, but where's the outrage? In the U.S., wealth inequality is too big to ignore. The adjusted median family income was lower in 2012 than in 1998. The disturbing fact of the matter is that the bottom 20% of the population is not getting better, but rather, it is getting worse. Overall, while the average growth from1993 to 2008 in real household income was 1.3% per year, the bottom 99% had only 0.75%, leaving a gap of 0.55%. As much as a quarter to a third of children is living with single or no parents in chaotic neighborhoods with failing schools. According to UNICEF, in the developed world (including the U.S.), there are 77 million children living in poverty. In the U.S., the Census Bureau's 2014 annual report on household incomes and poverty indicates 1 in every 8 adults (and about 2 in 5 children), spent at least one year in poverty; and 3 in 4 black children were in poverty at some time before the age of 18. In two independent studies, researchers found that acute poverty in early childhood is linked to smaller brain size and less efficient processing of certain sensory information. Poverty contributes to compromised cognitive function and low performance in schools, and researchers using fMRI demonstrated a measurable change in the brain. For adults too, financial woes change the brain—just thinking about shaky finances can drop one's IQ by an equivalent of 13 points. Poverty, in and of itself, is a vicious cycle—as, in one instance, lower-income people tend to make seemingly irrational and poor decisions when it comes to money.

A gigantic slice of human resource is vastly underused, and it has been that way for generations. It drives down the health in all sectors of the whole country. The study shows that the poor lifestyle is causing high mortality—unhealthy diet, smoking, poor management of chronic illness, drug and alcohol abuse, and other psychosocial problems are more common in low-income people. At the global economic level, especially with shifting political winds, the changes that are underway do not show a better picture either.

Being born with a silver spoon in the mouth, it works—being born with a plastic spoon, it breaks. Old-school philosophies like "succeeding by working hard" and "playing by the rules" are disappearing. The only good news is that one can still elbow out the crowd through education or competence at the workplace or by some other means. In America, those leverages are available; but in most countries, they are barely visible or nonexistent. Per WHO, an average female can expect to live twenty-four more years in a high-income country than in a low-income country. The poor die young.

- *Education:* Education is the proxy for wealth that leads to health. It could be that richer parents can provide their children better nutrition, better medical, care and better education. And in turn, the children, by virtue of being wealthy, usually live healthier and longer lives. Education, in and of itself, is reliably linked to longer lives geographically and demographically where it has been studied. It is almost to say that education is more important than income and wealth. Some sociologists are so convinced to acknowledge the primacy of education that they want to put it at the top of the list. They believe that a big difference can be gained by keeping young people in school. The more years in school, the more years of good life and life expectancy. The education effect never wanes! Research data comes to light in such a way as to make us believe that years in school are directly proportional to extra years of life with improved health decades later, in adult life and in old age. A nation in the long run can be better off by investing in education than by investing, say, in social welfare. The study highlights that women who are better educated and wealthier are less likely to be obese than their lesser counterparts. The similar effect, however, is not noticed in men. Data from sixty key data sources in the federal government and in the private sector show that if the head of the household has a bachelor's degree or higher education, then there are only 11% of boys and 7% of girls who are obese compared to 24% and 22%, respectively, if the head of the household has lesser than a high school education. Women over 25 with less than a bachelor's degree tend to be more obese (43%) than women with a bachelor's degree or higher (25%).

- *Conscientiousness:* Synonyms as meticulousness, carefulness, and neatness are the quality of a prudent, persistent, and well-organized person who is somewhat obsessive but not at all carefree. Surprising discoveries of eighty years of studies of health and long life in *The Longevity Project* indicate that the childhood personality of conscientiousness is the predictor of longevity. What keeps a kid in school is often conscientiousness! Another study claims that it is the smart kids and conscientious types who live longer. Not only that, they suffer fewer diseases before they die. The study compiles data from millions of people studied in dozens of academic articles. The conclusion is that people who are educated and intelligent take more conscientious decisions, acquire fewer illnesses, and also, as a result, die later than those who are less educated. However, neurobiologists—in one new research—have noticed some surprising and stunning outcomes about how older people make financial decisions. They say even very highly effective and functional people (but older) tend to be poor decision makers; they get it wrong more often than the younger people do.

While how these relationships work is wildly complicated and controversial, one very simple association between intelligence and health is always there. Highly conscientious people assume lower likelihood of developing all kinds of illnesses: diabetes, high BP, hernia, bone problems, sciatica, stroke, Alzheimer's, and tuberculosis. Smarter people are more careful avoiding accidents and are more likely to adapt four crucial lifestyle habits associated with longer life. They (1) quit smoking, (2) drink alcohol moderately, (3) exercise regularly, and (4) eat healthy food. While tracked up to their middle age, there has been a strong relationship (a) between low IQ and higher rate of hospitalization, after adjusting for socioeconomic factors, and (b) between low IQ and higher rate of illness, including non-brain illnesses such as cardiovascular diseases. The researchers hypnotize that the mechanism at work may be that less intelligent people have a harder time understanding the importance of physical activity, a heart-healthy diet, and the risks of smoking. They make foolish decisions and like to stay foolish. They love the fool's paradise.

When faced with physician's or nurse's advice to change his or her paradise (say, comfort items like diet or smoking), they would not be able (a) to comply with high self-directed effort, (b) to delay gratification, and (c) to go with long-term incentives.

- *Lifestyle (Smoking and TV):* Smoking burns the life quickly. Smokers at any age are typically twice as likely to die sooner than people who never smoked. Smokers who are overweight and obese die even sooner. As a group, smoking rate is more prevalent in less educated people than educated ones. Less educated people are less liable to think ahead and to delay gratification. (Read more about smoking in the chapter "Quit Smoking.")

  Sitting in front of the TV may be a relaxing way to pass an evening, but whiling away too much of one's time sitting may take years away from one's life as well. The American Time Use Survey reports that Americans watch TV 2 hours and 31 minutes each weekday. Another study in 2014 reports that American adults who watch 3 or more hours of TV a day do double their risk of premature death. From another survey in 2014—following the health habits of almost 12,000 Australian adults and using complex actuarial tables and adjusting for smoking, dietary quality, slenderness, exercise habits, and other variables—the scientists established that for every hour of television watched after the age of 25, it cuts life expectancy by 21.8 minutes. In 2016, on average, American adults watched 5 hours and 4 minutes of television per day. It's a lot of sitting. Sitting is the new smoking. For reference, smoking one cigarette a day cuts life expectancy by 11 minutes. Over a lifetime, a study found that people who watched an average 6 hours a day lived an average 4.8 years fewer than those who did not watch any television.

Instead of thinking of a far-off loss of a year or two after the seventies or eighties, one statistician cleverly interprets lifestyle choices more in immediate terms of adding or losing life hours—today, now. Assuming average life spans of about 80 years, one adult of 35 years and older will have nearly 1 million "half hours." The statistician assumes each half hour as a unit of life (normally, we count in one year) and names it intelligently "one microlife," hinting at a chance to live longer. So, each microlife represents one-millionth of life expectancy after age 35. Then he assigns, for example, smoking eats up approximately 10 microlives (5 hours) for every 20 cigarettes smoked a day—as if you are literally rushing toward your death spending 24 + 5 = 29 hours a day instead of 24 hours. It gives a feeling of clear and present danger! On the negative side, he linked other lifestyle factors to the loss of 1 microlife each for eating red meat every day, eating a burger, being overweight by roughly 11 lb. drinking an extra alcoholic beverage, watching 2 hours of television, and as mentioned, smoking 2 cigarettes. On the positive side, you gain microlife units by drinking 2–3 cups of coffee (1), taking statins (1), taking cholesterol-lowering drugs (1), eating fruits and vegetables (4), and exercising

20 minutes per day (2). Demographically, just being a woman is a gain of 4 microlives (2 hours) a day, being born in 2010 compared to 1910 is a gain of 21 microlives, and living in Sweden rather than Russia is a gain of 21 microlives. One interesting premise is that the tallies for additional microlives and those for lost microlives are not interchangeable: a microlife lost due to smoking 2 cigarettes can't be regained by exercising for 20 minutes extra. The idea here is to earn as much additive behaviors as possible to ensure that it outpaces the microlives you lose at the same time. However, remember, an individual reacts to any harmful or beneficial behavior, so differently.

- *Family and Friends:* There exists a strong relationship between having a network of family and friends and living a long and healthy life. We humans typically feel glad if someone talks to us; we feel sad otherwise. The biological impact of such a social connection is so much more than what we ordinarily understand. Researchers indicate that there are those lonely people who are more likely to become victims of cancer, heart ailments, and insomnia; and they die at a young age. Loneliness has become one great tragedy in a profoundly sick society. It is the sad reality of modern life. Especially for the older adults, the phenomenon called "shame in aging" sets in. They are ashamed of feeling useless and are ashamed of their appearance. They are ashamed of asking any help from others, which leads to more isolation. Loneliness harms insidiously and wreaks havoc on metabolism. It changes the way our genes work and alters the internal process through which a normal healthy person responds to external situations. There is hardly any prescription to cure loneliness. Some are lonely; some are very lonely.

- *Job We Do:* From age 20 to 60, half of our wakeful time is spent at our jobs. One entire chapter ("Job We Do") is addressed to cover this issue. Basically, job satisfaction contributes to a healthier and longer life. People with more powerful jobs most likely have more control over their work and life, and therefore, they have less work-related stress and anxiety. They are healthier, and they live longer. Even 40% of young adults ages 16 to 24 in the U.S. who don't have a job are fine with it.

- *Demography:* Demography is destiny! Longevity is related to where a person is born, brought up, and lives. The data finds that some countries like Japan, Switzerland, Sweden, Singapore, and in some specific places in those countries—say Japan's Okinawa Island—contribute to substantially healthier and longer life. In general, the lower death rates are in wealthier places. Among thirteen industrialized nations, however, the U.S. ranks twelfth based on the statistics of sixteen vital health indicators, such as, life expectancy, obesity, low birth-weight averages, and infant mortality. One research on mortality rate of immigrants living in the U.S. has revealed a few interesting points: (a) the longer the immigrants stay in this country, the worse their rate of heart disease, high BP, and diabetes; and (b) their American-born children tend to live even shorter lives than themselves, perhaps due to the fact that the immigrant advantages wear off with the adaption of the American lifestyle—high-calorie diets, drinking, smoking, and sedentary lifestyle.

- *Stress:* Light stress is good for health. Heavy stress is harmful to health and is perhaps a silent killer. Stress is so important a lifestyle factor that an entire chapter ("How to Deal with Stress") is devoted to its basic understanding.

- *Gender:* The life span of women, on average, is about 5 years more than men. Women, in general, have a 1% chance of reaching 100, while for men, it is only 0.1%. Men's immune systems are not as strong as women's, in part because, throughout evolution, living beings are prioritized in procreation over immunity. Therefore, females are protected better than males. Males are more susceptible to illnesses and suffer severely as a result.

- *Race:* Race is not skin deep! Social science experiments have shown that human beings feel, in general, greater sympathy for those who resemble them, than for those who do not. Apparently, the race stands out. The effects of racial bias rather than respecting to them are a legitimate form of loyalty and legality. It was dissimilatory then, it is discriminatory now. Study after study has acknowledged being a racial minority and thereof living below the poverty line, are vital factors that consequently contribute to higher mortality. It has an insidious effect on their lives on a day-to-day basis, even when it is not intentional. In the United States, being passed over for jobs for which they are qualified, shut out of housing and neighborhood they can afford, being treated with less courtesy than others, receiving poorer service at restaurants or stores, being treated with less respect than others, prejudice and overt bias, stereotyping, racial profiling, and law enforcement affect as much as 92% of African-American respondents in 2017. Half of them do experience themselves at work or during interaction with police. Pregnant women who report discrimination give birth to babies lower in birth weight. There are intentional and institutional discriminations as well. Black Lives Matter (BLM) movement by the African-American community is now an international campaign against systemic racism and violence towards black people. While primary causes—like, limited access to quality health care, diet, smoking, professional hazard and being vulnerable to violent crimes—can vary, most of the researchers have identified that race and poverty, separately and together, stands out.

According to one study published in *JAMA Internal Medicine* in 2016, scientists at the National Institute on Aging (NIA) examined the effects of race and economic status on mortality separately. They separated African American men and women who were 125% above and 125% below the federal poverty line and similarly did for the whites—a total of eight categories. When they compared their death rates over six years, they found that African American men below the poverty line had nearly three times higher risk of dying early than African American men above the poverty line; while among whites, the death rates remained about the same. Among women, both African American and white women below the poverty line had nearly two times higher risk compared to those above the poverty line. Subtle forms of racial discrimination in employment, normal differences of opinion, or failing to get along with coworkers at the workplace, in housing, in renting, in services, and in other facilities, including restaurants, are bad for overall well-being and normal health. Racial discrimination is a constant reminder that you are separate, not equal. Even in secondhand race discrimination, it is associated with genetic markers that may affect the risk for higher blood pressure. Race-based trauma is deeply rooted. Race discrimination is constantly felt by the blacks—not the incidence itself so much as the fact that there is no help on the way. Black people are not *white* people with *black* skin.

In the U.S., however, the race itself is now not a big factor, but the lifestyle associated with it is. In 2015, the federal authority reported a prevalence of demographic racial disparities in health issues. Whites die of drug overdoses more than any ethnic groups. Blacks are disproportionately hard-hit by AIDS, stroke, and heart disease. American Indians die in car crashes. Overall, the poor, the less educated, and the uninsured tend to live shorter, sicker lives. Children born to black women are three times more likely to die in infancy compared to those of other races. High

BP is twice more prevalent among blacks compared to whites. In the high-income category, unexpectedly, it is reverse the case for men of color, especially blacks and Mexican Americans: the higher the income, the higher the chances that they become obese. Over a five-year follow-up, one research finds that people who feel more racial discrimination tend to have a greater decline in kidney function—and the main reason is mental stress. Chronic stress leads to the release of the stress hormone. The stress hormone increases blood pressure, and that high blood pressure is responsible for heart and kidney disease.

- *Dieting:* Humans (as well as other animals) have fasted short-term and intermittently for much of their time on Earth. Compared to that, our present-day eating habit—three meals plus snacks every day—is too much. A sizable camp of nutrition experts recommends cutting back on how much we eat overall, and some recommend intermittent fasting—alternating between regular food consumption and short periods of eating almost nothing. Others offer reasons: even a typical diet with about 25% fewer calories than normal extends life span significantly. However, all the experts agree on one thing—that we'd all benefit from less sugar, mainly added sugar.

- *Obesity:* Doctors have warned for ages that obesity has unhealthy consequences, like the risk of heart disease, diabetes, and many types of cancer. All of that is responsible for an early death. One study, covering nearly four million people from thirty-two countries who were part of the Global BMI Mortality Collaboration, measurably demonstrates that an increase in BMI (even a slight increase) can cause harm to health. People with BMI above 25 and below 30, who are considered overweight, have an 11% increased risk of dying early before age 70, compared to those with a normal BMI of 25. For people with BMI between 30 and 35, who are the first category for obesity, they have a 45% risk; and for people with the highest level of obesity, or BMI of 40 or more, the risk is nearly triple. The researchers found differences between men and women who are overweight or obese: risk to men, in general, is three times more than that of women.

- *Mental Health:* The new model for assessing longevity now includes people's mental health. One ongoing study covers a population of three thousand people aged 57 to 85 years who enrolled in the National Social Life, Health, and Aging Project, which follows them for more than five years about various physical and mental health characteristics. The scientists monitor fifty-four health variables (like mobility, hearing, and eyesight), and they found that people with stable mental health are deemed the healthiest (with normal BP), the next healthiest being those with normal weight who did not have cardiovascular problems or diabetes. The unhealthiest group includes those with uncontrolled and untreated diabetes and people who are relatively sedentary. Obesity and being overweight are certainly the risk conditions, but if they aren't suffering from those conditions, they might be relatively healthy.

Even though huge progress has been made in reducing deaths from cardiovascular disease thanks to new drugs, procedures, and prevention, the years gained is outpaced by the climbing mortality from lung cancer, chronic obstructive pulmonary disease, and diabetes. Today's overweight children are tomorrow's potential heart and diabetic patients, terminating the nation's gains in health and well-being, so much so that the future life expectancy would settle down or even decline within the first half of this century. While the elderly disability rate has continued to decrease, disability rates among young people have begun to increase. The usual suspect is obesity. Another big factor is smoking, which is assumed to be a killer parallel with obesity and hypertension. These are the storm clouds on the horizon. A small adjustment in lifestyle can make a big difference and can improve the quality of life significantly. In spite of all these, people, however, hold the optimistic view that life spans will continue to increase. It will not. The seemingly inevitable rise of life expectancy of humans cannot go on, and it might have hit a ceiling of about 115 years, according to the conclusion on an analysis of decades of longevity records from around the world, including the Human Mortality Database and the International Database on Longevity. The absolute life span may be as high as 125, but the chances of anyone actually living that long are less than 1 in 10,000. For reasons, scientists state that parts of the body, including the brain, are not designed for long-term use, and that the consequences of pushing the limits of survival, is only to raise the prevalence of dementia, Alzheimer's disease, cancer, arthritis (joint and hip problems), loss of muscle mass, which are, however, not actually a consequence of failure, but of success living long. More than ever, however, we are now very close to a promising healthier old age: extending the health span, rather than the life span.

Poets have sung paeans to youth. They have lamented the passing of youth. Behind the yearnings for youth is the thought that with the passing of youth, a glory passes from life. Robert Browning, who was a worshipper of life, in his youthful passions and acts of courage as much as in the wisdom and kind spirit of old age, however, thought growing old was a gradual distilling into the quintessential values of life.

It is true that as the years roll by, it takes a toll on the simplicity, honesty, and straightforwardness of childhood. A man will not see and respond to the external world always with the mind of a child, but he can retain an attitude that is positive, optimistic, enthusiastic, fair, and kind, lasting till he breathes his last. Otherwise, falsehood and sickness of mind are as pathetic as the sickness of the body, if not more. If you are not afraid to die, you sure are fit to live. If you want to live long, open your heart. The heart that loves life is always young. He lives long who lives young.

He who prays young stays young! People who sincerely adores youth, find ways to avoid illness, and stay well and thrive. Youth sheds many a skin. Even the devil was not so evil when he was young. That's the essence of living young. It manifests in love, respect, and relationship. No one can turn the tide of time. Time will leave the ravage on our visage. But the aging process can be slowed down as long as the mind remains fresh and young. The secret of our youthfulness lies more in the brain than in the body. In general, the memories of one's youth make for long, long thoughts; and as we grow older, thinking through the thoughts, evergreen thoughts keep us younger. A sensible man never loses his child-heart. Albert Einstein once said, "The pursuit of truth and beauty is a sphere of activity in which we are permitted to remain children all our lives."

Youth is noble; old age is honorable. A man who carries this conviction of the blessings in existence will tide over the small difficulties that will never give him wrinkles on his face before his time. The conviction carries the courage. Have the courage; face the fact. Forgetting that which could have been but what is not, we can enjoy and celebrate our life many times over. But the paradox is that many of us do not live even once. The secret of living young is to think of our existence on earth as a wonderful blessing and to make the best use of it in our thoughts, beliefs, and actions. Know thyself. Life is so beautiful—today and every day.

He is young and perhaps right. A man's youthfulness in mind, as well as in body, depends on—to a great extent—how happy he is in life and how much he is enjoying it. Of course, enjoying does not mean living life abundant in the epicurean style. For example, a nice idea of living for others is not a typical set mentality, but it brings the satisfaction that gives vigor to our lives. People who believe that their lives have a purpose live longer than people who don't.

Faith helps to restore health. Sociologists noticed a connection between faith and health. Religious belief, faith, and worship can influence people at a far more basic level than any pharmacology. The mental and spiritual health of a regular churchgoer is more secure and at a higher level than that of a non-churchgoer. People rooted in religious communities presumably rely on one another for friendship, support, and mutual enjoyment for a good life overall. They reciprocate social support in their church. Receivers maintain a sense of gratitude, and that, in addition, reduces the incidence of depression. It is also noticed that those people who give help feel even better than those who receive it. Religious beliefs do not just uplift mind and spirituality but effect a total body overhaul. It is the same thought process that triggers the brain for instant healing—like visiting the doctor's office or walking into a temple.

Living within one's means is a great idea; its value is unquestionable even in these present times of consumerism. Similarly, the concepts of living simply—the old advice that we are often told by our elders from the time of our childhood—have great wisdom hidden within. These prudent ideas are always ageless. Simple living makes a natural living; natural living makes a complete living.

The face is the mirror of the mind. This is true in more than one sense. A face reveals the calm or turmoil inside. One of the secrets of youthfulness is calmness within. It is true that the state of mind essentially decides how young a person will appear. One should understand and practice this early on. It should not be that we neglect those in our youth's euphoria and suddenly become awake to the footfalls of aging. Live fast, die fast! Avoid fast life. Stay calm, composed and contempt. Happiness will follow. To a live long, go slow. Live slow, die slow!

Face-lifting! Yearly, thirteen million Americans get elective plastic surgery: breast augmentation, rhinoplasty, and face-lifting. Cosmetologists report that a lot of people past the prime of life come for plastic surgery for overhauling their face. Ageism is a problem; plastic surgery is the symptom (the thinking here, graceful aging does not mean that one should do nothing). If they had taken proper care of their lifestyle at the appropriate time, a lot of these surgeries could have been avoided. After all, it is the state of the mind that reflects one's face and bearings. Enjoy reality, reject the expensive antiaging fantasy.

Breast-lifting! According to the American Society of Plastic Surgeons, in the United States, about 290,000 women had implants for breast enlargement, and 109,000 for reconstruction after breast cancer in 2016. The FDA cautions that the implants cause a rare malignancy in the immune system, called anaplastic large-cell lymphoma. The breast cancer grows typically in the capsule of scar tissue that forms around an implant; it is usually treatable and not often fatal. Before gel silicone implants were introduced, the risk of developing a hole in the outer layer of silicone, due to wear and tear, was around 10% during the first decade. Health regulators warn that up to 93% of silicone breast implants ruptured within ten years. For women who had silicone breast implants before 2006, 20% to 40% of them had subsequent surgery to deal with the problems. In one legal fight in France, prosecutors appealed that Poly Implant Prothèse (PIP) used a cheap industrial-grade silicone. Now a new technique of breast reconstruction may reduce the pain: the technique places implants on top of muscle, instead of under it. Another research finds that there could be a possible link among saline, silicone breast implants and one very rare type of cancer called anaplastic large-cell lymphoma (ALCL). Research cautions that women with implants are more likely to die from lung cancer and respiratory complications. One factor could be that they are typically smokers and that some could have even as much as tripled the risk of death from alcohol and drug use. They have a greater risk of suicide, which is not apparent until after ten years of implantation. Typically, women who get implants may have a psychiatric problem to start with, which is linked to their lower self-esteem, especially body shaming. In one study, social scientists revealed a higher risk of suicide among women with breast implants. All things considered, getting a breast implant is surely a coarse decision—the view of *silicon valley* hardly justifies the risk.

Lifestyle is always associated with good health. The important ones are quitting smoking, weight loss, BP control, diabetes control, regular exercise, and a balanced diet. A new study indicates that these activities are significantly correlated to a healthy and longer life and well up to extreme old age and that these behaviors in the early years are adaptable and sustainable. Listen to your body's cues and plan to give certain parts some extra care as early as possible:

- **Skin:** From the age of 18, the resilient collagen and stretchy elastin declines at about 1% per year. Slow the process. Quit smoking, eat healthy and sleep well.
- **Lungs:** From the age of 30, lung function drops 1% per year. Do exercise.
- **Bones:** From the age of 35, bone mass drops up to 1% per year. Do weight-bearing exercise.
- **Eyes:** From the age of 40, eyesight declines. Don't smoke and keep out UV radiation
- **Muscles:** From the age of 40, muscle loss and fat gain happen. Routine physical exercise is a must.

- **Kidneys:** From the age of 50, kidney function declines. Drink plenty of water.
- **Ears:** From the age of 60, hearing loss begins gradually. Just avoid loud music or noisy industrial places.
- **Gut:** From the age of 60, the total number of villi in the intestine tends to flatten out and absorb fewer nutrients
- **Heart:** From the age of 65, the aerobic capacity drops by about 10% per decade, and heart disease typically starts.
- **Brain:** From the age of 70, age-related brain damage speeds up.

An individual does have control over his lifestyle, which can give him not only a long life but also good health and less chronic problems as late as in his nineties. Here are a few clues from the people who lived long. They are surprisingly so few and so basic that anyone can practice them without even trying: (a) eat less [Hint: Harvard research has identified genes that allow yeast to survive on fewer calories and extend its life span by about 30%], (b) make family a priority, and (c) reduce stress.

Mortality is negotiable! You are going to die, though. Immortality is not negotiable. Will happen, whenever it will. However, "living better and thereof living longer" is the idea, here. Your daily habits can either *add to* or *subtract from* potential years of your life. To live young and to live long, here are a few quick tips that longevity researchers recommend:

- Lose some weight somehow. Otherwise, the allied risk of diabetes, cancer, and heart disease can possibly cut twelve years off from your life.
- Ease your stress. Chronic stress makes you feel old. Work-related tension harms DNA in our cells. Pray, practice yoga, meditate, relax in the shower, walk, or do whatever feels good to you.
- Quit smoking.
- Sleep well.
- Work out often—ideally three days of cardio and two days of strength training a week.
- Eat more plants. Avoid red meat and processed food and sugary drinks. Go Mediterranean diet. Research claims that those who eat a diet that is 70% plant-based—fruits, vegetables, nuts, whole grains, beans, olive oil—benefit from a 20% lower risk of dying of cardiovascular disease. And another similar research says you're 30% less likely to have a heart attack or stroke than those who don't.
- Eat less. Several studies on both laboratory animals and humans have shown that caloric restriction—roughly 25% below the recommended adult daily calorie intake—does have a life-extending benefit.
- Connect to family, friends, and relatives and do volunteer for a cause. People most connected (having positive, meaningful, intimate relationships) lived 22% longer than those who were least connected. (And this lowered blood pressure in separate research.)
- Have more sex. The feel-good rush helps you fight stress and depression, jolts the immune system, and lowers blood pressure.
- Drink moderately.

- Stay curious, think positive, discover new things, keep learning, and be better informed about how to live a healthy life and stay engaged with the world. This can help up to a remarkable 7.5-year boost in life span.

We know nothing about the afterlife, if it exists at all. All that we know is that we are alive on this earth amidst its myriad beauties. Nature has provided us with the beautiful canopy of the sky with the air, water, plants, and flowers to make our life so immensely pleasurable. But instead of enjoying the abundance, we only pine for what it has not. We forget our Mother Nature. No matter how youthful and amiable you may feel, identifying yourself with nature is most important. Nature will nourish your mind. When you walk through the rows of pines or when the eucalyptus enthralls you, when the chirping of the early birds delights you, when the sunlight falling upon the scintillating peaks of the mountains looks glorious to you—you know that you are in the spring of life regardless of your age. Instead of a "fear of dying," envision the "joy of living." Do this to feel better, not just to live longer. Anticipate the sense of Mother Nature. You enjoy life when you enjoy nature. Let us rejoice while we are alive. Long live life!

3 Enjoy Good Food

> Let thy food be thy medicine and thy medicine be thy food.
>
> —Hippocrates (460–377 BC), Greek father of natural medicine

Humans eat food, not diet or medicine. Food is the most primitive form of life support, survival, and comfort. It is our source of nourishment that can be metabolized by our body. Food is the most powerful drug for the body that inherently works as protective, preventive and curative medicine. Deciding what to eat—in fact, deciding what food really is—is not so easy. Food can be friend, food can be enemy—frenemy. Life is good where eating is a pleasure. Also, food is not just a food, fuel or nutrition; it's a part of our ritual, culture and tradition. When American eat turkey on Thanksgiving, or Muslims eat sheer khurma (warm sweet vermicelli milk) on Ramadan, or Dutch eat oliebollen (doughnuts) on New Year, they are actually taking part in a ritual shared by millions of others. The food on the table is one attraction of the occasion to pull together the friends, family, and federation. Food plays one important part of our social insurance and social security. The social importance of food took precedence around one to two million years ago. After that, there have been four major milestones in human food culture:

1. Fire tamed by *Homo erectus* around 500,000 BC. In the northern Jordan Valley in Israel, archeologists have uncovered one new and surprising clues. The discovery was published in the *Proceedings of the National Academy of Sciences* in 2016, that ancient humans cooked on a wide variety of plants along with their fish and meat as early as 780,000 years ago.
2. According to the *Journal of Archaeological Science*, hominins used tools to butcher and prepare animals for eating about 250,000 years ago, or at least 50,000 years before the earliest modern humans appeared in Africa. And it was an absolute necessity to make the right tools and eat the proper diet to get smarter and smarter still.
3. Agriculture came along in 8,000 BC for mass production of crops, fruits and vegetables for a stable supply of basic foods.
4. The invention of pottery in 7,000 BC. Although ancient human cultures sought food items through hunting and gathering, today, that culture has been replaced by agriculture and farming.

Food is remarkably a bonding force. It is the human bondage sharing food with friends and families. Survey finds that in more than a quarter of families, food is considered to be an emotional response and a meaningful way to show affection. Scientists interpret: food is one very fundamental way how humans have been evolved. In fact, evolutionarily speaking, it was the use of fire by humans that has long been considered as a defining property of intelligence, separating humans from other animals. The ignition of fire before humans appeared during lightning strikes and the oldest recorded fire recorded on planet Earth has been identified from charcoal in rocks formed around 420 million years ago. The first human interaction with fire was perhaps 1.5 million years ago in Africa when humans started conserving by adding fuels to the fire, such as woods and dungs. This "stretch" fire was a novel achievement. The slow burning of the fire was useful not only for light and warmth at night, especially in the long winter nights, but also to frighten off predatory animals, and the smoke to keep off the insects. However, routine use of a single hearth with indications of roasting meat dates back only between 400,000 and 300,000 years ago from the caves in Israel. With food, they developed a relationship to the taste and flavor, in a way to sense what was going on around them and to chase down the preferred animals and to consume them as food. For a sharper sense of food, they required a bigger brain to process those senses. Compared to botanical diets, now the bigger brain emerged as they started eating meat packed with fat and protein. Proteins are useful to rebuild or replace dying cells, protect against viruses and bacteria, regulate body chemistry, copy DNA to form new molecules, release hormones for signaling and repair tissues and organs.

The proto-humans (hypothetical prehistoric primate, resembling humans) were eating enough root food to stay alive. It was around 2.6 million years ago when meat became the significant part of the pre-human diet. Killed prey was prepared either by slicing, pounding or flaking. It provided them a much more calorie-rich meal with much less chewing than root foods boosting nutrient levels overall. Cooking with fire come long after into vogue until only 500,000 years ago. Now with fire, our hunter-gatherer ancestors could cook a lot of plants that are safe to eat and more palatable like roasting nuts and roots for example, otherwise toxic or inedible as raw. They eat various parts of the plants. There was no single balance between meat and plant; they cooked a wide variety of plants—including veggies (like water chestnuts and acorns), fruits, nuts, and seeds—along with fish and meat. Although they had a variety of diets, they were never picky eaters. They perhaps used to eat in-season, which might have allowed them to stay in one place for some time.

With fire, cooking was made easy, especially for meat. Cooked meat was more comfortable to chew and digest, and its calories were more readily available to fuel even bigger brains. The cyclic evolution encouraged within the community an appreciation of food and, along the way, taste and love of the food. It then gradually became a social matter. Our animal ancestors (chimpanzees and monkeys) were like people in the sense that parents and siblings helped raise the offspring by providing food in the family. The concept of "food is love" followed next. They shared food with individuals even outside of their family circles. Sharing food has been a practice in strengthening the alliance and for future cooperation. Like today's Thanksgiving (unlike the business lunch), they shared food to make new friends, not just to keep old ones. Somewhere along the course, the brain got wired to remember the food events and the people associated with them—the "food memory." It is, therefore, no accident that our digestive system produces hormones like insulin, leptin, and ghrelin in such a way as to act on the hippocampus, enabling the brain to play an essential role in food memory. The gut-brain connection strengthened probably because our ancestors were more likely to survive if they remembered clearly where they got their last good meal. Today the same link between gut and brain exists, and that is probably the reason why we are conditioned to a particular dish—for example, what your mother used to make when you were a kid. Researchers observed, through brain scans, that the dopamine system gets activated when people look at someone they love or look at the food they love. In our brain, food is really connected to love. Food is the currency of love. We love to love food!

Therefore, when it comes to food, most of us have already fallen in love with food. We are terrible at judging how much we eat. About half of U.S. families surveyed said they treat celebrations as a time to take a break from concerns about overeating. With all the talks and cheers in the air, it's easy to overlook how much we eat and how good the food is. We indulge till we bulge. The food we eat and the content of our meals have been a subject of intense focus and constant speculation ever since we have woken up to the fact that eating the wrong kind of food is constantly adding to the various health disorders that we already suffer and which is further complicating our problems.

America is a land of not only immigrants but immigrant foods as well. Almost every food is an immigrant one. Apples come from Kazakhstan, pineapples from Brazil, bananas from New Guinea, and oranges and lemons from China. Immigrants and food explorers have brought rice, cotton, soybeans, mangos, quinoa, dates, bamboo and hundreds of seeds, plants and trees that transformed varieties of food (and food preparations) what Americans eat today. The average number of products (mostly food items) carried by a typical supermarket grocery store has tripled since 1980—from 15,000 to 50,000 SKU (stock-keeping unit). Yet, the downside is too many choices tend to poor selection. When there are many choices, shopping can actually cause fatigue and regret. [Hint: Regret, not picking the right one! Regret, you could have owned the other one! Regret, you have lost the other one! People tend to regret to lose the stuff they had owned or could have owned. It is one innate human trait, psychologically known as the endowment effect. It is perhaps inherited through evolution because it is noticeable cross-culturally in human and in nonhuman primates as well.]

One study shows that while 30% of people buy from a pool of 3 types of items, only 3% buy from a pool of 24 types of items. Selection needs a decision, which needs brain activity. An average American makes about fifty to seventy decisions a day, starting from which breakfast cereal to eat to how to reply to an email to career selection. Social science experiments conclude that decision fatigue reduces people's control over everything from aggression to tolerance to pain. Yet very few people are aware of it. Supermarket shelves are loaded with all kinds of fattening food and inebriating drinks. We indulge ourselves, but immediately afterward, we start feeling guilty and try to practice abstinence for a while. So, try to be mindful before each mouthful.

During the terrifying cholera epidemic in the 1830s in the U.S., Sylvester Graham advocated a particular type of diet consisting largely of Graham wheat. He asked people to refrain from having meat. His diet could protect people from the disease. Grahamite clubs sprang up, where people had Graham bread and crackers. In practice, food denial for the sake of health got tangled with food denial for the sake of holiness. However, today, our health advice has become much more scientific, even though it keeps shifting—for what is considered healthy at one time may not be so some time later. More often than you'd think, the trouble is that people just don't know what healthy food looks like. And why should they? The rules just keep changing. Common people need reference and guidance.

In 2015, one survey compared consumption of thirteen healthy foods (like fruits, vegetables, and whole grains) and seven unhealthy foods (like sugary drinks and trans fats) in 187 countries and found that even many poor countries, where alternatives were hard to come by, scored well in food choices. But the United States remained below average. This is despite the abundance of food resources, which is another puzzling statistic. The conventional wisdom is that a person is better off if he has more alternatives to select from. Most health advice focuses on eating a variety of foods from a range of diverse food groups to get most of the compounds, vitamins, and minerals that our body needs. But it does not work that well in food selection. In the land of plenty, people consume the food of empty. In one 2018 review of this topic, food researchers find that having a diverse diet may not necessarily lead to a better health. In their statement of review, published in the journal *Circulation* in 2018, the American Heart Association find little scientific evidence for the idea that a varied diet leads to good health outcomes—especially controlling the risk of chronic conditions like heart disease, obesity and diabetes. In fact, it turns out to be the worse outcome. Why? The reason is quite intriguing. Food researchers find that when Americans eat a wider range of foods, they also tend to eat more unhealthy foods, including snacks, fries, cakes and sweets, where it's quite possible that the unhealthy effects of the poor-quality foods might outweigh the health effects of the healthy foods. People are interpreting the word "variety" to include a variety of foods which may not necessarily be healthy.

One significant aspect of food is food waste! It cuts a sorry figure. According to a report from the Institution of Mechanical Engineers, 1.2 billion tons of food—as much as 50 percent of the total world production—get thrown away each year. In other words, 240 billion pounds of food is wasted in America each year. That 240 billion divided by 310 million U.S. population works out to 770 pounds per person per year or about 2 pounds of food per person per day. By most estimates, 25 to 50 percent of all food produced in the U.S. goes unconsumed, either left at source or spoiled in transit or discarded at the grocery store or scraped into the garbage can at home. Dollar-wise, Americans waste $640 of food per person per year. Though more than half say they reuse leftovers for new meals, more than half say they throw away leftovers at least once a week. People have started vacuum packing to extend the life of food. According to the U.S. Agricultural Department, food waste is the single biggest waste in U.S. landfills. The EPA notes that food waste makes up to 20 percent of landfill content; it rots, releases obnoxious gases. (Every year, four billion pounds of returned clothing (including online returns) ends up in the landfill. That's like every resident in the U.S. had a load of laundry—12 pounds of brand-new clothing—and then decided to throw it away.) One study says misinterpreting the expiration date is responsible for 20 percent of food waste. The total edible seafood supply in the U.S. is about 4.7 billion pounds per year; half of that gets wasted as a result of disorganization, poor logistics, and consumer refusals: consumers discard 1.3 billion pounds, fisheries toss off 570 million pounds when they catch the wrong species, and transport and distribution throw away 330 million pounds. A report commissioned by the UN estimates that, globally, one-third of food intended for human consumption—some 1.3 billion metric tons—is lost or wasted.

Wasted food contributes to environmental toll, making up to 20 percent of all the waste dumped in landfills, according to EPA. It helps to grow pests, cockroaches, and rats. It produces methane, a greenhouse gas. In U.S. homes, as much as 40 percent of food is wasted, the major cause being over-clutter of fresh foods and leftovers in massive refrigerators. Foods are not used for a long time and eventually go bad. [Hint: One good news is that technology like vacuum-sealed pouches is now the techniques in food preservation that keep food fresh longer—much longer. The idea aims at longer shelf lives, better logistics, and food management.]

People often choose the terrible food. As a matter of fact, much of the time, they choose the very worst one—the junk one. America is a fast-food nation. Fast-food joints have sprung up (now 160,000) like mushrooms in spite of their effect on the health and well-being of the general population. It is a nation of mindless eaters—50 million (1 in 7) people eat fast food every day. Nearly 40 percent of Americans eat fast food during the past 24 hours, according to 2018 report from CDC. Fast food and junk food are synonyms to each other. They all are bad food. Good food is good; but even good food, in excess, is bad. Bad food, in and of itself, is very bad; and then bad food in excess is very, very bad. Junk food—which was initially intended to be an occasional treat—is now a staple food for many on a daily basis, which is too bad. The average American spends about $70,000 on takeout over their lifetime. Junk is not a food, and a food should not be junk.

For here or to go? That is the standard question in any food outlet. Today, Americans consume one-third of their daily calories outside the home. Fast-food restaurants play a significant role in how families feed themselves. Fast-food frequenters apparently have no clue how many calories they're consuming. On average, with each order, an adult consumes 836 cal, adolescents 756 cal, and kids 733 cal. Even meals from large chain and local restaurants, 92% have more calories than is recommended, according to a new study published in 2016 in the *Journal of the American Academy of Nutrition and Dietetics*. Per the U.S. Department of Agriculture's Healthy Eating Index 100-point scale, the nutritional quality of fast food improved barely, with scores hovering below 50 points and worse for dairy and sodium. The average American's diet score is 55 points. In America, hyper-processed carbs and sweeteners constitute as much as 80% of all food products. Even though people have been cautioned for decades not to eat excess meat and fat, Americans recklessly consumed 67% more added fat, 41% more meat, and 39% more sugar in 2000 than they did in 1950—and calorie-wise, almost 25% more than they had in 1970. So, not surprisingly, people are fatter and unhealthier. The issue is not as simple as low-fat versus low-carb, but one primary factor is that animal protein does significantly increase the risk of premature mortality from all causes, including cardiovascular disease, cancer, type 2 diabetes, and Alzheimer's disease. The recommended amount of protein for a healthy adult a day: 56 grams for man and 46 grams for woman. American adults eat about 100 grams per day on average, and those even on a vegan diet, about 60 to 80 grams (from foods like whole grains, beans, legumes, nuts, fruits, and vegetables). Doctors, hospitals, clinics, schools and even some workplaces are showing, not just telling, people how to lead a healthier life by selecting nutritious food.

Weight gain is one major source of ill health. What causes weight gain? The usual suspect is the trio: fat, sugar, salt. Yet that's not the whole truth. The Institute of Medicine and the Department of Agriculture says it's the lack of real food. Real food solves the fat/sugar/salt problem. The main offenders are hyper-processed food and added sugar. To this effect, the combination of the USDA recommending a food guide and, at the same time, allowing fast food to thrive is like lighting one candle to God and another to the devil. The ratio of fast-food joints to supermarkets is now 5:1. The fast-food chains sell fatty, high-calorie packaged and processed foods that contribute more to obesity, diabetes, and cancer. Surveys show that while living near a supermarket has little impact on how healthily people ate, living close to a fast-food restaurant does. Paradoxically, local residents are reluctant to travel even a mile to access better, fresh, healthy foods. Such is the culture.

The CDC says about 5,000 Americans die every year of heart disease linked to only one item: the artificial trans fats. Because the Food and Drug Administration (FDA) allows food producers to put "0 g" on the package label even if it contains up to 0.5 g (the weight of a quarter is 5.67 g or 0.2 oz.) of trans fat per serving, 84% of food products are still found to contain the problematic oil, and the label on these are misleading. A typical regular/classic small 1½ oz. (42.5 g) potato chips label may read thus: Total Fat 16 g (Saturated Fat 2 g, Trans Fat 0 g).

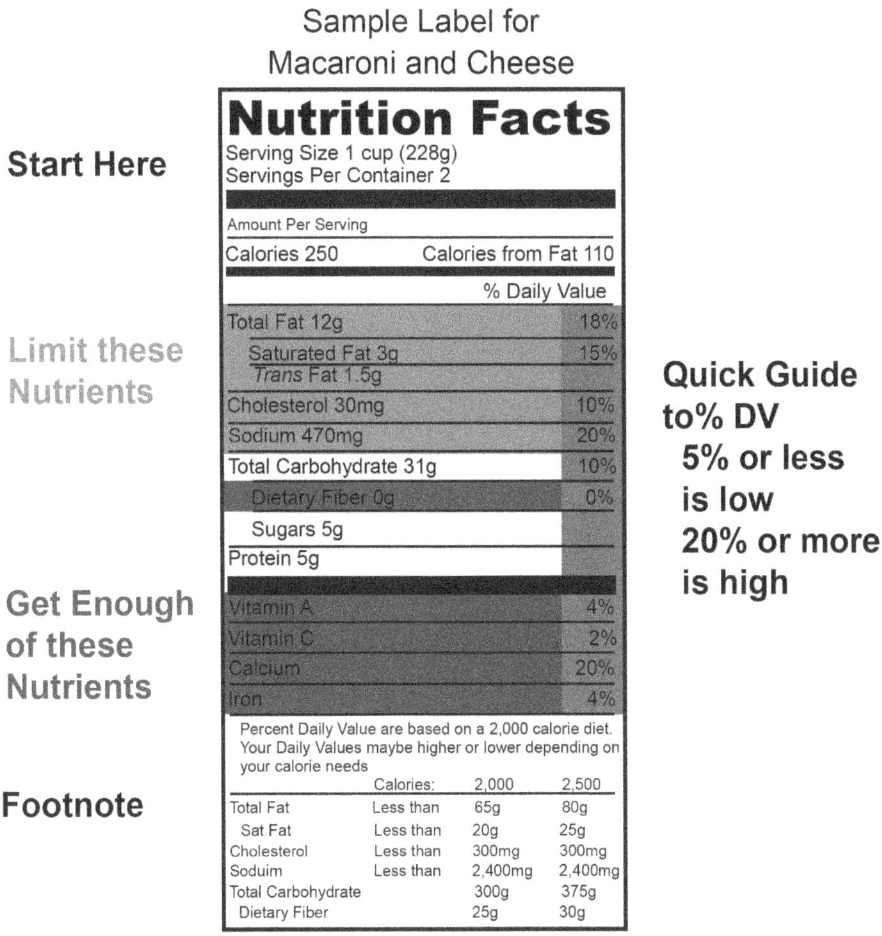
Sample Label for
Macaroni and Cheese
Nutrition Facts
Start Here
Serving Size 1 cup (228g)
Servings Per Container 2
Amount Per Serving
Calories 250
Calories from Fat 110
% Daily Value
Limit these Nutrients
Total Fat 12g 18%
Saturated Fat 3g 15%
Trans Fat 1.5g
Cholesterol 30mg 10%
Sodium 470mg 20%
Total Carbohydrate 31g 10%
Dietary Fiber 0g 0%
Sugars 5g
Protein 5g
Quick Guide to% DV
5% or less is low
20% or more is high
Get Enough of these Nutrients
Vitamin A 4%
Vitamin C 2%
Calcium 20%
Iron 4%
Footnote
Percent Daily Value are based on a 2,000 calorie diet. Your Daily Values maybe higher or lower depending on your calorie needs
Calories: 2,000 2,500
Total Fat Less than 65g 80g
Sat Fat Less than 20g 25g
Cholesterol Less than 300mg 300mg
Soduim Less than 2,400mg 2,400mg
Total Carbohydrate 300g 375g
Dietary Fiber 25g 30g

Sample Label for Macaroni and Cheese

How to read the Nutrition Facts in a food label! When Nutrition Facts was first published in the '90s, it was the fat treated as the culprit of poor health and cardiovascular disease. Today, based on research and trial, perspective has changed, there are many other factors to our concerns. Reading the food level right, is the right way to go.

Serving Size: The amount typically consumed at once. Their amount of recommendation may not be your consumption. Listed serving size may not be your serving size. So, pay attention to it—because all other numbers proportionately vary.

Calories: This is the number of calories provided by a single serving. A diet of 2,000 calories per day is recommended for average American healthy adult man. It varies widely based on factors like age, sex, activity level, weight, height, health goal, and individual metabolism.

Percent Daily Value (% DV): Depending on the frequency of consumption of this food and other foods, three (+/-) meals per day, a reasonable % DV is to stay between 5 and 20.

Nutrients and other Items: The amount of carbohydrates, fats, protein, cholesterol, sugar, dietary fiber, vitamins, and minerals, primarily depends on your diet plan—per day (per week, per month). However, a quick reference per day: saturated fat less than 20 grams (go as low), trans fat should be 0g (it is eliminated from all new food products sold in the United States since 2018 and those in other parts of the world by 2023, as recommended by WHO), sodium less than 2,300 mg, added sugar between 25 and 36 grams, and dietary fiber more than 28 grams (go as high).

As consumers eating multiple products don't know how much they're consuming, over time, the trans fats adds up. Denmark banned trans fat in 2004, and after a decade, in 2014, it shows a remarkable decline in mortality rates involving cardiovascular disease. In the U.S., the FDA has now proposed a revision of the nutrition labels that appear on something like 700,000 packaged foods—many of which only pretend to be foods. Higher in the category are doughnuts, crackers, movie-theater microwaveable popcorn, frozen pizza, coffee creamers, refrigerated dough products, and canned frostings.

Trans fats are the silent killer. According to the World Health Organization (WHO), eating trans fats (margarine or shortening)—common in baked and processed foods (french fries or doughnuts)—leads to the deaths of more than 500,000 people worldwide every year. In case studies, researchers cite some findings: (a) the process of reheating Vanaspati, which is made from palm oil, makes it more lethal contributing soaring rates of heart disease among South Asians; and (b) Pakistani men have a 62 percent higher mortality rate from heart attacks than men in England or Wales. The world does not need trans fats. Most people—in developed and developing countries—are not aware of it and can comfortably live without it. In the U.S., the first trans fat food came to market in 1911 and the last, in June 2018. In 2018, WIO releases a plan to help governments around the globe to eliminate trans fats from the global food supply by 2023. The ban is an easy call and the WHO initiative is right to do so. However, WHO may not be in the power of enforcement, but its efforts are now being taken seriously by the governments across the world.

U.S. studies show that on average, nutrition and food labels don't make much of a difference in what people ultimately buy. People don't even bother to check the "sell by" date. In food-buying behavior, the posted calorie counts are largely disregarded by both teens and adults. The effect of caloric information is marginally adequate in improving eating habits. However, it makes a difference to the people who pay attention. Today, calorie counts have been required on menus in restraints, and it is just starting. The whole idea behind the calorie counts is to help Americans be better informed—from supermarket to convenience store to restaurant—about what and how much to eat. Hopefully, it will be lighter and healthier food. Just for illustration, here are few smart choices: (1) cereal—choose 100% whole grain with more fibrous option, like bran; (2) vegetables—choose cruciferous vegetables (broccoli, brussels sprouts, cabbage, cauliflower, collard greens, kale), which are good for inflammation and diabetes and joint disorders; (3) yogurt—choose Greek, which has less sugar and more protein, and (4) peanut butter—a great nutritional package with protein, fiber and many minerals and vitamins; the high fat content may appear to be unhealthy, but peanut butter consists of mostly healthy unsaturated fat that reduces blood cholesterol and risk of heart disease—a standard serving of two tablespoons, about 200 calories, goes better with sandwich, crackers, baked goods, or as a dip.

Surveys suggest that some items are simply to be crossed out from your grocery list. They are fake rip-offs, drastically unhealthy, and outright not a food. Buy them with caution. Here are a few examples:

- Smoked and cured meats, preformed meat patties (packed with artery-clogging grease)
- Blueberry-, blackberry-, and strawberry-flavored items (Most of them do not contain actual berries, just artificial flavors.)
- Multigrain bread (mostly white bread with few grains mixed—check the list of main ingredients)
- Reduced-fat peanut butter (high in sugar)
- Aged large bottom-feeder fish, such as tuna, swordfish, shark, king mackerel, tilefish (high in mercury—choose smaller fish)
- Bottled tea and coffee, powdered ice tea mixes or prepared flavored ice tea (have more grams of sugar than a soda or slice of pie), bottled coffee
- Energy drinks (are sugar toxins—linked to diabetes, cancer, heart attack, convulsion, and even death)
- Gluten-free baked foods like bread, cookies, and crackers—which are often made with refined flours, sugar, and artificial ingredients more than traditional baked foods (Gluten is a protein found mainly in wheat. But it is also found in wheat varieties like farro and spelt, rye, barley, and triticale (a cross between wheat and rye). The Food and Drug Administration has set the standard in 2013, which is food's gluten level below a regulated threshold of 20 parts per million. Oats, which does not contain gluten itself, has some concern of cross-contamination with other gluten-containing grains. However, market hype does not spare bottled spring water that are innately gluten-free and yet advertised as "gluten-free." If you are not diagnosed with celiac disease or gluten intolerance, gluten-free does not necessarily mean healthy.

Demographically, only less than 1% of the general population has celiac disease; but paradoxically, 30% of American adults try to avoid gluten. Gluten-free has become a marketing trick in recent years.)

- Flavored nondairy milk (It is no better than unsweetened versions or skim milk.)
- Food made of wood—high-fiber cereals or snack bars (Most probably, they have an ingredient called "cellulose," which is simply a code word for "wood pulp.")
- White rice (has a 17% higher risk of diabetes)
- Gourmet frozen vegetables (worse than non-gourmet)
- Microwave sandwiches, snack or lunch packs (packed with whole lot of salt, fat, and unnecessary additives)
- Premium frozen fruit bars, gourmet ice cream (These have lots of sugar.)
- Spice mixes (Instead, buy them separately and mix them yourself.)
- Bottled water

In most countries, home food is the culture; in the U.S., fast food is the culture. Nearly 40 percent of Americans eat fast food during the past 24 hours, according to 2018 report from CDC. But why do we love fast food in the first place? Besides being fast service and some individual's reasoning like the convenience and fast hunger suppression, here is what the biological factor is. Like a treat, junk food (as most fast foods are) is tasty—no doubt about it. Typically, we crave certain foods so much that they seem to be addictive. Just the thought of pizza or ice cream rouses the release of the neural chemical dopamine. (Dopamine, an essential for normal functioning of the central nervous system, is one kick-start chemical compound that acts as a neurotransmitter in the brain and makes us feel happy. The dopamine neurotransmitter is responsible for transmitting signals between nerve cells [neurons] of the brain. It is one brain's pleasure signal, which is linked to neurological and psychiatric health.) It causes the brain to override the biological brakes that try to prevent eating or overeating. If you can have that person somehow in a brain scanner, you will notice dopamine release in part of the pleasure circuit, a part called the striatum. The striatum is involved in planning and decision-making, which is important for relating to action and reward. Researchers theorize that dopamine is not so much of the pleasure itself but the expectation of pleasure or prediction of pleasure (that you will be eating). However, if that person actually gets a chance to eat the food that he enjoys while in the scanner, you will also notice a greater release of dopamine. Overloaded with dopamine, the brain registers pleasure with a huge synergistic bang primarily due to (1) sensation and (2) calorie intake from the food—which is predominately a mixture of salt, sugar, and fat. The affinity to high-calorie food has a hereditary root that goes back to evolutionary hunter-gatherer days of primates for survival. So, as the fast food is typically high-fat, high-calorie tasty food, we flock there like flies.

It's not all a matter of poor willpower, not to resist fast food on the part of consumers; and at the same time, it is also not a modest matter of give-the-people-what-they-want attitude on the part of food producers. Years of research, investigation, and awareness on food production and consumption that is taking place in farms, factories, labs, marketing meetings, selling campaigns, and grocery aisles, common people are still hooked on some foods that are convenient and inexpensive. It needs a sincere effort for all good men to come along—from firms to food industries, from scientists to marketers, from mothers to policy-makers, and from whistle-blowers to the country's lawmakers.

Fast food—except being fast and ready to eat—has hardly any health benefits. Slim benefits, if any, come from the chemically added nutrients. Fast food often contains multiple forms of sugar, highly refined carbohydrates, chemically extracted fats, and perhaps most interesting of all, some secret ingredients that only food scientists know. This is not a food, but a food-like food. Some industries acknowledge the problem and say they are working on it. Sometimes, they come up with some gimmicks like creating "smaller" portion sizes and renaming healthier versions of classic junk foods. They argue about consumers' self-responsibility, as if their own marketing strategies do not play any covert role in these self-destructive ways. Of course, people have the self-responsibility; they have certain rights as well, including the right to eat junk food, to drink soda, to avoid exercise, and to gain weight. But at the same time, the government has its responsibility too, as most of the time, voluntary guidelines do not work. As a country, when a certain health-related issue reaches a certain point of importance, the government has a duty to step in. For example, people are advised to drive within speed limits, be safe, and not to fall asleep at the wheel. On the other hand, the government (DMV) can enforce safety traffic laws. Parents are needed to immunize their children before they go to school; on the other hand, laws just require it. Similarly, food authorities like the FDA and USDA must demonstrate their leadership, authority, and accountability and must provide citizens with a collective sigh of relief.

One food critic remarked, "In America, we eat collectively with a glum urge for food to fill us. We are ignorant of flavor. We are, as a nation, taste-blind." In contrast, for instance, French culinary traditions are often credited with keeping people trim even though the shops and the food markets are filled with pastries, cheeses, and meats; and people are talking about food all the time. Because they love to eat food! It turns out that it's not only what the French people eat but culture-wide. It is how they eat that seems to make a difference.

If you want your baby to love food that you love to eat, try early! Very early! The baby's palate and food memory are formed well before the birth! Research shows that what the mother eats during pregnancy not only nourishes herself and her baby in the womb but also shapes the food preferences for the baby later in life. It starts after twenty-one weeks of conception, when the fetus is only about 7 to 8 inches long. Besides vital systems fully functional—like rapid eye movement, blink-startle response, and responses to pressure, movement, pain, hot, cold, and light—the developing fetus can taste as well. A fetus drinks several ounces of the surrounding amniotic fluid, which is essentially flavored by the foods the mother has eaten in the last few hours. The scent of amniotic fluid—like garlic, chili, and ethnic spices—slowly builds the food memory. After the baby is born, the mother's breast milk, flavored by the food, reinforces the taste. Even in kidney transplant, donner taste (of burger) is sometimes passed on to the recipient who later urges for the taste (of burger). All these make lot of evolutionary sense as to why the Chinese love Chinese food and the Indian love Indian's. Different countries and cultures have different perceptions with different types of foods: delicious, tasty, ceremonial, religious and so on. In the 1800's America, feeding lobsters to the prisoners was considered to be cruel and unusual punishment, like making them eat rats. Worldwide, based on their religion, culture, custom, tradition, geography, weather and economy, people grow their food habits and food taste, so culturally, so ethnically and so differently. Therefore, for infants and toddlers early on, expose them to different foods, make it fun, and be patient. Give them healthy snacks—nutritionally similar to meals. Happy meal treats once in a while are not regular snacks, so don't go crazy about the no-junk-food rule. Get the whole family involved and lead by example. Research says that the kids' preferences do not change much from age 2 to 8. The foods we come to relish as children are the foods that cry out to us for the rest of our lives. The taste of junk food at an early age can carry over to the adult age as well.

Meat is known to be a source of complete protein, vitamins, and many other nutrients. According to sociologists and anthropologists, meat played a significant role in the evolution of the human species. In spite of the increasing popularity of vegetarianism, the demand for meat for human consumption has not dwindled. One study measured the human trophic level—where humans were placed on the food chain hierarchy—in 176 countries for each year from 1961 to 2009. It found that the global median human trophic level has jumped 3% in only fifty years. The early men had to struggle hard to gather their daily share of meat by hunting and sometimes risking their lives in that process. Now meat comes from local stores, nicely processed and neatly packaged. As a result, we often end up eating more meat than what is good for our health. On average, an American eats 225 lb. of meat a year. An excess of meat can have a deleterious effect on the liver and kidney. Many types of meat—red meat in particular—have a high quantity of saturated fat, an ingredient which is known to cause cardiovascular ailments. It is better to avoid red meat as much as possible. However, two to three servings a week is a good guide and rather beneficial. Knowing the nutrition value of meat, doctors these days do not suggest an entirely meat-free diet. Red meat is a rich source of iron in the body, which plays a vital part in blood and building the muscles. It is also known to be rich in vitamin B, which has an important function in controlling energy production. For such reasons, some dieticians recommend that we take small quantities of beef, lamb, or pork about twice a week; small quantities of chicken once or twice a week; and fish on the remaining days. According to some studies, eating an excess of meat may make a person vulnerable to cancer.

Seafood is a very good substitute for red meat. It has the advantage of being low-fat. Besides the benefits of omega-3 fatty acids, seafood lowers the risk of cardiovascular diseases and prostate cancer. There is, however, one risk in fish. Oily fishes can contain high levels of toxins in their flesh. A high level of mercury is another matter of concern as regards to big and aged fish. Some fishes that contain high levels of mercury are mackerel, swordfish, shark, and tilefish. Even freshwater fish that are raised in farms, rivers, or lakes may be risky due to contaminated runoff water by environmental pollutants, industrial waste like dioxins and PCBs. Still, the benefit outweighs the risk. Even though expected mothers are scared of sea fish because of mercury, but they can take smaller sea fish instead. On the benefit side, one study published in the *Journal of Clinical Endocrinology & Metabolism* in 2018, finds that 92 percent of couples, both eat fish twice a week or more, get pregnant in 12 months' time compared with 79 percent among those who ate less. While the mechanism, for the most part, remains unclear, researchers hypothesized that seafood might help in semen quality, ovulation and other key factors. Omega-3 polyunsaturated fatty acids are mainly eicosapentaenoic acid (EPA) and docosahexaenoic acid (DHA). EPA and DHA and their metabolites aid in gene expression, do help in cerebral blood flow, oxidative stress, levels of neurotransmitters, and production of new neurons. DHA, in particular, is one essential building block of the brain's cell membranes. Doctors have long been advising their patients to eat more fish because it is so rich in omega-3 fatty acids. But, not omega-3 supplement. One analysis analyzed medical records from 10 randomized trials covering 77,917 people with average age 64, having cardiovascular disease or at high risk for it. Subjects were given a dose of omega-3 supplements ranged from 226 to 1,800 milligrams a day. (1 pennyweight is 0.055 ounce, or 1.555 gram, or 1555 milligram.) After the trial for average 4.4 years, researchers published their findings in JAMA Cardiology in 2018, claiming that there exists no association between the supplements and lowered risk of deaths from heart disease, nonfatal heart attacks or other major cardiovascular events. Omega-3 fatty acids are essential in controlling heart disease by lowering blood pressure, inflammation, and cell damage. Oily sea fish—such as salmon, tuna, mackerel, sardines, black cod, oysters, rainbow trout, halibut, and bluefish—have higher omega-3s. Research shows that women who eat five or more servings of fish per week have a 30% lower risk of developing heart failure than those who eat fish less than once a month. Another investigation analyzed twenty-six observational studies published from 2001 to 2014. It found that people who eat fish a lot have a 17% lower risk of depression compared to those who eat fish the least. So, add a fish menu to the diet. The benefits from omega-3 fatty acids help those who started out eating very few fish and increased the intake to about 400 mg daily, which is equivalent to consuming about two servings per week. This is what the latest dietary guidelines from the American Heart Association suggest. The only concern is how the fish is cooked. Fish baked or broiled is heart-healthy, but not the fried ones—especially deep-fried. Researchers have discovered that people who eat broiled or baked fish weekly have more gray matter in the part of the brain that controls memory, according to one study in 2014. Fried fish has no heart-protective effect. The act of deep-frying fish can cause healthy omega-3 fatty acids to turn into unhealthy oil in which the fish is fried. The woman who eats even one serving of fried fish a week exhibits 48% higher risk of heart failure compared to women who rarely or never ate fish (after adjusting women's overall diet and other medical histories).

Eat shellfish once or twice a week. Shrimp, lobster, crab, mussels, oysters and mollusks are healthy food for various reasons:

- Shellfish, like land animals, are high in protein, meaning they have all the essential amino acids.
- They, like any fatty fishes (salmon or maceral), are high in omega-3 (about 25 to 50% of fatty fish).

- They have a range of cholesterol levels, but much lower than that of land animals, like chicken, cow or pork. However, dietary cholesterol does not necessarily contribute to unhealthy levels of blood cholesterol.
- Shellfish have varying amounts of *hard-to-get* healthy minerals: (i) selenium—a trace mineral important for cognitive and immune function; (ii) zinc—for immune function, cell growth, wound healing, metabolism, appetite, and sperm concentration and total sperm count for men; (iii) copper and iron—trace minerals—needed for blood and for major body functions; (iii) vitamin B—that helps to support nerve structure and cell function.

On the downside, there are some potential contamination concerns. Shrimp, lobster and oysters can accumulate heavy metals, namely lead and cadmium. So, get shellfish from right sources, prefer wild caught than farm-raised. Eat once or twice a week.

Nuts and beans, although not so widely known, are a rich source of proteins, vitamins, and minerals. Among the vitamins, nuts and seeds have a high level of vitamin E. Vitamin E, per recent findings, reduces the risk of Alzheimer's disease considerably. Nuts have higher nutritional density. The oils contained in nuts and seeds are of the less harmful type, less in saturated fat. A seed (commonly available in fruits and vegetables) is the embryonic plant enclosed in a seed coat; a nut is a hard-shelled fruit that contains one seed. A seed has everything needed to grow a tree or plant. Taking more of nuts and seeds and correspondingly reducing the intake of meat may go a long way in reducing the risk of cardiovascular diseases. Daily, a fistful of almond, walnut, or cashew is suggested. Add seeds such as sesame, sunflower, and pumpkin to your diet. Beans make some people gassy, but that is not any reason to avoid them. Experts recommend three cups of legumes a week; they are so good for your health. Beans have a lot of fiber and are good for digestion. It can help regulate blood sugar and lowers cholesterol. It is a good source of iron and vitamin B. Eat plenty of kidney beans, lentils, chickpeas, and their brother beans; they are all low in fat and calories and are packed with fiber, protein, and minerals.

Grains like rice, wheat, and millet account for a larger part of the calories we consume. One important fact about the grains that we should bear in mind is that the more we grind, mill, and refine the grains, the more we reduce their nutrients. The whole grain contains the whole kernel, which has three layers: (1) the fiber-rich bran outer layer, (2) the endosperm middle layer, and (3) the germ, the grain's nutrient-dense embryo. These nutrients are the complex carbohydrates and vitamins E and B. So, a compromise between the nutritional value and digestibility is what is recommended. Dieticians are in favor of what they call the "cereal alternative," where whole grains are either cut into pieces or the kernels flattened by rollers. For many, cereals are almost an integral part of the morning breakfast.

Milk, yogurt, cheese, and other dairy products are rich in protein and calcium. Calcium is an essential element for bones and teeth; therefore, one cannot overemphasize the importance of milk or dairy products for growing children. It is good for adults as well, who become prone to osteoporosis as they grow older. But one has to add a note of caution. Milk and milk products are high in saturated fat, which is not good for the heart. The bone-strengthening power of milk has been claimed over and over again in medicals, in ads, pop culture, and around the dinner table. But one study in 2014 suggests that the huge claim may not be all true. High milk intake, the study finds, doesn't appear to protect against bone fracture but rather escalates it. Researchers—after surveying more than 100,000 people in Sweden on their dairy consumption habits over a period of eleven to twenty years—find that higher milk intake is associated with higher bone fracture, especially in women, and higher mortality rate in both men and women. One possible explanation they provide is that higher levels of the sugars lactose and galactose in milk may cause bones to undergo changes (similar to inflammations that resemble aging), leading to falls and fractures.

The benefits of fruits and vegetables can never be underestimated. The USDA recommendation is five servings of fruits and vegetables a day. The fruit juice may have all the benefits of the fruit, but it will have no fibers, which the raw fruit has. The seasonal items are rich in content that are particularly beneficial for the body in that season.

FRUIT AND VEGETABLE
AVAILABILITY CALENDAR
JAN
FEB
MAR
APR
MAY
JUNE
JULY
AUG
SEPT
OCT
NOV
DEC
APPLES
ASIAN PEARS
ASPARAGUS
BEETS
BLACKBERRIES
BLUEBERRIES
BROCCOLI
CABBAGE
CANTALOUPES
CUCUMBERS
EGGPLANT
GRAPES
GREEN BEANS
GREENS/SPINACH
HERBS
NECTARINES
ONIONS
PEACHES
PEPPERS
POTATOES
PUMPKINS
RASPBERRIES
SQUASH
STRAWBERRIES
SWEETCORN
SWEET POTATOES
TOMATOES
WATERMELONS

Seasonal Fruits and Vegetables Availability Guide

One may say it is Mother Nature's own way of protecting and nourishing her children. Therefore, we should not miss the seasonal varieties in fruits and vegetables. After all, our primates had once lived on a botanical diet, wholly on grains, roots, fruits, and vegetables. Piecing together a long dataset of 140 primate species, including chimpanzees, orangutans, and gibbons, researchers established a relationship between their eating habits (fruits and vegetables) with respect to the size of primate brains: fruit-eating primates (frugivores) tend to have bigger brains than leaf-eating primates (folivores).

Researches have been conducted on the nutritional content of the food we eat; and while several myths have been dispelled, several facts have also been highlighted. Thus, we have become more conscious of the nutritional content of our food intake. Also, new studies continue to bring various interesting outcomes previously unknown. A quick list of heart-healthy foods includes salmon, oatmeal, blueberries, dark chocolate, citrus fruits, soy, potatoes, tomatoes, nuts, legumes, extra-virgin olive oil, red wine, green tea, broccoli, spinach, coffee, flaxseeds, avocados, and pomegranates. Researchers have been identifying what may be hundreds or even thousands of natural chemicals in foods that seem to have powers to prevent disease. They are not just vitamins and minerals but a whole array of strange-sounding compounds (like phytochemicals)—one research superseding the previous.

Fats

Our hunter-gatherer ancestors essentially lived on hunts. Hunted animals were their primary source of food. They required plenty of fat—more than many other contemporary primates—because they not only had to survive during the periods of food scarcity, but also, at the same time, they had to provide enough energy for their large, expensive brains and enough provision for the evolutionary reproductive process.

Fat is a natural oily, greasy or waxy organic compound occur in plants (cooking oils, nuts, avocado, soy, chocolate, palm and coconuts) and in animal bodies deposited as a layer under the skin and around the organs. All fats are not created equal. There are many types of fats. All fats are not good, all fats are not bad. Fats belong to a wide range of organic compounds, which are usually soluble in organic solvents. Fats are largely insoluble in water solvent. Chemically, fats are fatty acids and triesters of glycerol (three-carbon trialcohol). Fats are either liquid, soft, semisolid, sold at room temperature depending on their composition and structure. Fats are categorized as good fat and bad fat. Current federal guidelines recommend no more than 35% of calories from fat.

For years, food authorities have been recommending low-fat dairy products over the full-fat versions, because: (a) they are higher in calories that increases body weight, and (b) *more importantly,* they are high in saturated fat that increases LDL cholesterol. But that's not totally true; current research is trying to modify that recommendation. In one study, called Women's Health Study, covering 18,438 women, researchers find that people who consume full-fat dairy products, lose weight by 8% or at least maintain weight, and are less likely to develop diabetes. Another study was by the Population Health Research Institute of Canada, that tracked 136,000 adults from 21 countries of five continents for over nine years, during which period approximately 10,500 people either died or had a major cardiovascular issue, such as a heart attack or stroke. The result, now published in *The Lancet* in 2018, adds to the body of evidence suggesting that, that standard advice to avoid fat or eat low-fat dairy products may be misguided, and therefore, they now encourage people eating dairy products of all kinds: (a) full-fat dairy may actually be healthier than its reputation suggests, (b) people who eat full-fat dairy two servings a day, are more likely to lower the risk of total mortality rates (3.4% versus 5.6%), cardiovascular mortality rates (0.9% versus 1.6%), major cardiovascular disease (3.5% versus 4.9%) and stroke (1.2% versus 2.9%), (c) it prevents the onset of Type-2 diabetes, and (d) it may even prevent gain weight.

The case against low-fat milk is stronger than ever; because, when people try to reduce fat they eat, they tend to replace it with sugar or carbohydrates, both of which are worse on insulin and diabetes. While some researchers claim that replacing saturated fat with monounsaturated and polyunsaturated fats, can lower total risk of death, others feel more neutral about saturated fat. One study analyzed nine papers covering 600,000 people and concludes that consuming butter, which contains saturated fat, is not linked to a higher risk for heart disease, rather be slightly protective against type 2 diabetes. Even better is the ghee, a variation of clarified butter that originated in India. Clarified butter is unsalted butter heated gently causing the milk solids to separate out giving it a higher smoke point and making it ideal for high cooking temperatures. One international team of scientists tracked 135,335 people between 35 and 70 years old in 18 countries for 7 years of their self-reported diet and mortality records. After controlling key factors including age, sex, smoking, physical activity and BMI, they report in *The Lancet* in 2017 that (a) people in the highest 20% bracket in total fat intake (average of 35% of calories from fat) have 23% reduced risk of death compared with the lowest 20% (average of 10% percent of calories from fat); (b) consumption of higher saturated fat, polyunsaturated fat and monounsaturated fat are all associated with lower mortality; and (c) higher fat diets are also associated with a lower risk of stroke. In another study published in *European Journal of Nutrition* in 2017, researchers from China and the Netherlands analyzed data from 15 observational studies covering more than 200,000 people over 10 years, and now recommend that eating cheese about an ounce every day may actually be good for health. Cheese contains potentially beneficial ingredients like calcium, protein and probiotics, and hard-to-get B12. For general understanding, there are 20 slices of American cheese per pound; each slice is 0.8 ounce (23 grams) and has about 100 calories, 69% from fat, 22% from protein and 8% from carbs. However, here are few facts on the different types of fats found in food, and their effects on lipid profile:

Saturated Fat: We all talk about the deleterious effects of saturated fat. For that, we should have some idea as to what are the items that contain saturated fat. Any fat or fatty product naturally available in liquid state at room temperature does not have saturated fat (e.g., cooking oil or oily products). Butter, on the other hand, which remains in a solid state in room temperature, has saturated fat. That is the reason why dieticians warn against the consumption of a high volume of butter, which tends to increase triglycerides and cholesterol in the blood. If you eat butter, eat it in the morning or by lunchtime. "Butter is gold in the morning," as the saying goes, "silver at noon, and lead in the night." The same applies to cheese as well.

A fat that occurs naturally in living organisms (plant or animal) contains varying proportions of saturated and unsaturated fat. Saturated fat is composed of triglycerides, having only saturated fatty acids, which do not have double bonds between the carbon atoms in the chain. They are thus fully saturated with hydrogen atoms—as the name implies—and thereby cannot incorporate additional hydrogen atoms. It is solid at room temperature. It is mainly found in products made from animal fat, such as whole milk, cheese, butter, red meat, and ice cream. It occurs also in chocolate, palm, and coconuts. Saturated fats are not heart-healthy because they raise the LDL (bad cholesterol). Saturated fat comes from foods from animals and some plants: hydrogenated oils (palm, coconut), dried coconut, nuts and seeds, rendered animal fats, dark chocolate, fish oil (menhaden and sardine), processed meats (sausage, hot dog), and whipped cream. [Trivia: However, very few of us know that only 20% cholesterol is from the food; the rest comes from and is removed by the liver. So, having a good liver is the key to keeping the cholesterol level low in the blood. If the liver is malfunctioning, even a controlled diet may not help in keeping the cholesterol level within the limit. Also, very few of us know that high-cholesterol foods not necessarily raise the bad cholesterol.

All the evidence available so far reveals that saturated fat, not the dietary cholesterol per se, is the major contributor to serum cholesterol (serum gives the number of triglycerides present in the blood, normal being less than 150). Foods high in cholesterol, like eggs, cheese, shellfish (shrimp, lobster, crab), sardine, or full-fat yogurt, can raise blood cholesterol levels, but the net effect is relatively modest and varies from person to person. The landmark Harvard study in 1965 shows that saturated fat exerts a greater effect on serum cholesterol than dietary cholesterol does. The 20-year Western Electric Study that appeared in the *British Medical Journal* in 1997, supports this conclusion. Subsequent other studies support this conclusion as well. Ultimately, the weight of evidence leads to the changes in the recommendations: in 2013, the American Heart Association states, "There is insufficient evidence to determine whether lowering dietary cholesterol reduces LDL-C, or "bad" cholesterol," and the Dietary Guidelines Advisory Committee, removes its previous recommendation to limit dietary cholesterol, and conclusively states, "cholesterol is not a nutrient of concern for overconsumption."]

Unsaturated Fat: Unsaturated fat is available in nuts, avocados, sunflower, corn, soybeans, and olives. They are liquid at room temperature. Its chemical structure has double bonds between the carbon atoms. A monounsaturated fat contains one double bond. A polyunsaturated fat contains more than one double bond. The lesser the hydrogen count per carbon, the more liquid it is—canola or sunflower seed oil. When more double bonds between carbon atoms are created, the common hydrogen atoms are eliminated. So, unsaturated fat with fewer carbon-hydrogen bonds is unsaturated with hydrogen atoms (hence the name), meaning that an unsaturated fat molecule can absorb one (mono) or many (poly) hydrogen atoms. Unsaturated fats get spoiled more easily than saturated fats. Food manufacturers heat up unsaturated oil (like sunflower seed oil), inject hydrogen into it under pressure, and make it more saturated (trans fat).

Monounsaturated Fats: Monounsaturated fats have the fatty-acid chain that has single double bond and has all other carbon atoms single-bonded. It is available in olives, olive oil, canola oil, sunflower oil, and various nuts, such as peanuts, cashews, and almonds. Monounsaturated fats are liquid at room temperature but turn solid when chilled. Monounsaturated and polyunsaturated fats have several beneficial effects when consumed in moderation. They are used to replace saturated fats and trans fats. Monounsaturated fats reduce bad cholesterol levels and, hence, reduce the risk of heart disease and stroke. They supply nutrients to build and maintain the body's cells. Monounsaturated fats are rich in vitamin E, which is essentially an antioxidant vitamin that most Americans need more of. Not only are these food sources a heart-healthy diet themselves, but the boost of monounsaturated fat from them does even more to benefit the heart by raising the levels of good cholesterol and lowering levels of bad cholesterol.

Polyunsaturated Fats: Polyunsaturated fats have fatty acid that has long carbon chains with many double bonds unsaturated with hydrogen atoms. In the molecular structure, it has two or more bonds capable of supporting pairs of hydrogen atoms not currently part of the structure. Typically, polyunsaturated fat is fluid at room temperature and remain fluid even when chilled. Like monounsaturated fat, this type reduces levels of bad cholesterol and increases good cholesterol. They provide essential fats that our body needs but cannot produce itself—such as omega-3 and omega-6.

Polyunsaturated fats are available in soybean oil, corn oil, and safflower oil, fatty fish, such as salmon, herring, mackerel and trout, and in nuts and seeds, such as walnuts and sunflower seeds. The American Heart Association tells that plant-based monounsaturated fats—like those found in vegetable oils, avocados, nuts and seeds—are associated with a lower risk of dying from heart disease and other causes. Omega-6s in nuts and seeds and vegetable oils, do benefit the heart. It has generally been recognized that omega-6 increases the inflammation, and omega-3 from the fats in fish oil, decreases it. While the long-term study suggests omega-6s can be good for the heart, high omega-6 intake may reverse the course and increases the risk for heart disease. One Finnish study tracking 2,480 men aged 42 to 60, for an average of 22 years, establish that overuse of animal-based monounsaturated fats—in meat, dairy and eggs—are associated with a higher risk for heart disease.

Trans Fat: Trans fat, also known as trans fatty acid, is one very unhealthy fat. It is artificially made through the chemical transformation process known as "hydrogenation of oils." During the process, hydrogen is injected to the boiling vegetable oils, resulting in the reconfiguration of fat molecules to create trans fat. Liquid transformed oil, after hydrogenation, solidifies and increases the shelf life. Additionally, it stabilizes the flavor of oils as well as the flavor of the foods that contain them. It helps vegetable oils suitable for deep-frying for hours together. Margarine is made in this way to produce a solid that you can spread. The oils subjected to hydrogenation create trans fats. Among the hazardous fast foods we eat, fries are prime in purveying trans fats. Trans fats inflict havoc in the body's ability to regulate cholesterol. One study finds that those eating more trans fats had (a) 34% higher rate of dying from any cause, (b) 28% higher risk of dying from heart disease, and (c) 21% higher risk of heart disease compared to those who eat less. On the contrary, saturated fat is not associated with a higher risk of early death, heart-related problems, stroke, or type 2 diabetes. In the hierarchy of fats, mono- and polyunsaturated fats, which are found in vegetables, are the good kinds. Saturated fat comes next. Trans fats are the worst kind. Trans fat raises the low-density lipoprotein (LDL), or "bad" cholesterol, and lowers the high-density lipoprotein (HDL), or "good" cholesterol—all increasing the risk for coronary heart disease and stroke.

Researchers find that 3.8% of the calorie intake from trans fat is sufficient to raise LDL. In a 2,000-calorie-a-day diet, that 3.8% translates to 76 cal. Considering 9 cal/g of fat, it is about 8 g of trans fat a day. An average french fry of 5 oz. contains roughly 3 g of trans fats, just to give you an idea. Trans fat has also been linked to a greater risk of developing type 2 diabetes. In the realm of dietary threats, trans fats rank very high. Trans fats are widespread in margarine, vegetable shortenings, cookies, crackers, snacks, and other foods. The American Heart Association recommends limiting the daily trans fat intake to less than 2 g. So, please take a closer look, read the fine print on the label. If you see ingredients referred to as "partially hydrogenated" or "shortening," you have found the trans fat. Avoid those. Instead, search for natural oils like olive, soybean, canola, and palm oils. Studies show that even though nutrition and food labels don't make much of a difference in what the typical consumer buys, for concerned consumers (with a food allergy), it makes a lot of difference. For them, besides fat content and calorie count, ingredient anxiety (what food contains—if it contains gluten, for example) is a very important issue.

Carbohydrates: Carbohydrates are starches, sugars, and fibers that the body uses for energy. Carbs have hydrophilic molecules, meaning that they soak water and make it more difficult for our body to release water from the kidneys through metabolism. When we eat particularly refined carbohydrates—which we normally do, like rice, pasta, white bread, and cookies—our bodies absorb them fast, and the hormone insulin escorts them into our cells fairly quickly. If we eat a lot of them, the body stores most of those calories instead of burning them, causing a weight gain on high-carb diets. That is why typical health-conscious Americans despised them, designing entire diets to cut them out. But carbohydrates are essential for the body—maybe not so much in the form of refined carbohydrates, but in the form of unrefined carbohydrates, a kind of carb called "resistant starch," assuring a way to help control weight. They occur naturally in foods and are also added. Resistant starches are named so because they resist digestion. After ingestion, they bypass the small intestine (where most foods are digested) and come to the large intestine to be metabolized. Whole grains, brown rice, legumes, beans, and unripe bananas have resistant starches. Also, if you cook starchy foods like white rice, pasta, or potato, and then cool it in the refrigerator, the food develops resistant starches; and then even if you heat them up again, they retain their new resistant starches. Whole-grain wheat may contain as high as 14% resistant starch, while milled wheat flour may contain only 2%. The estimated average intake of resistant starch intake in America ranges from 3–6 g/day, while in India and China, it is 10–15 g/day. Resistant starch is a healthy food for people with type 2 diabetes; it controls inflammation and lipid profiles. A combination of resistant starch with a hardboiled egg, pea protein, whey protein, chicken, or Greek yogurt is a good diet.

Protein: The notion "carb is enemy, protein is friend" is overblown. Health experts state that there is only a certain amount of protein the human body can digest at every meal, about 20 g to 40 g. An excess high-protein diet puts extra strain on the kidneys and can lead to kidney damage. Several large-scale studies have linked high-protein diets with an increased incidence of heart disease, cancer, blood pressure, and other health issues. According to the National Kidney Foundation, up to 1 in 3 Americans are at risk for kidney impairment. People need only enough protein in the diet because it supplies indispensable amino acids that our body cannot synthesize on its own. Amino acids are the essential building blocks needed to create and maintain our muscles, bones, skin, tissues, and an array of vital hormones and enzymes. An average adult can get the recommended intake (46 g of protein for women and 56 g for men) per day by eating standard meals containing moderate amounts of protein-rich foods, like dairy products, eggs, fish, meats, beans, or nuts. But according to an analysis of 2007–2010 by the National Health and Nutrition Examination Survey, American men consume much more, averaging nearly 100 g of protein a day. One study covering 170,000 people for 28 years found that people who consumed more plant proteins have a lower risk of dying than people who ate more animal protein. However, certain types of animal proteins—from fish and chicken—have a lower mortality rate than that from red and processed meat. For instance, eating 50 g of processed meat (meat preserved by smoking, curing, or salting, or addition of chemical preservatives, like in ham, bacon, sausages, hot dogs, and deli meats) every day can increase the risk of colorectal cancer by 18%. Another epidemiological study shows that cancer rates increase nearly 400% among those who get 20% or more of their daily calories from protein, compared to those who restrict their protein intake to 10% of their daily calories; and the risk of mortality jumps to 75% among the heavy protein eaters. The last nail in the coffin comes from the World Cancer Research Fund (WCRF) who in their 2018 Continuous Update Project (an ongoing effort to inform consumers about lifestyle habits), recommends cutting back, significantly or totally, on processed meats including hot dogs, sausages, salami, ham, bacon and turkey bacon, corned beef, pepperoni, smoked turkey, bologna and other luncheon and deli meats, biltong or beef jerky, canned meat and meat-based preparations, as these products are associated with an increased risk of colorectal cancer. According to the American Meat Institute, processed meats are often cured with sodium nitrite that fights with bacteria and gives the meat a pink color and a distinct taste. Sodium nitrite can damage cells and morph into molecules that cause cancer. According to the American Institute for Cancer Research, a 15 gram a day (which, for example, is a single slice of ham on a sandwich), can increase a 4 percent increase in the risk of cancer. So, eating a more traditional serving of 50 grams of processed meat a day would increase the risk of colorectal cancer by 18 percent, according to one review in 2011. By comparison, the risk is equivalent to 100 grams of unprocessed red meat a day.

Fat—along with proteins and carbohydrates—is a macro-nutrient. It supplies energy and transports nutrients. Of the two types of fat, as it is well known, saturated fat is more harmful than unsaturated fat. Of all the cooking oils, olive oil is known to have the least saturated fat. Coconut oil (coconut is not a nut), extracted from the carnal, is mostly saturated fat, and its beneficial claims, including weight loss, better metabolism and improved cholesterol, is controversial. One tablespoon of coconut oil has six times of saturated fat that of olive oil, which nearly meets the daily limit of 13 grams that the American Heart Association recommends. The plus point of saturated fatty acid in coconut oil is lauric acid, which increases HDL, or "good," cholesterol; but with it, it raises the LDL cholesterol as well. Proponents of coconut oil argue that it is rich in phytochemicals that have healthful antioxidant properties. While it is true that extra-virgin coconut oil, like extra-virgin olive oil, contains phytochemicals, but most of the cooking coconut oils available in the market are refined and therefore, provides far less antioxidants, and that even if you use extra-virgin coconut oil, the harmful effects of saturated fat outweigh the beneficial effects of the antioxidants. While there's hardly any data to support the consumer's hype, there's hardly any independent study to claim the benefits, either. So, if you want to use coconut oil for cooking, make sure you use virgin type, and of course, in moderation. However, coconut oil is beneficial for external use, on the body, as a moisturizer for skin or hair. Between the two, olive oil is a better choice for overall health. (However, to impart flavor, coconut milk is delicious and healthy in many Indian curry dishes. Green coconut water has therapeutic value: one serving of 200 ml of coconut water (7 fl. oz. 95% water, 4% carbohydrates, 1% protein and fat), has 40 calories.) Better quality 'extra-virgin cold-pressed olive oil' brings its taste and flavor, and health benefits to foods. Verities of recipe suggest that not just for last-minute dressing, but good for low-heat frying and other low-heat food preparations. Choose extra-virgin olive oil. Extra virgin olive oil (sometimes cold pressed) is the purest form of olive oil that contains the most health supportive oleic acid which is not only good for tasty salad dressing but also good for other food preparation. Prefer olive oil that is available in a dark-colored glass bottle or in a tin container. Keep them in a cool place, away from sunlight. Unless you use it fairly quickly, it's better to buy in smaller quantities. In consideration of which oil is right for you, depends largely on the type of cooking. One important point to consider is oil's smoke point. Smoke point is the temperature when oil starts burning and smoking. If your cooking gets overheated, temperature past its smoke point, it not only degrades the flavor, but depletes the nutrients in the oil—and also, the oil converts into harmful compounds called free radicals. Olive oil has a lower smoke point (around 410°F) than other types of olive oil—so, never deep fry. [Info: Plenty of studies support that extra virgin olive oil (EVOO) may help reduce the risk of stroke, heart disease, type 2 diabetes and osteoporosis. Investigative reports in 2016, concludes that as much as 80% of the olive oil sold as EVOO in the United States is not truly extra-virgin.]

Canola oil is inexpensive and neutral in flavor; also, it is very good for high-heat deep-frying and a good source of omega-3s. As heat obliterates the flavors of most cooking oils, it is effective and economical to fry with inexpensive refined oils (canola, soy, peanut, sesame) and then give the cooking a finishing touch with fresh green olive oil. Unlike other seed oils, olive oils are pressed—sometimes cold-pressed—from fresh fruits (much like fruit juice); so, their out-of-bottle flavors can vary widely, from pungent to smooth. These unrefined oils are more heat-sensitive than refined oils. Do not deep-fry with extra-virgin cold-pressed olive oil. Oil molecules start breaking down, develop unpleasant flavors, and give off smoke at lower temperatures between 375°F and 390°F, compared to 475°F and higher for refined oils. A fully hot oven is 400°F–450°F.

The food carcinogens are heterocyclic amines (HCA). They are compounds characteristically formed in the meat that has been cooked at high temperatures, like fried or grilled. One prevailing theory is that the iron in meat works as a catalyst that turns nitrites from meat preservatives into a particular kind of carcinogen in the body. Diets containing high HCAs from such meat sources increase the risk of stomach, breast, and colon cancers. The increased risk is real and substantial. Studies reveal that people who eat one serving of red meat (beef, lamb, or pork) daily have a 13% increased risk of mortality, compared to those who eat less. Processed meat can raise the risk even higher, as much as 20%; and for those who eat 50 g every day, it can increase the risk of colorectal cancer as much as 18%. Researchers measured HCA levels in eight popular ready-to-eat meat products: (1) beef hot dogs, (2) beef-pork-turkey hot dogs, (3) deli roast beef, (4) deli ham, (5) deli turkey, (6) fully cooked bacon, (7) pepperoni, and (8) rotisserie chicken. They found HCA in the top two: rotisserie chicken meat (1.9 ng/g) and cooked bacon (1.1 ng/g). [A nanogram (ng) = one billionth (10^-9) of a gram.] One popular ready-made food is the hot dog. From Memorial Day to Labor Day (100 days), Americans eat seven billion hot dogs, which accounts for over twenty per person on average. Hot dogs, bacon, pepperoni, and similar popular meat items are kind of tasty treats. Treat them as treats—once-in-a-while items. Eat your way, treat your way!

After analyzing the reviews of eight hundred studies on foods causing cancer by the International Agency for Research on Cancer (IARC), WHO declares in October 2015 that processed meat causes cancer and red meat "probably" does so. It does not call for prohibitions on meats, however, but considers carcinogenic items and urges caution in deciding what meats you eat and how often. Processed meat refers to those as meat products "transformed through salting, fermentation, curing, smoking, or other processes to enhance flavor or improve preservation." It includes hot dogs, corned beef, beef jerky, sausages, ham, canned meat, meat-based preparations, and sauces. Red meats are defined as mammalian muscle meats that include beef, pork, veal, lamb, mutton, goat, and horse. All it means is that it is better to choose fish, poultry, eggs, and beans as options. While on the subject, scientists also warn that french fries increase the risk of cancer. In 2017, the U.K. Food Standards Agency (FSA) found that when starchy foods (like french fries) are deep-fried at high temperatures, it produces acrylamide, a substance linked to cancer in animals.

There are two types of fatty acids—the omega-3 and omega-6—that are essential for the body. Essential fatty acids, as the name implies, are essential for the human body to function properly. Yet the human body does not produce them. Cold-water fish, fish oil, flaxseed oil, and canola oil have omega-3 fatty acids; evening primrose oil and black currant seed oil have omega-6 fatty acids. Average American diets have an excess of omega-6 but less of omega-3. Consumption of foods having omega-3 oils is recommended to help reduce the risk of cancer and cardiovascular diseases and to avoid rheumatoid arthritis, premenstrual syndrome, dermatitis, and inflammatory bowel disease. Here are a few conditions that arise from high-fat foods.

Obesity: High fat consumption leads to excess caloric and fat intake, which increase body fat.

Coronary artery disease: Saturated fats are the major source of coronary artery disease.

Diabetes: Overweight and obese people are more likely to develop diabetic conditions or worsen the existing ones due to decreased insulin sensitivity.

Breast cancer: A high fat consumption is linked to an increased risk of breast cancer.

Of all food items, fat has the maximum caloric density; it has about 8 to 9 cal per gram. Compared to this, protein (the next highest density) has half—only 4 to 5 cal per gram. We get the major portion of the fat in our diet from meat and dairy products.

No more than 30% of daily calories should come from the fat. Here is one illustration with an example. One adult male normally eats about 2,000 cal each day; then 30% is 600 cal. There are 9 cal in a gram of fat. So, eat no more than 600/9 = 67 g (or 67/28.34 = 2.36 oz.) of fat each day. For reference, whole milk 8 oz. (about 0.236 L or 247 g) has approximately 0.279 oz. (7.93 g) of fat.

Fiber

Fiber is the material that gives plants texture, shape, and support. It is typically the cell walls of plants. In the diet, fiber is mostly indigestible and moves through the digestive tract without being broken down by enzymes. Although fiber is generally made up of carbohydrates, it does not have much of the calories. It adds to the bulk of the stool and ensures smooth flushing of the body's refuse. Dietary fiber is available aplenty in plant foods, such as whole grains, fruits, vegetables, legumes, and nuts. There are two types of fiber: soluble and insoluble. Soluble fiber is soluble in water and gets a gel-like soft texture in the intestines. It is available in vegetables and fruits, oatmeal, oat bran, rye flour, and dried beans. Insoluble fiber—having high amounts of cellulose—is not soluble in water. It passes effectively unchanged through the intestines. It is available in the skin of the vegetables, the bran of grains, the skin and pulp of fruit, and foods from roots, stems, bark, and leaves. Food contains both soluble fiber and insoluble fiber in varying proportion. When fruits and vegetables are processed through the juicer, the soluble fiber stays soluble but the insoluble fibers discarded into smithereens. Therefore, lesser the insoluble fiber, lesser the fiber scaffolding that latticework needs to generate the gel inside of the intestine. One can actually see real time through electron microscopy that the gel is forming inside the intestine. So, lesser the processed the fruits and vegetables are, the better effective they are. Experts from the American College of Cardiology scrutinized several nutrition-hyped foods—including juice—and comment that "whole food consumption is preferred" over a liquid diet. Because, the juice is missing an important component of dietary fiber without which it is essentially water and natural sugar. As a matter of fact, juice may even contribute to gain weight due to extra sugar. Smoothies may be better than juices. A green smoothie that includes dark leafy greens, like spinach, kale, peas and Swiss chard, is even better that provides calories, fiber, calcium and vitamins A, C and K, along with other powerful phytochemicals. Smoothies don't involve chewing; so, in drinking smoothie quickly, one may feel a little bloated.

In general, most fibers have two shared characteristics. (1) It gets partially digested in the stomach and intestines, and (2) they have less calories. Each type of fiber has its own textures (feel, roughness, smoothness) and specific health benefits. Insoluble fibers add bulk to the stool and quicken the transit through the digestive system. Thus, insoluble fibers are useful to relieve constipation, to treat diarrhea, and to prevent colon cancer. Soluble fiber, on the other hand, is useful to slow down the rise of blood sugar levels for diabetes and to lower the cholesterol level. One main component of soluble fiber is beta-glucan, which has proven effective in lowering blood cholesterol. Beta-glucan is a spongy soluble fiber that neutralizes the chemicals that lead to the formation of cholesterol in the intestines. It absorbs—many times its own weight—those chemicals and whisks them out of the body. Thus, it prevents cholesterol from recirculation and thereby prevents reabsorption into the bloodstream.

Fiber-rich foods, such as unrefined whole grains, seeds, fruits and vegetables, reduce the risk of diabetes, heart disease and arthritis. As a matter of fact, overall, eating more fibers reduces mortality rate, whatever may be the cause. Fiber's role in human health is not direct. Instead, fiber feeds billions of bacteria in our guts and keep them healthy; and in turn, gut bacteria keep our intestines and immune systems healthy. The enzyme breaks down food molecules. Our body produces only limited number of enzymes; they cannot break down many of the tough compounds in plants, leaving them indigestible molecules. The term "dietary fiber" essentially refers to those indigestible molecules. Gut bacteria carry special enzymes needed to break down them in the form of short-chain fatty acids. Some of these fatty acids are absorbed by intestinal cells, where it is used as fuel and the rest is passed into the bloodstream where it travels to other organs and then act as signals to quiet down the immune system. Gut bacteria also release bacteria-killing molecules and send chemical signals that intestinal cells rely on to coordinate the digestion process, and to maintain a peaceful coexistence with human immune system. A low-fiber diet cannot do all that, and thereof cause a low-level inflammation in the gut, and throughout the body. So, eat more green vegetables, fruits, roots, nuts and whole grains.

Sources of fiber are cellulose in plants; foods from roots, stems, bark, and leaves; the bran of cereal grains; oats; the cell wall of baker's yeast; and certain fungi and mushrooms. Psyllium-based fiber products and a healthy diet rich in high-fiber plant foods prevent cancers. (Some high-fiber brand names: Organic Clear Fiber is a clear-mixing natural fiber supplement made from acacia fiber. Metamucil is a fiber supplement made from psyllium seed husks. Isabgol is a natural vegetable product of psyllium husk, which is the upper coating of *Plantago ovata* (Isabgol), purified by sieving and winnowing. Psyllium and ispaghula are commonly used for several members of plant genus *Plantago*.) Researches that have been carried out since the seventies have confirmed the fact that a diet rich in fruits and vegetables lowers the risks and prevents or treats the following health conditions:

Cholesterol: Controls cholesterol levels.

Constipation: A high-fiber diet is recommended as a nondrug treatment for constipation.

Hemorrhoids: Bulkiness and softness in the stool relieve painful hemorrhoid symptoms.

Diabetes: Soluble fiber controls diabetes by slowing down the rise of blood sugar levels.

Obesity: High-fiber food helps the stomach feel full faster, which results in less calorie intake.

Cancer: Insoluble fiber adds to bulk, softens the stool, and quickens its movement through the gastrointestinal tract. The faster it travels, the lesser time there is for potential cancer-causing substances to damage the lining. It prevents the buildup of toxic chemicals that cause cancer in the colon. In general, fiber reduces fat absorption in the digestive tract and thereby indirectly helps to prevent other cancers as well (like breast cancer).

Here are few familiar foods that food scientists say can do a world of good:

Nuts

For many years, the nut was getting the beatings of nutritionists for its supposedly high fat content. It never found a place in the nutritionists' lists. But opinions have steadily veered in the other direction after researches revealed some of the hitherto unknown facts about the nuts. Not all nuts, but some of those like walnuts, almonds, cashews, Brazil nuts, hazelnuts, pecans, and pistachios are now among the favored items in the list. Being rich in vitamins, minerals, and antioxidants, their nutritional values are not questioned anymore. They have the potential to promote heart health. Studies have found that women who ate at least 142 g (about 5 oz. [1 oz. = 28.35 g]) of nuts a week (one fistful a day) were 35% less likely to have a heart attack than those who ate less than 1 oz. (or 28 g) a month. Nuts have monounsaturated and polyunsaturated fats. They are the good fats. Walnuts and flaxseed have some types of polyunsaturated fats—namely, the alpha-linolenic acid that can improve people's response to stress. Many nuts contain a phytochemical called ellagic acid. Ellagic acid acts to trigger a process known as apoptosis, in which cancer cells kill themselves. Nuts contain vitamin E, an antioxidant that may help prevent heart disease and cancer. Nuts have magnesium, manganese, protein, fiber, zinc, and phosphorus. Simply eating nuts improves one's diet without making any weight gain. Fat and fiber give a satisfying and filling feeling and thus prevent overeating. People are less likely to overeat and more likely to control calories because they already feel full. The recommended portion or serving size of 1 oz. (28 g) of cashews, pistachios, peanuts, or almonds have about 150 cal. Hazelnuts, walnuts, Brazil nuts, or pecans have a little more—about 180 cal. An ounce contains about 23 whole almonds, about 7 shelled or 14 half walnuts, or about 16 to 18 cashews. However, with each ounce providing about 150 cal, one has to be careful about eating them—by the fistful, not by the bowlful. The FDA recommendation suggests up to 1.5 oz. of nuts daily or one and a half "handful"—i.e., 35 shelled whole almonds or 20 whole walnuts. Pistachios have beta carotene, phosphorus, potassium, magnesium, vitamin B6, thiamine, and fiber. Compared to other nuts, they are high in carotenoids, a type of antioxidant that helps reduce the risk of chronic disease and improves heart health. One serving, which is one ounce, contains about 50 pistachios. Because nuts have plenty of nutrients, proteins, vitamins, fibers, healthy monounsaturated fats, and antioxidants, nuts deserve an honored place in the food plate. Stick to only the raw, unsalted variety. Try at least one fistful a day!

Tomatoes

In the United States, tomatoes are the second most commonly consumed vegetable, accounting for 18% of all vegetables (after potatoes at 21%). Studies consistently show that the more tomatoes and tomato products people eat, the lower the risk of many types of cancer. Tomatoes are full of lycopene, which is an antioxidant that protects cells from oxygen damage. It helps to fight cancers like breast, lung, prostate, colorectal, and pancreatic cancer; and it prevents heart diseases. As the tomato is high in potassium and, at the same time, very low in sodium, it helps to combat high blood pressure and fluid retention.

Tomatoes—if eaten with a little fat, say a sprinkle of olive oil—would more likely be absorbed (all its nutrients) into the body. Tomatoes that are chopped and cooked with oil allow the lycopene to be more readily available to combine with the good fats to be absorbed into the body. In one study, ten healthy women were fed a diet containing 2 oz. of tomato puree a day for three weeks, either preceded by or followed by a tomato-free diet for another three weeks. The researchers measured the difference in blood levels of lycopene and thereby evaluated oxidative damage to cells before and after each phase. They noticed that cell damage had dropped by 33% to 42% after consuming the tomato diet. Tomatoes are rich in vitamin K, which is good for the bones. Dark red organic tomatoes contain up to three times the lycopene of the regular brands. They should be smooth without wrinkles or bruises. Store them at room temperature; they smell pleasing when ready. Tomatoes—when cooked with broccoli—give a double dose of nutrients that protect against prostate cancer. Green tea is also a good partner in the fight against prostate cancer. Drinking tomato juice also helps with stopping blood clots. One serving of tomato juice per day takes care of this. Tomato juice is also an anti-inflammatory and is recommended to smokers and to those who are not active for long periods at a time—say, while flying. It is especially good for people with type 2 diabetes.

Spinach

Spinach is a green flowering plant consumed green or cooked. It is native to Asia. It has been cultivated since the seventh century in China, which remains the largest producer of spinach. The U.S. comes next. It is a seasonal plant in winter; it grows on soil up to ten to twelve inches in height. Spinach is a rich source of iron. Weight-wise, it has a relatively high level of iron when compared with other vegetables and some meat sources: a 170 g serving of boiled spinach has 6 mg of iron, compared to a 6 oz. (170 g) ground hamburger patty, which contains, at most, 4.4 mg of iron. Spinach has folate, a vitamin B that is so beneficial that it is now routinely added to flour. For expected mothers, folate inhibits neural-tube defects in babies. Spinach lowers blood homocysteine, an amino acid that irritates blood vessels and is associated with heart disease. Spinach is also rich in another valuable compound, known as lutein. Lutein helps to slow down the natural degeneration process.

Broccoli

Though it more closely resembles the cauliflower, broccoli belongs to the cabbage family. There are three commonly grown types of broccoli. (1) Sprouting broccoli has a greater number of heads with thin stalks. It is very popular in the U.K. and is sometimes called "calabrese." In the U.S., it is simply "broccoli." (2) Romanesco broccoli is yellow-green in color. (3) Purple cauliflower found in southern Italy, Spain, and the U.K. is another type.

Broccoli is low in saturated fat and cholesterol. It has protein, iron, calcium, magnesium, potassium, manganese, and phosphorus. It is a very good source for dietary fiber, vitamin A, vitamin B6, vitamin C (1 cup contains more C than an orange), vitamin E, vitamin K, and folate. Broccoli contains phytochemicals, including anticancer substances like sulforaphane and indole-3-carbinol (I3C). I3C is produced by enzymatic hydrolysis (breakdown) of the glucosinolate glucobrassicin, which is found aplenty in cruciferous vegetables, such as broccoli, cabbage, cauliflower, brussels sprouts, collard greens, and kale. It aids to control the estrogen associated with breast cancer into a more benign form. These I3C chemical compounds detoxify cancer-causing substances before they get a chance to cause harm. Consumption of cruciferous vegetables regularly reduces the risk of breast, colon, and stomach cancers. Broccoli has a lot of beta-carotene. The best way to get most nutrients to your body is to cook light and to chew hard. One study recommends that eating tomatoes and broccoli together offers better protection against cancer than eating either vegetable alone.

Mushroom

Mushroom is a fleshy, spore-bearing fruiting body of a fungus. It is grown above ground on soil or on its food source. Mushrooms have a stem, a cap and gills. The gills produce microscopic spores which help the fungus spread across its occupant surface. Mushrooms are a "powerhouse of nutrition." Not being a green or brilliant color of typical vegetables, and mostly being white, consumers should not avoid on the pretext of white food. They are low in calories and fat, and are cholesterol-free. They contain a fair amount of fiber and over a dozen of minerals like potassium, magnesium, copper, zinc and a number of B vitamins such as folate. They are very high in antioxidants like selenium and glutathione, which are known to protect cells from damage and reduce chronic disease and inflammation.

Salad and Salad Dressing

The salad is a botanical diet. Fat-free, low-fat, and oil-based salad dressings are mixed with salads for taste and health benefits. Food researchers, by analyzing the blood samples of the participants, found that (a) those who had eaten salads with low-fat or fat-free dressings did not absorb the beneficial carotenoids from the salad, but (b) those who had salads with an oil-based dressing did get the carotenoids. Other ways to help maximize the absorption of the carotenoid nutrients is by chopping or grating, which breaks down the plant material—the finer the chopped size (and sharper the knife), the better the absorption of beta-carotene. Eating a salad containing a lot of raw vegetables has considerable health benefits, not just for the nutrients but also for the high fiber content. Classically, a salad dressing is mixed to make the salad more palatable. But most of the dressings are high in sugar and salt, which only aggravate heart problems and diabetes. Even very "light" salad dressings are too much on sugar and salt and too little on nutrition. So, a wise choice is a simple one: oil-and-vinegar dressing, which—although packed with calories—contains various heart-healthy monounsaturated fatty acids and no saturated fat. Salad-bar dressings and fixings can be a junk-filled vegetarian nightmare unless one is careful.

Oats

The common oat is a cereal grain, grown for its seed. Oats are good for consumption as oatmeal. Oatmeal is the product of ground oat groats. (Groats, in general, are the dried outer covers of various cereals, such as oats, wheat, barley, or buckwheat.) Oat bran is the outer husk of the oat grain. Sometimes, the bran of the grain is discarded during the milling process—which is unwise; since, it contains the bulk of the dietary fiber of the grain, along with wholesome vitamin B and E, and useful source of minerals, such as magnesium. Oats are sold in the form of steel-cut, rolled, quick-cooking and instant type. Steel-cut oats are groats that are cut into small pieces. Rolled oats are groats that are steamed and rolled flat. Quick-cooking and instant oats are also rolled oats that are further flattened, steamed or precooked to cut down on preparation time. All types of oatmeal are considered whole grains, and are more or less equal in terms of their basic nutritional ingredients. Only concern is high sugar content in some instant oatmeal. Oatmeal and oat bran are important sources of dietary fiber.

One cup (1½ oz. to 3 oz.) of oats, raw in granola or cooked in porridge, consumed daily, can help to lower cholesterol. The dietary fiber is a measure of a mixture of about half soluble and half insoluble fibers. Fiber is oatmeal's main health characteristic. Also, unlike wheat and most other grains, oats contain large amounts of a specific type of fiber, called beta-glucan, which is consistently linked to healthier cholesterol scores and a reduced risk for diabetes and cardiovascular disease. Along with high fiber content, oats have many phytochemicals and antioxidants, which can help to prevent inflammations related to chronic diseases.

One key compound of the soluble fiber found in oats is beta-glucan. Beta-glucan has proven effective in lowering blood cholesterol. It adds bulk to the stools, makes it heavier, and speeds its transit through the gut, relieving constipation. For hypertensive patients, oats can aid to lower blood pressure. A daily serving of whole oats reduces high blood pressure and thus reduces the need for antihypertensive medication. It is one of the few grains that contain some rare antioxidants, such as vitamin E—like the compounds called tocotrienols. The dietary fiber and protein in oats make us feel full fast. That keeps us away from more fattening foods and helps in controlling weight. Kids who eat oatmeal regularly are 50% less likely to become overweight when compared to those children that don't. Similar to other grains and vegetables, oats have a host of phytochemicals (plant chemicals), most of which are considered to reduce the risk of cancer.

Salmon

Salmon are spawned and born naturally in freshwater streams. They migrate to the sea and then return to fresh water to reproduce. This is due to the domestication of certain types of salmon. In the Alaska area, the crossing over to various streams allows the salmon to populate new streams, such as those that emerge during glacier retreats. Salmon is a tasty and very popular fish. Eating salmon is healthy because it is high in protein and vitamin D. A 4 oz. serving of wild salmon serves enough for a full day's requirement of vitamin D; it is one of the few foods that can make that claim. One serving has more than half of the necessary B12, selenium, and niacin. Salmon is the source of B6 and magnesium and an excellent source of omega-3 fatty acids. The reason is that the smaller fishes that salmon eat in turn eat algae, which contain a high degree of omega-3 fatty acids. Omega-3 helps to prevent platelets in the bloodstream from clumping together and sticking to the arterial walls in the form of plaque. They also flush out triglycerides and LDL (bad) cholesterol. Omega-3 blocks the production of inflammatory substances, which are associated with autoimmune diseases like lupus and rheumatoid arthritis. It is also, at times, used as a dietary supplement in a nutritional approach to treat mental disorders. The docosahexaenoic acids (DHA) available in the omega-3 is one main constituent of cell membranes in the brain. Dietary deficiencies of DHA—not quite uncommon in America—may be a factor in childhood autism, attention-deficit hyperactivity disorder (ADHD), depression, and bipolar disorder. Treating these conditions with supplements of omega-3 fatty acids is one growing area of mental-health research. Salmon flesh is naturally orange to red in color. The natural color results from its own carotenoid pigments. Farm-raised salmon are naturally white, but farmers add coloring chemical in the feed to turn it reddish-pink.

Garlic

Garlic is used around the globe to add its pungent flavor and taste to a wide variety of dishes or as seasonings and condiments. Garlic has been used both in foods and in medicines since the time of the Egyptian pyramids. It was used by the ancient Greeks and Romans. Depending on the type of cooking method and how much is used, garlic may either present a mellow or intense flavor. It is often paired with onion, tomato, or ginger. The garlic bulb may be eaten raw or cooked, while the green leaves (raw or cooked) may be chopped up and added to salads. What makes garlic breath smell so bad is precisely what imparts its nutritional value. The odor aspects are due to sulfur-based compounds known as allyl sulfides. Garlic is a source of manganese and vitamin B1, B6, and C. It has protein as well as other minerals, like phosphorous, selenium, calcium, potassium, copper, and iron. Garlic contains allicin, which experts believe has antibiotic and bactericidal effects. Alliin is a sulfoxide compound that is a natural constituent of fresh garlic.

Garlic helps to boost cardiovascular activity. It has a soothing effect on the respiratory system. Health experts promote garlic as a cure-all, which may be a tall call, but many scientists agree that allyl sulfides and other phytochemicals in garlic do help protect the heart. This may be due to the fact that the sulfides can reduce cholesterol and make the blood less sticky. Garlic has antibacterial and antifungal powers. It aids to control blood sugar levels and thus prevents the complications of diabetes mellitus. Garlic was used as an antiseptic to prevent gangrene (body tissue dies [necrosis]—may occur after an injury or infection) during World War I and World War II. It is proven, from clinical trials, that a mouthwash containing 2.5% fresh garlic can aid to diminish antimicrobial activity. To make use of garlic's effective compounds, we need to smash or mince it. Raw garlic is more potent and effective; cooking garlic reduces its effect. If cooked for a long time or at high heat, its beneficial effects are lost. Side effects of garlic may include indigestion, halitosis (nonbacterial bad breath), nausea, emesis, and diarrhea.

Onion

The onion is one of the most common and oldest vegetables known to humans and is used in a large number of cuisines, recipes, and preparations spanning almost the totality of the world's food culture. The onion has a very distinctive pungent smell, and its taste fills up the flavors of almost every type of cuisine imaginable. Onion bulbs have multiple layers of dark, thick, papery skin with a higher percentage of solids and have flavors of varying intensity. They are a favorable choice for savory dishes that classically take a longer time to cook. They are widely used in the Indian subcontinent (called "pyaaz" in Hindi) and are fundamental to the native cuisine. The onion was first introduced in North America by Christopher Columbus during his 1492 expedition to Hispaniola. Typically, the onion is harvested annually, and its use can be separated into two categories: spring/summer (March through August) fresh onions and fall/winter (August through April) storage onions. Spring/summer fresh onions are available in red, yellow, and white. They can be marked by their thin light-colored skin. Because of higher water content, they are typically milder and sweeter than storage onions. Higher water content makes them susceptible to bruising and rot. Due to its delicate taste, the fresh onion is an ideal ingredient for salads, sandwiches, and lightly cooked dishes. Fall/winter storage onions are available in yellow, red, and white.

Onions have vitamin C. It is very rich in chromium, which is needed as a trace mineral in the human body. It helps cells respond to insulin. Similar to garlic, regular consumption of onions aids to lower cholesterol level and blood pressure, both of which, in turn, help prevent atherosclerosis and diabetes, heart disease, and stroke. These beneficial effects primarily come from the onion's sulfur compounds, chromium and vitamin B6. The casual consumption of onions (two to three times a week) is associated with a significantly reduced risk of developing colon cancer. Onions have a large number of flavonoids, and the most notable is quercetin. Quercetin aids to halt the growth of tumors and to protect colon cells from the damaging effects of cancer-causing substances. Cooking fish and meat with onions at a moderately high heat may help reduce the amount of carcinogens produced. Strong-flavored raw onions may give smelly breath when eaten fresh, but they hold great potential for fighting cancer with their high antioxidant activity.

Onions destroy osteoclasts (multinucleate bone cells that absorb bone tissue) so that they do not break down bone; and that is why the onion is very good, especially for women who are generally at increased risk for osteoporosis during and after menopause. While it is unknown, for the most part, as to how many daily servings of onions one has to eat to maximize protection against cancer, it is generally suggested that health-conscious people might well go for as much as possible—and choose the stronger-flavored onions rather than the mild ones. Making the onion and garlic a staple in one's diet may greatly lower the risk of several common cancers.

Apples

The apple is almost a symbol of good health. In Greek mythology, the apple is associated with the healing power of the god Apollo. Thanks to the then renowned physicians Hippocrates and Galen for promoting the ritual of serving fresh fruit (particularly apples) at the end of a meal because of the favorable effects of apples in digestion. Apollo is perhaps the source of the name and of the age-old saying "an apple a day keeps the doctor away." An apple a day may not keep the doctor at bay, but it is an excellent idea for good health. In fact, one apple a day is one basic defense for good health. In medieval times, doctors were taught that cooked apples could relieve bowel disorders and protect the lungs and nervous system. The apple is a source of both soluble and insoluble fibers. Pectin (typically present in ripe fruits) as soluble fiber benefits to prevent cholesterol buildup in the lining of the blood vessels, thus reducing the risk of atherosclerosis and heart disease. Insoluble fiber adds bulk to the stool in the intestinal tract, holding water to cleanse and move ingested food quickly through the digestive tract. Apples have antioxidants. Natural antioxidants are more effective than vitamin supplements. To get the most benefit, do not peel the skin off; almost half of the vitamin C content is just underneath the skin. Eating apples with skin increases insoluble dietary fiber content. Apple skin is packed with polyphenols, an antioxidant that prevents cellular damage from free radicals. [Info: When an apple is cut into pieces and is exposed to the oxygen in the air, it oxidizes polyphenols to form polyphenol oxidase (PPO) in color brown. Enzymatic browning happens to pears, bananas, and eggplants fairly quickly when cut.] In a study, 160 women were randomly asked to eat about 2.7 oz. (75 g) of dried apples or dried plums daily. After a year, the study found that the women who ate the dried apples had (1) lowered total cholesterol by 14%—lowered LDL (or "bad") by 23% and increased HDL (or "good") by 4%—and (2) decreased C-reactive protein by 32%. All these are good indicators of heart health and reduced inflammation. The Red Delicious apple is a wise selection of all the varieties.

One apple a day keeps the stroke at bay. White-fleshed fruits like apples, bananas, pears, and honeydew are very good for a significant decrease in stroke risk. A ten-year study tracked intake of fruits and vegetables grouped by the color of more than 20,000 men and women aged 20 to 65 who were healthy and free of cardiovascular disease at the start. The colors were green (broccoli, kale, spinach, and other leafy greens), orange/yellow (citrus fruits, carrots, peaches), and red/purple (tomatoes, beets, cherries), and white (apples [including applesauce], bananas, pears, cauliflower, cucumbers, chicory). The study noticed that overall, the white category was widely consumed of all the color groups, accounting for 36%. The most common fruits and food items of the group were apples, pears, and applesauce. In a decade-long period, the study logged a total of 233 strokes that people suffered. When the rate of stroke was matched to the color of the diet, researchers found no extra benefit with the amount of brightly colored fruits and vegetables they ate. This was quite of a surprise considering the fact that the phytochemicals that lend these foods their color have so long been associated with a lower risk of cancer and good heart health.

Oranges

The orange is probably the largest citrus crop across the world and is well-known for its vitamin C content, especially for cold, cough, and influenza. Broadly, there are three varieties of oranges: (1) the sweet orange, (2) the sour orange, and (3) the mandarin orange, otherwise known as a tangerine. The United States is known to produce the sweet variety. A hundred grams of oranges contain 47 cal, 12 g of carbohydrates, 1 gram of protein, and absolutely zero fat. A hundred grams of oranges also contain 89% of the recommended dietary allowance (RDA) of vitamin C, 4% of vitamin A, 4% of calcium, and 1% of iron. Due to its high content of vitamin C, the orange helps to absorb calcium into the body and to maintain the health of teeth and bones. It also contains vitamin A and vitamin B. The orange is a good source of minerals, such as iron, sodium, calcium, copper, phosphorus, potassium, magnesium, and sulfur. For its admirable therapeutic values, the orange is good for cold, cough, influenza, constipation, bowel disorders, indigestion, dyspepsia, dental care, pyorrhea, bone health, heart diseases, respiratory problems, skin care, pimples, acne, fever, measles, typhoid, and tuberculosis (TB).

Oranges are full of bioflavonoids and carotenoids, which are well-known to fight off cancer. They also contain phytochemicals, which are very helpful for heart disease. As oranges are high in fiber and water content, it contributes to the fullness factor, which is a key strategy for any weight-loss program because it dampens craving (for smoking as well) and helps prevent overeating. Like oranges, other citrus fruits have similar benefits as well: (a) adds fiber for the diet; (b) has vitamin C to reduce the duration and severity of cold; (c) has potassium to counter-regulate the salt in your diet by helping the body to flush out sodium; (d) helps the body to absorb iron; (e) provides vitamin C, which plays a role in collagen production that keeps skin looking supple, smooth, and bright; and (f) is extremely diet-friendly for weight loss.

Berries

The blackberry, blueberry, cranberry, black raspberry, red raspberry, and strawberry have long been a part of any healthy diet due to their anthocyanin content. Anthocyanins give them vibrant bright colors and act as antioxidants to fight off any damage to the cells. Berries are a favorite for their sweet tart taste, their spicy aroma, and their unique color. They are a very good source of vitamins A, C, E, and beta-carotene—and for minerals like magnesium, potassium, and manganese. They are high in fibers and are low in cholesterol, saturated fat, and sodium. These fruits contain more antioxidants than many other fruits or vegetables. Antioxidants—especially polyphenols—protect from free-radical damage that cause heart disease and cancer. Preliminary research shows that polyphenols can break down fat or inhibit fat cells from forming adipose tissue in the body, assisting us in our weight management. The benefit of blueberries is that they, like cranberries, seem to fight off urinary tract infections by preventing *E. coli* bacteria from sticking to the bladder walls. Blueberries have the most powerful health-promoting compounds—namely, anthocyanins, phytochemicals that belong to the falconoid family. Anthocyanins boost brainpower. Blueberry juice improves memory; it aids to prevent or delay the onset of dementia or other age-related memory problems. For all these benefits, blueberries are called a superfood. Strawberries and blueberries can build up a healthy heart over a lifetime. Research confirms and quantifies that women who ate three or more servings of strawberries and blueberries per week reduced (by up to one-third) their risk of heart attack. The raspberry appears to be potential support to body fat reduction. Eating blueberries in a fair amount (one cup a day), or for a longer period of time, lowers blood pressure—the effect is compatible with blood pressure medicines.

Watermelons

A sweet, soft, juicy watermelon is not only a great treat on a long hot summer day as a delicious thirst-quencher, but it is also a deliberate quencher to quench the inflammation from conditions like rheumatoid arthritis, asthma, diabetes, and colon cancer. Watermelon is a heart-healthy fruit. Besides being naturally low in fat and cholesterol, it has important natural antioxidants and vitamins C and A, especially its concentration of beta-carotene. It has plenty of lycopene compared to any other fresh fruits and vegetables, even tomatoes. Lycopene lowers the risk of many different kinds of cancer, especially cancers of the prostate, lung, and stomach. Research on watermelon suggests it is helpful for cancers of the colon, rectum, breast, pancreas, esophagus, oral cavity, and cervix. Watermelon has one special ingredient called citrulline, an α-amino acid—which boosts production of a compound that helps relax the body's blood vessels and thus reduces muscle fatigue. Citrulline—found in the flesh and in the rind of watermelons—reacts with the body's enzymes and gets transformed into arginine, an amino acid that benefits the heart and the circulatory and the immune systems. Circulating citrulline concentration is one biomarker of intestinal functionality. Watermelon is cleansing, alkalinizing, and a diuretic (promotes the production of urine). It was used in homeopathy for the treatment of kidney patients before dialysis became widespread. Watermelon is rich in nutrients—including vitamins A, B, and C and potassium—but the most important ingredient is lycopene, the antioxidant pigment that gives the flesh its deep red color. It has cardiovascular benefits, reduces the risk of stroke, and slightly lowers blood pressure and perhaps plays a role in protecting against some cancers. Red-flesh watermelon has more lycopene than other varieties, and seedless ones have even more. Lycopene from watermelon is easily absorbed into the body. Since watermelon is sweet, people do worry about the amount of sugar in watermelon, but that's (experts say) a bit of a misconception, because the sugar content is natural sugar (not added sugar) and is lower than other fruits, gram for gram. For example, while a cup of diced watermelon has about 9 g of sugar, a medium banana has 15 g of sugar, and so does a cup of blueberries.

Potatoes

Worldwide, the potato is the fourth largest crop, following rice, wheat, and maize. It is one very common food in our daily menu. It is filled with iron; calcium; vitamins C, B1, B3, and B6; and plenty of carbohydrates. In theory, as the textbook claims, a diet of milk and potato can provide all the nutrients human body needs. The annual average consumption on a global scale is about 73 lb. of potatoes per person. It is also most commonly consumed in the United States. According to Agriculture Department statistics, Americans eat 115.6 pounds of white potatoes a year on average, of which two-thirds are in the form of french fries, potato chips and other frozen or processed potato products. Potato accounts for 21% of all vegetables (second is tomato at 18%) in U.S. China is now the world's largest producer of potatoes. Nearly one-third of the world's potatoes are produced in India and China. Freshly harvested potato, out of the ground, contains about 80% water and 20% dry matter. Almost 60 to 80% of the dry matter is starch. The protein content of potato on a dry-weight basis, is close to that of cereals and considered very high in comparison to other underground roots and tubers. The potato itself is low in fat, but it gets fatty when cooked with oils and fats. It has several micronutrients, especially vitamin C. A single medium-sized potato of 150 g (about 5¼ oz, 1 oz. is 28 g), eaten with its skin, provides nearly half the daily adult requirement. The potato contains dietary antioxidants; this plays a role in preventing diseases related to aging. It contains enough dietary fiber, which benefits health. With potatoes, a balanced diet needs to include other vegetables and whole-grain foods.

However, there is a flip side. Potato ranks near to the bottom of healthful vegetables and it lacks the compounds and nutrients found in green leafy vegetables. Additionally, in preparation, if you take a potato, remove its skin (where most nutrients are), cut it, deep fry it in the oil, and top it off with salt, cheese, chili or gravy, then that starch bomb can very quickly turn into a weapon of dietary destruction. According to some scientists, potatoes—eaten in large quantities by the people with sedentary habits, and especially who are overweight—may invite heart disease and diabetes. The reason, as identified by food scientists, is that as we eat potatoes, the starch and other complex molecules in the potato combine with the saliva, and get easily converted into sugar, which then rushes to the bloodstream instantly. As glucose floods the bloodstream, insulin released by the pancreas joins in. The chain reaction causes the triglycerides in the blood to shoot up and the good cholesterol (HDL) to fall. This is a congenial pre-condition for heart disease and diabetes. This is not just a potato problem. It is a generic and lifestyle problem with all white bread, pasta, bagels, and most white rice. However, these ill effects could be minimized by eating them in moderation.

Milk

The U.S. Department of Agriculture (USDA) recommends that anyone older than age 9 should consume three cups of dairy products, which includes milk, yogurt and cheese, a day. Whole milk has significant amount of fat. However, some nutritionists advise skim milk, 1%-fat or 2%-fat versions, instead; it provides the same calcium and vitamin D for the bones, but without the gain of fat that can increase risk of heart disease and diabetes. Consumption of milk is one myth. Milk is not as nutritious as one might think! If you observe the nature, you will find humans are the only animal that consume milk outside of the infant period. Dieticians believe there is no need for it; there is hardly any evidence outside of the childhood period that milk is necessary. In the United States, it's a part of the politics; the government got involved in promoting milk, dairy products and, ineffectively, the whole dairy industry. If you love, of course, you eat but not necessary. However, recently, the consumption of alternative milks—the plant-based beverages made from almonds, walnuts, cashews, quinoa, peas, coconut, oats and soy (made through maceration and sometimes fermentation)—have risen rapidly, partly replacing conventional cow's milk. Even though the food label word "milk" confuses many consumers, these plant-based beverages have nutritional value similar to conventional milks, including cow's milk.

Cheese

The concept that "cheese is a healthy food" will come as a surprise to many, especially to dieters. Cheese has an ill reputation as fatty and sodium-high: an ounce (about a slice) of cheddar cheese has 9 g of fat and 180 mg of sodium. The magic lies in the cheese—in its other components and ingredients that are far more important than saturated fat and sodium combined. Food experts pinpoint some of its nutritional perks:

- Cheese is high in protein, bone-building calcium, and hard-to-get vitamin B12 that helps red blood cells for neurological functions.
- Cheese is not bad for the heart but rather beneficial. According to the 2016 report published in the *Journal of the American Heart Association*, eating an ounce of cheese daily is associated with 3% lower risk of stroke. Other research finds eating cheese moderately lowers levels of bad LDL cholesterol compared to butter, and it aids toward longer life.
- Cheese does not increase the risk of high blood pressure. As salty as it is, cheese is not linked to hypertension.
- Cheese is full of good bacteria. Eating moderately favorably changes the microbiota in the gut, which in turn improves metabolism.
- Cheese contains one wonderful fatty acid called palmitoleate, which neutralizes the damage caused by the saturated fatty acids and acts like insulin by getting excess sugar out of the blood. It helps protect against excessive lipids and type 2 diabetes.

Fish

Sea water fish (such as tuna, mackerel, salmon, herring, and sardine) and fresh water fish in lakes and rivers (catfish, tilapia, carp-fish), twice a week, are good for health. Other seafoods like shrimps, crabs, lobsters, and scallops should be taken in limited quantities, once a week. However, there are certain risks involved in consuming aged fish; because, it may contain certain toxins and mercury. But the benefits of eating fish in limited quantities seem to outweigh the possible harmful effects. The plant fruits and vegetables cannot provide as much iron, calcium, and vitamin B12 required by the body, that meat and fish can provide. Oily sea fish (such as salmon, tuna, sardines, mackerel, black cod, oysters, rainbow trout, halibut, and bluefish) have higher omega-3 fatty acids, which are good for heart. Make it a food habit getting protein from fish and reduced-fat dairy products rather than animal proteins. As ancient as Greece itself, the Mediterranean diet—high in fruits, vegetables, whole grains, fish, olive oil, and topped with a glass of wine daily—has been known for lower risk of vascular disease and Alzheimer's disease. Research claims that children who eat diets rich in fish, fruits, and vegetables tend to have lower risk for asthma and wheezing, compared to kids who don't. Several studies establish a link between early fish eating (starting around 12 months) and a lower incidence of allergic diseases. Pregnant women and nursing mothers are encouraged to eat at least 12 oz. of fish per week. It safeguards optimal brain development of babies. While omega-3 polyunsaturated fatty acids—healthy fats found in foods, such as fish, nuts, leafy greens and vegetable and flaxseed oils—are associated with a greater chance of healthy aging, omega-3s found in seafood seems to have the strongest effect of all. Healthy aging means living into very old age without any chronic conditions such as heart disease, dementia and cancer, rather than only on longevity. One study examined more than 2,600 older adults average age was 74 for 25 years by taking their blood samples to measure the levels of 46 different types of omega-3 fatty acids. After 25 years of follow-up, the study finds that only 11% of people meet the definition for healthy aging, and the omega-3 fatty acids seemed to be the clear winner to play a part in determining who fits into healthy aging, perhaps because these fatty acids are associated with enhancement of many aspects of health, including cardiovascular and cognitive health. Plant sources of omega-3s, such as flaxseed and walnuts, are healthy in their own right, but these compounds are "processed in the body differently" than fatty acids in fish, and thus likely to make the difference.

Eggs

An egg has everything needed to make a chicken. It is considered one of the healthiest foods available—with 13 essential vitamins, minerals, and high-quality proteins. Four out of five experts note that eggs are a fantastic source of vitamins:

- It is one of nature's most perfect foods. Unlike many other foods packed with vitamins, the fatty neon yolk makes many fat-soluble nutrients that are easier for our body to use. One large egg has about 6 grams of protein (for reference, 1 ounce of cooked meat has 7 grams of protein), and contains only 72 calories, providing a lot of nutrition in a small caloric package.
- Eggs are rich in nutrients: (a) choline (an essential micronutrient involved in metabolism, among other functions), (b) biotin (helps to convert food into

usable energy), (c) vitamin A (important for the immune system), (c) vitamin D (one of the only foods that occurs naturally), and (d) lutein and zeaxanthin (antioxidants that help protect our body from free radicals).

- Highly beneficial nutrients—like protein, vitamin B12, folate, and riboflavin—that are contained in an egg yolk, which counter the effects of cholesterol.
- Whole eggs are the source of highly bioavailable lutein and zeaxanthin, the two carotenoids that help to protect against oxidative stress, inflammation, and age-related macular degeneration. One egg contains one-third of your daily choline needs, a key component for cognitive function.
- Eating an egg in the morning helps to steer away from the carbs and protein-rich breakfasts, especially if one follows low-carb diets for a year or more.
- Though, carotenoids are available from other sources like carrots, fruits and green vegetables, but egg yolk has an edge: as because, carotenoids are to be eaten with fat in order for the body to absorb them fully, a whole egg comes in handy as a total package.
- The egg is a very good source of phosphorus, riboflavin, and vitamin B12. It is high in nutrients important for the brain and eyes and for the prevention of some eye diseases.

The cholesterol level in eggs is very high. One egg contains about 180 mg of cholesterol, while the recommended daily allowance (RDA) for cholesterol is less than 300 mg (or only 200 mg if the person has diabetes or heart disease). An egg increases cholesterol, but modestly. According to the 2015

Dietary Guidelines, dietary cholesterol should not be a cause of concern when it comes to raising person's blood cholesterol. Several experts pointed out—and some even suggest—that a limited amount of eggs is good for cholesterol. They help raise HDL "good" cholesterol: egg yolk is rich in carotenoids, lutein, and zeaxanthin (a yellow crystalline carotenoid) that helps eyes and protects against inflammation. Highly beneficial nutrients—like protein, vitamin B12 and vitamin D, folate, and riboflavin—that are contained in an egg yolk may counter the effects of cholesterol. In fact, research finds that people who eat about one egg a day has lower rates of heart disease and stroke, possibly because of eggs' high levels of "good" HDL cholesterol, which can help fight fat buildup in blood vessels. Eggs have been kind of vilified in the recent past, and the dietary cholesterol seems to have been unfairly slandered by the health community. According to research on heart disease at Harvard Medical School and Brigham and Women's Hospital, dietary cholesterol does not translate to high levels of blood cholesterol. National health officials seem to agree. The latest *Dietary Guidelines for Americans* do not have a cap on dietary cholesterol. Eating one egg a day—even for people whose genes place them at a greater risk for heart and cholesterol problems—isn't a problem, according to the study published in 2016 in the *American Journal of Clinical Nutrition.* Also, in another study that followed half a million people in China for nine years, the result published in the journal *Heart* in 2018, Chinese researchers reveal that people who eat one egg a day on average, tend to have 11% lower rates of heart disease, 26% lower risk of bleeding-related stroke and 10% lower risk of clot-related stroke than people who do not eat egg.

In contrast, another meta-study looked at data from six large prospective studies involving 30,000 participants, with an average follow-up of more than 17 years, and found that

- for each additional 300 milligrams a day of cholesterol in the diet, there was a 17% increased risk of cardiovascular disease and an 18% increased risk of premature death from any cause; and
- each additional half-egg a day was associated with a 6% increased risk of cardiovascular disease and an 8% increased risk of early death.

While the average cholesterol consumption of Americans—about 300 milligrams a day—has not changed much over the last few decades, even at that level, researchers caution that dietary cholesterol is tied to an increased risk for cardiovascular problems. The Dietary Guidelines for Americans 2015-2020, published by the Department of Health and Human Services (HHS) and the United States Department of Agriculture (USDA), bit confusing, cautioning that we "should eat as little cholesterol as possible while consuming a healthy eating pattern," and at the same time encouraging that "cholesterol is not a nutrient of concern for overconsumption," (rather avoiding eggs is not important).

Eating eggs with raw veggies is a very good idea; it boosts nutritional absorption. Cooked eggs increase carotenoid absorption in salads almost nine-fold, entailing a range of benefits including longer life span, fewer chronic illnesses, and a reduced risk of cancer. Cooking eggs— scrambled, hard-boiled, soft-boiled, omelet or poached—make the protein more digestible and increases the bioavailability of biotin.

Organic eggs or eggs from uncaged pasture-raised hens are the best. It eliminates the risk of consuming antibiotics, chemicals and heavy metals. [Info: There is no federal regulation for the use of the term "pasture-raised," but many farmers who market this claim, appear to raise their hens in pasture (open spaces). Technically, the term "free-range" only means that a hen may get only a few feet of outdoor space, while the pasture-raised hen gets more than a hundred square feet each on an open field, where the chicken can forage for plants and insects. They are not fed synthetic pesticides or fertilizers. The "vegetarian" label enforces further that the hens are not fed with any animal protein and have a diet consisting of corn and soybeans.] However, after all praises of egg, it does not mean that you have a heap of your favorite scrambled egg on your breakfast platter daily. For normal healthy adult, anywhere between three to four eggs a week is considered safe and healthy.

Tea

The benefits of tea, especially green tea, are so significant that one can say the key to a healthier and longer life may just be brewing in your cup! Before you make it a tea habit, make sure it is actually a tea. Real tea is harvested from a specific tea plant (*Camellia sinensis*) that has only four varieties: green, black, white, and oolong. Other than that, like an herbal "tea," it may be an infusion of a different plant, which is not technically a tea.

Green tea is a type of tea made solely with the leaves of *Camellia sinensis*, a small tropical evergreen shrub about one to two meters in height, extensively cultivated in China, Japan, India, and Afghanistan. In these countries, tea is the culture. People have documented the medicinal benefits of green tea to treat everything—from headaches to depression to weight loss to cancer—for at least the last four thousand years. In recent times, tea is in vogue in the West, where black tea consumption is on the rise. Several varieties of green tea have long been cultivated in many native countries. The taste, aroma, and quality differ substantially due to several variables, including growing conditions, harvesting time, and processing. In Asian cultures, green tea is consumed in about the same quantities as coffee is in the West.

Green tea is rich in polyphenols, a class of phytochemicals which has a hundred times the antioxidant power of vitamin C and is twenty-five times better than vitamin E in protecting our immune systems. In laboratory settings, experiments suggest that one group of polyphenols in green tea—called catechin polyphenols, particularly epigallocatechin gallate (EGCG)—kills targeted cancer cells without hurting healthy cells. EGCG is a very powerful antioxidant. Catechin in green tea—the amounts as well as the effects—are far higher compared to black tea. This is due to the fact that green tea undergoes minimal oxidation during processing, resulting in a fresh leaf holding the original quantity of intact catechin.

Green tea is effective in preventing the formation of abnormal blood clots and in lowering LDL cholesterol. Eliminating the formation of abnormal blood clots is so important when you consider that thrombosis (the formation of blood clots in veins or arteries) is the primary cause of heart attacks and strokes. Heart disease among Japanese men is very low, even though almost 75% are smokers. The reason? Green tea! Common black and green tea leaves consist of about

25% to 30% flavonoids, including quercetin and gallic acid. Flavonoids (also available in apples, bananas, grapes, tomatoes, and many other fruits and vegetables) protect against heart disease. Scientists hypothesize that green tea works on the lining of blood vessels, helping local cells there to secrete the substances needed to relax the vessels and allow the blood to flow more smoothly. Flavonoid in the tea works as an antioxidant and helps prevent inflammation in body tissue, which keeps the vessels pliable. Studies show that five servings of black tea per day reduce LDL cholesterol by 11% and total cholesterol by 6% in mildly hypercholesterolemic (high blood cholesterol) adults. Green tea contains fluoride—an element that helps prevents cavities and strengthens tooth enamel. One cup a day is suggested to reduce the plaque formation and bacterial infections in the mouth. While both green tea and coffee can help to cut the risk of stroke, but from a study that tracked 82,369 men and women in Japan, researchers found that the more green tea a person drank, the better it reduced risk of stroke: about 20% who drank four cups of green tea a day, compared to those who did rarely.

To sum up, here are a few therapeutic conditions where drinking green tea is helpful: (1) antioxidants in tea helps protect against cancers, including breast, lung, colon, rectal, esophagus, stomach, small intestine, liver, pancreas, ovarian, prostate, and oral cancers; (2) cholesterol; (3) rheumatoid arthritis; (4) cardiovascular disease—reduces the risk of heart attack; (5) infection; (6) impaired immune function; (7) acne-free skin—making it healthier and prettier; (8) weight loss; (9) slows the aging process; (10) digestion; (11) bowel regularity; (12) boosts exercise endurance; (13) lowers the risk of Parkinson's disease; (14) protects from ultraviolet rays;

(15) counteracts some of the negative effects of smoking; (16) improves bone mineral density and strength; (17) prevents neurological diseases, especially degenerative diseases like Alzheimer's; (18) protection against tooth plaque and potential tooth decay; and (19) bone strengthening.

However, if you like tea, go for green. Otherwise, if you add milk with tea, the milk protein can bind with the beneficial flavonols in the tea, and (according to some scientists) the binding may make it hard for the body to absorb the flavonols that provide the health benefits. Sometimes, drinking tea is even better than drinking only water. Tea is water plus antioxidants: two steps in one go. Studies recommend drinking three to four cups of green tea a day, which can cut the risk of heart attack and cancer. However, for those at risk for anemia, there is counterevidence that tea can prevent iron absorption from food.

Also, according to WHO, drinking very hot beverages—above 149°F (65°C), which is significantly cooler than that of most coffee served in restaurants and cafés (hot chocolate and coffee are frequently served at temperatures of 160°F–185°F, or 85°C–71°C)—is linked to higher risk of cancer of the esophagus.

Coffee

Coffee is a casual, social, and recreational drink. When we taste coffee as being nutty, spicy, or chocolaty, it is actually just an aroma sensation that we get. The taste of coffee comes from climatic conditions, soil fertility, altitude, and even how the beans are dried. The caffeine it contains is both a scourge and a tonic. The average drinker takes two to three cups a day. The good time to drink coffee is after 9:30 a.m. It helps the body to produce less of the stress hormone cortisol, which regulates energy and generally peaks between 8:00 and 9:00 a.m. Researchers claim that it is healthy to consume a little caffeine in the morning and continue to take it in small doses throughout the day; though, in the afternoon (after 2:00 p.m.), caffeine may deter the quality of sleep at night. Never drink coffee in the evening or at night. Caffeine helps to prevent Parkinson's disease and type 2 diabetes. A caffeine novice may get a quake from as little as 20 mg of caffeine, an equivalent of 1.5 oz. of strong drip coffee. Food experts suggest that a person needs about 5 mg to 6 mg (μg or mg) of caffeine per kilogram of body weight per day. For instance, for an 80 kg (or 176 lb.) body weight, a person would need about 400 mg of caffeine (or 20 oz. of coffee or two small-size coffees). An average coffee drinker may consume up to 300 mg a day, or 15 oz. of coffee. (One cup of tea is about 8 fl. oz. 1 pennyweight is 0.055 ounce, or 1.555 gram, or 1555 milligrams)

One study analyzed diet versus health, tracking 130,000 adults over twenty-four years. It found no evidence that drinking coffee increases the risk of death from cardiovascular disease, cancer, or other causes. Another large study that tracked almost 400,000 people for a fourteen-year observational study concluded that the more coffee was consumed each day, up to a point, the greater the benefit of longevity. Contrary to previous belief decades ago that the coffee habit could harm health and shorten lives, this study establishes a link that the risk of death gradually drops as the number of cups increases to four or five. At six cups a day, there is a slight rise in death risk. The mortality benefit is not measurably enormous—a death rate of 10% to 15%

lower than those of abstainers. Contrary to earlier research, the usual level of coffee consumption is no more of a diuretic (increased excretion of urine) than the equivalent amount of water. Our body quickly habituates to the condition and requires even higher doses. Physical dependence can occur in three days. Higher consumption of up to 1,200 mg (60 oz.) a day or more may lead to jitteriness and sleeplessness. Blood pressure increases, and that can be dangerous for people at risk for hypertension or other cardiovascular problems. Both men and women who drink three to five cups of coffee a day have about 15% lower risk of premature mortality compared to those who do not drink coffee at all. Studies recommend that coffee consumption is so healthy that it can be incorporated into a healthy lifestyle. The key is moderation.

It's interesting to note here how much the perception about coffee and caffeine has since been changed in the last few decades. Surveys in the 80s found that many Americans were trying to avoid coffee because caffeine was thought to be harmful, even at moderate doses. The reason? The actual reason was not the coffee, but the smoking. Back then, coffee drinkers were generally heavy smokers as well, and in those studies, it was very hard to disentangle and measure individually the two habits. Newer studies have since been able to separate out the effects of coffee and tea independently; and a newer picture has emerged recommending the benefits, not the risks. One study, published in the journal of *Nature Medicine* in 2017, states that older caffeine drinkers do have low levels of inflammation—which drives many, if not most, major diseases; the more caffeine people consume, the more protected they are against a chronic state of inflammation and there is hardly any boundary, reasonably. In one large-scale epidemiological study in 2016 by the National Cancer Institute, researchers parsed health information of 400,000 volunteers, ages 50 to 71, who were free of major diseases at the start of the study in 1995. By 2008, about 50,000 had died. The result: for men who reported drinking 2 to 3 cups of coffee a day were 10% less likely to have died than those who didn't drink coffee, and for women who drank the same amount had 13% less risk of dying during the study period. The North American branch of International Life Sciences Institute (ILSI) is a nonprofit organization (with funding from the American Beverage Association and the National Coffee Association) primarily dedicated to advance the understanding of nutrition and food safety. They examined more than 700 studies published between 2001 and 2015, which were conducted on humans with primary focus on how caffeine is related to 5 important factors: (1) toxicity, (2) bone health and calcium intake, (3) cardiovascular effects (including B.P. and heart rate), (4) behavioral health (including sleep, headaches, and mood), and (5) reproduction and development (including fertility, miscarriage, and birth defects). Their conclusions remain generally the same as those of previous reviews: 90% adult Americans consume less than 400 mg a day of caffeine, and it supports the safety of standard consumption practices in the United States. From another analysis, published in the BMJ in 2018, researchers scanned nearly 220 studies on coffee and found that compared to people who did not drink coffee, overall, the coffee drinkers may enjoy more health benefits: (a) 17% less likely to die early from any cause, (b) 19% less likely to die of heart disease, (c) 18% less likely to develop cancer, and (d) lower rates of diseases like liver cirrhosis, type 2 diabetes and even neurological conditions like Parkinson's and Alzheimer's disease. The only negative health effects related to pregnant women: the higher the coffee consumption, the higher the rates of miscarriage, premature births and low birthweight babies. And because of this and despite its long list of health benefits, businesses are required under Proposition 65, to put warning label to notify consumers if their coffee contains any of 65 chemicals, including acrylamide, that are linked to birth defects, reproductive issues and cancer.

Caffeine is an athletic performance enhancer, and it is legal. Sports stars like baseball players, cyclists, sprinters, runners, tennis players, rowers, and swimmers do take a cup of coffee (or a can of soda) one hour before the event for better performance. Researchers have been publishing caffeine studies for many decades, concluding that caffeine actually improves performance as high as 20%–25% in controlled laboratory settings and up to an average of 5% in real-world track and field. Caffeine helps pretty much in other kinds of endurance exercises as well, giving a performance boost of 1.5% to 5%. One reason people could endure exercise longer and harder after taking caffeine is that the compound helps muscles use fat as fuel. It spars the glycogen stored in muscles and, therefore, increases endurance. The other reason could be that caffeine upsurges the power of muscles by releasing calcium, which is stored in the muscle.

In theory, caffeine activates the cells, and sugar provides the energy to fuel that activation. They both work together, complementing each other. In practice, coffee with sugar can have beneficial effects on cognitive performance that can boost brainpower, memory, attention span, judgment, and reasoning throughout the day. However, some versions of coffee are so sugar-laden that a regular tea habit is just as unhealthful as a soda habit. Caffeine has long been known as a stimulant, but the overall health effects of either caffeine or sugar depends on quantity and duration. Coffee and tea are essentially volume of fluid that your body absorbs as much and expel the rest.

Because of its insulin-lowering effects, because of its antioxidant qualities, and because of other allied effects yet to be discovered, coffee reduces the risk of liver disease, diabetes, and Parkinson's disease. Now added to the list, for men, coffee lowers the risk of prostate cancer. While previous studies were relatively small and with mixed results, new studies show that for the men who drank the most coffee (six cups a day) for the last eight years, their risk of getting lethal prostate cancer was about 60% (30% for three cups a day) lower compared to that of men who drink almost no coffee at all. Epidemiologists (who deal with the study of the causes, distribution, and control of disease in large populations) noticed that the benefit comes from the coffee (caffeinated or decaffeinated), not from the caffeine, and that the benefit is independent of other lifestyle factors, such as sedentary lifestyle, smoking, and obesity. One study revealed that women who drank four or more cups of coffee a day over twenty-six years had a 25% lower risk of endometrial cancer compared to those who consumed less; and those who drank two to three cups a day had a 7% lower risk. However, remember that too much caffeine is injurious to health.

Red Wine

Wine wins the drink. It is an alcoholic drink and comes under alcoholic beverage. It is classically made out of fermenting grape juice. Grape juice, in and of itself, has its natural chemical balance in a way that it can ferment without added sugars, enzymes, acids, or other ingredients. Wine is produced by smashing grapes into mush and then fermenting using various types of yeast. Yeast ingests the sugars in the grapes and converts them into alcohol. Different kinds of grapes and different strains of yeasts produce different varieties of wines with a wide range of tastes. Archaeological evidence at sites in Georgia and Iran indicate that the earliest production of wine was as early as 6000 BC by fermenting the grapes.

In wine making, alcoholic fermentation occurs when yeast metabolizes with sugar (glucose, sucrose or fructose), forming ethanol (alcohol) and carbon dioxide. The sugar comes from grape juice. (In beer, it is from starch in the malted cereal grains, classically barley.) Grapes that are ripen have higher sugar content than those that are not as ripen. Winemakers add sugar to aid in fermentation, and to achieve the desired properties and flavor profiles. A five-ounce red wine typically contains about 0.9 grams of total sugar. Winemakers add sulfites as a preservative (not listed on the label) as well as 60 other additives which are legally be used without being disclosed. Wine is acidic by nature and adjustments are made carefully to balance the sweet and sour.

While excessive consumption of alcohol increases such hazards as alcoholism, high blood pressure, stroke, obesity, breast cancer, suicide, and accidents, epidemiological studies have persistently demonstrated in favor of moderate consumption of alcohol and wine. [One drink a day for women and two drinks a day for men. One drink may be defined as one (a) 12 oz. of beer (has 150 cal, same as 12 oz. soda), (b) 6 oz. of wine (half of a small can, 170 cal), (c) 1.5 oz. of 80-proof spirits (90 cal), or (d) 1 oz. of 100-proof spirits (the proof number is twice the percentage of the alcohol content measured by volume—i.e., in gin rum, vodka, whiskey, scotch, cognac, 90 cal). The pH acidity level of beer is 4, which is the same level as wine—vodka pH 4, whiskey pH 5, fresh cow's milk pH between 6.7 and 6.5, distilled water pH 7 (1 oz. = 30 mL). Usually, a glass of wine will be around 5 oz. to 6 oz., which is about half of a 12 oz. small Coke can. If you like to enjoy a glass of wine with dinner every night, then make sure a bottle of wine lasts five nights: there are five glasses of 5 oz. pours in every 750 mL bottle of wine. One study in 2015 claims that a glass of wine every night for two years increases the HDL level by about 10%.]

One study claims people who drink three to four days a week are 30% less likely to develop diabetes than those who drank less than once a week. Wine is linked to a decrease in death due to cardiovascular events such as heart failure. White wine is not a diet wine; it is basically colorless red wine. Red wine helps to avert further heart attacks if you have suffered from one. A new study finds that moderate alcohol consumption (preferably wine) may help women in their 50s and early 60s to lesser bone loss due to menopause when compared with heavy drinkers and people who don't consume alcohol at all. Alcohol influences the oral microbiome. Study finds that alcohol aids to strains of oral bacteria that are associated with heightened risk of some types of gum disease, cancer and heart disease, while simultaneously suppressing other strains of bacteria that protect the body from infection. In food combination of pairing the wine and cheese, the fat in the cheese coats the mouth and reduces the tannin-induced drying influence (wine's aromatic increasing while sour notes decreasing) and thereby change the dominant taste of wine in ways as to yield a better taste of the both. Red wine is a part of Meditation diet.

The effect, in part, is due to the large intake of Red Wine, as many nutritionists validate, for instance, the French suffer from fewer heart diseases than the Americans, in spite of their richer diet. When skins of the red grapes are used to make red wine, it is concentrated with supercharged antioxidants known as polyphenols, including one called resveratrol. Red wine drinkers: (a) have significantly increased levels of good HDL cholesterol; (b) have more beneficial cholesterol ratio; (c) experience a significant drop in components of metabolic syndrome; (d) get a better quality of sleep; and (e) have no significant adverse effects. Resveratrol is naturally available in the skins of red grapes. Some scientists and wine lovers tend to believe that drinking wine does good—helps to fight cancer and maintain overall well-being. Resveratrol boosts heart health in two ways: (a) by lowering cholesterol levels and (b) by functioning as an antioxidant in fending off toxic free radicals that can, otherwise, blockage in heart vessels. Indeed, the metabolic profiles of regular wine-drinkers look like those of people who maintain calorie-restricted diets, a strategy in which people cut the amount of calorie intakes in order to improve their cholesterol and insulin levels and heart-related function. Therefore, all it suggests is that resveratrol can mimic: it mimics the same pathways as caloric restriction.

Now, what is the dose? how much resveratrol does it take to trigger the good-for-you benefits? A lot. In one study, participants had to take about150 mg daily. As red wine contains only 15 mg of resveratrol per liter, it amounts to about 10 liters of wine a day. So, trying to get that much by drinking red wine, would be unwise, leaving an alternative, to reach the same blood levels of resveratrol, by taking supplements.

Wine is food. Like any other food, several studies have come to the conclusion that moderate consumption of wine is good for health and longevity. It cuts death rates by up to 40% per year. But the theory behind it—if purely due to the function of resveratrol—is in doubt. Some scientists also believe that drinking wine alone does not provide the human body with sufficient resveratrol for a significant positive effect. It should be noted thus far that the effects of resveratrol have been successfully tested only on rodents and cell cultures. In humans, resveratrol could potentially be a treatment for ailments like (a) Alzheimer's, (b) cancer, (c) cardiovascular disease, and (d) spinal cord injuries. It could also have some other benefits like (e) increased longevity, (f) enhanced athletic performance, (g) radiation exposure protection, and (h) stroke damage protection. The concentration of resveratrol (and polyphenols), is 10-fold higher in red wine than in other alcoholic drinks. Also, because there are numerous chemicals in other alcoholic drinks, it is entirely possible that wine consumption has more added benefits.

Liquors

Studies suggest that alcohol, when consumed in moderation, may promote heart health and even ward off diabetes and dementia. Could it be that moderate drinking is just another behavior that healthy people tend to do, not something that makes people healthy? The moderate people tend to do most things moderately—they exercise, they sleep, they don't smoke, they eat right, and they drink moderately. Whatsoever the reason, the evidence is so plentiful that some experts consider moderate drinking is one of the central components of healthy living. However, research suggests that alcohol impairs inhibitory control, which leads people to eat more. [Note: The National Institutes of Health is now starting a $100 million clinical trial to check first hand, if one drink a day really prevents heart attacks, where most of the financial contribution comes from 5 companies that are among the world's largest alcoholic beverage manufacturers.]

New studies find that alcohol is believed to reduce coronary disease because it has been found to increase the good HDL cholesterol and to have anticlotting effects. One study in Europe followed 14,629 people for twenty-four years, starting at an average age of 54. There had been a total of 2,508 cases of heart failures during the study. After taking into account the factors such as age, race, smoking, hypertension, and other variables, researchers found that moderate drinkers—who drank a glass of wine, a 12 oz. beer, or a peg of liquor a day—had a lower risk of heart failure than either heavy drinkers or abstainers by as much as 20% for men and 16% for women. The advantage gradually declined with heavier drinking. Other benefits have been noticed in other aspects as well. For cognitive advantage, elderly impaired patients who drank alcohol in moderation did not deteriorate as quickly as abstainers. Orthopedically, moderate drinkers had a higher mineral density in their hipbones than nondrinkers. Dietetically, light drinkers, to an extent, were less likely to develop diabetes than abstainers; additionally, people with type 2 diabetes who drank lightly were less likely to develop coronary heart disease.

The shocking news is that even heavy drinkers outlive nondrinkers. The study confirms that abstainers' mortality rate is generally higher than that of heavy drinkers and that moderate drinkers' mortality rate is the lowest. Another research in U.K. covered nearly two million men and women (half and half) with no cardiovascular disease to start with, followed them from 1997 to 2010 (median follow-up six years), based on cohort study of linked electronic health records covering primary care, hospitalization and mortality, and finally established the link between alcohol consumption and 12 different heart ailments. The study appeared in the *British Medical Journal* in 2017, state that people who did not drink had an increased risk for eight of the twelve heart ailments, such as heart attack, stroke and sudden heart-related death, with varying degree ranging from 12% to 56%, compared to people who drank in moderation. Yet another study, covering more than 333,000 people who were surveyed about their alcohol consumption and lifestyle habits and were tracked for an average of 8 years, finds (a) that light and moderate drinkers (14 or fewer drinks per week for men and 7 or fewer for women) are 20% less likely to die from any cause during the study period, compared to those who have never consumed alcohol, (b) that they were 25-30% less likely to die from cardiovascular disease, and (c) that these protective effects are more noticeable in white participants, women, middle-aged and older people and non-smokers. Alcohol in moderate use—1 to 3 drinks per day especially red wine—is considered to improve heart health, circulation and not to mention, the sociability. But why would alcohol free lead to a shorter life? Puzzle indeed! Here is one circumferential hypothesis. It's usually true that those who stay away from alcohol, also tend to stay away from their friends; they typically come from lower socioeconomic classes; to them, drinking is expensive. They undergo daily stresses of job, finance and child-care that might not only prevent them from drinking for a relax but cause them stress-related illnesses over long periods. They hardly get the stress-reducing benefits of any kind. Under such circumstances, even after taking into account for nearly all imaginable variables—socioeconomic status, number of close friends, level of physical activity, quality of social support, and so on—the researchers noticed that over a period of 20 years, mortality rates were: (3) highest, for those who were not the current drinkers, irrespective of whether they used to be alcoholics, (2) medium, for the heavy drinkers, and (1) lowest, for the moderate drinkers. Nondrinker displays greater signs of depression than those who jolly well allow themselves to join the party. Moderate drinking is not only fun and relaxing, but healthy.

Yet, another caveat! The hypothesis that moderate consumption of alcohol is good for one's health was first floated by the scientists of Johns Hopkins nearly 100 years ago, when they published a graph showing that modest drinkers lived longer than not only heavy drinkers, but also abstainers. Now critics of the alcohol hypothesis argue that moderate drinking is just something that healthy people tend to do, not something that makes people healthy. They cite plenty of studies that have linked moderate drinking to more health problems, not less. The World Cancer Research Fund (WCRF) in their 2018 Continuous Update Project (an ongoing effort to inform consumers about lifestyle habits), cautions that drinking is linked to cancers of the breast, mouth, throat, esophagus, liver, stomach and colon. Even though moderate drinking may actually help protect against kidney cancer, but for cancer prevention, they recommend not to drink alcohol, at all. According to the American Society of Clinical Oncology (ASCO), a body that represents the nation's top cancer doctors, is now cautioning that there exists a link between alcohol and cancer. They published their finding in 2017 in the *Journal of Clinical Oncology*. It reveals that heavy drinkers have higher risks of mouth and throat cancer, cancer of the voice box, liver cancer and, to a lesser extent, colorectal cancers, and that for women, even light drinking have a higher risk of breast cancer and esophageal cancer. In their explanation why alcohol leads to cancer, ASCO researchers describe that our body metabolizes alcohol into acetaldehyde and the formation of acetaldehyde starts when alcohol comes in contact with bacteria in the mouth, which explains the link between alcohol and cancers of the throat, voice box and esophagus. They estimate that worldwide 5.5% of all new cancers and 5.8% of all cancer deaths are attributed to alcohol use. About alcoholic weight gain, they explain that unlike carbohydrates, fats and protein, alcohol is a toxic substance that our body rejects—does not like to store, rather use it first. As alcohol is a source of calories, the alcohol calories are used for fuel, which means that people who drink must eat less or exercise more to maintain their body weight.

Moderate drinking may help you to live longer. In their annual conference in 2018, the American Association for the Advancement of Science, claims that drinking two glasses of wine or beer a day is linked to an 18% drop in person's risk of early death—the effect of which is even stronger than exercise. Red wine is often preferred for its anti-aging benefits. Other studies also reinforce moderate drinking protects heart attacks, strokes, chest pain and fatal heart disease. However, one warning underscores associations between drinking and at least seven types of cancer, especially for women, the breast cancer. For causes, researches find alcohol tends to disrupt DNA in a way that potentially leads to the development of cancers of the breast, mouth, esophagus, liver and colon. The risk gets fatal if you have other bad habits, such as smoking, drinking hot tea, and lack of physical activities. Alcohol calories contribute to alcoholic fat, which is a very common problem and thus, weight gain and obesity which then sets of other health problems, ranging from heart disease to type 2 diabetes.

One new study claims that any amount of alcohol is bad! The study is based on a review of nearly 700 existing studies on global drinking habits including 600 only on alcohol and health. Published in The Lancet in 2018, it calls into question the long-held benefits of moderate drinking which has been federal Dietary Guidelines for Americans and supported by the American Heart Association and the American Cancer Society. They assert statistical prevalence as: (a) alcohol is the seventh leading cause for premature death in 2016, resulting in 2.8 million deaths worldwide (2.2% of all female deaths and 6.8%, male); (b) in any given year, compared to non-drinkers, the risk increases starting from one drink a day at 0.5% increased risk of one of 23 alcohol-related health issues, including cancer, road injuries and tuberculosis (which in absolute number is 4 per 100,000 people), 2 drinks at 7% (28), and 5 drinks at 37% (148); (c) only a modest cardiovascular benefits are associated with the moderate drinking; (d) especially for women, the effect is overshadowed by numerous risks including breast cancer—the condition also conforms to (i) World Cancer Research Fund's recommendation which says that, as far as cancer prevention, it's best not to drink alcohol at all, and (ii) U.K. government's similar recommendation in 2016.

But, this is a big but, some nutritionists and epidemiologists counter argue that the statistics is misleading the fact; it is business as usual and much less news worthy for few reasons: (1) Limitations in study design. It's not any new study on alcohol. It is a meta-study by merging data from other observational studies on drinking done to estimate the risks for 23 different alcohol-related health problems. (2) The study combines almost 700 existing studies to calculate the levels of alcohol consumption worldwide, and thereafter, deduce statistically that ill effect starts increasing with each additional drink per day, and that the overall harm is lowest only at zero. (That's how it gets the news headlines.) The techniques to analyze the observational data is more of a casual fashion, and when the study compiles an observational study on top of another observational study, it gets more statistical significance than clinical significance: the very difference may be small but real, but that doesn't necessarily mean the difference is critical. (3) By interpreting the data, for each set of 100,000 people who have one drink a day per year, 918 are likely to have one of the 23 alcohol-related problems in any year, compared to 914 of those who drink *zero* drinks. In other words, it means that with one drink, 99,082 are unaffected while 914 will have at least one problem from 23 different alcohol-related health problems, leaving a difference of only 4 in 100,000 people having one drink and zero drink. The risk 4 per 100,000 (0.004%) for one drink increases to 977 (0.977%) for 2 drinks. While the individual risks and the heart-health benefits associated with light drinking vary, but because of the fact that a higher risk of cancer is associated virtually with any amount of alcohol consumption, the population-level recommendation is *no drink.* (4) For cheerful drinkers, however, here is separate analysis: according to National Health Interview Survey (NHIS) coupled with medical records of Veterans Health Administration (VHA) patients, *having one or two drinks for three times a week*, is associated with lowest overall risk of mortality, compared to those who drank even lesser than that. Therefore, comes the cautionary recommendation: drinking more than three times a week may be harmful to your health. (5) In the United States where there is hardly any prevalence of tuberculosis like other parts of the world, the statistics even lesser for moderate drinking. While it is no way advocating that people indulge in drinking and ignore the risks, but at the same time the risks are much smaller than many other risks in our lives. Since many other studies endorse with plenty of evidence that there exist the links between moderate drinking and lower total mortality and a decreased risk of heart disease, the endorsement is that *if you drink*—and that's the key—and if you enjoy, drink moderately. Alcohol is not medicine. Alcoholism is terrible. The danger of heavy drinking is very real. Everybody agrees that there's no question, heavy drinking is always harmful.

The researchers at the *Global Burden of Diseases* studied the levels of consumption of alcohol and its effects on health in 195 countries from 1990 to 2016. They evaluated a range of risk factors caused by the consumption of alcohol, including diseases, driving accidents and self-harms: alcohol led to 2.8 million deaths in 2016 alone, making it a leading risk factor for disease worldwide, accounting for almost 10 percent of deaths among people ages 15 to 49. About 5 percent of cancers cases were linked to alcohol. While moderate drinking may safeguard people against heart disease, they argue that the potential danger to developing cancer and other diseases overall, offsets these potential benefits, as do other risks of harms. So, they finally conclude worldwide population-level recommendation: no amount of alcohol is safe.

Cirrhosis is the formation of fibrous tissue (fibrosis) replacing liver cells that have died due to a variety of reasons, like liver toxicity, alcohol over consumption, and viral hepatitis causing long term irreversible damage to the liver and chronic liver failure, the liver does not function properly. Deaths from cirrhosis and liver cancer have risen dramatically in the United States in recent time. One study published in the journal *BMJ* in 2018, reports that the annual cirrhosis death has increased by 65 percent from 1999 to 2016, primarily due to alcoholic over consumption among adults ages 25 to 34 years old.

Now, let's go back to our general topic of food. In the selection of food, one important point not to be lost sight of is that while the content of our meals may be important, the source from which we get our food is no less important. For example, American's fondness for the turkey is well known. But the turkey that they get on their platter may hardly be the one of the pastures nibbling the green grass under the rolling hills. In 2010, 99% of all turkeys produced in the United States are the 'Broadbreasted White' a.k.a. 'Large White' variety. They are raised for their large, white meaty breasts. These artificial breasts are so large that they are unable to sex naturally and therefore they are artificially inseminated, performed by humans; otherwise, if it is not done so, according to Food and Agriculture Organization of the United Nations, this variety of bird would become extinct in just one generation. These birds are grown in an extremely packed condition of indoor factory farms. They live a life of unnatural, uncomfortable and are fed constantly grains rather than the grubs, bugs and grasses they should, and supplemented with a steady dose of antibiotics.

In America, over 300 million turkeys are raised in factory farms, where they are cooped up in windowless buildings. The nutritional value of these turkeys is far less compared to pasture-raised turkeys. Pasture-raised turkeys stay healthier by drawing in more nutrients, eating certain nutrients in different parts of the year. They grow naturally—more slowly than the factory birds. They have 25% less saturated fat, 35% more vitamin A, four times more omega-3 fatty acids, and about 40% less cholesterol than factory-raised turkeys. However, the good news is that in the U.S., the demand for antibiotic-free, pasture-raised meats (chicken, beef, ham, and lamb) is increasing, not from few but from plenty of big players in food industries. The current trend of transition to antibiotic-free, naturally pasture-raised pork, chicken, and beef that meets FDA recommended standards seems to be encouraging. In 2014, lawmakers were making new laws to require U.S. firms to release relevant information about their use of antibiotics. President Obama issued an executive order for creating a task force and an action plan for implementation.

Antibiotics can cause animals to grow fatter, faster. In commercial farming, time is money. A grass-fed cow requires 27 months to get to the market without antibiotics—which is more than double the time for a cow pumped with full of antibiotics. The bacterial strains can easily be transferred to humans by contact with animals or raw meat and more probably through the consumption of undercooked meat. Over time it becomes resistance to antibiotics. In one estimate by CDC, the growing resistance of bacteria to antibiotics is responsible for some 23,000 American deaths a year incurring financial losses of $34 billion a year. Antibiotic need to be avoided. The antibiotics human takes as medicine, do disrupt the so-called gut microbiome; and such disruption leads to an increase in the incidence of autism, Alzheimer's and Parkinson's disease. To curb the breeding of drug-resistant bacteria from antibiotic overuse, the Food and Drug Administration (FDA) has finally enacted rules in 2017 banning the use of human antibiotics in animals—chickens, pigs and cows—purely for growth promotion.

Food imports grew from $41 billion in 1999 to $86 billion in 2010. Overall, 16% of the food eaten in the U.S. comes from other countries. About 70% of fruits and vegetables come from abroad. Regulators and government agencies inspect only a tiny sample of the imports. However, proposals are being floated to create global coalitions of regulators and global databases to identify problems at sources like food manufacturing plants and to save resources by consolidating inspection efforts. The CDC epidemiologists studied foodborne illness outbreaks from 2005 to 2010 and reported that 39 outbreaks and 2,348 illnesses were associated with imported foods from fifteen countries. Nearly half of the outbreaks occurred during the latter part, between 2009 and 2010. Fish was the single biggest source of outbreaks, followed by spices. Nearly half of the outbreaks originated in Asia.

In the U.S., 80% to 85% of seafood is often imported from fish farms. Commercial seafood—as reported by food inspectors using DNA bar coding—has rampant labeling fraud in supermarkets and restaurants. One in five—out of 25,000 samples of seafood tested globally—is mislabeled, according to a 2016 report from the ocean conservation advocacy group Oceana. Sushi is mislabeled nearly 50% of the time in the United States. Cheap fishes are often substituted for expensive ones or labeled endangered species. While environmentalists, scientists, and fish geneticists claim that as much as 20% to 25% of the seafood products are intentionally and fraudulently labeled, regulators are yet lax in regulating seafood, and they are slow to implement the tools of the current technology. In 2012, an ocean conservation group, using genetic testing, found that nearly 40% of the seafood from eighty-one grocery stores and restaurants was not what they claimed it was. In 2013, there was one study of fish samples bought from twelve metropolitan areas. After genetic testing, it was found that about one-third of the samples were mislabeled. Between December 2014 and January 2015, Interpol (the International Criminal Police Organization) seized fraudulent and inappropriately mislabeled food in forty-seven countries from shops, markets, seaports, and airports; and they eventually removed 2,500 tons of food and 275,000 L of adulterated drinks (the most counterfeited product of all) out of the food supply.

As the U.S. food supply gets more and more global, so do the potential germs from all over the world. There are more occurrences of outbreaks from imported foods due not from more foods but from more countries. The CDC estimates that one in six Americans—about 48 million Americans—suffer from some kind of foodborne illness annually. About 128,000 people are sick enough to admit to hospitals for symptoms like nausea, vomiting, and diarrhea. Foodborne illnesses account for $9 billion in medical costs and $75 billion in food costs that are recalled and thrown away annually. Leafy vegetables, especially spinach and cabbage, are responsible for the majority of the illnesses caused by the norovirus, which comes from water contaminated by fecal matter. A single-stranded RNA, the norovirus—incorrectly called "stomach flu"—is technically known as viral gastroenteritis. Regulatory authorities do acknowledge that more needs to be done. IBM steps forward and plans to sequence the microbiomes of food ingredients to prevent outbreaks earlier. Their goal is to create a consolidated database on the sequence of the makeup of various foods at the molecular level; and once they can establish what a given ingredient is supposed to look like, the expert systems can be put in place to detect the problems before the contaminated food hits the dinner table. The process offers a microscopic view into what's happening in our food environment.

Today, it is disturbing to see headlines about intentional food adulteration. But how common is the problem? Experts say it is very common and rampant—more common than one can expect. The major one is economic adulteration, which is a deliberate substitution or addition of cheap compounds—lookalike or tests alike—to sell it cheaper. Carbohydrate-heavy foods like fruit juices are popular targets; anywhere from 5% to 25% of these foods are adulterated.

Yet the bigger truth is that industrial food production, in and of itself, is unhealthy, especially the meat. In the U.S. during the last half century, small farms have been replaced by massive industrialized operations that treat animals as nothing but commodities. Industrial operations may yield manufacturing cheap food for the supermarkets, but its economically viable model can only exist as it passes health costs to the public—the cost in the form of obesity, heart problems, antibiotic-resistant diseases, the occasional salmonella, polluted water, food poisoning, and possibly certain cancers. The food is cheap only in a shortsighted way. Like cigarette warnings, mass-marketed junk foods, sugar drinks, and the like should come with prominent health-warning labels. Food-regulating authorities should make it illegal to advertise such highly fattening food as "fat-free." Processed-food industries employ scientists to dissect elements of the palate and tweak ratios of salt, sugar, and fat to optimize taste so that they can hook consumers on their products in the same way the cigarette industries do to smokers on nicotine. Government regulation is warranted to implement industrywide standards for the interest of public health.

Evolutionarily speaking, we humans have not been evolved to eat healthy and go to the gym until recently; but we evolved to cooperate with each other to survive and thrive. For cooperation, we need our government "for the people"—not "for the corporations," who want to make money by stoking our craving. In the illegal trade practice, food industries thrive today, for the most part, by practicing collaborative marketing, collective lobbying, manipulative taste craving, gaming the billion-dollar deals, and worst of all, manipulating the support from the very government that we have elected. Thousands of companies, corporations and trade associations hire lobbyists who outnumber members of Congress 20 to 1, just to give you an idea.

Today, goods and good cooperation is needed more than ever. Now we live in a world where perfect strangers with global backgrounds open doors to each other on a regular basis. They swap goods for foods and foods for goods in global trade. One scratches the other's back on a daily basis. We are each other's partner and competitor. Corporations are cooperating and competing, friend and enemy (frenemy) at the same time. The idea is to share your idea, not protect your idea. In cooperation, we thrive! The food industries take this opportunity to their advantage. They thrive today with methodical marketing, manipulative taste craving, trading deals in billions of dollars—and worst of all, with the support from the very government that we have elected.

Enterohemorrhagic *E. coli* (EHEC) is a bacterium with frequent outbreaks in raw milk and milk products and raw meat and undercooked ground meat products. They cause severe foodborne illness. In 2015 in the U.S., 80% of the reported *E. coli* illnesses were traced back to beef and vegetables. In most cases, however, the illness was self-limiting; but that could have led to a life-threatening disease, especially in children and the elderly. *E. coli* is heat-sensitive, suggesting that *E. coli* can be removed if the food is prepared following basic food hygiene practices, such as cooking thoroughly at a high temperature. When it comes to eating raw fish, as in sushi, there exists some inherent risk of getting sick from bacteria and parasites. Survey reveals, half of sushi sampled from supermarkets contains an unsatisfactory level of bacteria. According to the U.S. Food and Drug Administration, sushi containing raw tuna, salmon, shrimp, scallop and oyster should not be left out for more than two hours, or more than one hour if the temperature is 90°F (32°C) or higher. Young children and pregnant women should refrain from eating raw seafood (even some cooked fish) that have high levels of mercury, like ahi tuna, king mackerel and swordfish. Sushi may be the halo of being healthy, but it is mislabeled nearly 50% of the time in the United States. Cheap fishes are often substituted for expensive ones. So, it's your judgement call and perhaps a good idea, 'to sniff before you eat,' and ask what the sushi roll is made of, and how and when prepared.

Aside from foodborne diseases from environmental contamination (including pollution of water, soil, or air), an investigative study by *Consumer Reports* has found that two out of three whole broiler chickens are contaminated with illness-inducing bacteria or infections with foodborne pathogens such as EHEC, whereas certain types of "organic" chickens posed the lowest risk. The study examined whole broilers bought from more than one hundred stores in about two dozen states and found salmonella in two-thirds of the chickens tested. While store-brand organic chickens were found to be free of salmonella, only less than one-half was free of campylobacter (appear comma or S-shaped).

It is an emerging man-made health crisis that is occurring not only with the overuse of clinical antibiotics in human bodies but by the overuse in livestock production. Animal antibiotics are added to animal feeds for healthy animals, to promote growth and prevent disease—about twenty-nine million pounds of antibiotics each year. Bacteria resistant to antibiotics—such as *E. coli* and salmonella—do make their way back to humans through the meat that we consume and through the environment that we live in, like one instance where waterways were contaminated with runoff. It is estimated that our indirect share of these antibiotics is over an ounce (2 tbsp) per year. Investigative studies reveal that nearly 20% of ground beef tested from conventionally raised cows has bacteria resistant to three or more classes of antibiotics. In 2013, the CDC issued statistics to the extent of the problem for the first time: at least two million Americans fall ill from antibiotic-resistant infections each year, and at least twenty-three thousand die from it. Once you fall ill, there are not many options left. The preventative or prophylactic use of antibiotics is banned in several European countries exactly for this reason. There is a dramatic difference in the levels of antibiotic resistance. Microbes typically go away once farmers reduce the use of antibiotics. In their first sincere attempt in decades, the Food and Drug Administration (FDA) have put in place one major policy in 2014 to phase out all systematic overuse of antibiotics in cows, chickens, and pigs. The first World Antibiotic Awareness Week was pledged on November 16–22 in 2015.

Worldwide, people are still continuing to use far more antibiotics than before. According to one most comprehensive study to date, published in the journal *Proceedings of the National Academy of Sciences (PNAS)* in 2018, researchers examined human consumption of antibiotics in 76 countries over time, and find that for every 1,000 people, antibiotic consumption increased by about 40% from 11.3 doses per day in 2000 to 15.7 does per day in 2015, including penicillin—the most common type of antibiotics—increased by 36%. One study highlighting how rampant overprescribing and inappropriate prescribing of antibiotics still is, cautions that 25% of the time antibiotic prescriptions are not only unnecessary, but harmful and hazardous. From 2015, if nothing major change happens, it will continue to contribute up to 10 million deaths every year due to its antibiotic resistance. Antibiotics still remain one of the most powerful classes of drugs, which in many cases, is a life saver.

The effectiveness of antibiotics depends primarily on how we use them, how well we manage the antibiotic in clinical practice and outside it, and how well we control the spread of antibiotic-resistant bacteria without drugs. A survey in 2016 suggests that hospitals are also cracking down on antibiotic-resistant infections, and for the first time, Medicare is also joining hands to penalize hospitals with too many avoidable patient-safety complications tied to the prevalence of two types of bacteria resistant to drugs. Quite simply, microbiologists tell us how an antibiotic works is not complicated. In fact, it is one simple demonstration that we inherited from evolution. When you get a bacterial infection, you take an antibiotic to treat it. The most susceptible bacteria die off first; they're the ones that get killed most easily by the drug. But if there remains any minor genetic variation among the bacteria that are causing the illness, or if some of these genetic differences happen to make one particular bacterium (singular of bacteria) more or less susceptible to the drug than the other bacteria are, then when you take antibiotics, that leaves behind the more robust bacteria. This is the reason why when prescribed a course of antibiotics, it's important to finish the entire course of the antibiotics. But, in a new study published in the *BMJ* in 2017, health experts from Brighton and Sussex Medical School, the University of Oxford and other institutions argue that "cutting short a course of antibiotics will encourage drug resistance" is not supported by evidence, and that taking more antibiotics than needed does lead to resistance. Their concept is in line with one of the most fundamental medication concepts that we should take as little medication as necessary.

Bacteria (previously thought brainless) are really brainy, and they demonstrate a highly effective "collective intelligence," like how to survive the antibiotics. These robust bacteria then reproduce themselves so that the next generation of the infecting bacteria is more likely to carry the genetic trait that confers resistance. If this process goes on for several generations—just as evolutionary theory would predict—the bacteria can become entirely resistant to the antibiotic. In fact, bacteria are quickly growing resistant to the antibiotics the U.S. currently has, which is breaking the model for making new drugs. For example, drug-resistant tuberculosis has a fatality rate down to 50% only. The patient dies due to infection resistant to antibiotics. Paradoxically, the U.S. has been creating even multidrug-resistant organisms that are now gradually showing up in top-flight highly guarded hospitals.

Immunologists estimate that more than sixty thousand American families go through such experiences each year, and the prospect of developing new drugs is so discouraging that few companies bother to try anymore.

All it means is that the overuse of antibiotics will lead to drug resistance. The U.S. has a much greater nontherapeutic use of antibiotics; some 70% of American antibiotics—weighing tens of millions of pounds of drugs every year—are used in animal feed. Because the factory farms where cattle, pigs, turkeys, or chickens are grown in close quarters cannot operate without the use of drugs in order to keep animals healthy. Furthermore, some drugs and hormones are used to plump up animals for more meat. A decade ago, the European Union banned the routine use of antibiotics in animal feed because of the evidence that its drug-resistance consequence on humans is enormous. Of late, the U.S. Food and Drug Administration (FDA) endorses abstinence for the same reason.

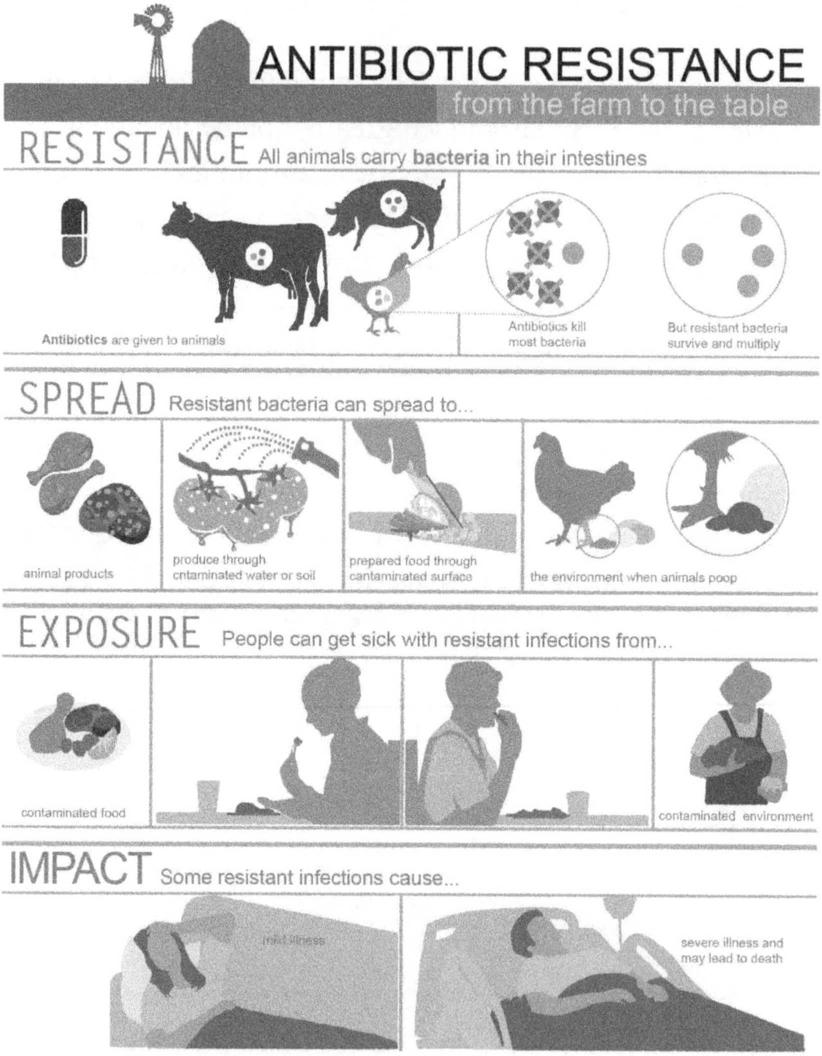

ANTIBIOTIC RESISTANCE
from the farm to the table
RESISTANCE All animals carry bacteria in their intestines
Antibiotics are given to animals
Antibiotics kill most bacteria
But resistant bacteria survive and multiply
SPREAD Resistant bacteria can spread to...
animal products
produce through cntaminated water or soil
prepared food through cantaminated surface
the environment when animals poop
EXPOSURE People can get sick with resistant infections from...
contaminated food
contaminated environment
IMPACT Some resistant infections cause...
mild illness
severe illness and may lead to death

Antibiotic Resistance

What about antimicrobial resistance? The World Health Organization (WHO) answers with a few facts: "Antimicrobial resistance (AMR) is resistance of a microorganism to an antimicrobial drug that was originally effective for treatment of infections caused by it. Resistant microorganisms (including bacteria, fungi, viruses, and parasites) are able to withstand attacks by antimicrobial drugs, such as antibacterial drugs (e.g., antibiotics), antifungals, antivirals, and antimalarials, so that standard treatments become ineffective and infections persist, increasing the risk of spreading to others." Here are some of their key facts:

- Antimicrobial resistance (AMR) threatens the effective prevention and treatment of an ever-increasing range of infections caused by bacteria, parasites, viruses, and fungi.
- AMR is present in all parts of the world. New resistance mechanisms emerge and spread globally.
- In 2012, there were about 450,000 new cases of multidrug-resistant tuberculosis (MDR-TB). Extensively, drug-resistant tuberculosis (XDR-TB) has been identified in ninety-two countries. MDR-TB requires treatment courses that are much longer and less effective than those for non-resistant TB.
- There are high proportions of antibiotic resistance (ABR) in bacteria that cause common infections (e.g., urinary tract infections, pneumonia, bloodstream infections) in all regions of the world. A high percentage of hospital-acquired infections are caused by highly resistant bacteria.
- Treatment failures due to resistance to treatments of last resort for gonorrhea have now been reported from

ten countries. Gonorrhea may soon become untreatable as no vaccines or new drugs are in development.

- Patients with infections caused by drug-resistant bacteria are generally at increased risk of worse clinical outcomes and death, and they consume more health-care resources than patients infected with the same bacteria that are not resistant.
- Resistance to earlier-generation antimalarial drugs is widespread in most malaria-endemic countries.
- It is an increasingly serious threat to global public health that requires action across all government sectors and society. Experts estimate that about ten million people will die each year by 2050, from infections that are resistant to antibiotics.

The United States federal government has quietly released some data on this in 2012, indicating that a ferocious germ that is resistant to many types of antibiotics had been increased by as many as tenfold on chicken breasts. It is a very serious and troubling trend. Roughly 80% of the antibiotics sold in the U.S. are consumed by the chickens, cows, and pigs that are then consumed by the Americans. Yet producers of meat and poultry are not bound by law to account for how and how much they use the drugs and antibiotics. Therefore, extracting data from the producers is so difficult to establish the link between routine antibiotic feed in animals and antibiotic-resistant infections in people. The overwhelming epidemiological evidence that is already available linking the two is something that even the FDA acknowledges to be true. Resistant bacteria now appear to be the major health threat for the general population. Common infections that have been routinely cured with penicillin pills now require intravenous-drip antibiotics.

At the individual level, one good advice is that one should not take antibiotics when not needed. For example, antibiotics don't help against nonbacterial infections like colds, sinusitis, or flu (both caused by viruses, NOT by bacteria). In case of the common cold (an upper respiratory infection), it is caused by more than 200 different subtypes of the respiratory virus; it usually takes few days to build up and lasts about three to five days. It has no medicine; so, no medicine is the best medicine. In case of flu (influenza) which comes more abruptly and lingers twice as long, people are better off just weathering the illness at home; taking time-off, rest and plenty of water are the true cures. Typically, for healthy adults and kids, colds and flu don't require a doctor's attention; but if a flu patient goes from well to very sick in a matter of minutes, then see doctor immediately. Flu is common cause of pneumonia and death. In one study of 166 sinusitis patients, when half the patients were dispensed with the antibiotic amoxicillin and the other half with sugar pills (almost all offered with other basic remedies to relieve symptoms), researchers noticed no difference whether they got the antibiotic or not. Yet, 58% prescriptions are written for antibiotics for patients aged 14 and under, for 5 upper respiratory infections: (1) sore throat, (2) common cold, (3) ear infection, (4) bronchitis and (5) sinus infection. Common colds thrive in cooler temperatures. One study by Yale University establishes that a 7°C drop in ambient temperature, can interrupt the body's ability to stop cold viruses from proliferating. So, if you cool down the room temperature from 98.6°F (36.2°C) (average normal body temperature) to 91.4°F (33°C), it can dampen your immune system allowing viruses to replicate and thrive. Keeping your nose area warm, helps. Washing hands often—especially before eating or touching eyes, nose or mouth—is the best way to keep at bay the illness-causing microorganisms from getting into your body. General fitness and stress-lowering meditation are clinically proven ways to lower the risk for colds. Some studies claim vitamin D supplements do help in colds and flu.

Respiratory infections are caused by viruses (not by bacteria), which do not warrant for antibiotics. So, do not ask the doctor to prescribe antibiotics when you have (or your child has) a mere cold. Another important thing is to make sure that you follow your doctor's advice correctly, especially when you use antibiotics. You have to take the full dose of antibiotic medication that the doctor has prescribed for you, even when you feel better just after a few doses. This is to make certain that you kill as much of the bacteria as possible the first time around. Otherwise, if you kill only just a fraction of the bacteria—enough to feel better, for example, with natural immunity to fight the infection comfortably—you still have the surviving bacteria and could still spread them. And now they are even more robust and more antibiotic-resistant than usual. So, for the next time, the antibiotic does not work that well. Therefore, you should not take antibiotics when these are not needed. Or if you have to, follow all the way as the doctor prescribes. [Info: According to a study, one special type of honey—manuka honey—from New Zealand has shown promise against bacteria. It lowers the risk of infections among people using medical devices like catheters. The study finds that the honey, even at a very low concentration, inhibits the bacteria's ability to develop into a biofilm.]

Antibiotic-free large-scale organic poultry has significantly lower level of drug-resistant bacteria than that of their conventional counterparts. Both types of bacteria are accountable for the large-scale food-borne illness in the United States, infecting at least 3.4 million people annually. Farm workers who handle those animals get sick, constantly. Drug resistant infections in general population have been sky-rocketed since the 90s, now killing at least 70,000 a year. Now, a new type of pneumonia emerging in China, which is both highly drug-resistant and extremely lethal. It spreads easily and quickly. A fatal outbreak happened in one brand-new hospital in China with very good hygiene record. The drug-resistant microbe strain is so lethal that there is no drug available to quell, not only in China but also in the U.S. Current food safety and hygiene practices among poultry producers and handlers are not adequate. No chicken is completely free of pathogens. So, in preparing poultry, be cautious of cross-contamination on the cutting board, and cook it well at an elevated temperature. Consumers are required to be vigilant both at the grocery store and at home to cook chicken properly: thaw chicken at room temperature (not in a microwave oven) and cook it in a hot oven (consult oven temperature).

However, these examples are not limited only to chickens and turkeys. When compared with most commonly available American beef (which is raised on a grain-intensive feed), pasture-raised beef offers 400% more vitamin A and E. The beta-carotene and conjugated linoleic acid content—all of which are known to prevent cancer—is also much higher. It is rich in omega-3 fatty acid, which is a major inhibitor of heart disease. Animals that are raised on an unvaried and unnatural diet are much poorer as far as these nutrients are concerned.

The same pattern holds true for vegetables as well. Vegetables such as broccoli, brussels sprouts, cabbage, turnips, kale, and mustard greens are mostly grown in a soil where only these vegetables are grown with the help of large amounts of chemical fertilizers and pesticides. Fertilizers are used copiously in these large farms, especially synthetic nitrogen. The chemicals enable the vegetables to grow sturdy and quickly, enabling them to withstand the rigors of long-distance travel. When they arrive at the supermarket, they look fresh and have the same luster as when they were picked. But the combination of different factors, like being raised in an industrial farm, shipped over a long distance, and stored days before and after being delivered to the supermarket makes the vegetables lose up to three-fourths of their vitamin C and almost all of their calcium, iron, and potassium. They are much inferior in taste compared to the naturally grown ones.

Here is one example of how industrial farming in the U.S. has destroyed the taste and nutritional value of the tomato. Florida accounts for a third of all fresh tomatoes produced in the United States and virtually all the tomatoes harvested during the fall and winter seasons. Tomatoes mass-produced in Florida differ radically from the garden varieties that you grow in your backyard. Why? First, farm tomatoes are grown in the sand that contains less nutrients and organic materials. Second, tomatoes are pacified by pesticides, transported, and artificially ripened. The extreme humidity of Florida breeds such large populations of insects that farmers have to apply vast and various pesticides on a weekly basis. Take, for instance, tomato growers. The official Florida handbook lists as many as 110 different pesticides, fungicides, and herbicides that can legally be applied to a tomato field over the course of a growing season. The Pesticide Action Network nicknamed them as "bad actors" since they are really the worst in agricultural chemical arsenals. Florida growers apply pesticides and herbicides eight times more than that used in California, the next leading tomato-growing state in the country. Because farmers are paid by the weight, they plant tomato plants that yield as much as possible and produce tomatoes that are able to stand up to being harvested, packed, artificially turned red or orange (in an ethylene gas chamber), and then shipped without breaking across the U.S. to reach supermarkets after a week or ten days later. The mass-produced tomatoes available in today's supermarkets really lack the flavor, taste, and value. One ambitious experiment, which is supposed to spread over a hundred years, compares plots of organic and conventional tomatoes; and now, at the ten-year mark, they have observed that tomatoes grown in organic lands contain significantly higher levels of beneficial antioxidant compounds. The same observations apply to most root vegetables as well, whether potatoes, beets, parsnips, or carrots.

For the great flavor and health benefits, the right thing is to eat vegetables grown in nutrient-rich soil. Most organic farmers try to develop complex relationships between crop roots, soil microbes, and minerals. These relationships are upset by chemical additives. It is an occult relation between humans and vegetation. To avert such situations, we need to have a radical change in our culture and paradigm shift in agriculture planning. Organic (rather than inorganic) should be the norm—not the other way around. Some produce should be labeled as "inorganic produce," and that "organic produce" should be labeled as simply "produce," as it is logically obvious. Our "organic life" should default to "Life." Organic eaters should demand benevolence in their food!

Yet some researchers still claim that fruits and vegetables labeled "organic," on average, are no more nutritious than their conventional inorganic counterparts; nor are they any less contaminated by such bacteria as *E. coli*. Inorganic conventional produces have more pesticide residue; they admit it to be true. But the levels are almost always under the allowable safety limits set by the Environmental Protection Agency. They claim, at the same time, that conventional fruits and vegetables are far less expensive and do no harm to humans and that there is no obvious health advantage to the organic meats as well. But that claim is hard to swallow. The reason, their studies have a real hard time in taking into subtle effects of our environment on our health or what we eat, or any other powerful influences get in the way (as many studies are often funded by the food manufacturers). Also, the typical study time of two years or less is hardly enough to determine and document any particular health hazard or benefit.

According to the Environmental Working Group's 2018 report, 70% of conventionally grown fruits and vegetables contain up to 230 different pesticides or their derivatives. According to market sample analysis by the U.S. Department of Agriculture, the "Dirty Dozen List of Fruits and Vegetables" with high pesticide include: (1) strawberries, (2) spinach, (3) nectarines, (4) apples, (5) grapes, (6) peaches,

(7) cherries, (8) pears, (9) tomatoes, (10) celery, (11) potatoes, and (12) sweet bell peppers. To give a bare idea about the intensity of contamination, one sample of strawberries, for instance, tested positive for 20 different types of pesticide, and one sample of spinach contain twice the pesticide residue by weight than any other fruit or vegetable. According to the CDC, though foods of animal origin are the most likely to be contaminated, raw fruits and vegetables can easily be contaminated and spread food-borne illness as well. While fruits and vegetables are considered to be healthy nourishment, but in reality, it is just the opposite. Now, it's your call. In the meantime, to remove the pesticide and E. coli bacteria, wash fruits and vegetables thoroughly with water. Produce are produced in the soil, so there could be dirt on it. Produce, sold in loose or sold in the open, are exposed to contamination. Rinse or submerge leafy vegetables in water, scrub with the clean brush, use baking-soda to clean away pesticides. Yet, if you are not sure, switch to organic, which will significantly reduce pesticide and E. coli. However, you need not wash items that are labeled "pre-washed" or "ready to eat."

Almost all corns, soybeans, pluses and minuses are now grown in the U.S. contain DNA derived from bacteria. The foreign gene empowers these GMO (genetically modified organisms) crops to produce their own insecticide to fight off pests resistant to herbicides and to withstand drought. Unlike any of their previous predecessors, these cornstalks, to give an example, are so tough that when you cut them off to harvest them, they are like little spears stabbing, bumping, and flattening tractor tires (in some instances, flattening just in two years as against normally five or six years). They spoil the soil! You can't grow any other crop in there. Naturally, the quality of GMO crops for human consumption is open to discussion. In a real-world situation, while the Scottish government passed a law to prohibit genetically modified crops, here in the U.S., the government approved genetically modified salmon as safe for human consumption. [Info: A new gene is inserted into fertilized salmon eggs to boost the production of growth hormones, making a fish grow twice as fast as its conventional farm-raised counterpart.]

Almost all processed foods in the U.S.—cereals, snacks, salad dressings—have ingredients from plants whose DNA have been manipulated or genetically modified (GM) in the laboratory. Technically, GM foods are the foods that are produced from organisms whose genetic materials (DNA) have been modified (e.g., by introducing a gene from a different organism) in an important way that does not occur naturally. It changes the DNA architecture and designs life by synthetic biology. Researchers are now engaged in this to improve the yield by introducing one or many resistance elements to the plant to protect from diseases, and by enhancing the plant's tolerance to herbicides. Very soon, they aim to add nutrient contents of the food by reducing the plant's allergenic potential, or by improving the production process. While food scientists and regulators claim that it does not pose any danger, a fierce debate is going on over labeling the GMOs. Enlightened consumers and informed supporters in favor of labeling argue that consumers do have the right to know if foods have been genetically modified with genes from another species. The FDA says that GMO labeling is generally not necessary because such genetic modifications do not materially change the food. Farmers, food companies, and biotech scientists are afraid that GMO labels might upset consumers to reject genetically modified food along with the technology that started it—linking the genetic engineering to health hazards that many scientists have discredited. Until now, Americans are quite about genetically modified crops on the market compared to Europeans, who claim that such foods must be labeled. Protesters in Britain are threatening to remove some genetically modified wheat being grown in a research trial near London. Rather than genetically modified crops, a new generation of crops is coming to the market—known as gene-edited crops. Unlike the older methods of engineering the genes, the method uses a gene-editing tool like CRISPR to snip and tweak the DNA at precise locations. As the gene-edit does not introduce foreign genes from plants or pests into the crops, it largely falls outside the current regulations. Genetically modified crops and genetically edited crops are mostly more of a political issue than science.

The dairy industry has also not remained unaffected by the process of industrialization of the food supply. Pasture-raised cattle give far more nutritious milk. A pasture-raised hen gives eggs that have up to three times the amount of cancer-fighting omega-3 than that of eggs that come from factory hens. Consumers are now increasingly concerned about the origins of the products they buy, and as their purchasing habits change, the businesses have also respected the customers' loyalty by sourcing sustainably produced goods.

World consumption of animal-based protein jumped from 150 billion pounds in the 1960s (when the population was 3.5 billion) to 550 billion pounds in the 2010s (when the population was 7 billion). North Americans top the list at 260 lb. of meat per year. Today, food scientists are working on a number of meat substitutes: (a) in vitro meat, (b) growing certain parts of the animal (edible meat) under a suitable medium, and (c) meat made from vegetable compounds, all of which could one day produce an end product that is sufficiently meat-like in appearance, texture, smell, taste, and after-eating satisfaction.

Like any good ecosystem, our diet should be varied, dynamic, and interrelated. Twenty years ago, Americans were spending roughly 10% of their disposable income on health care and about 15% on food. In 2014, those numbers were essentially reversed. There is a tendency to ignore the plant and animal systems loaded with genetic complexity. We forget the benefits that complexity passes down to us. Food should be such as would reduce, if not eliminate, the need for medicine.

We should remember that we can't be healthy unless our food production and firms are healthy. We cannot afford to forget that the diversity of food culture is at the root of healthy agriculture, which is in tune with the natural ecosystem. We also cannot forget that we cannot tinker too much with the food chain without incurring the wrath of nature.

With the influx of modern trade and the advent of modern supermarkets, it has become more difficult to stick to the right diet. Every trip to the supermarket is like an unwinding exercise after a hectic day. This means a person invariably ends up buying all the wrong things to indulge himself in a way he thinks he really deserves after a hard day's work. What is necessary before we enter the supermarket is a healthy shopping list so that we don't lose our way, lured by the colorful arrays of items on the shelves. For reference, a typical supermarket food store has an inventory of about twenty-five thousand types of items, mostly food. Items kept on the shelves are nicely packaged to make them visually attractive so that buyers tend to pick up things while walking around. However, this is discouraged by health scientists as this leads to increased purchases and consumption of junk food. Some food experts recommend that packages should be labeled as simply as color codes—like traffic light symbols—so that consumers can easily figure out with a glance which food is a go (green), a go-slow (yellow), or a stop (red). In contrast, the food industry's efforts to make selecting food easier may instead make it more confusing for consumers to understand. However, to make sense of food labels, here are the key words, defined with statements:

- **Organic:** Organic products are produced without synthetic fertilizers and antibiotics, sewage sludge, irradiation, and genetic engineering. They do not contain GMOs. Products with "organic," "100% organic," or "made with organic [ingredients listed here]" labels are certified by the U.S. Department of Agriculture (USDA). The USDA organic livestock standard prohibits antibiotics and growth hormones and requires 100% organic feed. According to the organic trade group, such items account for 5.5 percent of all food sold in retail outlets in 2018 in the United States. One study claims that people who ate more organic produce, meat, egg, dairy, and other products, have 25 percent fewer cancer diagnoses overall especially lymphoma and breast cancer; though, the study does not prove an organic diet is the factor that causes the reduction in cancers. One French study that followed 70,000 adults, most of them women, for five years, report published in 2018 in *JAMA Internal Medicine,* strongly suggests that people who eat more organic produce, grains, fruits, vegetables, meat and dairy products can have 25 percent fewer cancer diagnoses overall, especially lymphoma and postmenopausal breast cancer.

Now greenhouse-grown "hydroponic" vegetables are using organic label as well. In fact, hydroponically grown vegetables, produced on an industrial scale, are taking over organic vegetables grown organically. National Organic Standards Board argues that when you can produce, take for example of tomatoes, per pound hydroponically with 3 to 5 gallons of water, why growing the same in an open field that uses anywhere from 26 to 37 gallons of water. Most organic labeled tomatoes sold in supermarkets in 2017 are grown without touching the soil. Very soon virtually all tomatoes, peppers, cucumbers, lettuce and berries will be hydroponic. Longtime organic farmers consider it a betrayal of true organic principles.

- **Natural or All-Natural:** These terms are the most dubious and misleading of all. There is no government regulation from the FDA or USDA for using the words on the labels; they can't or won't define it. Yet consumers search for the word, and food companies love to print it on the labels. "Natural" is a generic term for foods that do not have synthetic preservatives, additives, and artificial sweeteners. The word "natural" is regulated only in meat products, where the regulation requires meat products have no preservatives and undergo minimal processing. The FDA objects to calling it a "natural" food only if it contains synthetic additives, artificial flavors, or colors. Food producers can add sugar or cornstarch, oil, or anything else naturally derived from plants or animals to their products. It's all "natural." Surveys show that most consumers perceive the label as equivalent to "organic." According to *Consumer Reports*, 62% of consumers believe that the "natural" label means no artificial ingredients, pesticides, or chemicals, and it hasn't been genetically modified. But, in fact, it is not: there is no agreed-upon definition or regulation for the label "natural" universally.

- **Regenerative:** Not official yet! It's not about the food, but about the soil where food grows. It's a grass-root movement by the organic farmers—to keep roots of all kinds in the soil. Over time, the soil grows darker and more fertile with chock-full of microbes and fungi. The aim is to promote "healthy soil" that is full of life. The soil culture was not in mainstream American agriculture. But now, the big food companies are on board and appealing for a new eco-label for their products, alongside "organic"—calling, "regenerative."

- **GMO or Bioengineered (BE):** Not official yet, which one! Based on feedback from 112,000 responses from consumers, farmers and manufacturers, among others, USDA unveils forthcoming prototypes for more commonly used phrases like genetically engineered or GMO.

- **Cage-Free:** To describe poultry and eggs with reference to the animals (chickens and turkeys), whether they are given relative freedom to move around.

- **Free-Range:** To describe livestock and poultry—anything from cows to pigs to chickens—permitted to graze or forage for grass, plants, grains, and the like, rather than being confined to feedlots or small enclosures. "Free-range" does mean organic.

- **Grass-Fed:** A grass-fed livestock is one that has eaten nothing but its mother's milk, fresh grass, and hay—i.e., cattle raised in grass pastures.

- **Pesticide-Free:** "Pesticide-free" means no pesticides (including herbicides) are used—at all. However, there are some caveats; some products that have ingredients that are technically considered pesticides but are of low concern are considered to be compatible with the "pesticide-free zone" label. Unfortunately, that is not always the case. Investigative studies have found that even some organic produce contain pesticide residue. So, for true pesticide-free products, go for only "pesticide residue-free" labels.

- **Hormone-Free and Antibiotic-Free:** To describe a general claim that no growth hormones and no antibiotics were used in the production of beef, poultry, pork, and more. Grass-fed, pasture-raised animals are typically antibiotic- and hormone-free. It's a little confusing, but for a quality choice of meat, the best way of finding hormone-free and antibiotic-free meat is to look for the "USDA Organic" seal.

- **Whole Grain and Multigrain:** A grain is a small hard seed—a seed from a food plant such as corn, wheat, rice, rye, oats, barley, maize, or millet. A whole grain is defined as a cereal grain that contains the cereal germ, endosperm, and bran; in contrast, a refined grain retains only the endosperm. "Whole grain" contains all the natural nutrients in the grain and has not been refined. The term "multigrain" refers only to the fact that more than one grain is used in the product, and the grain used may be whole grain or a refined grain. All grains in multigrain may not be nutritious. By monitoring diet habits and food intake every two to four years, one study tracking about 118,000 men and women with no cancer or cardiovascular disease to begin with, concluded that higher whole-grain intake was associated with lower cardiovascular mortality and the mortality overall: for every 28 gram-per-day serving of whole grains was measurably linked to 9% lower rate of death from cardiovascular disease and 5% lower rate of death from any other cause. Whole-grain consumption helps in disease prevention.

  Eat whole grain and extend your life span! According to one report in the *BMJ* in 2016, whole-grain consumption is associated with a considerable reduction in the risk of death from cancer, coronary heart disease, infectious disease, respiratory disease, and diabetes. Analyzing collective data from forty-five studies, researchers report that eating 90 g of whole grains a day reduces the risk from all-cause mortality by 17% when compared with eating none. In another analysis, researchers using data from fourteen prospective studies covering 786,076 participants report that eating whole grain reduces the risk from all-cause mortality by 16% (each 16 g increase by 7%) and from cardiovascular mortality by 18% when compared with eating none. Whole grains are still good when lightly processed, for instance, in steel-cut oats, barley, brown rice, buckwheat, whole wheat, more unrefined forms of oatmeal, whole rye, and millet. The human body responds very differently to milled grains than to whole grains with the kernel intact. Whole grains that are less processed take longer to digest and therefore lead to more gradual rises in blood sugar. In general, whole grains contain more fiber; however, many products with whole grains that claim to be high in fiber contain added fiber in the form of cellulose, which is not desirable. Also, all whole-grain foods are not necessarily healthy; some may be loaded with salt, sugar, preservatives, and very little fiber.

- **Gluten-Free:** Gluten (from Latin *gluten*, "glue") is a generic name for the protein composite (glue) present in the foods that are produced from wheat and other grain species, including barley and rye. For more than 93% of the world population, gluten is perfectly fine; but food manufacturers and marketers twist it otherwise. Gluten is not entirely perfect, however, because of its reaction to celiac disease—an immune reaction to gluten that damages the small intestine. This is very real; it affects two to three million

Americans. Gluten ataxia is a neurological condition characterized by loss of coordination and balance. It is one scarier condition that attacks the brain, which in turn cause problems in gait and muscular control. Approximately, an additional eighteen million Americans may also have some lesser forms of gluten sensitivity that cause intestinal discomfort but no damage. For those with celiac disease (who have to maintain a strict gluten-free diet) or for those with gluten intolerance, all products labeled "gluten-free," unfortunately, aren't always entirely gluten free; there persists a trace of gluten, which is typically present in wheat, barley, and rye. Gluten-free products—such as bread, crackers, and cookies—are often packed with more refined flours, sugar, and artificial ingredients than traditional baked products. So, if you aren't clinically diagnosed with celiac disease or gluten intolerance, "gluten-free" doesn't necessarily mean healthy.

Serving size matters. While eating calorie-rich items like ice cream, milkshake, or junk food like chips, crackers, or cookies, it is advisable to pour them on a plate instead of having them straight out of the container. Treat them as a treat, not as part of your normal meal. Also, it is advisable to have ample quantities of water, at least eight glasses (of 8 fl. oz.) a day, to flush the toxins out of the body. Drink room-temperature or lukewarm water. Chewing ice or drinking ice-floated cold water is a lure to fatness. Drinking water just before bed indulges fat and is not a good practice. Alcohol consumption should be restricted. Also, even while eating fast food, one can choose healthful items by avoiding fried food or large portions. While cooking, it is better to broil, bake, or roast. Light stir-fry is better than deep-fry. Sautéing is frying the food first on one side and then on the other, and one should ideally use a nonstick frying pan to reduce the amount of oil required. Also, one can try using flavorful oils like sesame oil or olive oil. Adding a pinch of parmesan or blue cheese to the recipes can add flavor without adding too much calories. Add olive oil and vinegar to salads. Another quick way of spicing up meals without adding fat could be to try out some fresh herbs. Ethnic foods and seasonings often add a lot of flavor without adding sugar, fat, or calories.

While two-thirds of Americans are considered overweight and when many acknowledge a desire to eat healthier, fierce competition is raging among the food producers to discover the Holy Grail: products that will have less of the bad stuff (fat, sugar, salt, white flour) and more of the good stuff (whole grains, fiber, and fish oil). Yet business remains business for the most part. Consumers are regularly fed bad stuff as ever, like preservatives, flavors, colors, chemicals and compounds which are commonly used to protect the integrity of food, and in safe transportation and storage. Few chemicals are specially of health concern: nitrates and nitrites, used as preservatives primarily in meat products; phthalates, used to make plastic packaging; bisphenols, used in the lining of metal cans for canned food products; perfluoroalkyl chemicals (PFC), used in grease-proof paper and packaging, and perchlorates, used in plastic packaging as antistatic agent.

Given the easy availability of ready-to-eat processed food marketed as "healthy," Americans end up consuming large quantities of these processed foods, blissfully unaware of the fact that what they were eating might not be that healthy. In reality, it is. Approximately 60% of an American's daily calories come from "ultra-processed" food that contains ingredients such as preservatives, flavors, colors, hydrogenated oils, emulsifiers, sweeteners, and other additives that you wouldn't cook with at home. The higher the degree to which a food item is processed, the further it goes from the origins of the food chain. So, one of the most important prerequisites for staying in good health is to stay as close to the original as possible. We are not obliged to eat preservatives.

Another piece of news that breaks the traditional notions of eating healthy is that refrigerated food is susceptible to a poisonous bacterium called listeria. Thus, it may not be safe to store large quantities of leftovers in the refrigerator for consumption later, as is the general practice. At least, one should not do it very often. A variety of dairy and poultry products—as well as some vegetables—is susceptible to this bacterium, which has been shown to survive low temperatures and longtime pasteurization. In dairy products, *Listeria monocytogenes* are normally concentrated in curd (naturally contaminated cheese) and in smaller amounts in cultured buttermilk, butter, and yogurt. The organism is quite capable of surviving in meat and also in raw eggs regardless of typical aftertreatment. Freezing, surface dehydration, and simulated spray chilling have been shown not to affect the survival of the bacteria. Among vegetables, only the potato and radish appeared to be regularly contaminated, while new studies have further shown that small quantities of bacteria were present in salad ingredients and even in prepacked mixed salads. Listeria grows well at 70°F (15°C) on fresh vegetables stored under a controlled atmosphere, as well as in refrigerated cooked items. Keeping in mind these findings, one must try to eat as much freshly cooked food as possible.

In the U.S., new estimates of food poisoning cases tracked by the CDC indicate that about 48 million people a year get sick from tainted food. This estimate is way down from the previous figure of 76 million in 1999. The number of deaths is also down to about 3,000 a year from 5,000. Yet this tells us that one in six gets sick each year from tainted food. The illnesses, hospitalizations, and deaths to this extent also tell us that the government needs to do more.

Save thyself! Unless you are cautious enough, food is unsafe practically at any meal. About 200,000 Americans are sickened every day by contaminated food. Approximately 325,000 Americans are hospitalized every year due to foodborne illnesses. The economic cost is passed on to society instead of the food producers. The economic cost is huge. According to one estimate, the annual health-related cost of foodborne illnesses in the U.S. is about $152 billion. Perverse economic incentives without secured food safety rules now guide the food market. Adulterated foods are cheaper to produce than safer and quality foods. Since consumers cannot make out the difference between the two, good producers that try to do the right thing are forced out of the competition. Food surprises are reminders that almost every bite we take is with a leap of faith. The law of the jungle prevails. A great deal of harm can be avoided with a few simple reforms by the government authorities and custodians. Nobody should lose a child because the government lacks the will and power to act.

Although humans are omnivores, each culture and religion hold some food preferences. Despite all the authority we grant to science in matters of nutrition and nourishment, culture still has a lot to tell us about how to choose, prepare, and eat food, and especially the taboos we invoke to organize our eating lives. Some of these food habits have withstood the test of time and have been established by food science, but all of them have something to teach us about our continuing efforts to pick a healthy and wholesome path every step of the way through the minefields of modern food, from markets to menus. In one survey, while most Americans didn't consider their diets as healthy, 56% of them haven't changed their eating habits even with all essential health information.

Roasting or baking is one way to make vegetables tasty by removing water content without losing much of their nutritional value. Roasting or baking vegetables with a modest amount of olive oil and sea salt, until they are a little dark and crispy—like crunchy cauliflower, crispy brussels sprouts, or caramelized root vegetables. They can be almost too tasty and too good for you. While some nutritional values may deplete, others may boost and still remain veggies at heart: full of fiber, filling, low in calories, and rich in minerals.

Preparing food or preheating food in a *microwave oven* is another area where science and business are mysteriously silent. Convenience—especially in the use of microwave ovens—comes at a significant harmful threat to health in general. Microwaves are electromagnetic radiation where waves of electrical and magnetic fields move together through space. They are on the low end of the distribution of energy in the radiated spectrum, which includes visible light, radio waves, gamma rays, and X-rays. The microwaves' electromagnetic radiations have a wavelength of about 10 cm next to radio waves, which run in a few mm. It generates heat by triggering water molecules in the food to resonate at very high frequencies. If the food does not contain water, it won't heat. The radiation is nonionizing, meaning that it does not carry enough energy to ionize atoms or molecules, but it can change the position of atoms without altering their structure, composition, and properties. It does not happen in conventional ovens (gas or electric). Nonionizing radiation also occurs in our usual living environments, such as those from cellular phones, home electronic devices, visible light, ultraviolet and infrared waves, waves from radio or television, and electric blankets. One example can be prolonged exposure to sunlight that can damage your skin (which is obvious) and the surface of the eyes (which not many people know). The effect of radiation is cumulative. Exposure to radiation from multiple sources can hurt tissues by causing molecular damage, including DNA mutations. [Mutation is a sudden alteration in one or more heritable characteristics from the parent type. It occurs due to alteration or damage in a gene or a chromosome in such a way as to permanently alter the genetic messages of the nucleotide sequence of a genome of any organism, virus, or any other genetic element.]

While a microwave oven can conveniently and rapidly heat the food, it can cause a change in the food's chemical structure. It deforms, distorts, and damages the molecules of the food. Microwave technology, first discovered in 1945, was put in use for microwave ovens and were introduced to household consumers in the late 1970s. Since then, numerous health issues have emerged. Besides depleting the nutritional value of food, numerous carcinogenic toxins leach out of plastic and paper containers, including popcorn, pizzas, and chips. And these toxins mix into the food that we ingest. Radiation leakage occurs while operating—mostly in defective models. Even when it operates correctly, the microwave levels within the kitchen area tend to be significantly higher. Microwaves travel through walls. Studies demonstrate that a 2.4 GHz radiation (which is a typical frequency of radiation emitted by microwave ovens and by the Wi-Fi routers) can harm the human heart at nonthermal levels. For some, the radiation causes blood sugar to spike, which can be a cause of one type of diabetes. Studies generally agree that microwaving food damages its nutritional value. Broccoli can lose up to 97% of its beneficial antioxidants. As short as sixty seconds of microwaving can make raw garlic deactivate its alliinase, its principle beneficial ingredient. Microwaves cause a greater degree of "protein unfolding" than conventional heating. It destroys vital disease-fighting agents in breast milk that offer protection for the young baby. The vitamin content of infant formulas gets depleted by microwaving, and some amino acids get converted into other substances that are biologically inactive. By informing all these, the perspective here eating microwaved foods over months and years, what is the collective effect on the body and the health? Think about it. Just imagine that you get your beautiful organic veggies at a premium price or out of your labor, and then you ruin it into a "dead" food that can even cause disease! So, instead of microwaving—steaming, boiling, or light cooking is best.

Just six minutes of microwave heating turns 30% to 40% of the vitamin B12 in milk into an inert (dead) form and is unusable by mammals. Mysteriously, there has been little research done on how microwaves affect the organic molecules, or how the human body responds to consuming microwaved foods. Some twenty years of Russian research—the result of which was convincing enough to ban the microwave ovens in Russia in 1976 (but lifted during Perestroika)—issued a global warning about the biological and environmental damages associated with the use of microwave ovens. Some of those concerns are as follows:

- Carcinogens are formed in varying degrees from microwaving of nearly all foods.
- Microwaving of milk and wet grains converts amino acids into carcinogenic substances.
- Microwaving cooked or prepared meats causes the formation of cancer-causing agents like d-nitrosodienthanolamines.
- Thawing frozen fruits in a microwave woven converts their glucoside and galactoside fractions into carcinogenic substances.
- Even extremely short exposure for raw, prepared, or frozen vegetables convert their plant alkaloids into carcinogens.
- Microwaving plants—especially root vegetables—form carcinogenic free radicals.
- Structural degradation leading to decreased food value is found to be 60%–90% overall, with a significant decrease in bioavailability of vitamin B complex, vitamins C and E, and lipotropics (substances that prevent abnormal accumulation of fat).

As you cook, so you eat. From time to time, you should pause and devote your attention to what you are eating. Cooking should be considered neither a chore nor a recreation. It is just like any other household work—a work to be done. Simple cooking done with fresh, well-selected ingredients is a joy and returns us to the basics. Yet the growing trend is that people are relying on convenience: buying foods such as pre-chopped vegetables instead of buying the whole raw ingredients and doing the kitchen work themselves. Instead of microwaving or boiling, steaming the vegetables is best. One survey estimates a trend of about a 17% increase in all types of prepared veggies over 2010 to 2011. Obviously, chefs and food lovers don't exactly embrace the trend. Cooking from scratch is getting out of the usual run.

Cooking changes our lifestyle. Home cooking is the one single most impactful task we can do as a family to improve health and general well-being. Aside from the fact that cooking is considered a "moderate exercise," it enables us to take care of our nourishment, nutrition, pleasure, relaxation, health, environment, and culture. The wisdom and the pleasure of getting children interested in cooking early on is also a good idea. Consequently, it helps our children—the next generation—to take care of these things and to think critically. If you neglect, if you use a smoke alarm as a timer, you miss the point. You miss the dinner. So, be thoughtful about your meal. Food should be homemade, not machine-made. So, love cooking! Cooking is a performing art!

The state of the Standard American Diet (SAD) is really sad. Transgenic corn grains, high-tech cereals, miracle milk laced with growth hormone, mysterious milk, super squash, diet colas sweetened with aspartame, TV dinners, super-fast breakfasts—this is the food inventory of America!

Are we supposed to eat all these, or are they going to eat us? We are not even talking *E. coli* poisoning, bisphenol A (BPA) contamination in food (more than two-thirds of cans on U.S. grocery store shelves contain BPA; more than 92% of Americans have BPA in their urine), mercury in fish, or dioxin in drinking water. A blood test of pregnant mothers shows dozens of chemicals, called environmental organic acids (EOAs), some of which have never been documented, that are linked to cancer, genetic defects, and fetal damage. Bisphenol-A have the chemical structures very similar to hormones, implying that they can disrupt the endocrine system of the fetus and interfere with its development. Genetically engineered pharmacorn is getting inadvertently mixed in all kinds of food from cornflakes to baby food. Genetically modified (GM) food—the food that is derived from organisms whose DNA has been modified through genetic engineering—and biopharmaceuticals are wreaking havoc in food industries. Where are we going? Are we not going away from Mother Nature? The official modes of talking points about food are suffering a serious loss of credibility. If you seek a medical guide from the food authorities, more often than not, you get the wrong directions. There is nobody to rely on. If we can't rely on the producers or on the government or even on the nutritionists to guide us, then who can we rely on?

The food contains instructions for our metabolism. Our relationship with food is a mirror to ourselves. We are what we eat. We live by the food, we die by the food. So, eat well, live well, and thrive! Good food strengthens us; bad food hurts us. Treat it like a task that deserves attention, devotion, and dedication so that every meal will turn into a feast. The joy of a homemade meal, modest as it may sound, is another way to enjoy Mother Nature. Food is the most primitive form of solace. Turn to Mother Nature. We need to gather and prepare our own food. All plants and animals gather their own food from Mother Nature. Nature is our mother.

3.1 How Food Works

> One should eat to live, not live to eat.
> —Cicero (106–43 BC), Roman philosopher and orator

From an evolutionary perspective, human settlers—like most animals—were hardwired not just to eat but to gorge. It's because living in the wild means you never know how much sweat you have to shed to get the next meal or when the next famine is going to strike. So, the best way to survive is to load up on calories when you can, even if that starvation never comes. We are not only programmed to eat a lot, but we also prefer to eat fatty foods that are high in calories. Deliberately, being a fat lover is a big advantage. The appetite causes animals to long for and consume high-calorie fatty foods, storing away the energy reserve for times of starvation. Since then—and perhaps more after the invention of pottery around 12,000–7,000 BC—humans started eating twice as much, risking injury to kidneys, damage to the liver, and falling sick.

Eating is not an entertainment. Yet it is. We love to eat. We enjoy the food. We indulge food in the same emotion as love, affection, or reward. Emotions are rapid delivery systems in the brain, and food drives emotions. But food is primarily a health issue. Food is energy—partly necessary for the wear and tear of our daily lives and partly necessary for ongoing maintenance and to avoid sickness. At the same time, food in excess may cause illness. We need food for survival and to remain fit, but not as much to be food-sick. Not a mindless eating but a mindful eating!

Eat what you like to eat. Even more importantly, do not eat what you do not like to eat (in quality and in quantity). I repeat: Do NOT eat what you do not like to eat. You might think that's easy but think again. It's not. Even if you can recall it while eating that you should not be eating, it is still good enough. Here is one joke. On his way to work, a man stepped on a banana skin and slipped on the road and got hurt. He managed somehow and went to work. Come the next day, being more careful, he saw another banana skin at the same spot. Then he panicked, for he had to step on it, slip over it, and get hurt again that day. The same goes for the analogy here: "Oh! I have to eat that junk again today!" You might be eating the same dinner leftover from yesterday or the only meal you have or the only few meals that you can cook. You knowingly eat the same junk today like stepping on the banana skin and getting hurt again today, knowingly. Food that you like to eat is really hard to find, even in a banquet. Anyway, try to eat what you like to eat, and don't eat what you don't like to eat.

Your gut instinct tells you what and when the food is good for you, or not good for you. (Actually, it is your gut ~~instinct~~ bacteria that tells you what and when the food is good for you, or not good for you. Gut is considered as our second brain.) Our gut is jam-packed with microbes. Gut bacteria react to what we eat. One of their actions is to digest some parts of the food that we can't digest on our own. The apparent nutrient value of food may not be an absolute one, but the one that is since modified in part by these microbes Trillions of bacteria that live in the gut influence our physiology wildly from one person to another. It sounds funny but true, that these microbes in our digestive tracts do influence our food taste and food choices by manipulating our dietary desires by releasing distinct molecules that affect certain organ systems or influence our brain through the vagus nerve.) When you ingest what you like, you digest with ease. Food value is not what you ingest but what you digest. Our metabolism-cum-hunger affiliates the food, the saliva, the taste produced in our mouth, and the digestive enzymes in the stomach. Mechanical crushing, crunching, grinding, and breakdown of food begins in the mouth, and the chemical digestion begins as soon as the food is mixed with saliva to break down the starches. When you do not get the pleasure of eating, enough saliva is not secreted, and ingested food does not get digested. The result would be stomachache, heartburn, slow bowel movement, and so forth. So, eat what you like to eat. Also, eat when you like to eat, especially when you are hungry; do not eat because it's time to eat. Food tastes better when one is hungry; hunger is the best sauce. However, while hungry, never wolf down the food quickly. Mindful eating helps to achieve that. One weight-loss study covering nearly 60,000 people finds that about one-third of the people eat fast, more than half, at a normal speed, and only about 7%, at a slower speed. The final result: compared to fast eaters, those who eat at normal speed are 29% less likely to be obese while slow eaters, at 42%.

You eat; therefore, you are! The foods you eat, the liquids you drink, the drugs you take—all leave a mark on your body. Everything affects the internal workings of your gastrointestinal tract for the better or for the worse. The importance of a healthy digestive system is both to nourish and cleanse the body. If your digestive system performs at its best, you feel strong and healthy.

Eat regularly. Typically, three meals a day—breakfast, lunch, and dinner. It works well with the basic physiology of the human intestinal tract. Do not skip a meal. The stomach takes about four to six hours to processes a meal. When digestion begins, cell linings of the stomach and intestines release gastrointestinal hormones that stimulate the gallbladder, the liver, the pancreas, the intestines, and the brain. These hormones are routinely released according to a three-meal time schedule and are consistent with 24-hour body's cardinal clock which is linked to the metabolic processes of the body, that keeps our organs running, functioning and even thriving. The number of circadian clocks controlled by "clock genes" is not one, but *several*. Each organ—heart, liver, kidney, gut—has its *own clock* that governs their daily cycle of activity. They are synchronized with one master-clock in the brain that coordinates all other biological clocks in the whole body. The gut clock, for instance, regulates its daily routine, a flow of enzymes, absorption of nutrients, and the removal of waste. The microbiomes in our guts (the communities of trillions of bacteria) also operates on a daily rhythm as well. These daily rhythms are so integrated that they are programmed in the DNA, and at cellular level of each organ, thousands of genes are switched on, and switched off roughly at the same time every day. So to speak, we are made to have a 24-hour rhythm in our physiology and metabolism system. The daily rhythms are very important and are important because, just as our brain needs sleep each night to repair, reset and rejuvenate, every organ needs to have a down time to repair, restore and reset. During the day, much of its effect from the sunlight, the pancreas increases its production of the hormone insulin, which controls blood sugar levels, and then slows down at night. During the night, much of its effect from lack of sunlight, the brain releases melatonin, which prepares tired body to sleep. Experimental evidences in the human also suggest that consuming the bulk of the food earlier in the day is better for health. This early eating approach, also known as early time-restricted feeding, originates from the idea that human metabolism follows a daily rhythm, with enzymes, hormones and digestive systems primed for food intake in the morning till evening. Eating late in the night, on the other hand, sends a conflicting signal to the biological clocks that it's still daytime. After all experiments, trialed and tested, researchers are now sanguine that people can improve their metabolic health when they eat their meals in a daily 8- to 10-hour window—starting in the morning and finishing early in the evening. But in practice, the survey shows that most people eat over a period of 15 hours or longer each day. Thus, by changing and disrupting our normal daily cycles, we increase our risk of many illness. This is one of the reasons why night shift workers are so vulnerable to obesity, diabetes, cancers and heart diseases. While many socioeconomic factors are more likely to play a role in our wellbeing, researchers assert that circadian disruption is one key factor, which can be avoided, is responsible for the outcome of poor health. So, eat three meals a day at a certain time regularly; and, do not skip a meal.

A colloquial saying goes like this: Eat your breakfast like a king, lunch like a prince, and dinner like a pauper. Make morning meals a priority and heavy. Even dieters are often told to have a heavy breakfast, because it reduces the quantity of food consumed during the rest of the day. But one study reports otherwise. German researchers tracked the food intake of 100 normal-weight adults and 280 obese adults in two groups, who were asked to keep detailed records of everything they ate over two weeks. In both groups, a large breakfast did not affect subsequent meals; it simply added to the daily calories they consumed. It practically did not matter if they had a large breakfast, a small one, or none at all; their non-breakfast intake remained nearly the same. This means exactly the opposite of the commonly believed counsel. So, eat your breakfast normally; a heavy breakfast does not compensate for any subsequent meals. Plain oatmeal, traditional pita bread, whole grain breads, eggs, fruit, nuts, plain yogurt are common breakfast items.

Breakfast jump-starts the metabolism process of the day. So, don't mess it up. As breakfast appetizer, experts advise two good habits immediately after you woke up and before you take breakfast: (1) drink a glass of cold or room-temperature (20°C or 68°F) water (if possible, add a touch of lemon for extra metabolic boost and a zest of flavor) which activates a process called water-induced thermogenesis, where your body starts burning calories to heat the ingested water up to your body temperature (normal: 36.5–37.5 °C or 97.7–99.5 °F), and (b) go for a brisk walk (if possible, some cardio or strength training). Skipping breakfast is a not at all a good idea; because, skipping a meal, especially the first meal after overnight fast, affects hormones which are linked to appetite. Insulin action is more efficient in the morning. Metabolic rates (the rate of energy consumption) are higher early in the morning. So, people, who skip breakfast, do not get these benefits. If they go too long without eating, they slow down everything, and then when they eat later in the day, they introduce calories when glucose level has already dropped. Breakfast eaters tend to manage their weight down, compared to breakfast skippers. Studies after studies establish that eating breakfast, eating especially in the morning before 8 a.m., does the body good, improve attention and concentration. Some people are not hungry until a few hours after wake up. But, people who do not break fast soon after rising (half an hour or so), or take breakfast later in the morning, typically consume more calories over the course of the day and run a higher risk of type 2 diabetes and obesity. Without an a.m. meal, the brain reward centers lit up craving for high-calorie foods.

One Spanish study over 5 months—involving 420 overweight and obese volunteers, half men and half women, with average age 42—found that (a) dieters who ate during early part of the day—breakfast in morning and main meal before 3 p.m.—lost more weight, an average of 22 pounds over 5 months, compared to 17 pounds that of the late eaters, and (b) that what they ate in the morning was even more important than when they ate. On the contrary, another research in Canada who tracked the habits of about 12,000 adults concluded that breakfast is not consistently associated with overweight or obesity prevalence. Another study published in 2016 in the *American Journal of Clinical Nutrition* reveals that when it comes to weight loss, breakfast eaters do no better—or worse—than people who skip. High-protein breakfast generally helps to control appetite and eat less in remainder of the day. However, avoid high-carb foods (bakery muffins packed with added sugar) for energy. People burn more calories over a 24-hour period when they extended their overnight fast by skipping either lunch (41 more calories) or dinner (91 more calories), compared with the 3-meals-a-day schedule. May sound like a good thing, but the glucose concentrations, insulin resistance and markers of inflammation get higher after lunch on breakfast-skipping days. As because chronic inflammation is known to affect insulin sensitivity, researchers therefore, conclude that skipping breakfast is not a good idea, it could contribute to "metabolic impairment," which could potentially increase the risk for obesity and type 2 diabetes.

Another surprising reason that you should not skip breakfast is the increased risk for cardiovascular disease: people who skip breakfast are more likely to have higher cholesterol level, dangerous plaque build-up in their arteries, hardening and narrowing of arteries, according to one study, published in the Journal of the *American College of Cardiology* in 2017. Occasionally skipping breakfast may be permissible, but for many of us, eating daily three "square meals" does no longer fit our lifestyle; and as a society, we are slowly moving toward more continuous snacking and eating on-the-go, especially among millennials. Young adults skip breakfast twice as much compared to older adults. It is a huge cultural shift. Breakfast deserves the glory, as the most important meal of the day.

In the U.S., the concept of breakfast-specific food didn't exist until the mid to late 1800s. The breakfast was more like a meal or a dinner—that still exists in many other countries. In the U.S., the fact remains that 31 million do not eat breakfast in the morning. Eating breakfast is essential. It is also essential to stay on a three-meals-a-day course. Popcorn for breakfast or for lunch is nothing but skipping the meal. However, yogurt, and even dessert, for breakfast is a very recent phenomenon in the U.S. Contrary to the view of skipping meals, some well-publicized studies suggest that eating numerous snack-like meals throughout the day might stimulate weight loss; but it will NOT. A recent study conducted on overweight men refutes that. In that study, the control group of overweight men ate three meals of 750 cal each, and the experimental group of overweight men had six meals of about 375 cal. Over the period of the twelve-week study, the experimental group complained feeling less satisfied after smaller repasts. The study finally concluded that the pattern of eating three-meals-a-day is very optimal, and any exception to that does not yield a better metabolism in normal, overweight, and obese people.

You should eat breakfast in the morning, not in the late morning or in the afternoon. In 2014, Harvard School of Public Health researchers monitored 26,902 male health professionals aged 45 to 82 over a sixteen-year period and found that a good meal in the morning is essential to help your body prepare for the day to come and lower your risk of heart disease, diabetes, and obesity. For the rest of the day's meals, here's what they found: men who skipped breakfasts had a 27% higher rate of heart attack or death. The reason is that skipping breakfast will make people hungrier and will allow them to eat a larger lunch or dinner; it causes a surge in blood sugar, and over time, this can lead to diabetes, high cholesterol, and high blood pressure—all the risk factors that can snowball to a stroke and heart attack. One 2008 study published in the journal *Pediatrics* reveals that teenagers who ate breakfast regularly had a lower body mass index than those who did not. But another recent study for weight management, according to a short-term experimental study (published in 2016) that randomly assigned people to eat or skip breakfast for six weeks, researchers found no difference in weight change and other health outcomes. For overall health management, however, breakfast is good for health. Experts from various committees of the American Heart Association, based on studies that compared breakfast-eaters to non-eaters and their heart disease events, put out a scientific statement in 2017 that supports the existing advice about the benefits of breakfast. Breakfast-eaters are more likely to have a lower risk of heart disease and are less likely to have high cholesterol and high blood pressure. And they tend to have more normal blood sugar levels and sugar metabolism, resulting in lower risk of diabetes than those who didn't eat breakfast.

And health authorities are also taking note of this. The American Heart Association has endorsed this idea that the timing of meals does help reduce the risk factors like heart disease, high blood pressure and high cholesterol. While occasional fasting is associated with weight loss, at least in the short term, the heart association issued a scientific statement in 2017 highlighting the fact that skipping breakfast—which 20 to 30 percent of American adults do on a regular basis—is linked to a higher risk of obesity and impaired glucose metabolism or diabetes. Also, since our digestive system and the action of insulin, the pancreatic hormone our body uses to process sugars into carbohydrates and store glucose, appear to be at its peak early in the day, having large meal in the morning appears to have definite advantages on weight control, than large meal in the evening, especially in late night, say, after 10 pm. Doctors say that pancreas is literally sleeping after sunset and cannot produce enough insulin, and therefore, evening eating pushes blood glucose high in the blood-stream and stay high what doctors once call it "evening diabetes." One small clinical trial by Wolfson Medical Center in Tel Aviv, finds that large-breakfast eaters lose more body fat especially in belly fat and gain more benefits in the improvement of metabolic factors like fasting glucose levels.

To sum-up all pros and cons about breakfast, irrespective of losing weight or not, according to science, most dieticians are in the opinion to have breakfast in the morning within half an hour to one hour of waking—for a host of reasons including health benefits and good lifestyle.

Also, what you eat for breakfast is as important for setting the blood sugar level for the rest of the day. If you eat something whole grain with some fat and protein to it, your blood sugar rises slowly and falls slowly. If you eat something refined, like overly sweet pastries, your blood sugar rises fast and falls fast, which you do not want. Filling up earlier in the day also makes sense, when the body needs its most calories for energy. In European countries, usually, the very large meal of the day is eaten during the daytime. But don't overeat, because consumed calories have to be used up no matter when you eat. What you cannot use up is more likely to be stored as fat. Therefore, paying attention and being mindful to both what and when you eat is important.

A trend that could lead to eating disorders and subsequent health problems is the pressure of modern living and demanding careers that are forcing people to skip their breakfast for a delayed or postponed meal. Chained-to-office-desk worker delay eating until they get to their desks—a norm called "deskfast." Breakfast is one important meal of the day. Studies have established that eating breakfast (eating in the morning) does the body good and improves attention and concentration. In practice, few of us do, just the opposite. Nationwide, around 15% of adults report that they have fasted to slim down. A number of popular diets encourage intermittent fasting as well. A new study shows that people who eat after an overnight fast are more likely to ignore protein, fats and vegetables and immediately reach for high-calorie carbohydrates and starches. Hunger intensifies food craving. After a long fast, by skipping a meal or two, people naturally consume more calories at a time than they otherwise would. High-calorie food stimulates greater activity in the reward centers of the brain when people get the chance to eat after missing breakfast. One study finds that those who fasted eighteen hours are more likely to begin their meal with starches, eating bread or french fries before anything else. And they are less likely to eat vegetables or, for that matter, any healthy food first. In other settings, some people are in the habit of eating a heavy dinner with plenty of carbohydrates to have an urge of night's sleep. In the night, we should eat as light and sleep as sound. Eat less when you dine; live to age ninety-nine.

Studies suggest that it is healthy not to have too much food late in the day. To maintain a healthy weight, it is also important that you eat when you are hungry. Most importantly, do not eat when you are not really hungry or just in response to food cravings or just to maintain an eating schedule. Hunger peaks when you routinely expect the food. It peaks during breakfast, lunch, and dinnertime. Craving peaks after dinner. Avoid eating, especially when you are doing something and are unmindful about eating (like watching TV). You forget to stop and thus overeat.

Eat, but don't overeat. Eating too much at one meal causes pain and indigestion. It is important to eat according to your appetite. Avoid the "clean plate habit" (which is drilled into us during childhood by our parents)—not only for yourself but also for all family members, especially children. When they don't want to eat, or don't want to eat any more, don't scold them for this. (And in fact, don't scold them for any reason during mealtimes in general). Avoid too-large servings at home or in restaurants. Eat out, but not every day—leaving the dining table abandoned. According to the Commerce Department, Sales at food-service and drinking establishments rose in 1018 bringing the three-month annualized gain to 25.3 percent, the fastest pace in figures going back to 1992. When you eat out, you typically tend to eat more, sometimes worse than when you eat at home. Restaurant serving sizes have increased as well. Studies show that women in their fifties and early sixties do succeed at long-term weight loss when they practice mindful eating, especially when eating out. By cutting back on meat, cheese, butter, dessert, soda, and sugary drinks, they consume at least 300 fewer calories a day. Also, avoid eating between meals; this is often where the calories add up, and fat piles up. If you must, have a good snack. Make it a nutritious one: fresh fruit or raw vegetables.

There's a difference between getting hungry and feeling hungry. Getting hungry at meal time—breakfast, lunch or dinner—is regular. Feeling hungry—in between the meals—is irregular. While getting hangry is a real thing, feeling hungry is a fake thing where snakes fill in as a filler. Americans love snacks. They eat snacks at home, at work, at movie theaters, in the car, and especially in front of the

TV. While the typical snack time is around 3:00 p.m., when cravings are most difficult to ignore, there's hardly any time yet when they don't put something in their mouth. The mouth is in motion. Over the past thirty years or so, compared to three meals a day, the habit of eating meals has increased from 3.8 to 4.9 meals a day. Food is available everywhere, and snacks have become an acceptable norm. Snacks have now become the fourth meal of the day. Snacks account for 580 extra calories per day. And sadly enough, the majority of calories comes from beverages. While men have a better handle on self-control over food cravings, women don't—the reason is that they usually tend to snack or binge to cope with endless stress, anxiety, sadness, and exhaustion. So, if you eat snacks, be mindful and select healthy (not the junk) snacks: roasted and lightly salted pistachios, popcorn or peanuts, or pita breads, chips or crackers with two-tablespoon of hummus or avocado dip. Hummus is a chickpeas base with olive oil, tahini (sesame paste), lemon juice and spices, and avocado dip is avocado base with sour cream, lime juice, ground cumin, black beans, and chopped tomato. The snacks may be nutritious but high in calories, easily 100 to 300 calories per sitting. To men and women, however, it is one single most damaging contributor towards weight gain. "I don't snack. I don't generally eat sweets or drink soda. I never eat between meals or even before big ones."—Anthony Bourdain (1956—2018), an American celebrity chef, author, and TV host of *Parts Unknown*. Snacks—the filler—is a killer.

Eat as you wish; dress as others wish. Eat what you like best; otherwise, you will eat what others will like best. Don't eat food that you dislike. A fast is better than fast food. A fast food is a junk food, a bad meal. If you like the food you enjoy eating, the body accepts it and digests it better. The reverse is even more true. If you do not like the food and you don't enjoy eating, the body does not accept it. Indigestion and upset stomach results, and leads to many ailments. Some parents eat and force their children to eat some healthy foods that they actively dislike. This practice—typically cultural or sometimes personal—can result in a digestive disorder, because the appetizing stimulation of enzyme secretion is, for the most part, dependent on the taste, flavor, and texture of the food. Spices, herbs, and aromatic leaves—which may or may not have any food value—are added to the food preparation, primarily to enhance the taste. If you do not find the food appetizing (or worse, actively dislike it), you may find that your digestion is deterred. A strong dislike of common food may also be a sign that you have an allergy or intolerance to that food.

We are born and brought up with individual taste preferences that are influenced by culture, age, gender, genes, and most of all, exposure to a variety of tastes since our infancy. One study experimented with overweight and obese kids and found that those kids have less-sensitive taste buds than their normal-weight peers. Taste buds get dull, as researchers observe, primarily due to a biological withering of taste buds as people starts gaining weight. Obese people have about 25% fewer taste buds: the older cells die off more quickly than replacement new cells that grow more slowly. However, this is a two-way mechanism: taste buds do come back once they lose weight. Studies on bariatric surgery patients show that they regain food tastes better and intense. Therefore, for obese people, to have the same flavor sensation, they eat more food. In general, girls and older children have a better ability in correctly identifying the various tastes. As most kids get older, their ability to differentiate between taste sensation improves, but not among the obese kids. Previous studies have proven that people with more sensitive taste buds tend to eat less, apparently because they don't need as much food to get the same taste sensations. Biologically backed, overeaters have a lesser number of receptive buds, as a matter of fact. As the taste sensitivity plays a sensitive role in childhood obesity, it is obviously a better strategy to focus on mindful eating and on taste preferences for prevention of overweight and obesity rather than counting the calories alone.

Good digestion is one important factor in ensuring good health and the prevention of disease. It is, therefore, important to eat a wide variety of fresh produce and, at the same time, to limit the consumption of highly refined foods and junk foods in general. Avoid the foods and beverages that cause indigestion and irritation to the digestive tract. Avoid or limit alcohol, vinegar, caffeine, spicy, greasy, refined foods, or hyper-processed junk foods. If the food is not digested completely and properly, it leaves the stomach with partially undigested food, and that enters the small intestines, where it can ferment and produce, among others, hydrogen and carbon dioxide, causing the discomfort of indigestion. Certain psychological factors—such as worry, anxiety, and stress—can further disturb metabolism and digestion, either by weakening the mechanism that controls stomach contractions or by dropping the amount of digestive enzymes the body secretes.

Eat well, live well, and thrive! Nature has created with care thousands of different varieties of edibles for our nourishment. Each variety is replete with several types of nutrients. Some are rich in protein, some in carbohydrates and fat, some with minerals and vitamins. Eat the right foods. It is rarely possible for any individual to know the contents and value of each, but there are certain basic things we should know. Choosing the right food and in the right amount in proportion with one's age, activity, and constitution is a wise way to go. Eat a balanced diet and keep your protein intake down. Increasing intake of fruits, vegetables, nuts, and grains significantly increases your intake of fiber. The key to being healthy is eating a varied and balanced diet that contains the widest possible variety of natural foods and provides a good balance of carbohydrates, fats, proteins, fiber, and recommended amounts of all the vitamins and minerals.

Is it good or bad to stay in a limited number of foods? No one food or a limited number of foods has all the nutrients and minerals we need, in heavy to trace amounts. Naturally, eating a variety of foods helps us to get enough of each. But how much variety of food is enough, and how much are too much? One study in 2015 finds that women who regularly eat sixteen to seventeen items from a healthy list of foods benefit with a considerable 42% drop in death rate from any cause, compared to women who eat fewer than nine. Here is a list of some healthy foods: bananas, raspberries, oranges, kiwifruits, pomegranates, blueberries, grapefruits, tangerines, avocados, tomatoes, eggplants, Swiss chards, mushrooms, kales, broccoli sprouts, fennels, garlics, sweet potatoes, beets, spinaches, cauliflowers, collard greens, onions, winter squashes, tunas, sardines, anchovies, salmons, poultries (dark meats), whole wheat breads, quinoas, hemp seeds, rolled oats, kamut, lentils, farro, walnuts, almonds, chia seeds, flaxseeds, eggs, kefir, 2% Greek yogurts, olive oils, cumin, turmeric, cinnamons, rooibos tea, and red wine. Here is a short list of assorted healthy foods: legumes (peas, beans, and peanuts), spinaches (salad type or cooked type), quinoas (instead of rice and bread), tomatoes, vitamin-D-fortified milks, apples, salmons, enriched cereals (fortified with folic acid), berries, eggs, clams, oranges, extra-virgin olive oils, turmeric, peppers, green tea, and red wine. And, very finally, not included in the list are, the very foods you like the most. If you find you cannot eat heavy or spicy dishes, then don't. Many old people should eat foods of their liking for the benefit of their health with no harmful effects. So, eat what you like to eat; otherwise, you will eat what others will like you to eat.

On the other hand, eating too much of a varied diet may have not-so-good health effects that come from your microbiome. The networks of microorganisms live inside our body and support our digestive system, help control the appetite, and perform many essential functions. It is interesting enough to imagine that your surrounding personal cloud of microbes stays with you and follows you wherever you go. You literally move around in a plume of airborne bacteria and other microbes that are unique to you. Typically, the more diversity the gut microbes have, the better it is for the gut. Mixing too many foods actually reduces the number and variety of gut microbes, thereby reducing their health benefits. Also, one thing's for sure—that, as a species, we humans eat a far greater variety of food than any other animal. And today, we even eat more varieties than we used to a century ago. Besides, the more the variety of foods, the more we eat—obviously, no question on that.

Typically, anything that has the plant origin does not contain cholesterol. Food specialists suggest consumption of 2 servings of fruits and 3 servings of vegetables, totaling 5 servings a day. The USDA's Food Guide Pyramid recommends slightly higher: 2–4 servings of fruits and 3–5 servings of vegetables daily. Because of our origin that goes back to the evolutionary days of primates, our bodies are still adaptable to the Stone Age diet of roots, vegetables, and fruits.

One serving of fruit may contain the following:

1 medium apple, banana, or orange
1 melon wedge
¼ to ½ cup berries or chopped fruit
1 to 2 oz. dried fruit (raisins, dried cranberries, prunes, etc.)
¾ cup fruit juice—6 oz. of 100% fruit juice, NOT fruit drink

One serving of vegetables may contain these:

1 cup, loosely packed raw green leafy vegetables or ½ cup cooked greens
½ cup chopped of any other vegetable, cooked
6 oz. of 100% vegetable juice (low sodium is a better option)

About the number of servings and the total amount of servings per day! While federal authorities, health scientists and nutrition experts have recommended eating 5, 7, or even 10 servings of fruits and vegetables a day for optimal health, a new study claims that just 3 to 4 servings a day of combined fruits, vegetables, and legumes may be enough. The study published in *The Lancet i*n 2017, researchers analyzed health records and diet reports of more than 135,000 people across five continents. When the researchers associated how much fruit, vegetables and legumes people ate, with the mortality rates, they find that those who are eating 3 to 4 servings a day are 22% less likely to die during the study period of 7 years, compared to those who eat less than one serving a day. Surprisingly, the benefit stops there abruptly: people eating more than 4 servings a day, do not get any better in mortality rate. The outcome remains strong enough even after adjustments of factors like age, gender, health status, physical activity, and meat and grain consumption. Amount wise, it is approximately 375 to 400 grams per day, the optimal. For common people, it amounts to: 1½ to 2 cups of fruits and 2 to 2½ cups of vegetables a day. For reference, one medium-size apple is about 180 grams.

Excessive fruit consumption has its downside! You may suffer from diarrhea. One 2013 Harvard study links fruit juice to an increased risk for diabetes (while recommending smoothie instead). A full-blown fruitarianism is injurious to health; it is linked to nutritional deficiencies in many people, and may be unsafe for children and those with certain medical conditions, like diabetes. The main concern is its sugar content. However, while most fruits are high in sugar, researches have consistently linked, on the contrary, that whole fruit consumption reduces the risk of obesity and other metabolic diseases. Here it's why. Whole fruit has both soluble and insoluble fiber; together, they form a gel-like "latticework" on the inside wall of the duodenum in the small intestine. It's like preventing a tsunami by building an underwater wall.

This gel barrier limits the rate of sugar absorption, so that the liver is not overwhelmed. The benefits of eating whole fruits seem to mitigate any sugar-driven health risks. Also, as the dietary fiber is indigestible, the bulk of the fruit fiber moves down quickly to the small intestine, jejunum and ileum, where the gut signals to the brain that you're full. As you tend to feel full more quickly, thus, normal fruit consumption is *self-limiting*, overeating whole fruit is relatively low.

The CDC survey tells us that only 32.5% of American adults ate 2 daily servings of fruit in 2009—a slight decline from 34% in 2000. And when it comes to 3 daily servings of vegetables, the Americans' performance is even shameful—only 26%. One survey in 2016 indicates that 87% of Americans consume less than the 2½ cups of vegetables per day. To those people especially, here are some low-stress, bare-minimum ways to become a healthier person: get any form of exercise every week, and eat colorful meals (that contain two or more different colors) with friends. This can be an enjoyable way to live a healthier life.

Eating vegetables of all colors is good because each has a particular nutrient that the others may not have, with each nutrient being necessary for our health. Vegetables green in color is anti-obesity and antidiabetic. These are a few of the many reasons why we should take large quantities of green vegetables. These are forbidden to diabetic patients: no white after night—white rice, white bread, white pasta. Any edible that splits into two parts (split peas, lentils, pulses, grams, etc.) causes the generation of gas in the stomach. So, whenever you eat these items, eat in limited quantities. Eat fruits of different colors as well. Fruit is a vegetable with a diverse look and feel.

Fish is good as it contains high amounts of omega-3 fatty acids, which protect the heart. On the other hand, there are certain risks in consuming aged fish as they may contain certain toxins and mercury. But the benefits of eating fish in limited quantities seem to outweigh the possible harmful effects.

Daily fluid intake is one single important factor. Besides water, it is important to know that we get our fluid requirements from the other fluids we drink and from the food we eat. For instance, an orange contains about 87% water. Good sources of water include (a) water, (b) food (most food has water in it), (c) fruits and vegetables, and (d) drinks, especially non-caffeinated, nonalcoholic beverages like fruit juice.

There are a few ways to evaluate the daily fluid requirement. A simple rule of thumb for adults is ½ oz. of fluid per pound of body weight per day. For a body weight of 150 lb., it is $0.5 \times 150 = 77$ oz. A Coke can is 12 oz.—so about six cans. One gallon of water is 127 oz.—so about half a gallon every day. The other way to evaluate daily fluid requirement is to base the fluid need on caloric intake. A milliliter (0.034 oz.) of fluid for every calorie ingested. Recommended calories needed for an adult of 150 lb. consuming 1,950 cal a day is $0.034 \times 1{,}950 = 66$ oz. However, it is equally important to realize that fluid requirements may vary noticeably under varying degrees of conditions, such as exercise, extreme climates (especially in hot and humid environments), and during illnesses associated with fever. These situations require more fluid intake.

What we eat, how much we eat, when we eat, and even how and where we eat (the environment) are all important. There are certain considerations for healthy eating, which we shall try to recount one by one as follows:

- We should eat only when we feel hungry. Our hunger is an indication that the system requires refueling. We should restrict eating to three meals and avoid munching (except fruits) in between. Eat in proportion so that you comfortably maintain the three-meals-a-day routine at the scheduled time.
- We should stop eating before we are full. The fullness does not mean that we should gorge up to the throat level. We should always leave some room in the stomach when we stop eating. In a good eating habit, one-third of the stomach should be filled with food, one-third with drink, and the rest left empty. One better way is to take raw food with the other items for a balanced diet. Raw foods also rein in our appetite—without which we tend to binge. In fact, we should eat some amount of raw vegetables with every meal as they contain enzymes, vitamins, and minerals—all essential nutrients for the body.
- Follow the routine. We should eat, sleep, and wake up at routine times (to be consistent with our biological clock) on each day every day. Two research papers published in 2016 in the *Proceedings of the Nutrition Society* suggest that it's not just what you eat but when you eat that affects your health. They demonstrate that people consuming more calories overall during regular meals are less obese than those who have irregular meals. Many metabolic processes in the body—such as hunger, digestion, metabolism, cholesterol, and

glucose—follow the internal body clock that repeats every twenty-four hours.

- The important thing to remember is that when we leave the dining table, we should leave content and not with a feeling of satiety and being overstuffed. If due to extreme craving we have eaten something that is not supposed to be good for us (like in a dinner party), we should not ruminate over the matter and feel guilty about it; but rather, we should try to forget it and not do it the next time. Worrying over the matter will only leave the good food undigested.
- We should invariably include some whole food in the diet. Whole food has one ingredient. For example, sugarcane is a whole food, but its derivative (like sugar) is not whole food. Crushed wheat is whole food; fine flour is not.
- We should avoid, as much as possible, processed food or the food kept in the fridge for quite some time. By processing the essential nutrients in the food, the enzymes, vitamins, and minerals are often destroyed. So, when we eat, we are only under the illusion that we are taking the food with all its natural nutrients. On the contrary and in fact, it is found that a large number of calories in the processed food and fast food may lead to many health problems, such as increased risk of cancer, allergy, auto-inflammatory disease, and reduced immunity control of infection. Even a small amount of processed food alters the chemical balance in our brains as to cause negative mood swings along with a noticeable dip in energy. Of course, there are exceptions.

We should have sufficient quantities of high-fiber food in the diet. Fibers are of two types. Fruits and vegetables like beans have soluble fibers, while the bran of wheat has insoluble fiber. Specialists suggest that we take both types of fibers in the diet, and the average intake should be about 30 g daily. (Some high-fiber brand names: Organic Clear Fiber is a clear-mixing natural fiber supplement made from acacia fiber. Metamucil is a fiber supplement made from psyllium seed husks. Isabgol is a natural vegetable product of psyllium husk, which is the upper coating of *Plantago ovata* (Isabgol), purified by sieving and winnowing. Psyllium and ispaghula are commonly used for several members of plant genus *Plantago*.) There are many benefits of fibers in the diet. Some of these are as follows:

It reduces cholesterol.
It absorbs and removes toxins from the system.
It promotes the growth of good bacteria in our body.
It reduces hemorrhoids.
It reduces constipation.
It prevents cancer.
It prevents heart diseases.
It plays a big role in promoting good bacteria.

- Better not to have more than three items in a meal. When we take a few items, we take more of each item to fill our stomach. A limited number of items in the meal enables the stomach to digest faster, putting less strain on the digestive system. Proper "food combination" matters.

- Never hurry, while eating. We should chew the food properly before we swallow. Chewing causes saliva to mix with the food, which makes it easier for the digestive system to digest. The food in the mouth should be chewed long enough to make it almost like a liquid before it is swallowed in.
- It is always a good practice to eat fruits by themselves, not prepared or sided with other items. Never eat fruits in an empty stomach (one simple rule of thumb: empty stomach is considered two hours after eating). The afternoon (4:00 p.m.) is the preferred time for eating fruit. It enables the digestive system to digest better.

A botanical diet—plant-based food (the green energy)—is good because it prevents most of the diseases like heart ailments, cancer, diabetes, obesity, and the like. That is why dieticians always put emphasis on fruits, vegetables, grains, nuts, and legumes. At the same time, we should be careful enough to ensure that we take the required quantity of protein in the food. A low-protein diet may impede calcium absorption in the body, which may cause osteoporosis to set in early.

A few words about vegetarianism are needed here. The obvious dangers of a diet rich in animal protein has made many people all over the world switch over to a complete vegetarian food as a conscious choice. In some families, vegetarianism is rooted in religion and on matters of principle; vegetarian foods have been eaten through the generations, and any kind of animal protein is a taboo. Young children who are nurtured in the culture of an all-vegetarian diet later find even the idea of an occasional foray into the non-veg world an anathema. On the contrary, some dieticians like the idea of a flexible vegetarian who, for example, sitting with friends and family in a Thanksgiving dinner—even if he or she is mostly vegetarian—will jolly well enjoy the turkey with everyone. Do not be stubborn, bend the rule once in a while. Unless the choice of food is circumscribed by religious or cultural norms, be courtship with food—treat your body, not as a *temple* but a *food court* (an area within a building (such as a shopping mall) set apart for food concessions) and enjoy the varieties. As everybody knows, eating is not exclusively for nutrition or nourishment, but also for social reasons, fitting in and having fun with family and loved ones, on occasions. Hot dogs taste better at the ballpark, popcorn in the movie hall. Tasty food as treats is enjoyable. The idea here is: relish the food! It is good for your health.

While there cannot be any two opinions about the values of vegetables and fruits in the diet, a few words of caution are also necessary. The plant products obviously have much less protein content than the meat and fish. Therefore, to meet the body's protein requirement, the vegetarian has to look for a suitable alternative source. Sometimes the substitute—particularly for young kids—leads to a wrong choice. The vegan may gravitate toward such items as cheese, sandwiches, pastries, and other dairy products—which are, again, very high in fat content.

The plant products also cannot provide as much iron, calcium, and vitamin B12 required by the body, which meat and fish can provide. Therefore, the vegetarian has to supplement calcium from outside; and as in many cases, it could not be correctly calibrated and supplied to the body. [Almost all calcium in the body is stored in bone. The normal level of calcium in the blood—for adults 8.5 to 10.6 mg/dL—is automatically and carefully controlled. When calcium level in blood gets low (hypocalcemia), the bone releases calcium to balance a good level; and when it gets high (hypercalcemia), the extra calcium is absorbed in the bones or drained out of the body with urine and stool.] Osteoporosis due to low bone mass remains a threat to vegetarianism. Similarly, the need for vitamin B12 also cannot be met fully, and its deficiency can cause complications.

Unless for unavoidable reasons, a prudent amount of animal protein is always desirable. Sometimes we do not know what the prudent amount is. For example, it has been statistically reported that on average, an American takes about 120 g (4.5 oz.) of protein daily (1 oz. = 28.35 g). This is about double the quantity actually needed by the body. [Hint: The livestock count—chicken, turkey, cow, etc.—which has to be reared in the U.S. to meet such demand is an astronomical number of 7 billion. The grain they eat daily is enough to feed 700 million people.] Now the question is how much protein is good for our health. Dieticians prescribe a range from 70 g to 90 g of protein daily. They warn that more than this level of protein may cause the bones to be denuded of the calcium, which can be dangerous. Moreover, if we take more protein—particularly the animal proteins—we tend to pile up more fat in the body.

Watching for the carbohydrate intake is not less important. For past decades, carbohydrates were looked upon as the main culprit. People believed that carbohydrates cause more calories to be pumped into the system than what is required. Researches of late suggest that there is an optimum level of carbohydrate below which the level of insulin in the blood may fall, triggering complications. This knowledge has made dieticians in weight reduction clinics sit up and reconstitute the diet for weight reduction. There was a tendency to reduce it as much as possible. The diet plan has been changed now. At the beginning of the program, the carbohydrate intake was reduced to about 25 g; but after the first stage of reduction, the diet was modified to contain a higher level of carbohydrates (say about 40 g), and then the level was slowly adjusted further on.

Among the carbohydrates that we take, sugar, white rice, and white bread are less preferable to brown rice, whole wheat bread, beans, and so forth. The reason is that the former contains less fiber and causes the sugar level in the blood to spike. Eat whole wheat pasta, not refined white pasta. A one-cup serving of cooked whole-wheat spaghetti has about 23% of daily fiber (white pasta has only 9%) and 16% of your protein requirement. The body responds by producing more insulin, and that causes more of the calories taken in to be converted into fat. On the other hand, whole wheat bread, brown rice, beans, and the like, contain more fiber, which break up slowly and do not cause the blood sugar to spike.

Proteins and carbohydrates contain only 4% fat content. In contrast, most dairy products contain much higher fat content. Therefore, avoiding the animal protein and carbohydrates to binge on dairy products and pastries does not make any dietary sense. Moreover, it is beyond our capacity to know the nutrient content of all the edibles as the information will make a huge tome above our capacity to remember. Not only that, every day we are confronted with new findings about the nutrient content and dietary values of the food we eat. We are often baffled as the new findings contradict the beliefs we have held for a long time. We do not know if even the most recent finding will not be overturned by some other researches later. But all that we can safely believe is that it is good to have as much food from natural sources, such as plants. As for the grains, the whole wheat products and unrefined rice are better than the white ones. While going for our protein to sources alternative to the animal protein, we should not make any wrong choice that may result in quite the opposite of what we aimed for. Also, we may not know when we take calories in excess of what we need as, most of the time, we tend to believe that we eat less than what we need. We should be mindful and conscious of the calorie count. So, go for the balanced diet! Each calorie counts.

What is calorie, or Calorie? The *Calorie* was first scientifically defined in 1824 by the French chemist and physicist Professor Nicolas Clément. He defined *Calorie* as a kilogram-calorie (or a kg-calorie, which is the modern kcal). Historically, the unit of calorie has been used following two major definitions—calorie and Calorie—which are two different units by a factor of 1,000 (1 Calorie = 1,000 calories). In *food and health* industries, the calorie used are actually "Calorie" (sometimes interchangeably written as calorie), for example, an average woman needs to eat about 1500 Calories per day or a boiled egg has 80 Calories.

The calorie or the gram calorie, the small calorie, or simply "calorie (symbol: cal)" is the amount of heat (energy) required to raise the temperature of one gram of water by 1°C (Centigrade). This theoretical term—*calorie*—is commonly used in *physics and chemistry.*

The Calorie, or the kilogram-calorie, or kilocalorie (symbol: kcal), or Calorie (capital C) is the amount of heat (energy) needed to increase the temperature of one kilogram of water by 1°C. It is exactly 1,000 small calories. This unit is from the International System (IS) of Units.

Recommended daily calorie intake: Here's the daily Calorie (big C) intake for men and women. Daily calorie requirement is determined by three factors:

> **Weight**—Weight matters because you burn up calories just to keep your body going.
>
> **Muscle**—Based on your height and weight, your muscle mass is an important factor. A pound of muscle may burn up to extra 50 cal per day compared to that of a pound of fat.
>
> **Activity**—Your activity level needs to be taken into account, for obvious reasons.

This data is taken from the U.S. Department of Health and Human Services. If the average U.S. male is 5 feet 9.1 inches tall and weighs 180 lb., the average body mass index (BMI) is 26.5; and if the average U.S. woman is 5 feet 3.7 inches tall and weighs 152 lb., the average BMI is 26.3.

Basal Metabolic Rate (BMR) for a thirty-year-old man is as follows:

$$66 + (6.3 \times \text{weight in pounds}) + (12.9 \times \text{height in inches}) - (6.8 \times \text{age in years})$$

$$66 + 6.3 \times 180 + 12.9 \times 69.1 - 6.8 \times 30 = 66 + 1{,}134 + 891 - 204 = 1{,}887 \text{ BMR}$$

Basal Metabolic Rate (BMR) for a thirty-year-old woman is as follows:

$$655 + (4.3 \times \text{weight in pounds}) + (4.7 \times \text{height in inches}) - (4.7 \times \text{age in years})$$

$$655 + 4.3 \times 152 + 4.7 \times 63.7 - 4.7 \times 30 = 655 + 654 + 299 - 141 = 1{,}467 \text{ BMR}$$

The formula gives you the BMR. Now you have to factor the percentage for your activity level.

Sedentary (no exercise, desk job most of the day):	BMR × 20%
Light Activity (no exercise, some leg work during the day):	BMR × 30%
Moderately Active (exercises 3 or more days a week, each 30 minutes or more):	BMR × 40%
Highly Active (exercises 5 or more days a week, each 30 minutes or more):	BMR × 50%

The calculation gives you a fair idea about how many Calories you need to maintain your current weight. So, from the above example, the recommended intakes for light activity are 1,887 × 1.3 = 2,453 cal for a man and 1, 467 × 1.3 = 1,907 cal for a woman. [Hint: Here are some food samples that 2,000 cal spread over a typical American meal: steak (1,700), sausage (1,800), burger (500), orange juice (100), chips (200), cookie (400); shake (700), wine (200), and soda (300).]

For Olympic athletes, food is the fuel for exceptional athletic performance. One of the secrets of Michael Phelps's (all-time records for Olympic gold medals) astonishing performance in the 2008 Beijing Olympic Games is surely the consumption of as much as 12,000 cal in a day. Athletes—marathon runners, cyclists, and rowers—typically eat eggs, pancakes, and pasta before competition to fuel their super-intense stamina. However, calorie consumption is very subjective. It depends a lot on the type of sports; and even within a sport, it differs as to body frame, age, and sex.

Technically, heat is called thermal energy. A list of major forms of energy includes: mechanical energy (kinetic and potential), electrical energy, chemical energy, thermal energy, sound energy, light energy, and magnetic energy. The energy of any form can be transformed into another form, yet, the total energy (the sum of two forms of energy) remains always the same. This principle is called the conservation of energy. It was first postulated in the early nineteenth century. The human body system (as a metaphor of an auto engine) takes chemical energy in the form of food and produces mechanical (walk), thermal (about 100 watts average to raise and maintain body temperature at 98.2°F ± 1.3°F), and sound (talk) energies. The body temperature differs in hot deserts or cold polar regions. In hotter regions, the body uses energy to cool it down, like an air conditioner needs electrical energy; and in cooler regions, the body needs the energy to heat up to the normal body temperature, like a heater needs electrical energy. In both cases, the body needs energy and thereby increases the metabolic rate by burning more energy. Prolonged exposure to extreme climates (hot, cold, humid, polar, altitude) increases basal metabolic rate (BMR) permanently. Basal metabolic rate (BMR) is the optimal level of energy required to perform basic, life-sustaining functions such as breathing, digestion, and circulation. It is the amount of energy that our body (any organism) needs to carry out daily activities, all of which are beyond your control. However, it is observed that people who live in extreme climates often have BMRs that are 5%–20% higher than those in normal climates. Also, physical activities significantly increase the body temperature—which, in turn, burns more calories.

Food is chemical energy that is available through digestion. The quantities for food energy are expressed in kilojoules (kJ) or food Calories (kcal)—capitalizing the C so that one food Calorie is equal to 1,000 cal. One food Calorie (1 kcal or 1,000 cal) is equivalent to digestively available food energy (heat) that will raise the temperature of one kilogram of water 1 degree Celsius. [Hint: 1 plastic can of gallon water is 3.78 L or 3.78 kg, which means that it requires 3.78 Calories to heat up by 1 degree Celsius. A typical burger contains a total of 540 Calories.] Food calories are typically called kilocalories on the basis of theoretical use of small calorie in physics and chemistry. The term *kilocalorie* representing "Calorie" is less often used by laypersons; and for that matter, food Calories is often printed (labeling: EU kcal, U.S. calories) and spoken as "cal," "calories," or simply "calorie." The word "calorie" is now a placeholder for many generic expressions, all representing Calories (kcal).

If you plan to lose weight, you take less calories from food or burn more calories or do both. Theoretically, to lose 1 lb. of body weight, you need to under-eat by 3,500 food Calories. This conventional wisdom is not exactly right. The body's metabolism changes as you lose weight. Moreover, there is a time lag; because if you cut your caloric intake, after a while, your body reaches its equilibrium—not immediately but after some time. For such time lag, it actually takes approximately two to three years for a dieter to reach their new "steady state." One obesity model predicts that if you eat minus 100 cal a day, in three years, you will, on average, lose 10 lb. Wide variation in your day-to-day food intake does not cause wide variation in body weight as long as your average food intake over a year is about the same. This is because the body responds very slowly to food intake. Caloric restriction has its evolutionary root as a survival mechanism (survival is an extreme motivation), allowing species to survive on scraps when food is scarce. The survival mechanism works and produces lasting positive effects only if the overall diet is balanced. The complex relationship between caloric processing and metabolic functions explains why anorexia (lack of appetite) is so unhealthy and so hard to treat. The dieters simply starve themselves to malnutrition and aging. So, if you want to remain healthy and live long, then a balanced diet—not the caloric restriction—is the best practice.

Most diet plans work—as planned. But the reaction time is very slow, in the order of one year. The beauty of the diet phenomenon is that every diet promises miracles, but there's hardly any regulation. There is a growing clientele of people running from pillar to post, trying one program after another after another in a hope that something might click. It's a funny paradox that every diet works, or no diet works. A diet works (what you typically see in ads) in the short term, but not in the long term. Most people don't stay in the program long enough—one to three years—to see the weight stabilized. For example, as a cautionary to obese people, a study indicates that the fatter a person is, the easier it is to gain weight. An extra 10 cal a day, which is practically nothing, puts more weight on an obese person than on a thin person.

For a typical obese person to lose weight, all it means is that he/she cuts and/or burns the daily intake by 500 cal, which is an achievable amount for most adults. You can attain that by reducing caloric intake (eating fewer calories) and/or increasing caloric output (exercising to burn more off), or both. If you cut out your daily junk food and soda, you will be eating 500 cal less. If you exercise an hour in the gym, you will also burn 500 cal. You will find it less stressful if you do the diet control along with some form of exercise. If your aim is to reduce 500 cal per day, then you may try a middle path: eating 250 cal less and doing an extra 250 cal of exercise (about half an hour of cardio). In contrast, an average American takes typically 500 more Calories (kilocalories) than what he used to take fifty years ago. Besides, today, an adult is not getting enough time for exercise or a simple walk to burn any extra calories. A man has to walk for over an hour to burn this extra 500 Calories. Less of intake by 300 to 500 Calories per day may slow the aging process as well, resulting in a longer life.

Less is more! No diet has ever been planned to defy the law of thermodynamics. No matter what you do—low carb, low fat, low this, low that—the only realistic way to lose weight is to consume less and to burn more calories than you consume. By eating, we adults mainly replenish the necessary wear and tear of our body on a daily basis, and the excess of it is stored away, mostly as fat in the fat tissues. From an evolutionary perspective, human settlers, like most animals, were hardwired not just to eat but to gorge. Since then—and perhaps more after the invention of pottery around 12,000–7,000 BC—humans started eating twice as much, risking injury to kidneys and livers, and falling sick. Less food, more good!

Nutritionists usually deal with caloric density (CD)—calories per gram of food: carbohydrates (calorie density 4 Calories per gram or kcal/g), fiber (2), proteins (4), fats (9), organic acids (3), polyols (sugar alcohols 2.4), and ethanol (drinking alcohols 7). All foods are made up of varying combinations of these components. Everything else in food is non-caloric, and that includes (but is not limited to) water, vitamins, minerals, antioxidants, caffeine, spices and natural flavors, and enzymes. Tea and coffee have no calories of their own. Some carbohydrates that are hard to absorb—for example, fiber or lactose in lactose-intolerant individuals—contribute very few calories. A typical burger contains a total of 540 Calories: fat (260), carb (180) and protein (100). To burn these 540 Calories, you need to do any one of the following:

150 minutes (2½ hours) of walking
90 minutes of cycling
60 minutes of jogging
45 minutes of swimming

When we eat, the body's digestion system breaks down the food into a stream of nutrients, including glucose (sugar), lipids (fats), and amino acids (the building blocks of protein). If our food happens to be a burger meal—a processed fine wheat flour bun, one beef patty, fries, and a soda—it causes a rush of sugar, creating a condition (medically called as postprandial hyperglycemia—a big spike in blood sugar levels. This is a poor diet and not good for health as because of the pre-meal blood glucose 90–130 mg/dL (dL is an acronym of deciliter—a metric unit of volume equal to one-tenth of a liter) spikes beyond 180 mg/dL on post-meal after one to two hours of eating.

Poor diet over a long period of time leads to hypertension and builds up gunk in blood vessels that increases the risk of heart attack. The postprandial hyperglycemic spikes are relevant in the sense that it is an indication for the onset of cardiovascular complications, which are direct and independent risk factors for cardiovascular disease (CVD). Tissue becomes inflamed, just as it does when it gets infected. Blood vessels constrict. Blood pressure rises higher than normal. It is generally noticed that there is a crummy feeling a few hours after eating junk food. A sudden gush and then drop in insulin (insulin is a hormone that spurs your body to store energy) gives a hungry feeling again soon after eating, despite having a large meal with plenty of calories. Junk food disturbs the hormonal profile. Sugar in food stimulates the stress hormone cortisol, which tends to further stimulate an appetite for calorie-dense foods. The big post-meal surges in blood sugar are more likely in people who don't exercise or those who carry fat around their abdomen.

Human Digestive System

Now here is an illustration as to how our digestive system works, how food gets transformed into energy. For humans, the digestive system plays a vital role in the functioning of the body overall. In its entirety, the human digestive device is about thirty feet (nine meters) of convoluted pipework starting at the mouth and ending at the anus. Along the digestive tract, food is broken down, split up into basic constituents—carbohydrates, proteins, fats, vitamins, and minerals—and then sorted out and channeled around the body to nourish and replace cells and supply energy to our muscles. In brief, here is how the human digestive process works.

In the mouth: The process initiates at the mouth with ingestion (eating). Our mouth, teeth, and tongue chew and grind up each mouthful; the tongue prepares it into a ball-shaped bolus for swallowing. Food is partly smashed down by the process of chewing and by moistening with saliva. Saliva is secreted in large amounts, about 1 L to 1.5 L a day (enough to fill two large-size swimming pools during a lifetime) by three pairs of exocrine salivary glands in the oral cavity. Saliva secretion controls pH in the mouth—the pH is typically 6.8, slightly acidic (distilled water having pH 7.0 is neutral; lower values are acidic and higher values are alkaline). An enzyme in the saliva begins to digest the starch from food into smaller molecules. Enzymes, proteins by themselves, primarily digest protein and help various chemical reactions in the body. They are secreted at several places along the digestive tract and break down large molecules of food into smaller molecules for the body to absorb. Enzymes like ptyalin, which initiates sugar digestion, are introduced early in salivary secretions. It provides adequate lubrication to facilitate chewing and swallowing.

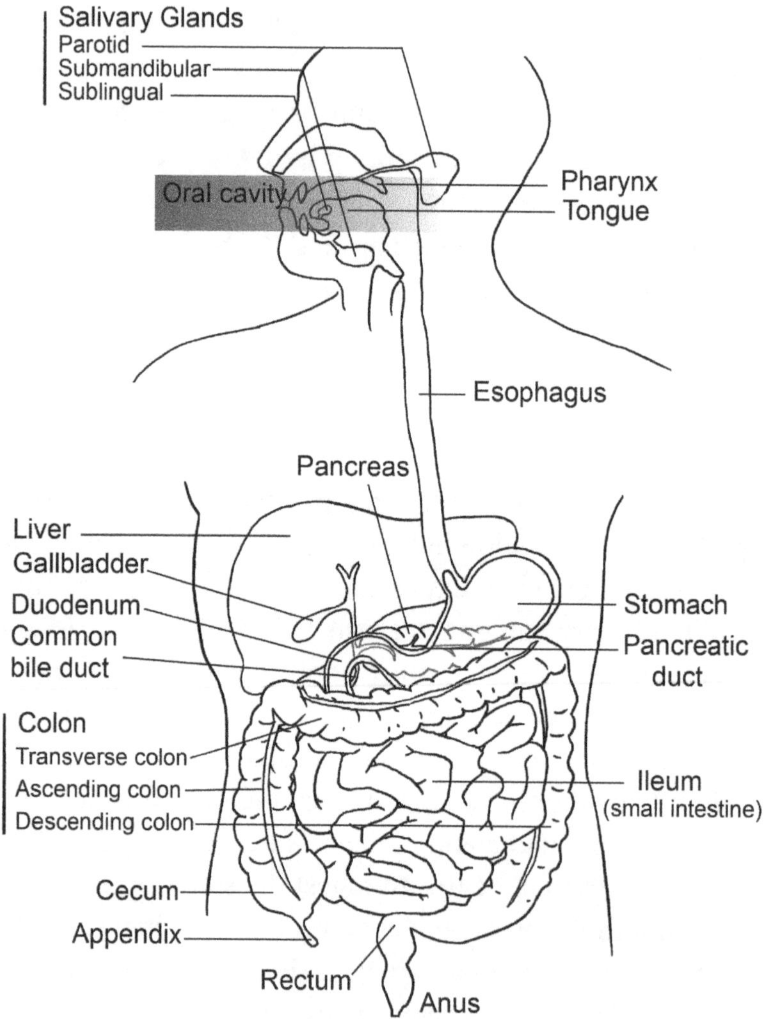

Digestive System

On the way to the stomach (esophagus): The food is chewed in the mouth and then swallowed. It enters the alimentary canal—called the esophagus—that channels the throat to the stomach. The esophagus is the first part of successive hollow organs that transports the ingested food through muscular contractions known as peristalsis. It funnels the food from the throat into the stomach. Essentially, it transports the food into the stomach. [Info: According to WHO, drinking very hot beverages—above 149°F (65°C), which is significantly cooler than that of most coffee served in restaurants and cafés (hot chocolate, and coffee are frequently served at temperatures 160°F–185°F (85°C–71°C)—is linked to higher risk of cancer of the esophagus.]

In the stomach: An empty stomach is about 12 inches long and at its widest about 6 inches across. It's about the size of a clenched fist which can expand up to 3 or 4 times its size during a large meal, but when empty, it returns back to the size of a clenched fist after food passes into the small intestine. The stomach is the major part of the digestive system. It is located behind the lower rib cage, left side. It is one large sack-like, pear-shaped, muscular enlargement chamber. It performs three mechanical tasks. First, it receives just-swallowed food. While receiving the food, the muscle of the upper part of the stomach enlarges enough to wrap the volume of the food. The second task is to mix the food up with the digestive juice produced by the stomach. It is the lower part of the stomach in action to muddle these materials by its muscle action. The third task is to squeeze the food slowly into the small intestine. The stomach has food-digestive glands on the stomach lining. They produce and secrete digestive hydrochloric acid. The stomach environment gets very acidic [pH of 0 is most acidic; pH of 7 is pure water; pH of 14 is most basic; the resting stomach runs slightly acidic with a pH level of 4 to 5. The stomach can go as acidic as pH of 1 in the scale of 7 to 0; for reference, a pH of 1 stays in between (a) lemon juice with pH of 2.4 and (b) pure hydrochloric acid with pH of 0].

The stomach environment provides a suitable pH level for the reaction to occur by enzyme pepsin. The environment kills as many microorganisms that are ingested with the food. The enzyme helps to digest protein. The stomach contracts slowly (about three times a minute), churning the food and mixing it with digestive juices. Enzyme pepsin targets proteins. Enzyme lipase targets fats. Hydrochloric acid dissolves the contents in the stomach and kills potentially harmful bacteria. In four hours or less after the meal, the food is processed by the stomach, resulting in a semiliquid paste called chyme. Chyme is pushed down by the muscular pumping motion of the peristalsis, into the first part of the small intestine (called the duodenum).

In the small intestine: The small intestine is comparatively narrower, about one inch in diameter and a twisting tube measuring about twenty feet (six meters) in length. The small intestine is divided into three segments: the duodenum, the jejunum, and the ileum. The small intestine occupies the most part of our lower abdomen. It is in the small intestine where most of the digestion and absorption of nutrients take place. The duodenum, the first of three segments, produces large amounts of mucus to protect the intestinal lining from acid in the chyme. Here, most of the chemical digestion takes place. The pH level changes: the acidic slowly becomes slightly basic (pH about 8.5). In the duodenum, the food gets mixed with fluids from the other two digestive organs. The first digestive organ is the pancreas; it produces complex digestive fluid that contains an array of enzymes that break down the carbohydrates, fats, and proteins in the food. Some other enzymes that are secreted from the glands in the intestinal wall take active part in the digestive process as well. The second organ is a very important one: the liver. The liver produces yet another important digestive fluid, called bile acid. Bile acid is produced during the interval of meals and is stored in the gallbladder. While eating, the gallbladder squeezes bile acid out through the bile ducts into the intestine, to mix with the fats of the food. It dissolves the fat into the watery contents of the intestine, much like liquid detergent that dissolves grease from a cooking pot into the water. Once the fats are dissolved, the chyme is then mixed with the enzymes secreted from the pancreas and the lining of the intestine. Over a period of three to six hours, the muscular pumping motion of peristalsis moves the chyme into the next segment of the small intestine, the jejunum. Here in the jejunum, most of the digested carbohydrates, proteins, electrolytes, water-soluble vitamins, and minerals are absorbed. The leftover chyme is then pushed into the last segment of the small intestine, the ileum. In the ileum, fat and fat-soluble vitamins A, D, E, K, and B12—along with the bile salts—are absorbed. [Info: Bad things happen when you indulge greasy foods: (1) Out of fat, carbs and protein, fat is digested most slowly. To break it down, it requires enzymes and digestive juices, like bile and stomach acid, which many people are deficient to begin with. Added fat in the food strains digestive system even harder, often leading to bloating, nausea and discomfort. (2) Fat not only sits longer in the stomach resulting in stomach pain, but also enters intestines inadequately digested resulting diarrhea. (3) It throws the gut bacteria (microbiome) out of balance due to hormonal imbalances and bacterial imbalances causing acne. (4) People who eat fried foods between four to six times a week carry a risk for type 2 diabetes up to 39%, and coronary heart disease, up to 23% compared to who don't.]

Lipase and other digestive fluids break down the fat molecules into fatty acids and some types of glycerol. Absorption of fat into the body takes about ten to fifteen minutes. It occurs in the villi (Latin: *villus*, "shaggy hair"—plural *villi*), the millions of fingerlike projections that cover the walls of the small intestine. Inside a villus, there is a series of lymph vessels (lacteals) and blood vessels (capillaries). They protrude into the small intestine. The mucosa area (a layer of smooth muscle) is increased by the cumulative surface of each absorbing cell of the mucosa, which also has its own microscopic brush like projections called microvilli. This creates an enormous absorbing surface, called the mucosal epithelium. These factors increase the absorbing surface up to 600-fold—astonishingly equivalent to the surface area of half a basketball court. The lacteals move glycerol and fatty acids into the lymphatic system, where it is ultimately passed into the bloodstream. The fatty acids are then transported by the bloodstream to the membrane of adipose cells or muscle cells. There they are either stored or immediately oxidized for energy. After absorption, lipids are repackaged with proteins, and the digested product moves to the liver.

Liver: Out of the small intestine, the digested product moves into the liver. In the liver, digested products are repackaged with a coat of cholesterol and protein. This coating allows the fat to be dissolved in the blood and thereby enables the fats to be transported to various parts of the body, where fatty acids are extracted to provide energy for cellular components.

What functions does the liver perform? The liver is considered to be the body's most versatile organ. Astonishingly, it performs more than five hundred functions of the body. Here is an important one. *Carbohydrate* means one of many combinations of carbon, hydrogen, and oxygen, whose various molecular sections join and break by taking on or releasing water. To build complex carbohydrate glycogen, the liver—with help from some specific enzymes—puts the simple sugars back together by rejoining them using water. The liver plays this trick with insulin, which is secreted by the pancreas. (Insulin is an essential hormone that helps metabolism by playing the role of a chemical messenger that regulates the level of glucose in the bloodstream; the lack of insulin causes a form of diabetes.) The process is named glycogenesis ("glyco" means sugar; "genesis" means creation).

Glycogen is typically stored in the cells of the liver, in the muscles, and to a lesser extent, in various other tissues in the body. And if glycogen is not needed because the cells are "full," the glycogen is converted to body fat. Two reversible processes go on: (1) the liver makes glycogen from the sugar, and (2) the liver makes sugar from the glycogen. The liver accrues and then dispenses sugar as needed, maintaining the sugar level, much like a thermostat. The control is performed by the balance of a few hormones: insulin (which instructs the liver to store the sugar), glucagon (which instructs the liver to release the sugar), and other hormones released from the pituitary, thyroid, and adrenal glands. Low sugar level triggers the release of glucagon, while high sugar level triggers the release of insulin from the pancreas. [Trivia: However, very few of us know that only 20% cholesterol is from the food; the rest comes from and is removed by the liver. So, having a good liver is the key to keeping the cholesterol level low in the blood. If the liver is malfunctioning, even a controlled diet may not help keep the cholesterol level within the limit.]

The chain effect of sugar is quite vicious. Sugar raises insulin level; a higher insulin level constrains release of growth hormones, which, in turn, depress the immune system. An excess inflow of sugar into the bloodstream upsets the body's blood sugar balance, triggering the release of insulin, which the body uses to keep blood sugar at a consistent safe level. Insulin is the hormone of feast. Insulin prompts the body to store excess sugar floating around the bloodstream as fat. Insulin was primarily important in our ancient caveman days, when we needed the energy from one meal to the next meal as long as possible, until we had hunted down the next meal. But today, as we have the next meal ready, insulin still promotes the storage of fat. Or in other words, when we eat in excess or when we eat the sweet stuff that is high in sugar, we are aiding to gain weight and to elevate triglyceride levels—both of which are inherently linked to cardiovascular disease.

As the amount of sugar in the body is reduced by the disbursement of energy, it is replenished by the intake of food. Since we do not eat constantly but, rather, eat at intervals, the level of sugar in the blood is kept in line by several hormones that tie up and release the sugar on an as-needed basis to maintain the sugar level. All types of tissues of the body use the sugars as a source of energy, and at the very end of the process, there is nothing left except carbon dioxide (CO_2) and water (H_2O). The CO_2 is expelled through the breath, and water is either reused or excreted as urine. The liver is at the center, for disease control! What a great system the liver is!

The steroid is a large class of organic compounds (hormones, alkaloids, and vitamins) that promote the storage of protein and the growth of tissue; it is occasionally used by athletes to enhance muscle strength. Cholesterol is a compound of sterol type found in body tissues, blood, and nerves. It is a white waxy steroid of fat that is produced in the liver or intestines. It produces steroid hormones to build healthy cells and cell membranes to establish proper membrane permeability and fluidity. Cholesterol is transported into the blood plasma; it is one main component required for the manufacture of bile acids, steroid hormones, and vitamin D.

In the liver, chyme is wrapped with a coat of cholesterol and protein. The demand to make cholesterol by the liver for such coatings is greater for saturated fat than polyunsaturated fat, which translates to the fact that the former demands and contributes to a higher blood cholesterol level than the latter. Liver cells are responsible for filtering the blood of harmful substances (such as alcohol and ammonia) and storing fat-soluble vitamins and other excess substances such as glucose (sugar) for release when the body requires extra energy. Undigested products remain in the digestive tract. These are some fluids, indigestible residues, and cellular debris. The remains are passed into the large intestine.

In the large intestine (colon): It is about five feet (1.5 m) long. It has six parts: (1) cecum, (2) ascending colon, (3) transverse colon, (4) descending colon, (5) sigmoid colon, and (6) rectum. The appendix, a tube-shaped sac, is connected to the cecum; it contains lymphoid tissue that intercepts pathogenic microorganisms entering the digestive tract. Sometimes fecal matter (solid excretory product) may get trapped in the appendix, resulting in appendicitis, which is an infection and inflammation. The large pouch-shaped cecum is the beginning of the colon. Here the remains are eaten by billions of harmless gut bacteria. In the colon, extra water is extracted; extra sodium and potassium are excreted to maintain electrical neutrality. The bulk gets thickened to form the stool. The stool travels upward in the ascending colon and then crosses over to the abdomen in the transverse colon. And then it gets down the other side of the body in the descending colon. It then transits through the sigmoid colon, arrives at the rectum, and finally gets expelled through the anus.

Colonic transit time is defined as the time required for the stool to transit through the large intestine. While constipation is common in general, irregularities and erratic lifestyles contribute to the problem, especially for the travelers. According to the standardized methodology that measures colonic transit time by ingesting radioactive tracers, constipation seems to be a real phenomenon for inter-time-zone travelers: the average frequency of bowel movement slows down from once a day to about once every day and a half, particularly during the first days of travel. The degree of constipation associates with the degree of jet lag; anywhere from 12 to 19 percent of people suffer from such constipation. Besides colon cancer, the vast majority of illness comes from constipation. Diet is one prime importance to tackle the problem.

Passing gas, farting or flatulence (intestinal gas expelled through the anus) is a normal body reaction. Gas may be uncomfortable, but not harmful. Some food gives out gas. Gas—hydrogen, carbon dioxide, and methane—is produced by the gut microbiota that live in our large intestine. The odor is from other waste gases, particularly from skatole (of bacterial decomposition) and sulfur-containing substances. Few fiber-rich plant foods—broccoli, cabbage, legumes, wheat, onion, beans, rye, nuts, seeds and any edible that splits into two parts (split peas, lintels, pulses, gram)—are not easily digested. These foods when ingested, tend to pass through the gastrointestinal tract and arrive undigested at the large intestine where gut bacteria chew them down. Among other things, gut bacteria do two things: (1) separate nutrients from the food and make it available to the body to use, which is good; and (2) produce gas as a byproduct, which is bad. While, for the most part, this is a normal process of bowel function, but the nutrition scientists add to it that (a) the production of gas varies from person to person, as they do in many other aspects; (b) people, who lack gut enzymes, which is needed to digest certain nutrients, allow more of those ingested foods undigested and let slip through to arrive at the large intestine; (c) eating too much or too quickly, overloads the digestive system, allowing foods to slip through; (d) for people who are lactose intolerant (lack of a digestive enzyme needed to break down milk sugars), eating dairy products produce gas and bloating, and perhaps, diarrhea, constipation, bloody stools, stomachaches and vomiting; (e) being sick aggravates the condition further; (f) for older people, (i) the digestive process slows down leading to constipation and flatulence, (ii) as they take more medications, and some of those medications (blood pressure medications, certain narcotic pain relievers and antibiotics) have side effects of flatulence; and (iii) loose dentures, difficulty in chewing and swallowing food, can cause to swallow air during normal activities, it is then released as gas; and (g) finally, for relief, (i) consumption of probiotics boost development of "friendly bacteria" in the digestive system, which can be helpful in treating flatulence; and (ii) over-the-counter anti-gas supplements do work in most of the time, they contain enzymes that aids to break down the gas-producing foods before arriving at large intestine.

Carbohydrate Digestion

The *2005 Dietary Guidelines for Americans* recommends that a little over half (45% to 65%) of total daily calories should come from carbohydrates. Carbohydrates include breads, pasta, rice, potatoes, peas, beans, fruits, and vegetables. Many of these foods contain both starch and fiber. In the stomach, carbohydrates stay the least time, while protein stays longer. The fat stays the longest. The way carbohydrates are digested is different from the way protein or fat is digested.

There are two types of carbohydrates: simple carbohydrates (sugar, fruit juice, honey) and complex carbohydrates (whole grains, green vegetables, beans, peas, or potatoes). In energy transferal, simple is immediate absorption, complex is gradual. Complex carbohydrates are preferable because the foods are more nutritious and yet with lesser calories per unit weight when compared to fat. Overeating carbohydrates is less of a problem compared to that of fat or sugar. Complex carbohydrates are processed, digested, and absorbed by the body gradually, lessening the fluctuation of blood sugar level. They are preferred over simple carbohydrates in a condition like diabetes, where stable blood sugar level is essential over time. A high-carbohydrate and high-fiber diet consists of a high quantity of vegetables, fruits, nuts, and whole grains. This diet is moderate in protein, but the protein content of the items as a whole should not be so low as to be nutritionally inadequate.

Of the recommended carbohydrates consumed daily, about 60% is starch, 30% is sucrose (also known as table sugar), and 10% is lactose and incidental amounts of other sugars. (Milk has a lactose type of sugar.) The digestion of carbohydrates starts right from the mouth. The enzyme in saliva breaks down the digestible carbohydrates in simple sugar molecules. When a simple sugar molecule reaches the small intestines, no matter what carbohydrates are the sources, they all have become simple sugars. Food must be transformed into simple sugar first before it can be absorbed. Sugar diffuses through selective membranes of the small intestines and then enters the blood.

Starch is digested in two steps. In the first step, enzymes in saliva and pancreatic juice break the starch of larger molecules of carbohydrates into smaller molecules of maltose. In the second step, enzymes from the lining of the small intestine splits the maltose into half, smaller molecules of glucose that are subsequently absorbed into the blood. Digestive enzymes break down food into smaller manageable molecules. Some major digestive enzymes are as follows:

- amylase—hydrolyzes (breaks down) the carbohydrates, starches, and sugars that are available in potatoes, fruits, and vegetables
- lactase—hydrolysis of lactose (milk sugar)

- diastase—digests vegetable starch
- sucrase—catalyzes the hydrolysis of sucrose and maltose to produce glucose and fructose; it digests complex sugars and starches
- maltase—catalyzes the breakdown of maltose and similar sugars to form glucose; it transforms disaccharides to monosaccharides (malt sugars)
- invertase—catalyzes the hydrolysis of sucrose, forming invert sugar; it breaks down sucrose (table sugar)
- glucoamylase—hydrolysis of starch to glucose
- alpha-galactosidase—simplifies digestion of beans, legumes, soy products, seeds, roots, and underground stems

Lactase hydrolyzes (breaks down) the lactose into glucose and galactose, which are then transported across the intestinal cell on a glucose carrier in combination with sodium ion. In the cell interior, the sodium is stripped off from the carrier and pumped out of the cell, leaving the sugar within the cell and freeing the carrier (sodium) to repeat the process. Sugar is, however, digested in one step. The enzyme secreted from the lining of the small intestine wall digests sucrose into glucose and fructose, which are then transferred through the intestine into the bloodstream.

The deficiency of one or more of the digestive enzymes (maltase, cellulase, lactase, or sucrase)—most commonly lactase—causes intolerance to foodstuffs. When it does, sugar remains undigested in the gut cavity and accumulates water, which then leads to bloating and pain. In the colon, bacteria utilize undigested sugar to produce acid and gas; and that leads to symptoms of diarrhea, abdominal distension, and cramp.

There are two major problems in consuming too much sugar: (a) it adds up quickly to a lot of calories consumed, and (b) it contains very little nutritional value. If you replace any nutritionally rich carbohydrates like beans, grains, vegetables, potatoes, and the like with refined sugar (sweet drinks), you get poor nutrition, and you are likely to gain weight from the extra calories. Sugar has a higher tendency to be converted to fat by raising the insulin level. Here are a few factors, including some lifestyle ones, explaining how sugar adds up so quickly:

- Sugar is a very concentrated source of carbohydrate by weight; and it is easier to eat more (unseen) sugar than other forms of carbohydrate and, thereby, more calories.
- Sugar has a very appealing sweet taste; it is easily overeaten out of pleasure and comfort.
- Sugar is associated with and consumed with other equally bad fatty foods, such as pastries, cookies, ice cream, and sweet stuffs.
- Sugar is often consumed in large quantities as beverages—sodas, juices, punch, and so forth. A large soda can easily contain more than 300 cal alone!

How does sugar affect the blood? The blood from the capillaries is carried directly into larger blood vessels that lead to the liver. At the peak of absorption, the sugar concentration in the blood rises. This higher concentration of sugar increases the blood density and, in turn, increases the "thickness" of the blood. As the blood density or thickness increases, it tends to pull water from the body tissues (causing dry tissue or tissue dehydration) to dilute the blood (causing increased volume). If this is allowed to continue (when consumed too much of sugar), it would result in (a) increasing heart action (to handle increased volume) beyond that which the heart can tolerate, and (b) in tissue dehydration (cracked lips, sunken eyes, lethargy). To check these things happening, some sugar is withdrawn from the bloodstream by the liver and is converted into a new complex carbohydrate called glycogen. Blood sugar (concentration), glucose level, or simply sugar refers to the amount of glucose present in the bloodstream. Normal blood sugar level is about 90 mg/dL.

Carbohydrates are ranked on a scale from 0 to 100 depending on how they raise the blood sugar level after eating. It is called the glycemic index (GI).

- **Low GI (55 or less):** beans (lentil, pinto, peanut, chickpea, black kidney); small seeds (sunflower, flax, pumpkin, poppy, sesame, hemp); fructose; walnuts, cashews, most whole intact grains (durum/spelt wheat, oat, rye, brown rice, millet, barley); most sweet fruits (apples, bananas, strawberries, peaches, mangos); tagatose; mushrooms; chili and most vegetables.
- **Medium GI (56–69):** enriched wheat, pita bread, pumpernickel bread, basmati rice, unpeeled boiled potato, raisins, and prunes.
- **High GI (70 and above):** high fructose corn syrup, glucose (grape sugar, dextrose), maltose, white bread, white rice, waffles, chips, potato, tofu, corn flakes, extruded breakfast cereals, sweet potato, white potato, pretzels, and bagels.

Foods with a high GI are quickly digested and absorbed, resulting in a quicker rise and fluctuation in blood sugar level. Foods with low GI, in contrast, because of their slow digestion and absorption—the rise in the blood sugar level and the insulin level is gradual, which is beneficial to health. According to a study, a fiber-rich diet helps to reduce the risk of death from heart disease and infectious or respiratory disease by as much as 22%. Low GI food helps to improve both the glucose level and lipid level in people with diabetes (type 1 and type 2). They help with special benefits for weight control because they aid to control appetite and suppress hunger. They also aid to lower insulin level and insulin resistance. So, give it a try: switch without hitch! Switching to a low-GI diet is simply a "this for that" approach—swapping high-GI carbs for low-GI carbs. So, use breakfast cereals based on brans or oats, eat a variety of fruits and vegetables, and reduce the amount of potatoes, white bread, and sweetened beverages.

Caloric intake is linked to caloric density (CD) of the food. Caloric density is calories per gram of food. Some examples are pork bacon (5.8), potato chips (5.3), yellow cake with chocolate frosting (3.8), apple (0.52), green beans (0.35), strawberries (0.3), and spinach (0.23). To be contentedly full, one needs to eat a sufficient amount of food by weight and by volume. So, eliminating or reducing too much on a certain category of food is a wrong approach for weight loss. The better approach instead is to follow a balanced diet in order to reduce the caloric intake by reducing the caloric density of each portion. Increasing "energy expenditure" can be done in two ways:

1. Increase of basal metabolic rate (BMR) by being active, thereby increasing daily energy expenditure. Our body burns a certain amount of calories on a typical day by doing virtually nothing or without additional exercise.
2. Increase baseline output by exercise and developing more lean body mass (muscles). The recommendation is a fitness program that combines muscle strengthening and aerobic (cardio) activity in a very powerful synergistic way.

Protein Digestion

Proteins belong to a class of nitrogenous organic compounds. They are large molecules of amino acids arranged in a linear chain and joined together by peptide bonds. Protein digestion does not start until food enters the stomach. The hydrochloric acid secreted in the stomach "denatures" the protein—meaning that hydrochloric acid helps to break the protein down into short chains of amino acids (peptide chains) joined together. This also happens when hydrochloric acid from the stomach recreates the enzyme (called pepsin) to participate in the breakdown of protein. The broken proteins—now in small peptide chains—enter the small intestine, where they are broken down into di-peptides (two amino acids joined together) by pancreatic enzymes. Di-peptides are broken down again into individual amino acids by other pancreatic enzymes. The amino acid is soaked through the small intestine and then travels in the bloodstream and ultimately reaches the liver. The amino acid functions within the liver for lipid metabolism (to detoxify the liver) and the manufacture of glutathione (that helps in our coordination ability and solving mental problems), among others. However, consuming too much protein is harmful for people with liver problems.

Fat Digestion

Fat belongs to the class of organic compounds called lipids. Lipids are fatty acids or derivatives of fatty acids. They are not soluble in water and thus not easily hydrolyzed (broken down) by fat-digesting enzymes (lipase) in watery content in the gastrointestinal tract. That is the reason why fats take a longer time to digest than carbohydrates or proteins. They are only soluble in organic solvents. Fats are made primarily of triglycerides, where each molecule contains a chain of three fatty acids. Dietary fats have saturated fats (which are usually solid at room temperature, such as butter and animal fat) and polyunsaturated fats (which are liquid at room temperature, such as vegetable oil and fish oil). Fats in cooking oil, cheese, butter, and meat are essentially organic compounds composed of complex molecules and are a very concentrated source of energy in our daily diet.

Short-chain fatty acids and a few medium-chain fatty acids are absorbed by the bloodstream directly through the intestine capillaries and through the portal vein, just as other nutrients get absorbed. The rest (majority) of the medium-chain fatty acids and all the long-chain fatty acids are too large to be absorbed directly through the tiny intestinal capillaries. Completion of fat digestion and absorption thereafter requires these medium- and long-chain fat molecules be broken down into smaller manageable molecules. During the digestion process, fats are broken down partially to free fatty acids and molecules with one, two, or three attached fatty acids—namely, mono-, di-, and triglyceride. It is done by mixing the fat with the digestive enzyme lipase from the pancreas. "Very high triglyceride"—normal is less than 150 mg per deciliter (mg/dL)—is a medical term, which is something serious, meaning too much fat in the blood. Two studies independently identified the mutation process in a single gene (APOC3) that helps to protect against heart attacks by keeping the triglyceride levels very low for the lifetime. Americans (20% of adults have over 200 mg/dL) might be suitable candidates for triglyceride-lowering drugs. Researchers at the Broad Institute of Harvard and MIT—after analyzing seventy studies involving two hundred thousand people—establish that people with a genetic predisposition to higher triglyceride levels are more likely to have more heart attacks and that those with genetically lower triglyceride levels are more likely to have fewer. A higher triglyceride level is one prime cause of heart attacks.

The pancreas is the main source of digestive enzymes (called lipase) for digesting the fats and proteins. Lipase catalyzes the breakdown of fat, lipid, and glycerol molecules into fatty acid molecules and glycerol molecules. The food is moved to the duodenum, the first part of the small intestine. However, as the fat is not dissolved in water, the fat molecules remain intact and enter the duodenum in a congealed mass, which makes it impossible for the pancreatic lipase enzymes to break them down. Lipase is a water-soluble enzyme; but it can react only to the surface of the fat molecules, not the inside. To surmount the problem, the digestive system uses a substance called bile, which is produced in the liver and stored in the gallbladder. Bile moves in the duodenum via the bile duct. Bile emulsifies fats and disperses them into small droplets that are then suspended in the watery contents of the digestive tract.

People need to know this mechanism to appreciate the need for maintaining a proper balance of the diet to include both varieties: the acidic and the alkaline. Unless a proper balance of the acid alkali ratio (of pH) is maintained in the intestinal tract, complications will arise in the digestion of food. Proteins—particularly the animal proteins—are known to be acidic in nature as they contain a high proportion of chlorine, phosphorus, sulfur, and nitrogen. To maintain the correct pH ratio (acidity or basicity), we should eat sufficient quantities of food that contain (basic or alkaline) potassium, sodium calcium, and magnesium. These elements are available in abundant quantities in fruits and vegetables. Almost all vegetables (barring a few such as broad beans, asparagus) are known to be alkaline in nature. All nuts (except walnuts and hazelnuts) are alkaline in nature. Whole milk and skimmed milk are known to be mildly alkaline.

A blood sugar spike is rather easy to control. Blood sugar rises and falls quickly if a person eats some easily digestible meal rich in sugar and carbohydrates like white bread with jelly. Eating some vinegar with the bread, however, dampens the impact. The same effect ensues if a person takes bread with nuts or with a glass of wine. However, for the wine—or, for that matter, any alcohol—the dampening effects reverse the course after a couple of drinks, which may help to explain why moderate drinking (not heavy drinking) is associated with a longer life span. To drink less and still have fun, follow a simple trick: use a smaller glass. Keep your glass on the table while you pour, and never fill it over half full. Survey after survey submits that alcohol in moderation promotes heart health and even wards off diabetes and dementia. The evidence is so ample that some experts go one step further and advocate moderate drinking: about one drink for women, about two drinks for men a day. It is really a wishful drinking.

One drink may be defined as any one of (a) 12 oz. of beer, (b) 6 oz. of wine, (c) 1.5 oz. of 80-proof spirits, or (c) 1 oz. of 100-proof spirits (the proof number is twice the percentage of the alcohol content measured by volume—i.e., in gin rum, vodka, whiskey, scotch, cognac). The pH acidity level of beer is 4, which is the same level as wine. Vodka pH is 4, whiskey pH is 5, fresh cow's milk has a pH between 6.7 and 6.5, and distilled water has a pH of 7.

But when you go overboard per day or per week or even per month, your chance for developing alcohol dependence increases dramatically. One study followed more than eleven thousand Swedish twins for nearly half of their lives and concluded that drinking more than two drinks per day increased a middle-aged person's stroke risk more than the traditional health dangers, like high BP and diabetes. From another large-scale study covering more than forty thousand people, researchers additionally found that people who are "at risk" drinkers (daily or nearly daily) have seven times the risk of developing alcohol dependence compared to low-risk drinkers. Per the CDC, heavy drinking costs the U.S. $223 billion annually—75% lost productivity, 11% health care, 9% criminal justice, and 8% alcohol-related syndrome and associated disorders. Approximately half of the burden is passed on to the government.

Fruits and Vegetables

In general, we should eat as much fruits and vegetables, favor whole grains over highly processed food, and choose red meat as an occasional menu rather than the daily focus of the meal. And finally, we should not eat any more than our body needs!

The fact is not that fruits and vegetables are good for you—the fact is that they are so good for you that they could save your life. It needs only some understanding and mental setup. No matter how much we think that we know about what goes into a healthy meal, we often miscalculate. Some vegetables are healthier than others, some whole grain products are less processed than others, and some fish are safer to eat than others. You might be thinking you are eating right, which perhaps is not the case. By making slight changes based on dietary guidance in what you eat and how you eat, you could practically start eating considerably healthier. Yet the fact remains that Americans most often eat only six types of fruit out of the more than sixty types commonly available in the open market. Out of about 300 lb. of fruit consumed on average per person in the U.S. each year, 44% is fresh, and the rest is in drinks, cans, sauces, jams, and jellies.

Studies after studies have cautioned that as much as 80% of heart disease and 90% of diabetes is associated with unhealthy eating and lifestyles. Doctors have proved that a diet with more fruits and vegetables—as well as small amounts of nuts and dairy products—can lower blood pressure and "bad" cholesterol as effectively and efficiently as medications. Additionally, adding fibers from fruits and vegetables and avoiding highly refined food can prevent or at least delay the onset of type 2 diabetes.

When the nutritionists ask us to replace the fat intake with complex carbohydrates, it imposes some conditions as well. Just as we get the complex carbohydrates in fruits, leafy green vegetables, whole grains, beans, broccoli, and the like, we also get the same from fried chips, rice, and pasta. The question is what kind of complex carbohydrates we should bring in the diet. For example, when we go for fried potatoes, we not only take a higher volume of food than we need but also tend to put in more calories. The depletion of some valuable nutrients—such as antioxidants, which are found in some of the vegetables—is another factor. Also, it is known that the skin of the potato is rich in potassium; but when we take it in the form of fried chips, we do not get that benefit. What gives us little pleasure of the palate is only at the cost of the waist.

A compound called a phytochemical is available in all plant products, such as broccoli, cabbage, tea, and the like. Phytochemicals prevent the disintegration of the cells by free radicals. By curbing the activity of the free radicals to cause cellular damage, phytochemicals protect the health in us. Many food experts say that phytochemicals are a wonderful gift of nature. Besides vegetables—such as broccoli, brussels sprouts, cabbages, and the like—it is found abundantly in the form of a compound called flavonoids in citrus fruits and onions. Flavonoids protect the heart from many chronic diseases.

Besides the flavonoids, there is yet another type of phytochemical known as carotenoid. This is abundantly found in carrots and other yellow and orange vegetables. The beta-carotene—as these are often called—are renewed into vitamin A inside the body. They save the body from the onslaught of several diseases, such as coronary diseases, cataract, cancer, and muscular degeneration. As regards the amount of fruits and vegetables, a minimum of five servings (both put together) is considered to be the guide. Besides being high in phytochemicals, vegetables are high in fibers as well. As we know, the fibers save us from a number of diseases like heart disease, cancer, diabetes, and so forth. Due to the combined effects of the phytochemicals and the fibers (besides many other nutrients), vegetables become one of the most essential ingredients of the diet.

Now the question is what the best form of taking vegetables is. It depends on one's taste, choice, and convenience. One may go for fresh fruits and vegetables as much as possible. It is important to know that frozen items are not any deficient in the nutrient content. Do not assume that vegetables fresh from the garden are the only vegetable you should take. Frozen vegetables can be just as good and are occasionally better. Because frozen vegetables are chilled immediately after being harvested, they often contain more nutrients than produce that has latency in transportation and have been sitting on the shelf of supermarkets for a few days.

Freezing does alter the nutritional composition of fruits and vegetables slightly, and so does the fresh ones in latency. There is no clear winner. The difference in nutrient levels between fresh and frozen are so minor that they have hardly any impact on overall health; and for that reason, dietitians generally encourage people to eat as many and as much fruits and vegetables from whatever sources. Plus, minerals like iron, zinc, calcium, and magnesium are almost bulletproof; and so are the fibers. They hardly matter, fresh or frozen.

University of California researchers compared the vitamin content in eight commercially available fresh and frozen fruits and vegetables—broccoli, spinach, peas, green beans, corn, carrots, strawberries, and blueberries—and found no consistent differences. The vitamin content is occasionally higher in some frozen foods.

An intuitive idea of taking vegetables raw and fresh may not be attractive to many people. For some people, even the idea of taking vegetables in a boiled condition may become quite daunting because of its blandness. For that, one may try different varieties and eat in any other form, such as in soups or salads or as an ingredient of the pasta that one eats. It goes without saying, however, that eating vegetables only in fried form will take away much of their nutrient value. Stir-frying is not that bad compared to deep-frying.

Some people suggest that taking vegetables in raw form is the healthiest. Some research into the matter recently done, however, suggest that while eating raw vegetables may help us fully absorb the nutrients from the vegetable, some of the nutrients, however, are more effective after cooking and processing. Eating raw vegetables may enable us to absorb a high level of the vitamin A and beta-carotene contained in the vegetables, but another antioxidant called lycopene (found in good quantity in tomatoes) is ready for absorption only after processing. Cooking breaks down the cell walls, making the nutrient ready for absorption by the human body. Processed tomato contains lycopene, which is more ready for absorption. Tomato paste has lycopene, which is four times more in quantity volume-wise than a fresh tomato.

Organic fruits and vegetables contain 40% more nutrients on average than their chemical-fed counterparts. Pasture-raised cattle produce meats and dairy products that have more beta-carotene and at least three times more CLA (conjugated linoleic acid that reduces the risk of cancer) than conventional grain-fed cattle. Where nutrition goes, flavor follows—thanks to Mother Nature. The taste, the aroma, and the feel-good effect should come from satisfying and enjoying the food. Economists noticed public perception between organic products and something social psychology calls the "halo effect" (why we like what we like). A halo effect, in theory, is a cognitive bias that involves one trait influencing the other: if you favor a politician's politics, you are likely to think he is a statesman too. In this way, we get the things systematically wrong. If it is pricey, it must be better; or it is better because we are told that it is. These are all fabrications our brain gets confused with. Researchers using an fMRI scanner show that it's not only when you feel more pleasurable but also when you say you like it more. You actually experience it then and there; the part of the brain connected with pleasure and reward lights up. When people are told food is organic, they tend to believe it is more nutritious and better-tasting as well. Aside from the halo effect, however, organic products really taste better, according to the taste test by professional chefs; and most importantly, it stops the spread of antibiotic-resistant bacteria that usually cause serious infections. In 2014, there were two million infections in the U.S., causing twenty-three thousand deaths from antibiotic-resistant bacteria. The foods are antibiotic-free but rich in bacteria—and that's a good thing. In the U.S., a current trend of transition to antibiotic-free, naturally pasture-raised pork, chicken, and beef that meets FDA recommended standards seem to be encouraging. In 2014, lawmakers were making new laws to require U.S. firms to release relevant information about their use of antibiotics. President Obama pronounced an executive order for creating a task force and an action plan for implementation.

Nutritionists say that vitamins A, D, E, and K and antioxidant carotenoids do not lose their nutritional value by boiling and steaming. But vitamin C contained in the vegetable may lose its value by a large percentage. Spinach, for example, loses over 50% of its vitamin C by cooking. The carrot also gives its entire nutritional value when eaten raw. Processed and canned carrots will have less than 10% of their nutritional value. Even when it is boiled and eaten, it loses some of its nutritional value. Steaming and frying makes it lose its food value even more. Deep-frying is the worst of all. Because the nutrient content and the taste widely vary depending on the cooking process, the sensible way to go is to eat a variety of vegetables prepared in a variety of ways.

Let us say that nothing nourishes us as much as what we take directly from Mother Nature. There is always a joy harvesting the grains, fruits, and vegetables fresh from her garden. Nature brings in various fruits and vegetables in different seasons throughout the year, which we humans need to acknowledge as the requirements of our bodies vary to an extent according to the seasons. After all, our ancestors had once lived wholly on foods provided by her. All she yields on earth vary from season to season as she knows that the needs of her children also vary according to the climate. What she produces in the tropics are not the same as what she grows in deserts. She has stored all the nutrients that we—living in different climates—need. The prudent thing is to take this cue from her and choose our diet from what She brings forth in the different seasons and in the different places we live. With little inspiration, we can make a wonder of food with the help of Mother Nature.

3.2 Diet and Nutrition

> The chief pleasure in eating does not consist in costly seasonings or exquisite flavor, but in yourself.
> —Horace (65–8 BC), the classic Roman lyric poet

The archeological discovery of "Ardi" of 4.4 million years ago and "Lucy" of 3.2 million years ago reveals that our common ancestors lived on a botanical diet, mostly on plants and vegetables. It is also an established fact that our ancestor primates could never have evolved as big, strong, intelligent, and socially active hominids if they hadn't turned to meat. One agreement could be the vegetarian primates like gorillas and orangutans are less so than more omnivorous chimpanzees. The early hominids started eating the meat of other animals about 2.5 million years ago since the time of the Stone Age. Apelike African humans then started evolving. The control of fire as early as 1.8 million years ago by *Homo erectus* was a turning point in human evolution. Fire—tamed by *Homo erectus* about 1,500,000 to 500,000 years ago—was used to prepare the raw meat and vegetables. This protein of meat and the glucose of the botanical diet, gave early man an edge in the expenditure of energy on demand. This energy was used to collect more food, to build shelter, to play, to relax, and to socialize. Agriculture was invented around 8000 BC, and pottery followed soon after, 7000 BC.

Humans evolved to eat. Anthropologists looked at the diets, habits and physical activities of hundreds of modern hunter-gatherer groups and small-scale societies, whose lifestyles are very similar to those of ancient populations, and find that they all generally exhibit excellent metabolic health while consuming a wide range of diets. Their diet varies from food that contains 80 percent of daily calories from carbohydrates to food that contains mostly the meat; but, almost all of them eat a mix of plants and vegetables, meat and fish, and grains and lintels, consuming foods that are generally nutritious. Sugar is not uncommon for them, which they consume largely in the form of honey. They rely on a fairly small number of types of food; yet, the amount of daily calories they consume on average, is similar to that of an average American. Life in hunter-gatherer societies is tough, especially for infants, who die of infectious disease, gastrointestinal illness, acute infections, and accidents. But those who survive to adulthood would often live up to their very old age relatively free from degenerative diseases, which are now very common in our modern-day society.

Humans eat food, not diet or nutrition. The food is to regulate the purpose of maintaining and improving one's physical condition. Diet is the food that is balanced. The key facts relating to a healthy diet (and some allied facts), as defined by the World Health Organization (WHO), are as follows:

- A healthy diet helps protect against malnutrition in all its forms, as well as noncommunicable diseases (NCDs), including obesity, diabetes, heart disease, stroke, and cancer.
- An unhealthy diet and lack of physical activity are leading global risks to health.
- Healthy dietary practices start early in life. Breast-feeding may have longer-term benefits, like reducing the risk of overweight and obesity in childhood and adolescence.

- Energy intake (calories) should balance energy expenditure. Evidence indicates that total fat should not exceed 30% of total energy intake to avoid unhealthy weight gain, with a shift in fat consumption away from saturated fats to unsaturated fats and toward the elimination of industrial trans fats.
- Limiting the intake of free sugars to less than 10% of total energy is part of a healthy diet. A further reduction to less than 5% of total energy is suggested for additional health benefits.
- Keeping salt intake less than 5 g per day helps prevent hypertension and reduces the risk of heart disease and stroke in the adult population.
- The WHO member states have agreed to reduce the global population's intake of salt by 30% and halt the rise in diabetes and obesity by 2025.

Diet plans are planned on adapting the intake of any one or more of the macronutrients (carbohydrates, proteins, and fats) that constitute the major portion of food that a person eats (other than water). Food is a necessary source of energy. They provide adequate amounts of nutrients, along with weight-maintenance regimens that are designed for long-term use. In the U.S., diets and dieting are interpreted in as many ways as dieters are. It is so subjective and so confusing. An obsession to diet is a sickness in its own way—as if you pay the penalty for crossing the feed limit. It makes you feel lesser about yourself and probably does more damage than good to your health. Even kids (besides adults) who are frequent dieters gain as much as 2.5 lb. more each year than their peers who do not diet. The reason is that an overly restrictive diet leads to cycles of binge eating. The CDC announces that poor eating habits and inactivity are the serious causes of preventable deaths in the U.S. Obesity is a major health threat.

Researches and studies on the nutritional properties of different types of food have been going on for many decades. The results are not always consistent with one another. Sometimes they are too bafflingly contradictory for the common man, who is often at a loss as to what is the proper diet to ensure a healthy life. But as researches are conducted extensively at different parts of the globe by different groups of scientists, researchers have been successful in breaking some common ground where the opinions are not so contradictory. In other words, the good and the bad effects of a large variety of edibles have been established beyond any reasonable doubt and dispute. To this effect, let us compile some information about six basic categories of nutrients that our body needs to acquire from food: (1) protein, (2) carbohydrates, (3) fat, (4) fibers, (5) vitamins and minerals, and (6) water.

Proteins

Proteins belong to a class of nitrogenous organic large molecules of amino acids arranged in a linear chain and joined together by peptide bonds. Proteins are essential elements for any organism. They play a key role in every process within the cell. Many proteins are enzymes (catalysts for biochemical reactions). They catalyze (assist) biochemical reactions and are essential to metabolism. Proteins are essential for the body because they build up the muscles and give the body its strength. There are twenty amino acids considered to be essential for the body. To function properly, the body needs all of them, and in the right amounts. Twelve of them are manufactured in the body, and eight are to be accrued from the diet. The most abundant source of protein is meat—beef, chicken, pork, mutton (goat meat), lamb, and so forth. Besides meat, another rich source of protein is milk. An excess of protein in the body, however, will create complications. Scientists have researched the safe limit, and it is generally 0.8 g to 1 g of protein per kilogram (2.2 lb.) of the body weight per day. For 160 lb. of body weight, one needs 72 g of protein, which one can get from 200 g (7 oz.) of lean beef.

Animal-based foods have complete proteins, while most plant foods, incomplete—meaning certain amino acids are missing. However, the Academy of Nutrition and Dietetics cautions that people should not be swayed away by the terms "complete protein" and "incomplete protein," for two reasons: (1) liver stores various essential amino acids over the course of a day for use later on; so, (2) if a person consumes varied healthful diets—animal-based and plant-based (even exclusively plant-based) foods—within a day, an adequate supply of essential amino acids is restored. As long as one eats a variety of nutritious foods, one need not consume complementary plant foods simultaneously. Rice and beans combination, is a perfect example of complementary proteins: the amino acids that are missing from rice are found in beans and vice versa.

In many middle socioeconomic classes in the developing and even developed countries, the average intake is less. For example, in India, it is less than 0.4 g of protein per kilogram. In contrast, the average consumption in the U.S. is 1 g to 2 g—which, without hesitation, is the usual suspect responsible for different types of avoidable health problems. Among several other deleterious effects, excess protein is responsible for high blood pressure and poor lipid profile.

Today, vegetarianism is projected as one healthy diet. Vegetarian food tends to keep the blood pressure under control. They suffer much less from hypertension. The vegans are often leaner than the non-vegans, and that might be one reason for their blood pressure. The other reason is that vegetables ensure a higher intake of potassium, which causes the BP to remain at an optimum level. Many Americans fall short on potassium because they don't eat enough fruits and vegetables. Some plants are also known to lower blood viscosity. For these reasons, vegetarian people usually have a lower risk of heart attacks and kidney ailments. However, complete vegetarian food may not be able to meet all the protein requirements of the body. So, unless vegetarianism is on matters of principle and aesthetics, one can strike a balance of vegetables and some animal protein. One or two moderate servings of beef, pork, or mutton and two servings of chicken or fish per week—along with plenty of vegetables, fruits, grains, and cereals—will provide enough protein.

Supplements

Well-come to the wild world of mysterious dietary supplements—in the business of wellness! Dietary supplements occupy a broad range of (yet poorly regulated) space between two more defined consumables: food and drugs. Americans spend approximately $28 billion a year on dietary supplements, which is more than double what was spent in 1995. But do supplements really work? Well, it depends. Some work, some don't. Sometimes they do provide nutrition without eating notorious food and do cure and maintain wellness without medicine. Whether they can improve health and how is a matter of enormous scientific inquiry. DNA testing reveals as much as 80% of the supplements tested do not contain what the labels on their bottles claim. In 2015, the New York State Attorney General's Office conducted spot tests on popular store brands of herbal supplements and then accused four nationwide retailers of selling dietary supplements that were fraudulent, duplicitous, and contaminated with unlisted ingredients. As many as four out of five products contained none of the herbs listed on their labels; and in the majority of the cases, the supplements contained cheap fillers like rice and houseplants or some substances that could be detrimental to health. One review published in *British Journal of Clinical Pharmacology* in 2018 identified a number of common herbal supplements (including green tea and Ginkgo biloba) that can adversely interact with prescription medications, making them less effective—and may even dangerous or deadly. In general, vitamins or supplements do not provide an extra benefit that they claim, rather cause harm. More is not merrier! As a matter of fact, there are plenty of fortifications in the American food supply that getting multivitamins just from the foods is easy and sufficient enough. Also, supplements and vitamins are not the same things. Americans need to understand that most vitamins and dietary supplements available in America are not made in America; and, given the state of statutory regulations in place now, it is difficult to say if a supplement is safe, or of good quality. Some independent, nonprofit organizations (like United States Pharmacopeia (USP) or NSF International) set standards for medicine, food ingredients and dietary supplements. Only a handful of brands carry their seals of approval.

That supplements are "superfoods" is simply a marketing gimmick. There are over eighty-five thousand dietary supplements for sale in America, compared to only thirteen vitamins. While scientists know exactly what vitamins do in bodies and how much of a dose is needed, they have hardly any idea about the thousands of supplements. People commonly assume that all vitamins and dietary supplements are regulated and tested for safety and effectiveness before they're sold. But they're not. Supplements are essentially for people with restricted diets or health issues that make it hard to absorb nutrients from food. Following the passage of Dietary Supplement Health and Education Act of 1994, the market opened the floodgate for the industry to bring any supplements to the market without any certification from the FDA for safety and its efficacy. Surveys indicate that 52% of adults used one or more supplements in 2012. About 33% of children under 19 used dietary supplements or alternative medicines in 2018; multivitamins are the most common supplements, followed by vitamin C, omega-3 fatty acids, vitamin D and melatonin. Studies show that there is little benefit in supplements, and that no pill can supply the nutrients found in wholesome foods.

Yet Americans use supplements in the form of vitamins, energy drinks, mineral waters, and herbal medicines to treat a wide variety of conditions, including colds, arthritis, immune system issues, and weight loss. Common problems include children taking supplements meant for adults, and adults are choking on pills. Common complications include irregular or rapid heartbeat and chest pain. As many as three out of four ER visits are associated with the use of weight-loss and energy-boosting supplements. In 2015, the Department of

Justice (DOJ) and other agencies—like the Federal Trade Commission (FTC) and the Food and Drug Agency (FDA)—reviewed dietary supplements and their manufacturers for using any unlawful and fraudulent ingredients. They were surprised to see that some—from a list of 274 dietary supplements that the FDA recalled between 2009 and 2012—are still being sold in the market. They are now taking legal action. There are new studies emerging regularly, but many of them have tiny sample sizes and lack placebo controls. Sometimes the information is so contradictory that it's like trying to make your way through a fog. However, the view of the majority seems to be that we cannot meet the full quota of the requirement of all the nutrients through a normal diet while the ideal and recommended diet is 3 to 5 servings of vegetables; 3 to 4 servings of fruits; 6 to 10 servings of bread, rice, grains, enough of nuts and seeds; and 2 to 3 servings of meat, eggs, and chicken.

It is, however, rarely possible to follow the copybook of the ideal diet. The general experience in America and other countries is that people rarely take the prescribed quota of vegetables and fruits. There is a general preference for non-vegetarian items like meat and fish, particularly among young people. Therefore, taking supplements becomes unavoidable even for the healthy individual, not to speak of a person suffering from a particular ailment due to a vitamin deficiency. Even though virtually all experts agree with almost certainty that a daily multivitamin would not hurt anybody, the experts' opinion is also divided about whether people should be taking high doses of vitamins to cure and prevent chronic illnesses or to delay aging. According to a large-scale study among men, it is revealed that the daily multivitamin doesn't protect against stroke, heart attack, or heart-related death. However, some experts still believe that there is some evidence to justify taking moderate amounts of antioxidants.

Vitamins

Vitamins are organic compounds present in most of our foods in varying amounts and are required by the body in small amounts for the regulation of metabolism and upkeep of normal growth and bodily functions. The most common are vitamins A, B, C, D, E, and K. Vitamins B and C are water-soluble, the excess amounts of which are excreted in the urine. Vitamins A, D, E, and K are fat-soluble and are stored in the body fat.

Vitamins	Uses	Sources
Vitamin A (Beta-Carotene)	An antioxidant that protects against cancer, heart disease , stroke and night blindness. Supports healthy skin, vision, and formation of bones and teeth	Sweet Potatoes, Carrots, Dark Leafy Greens, Dried Apricots, Cantaloupe, Butternut Squash
Vitamin B1 (Thiamine)	For nervous system, body growth and body metabolism. Promotes healthy blood formation and circulation, carbohudrate metabolism, and increased brain function	Brown Rice, Peas, Pastacios, Macadanian Nuts, Pecans, Sunflower Seeds, Salmon
Vitamin B2 (Riboflavin)	Aids in the formation of red blood cells, antibody production and cell growth	Almonds, Dry Soybeans, Cheese, Fatty Fish, Spinach, Whole Grains, Poultry
Vitamin B3 (Niacin)	Supports healthy nervous system, the metabolism of carbohydrates, fats, proteins and digestion	Fatty Fish, Poultry, Broccoli, Carrots, Peanuts, Mushrooms, Avocados
Vitamin B5 (Pantothenic Acid)	The anti-stress vitamin. Supports proper function of adrenal glands, neurotransmitters, and GI tract. An aid for treating depression and anxiety	Fresh Vegetables, legumes, Mushrooms, Raw Nuts, Whole Wheat, Whey, Fatty Fish
Vitamin B6 (Pyridoxine)	Helps balance sodium & phosphorus.Supports the formation of antibodies and red blood cells, and normal brain function	Fatty Fish, Pistachios, Hazelnuts, Garlic, Wheat Bran, Sunflower Seeds, Walnuts
Vitamin B9 (Folic Acid)	Brain food. Promotes energy production and formation of red blood cells. Strengthens immunity by supporting function of white blood cells, healthy cell division and replication	Asparagus Mushrooms, Root Vegetables, Dark Leafy Greens, Whole Wheat, Dates, Oranges, Fatty Fish
Vitamin B12 (Cyanocobalamin)	Aids in formation of blood cells, helps with metabolization of iron and necessary for digestion. Protects nerve endings, supports memory, learning, enhances sleep	Soybeans, Mackarel, Salmon, Eggs
Biotin	Aids in cell growth and fatty acid production. Helps to relieve muscle pain	Egg Yolks Poultry, Fatty Fish, Whole Grains, Soybeans
Choline	Helps in nerve transmission, liver and gallbladder function, hormone production, and proper brain function and memory	Egg Yolks, Legumes, Soybeans, Whole Grain Cereals
Vitamin C (Ascorbic Acid)	A powerful antioxidant that supports the immune system. Help repair tissue and bone damage. Reduces symptoms of asthma and helps prevent cancer	Guavas, Kiwi, Papayas, Oranges, Strawberries, Dark Leafy Greens, Broccoli, Brussel Sprouts, Bell Peppers
Vitamin D	Required for the body to absorb calcium & phosphorus. Supports the nervous system and protects against muscle weakness, osteoarthritis, and cancer	Cod Liver Oil, Eggs, Mushrooms, Fatty Fish, Sweet Portatoes
Vitamin E	A powerful antioxidant that protects the body against free radicals. Improves circulation and promotes normal blood clotting and healing. Supports healthy nerves and muscles	Spinach, Almonds, Sunflower Seeds, Avocados, Broccli, Sqash, Whole Grains, Sweet Potatoes
Vitamin K	Aids with bone formation and promotes healthy function of liver and intestines	Broccoli, Cauliflower, Dark Leafy Greens, Oatmeal Rye, Safflower Oil, Soybeans, Yogurt, Prunes
Vitamin P (Bioflavinoids)	A power antioxidant that partners with Vitamin C to support good heart health and combat atherosclerosis	Sweet Peppers, Strawberris, Oranges, Broccoli, Brussel Sprouts, Garlic, Spinach

Vitamin Information Chart

Vitamin A

Vitamin A is fat-soluble. It helps in the formation and maintenance of healthy skin and hair, bone growth, tooth development, mucus membranes, and reproduction. It plays vital roles in many other functions throughout the body, such as vision, immune functions, and bone metabolism. It fights off viral infections and reduces the risk of heart disease and stroke. Vitamin A promotes healthy surface linings of the eyes and in the respiratory, intestinal, and urinary tracts. When a surface lining breaks down, it becomes open for bacteria to enter the body and cause the infection. Vitamin A is available in beef, pork, eggs, fish, milk, butter, carrots, sweet potatoes, spinach, leafy vegetables, pumpkins, collard greens, cantaloupe melons, papayas, mangos, peas, and broccoli. Green and yellow vegetables and yellow fruits provide half the required vitamin A in the form of carotenes. Grain products and milk and milk products each provide about 20% of the vitamin A needed. Vitamin A may be depleted from food during preparation, cooking, and storage.

Vitamin B

There are eight B vitamins, and all of them are water-soluble. They are spread throughout the body and play many essential roles from cell metabolism to maintaining muscle tone and healthy skin to promoting cell growth and division to boosting the immune and nervous system functions. And it also reduces the risk of pancreatic cancer. Historically, all eight B vitamins were once thought of as a single vitamin, and thus these were referred to as vitamin B (as people refer to vitamin C or vitamin D). Supplements containing all eight vitamins are generally referred to as a vitamin B complex. Out of the individual B-vitamin supplements, B1 (thiamine),

B6 (pyridoxine), B9 (folic acid), and B12 (cobalamins) are well-known. Sufficient intake of the folate (B9) vitamin is very important in preventing neural tube birth defects. [Caution: Some research has linked folic acid to breast cancer. They believe that women who take high doses of folic acid (in vitamin M, vitamin B9, vitamin B complex) supplements during pregnancy are predisposed to a higher risk of developing breast cancer at a later stage.]

Vitamin B12 is essential for red blood cell formation, neurological function, and DNA synthesis. B vitamins are available in all unprocessed whole foods. Processing food—as to the form of white flour and sugar—tends to significantly reduce vitamin B content. Vitamin B is concentrated in meat and meat products, poultry, dairy products, liver oil, turkey, and tuna fish. Additional sources are potatoes, lentils, bananas, chili peppers, beans, nutritional yeast, brewer's yeast, and molasses. Most of the B vitamins need to be replenished daily because any excess is not retained but excreted in the urine. A word of caution! Taking a large dose of certain B vitamins may cause harmful effects.

Vitamin C

Vitamin C is essential for the growth, repair, and maintenance of tissues in all parts of our body. It helps to produce collagen, an important protein essential to make tissues, tendons, ligaments, skin, and blood vessels. It plays a role in repairing and healing wounds, scar tissue, cartilage, bones, and teeth. All fruits and vegetables have varying amounts of vitamin C. Premium sources of vitamin C include citrus fruits and juices, tomatoes, broccoli, green peppers, berries, turnip greens, leafy greens, sweet and white potatoes, and cantaloupe. It is relatively easy to acquire vitamin C from food, especially if you eat the recommended 5 servings: 2 servings of fruits and 3 servings of vegetables each day. The USDA's Food Guide Pyramid recommends 2–4 servings of fruits and 3–5 servings of vegetables daily. High intake of ascorbic acid (vitamin C) can improve mood and stimulate sexual activity. Low intake, on the contrary, tends to a higher risk of many ailments, especially cancer. Vitamin C, vitamin E, and beta-carotene are all beneficial antioxidants. Vitamins C and E deter the development of cataracts, the clouding of the lens in the eyes of people over sixty-five. As vitamin C concentrates in the eye, it is very important, especially for older people, to consume more of it so that cataract development could be delayed by ten years—which means that about half of cataract surgery could be eliminated with the help of vitamin C. The human body does not manufacture vitamin C on its own, nor does it store it. So, it is important to consume ample amounts of vitamin C–containing foods daily.

Vitamin D

Vitamin D controls the crucial biological function by controlling the levels of calcium and phosphorus in the bloodstream. It helps the process of absorption of calcium and thus helps to create and maintain strong bones. Vitamin D belongs to a group of fat-soluble prohormones, and it is naturally available in very few foods, like egg yolks, salmon, tuna, mackerel, mushrooms, and fish liver oils. It is also produced endogenously when sun's ultraviolet-B(UVB) ray strikes the skin and triggers synthesis for vitamin D. Sunlight itself doesn't actually "provide" vitamin D; rather, your body internally produces vitamin D when the skin is exposed to UVB, which triggers vitamin D synthesis. The liver and kidneys convert this biologically inert form of vitamin D into biologically active forms. Only then your body can use it to promote calcium absorption and bone health. Here are a few important points to note: (1) ultraviolet A or UVA penetrates deep within the skin layers and can cause premature aging; (2) UVA can penetrate glass window; (3) ultraviolet B or UVB causes the redness of sunburn; and (4) UVB can *not* penetrate glass window, so you need the *direct* sunlight. In the summer, when the sun is directly overhead, a 10 minutes exposure a day to 10% of the body's surface, conveniently enough of arms and face, is enough. It's a pretty rough estimate for someone with light skin; however, many other factors affect vitamin D synthesis. People with darker skin need twice or more sun exposure to make the same amount of vitamin D. Synthesis declines with age. Environmental factors like ozone, air pollution, clouds and winter, do decrease vitamin D production. Our body stores vitamin D in fat tissues and the liver. So, there are ample opportunities to make sufficient vitamin D during spring, summer and fall time. While cause and effect yet to uncover, researchers linked that babies born in May have vitamin D levels that are 20% lower than those in babies born in November (and almost double the amount of potential harmful auto-reactive T-cells (T-cell helps other white blood cells in the immunologic processes) indicating higher risk of developing multiple sclerosis later in life).

Vitamin D gotten through the process of sun exposure, from food, and from other supplements is biologically inert and needs to undergo two hydroxylations in the body for activation. Various fortified foods commonly available in the U.S. provide sufficient vitamin D. For instance, almost all the U.S. milk supply is fortified with 100 IU/cup of vitamin

D (IU stands for international unit, a unit measurement of substance based on biological effect). A deficiency of vitamin D leads bones to become thin, brittle, or misshapen. The body always needs calcium for strong bones. Vitamin D is the essential element for adequate serum calcium and phosphate concentrations for normal mineralization of the bone. It plays a vital role in the modulation of neuromuscular and immune functions and for the relief of The chemical groups called phosphates within the cells trigger a cascade of chemical changes that amplify the dopamine signal. Vitamin D is available in fortified milk and fortified yogurt. Butter, cream, margarine, and breakfast cereals are also good choices. A glass of milk has 300 mg; a serving-size container of yogurt has 200 mg to 300 mg; and a two-thirds slice of cheese will give you 200 mg to 300 mg of calcium.

Earlier, the Institute of Medicine (IOM) released the first recommended dietary allowance for vitamin D and calcium that the average adult needs: about 600 IU of vitamin D and about 1,000 mg of calcium per day. Vitamin D and calcium levels go hand in hand to maintain bone health because vitamin D must be present for calcium to be absorbed in the digestive tract. But in actual need, daily intake of vitamin D could be as low as 200 IU to 400 IU for adults of normal health and as high as up to 800 IU for those 71 years or older, who are dealing with deteriorating bones. Now, the IOM expert committee, which includes bone specialists, not only concludes that most people do not need these supplements but it also warns that serious health risks may result from the high doses that people typically take. People need enough calcium, but not in excess, because the body can only handle 600 mg of calcium a day. Extra calcium in the blood—usually excreted through kidneys into the urine—can build up a kidney stone. [Hint: For removal of kidney stones, one simple advice is to drink more water. Physicians recommend fluid intake—as much as 8 to 10 glasses of water—be spread throughout the day. The aim is to produce at least two liters of urine a day.] Higher doses can cause heart disease linked to calcium supplements and balance instability, shaking (tremors), and coordination resulting in the very falls and fractures that vitamin D is actually meant to protect against. There is increasing skepticism on whether older adults need to increase calcium intake via supplements in order to prevent osteoporosis and bone fractures. For the daily intake of 1,000 mg to 1,200 mg of calcium per day for older adults, new research finds little evidence to support it—let alone the known side effects, like cardiovascular and constipation problems. In conclusion, the research suggests that policymakers, health organizations, and physicians should not recommend increased doses of calcium for fracture prevention, either through dietary sources or through calcium supplements.

Bone health depends on three things: (a) food and drink habits, (b) personal and family history of broken bones, and (c) lifestyle and habit that influence bone health. About a third of all osteoporotic fractures are linked to a nutritional root. What you eat since childhood is critical to the amount of calcium in your bones. However, the IOM finally recommends (a) 1,000 mg for children of 4 to 8 years, men and women 19 to 50, and men 51 to 70; (b) 1,300 mg for children 9 to 18; (c) 1,200 mg for women 51 and older and men 71 and older; and (d) the upper limit of safety is 2,000 mg a day for men and women over 51. In 2013, the

U.S. Preventive Services Task Force (USPSTF) drafted a recommendation that taking less than 400 IU of vitamin D and 1,000 mg of calcium every day doesn't reduce the risk for bone fractures among postmenopausal women and, therefore, recommended against consuming that.

Different health organizations, however, establish different interpretations and thresholds for what they consider to be sufficient levels of vitamin D, and that creates a misleading perception that more people are deficient and, therefore, is a consequential jolly good excuse to pop more pills. Most people get the daily requirement through usual sources like diet and sunlight. The committee, however, cautions against some practices of UV exposure as it can increase the risk of skin cancer, and that risk outweighs the need to boost vitamin D production in the body. For a three-month-old baby, doctors caution that low levels of vitamin D can increase the risk of repertory infection by as much as 100%.

Vitamin E

Vitamin E is an antioxidant that fights the production of toxic oxygen compounds that are formed when fat undergoes oxidation. It is fat-soluble. It is essential for preventing free radicals from injuring the heart. That is why some doctors suggest administering vitamin E to patients of heart attack to strengthen the heart muscles. Research conducted by the doctors involving a very large number of patients has shown startling results on the effect of beta-carotene (available in vitamin E) on heart patients. It was found that men with a history of cardiac disease who were given 50 mg of beta-carotene on alternate days suffered only half as many heart attacks as the patients who did not take any. Nuts, seeds, and vegetable oils are good sources of vitamin E. A significant amount is available in green leafy vegetables and fortified cereals.

Vitamin K

Vitamin K is long known to form blood clotting; it risks to make four out of thirteen proteins needed for blood clotting. Its role in forming blood clotting is so serious that people who take anticoagulants—such as warfarin (Coumadin)—must be very careful with their vitamin K intake.

Vitamin K helps bones to retain calcium. Rapid calcium loss is a major problem among postmenopausal women, giving rise to fragile-bones syndrome called osteoporosis. Researchers are of the opinion that vitamin K is involved in building the bone because (a) a low level of vitamin K is linked to low bone density, and (b) a supplement of vitamin K benefits quantifiable improvement in biochemical measures of bone health. Vitamin K is available in leafy green vegetables, such as cauliflower, cabbage, spinach, broccoli, and brussels sprouts. Fruits such as avocado and kiwifruit are high in vitamin K. The average diet is self-sufficient in vitamin K. Primary vitamin K deficiency is rare in healthy adults.

Minerals

Minerals are sourced only from the soil. Unlike vitamins and supplements, minerals cannot be produced by a living organism. Minerals from the soil are soaked up by the plants and then transferred to us as we eat the plants and plant-chain foods. Minerals are vital elements for our existence because they are the building blocks that make up our bones, muscles, and tissues. They are essential components in many of our life-support systems, such as hormones, enzymes, and oxygen transport.

The body does not produce any mineral. It must be absorbed through food. The best way to increase mineral intake is through the natural way. It means eating as many varieties as possible of unrefined foods like fresh fruits and deeply colored vegetables, whole grain breads and cereals, and lean meats as well as low-fat dairy products. If the diet is a balanced one with the right proportion of carbohydrates, proteins, and fat, one may get the required quota of minerals. As to the right proportion, some specialists suggest that calorie-wise, the proportion of carbohydrates to protein to fat should be 60:15:25. Stay moderate, follow the Federal Dietary Guidelines for Americans: 45–65% of calories from carbs 20–35% from fat, and 10–35% from protein. It is about similar to the USDA recommendation. If one is still deficient in any mineral, one may supplement it with the guidance of a doctor.

Minerals

Mineral Name	Major Functions	Deficiency Effects	Toxicity Effects	Food Sources
Calcium	Makes up bone and teeth; muscle contraction/re-laxation;blood pressure; clotting;nerve function	Children - stunted growth Adults - bone loss (osteoporosis)	Diarrhea, interference with absorption of other minerals	Dairy, fish with bones, tofu, greens, legumes, fortified foods
Chromium	Helps insulin move glucose (sugar) from blood into cells	Abnormal glucose metabolism	Possible muscle degeneration	Meat, whole grains, vegetable oils
Fluoride	Helps make bones and teeth stronger, helps teeth resist decay	Susceptibility to tooth decay	Fluorosis, discolored teeth, nausea, chest pain	Fluridated water, seafood, tea
Iodine	A component of thyroid hormone - helps regulate growth, development, metabolism	Goiter, cretinism	Low thyroid activity, enlarged thyroid	Iodized salt, seafood, plants grown in iodine-rich soil
Iron	Part of hemaglobin carries oxygen in blood, myoglobin carries oxygen in muscle	Anemia, weakness, head-aches, reduced immunity, low cold tolerance	Fatigue, infection, liver damage, colon cancer, bloody stools, fatal to kids	Red meats, fish, poultry, eggs, legumes, dried fruit
Magnesium	Mineralization of bones and teeth, helps enzymes function, muscle contrac-tion, nerve transmission	Weakness, muscle twitches, confusion, convulsions, bizarre muscle movements	Confusion, lack of muscle coordination, death(all due to overuse of laxatives, antacids)	Nuts, legumes, whole grains, dark leafy greens, seafood, chocolate/ cocoa
Phosphorus	Bones and teeth; DNA; Phospholipids(part of cell membranes)	Weakness, bone pain (Deficiency rare - usually a side effect of medication)	Low blood calcium, increased calcium excretion	All animal tissues(meat fish, poultry, eggs, milk)
Potassium	Maintains normal fluid and electrolyte balance, assists nerve impulse transmission and muscle contraction	Muscular weakness, paralysis, confusion (due to dehydration)	Muscular weakness, vomiting reflex	All whole foods, fruits, vegetables, grains, meat, milk
Selenium	Antioxidant, works with vitamin E	Keshan disease, muscle pain/degeneration, cataracts, low sperm, fragile red blood cells, heart damage	Nail and hair brittleness and loss, nerve, muscle, liver damage, nausea	Seafoods, organ meats, other meats, grains, veg depending on soil content
Sodium	Maintains normal fluid and electrolyte balance, assists nerve impulse transmission, muscle contraction	Muscle cramps, mental apathy, loss of appetite	Edema, acute hypertension, increased calcium excretion	Table salt, soy sauce, MSG, all processed foods
Zinc	Part of insulin, helps many enzymes function, DNA repair, taste perception, immune function, wound healing, sperm	Failure to grow (kids), dermatits, loss of taste, poor healing, sex retardation	Fever, Nausea, vomiting,dizziness uncoordinated, anemia, heart disease	Protein-containing foods, some grains and vegetables

Minerals Chart

Quantity-wise, the human body needs two types of minerals: macro minerals and trace minerals. Our body demands large amounts of macro minerals like calcium, sodium, magnesium, potassium, phosphorus, sulfur, and chlorine. They all are needed to build blood, nerve cells, muscles, teeth, and bones. They produce the essential electrolytes that our body needs to regulate blood volume and to balance an acid-to-base ratio. On the other hand, trace minerals are required in only very tiny amounts. Mainly, they participate in chemical reactions within the body and are especially needed to manufacture important hormones. A trace amount of gold, silver, and other metals have been detected in human waste. The following are classified as trace minerals: iron, zinc, copper, manganese, chromium, selenium, molybdenum, iodine, fluorine, and boron. Of the many minerals, iron is supposed to be the most vital for human life; it is an essential ingredient of blood. Zinc comes next.

If less is good, more will be better. However, this notion doesn't work for mineral supplements because absorbing more of one mineral can cause one to absorb less of other minerals. Such a problem typically arises when the different minerals race to compete in the pathways through the body, or when they interact with each other and form a mineral complex that is poorly absorbed. Daily supplements of multivitamins are, however, not known to cause any harm. Many people have been regularly taking doses of vitamins to combat chronic diseases or to delay aging. Taking moderate amounts of antioxidants as a supplement is not discouraged. What, however, has to be remembered is that an excess of vitamins has to be avoided. For instance, an excess of vitamin A may cause liver damage. Beta-carotene from food is converted to vitamin A inside the body; and therefore, when vitamin A is taken as a supplement, the limit should not be crossed. It is one of the reasons why supplementing minerals in the body should preferably be under a doctor's guidance.

Iron

Iron is an outright requirement for most forms of life, including humans and most bacterial species. In humans, iron is one essential element of red blood cells. Iron helps transport oxygen throughout the body and helps the metabolism. It aids in energy production and cell diffusion and helps the immune and central nervous systems. The human body has 0.00004% iron. Most well-nourished people have 3–4 g (less than the weight of two pennies) of total iron in their bodies. About two-thirds (2.5 g) of iron stays in hemoglobin, which is the protein in the red blood cells that carries oxygen throughout the body's tissues. If we have a lower level of iron, our muscles will receive less oxygen and produce more lactic acid. A buildup of lactic acid results in premature fatigue when we work physically. Common indications of iron deficiency are a rapid heartbeat, fainting, fatigue, weakness, and swelling of the tongue.

Anemia is a condition characterized by deficiency of red blood cells or of hemoglobin in the bloodstream. It occurs due to a decreased level of red blood cells (RBCs) or reduced normal quantity of hemoglobin in the blood. It is a condition where the person does not have enough red blood cells to carry adequate oxygen to tissues. Typically, anemia stays undetected for many people, and the symptoms are minor or vague, such as weakness, fatigue, general malaise, and poor concentration. Anemia is more common in women than men, primarily because women tend to lose iron through menstrual bleeding. Iron is the only mineral that a woman needs a higher daily requirement than a man. Especially during pregnancy, iron deficiency may result in increased risk of premature delivery, giving birth to infants with low birth weight, and maternal complications. Iron deficiency and iron-deficiency anemia are comparatively common in women of childbearing age, older infants, toddlers, and teenage girls. In the U.S., one in four women of childbearing age has iron-deficiency anemia. The recommended daily allowance (RDA) of iron is 15 mg for women and 10 mg for men.

As all plants and animals innately have iron, iron is available in a wide variety of food sources. Iron that is derived from animal food is easier to assimilate than from the plant foods. The reliable sources to maintain the right level of the mineral is to take lean meats, dried beans, whole grains, wheat germ, and breakfast cereals. Breakfast cereals that are fortified with iron are well-situated. Other sources include some fish, dried fruit, and spinach. Iron supplements are made in two forms: ferrous and ferric. Ferrous iron (e.g., ferrous fumarate, ferrous gluconate, ferrous sulfate) is better absorbed by the body and is the preferred form immediately when iron deficiency is first diagnosed. Ferric iron (e.g., ferric ammonium citrate, serum ferritin), is not well absorbed. Common side effects of both iron supplements are vomiting, constipation, nausea, diarrhea, constipation, dark-colored stools, and abdominal discomfort. The World Health Organization (WHO) theorizes that iron deficiency is the primary nutritional disorder in the world that affects more than 30% of the world's population.

Iron-deficiency anemia is a common type of anemia. (Other types include anemia of chronic disease, vitamin-deficiency anemia, aplastic anemia, anemias associated with bone marrow disease, hemolytic anemias, and sickle cell anemia.)

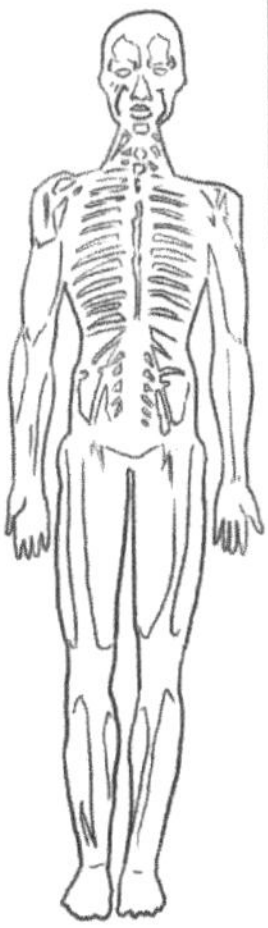

Element	% by mole
Hydrogen	63.0
Oxygen	26.0
Carbon	9.0
Nitrogen	1.25
Calcium	0.25
Phosphorus	0.19
Potassium	0.06
Sulfur	0.06
Sodium	0.04
Chlorine	0.025
Magnesium	0.013
Iron	0.00004
Iodine	0.000002

99% of atoms in a human body come from these 4 elements

Body Composition by Elements

Calcium

Mineral calcium is required for healthy bones, teeth, and better functioning of the heart, muscles, and nerves. The human body has 0.24% calcium. The recommended daily dose required for the adults is 1,000 mg for people aged 19 to 50 and 1,200 mg for those older than 50. The food sources for calcium are low-fat milk, yogurt, cheese, and calcium-fortified orange juice. An adult eats these foods at least three servings a day to meet the recommended dose. However, it is not clear that we need as much calcium as is generally recommended, because it is not clear if dairy products are really the good source of calcium for most people. While calcium intake from foods and dairy products may lower the risk of osteoporosis and colon cancer, a higher intake may result in the risk of prostate cancer for men and possibly ovarian cancer for women. Also, milk and dairy products are high in saturated fat and retinol (vitamin A), which, at higher levels, can paradoxically weaken the bones. So, limit your intake of milk and dairy products appropriately and certainly no more than one to two servings per day. Nondairy sources of calcium include fortified soy milk, almonds, tofu, collards, beans, leafy green vegetables, and broccoli.

Weight-bearing exercise, sports, walking, or jogging is an essential part of building and maintaining strong bones. The perfect time is during the young to youth adulthood years when bones build up to their peak strength. So, a healthy lifestyle with play and exercise, an adequate calcium-rich diet, and vitamin D can help keep strong bones through the adult years. An average woman does acquire most of her skeletal mass by the age of twenty. A rapid decline in bone mass occurs in older adults, increasing the risk of osteoporosis and fracture. Osteoporosis is an age-related thinning of the bones. Throughout life, bones constantly remodel themselves: build up new sections while dissolving old ones in turnover processes called "formation and resorption." As we age, the turnover progressively goes out of balance, making the bones thinner and weaker. For women, during menopause, the rate of resorption increases, but the formation of new bone does not keep up with the loss. The United States Preventive Services Task Force (USPSTF) has revised their guideline in 2018 recommending that all women over 65 and women under 65 but past menopause, should undergo bone density screening (DEXA scan, a brief, noninvasive, safe and inexpensive test) to prevent osteoporotic fractures. For men, the decision is inconclusive, no recommendation, yet.

One study finds that moderate alcohol consumption—about 1½ drink (preferably wine) per day—may help women in their fifties and early sixties to prevent bone loss. However, more than two drinks a day—especially drinking quickly—can obviously increase the risk of falls and fractures. Another study shows beer can be good for bone. Dietary silicon—usually found in grains, especially in oats and barley, which are the key ingredients of beer—can help to maintain bone strength and to keep the connective tissues in good condition. Barley is richer in silicon content than wheat. Beer consumption, in moderation, is another source of silicon and has been shown to be beneficial in halting bone degradation in conditions like osteoporosis.

Drugs are supposed to slow down bone loss and are a popular way to combat osteoporosis, particularly among women past menopause. Paradoxically, however, some commercial bone-boosting drugs actually increase, rather than decrease, the risk of some types of rare fractures. Some studies caution that while the medications do prevent fractures common with osteoporosis, they may increase, as side effects, break other, sometimes, stronger bones.

Sodium (Salt)

Sodium is a soft silver-white, ductile, extremely fast reactive metallic element of the alkali group. It is one chemical element represented by Na+. It is passed to our body primarily as salt, which is a chemical compound of 40% sodium and 60% chlorine (Cl—another chemical element, a toxic, irritant, pale green gas). Salt has 40% sodium by weight. Therefore, salt and sodium, by weight, are not the same measure; yet both are used interchangeably in typical usage. Taken from CDC website under heading, "Dietary Guidelines for Sodium" in 2017, reads as: "The 2015-2020 Dietary Guidelines for Americans recommend that Americans consume less than 2,300 milligrams (mg) of sodium per day as part of a healthy eating pattern." Sodium is listed on food labels as "Sodium," not salt. For 2,300 mg of sodium, salt is 5,7500 mg, which is about one teaspoon (1 teaspoon = 5,6900 mg) of table salt. Teaspoon (tsp, ts) is about 5 ml, 0.17 fl oz, or 4.2 grams (a nickel weigh 5.00 grams). Tablespoon (Tbsp, tbsp, Tsp or Ts) is 3x of teaspoon.

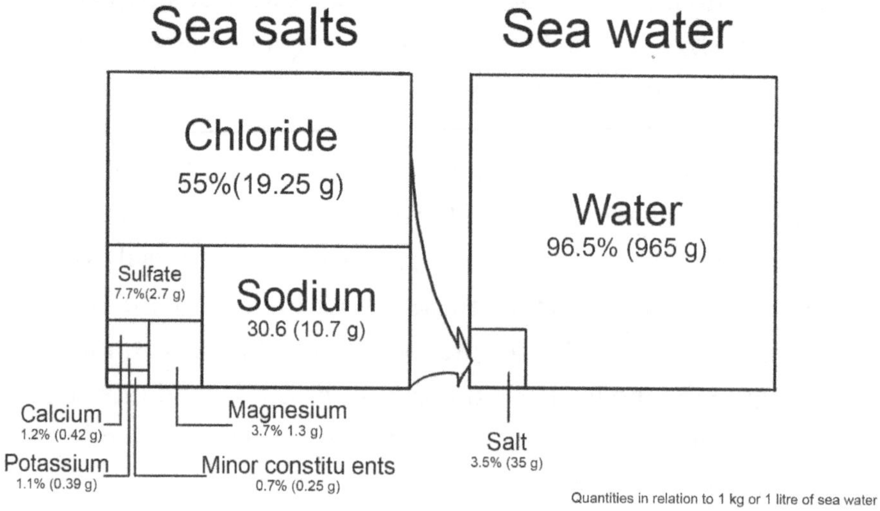

Salt and Seawater

The human body has 0.04% sodium. Sodium is both an electrolyte and mineral and is essential for the body (1) to maintain the electrolyte balance of fluids in our body, (2) to transmit nerve impulses, and (3) to regulate contraction and relaxation of muscles. Our kidneys control the sodium level in our bodies. When the sodium level is low, the kidneys preserve sodium. When the sodium level is high, the kidneys excrete excess amounts in the urine. If the kidneys can't eliminate enough sodium, the sodium starts to accumulate in our blood. To maintain the electrolyte balance, accumulated sodium in the blood attracts and holds excess water, and thus the total volume of blood increases overall. Increased volume of blood, in turn, forces our heart to work harder, to handle more blood volume through our blood vessels, thus increasing the blood pressure in the arteries. Besides high BP, high sodium intake is associated with osteoporosis, asthma, kidney stones, and gastric cancer. So, keep in mind that the lower the sodium intake, the lower the blood pressure. Certain diseases—such as congestive heart failure and chronic kidney disease—can lead to an inability to regulate sodium.

Here are the main sources of sodium in a typical U.S. diet:

5% added while cooking
6% added while eating
12% from natural sources
77% from processed and prepared foods

Here are the ten common daily foods that account for a total 44% of all sodium consumption: (1) bread and rolls (7.4%), (2) cold cuts and cured meats (5.1%), (3) pizzas (4.9%), (4) fresh poultry (has salt within) and processed poultry (4.5%), (5) soups (4.3%), (6) sandwiches like hamburgers and cheeseburgers (4%), (7) cheese (3.8%), (8) pasta dishes such as spaghetti with meat sauces (3.3%), (9) meat dishes like meat loaf with tomato sauce (3.2%), and (10) snacks, including chips, popcorn, pretzels, and puffs (3.1%).

Repeat, only 11% of the sodium comes from the average U.S. diet while cooking (5%) and eating (6%); the majority (77%) comes from breads, packaged or processed foods, sauces, soups, cured meats, pastries, cereals, salad dressings, and condiments. So, even though one may limit the amount of raw salt added to food, the base food itself may already be high in sodium. Recommended 2,300 mg of sodium, is 5,7500 mg of salt, which is about one teaspoon. (Hint: Now something about spoon size! It is fascinating to note that even in a small sample of homes, teaspoon size varies significantly. The largest spoon is three times the size of the smallest spoon. Even when the people are given a precise measurement as 5 mL for 1 tsp, only one in five people manages to pour the correct amount. The teaspoon is a unit of culinary measure in the U.S.

Our body relies on many essential minerals for a variety of functions, but sodium outstrips far. Sodium levels in the blood has to be carefully maintained in order to maintain blood pressure and the transmission of nerve impulses. Clinical investigations, which were meticulously done in recent time, contradict much of the conventional wisdom about how the body handles salt. Our body needs sodium for proper functioning, but our salt intake far outstrips the physiological needs. Per CDC report, 9 out of 10 Americans eat too much sodium: on average, 3,400 mg (as against 2,300 mg recommended) of sodium per day contributing to higher rates of heart disease and stroke. People with heart problems, including middle-aged and older adults, ethnically blacks and those with high blood pressure, should restrict salt to 1,500 mg or 1/3rd teaspoon a day. American Heart Association (AHA) re-affirms that it is the same 2011 recommendation that all Americans should limit their sodium intake to just 1,500 mg per day, which is little less than a teaspoon of table salt

Salt has a huge impact on the taste of food than any other ingredient. It's relationship to taste is multidimensional; it not only provides its own unique taste, but also enhances the taste of other ingredients. If you can use salt well, food will be tasty. Adding a pinch of salt to foods, like broccoli or cauliflower, can be one useful way to condition children's taste bud in order to liken such nutritious foods. The ill effect of salt content is negligible, except very young kids with lesser body weight. In many cuisines around the world, salt takes the bitter out and makes the food palatable. Once children associate vegetable's flavor with more of an appealing flavor, like a salty or cheesy topping, their taste buds become trained to like vegetable's flavor, even if the salt or topping is taken away. Recently there are some gimmicks in the salt market. Himalayan pink salt may have some decorative value, but nothing else. Iodized salt is of least importance, as the American diet provides plenty of iodine that body needs.

One study reviewed diet and blood pressure data of 6,235 kids aged 8 to 18 years and found that those with the highest salt intake were two times more likely to develop prehypertension or hypertension than those who ate the least salt. Additionally, kids who ate salt the most were seen as overweight or obese;

they had three times more the risk of high blood pressure. Another study tracked 4,283 Australian kids aged 2 to 16 to establish the relationship between salt intake and sugary drinks. Participant kids, on average, were taking about 6,000 mg of salt per day. Researchers noticed that about 62% of these kids regularly drank sugar-sweetened drinks—soda, sports drinks, energy drinks, fruit drinks, and flavored mineral waters. And those kids who drank more than one serving a day (26%) tended to be overweight or obese. This implies that excess salt may be a part of the chain of events contributing to overweight children. This also implies that the combined effect of both excess salt and excess weight has a significant effect on blood pressure than either will alone. Since both are major risk factors for heart disease and stroke in adulthood, it simply implies that this generation of children may be more vulnerable to these conditions than ever before.

According to the World Health Organization (WHO), following is their text that give the key facts relating to salt reduction:

- High sodium consumption (more than 2 to 5 g/day) and insufficient potassium intake (less than 3.5 g/day) contribute to high blood pressure and increase the risk of heart disease and stroke.
- The main source of sodium in our diet is salt, although it can come from sodium glutamate, used as a condiment in many parts of the world.
- Most people consume too much salt—on average, 9–12 g per day, or around twice the recommended maximum level of intake.
- Salt intake of less than 5 g per day for adults helps to reduce blood pressure and risk of cardiovascular

disease, stroke, and coronary heart attack. The principal benefit of lowering salt intake is a corresponding reduction in high blood pressure.

- The WHO member states have agreed to reduce the global population's intake of salt by a relative 30% by 2025.
- Reducing salt intake has been identified as one of the most cost-effective measures countries can take to improve population health outcomes. Key salt reduction measures will generate an extra year of healthy life for a cost that falls below the average annual income or gross domestic product per person.
- An estimated 2.5 million deaths could be prevented each year if global salt consumption were reduced to the recommended level.

However, there is a spin. When it comes to the consumption of salt, there are no rights or wrongs—at least none that have been determined yet. In the U.S., estimates have been made by different schools of thought that salt regulation could help improve the nation's preventable deaths from 44,000 to 150,000 annually while, at the same time, others believe that it will have no effect to adverse effect. That's the fallacy of the salt debate. There is so little reliable evidence that you can imagine just about any outcome. So, for all the outcry about the growing threat of salt in packaged foods, experts are not even sure yet if Americans today are eating more salt than they used to.

Now one provocative study suggests that moderate salt intake might be "no problem" and that, on the contrary, diets with very low salt could be a problem. Studying nearly four thousand Europeans, researchers found (1) that an increase in systolic blood pressure (the upper number in blood pressure readings) is associated with increase in salt in urine; (2) that the changes in diastolic blood pressure (lower number) do not have any relationship with salt; (3) that (the most interesting of all) the increase in salt and the increase in diastolic pressure are not associated with increased deaths from cardiovascular disease like heart attacks and strokes; and (4) that finally, on the contrary, people with less salt in their urine are more likely to die from cardiovascular causes. One more research in 2015 adds another twist to the weird benefit of eating salty food: salt is one ancient way for the living body to protect itself against and is an effective way to ward off microbes. The study finds that with salt, the level of sodium goes up around the infection site; and without salt, the bacteria tend to flourish and thrive.

In 2005, an expert committee—commissioned by the Institute of Medicine at the directive of the Centers for Disease Control and Prevention—found that, in consideration of increased rate of heart attacks resulting in an increased risk of death, there was no rationale for anyone to aim for sodium levels below 2,300 mg (about a teaspoon of salt) a day. The average salt-eating habit around the world, and in the United States, is approximately 3,400 mg of sodium a day, according to the Institute of Medicine. It is the very amount that has remained unchanged in decades.

Yet another spin! Danish researchers found that while reducing salt consumption can lead to a 1% drop in BP in people who had normal pressure and a 3.5% drop in those with hypertension, there are side effects that may offset these benefits. People who cut dietary salt can have a 2.5% increase in cholesterol levels and as much as a 7% spike in triglycerides. Cholesterol and triglycerides are the other two major factors for heart disease. Triglycerides contribute to diabetes as well.

The salt culture and the assumption thereof are based on the statistics. Statistically, the harder the experts try to save Americans, the worse were the results. Examples are like when the nation followed the admirable advice to quit smoking, smokers gained 15 lb. on average by some estimates. While the side effect extra weight was certainly a worthwhile trade-off for better health and longer life, the fact of the matter is that success comes with a new challenge. Another example is when authorities advised Americans to avoid fat, which became the official villain of the national dietary guidelines during the eighties and nineties. While the anti-fat campaign made a definite impact on the marketing of food, Americans, on the contrary, gobbled up all the new low-fat products and continued getting even fatter. Ultimately, in the 2000s, the experts had to revise the dietary guidelines. They acknowledged their mistake that the anti-fat advice might have indirectly contributed to obesity and diabetes by unintentionally encouraging Americans to eat more calories. The new system encourages fiber-rich and lesser-calorie-point foods like fruits and vegetables and discourages high-fat, low-fiber, and processed foods. In 2014 fall, the panel of experts that developed the country's dietary guidelines conceded that they got rid of the concept of the low-fat diet. In 2015 spring, they lifted the longstanding guideline on dietary cholesterol, explaining that there was "no appreciable relationship" between dietary cholesterol and blood cholesterol. Americans, as it reveals, have unnecessarily been avoiding shellfish, egg yolks, and liver for decades. Some believe that the food industry is partly responsible for the cause because they have muddied the waters through lobbying. Now, the new guidelines will administer everything from school lunches to doctors' dieting advice.

The salt habit is a hard nut to crack. In one study, researchers have had a hard enough experience getting people to cut back during short-term supervised experiments. The salt reformers believe that reform is possible if the food industries cut back on all the hidden salt in its products. They want the United States to follow Britain, where there had been a huge campaign to force industry, as well as consumers, to use less salt. As a result, there was about a 10% reduction in daily salt consumption from 2000 to 2008, as measured by surveys that analyzed the amount of salt excreted in urine collected over twenty-four hours. While at the same time, on the contrary, another group of researchers analyzed surveys from thirty-three countries around the world and reported that, despite wide differences in diet and culture, people generally consumed about the same amount of salt. Still the salt reformers argue that with the right help, people can maintain low-salt diets without gaining weight or suffering other problems. Alternative solution! There could be health benefits eating less sodium and more potassium by replacing sodium chloride as salt by potassium chloride. Potassium chloride, as a salt substitute—foods blind-tasted virtually identical (slightly bitter) compared to that made with regular salt—is already in use in some consumer products like processed meat.

Even if people are persuaded to eat less salt, would they end up better off? Are the estimates about all the lives to be saved just extrapolations based on the presumed benefits of lower blood pressure? A low-salt diet is associated with better clinical outcomes only in five out of eleven studies; while for the rest of the studies, the people on the low-salt diet remained either the same or got worse. Biologically too, when you reduce salt, you reduce blood pressure; but there can also be side effects and other adverse and unintended consequences. In fact, there can be a "reverse causality" effect, in which higher BP may actually be rolled over to lower BP as soon as people with hypertension limit their salt intake. According to the AHA, there are several studies published in recent years that found unusual associations between poor heart health and low sodium intake. One massive collaborative study was conducted by the 2010 Global Burden of Disease Survey collaborating researchers from fifty different countries. They analyzed 247 surveys of the adults, where the participant adults reported on their sodium intake from 1990 to 2010 in various food questionnaires, and they found that adults around the world consume as much as 4,000 mg of sodium a day, on average, either from the prepared foods or from the table salt or from the salt added to the foods while these are being prepared. It is approximately two times the amount recommended by the World Health Organization (2,000 mg per day) and nearly three times that of the AHA (1,500 mg per day).

Low sodium intake may even be harmful. One study reviewed four observational studies that covered 133,118 people who were monitored for four years. The researchers recorded their estimated sodium consumption by urinalysis corresponding to their blood pressure readings. The result of the review that came out in *The Lancet* (published in May 2016) is that (1a) among people without hypertension (without high blood pressure), consuming as high as 7,000 mg of sodium daily (about 3 tsp of salt), did not increase any risk for disease or death, but (1b) among people who had less than 3,000 mg (less than 1 tsp of salt), they had a 26% increase in risk for death or for cardiovascular diseases like heart disease and stroke, compared to that of those who consumed 4,000–5,000 mg a day; and (2a) among people with hypertension (with high blood pressure), consuming more than 7,000 mg a day increased the risk by 23%, but (2b) among people consuming less than 3,000 mg, it increased the risk by 34%, compared with those who consumed 4,000–5,000 mg a day.

A pinch of salt that adds the taste! Salt blocks sourness, bitterness, and rottenness; and it enhances sweetness. Salt is one cheap way to add taste to food. It is the third cheapest and most essential ingredient after air and water. So, in order to boost the consumers' taste, just add salt (and butter). Studies find that people eat more salt (and cholesterol) at dine-in restaurants than even taste-appalling fast-food joints. Elevated levels of salt in the body lower stress hormones and raise the level of oxytocin, a hormone involved in love and other social connections. Oxytocin stimulates the processes that allow love and social well-being to reduce stress. So, this explains why potato chips, french fries, ketchup, and other salt-rich treats are so appealing.

A desire for extra salt could be genetic. Some just can't help going for high-salt foods. Almost one in four has the genetic makeup that heightens their taste perception.

They are called “supertasters.” While supertasters value taste of the food, non-tasters value the “value of the food.” Typically, supertasters perceive more saltiness in table salt, more sweetness from added sugar, more chilliness from hot peppers, and more tingling from carbonated sodas. They can make out smaller differences in saltiness, sweetness, or chilliness than others. That may explain why most professional chefs are supertasters. The supertasters desire salt saturation to the max—max to the point where most people find the food not only salty but irritating in the mouth. After all, too much salt is bad for health, and it needs to be controlled. Because supertasters are more sensitive to changes in salt levels, they may have to go a little more slowly to lower their salt level. Instead of no-salt foods, perhaps they should choose reduced-salt food. The point is that genetics do matter, but it’s not fate.

After all is said and done, the take-home advice is this: don’t worry too much about the salt. The enduring salt limit of 1,500 mg a day is okay, but the blood pressure rises only when salt intake tops 3,500 mg daily. If your kidneys have no problem, you probably don’t need to cut salt from your diet. Instead, avoid processed foods (which are the real sodium suppliers) and choose more natural food. A food choice is exactly that—nothing but a choice!

Magnesium

Magnesium is another essential mineral that plays a vital role in a wide range of bodily processes, and that especially, interacts with an important neurotransmitter that favors sleep. Low level of magnesium is associated with higher levels of stress, anxiety and difficulty in relaxing, which are key factors for a good sleep at night. Studies find that magnesium deficiency, especially in older people, may cause certain disorders, such as type 2 diabetes, gastrointestinal diseases and alcoholism. Like sodium, our kidneys control the magnesium level in our bodies; and so, the deficiency is rare in healthy people. However, taking an excessive amount of magnesium in the form of supplements can cause stomach cramps, diarrhea and nausea. Magnesium is widely available in both plant and animal-based foods. Leafy green vegetables, legumes, nuts, seeds, whole grains, fish, chicken, beef are good sources of magnesium.

Zinc

Zinc is a trace mineral that is required for the body's defensive (immune) system to function properly. It plays a vital role in the process of cell division, cell growth, wound healing, and also aids to break down carbohydrates. Zinc (along with copper and nickel) is needed for our chemical-sensing system of smell and taste. Though in trace amounts, zinc is spread out in every tissue throughout the body and is an important element for metabolism. Metabolism is the sum of complex biochemical processes that occur within a living organism (i.e., yielding energy from food) that are necessary to maintain life. Zinc is essential in the process of making protein, which indirectly means it helps to grow muscles and other tissues. When you have a zinc deficiency, you may have rough, dry skin; you may lose your appetite; you may lose your head hair; your wounds may take a longer time to heal; and you are unable to smell and taste food correctly. Like iron, zinc is better absorbed from animal sources—beef, pork, lamb, whole grain cereals, eggs, and seafood (oyster)—than from plant sources. Studies indicate that deficiencies in zinc impede upon both male and female fertility. Too much alcohol may reduce zinc levels. A dietary allowance (15 mg of zinc a day) can help keep the reproductive system functioning suitably. Over-the-counter supplements for zinc do relieve the severity and duration of people's overall cold symptoms.

Do we need supplement? In the U.S., before 1920, iodine deficiency was common. Iodine is now available through salt and water. In the 1930s, vitamin D deficiency was associated with rickets (a disease of childhood; softening and distortion of the bones resulting in bow legs). In 1933, milk was first fortified with vitamin D. Over time, many foods were fortified with added nutrients—for example, niacin and iron were added to flour. Fortification was restricted to only a few select foods in order to prevent indiscriminate fortification so that, in part, the program would not create nutritional imbalances. The FDA restricted the number of foods that could be fortified to eight, and it specified which nutrients would be added. Over the years, Congress restricted the FDA's authority over fortification and dietary supplements. That opened a floodgate for an eventual explosion of vitamin-enhanced beverages, energy drinks, sports drinks, and the drink item you name it. Today it accounts for more than $18 billion in sales a year in the U.S. alone.

One very common and obvious question before us is whether our body requires vitamin supplements through tablets, capsules, and pills, or whether a proper planned diet can handle the need of the body totally. Opinions are divided. The majority believe that we can get all the vitamins, nutrients, and minerals we need from our daily diets, and taking supplements is just no more than making expensive urine.

Yet there has been an ever-growing consumer demand, and beverage companies are responding by adding vitamins and minerals to drinks, juices, sodas, and bottled water, even though the amounts of added nutrients are significantly small. Some products promise improvement in energy and immune functions and promote performance and emotional benefits relating to nutrient formulations that go beyond conventional nutritional science. In some cases, the ingredients are potentially harmful. People simply exceed the safe limits of vitamin and nutrient intakes set by the Institute of Medicine. One study in 2012 examined forty-six beverages sold in the supermarkets alongside bottled water, and they noticed that many of these drinks contained vitamins B6 and B12 and vitamin C in quantities "well in excess" of the average daily requirements for a young adult. In another large study in 2012, an analysis of seventy-eight clinical trials involving three hundred thousand people revealed that antioxidant supplements like beta-carotene, vitamin A, and vitamin E actually increased the mortality rate. One year later, the United States Preventive Services Task Force (USPSTF) followed suit but concluded carefully that there was "limited evidence" that taking vitamins and minerals could prevent cancer and cardiovascular diseases.

People have been gobbling vitamin C for twenty years in the certainty that it can cure a common cold, yet the evidence is still lacking. The same is true for vitamin E. If you feel you are doing well with your body by taking a daily dose of multivitamins or supplements with extra vitamin C or E, think again. Studies find that taking supplements can be linked to higher odds of early death, especially for older women. The researchers examined a variety of supplements and tagged higher odds of death commonly associated with six of them: (1) vitamin B has 10% higher risk of death compared with nonusers, (2) folic acid 15%, (3) iron 10%, (4) magnesium 8%, (5) zinc 8%, and (6) copper 45%. Vitamin supplements become increasingly important in old age as the body's ability to absorb vital nutrients from food diminishes. Then again, some studies also caution that dietary supplements (vitamin B6 and iron) may shorten life in women, and that vitamin E intake may increase the risk of prostate cancer in men. Several credible large studies report a higher incidence of heart attacks in both men and women who take calcium supplements. So, instead of vitamins, take real food. For example, vitamin A: sweet potatoes, root vegetables; vitamin B: eggs, dairy, nuts, tuna, chickpeas; vitamin C: citrus fruits (orange), which act as an antioxidant; vitamin D: salmon, fish, protein; vitamin E: almonds, nuts; calcium: kale, greens, vegetables, salads; magnesium: cashews; iron: spinach, greens, vegetables, salads; and multivitamins: pomegranates, fruits. The rest is your judgment call.

Antioxidants

The free radicals are products of our body metabolism. They are also created in the body by tobacco smoke, overexposure to sunlight, car exhaust, and other environmental pollutants. They are toxic molecules with harmful effects on health. They promote aging, impair tissues, and trigger cancerous growth. Here, the importance of the antioxidants lies in its capacity to neutralize free radicals in our body. Berries—blueberries, raspberries, and cranberries—are known to be high in antioxidant content. Beta-carotenes that have antioxidant properties are effective in the prevention of cancer. It has been observed that in countries where people take more beta-carotene in their diet, as in Japan, there have been less incidences of cancer of the lung, colon, prostate, and breast. Beta-carotene is found aplenty in carrots and sweet potatoes besides other edibles. It is the beta-carotene that turns into vitamin A inside the body, another important nutrient the body needs.

Because of the elixir-like qualities of the antioxidants, it has evoked a lot of interest in the scientific community to know more about it and its huge benefits that have so far been discovered from research. By controlling oxidation in the body, the antioxidant prevents cell and tissue damage while preventing cancer, heart diseases, and aging. Food scientists claim that apples of the red variety are rich in these antioxidants. Antioxidant chemicals extracted from apples is capable enough to stop the growth of colon cancer and liver cancer by almost two-thirds.

The earlier Food Guide Pyramid from the United States Department of Agriculture (USDA) was a guideline of a typical daily menu. It was not a rigid preparation but a general guide that allows choosing a healthy diet that is right for an individual. The food pyramid endorsed eating a balanced diet with a variety of foods to get the nutrients one needs and, at the same time, the right amount of calories to maintain healthy well-being. Use the pyramid to help you eat better every day. Start the base with enough cereals, breads, rice, and pasta; and take plenty of fruits and vegetables. Add 2–3 servings from the milk group and 2–3 servings from the meat group. And finally, go easy on foods in the small tip of the pyramid—oils, fats, and sweets.

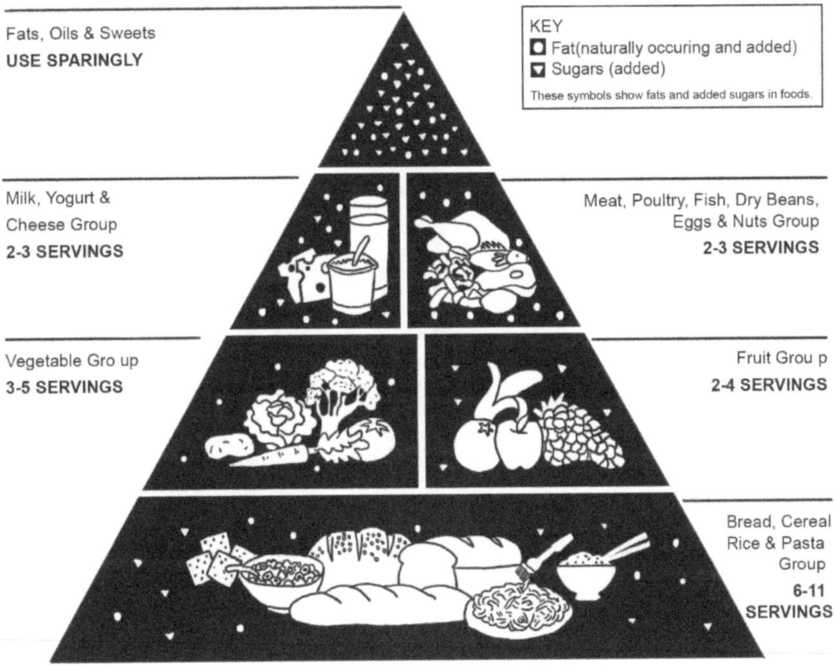

The original food pyramid from the USDA

GRAINS Make half your grains whole	VEGETABLES Vary your veggies	FRUITS Focus on fruits	MILK Get your calcium-rich foods	MEAT & BEANS Go lean with protein
Eat at least 3 oz. of whole-grain cereals, breads, crackers, rice, or pasta every day 1 oz. is about 1 slice of bread, about 1 cup of breakfast cereal, or 1/2 cup of cooked rice, cereal or pasta	Eat more dark-green veggies like broccoli, spinach, and other dark leafy greens Eat more orange vegetables like carrots and sweetpotatoes Eat more dry beansa and peas like pinto beans, kidney beans, and lentils	Eat a variety of fruit Choose fresh, frozen, canned, or dried fruit Go easy on fruit juices	Go low-fat or fat-free when you choose milk, yogurt, and other milk products If you don't or can't consume milk, choose lactose free products or other calcium sources such as fortified foods and beverages	Choose low-fat or lean meats and poultry Bake it, broil it, or grill it Vary your protein routine - choose more fish, beans, peas, nuts, and seeds
For a 2,000-calorie diet, you need the amounts below from each food group. To find the amounts that are right for you, go to MyPyramid.gov				
Eat 6 oz. every day	Eat $2^{1/2}$ cups every day	Eat 2 cups every day	Get 3 cups every day; for kids aged 2 to 8, it's 2	Eat $5^{1/2}$ oz. every day

Find your balance between food and physical activity

- Be sure to stay within your daily calorie needs.
- Be physically active for at least 30 minutes most days of the week.
- About 60 minutes a day of physical activity may be needed to prevent weight gain.
- For sustaining weight loss, at least 60 to 90 minutes a day of physical activity may be required.
- Children and teenagers should be physically active for 60 minutes every day, or most days

Know the limits on fats, sugars and salt(sodium)

- Make most of your fat sources from fish, nuts, and vegetable oils.
- Limit solid fats like butter, stick margarine, shortening, and lard, as well as foods that contain these.
- Check the Nutrition Facts label to keep saturated fats, *trans* fats, and sodium low.
- Choose food and beverages low in added sugars, added sugars contribute calories with few, if any, nutrients.

MyPyramid form USDA 2005

Any questions or comments? What's the serving size? Yes, that's the right question. The right quantity of food that amounts to one serving is listed below. You need to eat from all five major food groups—at least, least number of servings. You need all of them for the needed vitamins, minerals, carbohydrates, and proteins. If you can, try to pick the food with lower fat choices. For the oils, fats, and sweets group, no measure is given because the message is USE SPARINGLY.

- **Milk, Yogurt, and Cheese:** 1 cup of milk or yogurt; 1½ oz. of natural cheese; 2 oz. of processed cheese.
- **Meat, Poultry, Fish, Dry Beans, Eggs, and Nuts:** 2–3 oz. of cooked lean meat, poultry, or fish; ½ cup of cooked dry beans,1 egg, or 2 tbsp of peanut butter count as 1 oz. of lean meat.
- **Vegetables:** 1 cup of raw leafy vegetables; ½ cup of other vegetables, cooked or chopped raw; ¾ cup of vegetable juice.
- **Fruits:** 1 medium apple, banana, or orange; ½ cup of chopped, cooked, or canned fruit; ¾ cup of fruit juice.
- **Bread, Cereal, Rice, and Pasta:** 1 slice of bread; 1 oz. of ready-to-eat cereal; ½ cup of cooked cereal, rice, or pasta.

The USDA recommends that an adult should consume meat, eggs, and dairy products not exceeding 20% of total daily caloric intake. The remaining 80% should come from grains, fruits, and vegetables. For children age 2 and up, 55% of their daily caloric intake (a toddler needs 1,000 to1,400 cal a day) should be from carbohydrates, 30% from fat, and 15% from proteins. Also, saturated fat should not be more than 10% of total caloric intake. Such a low-fat, high-fiber diet is planned to promote health and to help prevent diseases, including heart disease, obesity, diabetes, and cancer.

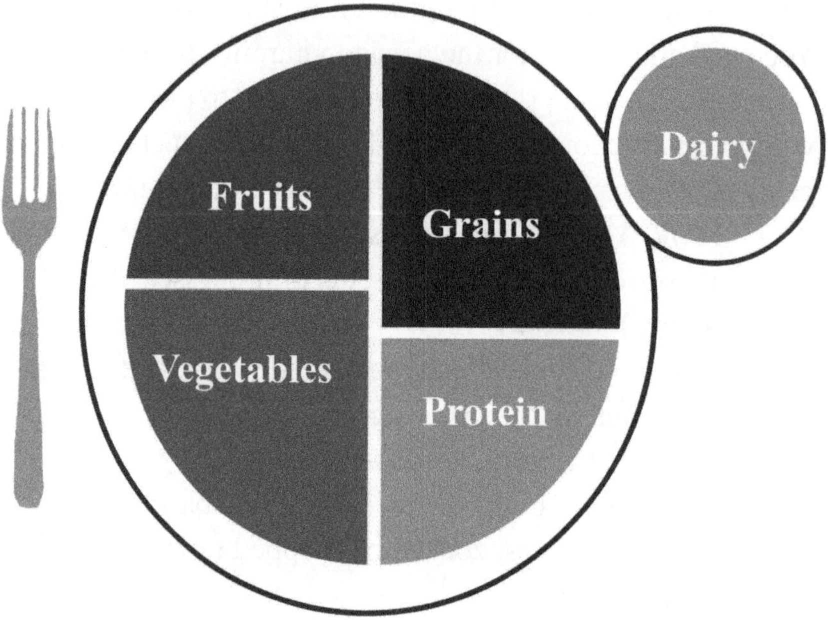

MyPlate

Pyramid lost! The twenty-year-old food pyramid, having a long and tangled history, is now officially retired. Now, pyramid regained! Rebuilding the pyramid per federal dietary guidelines! The new symbol in its place is a dinner plate known as "MyPlate." It is a plate (suggested by the CDC instead of a pyramid) divided into portions that convey the message in a simpler way that we all can understand better. It consists of four colored sections: (1) grains, (2) proteins, (3) vegetables, and (4) fruits. The plate values a lot, especially for fruits and vegetables. In fact, half the plate is filled with fruits and vegetables. Half the plate, in and of itself, is quite an effective communication. A smaller circle at the top-right corner of the plate is for dairy, suggesting a glass of low-fat milk or a cup of yogurt. The picture of the plate is very convincing and compelling. It is also very clear and straightforward. Less projecting on the plate is the meat. Curiously, the meat is not even mentioned. Another important item missing is, perhaps, water—highlighting the benefits of drinking water and the harm of soda water or sugary beverages. Americans should take the new dinner plate seriously. It tends to be crucial in the administration's crusade against overweight and obesity.

The dietary guidelines focus on a health-promoting eating pattern "across the life span." Moderate cholesterol intake from low-fat foods like eggs, shrimp, crab, and other shellfish is okay. Moderate drinking of coffee is part of a healthful eating pattern. For alcohol, up to one drink for women and two for men a day. For carbohydrates—like rice and breads, cakes, cookies, and pastries—at least half of the grains should not be refined and stripped of their essential nutrients. Earlier recommendations restricting low-fat diets may have led to an increase in carbohydrate consumption, causing the obesity epidemic to worsen. Restrict added sugar—much of which comes from soda and other sugar-sweetened drinks—to less than 10% of daily calories, saturated fats to less than 10% of daily calories, and sodium to 2,300 mg a day for adults and children 14 and older. Eat this, not that: eat more vegetables and fruits, more seafood (about 8 oz. of seafood per week, based on a 2,000-calorie-a-day diet), whole grains, nuts, and seeds. And eat less foods high in sugar, sodium, saturated fats, and refined grains.

Food combinations in a meal or subsequent meals are very important. Wait the following recommended lengths of time between meals—do not cartel those meals:

2 hours after eating fruit
3 hours after eating starches
4 hours after eating proteins

Following are charts of food combinations for better understanding.

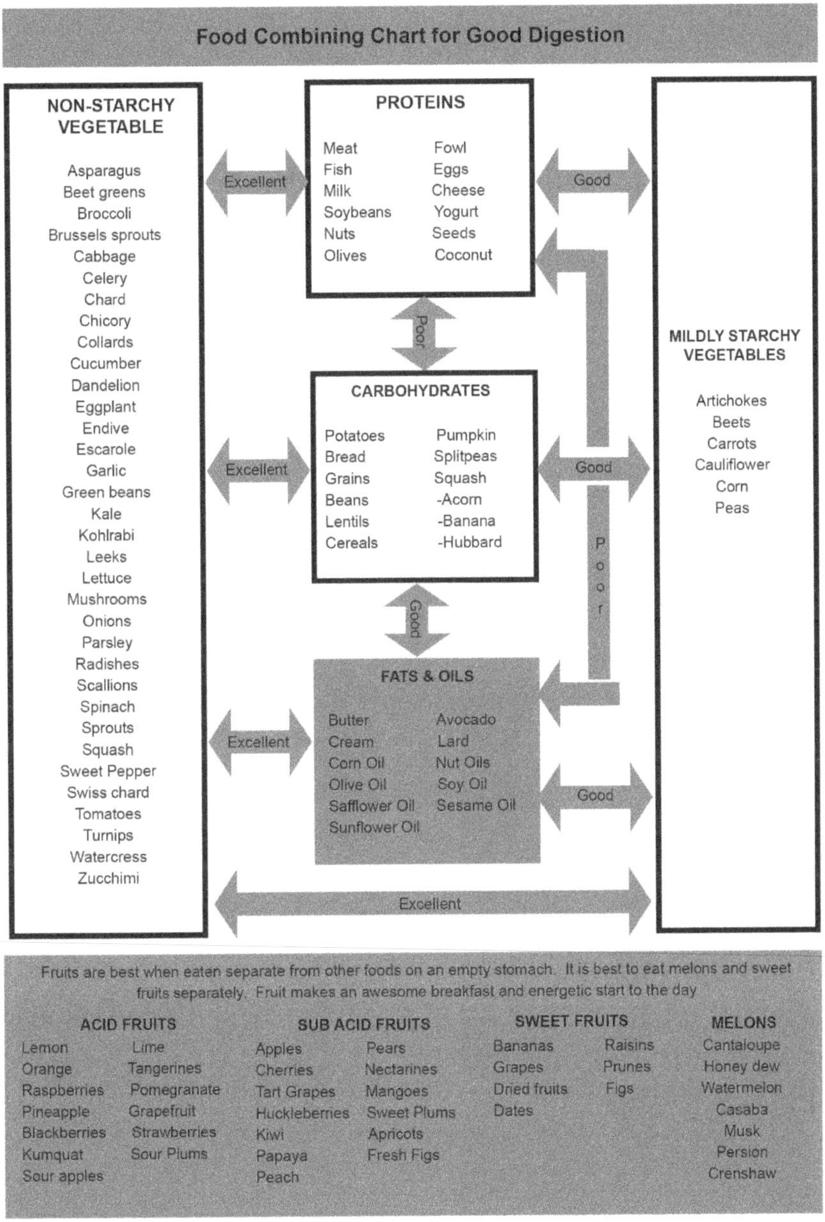

Food Combining Chart for Good Digestion

Diets

A dieting plan is one wishful scheme that everyone tried at least once for reasons hard to define. It is the bliss between hypothesis and theory. Typically, it is the promise of a short-term—not of a long-term—tenure. Surveys find that over a quarter of the dieting people are constantly fighting the bulge. They cannot sustain it for a long time. Over 40% of dieters admit that they end up giving in to temptation. A lot of diets—such as Atkins, South Beach, and the grapefruit diet—involve rigorous eating plans. People get fed up quickly and retreat to have few treats. Often, people do not integrate daily exercise in their weight-loss plan; so, in the event of abandoning the diet plan, they often put back the weight, sometimes even more than they lost. Women reveal that they are more likely to gain weight back after the diet. As a matter of fact, nearly 40% say they end up being heavier than before.

There was a time when red meat was healthy and pasta was unhealthy. Then pasta became great, and red meat turned terrible. Then the Atkins craze—the rules flipped again. There are now many familiar diets: the Mediterranean diet, the South Beach diet, the low-fat diet, the grapefruit diet, and the cabbage-soup diet. And all of them promise great things. With every diet comes a problem; with every new truth comes a part myth. The era of myth and marketing is leaving consumers disappointed, frustrated, and no healthier than they were before.

Diet lures and diet lies. When you diet, even the worst food begins to look good. The key to good health is a balanced diet. Diet becomes food when it is balanced. Eating balanced food supported with regular physical activity is the better way to improve your health and well-being. Here are a few well-known diet plans.

Atkins' Diet (Low-Carb Diet)

This is fundamentally a low-carbohydrate eating plan. The plan was founded by Dr. Robert Atkins (1930–2003) in 1972 with the goal of weight loss in mind. As carbohydrates are the primary reason for weight gain, this weight-reduction diet plan controls carbs and excludes refined sugars. Ideally, it improves overall muscle mass while shedding fat pounds from the body. The recommended foods include meat and meat products, whole grains, fruits and vegetables, and dairy products. This is a protein-based diet and is supposed to lead to more lean muscle mass and less body fat.

Advantages: It offers plenty of protein for muscle repair and strength training, and people who relish meat and dairy products may prefer this weight-reduction plan. It suggests consumption of fewer simple carbohydrates.

Disadvantages: There are no convenient appetite suppressants. People who love foods like white bread, pizza, and various other processed carbs may not find the plan suitable for them. It gives the biggest metabolic benefit initially, but there are long-term downsides; and in practice, people have trouble sustaining low-carb diets. So, instead of low carb, consider slow carb. While adults should get about 50 percent of their daily calories from the carbohydrates, consider slow carbs that have slow digestion and high fiber: fruits, beans and vegetables—and whole grains that include everything from whole wheat to brown rice to steel-cut oats.

Don't be too obsessed with calorie count! When you eat balance food, your body can do the rest for you. The problem with the food that makes people fat, isn't calories: it is the result of cascade reactions in the body that promotes fat storage and urge people overeat. Processed food, especially carbohydrates like chips, crackers, and white rice, digest quickly into sugar and increase the level of hormone, insulin. Insulin is like a booster for your fat cells to grow, it directs cells to snap up calories in the blood and store them as fat, leaving the body hungry in hurry. If it happens too many times and too often, your metabolism will start working against you, and then, when you try to reduce the calorie balance, the body fights back.

For half a century since the 1960s, it is a known fact that insulin signals fat cells in our body to accumulate fat, while signaling other cells to burn the carbohydrates for fuel. A slight increase of insulin level triggers switching from burning fat to burning carbohydrates for fuel, by necessity. This hypothesis of carbohydrate metabolism is uniquely fattening. Because, even a spoon of rice or a bite of ice-cream can raise insulin level that forces energy into fat cells while depriving other cells of the energy they would have otherwise utilized. This in essence, creates artificial starvation. You respond to hunger with more carbohydrates. The differential effect of insulin on fat and carbohydrate can easily lead to a binge: the more insulin you release, the more you crave for carbs. High insulin drives high carb-craving. Here, eating fat-rich food helps to extinguish binge behavior as opposed to high-carb food which exacerbates it. Therefore, the first and foremost strategy is to avoid the trigger, stay away from carb. One international team of scientists tracked 135,335 people between 35 and 70 years old in 18 countries for 7 years of their self-reported diet and mortality records. After controlling key factors including age, sex, smoking, physical activity and BMI, they report in The Lancet in 2017 that people who are in the highest 20% bracket of consumption of carbohydrates, have 28% increased risk of death compared to those of in the lowest 20% bracket. However, high carbohydrate intake is not associated with cardiovascular death. So, one advice to carboholics: be sober on carb—between 50% to 55% of caloric intake from carbs.

For life expectancy too, when it comes to carbs, here is another large study that claims just that: moderation. In the study, researchers tracked food consumption of nearly 15,500 middle-aged U.S. adults for 25 years. After taking into account of their demographic background, education, income level, smoking habits, exercise habits, medical histories and other lifestyle factors, and particularly after reviewing additional studies on carbohydrate intake, involving more than 432,000 people in total, they concluded that mortality risk is higher for those who are on the high and low ends of the carb spectrum—people who consumed more than 70% or less than 40% of their total calories from carbohydrates, compared to those who consume 50 to 55% of their caloric intake from carbs. According to the study, the result published in *The Lancet Public Health* in 2018, they provide possible explanations for this pattern: (a) people who are on the high end (more than 70%) of the carb spectrum, tend to consume large amounts of refined carbohydrates, which don't have much nutritional value resulting weight gain, obesity and overall health; (b) people who are on the low end (less than 40%) of the carb spectrum tend to eat more meat and dairy products, which increases the risk of heart disease, stroke and death; and (c) people who are on moderation, at the middle (50-55%) of the carb spectrum, tend to strike a better balance. Hence, their advice is: if you're going to cut carbs from your diet, think carefully about how you replace them: replace them with plant-derived proteins and fats, such as beans, nuts and seeds, fruits (no fruit juice) and vegetables (and eliminate sugary drinks).

There are not many large and rigorous studies showing the long-term effect of low-carbohydrate diets; and, in fact, there is not even a universal consensus on the definition of a low-carbohydrate diet, which varies from health expert to dietician to doctor. With very-low-carbohydrate diets, insulin secretion can drop up to 50%, meaning that much less insulin is required to maintain the normal blood glucose level. Since diabetes is a condition when the body can't produce enough insulin, apparently, eating very-low-carbohydrate diets makes sense; but some longer-term studies fail to prove that low-carbohydrate diets really benefit glucose control. Sometimes, diets are effective in the short term (does better on glycemic control), yet there is everyday difficulty in continuing the diet over the long term. And also, as time progresses, benefits disappear. Even if the diabetic patients actually continue their diet for years or decades, the insulin levels may be better, but the cumulative effects of a low-carbohydrate diet on lipoproteins and vascular biology, could offset such "benefit" like a lower insulin level would result in fewer heart attacks. Recommended level is 50 to 55% of caloric intake from carbs. One research published in the *European Society of Cardiology Congress* in Germany in 2018, finds that diets very low in carbohydrates, less than 26%, may raise individuals' risks of premature death over time and the risks get more dominant when that level dips below 10%. Another study, finds people who eat the lowest amount of carbs have roughly a 32% higher risk of total mortality, a 50% higher risk of dying from vascular diseases and a 36% higher risk of dying from cancer, compared to people who eat the most carbs, which translates the difference in absolute number as high as 6.4 years of life, on average. When it comes to weight loss, again, studies show there are hardly any differences among diets that restrict calories, fats, or carbs. So, stay moderate, follow the Federal Dietary Guidelines for Americans: 45–65% of calories from carbs 20–35% from fat, and 10–35% from protein.

There's been countless studies and lengthy debates over low-carb or low-fat diet, better for weight loss. The final verdict: Both—and neither! According to one study published in *JAMA* in 2018, the study tracked 600 adults, random half and half on each plan, for a year and found that the two plans helped dieters drop: 11 pounds in the low-fat group, 13 pounds in the low-carb group. Any dieter was able to succeed on either one. One interesting finding, however, was that the most successful dieters, regardless of which plan they followed, were those who reframed their relationship with new diet and began eating more mindfully, cooking at home more often and focusing more on whole foods. Researchers finally conclude that mindful about food, is more important than the diet itself, and for that matter, differentiating between the low-carb or low-fat diet.

Ketogenic Diet

The ketogenic diet is a low-curb, high-fat, adequate-protein diet. Due to low-carb, it forces the body to digest fats rather than glucose from carbohydrates. Sometimes a 90% fat diet is good for special treatment. The fat-based ketogenic diet is, in fact, a medicine, which is prescribed for patients with debilitating and hard-to-cure epilepsy. Because, there is very little carbohydrate in the food, the liver is forced to convert fat into fatty acids and ketone bodies in blood stream. The ketone bodies go into brain, replace glucose as an energy source and create a unique effect on the brain. Thus, an elevated level of ketone bodies in the blood, a state known as ketosis, leads to a reduction in the frequency of epileptic seizures. In food-medicine-therapy world, the benefits of food as medicine has never been new. There are plenty of foods identified to cure everything from cancer to heart disease to cataracts. It is a part of basic good health all the time. It is an enthralling reminder to all of us that drugs are not the only medicine and are certainly not the only strategy for improving health.

Dr. Andrew Weil's Wellness Diet

It aims for a variety of food types, which include as much fresh food as possible. Eat plenty of fruits and vegetables; and include carbohydrates, fat, and protein in every meal and less processed and preserved foods. The food aggregates similar in the line of USDA recommendation: for example, a normal adult of 150 lb. consumes 2,000 cal a day. The distribution—calories-wise—is 40 to 50% from carbohydrates, 30% from fat, and 20 to 30% from protein. [Hint: The Federal Dietary Guidelines for Americans: 45–65% of calories from carbs, 20–35% from fat, and 10–35% from protein. In comparison, low carbs diet is 28% from carbohydrates, 40% to 43% from fat (twice as much poly- and monounsaturated compared to saturated), and 28% from protein. The theory is cutting back on carbs, not fat, may lead to more weight loss.]

Carbohydrates: About 160 g to 200 g of whole brown rice, whole wheat or oat, and so forth (less refined); sweet potatoes; winter squashes; and beans. Try to avoid sweet foods made with high-fructose corn syrup. Six so-called bad carbs—corn, banana, breakfast cereal, white potato, sourdough bread, and green peas—are actually good for the health for various reasons. One selling point of a carbohydrate-restricted diet is that one can eat to satiety; counting calories is not important as long as most carbohydrates are avoided.

Fat: About 67 g (2 oz.). The ratio of saturated to monounsaturated to polyunsaturated fat should be in a ratio of 1:2:1. Use extra-virgin olive oil as cooking media. Diet includes less butter, cheese, cream, and other full-fat dairy products—and nuts, especially almonds, cashews, and walnuts. Try to avoid fatty meats, products made with coconut, chicken with skin, palm kernel oil, sunflower oil, corn oil, cottonseed oil, and mixed vegetable oil. Avoid vegetable shortening, margarine, and all products made with partially hydrogenated oils of any kind.

Protein: Protein should be 90 g to 120 g (2–4 oz.), lesser for the people with liver or kidney problems, allergies, or autoimmune disease. Make it a food habit to get protein from fish and reduced-fat dairy products rather than animal proteins. Vegetable protein is a better source, especially from beans in general and soybeans in particular.

Fiber: The more the merrier! Eat at least 40 g (1½ oz.) of fiber a day. The ideal source is from vegetables, fruits, and whole grains. Some ready-made popular cereals can be good fiber sources as well.

Phytonutrients: "Phyto" in Greek means plants. Phytonutrients (chemicals that help protect the plants from bugs, germs, fungi, and other threats) are defined as nutrients that have been scientifically proven to provide health benefits. For natural well-being and protection against age-related diseases, eat a variety of fruits and vegetables. Select fruits and vegetables from all colors of the spectrum, especially apples, tomatoes, berries, oranges and yellow fruits, dark leafy greens, and mushrooms. Prefer organic vegetables whenever possible, and avoid produce that tends to have pesticide residues.

Mediterranean Diet

As ancient as Greece itself, the Mediterranean diet—high in fruits, vegetables, cereals, fish, olive oil, and topped with a glass or two of wine daily—has been known for lower risk of vascular disease and Alzheimer's disease. Studies show that people from Mediterranean countries seem to have lower rates of heart disease than the general population, and the pattern appears in such a way as to attribute it to the diet.

One gigantic study spanning over five years and involving seven thousand people was carried out in Spain. One group was given four tablespoons of extra-virgin olive oil each week, and the other group with a combination of walnuts, almonds, and hazelnuts (1 oz. each day). Both groups' diets consisted of at least three servings of fruits and at least two servings of vegetables each day, fish at least three times a week, and legumes (which include beans, peas, and lentils) at least three times a week. They were swayed to eat white meat instead of red, and for those accustomed to drinking, to have at least seven glasses of wine a week with meals. They were persuaded to avoid commercially made cookies, cakes, and pastries, and to limit their consumption of dairy products and processed meats.

To monitor compliance with the Mediterranean diet, the study logged levels of (a) the urine marker of olive oil consumption (hydroxytyrosol) and (b) the blood marker of nut consumption (alpha-linolenic acid, an omega-3 fatty acid found especially in seeds). The whole effect of the Mediterranean diet was a single measure of its entire package, not just the olive oil or the nuts. The study did not look at merely the risk factors like cholesterol, hypertension, or weight; they looked at the hard facts that really mattered: heart attacks, strokes, and death. The study ultimately found that eating such a nicely balanced diet with fruits, vegetables, olive oils, and nuts—and by actually enjoying food and life at the same time—one can lower heart disease by 30%. The diet can help to reverse the metabolic syndrome. This is really a surprising welcome result that apparently compared the usual modern diet—with its regular consumption of red meat, sodas, and commercial baked goods—to a diet that shunned all that. To put the benefits on comparison, statin therapy lowers heart disease by 44%. So, the optimal choice for those at high risk of cardiovascular disease is to go for a combination of both diet and statins; and for those at lower risk, lifestyle measures including the Mediterranean diet. Another survey by the Department of Epidemiology covering more than twenty-three thousand people reveals that the fundamental element of Italians' Mediterranean diet is associated with reduced abdominal obesity. And also on the contrary, consumption of pasta is not associated with increased body weight but, rather, the opposite.

Having the Mediterranean diet most of your life may pay off with a disease-free old age and a longer life. Including staples like olive oil, vegetables, and nuts, the Mediterranean diet has been a game changer for health and longevity. Countless studies affirm lower risks of heart attack and stroke, and it even slows or prevents memory loss. The protective benefits are likely to stem from the united effect of the diet's healthy fats and nutrients. One study established that the Mediterranean diet alone is capable enough to reduce the risk of diabetes without even trying via losing weight or doing exercise.

Scientists at the Harvard School of Public Health—in collaboration with Brigham and Women's Hospital—reviewed dietary data collected from surveys and question-and-answer sessions involving 10,670 women in their late fifties and early sixties and found that, overall, women who stick to more plant-based foods—healthy fats like olive oil, fish, whole grains, moderate amounts of alcohol (preferably red wine), and very little red and processed meats—were healthier than those who did not have the Mediterranean diet. The elderly women showed no signs of impairment in their cognitive functions or any of the physical disabilities. One study on the Mediterranean diet claims that the diet perhaps has some beneficial effects for the brain, like slower rates of cognitive decline; but the claim has not been strong. Another study claimed that the diet could help to retain memory and perform better cognitive functions only in people without diabetes. Some research claims that children who eat diets rich in fish, fruits, and vegetables tend to have a lower risk for asthma and wheezing compared to kids who eat several hamburgers a week.

Here's the list of foods belong to typical Mediterranean Diet.

- *Grains:* oatmeal, quinoa, rice, barley, pasta, whole grain breads and cereals. *Fruits:* apples, apricot, peaches, plums, prunes, berries, cherries, figs, melon, red grapes, oranges and lemons.
- *Vegetables:* cabbage, broccoli, carrots, kale, spinach, brussels sprouts, broccoli, beets, red bell peppers, corn and eggplant legumes, leafy greens, onion, squash, tomatoes, split peas, lentils and peanuts, and beans like lima, black, red, kidney and navy.
- *Nuts and Seeds:* walnuts, hazelnuts, almonds, sunflower seed and sesame seed. Seafoods: salmon, tuna, bluefish, sardines, cod, crab, shrimps, mackerel and trout. Meat: chicken, turkey, and land animal protein of choice (serving size limited to 3 ounces, about the size of a deck of cards).
- *Dairy and Eggs:* cheese, low-fat milk, Greek Yogurt, and three to four whole eggs a week.
- *Oil:* olive oil, especially extra-virgin and virgin, avocado oil, grape seed oil, the least processed forms, or canola oil; avoid butter or margarine. Herbs and Spices: bay leaf, coriander, cumin, turmeric, mint, rosemary, sage and pepper.
- *Treats and Desserts:* pastries, cookies, pudding, cakes, doughnuts, french fries, potato chips and all sweetened

and diet carbonated soft drinks—are best avoided altogether.
- *Wine:* red wine, with a daily limit of five ounces for men and three ounces for women consumed with a meal.

However, all said and done, the Mediterranean diet is only half of the story. It is essentially the lifestyle that matters: food, exercise, nature (getting fresh air, blue sky, sunlight and sunshine) and social interactions. It is a prescription for a person as a whole, rather than food alone. It is the whole approach. It takes the whole village to make it work.

Anti-Inflammatory Diet

There is no anti-inflammatory (AI) diet as such. But the AI diet plan is based on most research-backed anti-inflammatory cred. It is essentially traditional Mediterranean diet emphasizing the effects of some selected foods for fighting the inflammation—top few are: berries, dark green leafy vegetables (like kale, spinach, Swiss chard), fatty fish, garlic and onions, green tea, ginger, turmeric, nuts, oranges, and tart cherries. The aim is to cut back on foods (like added sugar, sweet drinks, and refined grains) that trigger inflammatory response, and add more of the foods from the above and supplement with: (1) lots of omega-3s from fatty fish like salmon, mackerel, tuna, sardines, herring, and anchovies; (2) oranges, colorful berries and other fruits, mushrooms, summer squash, beets, cauliflower; (3) greens of all kinds, kale, spinach, Swiss chard, non-starchy vegetables, ginger, turmeric, Bell peppers, variety of hot peppers (like chili and cayenne); (4) monounsaturated fats like olive, avocado and walnut oil; (5) to focus on intact whole grains like quinoa, brown rice, and bulgur wheat; and (6) fruit juices, natural sweeteners like honey, low-fat and nonfat milk, soy milk, tofu, yogurt and green tea. The whole idea is to reduce pain and inflammation.

Vegetarian Diet

Researchers have analyzed the results of published studies and reached the conclusion that the vegetarian population has a lower rate of hypertension. Vegetarians are slimmer, on average—and that is one important factor why their blood pressure is often in a healthy range. Other benefits include vegetarians' higher intake of potassium as well as the tendency of plant-based foods to modulate blood viscosity, resulting in lower risk of blood pressure, heart attack, stroke, and kidney failure. One study involving seventy thousand participants established that vegetarians have a 12% lower risk of death compared with non-vegetarians. Vegetarians live longer. Some studies acknowledge that people following a vegan diet do lose weight more than people on conventional low-fat diets; and for diabetics, they do gain better control of glucose and cholesterol. The study highlights another special effect that eating plant foods high in carotenoid—a nutrient found in some fruits, leafy greens, and root vegetables—gives the skin a healthy glow. [Hint: The slight changes in blush by tinting the skin yellow and red is more appealing than the artificial skin color by suntan. For people who eat 1 to 3 servings (the USDA recommends 5 servings minimum) of fruit and vegetables a day, the skin color changes in just six weeks. Eating carrots a lot—or other foods (tomatoes, sweet potatoes) rich in carotenoids—can turn the skin orange. The color change in skin is due to two naturally occurring food pigments: (1) beta-carotene (the pigment that makes the carrot orange) and (2) lycopene, which makes the tomato red.]

Besides, the vegetarian diet is much more environment-friendly than the non-vegetarian diets, particularly when containing meat. [Analyze this. For every kilogram (2.2 lb.) of food grain-fed livestock meat, it consumes 100,000 L (3.78 *L* per *gallon—i.e., 26,000 gal.)* of water, which is just what a person drinks in a lifetime. I repeat—just for the production of 2.2 lb. of meat. It costs fossil-fuel energy eight times as much as for the production of an equivalent amount of plant protein. To put it in another way, the average non-vegetarian diet burns the equivalent of a gallon of gas per day, which is twice that of the vegetarian diet. The total livestock population in the U.S.—cattle, lambs, pigs, chickens, turkeys, etc.—consumes five times as much grains as that of the U.S. human population.]

The Okinawa Diet

The Okinawa diet follows the traditional Okinawan dietary composition for a delicious blend of East and West so that anyone can reap the very benefits as the leanest and longest-living people on earth in Japan's Okinawa Island. Their diet, on average, has no more than 1 cal per gram weight; and their BMI, on average, is 20. Their diet contains 30% fresh vegetables, small quantities of rice, sweet potato, soy, tofu, a small amount of fish, the occasional pork, other legumes, and virtually no egg or dairy products. The Okinawa diet plan is a revolutionary approach to health, longevity, weight loss, and weight maintenance. It is one very simple menu that is easy to continue.

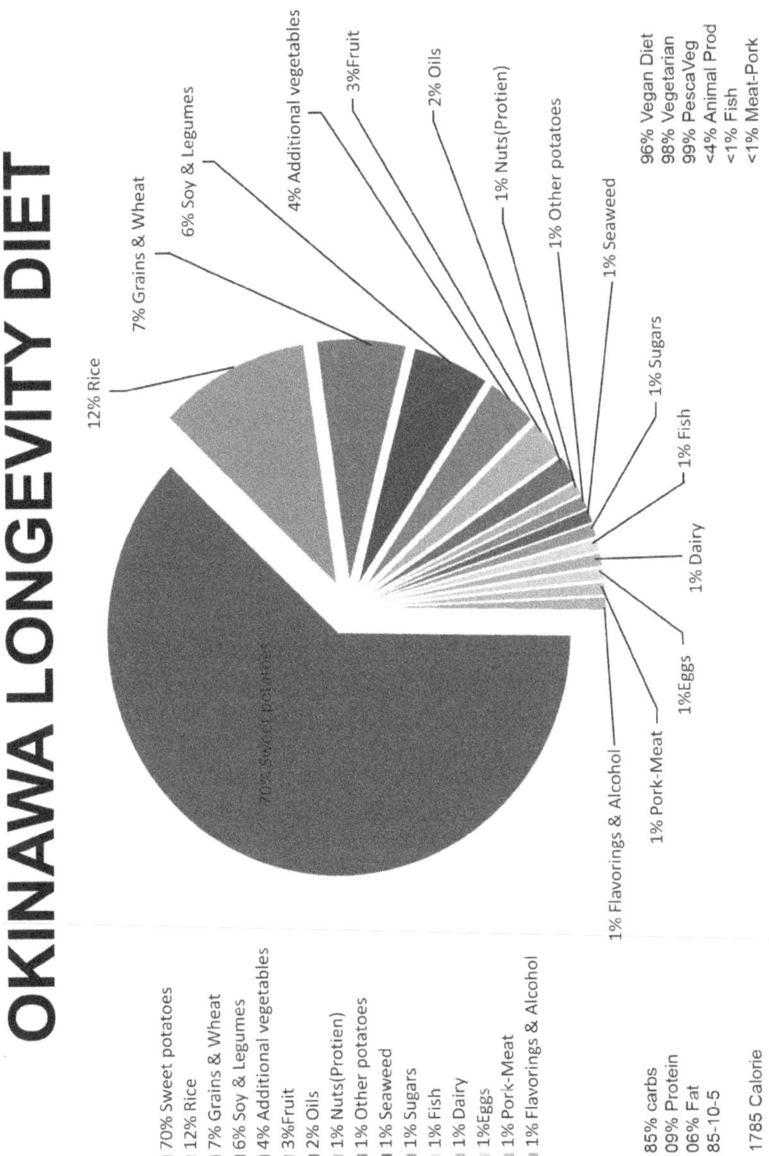

Okinawa Longevity Diet

Polymeal Diet

The "Polymeal" diet—a natural food alternative strategy compatible to the "Polypill" strategy, a multi-drug-based approach for reducing heart disease—is a prescribed diet consisting of (a) fish four times a week, (b) wine 150 mL (5 fl. oz.) a day, (c) dark chocolate 100 g a day (eat it by the bit, not by the brick—not every day, once or twice a week), (d) fruits and vegetables 400 g a day, (e) garlic 2.7 g a day, and (f) almonds 68 g (55 counts) a day. Scientists who designed the Polymeal used a computer model of the American adult population and calculated that the risk of heart disease would fall by 76%, women would live an additional 5 years on average and men 6.6 years—compared to the control group, which did not follow the diet. Their prognoses were based on previous research that identified the success rate of specific foods in lowering blood pressure.

Dr. Bradley Willcox, the coauthor of *The Okinawa Diet Plan*, commented on the Polymeal diet: "This is a very interesting study that supports the powerful potential impact of diet on longevity. This is consistent with what we see in the Okinawa Diet, where Okinawans are at 82% lower risk for heart disease than Americans, live about five years longer on average, and have four times as many people over the age of one hundred. On average, Okinawans eat fish (80 g per day), drink alcohol in moderation (1–2 drinks per day), and eat seven servings per day of fruit and vegetables (394 g per day).

"While the Okinawans are not huge consumers of almonds or chocolate, they do enjoy garlic, soy foods (such as tofu, miso soup), jasmine tea, and healthy oils such as a canola/soy oil blend that is popular all over Japan. Add to that a variety of spices that jazz up any dish, such as turmeric and a variety of chilies and other peppers, and you have a delicious way to eat yourself toward a healthy heart and long life."

Losing weight on a diet is tough! The problem is not the diet or willpower. It's the neuroscience factor. Some diets even evoke weight gain as an unintended consequence of our obsession with diets that plans for weight loss. Research finds that long-run dieting is rarely effective; it does not improve health, rather does more harm than good. Metabolic control is a powerful mechanism that the brain uses to keep the body within a certain weight range, called the set point. The range is subjective, varying from person to person; it is set by genes and life experience. Basically, when a person drops weight below the set point, the body goes into panic mode. It not only burns fewer calories but also produces more hunger-inducing hormones, which sends starvation signals to the brain; and in response, the brain alarms eating as urgent.

Prescription diet! Many doctors tell their patients honestly that a diet can act as a medicine, but that hardly works till they actually write the diet on the paper like a prescription. Most diet plans work, but the reaction time is very slow—in the order of months, if not years. Most people don't stay in the program long enough (one to three years) to see their weight stabilized. In dieting, there is no magic diet. Magic isn't a substitute for science. And not only does the stabilization of health (i.e., weight loss) take time, but also many more things are involved in it. For example, as a cautionary to obese people, studies indicate that the fatter a person is, the easier it is to gain weight. An extra 10 cal a day, which is practically nothing, puts more weight on an obese person than on a thin person. For some people, things happened early in life to set their food-sensing mechanism to demand more fat on their bodies. Another example, even though the study doesn't have enough data to back it up, is that dieting causes depression; it does show, however, that weight loss doesn't necessarily uplift mental health, as many people like to assume.

After all said and explained, here are five best ranking diets for 2019, according to the U.S. News & World Report:

#1: The Mediterranean diet (eat more plants, whole grains, healthy fats, olive oil, and lean proteins; eat less processed foods, red meat and refined sugars).

#2: DASH Diet (Dietary Approaches to Stop Hypertension, designed to lower blood pressure: eat more fruits, vegetables, low-fat dairy, whole grains and moderate amounts of lean protein; eat less items that contain minerals such as sodium, potassium, calcium, and magnesium, which can help lower blood pressure).

#3: Flexitarian Diet (diet for "flexible vegetarians" designed to lower heart disease, type 2 diabetes and cancer: eat more plant-based food; eat less meat).

#4: MIND Diet (Mediterranean-DASH Intervention for Neurodegenerative Delay) combines aspects of the DASH and Mediterranean diets, designed for improving brain health: eat three servings of whole grains, a salad, vegetable, and wine).

#4 (tie): WW (from Weight Watchers—a user is assigned a daily point total to eat foods based on their calorie, sugar, saturated fat and protein content).

Eating healthy may seem like a humble goal, but can you afford it? On the economy ground, studies find you can, you spend only marginally high. Based on one scientific survey, the Departments of Agriculture and of Health and Human Services released one guideline in 2011, which is sensible, attainable, and, for the general population, affordable. They give a wide variety of healthy dietary options with fewer calories and without excessive sacrifice of dinner pleasure. Here is their summary of the guidelines:

- Eat more plants. Choose vegetables and fruits at each meal—as much as half the plate.
- Choose lean meat and poultry and more seafood.
- Choose nonfat or low-fat milk and dairy products.
- Choose low-sodium food, and use less salt in food preparation.
- No need to cut out carbs. Choose fiber-containing—carbohydrate at all meals, at least a small portion of, for instance, sweet potato, quinoa, brown rice. Choose more fiber-rich whole grain foods and less refined and processed foods.
- Embrace fat. Choose unsaturated fats—monounsaturated and polyunsaturated fats: They are "good fats" and they reduce inflammation and aid in heart health. Incorporate into your meals and snacks nuts, seeds, avocados, fish, olive oil and less butter and margarine.
- Cook at home and eat at home. Sit down with family members when you eat. With food at the center of the table, you and your family members are happy to rally around. Establish table manners. Different cultures observe different rules for table manners. For example, take your portion of the food to your own plate while

seated at a table. Children learn lots of essential etiquettes from table manners. Try not to eat while working at the desk, watching TV, standing in front of the fridge, driving in a car.

- Listen to your body, your body's hunger cues. Be mindful about what, when and how much you're eating.
- Drink plenty of water. Drink calorie-free beverages like coffee and tea. Choose 100% fruit juice.
- Take occasionally, as a treat, regular sodas, fruit drinks, and energy drinks.
- Limit alcoholic drinks to 1 a day for women and 2 for men.
- Do regular exercise for a balanced caloric input-output.
- Eat less. [Hint: A professor of genetics at Harvard Medical School has identified genes that allow yeast to survive on fewer calories and extend their life span by about 30%.]

The key to good health is a balanced diet. Diet is food when it is balanced. Balance—rather than calorie constraints with constant criticism and desire denial—is the key to a wholesome diet plan that you can maintain, endure, and enjoy. Eating a healthy balanced diet and, at the same time, doing affordable physical exercise is the better way to preserve, protect, and defend your good health. And finally, remember the mantra from Mother Nature: "Eat what you like to eat; don't eat what you don't like to eat."

3.3 Herbs and Spices

> God made the earth yield healing herbs, which the prudent man should not neglect.
>
> —From Ecclesiastes, an Old Testament book consisting of reflections on the vanity of human life

An estimated 250,000 to 500,000 types of plant are here on earth today. So far, only about 5,000 of them have been identified and studied for their therapeutic values and, subsequently, for their medicinal applications. The herb is always of plant origin. It is not of animal origin; nor is it a supplement that was developed in a lab. They have been used in all cultures and customs since the beginning of recorded history. Herbal medical practice is an ancient way of health-care practice. Over the ages, herbal medicine has been an extraordinary influence on human health. Numerous alternative medicines and therapies treat their patients with herbal remedies. Some versions include the name as naturopathy, orthomolecular medicine, and Ayurvedic medicine. Because of its source of origin, herbal medicine is popular as a botanical medicine. In Europe, it is known as phytotherapy or phytomedicine. About a fourth of all prescription drugs are derived from trees, shrubs, or herbs.

The World Health Organization (WHO) calculates that out of 119 plant-derived popular pharmaceutical medicines, about 74% are used in modern medicine. They estimate that while the 80% world population is dependent on conventional medicine for primary care, herbal medicine constitutes a large part of what is practiced as traditional medicine around the world.

The herb contains various naturally occurring chemicals that have biological effects. It works pretty much similar to antibiotics and pharmaceutical drugs. Herbal medicine is ideally beneficial when it is used to cure ongoing chronic diseases. Typically, it is a slow treatment that takes time for a noticeable result. Quick action from herbs is a stretched expectation. Because the herb takes an indirect route to the bloodstream or target organs, it often reaches its destination slower than many conventional drugs that take direct routes. However, this is not always the case with all herbs, especially when they are taken in large quantities—mass effect kicks in. If diagnosed and medicated skillfully, they can cure a multitude of conditions with few or no negative side effects.

The herb is (not limited to) a small soft-stemmed plant with fleshy (rather than woody) parts that were once living. It can be a flowering garden plant or potherb, a seed-bearing plant, tree, or shrub without a permanent woody stem. The plant generally grows in the season yearly and dies after flowering. The herb may include leaves, flowers, seeds, roots, root bark, inner bark (cambium), berries, and other portions of the plant. They are often savory aromatic vegetation used in medicine or as a culinary seasoning or as a scent or dye in cosmetics; and sometimes, it is used for spiritual purposes. The majority comes from some plantlike organism.

Medical science assumes that there are many herbs yet to be discovered that can do miracles someday by curing some of the world's most debilitating, life-threatening diseases. Maybe! Maybe in the future, herbs might replace prescription drugs or antibiotics as a common treatment. Whatever it may be, there still remains a significant learning curve about the intrinsic value of the herbs, the ingredients that compose them, and the therapeutic features of many more herbs that are to be discovered yet. An international herbal reference center to this effect is essential to assess the composition and risks of products available to consumers for substantial health benefits for the public.

Prehistoric sites in Iraq reveal that Neanderthals used herbs such as Yarrow around sixty thousand years ago. Even earlier, humans were fascinated with the aroma of herbs; they used to rub strong-smelling herbs on their bodies to camouflage themselves from the animals they were hunting. They added herbs to mask the stink of rotting meat. By trial and error, they discovered the many remedial properties of herbs—sometimes learning the hard way because while some heal, others kill. Ancient medical manuals facilitate the identification of plants for medicinal purposes. In India, hundreds of medicinal plants were known before the Christian era.

Besides India, other parts of Asia have early records of medicinal plants and minerals, such as in ancient Chinese and Mediterranean civilizations. Manuals identifying and listing hundreds of plants for their therapeutic values have been prepared for over two thousand years. The Chinese have a collection of 1,892 ancient herbal remedies, which are still authoritative today. The school of alchemy flourished in Alexandria (now Egypt) during the second century BC; they prescribed and dispensed many medicinal agents. Since then, they remained popular methods of cure and prevention that considered being safe and healthy.

Before the establishment of universities during the eleventh and twelfth centuries, monasteries used to serve as medical schools. Monks used to copy and translate many of the works of Hippocrates, Dioscorides, and Galen. Thereafter, with the invention of the printing press in the mid-fourteenth century, medical manuals were printed and herbals were produced in mass; books and herbals were made available to people outside the monastery and university. Use of the herbals required no specialized skills: people simply gathered the herbs and applied them in the prescribed manner and dosages. Today, the resurgence of trust in herbal medicine is a worldwide phenomenon. The practice of herbal medicine ranges from mild-acting plant medicines, such as chamomile and peppermint, to very potent ones, such as foxglove (from which the heart-stimulant drug digitalis [notably digoxin and digitoxin] is derived). They provide a wide spectrum of plant medicines with diversified medical applications. This also demands, at the same time, the need for modern medical science to turn its attention to the plant world once again to find new medicines that can cure cancer, diabetes, AIDS, and many other conditions and diseases.

In concept, disease results from a disruption of the spontaneous flow of nature's intelligence within our physiology. In other words, when we disrupt nature's law and when we cannot adequately rid ourselves of the results due to disruption, then we have an ailment. In theory, Ayurvedic principles emphasize just that. By understanding oneself, by identifying one's own body constitution, and by recognizing the sources of aggravation, one can cleanse, purify, and prevent disease and also uplift oneself into a realm of awareness previously unknown.

The herb is extensively used in Ayurvedic medicine. Ayurveda is the medical practice that is the traditional medicinal system native to India, and it is progressively practiced in other parts of the world in the form of alternative medicine. The word *Ayurveda* is composed of two words in the Indian Sanskrit language: "ayur" (meaning life) and "veda" (meaning science)—life science. Continuing to evolve throughout its time, Ayurveda is still an active influential medical system in South Asia. Ayurvedic medicine has a legacy of using herbal preparations that have been clinically tested and are now being scientifically validated. Today in the Western world, it is considered to be a part of complementary and alternative medicine (CAM), where several of its methods—such as herbs, massage, and yoga—are prescribed in the form of CAM treatments.

Ayurveda is restorative, preventive, and curative. The method of healing includes, besides medicine, diet and natural therapies, along with dietary changes, herbal tonics, exercise, massage, yoga, meditation, medicated enemas, herbal sweat baths, and medicated inhalers. Ayurvedic treatment puts emphasis on body, mind, and spirit, and it tries to restore innate harmony. Therefore, a special effort is made by the Ayurvedic physician to involve different sensory organs. In diagnosing illness, the physician pays close attention to pulse, eyes, tongue, and nails; and the diagnosis is primarily based on observation rather than laboratory test results. The central idea of Ayurvedic medicine is to rid the body of indigestible toxins, which attract viruses and compromise the autoimmune processes and responses. The medical herbs or spices are sometime mixed with highly toxic heavy metals like arsenic, mercury, lead, and cadmium—to which modern medicals have questioned the safety of those concoctions. Manipulation of a patient's behavior and creating lifestyle changes are very common in Ayurvedic treatment.

Although the herbals' reduced side effects are generally true, if used inappropriately, some powerful herbs can cause adverse side effects. Qualified herbalists treat herbs with great care. They are educated and trained to know how to concoct remedies for specific symptoms and diagnoses. Most herbs are beneficial, but as they come from plants (and as some plants are noxious), they themselves are poisonous if used for long periods of time. Natural and good are the same thing. Typically, a bitter-tasting herb is a medicinal herb, and a pleasant-tasting herb is less toxic, and it is used for a longer period of time.

Alternative medications have become increasingly popular, and Americans spend billions every year on natural remedies for everything from arthritis to the common cold to heart health. Americans use them assuming that even if they are not effective, they are, at worst, harmless. But that is not the fact! The popular notion that anything natural can be considered to be safe is seriously questioned. Doctors now acknowledge that some natural supplements conflict with other treatments and medications they prescribe. Some supplements even interfere with anesthesia. For example, patients are advised to stop taking all-natural remedies at least two weeks before surgery, leaving the body plenty of time to clean them out. Even today, little is known about their interaction with pharmaceutical manufacturers and the reliability of their manufactured products. Moreover, in the past, there have been issues of adulteration and contamination in some natural medicines, which has given ethnic medicine a bad name. Doctors, too, have never quite figured out what to say about herbal supplements.

There are some other revelations about the effects of some of these. For example, *Ginkgo biloba* was used by eleven million Americans to improve memory and to increase blood circulation, assuming that ginkgo may reduce the number of platelets in the blood and could, thereby, prevent blood from clotting. However, taking ginkgo at the same time they are taking blood-thinning medications (like Coumadin or even aspirin) can make a patient dangerously vulnerable to bleeding. Another Chinese extract called *Aristolochia fangchi*, used primarily for weight loss, may now be linked to both systemic kidney failure and urinary tract cancers. The herb was tried and tested on a group in a Belgian clinic, and kidney deterioration was observed. These contradictions in researches and findings may leave one in a confused state of mind. A layman without up-to-date knowledge of all these medicines or of their possible benefits could end up feeling disillusioned. This is also partly true because in this line of medicine, there isn't enough dependable guidance available through certified practitioners or regulators or government agencies.

Yet there is another problem. Companies can legally sell herbal preparations without guaranteeing what's on the label or what's inside the bottle. Also, most of these herbal enhanced foods contain such small amounts of their active ingredients that they probably do not have any biological effect at all and are hardly healthy or worth the value-added cost. These uncertainties don't mean that one should never take a supplement. So, it is even more important now that one must discuss with one's physician whatever one is taking—something not enough patients do. A recent study shows that while sixty million Americans have taken alternative medicines, only a third of them have reported it to their doctors.

Another element often mentioned along with Ayurveda and herbs are spices. Spices play an elevated role in medicine. Obtained from completely natural sources, they too have curative properties and are currently used very often as a supplement to common drugs. Though more subtle and slower in their impact, they are said to be entirely free from side effects and are often very beneficial for health in more ways than one. Their flavor and fragrance are used in food, and they have lent a completely new dimension to the kitchen in food preparation. Like spices, culinary herbs are also separated from vegetables in the sense that they are used in relatively small amounts, especially for the purpose of flavor, aroma, and piquancy rather than food values. Most spices are cooked with the food; they are usually the dried parts of various plants that give aromatic, pungent, and otherwise different flavors. Spices and herbs consist of bulbs, barks, rhizomes, flower buds, stigmas, fruits, seeds, and leaves (green or dried). They are commonly passed as spices, spice seeds, and herbs. Spices are fragrant or pungent plant products of tropical and subtropical regions. The typical species for the usual diet includes cinnamon, cloves, ginger, cardamom, and pepper. Spice seeds are usually small aromatic kernels of herbaceous plants, including sesame, cumin, fennel, caraway, poppy, and anise. Herbs can be fragrant leaves of such plants like mint, bay leaf, cilantro, rosemary, thyme, and marjoram.

A spicy meal (not an oily meal) can not only enhance the taste but also lower the triglycerides by 33% and insulin by 20%. Keeping these levels low, yields the lower risk of metabolic syndrome, as well as diabetes and heart disease. Scientific spice researches on a range of herbal remedies—including traditional healing methods, many of which come from Ayurvedic medicine—were evaluated using modern scientific methods. They revealed some real benefits. These findings are based on examining diabetes treatments in India, wound-healing agents in Ghana, and cancer treatments in China and Thailand. For instance, one of the plants examined is the curry-leaf tree from India, which is believed to have potential benefits in treating diabetes. The cardiologists have discovered that the extracts from the curry-leaf tree restricts the action of a digestive enzyme called pancreatic alpha-amylase, which takes part in the breakdown of dietary starch to glucose. Like cilantro, curry leaf is almost always used green and fresh. It is good news for many of us who love a rich course made with plenty of turmeric and bold amounts of pepper, garlic, and ginger. Here are some common herbs along with their uses and benefits.

Bay Leaves: Fresh or usually dried whole bay leaves (not for eating) are soaked in the cooking dish for their distinctive flavor and fragrance (removed from the food before serving). They flavor curries, soups, stews, braises, and pâtés in Asian and Mediterranean cuisine. Indian bay leaf and Indonesian bay leaf are pretty much fixtures in the cooking of many European and North American cuisines.

Cardamom: Cardamoms are of two types, namely, *Elettaria* and *Amomum* of the ginger family. Both types are small and triangular in cross-section, a spindle-shaped seedpod with a papery outer shell and small black seeds inside. *Elettaria* pods are smaller (½ inch long) and light green, while *Amomum* pods are larger (1 inch long) and dark brown. Both are used as flavorings in food and drink, and also as a medicine. They both have an intensely aromatic fragrance (mouth freshener) and a unique taste. The use of cardamom is very common in Indian cooking.

Chives: The chive (Latin word for "onion," and it looks like an onion) is a bulb-forming herbaceous plant of the onion family Alliaceae, native to Asia, Europe, and North America. They grow 1 to 2 feet tall in a dense cluster from the roots. The bulbs are slender and conical, about an inch long and a half inch broad. Chive bulbs and leaves are shredded (straws) and used as a condiment for fish, meat, eggs, baked potatoes, and soups. Fresh chives are available year-round, making it a readily available herb; or they can be dry-frozen without much loss of its taste. The therapeutic properties of chives are very similar to those of garlic, but weaker.

Chocolate: Chocolate is a very good mood food. It is one favorite flavor that many people enjoy across the world. Chocolate is processed from the tropical (*Theobroma*) cocoa bean. Cacao trees are native to the lowlands in tropical South America and have been cultivated for the last three thousand years. Raw cacao beans are of intense bitter taste. They are fermented and then dried, cleaned, and roasted appropriately to develop various flavors. The shells are removed, and cacao nibs are then grounded and liquefied, resulting in pure chocolate in the fluid form (called chocolate liquor). Raw pure chocolate has cocoa solids and cocoa butter in varying proportions. The liquor is then further processed into these two products: low-fat expensive cocoa solid and high-fat inexpensive cocoa butter. The cocoa solid (60% to 80%) is used for chocolate bars for its characteristic flavor and color, while cocoa butter is used for its smoothness and low melting point. Majority of the chocolates are in the form of sweet chocolates mixed with sugar. Milk chocolate is a sweet chocolate with added powdered milk or condensed milk. Researchers claim that dark chocolate, eaten in moderation—100 g a day (not every day but once or twice a week)—is very good for heart health. Dark chocolates (having substantial amounts of antioxidants) have more health benefits.

By tracking food intake of a large group of Swedish people who consumed 1 to 2 servings of chocolate a week (the number of servings per week is the key factor, the amount not as much) over a period of nine years, researchers noticed an astonishing 32% reduced risk of heart failure than those who did not eat at all. While the biological aspects of how different cocoa components work is not entirely clear, research, however, provides some clues:

- Flavanols, the principal ingredient of cocoa, can actually reverse at least one aspect of memory loss associated with normal aging.
- Flavanols help keep blood vessels supple as opposed to hardening over time (which may be one reason they aid better function in the brain).
- Flavanols have anti-inflammatory effects (which might be another reason for better brain function).

One caution, however. People who eat chocolate tend to eat more chocolate calories; and thereby, the chocolate's benefit to promoting thinness starts to fade away—once they eat more and more. So, eat twice a week, no more than that. Researchers have shown that flavonoids found in cocoa and chocolate may enhance blood flow by relaxing blood vessels, thereby lowering blood pressure. Flavonoids, which are also polyphenol antioxidants, hold back clumping of platelets and thus reduce inflammation. Biochemical analysis has further identified a special component in cocoa that is responsible for reducing platelet clumping, thereby helping smooth blood flow. Both actions in tandem can lower the risk of heart disease. However, more recent researches have not turned up much proof in support that chocolate in any form is of any helpful.

Cinnamon: Cinnamon is one very old and common spice known to humans. The cinnamon tree (thirty to fifty feet tall) is evergreen. It belongs to the family called Lauraceae and is native to Sri Lanka (formerly Ceylon). Sri Lanka supplies 90% of the world's cinnamon, followed by China, India, and Vietnam. Cinnamon from Sri Lanka is considered as "true cinnamon," while the Chinese variety is known as "cassia." Cinnamon sticks (or quills) come in thin layers. Cinnamon bark can be used whole as is, in the cookery as a condiment or garnish for flavoring the food (removed before eating), or it can be mixed with the food in the form of powder. Cinnamon has a high antioxidant content and is therapeutically used in the form of essential oil, which gets its unique healing abilities from its three basic active ingredients: (1) cinnamyl acetate, (2) cinnamaldehyde, and (3) cinnamyl alcohol. Additionally, it has a wide range of volatile substances. Cinnamaldehyde helps to prevent risky clumping of blood platelets by slowing down the release of inflammatory fatty acid from the platelet membranes, thereby reducing the formation of inflammatory messaging molecules.

Cinnamon essential oils act as an "antimicrobial" food. Because of its capacity to stop bacterial growth as well as fungi and yeasts, it is very effective. It can be used as an alternative to traditional food preservatives. Cinnamon aids in food digestion. It is used to season some high-carb foods, where it can lessen the carb impact on blood sugar levels; it slows down the rise in blood sugar level after meals. Historically, it has been used to treat toothache and to fight bad breath and to provide relief during the onset of a cold or flu, taken mixed in tea with some fresh ginger. Two related studies suggest cinnamon (which contains a molecule with insulin-like properties) can reduce risk factors for diabetes and heart disease up to 30% by controlling glucose levels in type 2 diabetics and reducing inflammation and cholesterol levels. Like cinnamon essential oils, just smelling the wonderful odor of cinnamon bark itself boosts brain activity and enhances cognitive processing on tasks related to the attention process, virtual and working memory.

Coriandrum: Coriandrum is native to southern Europe and the western Mediterranean region. It is a soft plant, growing up to twenty inches tall. The lacy foliage is called cilantro, which—for its distinctive fresh fragrance—is used as a condiment in Mexican and Southeast Asian salads, soups, and meat dishes. The dried seed is coriander. It is a pleasantly aromatic, not very strong, spice that is much used in European and Middle Eastern stews, sausages, sweetbreads, and cakes.

Coriander seeds are used in perfumery and pharmacological industries in order to mask the taste of medicines. It is sometimes used to flavor gin and liqueurs. Coriander is grown worldwide for the leaves (cilantro) or the seeds (coriander), or both. Cilantro, like curry leaf, almost always is used green and fresh.

Chili (a.k.a. hot pepper, red pepper, cayenne, and *Capsicum annuum*): Chili, green chili, red chili, or chili pepper is the fruit of plants from the genus *Capsicum.* The first chili peppers grown by humans were in eastern Mexico. In botany, the plant is considered as a berry bush. There are numerous types of chilies that vary in size, shape, color, flavor, and hotness. It has been cultivated since the prehistoric era in Mexico and Peru. It was introduced to the Caribbean by Columbus, who named it "pepper" because of its similarity with the old-world peppers of the *Piper* genus. The chili peppers and their various cultivars are now grown throughout the world; they are widely used as spices like vegetables in cuisine, and even as medicine. Hot chili puts fire on your tongue and tears in your eyes. The compound that gives chili its pungency when ingested or applied topically (to body surfaces) is capsaicin. The chili peppers have several other allied chemicals collectively called capsaicinoids. The chili peppers (fresh, dried, or powdered) are eaten raw or cooked for its fiery hot flavor. Capsaicin is a very safe and active painkilling agent in the management of arthritis pain, herpes zoster–related pain, diabetic neuropathy, chronic pain, and headaches. Other benefits may include cancer cell death, weight loss, diabetes control, lower LDL, and reduced insulin to lower blood sugar.

Chilies are an exceptional source of vitamins A, B, C, and E with minerals like molybdenum, manganese, folate, potassium, thiamin, and copper. It acts as a gastrointestinal detoxicant in helping in the digestion of food. Chili peppers have a bad (probably mistaken) reputation for contributing to stomach ulcers. But the fact is that chilies not only do not cause ulcers, they, on the contrary, prevent ulcers by killing bacteria you may have ingested; and at the same time, they stimulate the cell lining of the stomach to secrete protective buffering juices. Chilies are powerful antioxidants to remove free radicals. It has vitamin C, folic acid, and beta-carotene—a combination that reduces the risk of colon cancer. Chilies have carotenoid lycopene, which is known for preventing cancer. Chilies provide relief for colds and nasal congestion by increasing metabolism. Its pungency and peppery heat boosts secretions that help clear mucus from a stuffed-up nose or congested lungs; and in turn, it dilates the airway of the lungs, thereby reducing asthma and wheezing. Chilies help to reduce triglyceride levels, blood cholesterol, and platelet aggregation and, at the same time, increase the body's ability to dissolve fibrin, an insoluble protein formed from fibrinogen (a soluble protein present in blood plasma) during the clotting of blood. It suppresses appetite and burns calories. Though too large a quantity may not be applicable to Americans, still, a reasonable amount may be helpful. One research has shown that one's personality seems to be a significant player in the lust for hotness or spiciness in the food.

A meal with a bolt scoop of chili! People who tend to enjoy adventure, extreme sports, and exploration are up to six times more likely to enjoy the spicy-hot meal. Women love spicy foods more than men. Hot sauce production in America is one of the fastest-growing industries. Home cooking—and the use of spices in general—has skyrocketed in recent years (among the millennials). One study tracked 16,179 American adults participating in a larger public health study where there were 4,946 deaths over a period of twenty-three years. After controlling factors like age, sex, blood pressure, cholesterol, diabetes, smoking, and other characteristics, they found that those who reported eating hot peppers had a 13% reduced risk of early deaths. The study was, however, an observational; and there was no information about the quantities of peppers people ate. Therefore, no connection can be drawn. Yet researchers still believe that capsaicin has the antimicrobial and anti-inflammatory properties that may somehow be associated with disease prevention. Another study of more than 16,000 American men and women finds that those who eat hot chili peppers tend to live longer than those who don't.

Cloves: Cloves are the automatic unopened pink flower buds of the evergreen clove tree. Ten to twenty feet tall, it is native to Indonesia and India. The buds are hand-picked (½ to ¾ inches length) when they are pink and are dried under the sun until they turn brown. Cloves are used as a spice all over the world. Cloves are important ingredients in Indian Ayurvedic medicine and Chinese medicine. It is applied in dentistry as an anodyne (painkiller) for dental emergencies. Cloves are used as carminatives—used either to relieve or to prevent the formation of (or to facilitate the expulsion of) gas in the gastrointestinal tract. Cloves are said to be a natural anthelmintic that expels parasitic worms.

Ginger: Ginger is the underground stem of the ginger plant. Ginger root, which is aromatic and pungent, is a spice that is used for cooking as a delicacy or is used raw for medicine or is used as a powdered supplement. Ginger can be boiled in water and then added to tea to make ginger tea, to which honey is often added as a sweetener (and in some cases, sliced orange or lemon for flavor). Ginger paste, minced, or juice is quite potent and is used as a spice in Indian and Chinese cuisine, such as mutton, chicken, seafood, and vegetables. In Western diets, it is used in sweet foods, such as ginger bread, ginger cake, ginger biscuits, ginger ale, and ginger snaps. Dried ginger root is ground into powder and put into capsules and sold in pharmacies for medicinal use. It is an herbal medicine to treat upset stomach, nausea, vomiting, osteoarthritis, and motion sickness, especially seasickness. Unlike anti-vomiting drugs, which sometimes cause severe birth defects, ginger is inherently safe, and only a small dose is required. With regular consumption, ginger provides numerous therapeutic benefits, including use as an anti-inflammatory and antioxidant. The anti-inflammatory compounds of ginger, called gingerols, help to reduce the pain with osteoarthritis and rheumatoid arthritis and thus improves mobility. Gingerols inhibit the growth of colorectal cancer and cause cell death in all the ovarian cancer lines. Regular consumption of ginger cleans the colon and stimulates blood circulation. It is familiar to travelers with weak stomachs, who use it to curb nausea. It is one instant home remedy for cancer patients undergoing chemotherapy and for pregnant women.

Ginger contains two types of chemical compounds, gingerols and phenols, which act as an analgesic (pain reliever). Raw ginger reduces muscle pain by 25%. Ginger has been successfully proven to prevent ulcers, to treat heartburn, and to aid with digestion. Almost 40% of Americans routinely suffer from gastroesophageal reflux disease (GERD), acid reflux, or severe heartburn. These are some of the reasons why ginger roots are used as herbs, as spices, and as medicine in so many centuries.

Mint: The refreshing aroma of mint is admirable. It is well-known for mouth and mouth freshener. Mint is scientifically known as *Mentha*. Mint has over two dozen species and hundreds of varieties. It is an herb with remarkable therapeutic values and medicinal properties. People love mint mostly for its flavor. The consumer market is full of mint-flavored products like chewing gums, candies, mouth and breath fresheners, inhalers, toothpastes, and cigarettes. While it is best known for its refreshing property, mint actually has much more to offer. *Mentha* (mint) has at least twenty-five species of flowering plants, collectively called Lamiaceae (Mint Family). The most common and popular mints for cultivation are the hybrid mints: peppermint, spearmint, and apple mint. Peppermint has more potential as an herb than spearmint, which is simply a culinary herb. Green or dried leaves give a pleasing fresh, aromatic, sweet flavor with a cool aftertaste. They are used in candies, teas, beverages, jellies, syrups, and ice creams. Mint is an appetizer and promotes digestion; in a way, it aids to break down the fats. It is an active operative in opening up congestion of the nose, throat, bronchi, and lungs, giving relief in respiratory disorders resulting from asthma or cold.

Turmeric: Turmeric, a perennial (all seasons) plant of the ginger family, is grown throughout India and other parts of

Asia and in Africa. Like ginger, the rhizomes are root-like horizontal stems of the turmeric plant underground. Known for its distinct golden color and bitter taste, turmeric is one fixture in Indian cooking. Raw turmeric that grows fingerlike underground stems (rhizomes) are boiled for several hours and then dried in hot ovens. Once dried, they are ground into deep orange-yellow powder. Turmeric powder is regularly used as spice in Asian and Middle Eastern cuisines. Turmeric can be used fresh, much like ginger. Turmeric has been in vogue for ages as one powerful anti-inflammatory compound in both the Indian and Chinese systems of medicines. It is used to treat a wide range of conditions, including jaundice, arthritis, hemorrhage, toothache, bruises, chest pain, menstrual difficulties, flatulence, bloody urine, and colic. Turmeric is usually applied directly to the skin for healing wounds, skin problems, and eczema. It is a ready-made antiseptic paste for cuts, burns, and bruises. Turmeric cures other conditions like heartburn, stomach ulcer, and gallstone. It reduces internal inflammation and thus helps to prevent cancer. It can be consumed by mouth as a powder or in capsules, teas, or liquid extracts.

The curcumin in turmeric gives it its yellow color and is used as a food additive to color food. Therapeutically, curcumin provides an anti-inflammatory effect, which is comparable to that of many potent drugs, and it provides powerful antioxidant effects to protect the colon cells from free radicals. Curcumin is highly capable to prevent oxidation of cholesterol in the body. That increases the liver's ability to clear LDL cholesterol by relying on turmeric. Numerous studies claim that regular consumption of turmeric helps to lower the risk of breast, prostate, lung, and colon cancer.

Turmeric teams up with cauliflower to halt prostate cancer. Turmeric is good for Alzheimer's disease.

There are ample varieties of herbal medications: herbal capsules, herbal compresses, herbal douches, herbal baths, herbal electuaries, herbal extracts, herbal implants, herbal oils, herbal plasters, herbal salves, herbal teas, herbal infusions, herbal ointments, herbal decoctions, and herbal wraps. Using herbal medicines has long been a therapeutic healing technique. Most prescriptions are typically mixtures of herbs, plant extracts, and other organic substances. Gentle herbs! Mother Nature's little helpers!

CPSIA information can be obtained
at www.ICGtesting.com
Printed in the USA
BVHW030954250419
546530BV00005B/15/P

9 781984 566874